COMPANION

STUDIES IN AMERICAN HISTORY

American Episcopal Clergy: Registers of Ordinations in the Episcopal Church in the United States from 1785 through 1904--with Indexes. Edited by Kenneth Walter Cameron.

The Anglican Episcopate in Connecticut (1784-1899): A Sheaf of Biographical and Institutional Studies for Churchmen and Historians with Early Ecclesiastical Documents. Edited by Kenneth Walter Cameron.

The Catholic Revival in Episcopal Connecticut (1850-1925). By Kenneth Walter Cameron.

Centennial History of Trinity Episcopal Church, Bridgeport, Connecticut, Missionary of the Catholic Faith 1863-1963. By Kenneth Walter Cameron.

The Church of England in Pre-Revolutionary Connecticut: New Documents and Letters, with a Detailed Index. By Kenneth Walter Cameron. [In progress.]

Connecticut Churchmanship: Records and Historical Papers concerning the Anglican Church in Connecticut in the Eighteenth and Early Nineteenth Centuries. Edited by Kenneth Walter Cameron.

Documentary History of the Protestant Episcopal Church in Connecticut, 1704-1789. Edited by Francis L. Hawks and William Stevens Perry. [Originally published in 1863.] (Re-edited by Kenneth Walter Cameron, 2 vols. in 1.)

Early Anglicanism in Connecticut: Materials on the Missionary Career of Roger Viets, Samuel Seabury's Communion Office, and Aids for Scholarly Research. Edited by Kenneth Walter Cameron.

Facsimiles of Early Episcopal Church Documents (1759-1789). Edited by Kenneth Walter Cameron.

The Genesis of Christ Church, Stratford, Connecticut: Pre-Revolutionary Church of England; Background and Earliest Annals... With a Detailed Index. By Kenneth Walter Cameron. An Appendix by Carolyn Hutchens.

Historical Resources of the Episcopal Diocese of Connecticut. Edited by Kenneth Walter Cameron. Index by Carolyn Hutchens.

Index of the Pamphlet Collection of the Diocese of Connecticut. By Kenneth Walter Cameron.

Letter-Book of the Rev. Henry Caner, S.P.G. Missionary in Colonial Connecticut and Massachusetts until the Revolution. A Review of his Correspondence from 1728 through 1778. By Kenneth Walter Cameron.

The Life of Eben Edwards Beardsley, Connecticut Churchman and Ecclesiastical Historian (1808-1891). By William Agur Beardsley. (Edited by Kenneth Walter Cameron.)

The Works of Samuel Peters of Hebron, Connecticut, New-England Historian, Satirist, Folklorist, Anti-Patriot, and Anglican Clergyman (1735-1826). With Historical Indexes. Edited by Kenneth Walter Cameron.

TRANSCENDENTAL BOOKS—DRAWER 1080—HARTFORD 06101

OLD CONNECTICUT

HISTORICAL PAPERS ON PEOPLE, PLACES, TRADITIONS, AND EARLY ANGLICANISM

By

SAMUEL HART

ANNOTATED AND EDITED WITH

BIOGRAPHICAL AND BIBLIOGRAPHICAL APPENDICES

By

KENNETH WALTER CAMERON

TRANSCENDENTAL BOOKS — BOX A, STATION A — HARTFORD
06106

TO

J. WARREN HUTCHENS

IN

SEABURY'S APOSTOLIC LINE

WITH THE SAME

CATHOLIC COMMISSION

INTRODUCTION

This gathering of the papers of Samuel Hart which bear upon the history of old Connecticut is based upon the resources of the Archives of the Diocese, which include other historical papers by Dr. Hart, about three hundred sermons, dozens of college themes and theses, a considerable correspondence, and important private journals--all of which will eventually invite scholarly attention. Though the present volume, indeed, must be considered only a sampling of the whole, it is large enough to indicate that the years between the two famous registrars--Dr. Eben Edwards Beardsley (1866-1874) and Dr. William Agur Beardsley (1917-1946)--witnessed a third competent and productive historiographer.

Samuel Hart's significance as a historian has been undervalued in the twentieth century largely because he followed the custom of publishing Connecticut history in the newspapers of the towns concerned and, when possible, in the centers of Hartford and New Haven, assuming that scholars and the historically minded would clip the newsprint, preserve it in scrapbooks, and by such means transmit to to posterity. From a bibliographical point of view, the plan was not ineffective, for most of Hart's addresses and papers have survived. From the standpoint of his reputation, however, the inaccessibility and awkwardness of old newspapers for researchers have until now encouraged our forgetfulness of his accomplishments. Thanks to the increasing use of microfilm, perhaps we may expect a resurgence of interest in these neglected and fragile resources for the recovery of documentary and historical fact. The index to the present volume, indeed, will point out such possibilities and list dozens of largely forgotten subjects, people and institutions in Old Connecticut, convincing the user that in offering this collection from the past we have rendered a service to historians of the present.

In behalf of the Diocese, I wish to thank Jeffrey Barbour, Esq., a member of the Hart-Bailey-Barbour family and currently curator of the Hart homestead in Old Saybrook, for many recent courtesies. Acting for the Hart heirs and especially for his aunt, Miss Elizabeth Bailey (now convalescent)--who for many years has generously contributed important historical papers to the Diocesan Archives--last year he helped deposit the last of the available Hart manuscripts-- in a concrete way continuing his aunt's dedication to Connecticut history and furthering the lifelong activities of his grandfather, the still-remembered and much beloved Dr. Melville Knox Bailey, who followed Dr. Hart in loyally supporting the purposes of the C. M. P. C. That organization, by helping the present volume into print, calls attention to Dr. Hart as one of its earliest and most devoted servants, its leader and vice president from 1891 until his death, and its principal editor for twenty-six years!

K. W C.

All Saints' Day, 1976.

The Market Place and the town plan.
A copy of the Brockett map of 1641.
The original has been lost.

NEW HAVEN
IN
1641.

TABLE OF CONTENTS

4

5

EARLY MAPS OF THE
NEW HAVEN GREEN

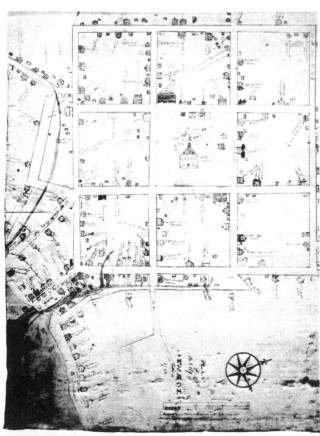

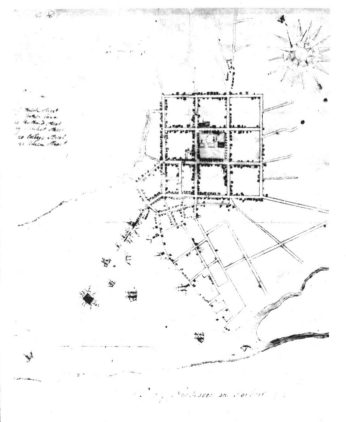

The Public Square and its surroundings.
The Wadsworth map of 1748.

The Public Square on the eve of the
American Revolution. The Ezra Stiles
map of 1775.

BRANTORD

MILTORD

STRATFORD

LONG ISLAND SOUND

TYPES OF COLONIAL SETTLEMENTS IN CONNECTICUT

[1] The colonies of New England have had from the first very much in common. Not only have they, in great part, the same material features and surroundings; but they were settled by substantially the same people, with substantially the same ideas, and for substantially the same ultimate purposes; and their growth has taken place under not very dissimilar conditions.

But no sooner do we note the points of resemblance among the settlements which finally made up the colonies and states of Massachusetts and Connecticut, than our attention is called to points of difference. There were two original settlements in what is now Massachusetts, which were after a time united by the provisions of a royal charter; and in Connecticut also there were two original colonies, besides the military post at the mouth of the river, one of which was absorbed by the other under the operation of a charter secured from the king. The earlier of the two colonies or settlements in Massachusetts was made by a company of Independents or Separatists from the Church of England--Pilgrims we call them--who had come out from that Church as from Babylon, had fled to Holland, and thence had sought a home in the new world. They came without the color of authority from the State, though they soon afterward obtained a patent from the Council for New England. As Independents, and as an entirely new government, they held to no connection between Church and State, and no religious test was ever required among them as a condition of exercising the franchise or of holding even the highest office of state. It was from Plymouth, as Dr. Bacon has reminded us, that the typical New England churches had their genesis. The other Massachusetts colony, that of Massachusetts Bay, dating at Salem from 1629 and at Boston from 1630, was a settlement of Puritans--that is to say, of men who declared that they were members of the Church of England as by law established, but of that church as reformed or in process of reformation from serious errors both of doctrine and of practice. We recall Mr. Higginson's apostrophe to England, in words which were eloquent and touching in their sound, as he set sail: "We will not say, as the Separatists are wont to say, Farewell Babylon, Farewell Rome; but we will say, Farewell dear England, Farewell the Church of God in England." But Mr. Higginson meant not the then actual England and Church of England, but ideals of them, such as he and his companions were trying to draw out from the corrupt realities, and such as they hoped to make realities in the lands across the seas. They had a charter, never intended, it may safely be said, to be a charter for a government or to be taken out of the kingdom--a charter for a trading company--which yet they were determined to use for their purposes somewhere in the vast country then known as Virginia. Upon this charter they engrafted provisions for the maintenance and carrying out of the principles which they deemed necessary for the perpetuation of a regimen in Church and State such as they approved. Not all of the original charter members were also members of their purified Church; but when they had made their settlements, and had matters practically in their own hands, they provided that no one should thereafter be admitted to take any part in the government, as voter or as office-holder, unless he were also a Church-member. Thus the colonists of the Bay were not separatists in their theory; Roger Williams, who was then one of the stricter sort and a Plymouth man, would not commune with the church in Boston, because it did not repent openly of its sin in that it had formerly had communion with the apostate Church of England. Practically, however, they soon became Independents; Roger Williams himself, though not without some vigorous protests, became for a while preacher to the church in Salem; Endicott at an earlier day sent back to England those who objected to the setting up of a new church; the Massachusetts Bay people were determined to establish a new state, and for their new state they must, on their own theory, have a new established Church.

It was the latter of these two colonies that became the stronger, very largely, no doubt, owing to the advantages of its position, but still more owing to the stern resolution and the remarkable ability of its leading men for more than one generation. There was a long struggle to retain the charter (to which reference will be made presently); and when it was declared forfeited and the Bay was made a royal colony, the earlier, Independent, more liberal settlement of Plymouth, which had had but a feeble existence for some seventy years, was incorporated into the later, puritan, close corporation of Massachusetts; but the latter in the process lost a large part of its closeness, inasmuch as the new charter, dating after the Revolution in England, forbade the application of religious tests for membership.

The settlers of the river-towns which were included in the original colony of Connecticut came from Massachusetts, the few Plymouth men who reached Windsor in 1633 having made no permanent settlement. They came as a colony from the Bay, bringing with them a constituted civil authority, and were one colony from the first, although they settled in three communities. The constitution which they adopted was not strictly a confederation or an entirely new establishment of government; it was rather such adjustment as seemed to them desirable and wise when they found themselves, or made themselves, quite independent of the Bay. But Mr. Hooker, who led the colony from Massachusetts-- as also, I believe, Mr. Cotton, who had come in company with him from England but stayed in Boston--was not a Massachusetts Bay Puritan. It was he who gave form--at least in part, for much must be attributed to the influence of Mr. Ludlow of Windsor (later the founder of this town)-- to the form of government adopted in 1639; and this was far more like that of Independent Plymouth than like that of Puritan Massachusetts, as is evident in the foundamental matter of the requirements for citizenship. There was never a religious test in the colony of Connecticut, except the one proviso that the governor must be a member of the church.

Our other colony, that of New Haven--I do not mention Saybrook, as it was practically a military garrison and was soon incorporated with Connecticut, the River Colony--was more Massachusetts-like than Massachusetts itself. Mr. Davenport and his colleagues expected to establish at the fair haven which they had discovered on the Sound, if not the millennial kingdom, at least a true theocracy; and certainly none but a member of the church could

have anything to do with even the secular matters of such a state. To be sure, Mr. Eaton thought, as did the separatists at Plymouth, that all free planters, "however they might delegate authority, should have" at least "power to resume it into their own hands." But Mr. Eaton was promptly suppressed; and the whole body chose twelve men, who out of their own number chose seven, and these seven pillars, thus hewed out by wisdom for the building of her New Haven house, founded a new Church and new State, puritan in principle even if it was very independent in fact. Thus it was determined that in that colony (or rather settlement) "church members only" should "be free burgesses"; it was not absolutely required that they should be members of the local church, though probably this would be nearly always the case.

The River Colony, the original Connecticut, was not, I maintain in spite of the assertion of some historians, a confederation of towns; it was one from the beginning, and came from Massachusetts sufficiently organized for all necessary purposes. The New Haven colony, on the other hand, did become a confederation, when the younger neighbor settlements at Milford and Guilford united with that at the mouth of the Quinnipiack. There was no time when Hartford and Wethersfield and Windsor were independent of each other; but Milford, though its church was organized at New Haven, became at once independent on its removal, and within three years it was administering its government on principles inconsistent with those which were maintained in New Haven. The Guilford settlers, who had come from England for the express purpose of founding a colony by themselves, had but sojourned at New Haven for a few weeks, long enough to ask--or at any rate to receive--advice from Mr. Davenport, and long enough also to detect certain faults in the theory or practice of the constitution of the colony which he had founded. Yet for some reason they waited a while; and it was not till nearly four years had passed that the seven pillars of Guilford were selected and a church founded. Then the original purchasers, who had held the title of the land until that time, magnanimously "resigned up their right into the hands of the church, and those four of them also which were chosen to the exercise of civil power did express that their trust and power for that work were now terminated and ended." And only members of that particular church, thus founded and established, were allowed to be burgesses and to have the right of suffrage in Guilford. This was enough to secure for the plantation admission on equal terms to the New Haven jurisdiction. But the further provision that all the planters, whether freemen or not, should have notice of all meetings with opportunity to bring forward weighty objections, shows that due consideration was had for those who professed the Connecticut rather than the New Haven form of government, and, in short, wished a democracy rather than an ecclesiocracy; and it was a satisfactory assurance that none of the planters should be really deprived of any of their rights.

Thus the colony on the River and the confederation on the Sound were organized on principles which differed, speaking generally, as did those of Plymouth and Massachusetts Bay. But here it was the Independent settlement-- at least that organized on independent or separatist principles--which prevailed. Before the union, neither Connecticut nor New Haven had a charter; each exercised a government in its own way; and from the first Connecticut was the stronger, not so much on account of position or mercantile advantages, as because of its form of government and the methods of its administration; and that too, although part of its towns lay on the Thames and part stretched along to the west of Milford until they touched at Stamford, another unit of the New Haven confederacy.

When the king "came to his own," Connecticut secured a charter for what was practically a free and independent government; and what is especially pertinent to our present subject, the limits which the charter gave to the colony were such that it included all the New Haven towns. New Haven did not yield to all willingly or very gracefully. Her protests and appeals would be really touching, if they were not so long. She pleaded broken faith; she lamented above all that she would not be able any longer to restrict the suffrage as she had done; but she had to decide and to decide quickly, whether she had better fall into the hands of Connecticut with its separatist and latitudinarian principles of government, which a large minority of her people, by the way, approved, or into the hands of the Papist Duke of York, who had a sort of claim to all the territory west of the Connecticut River, a claim which Connecticut could now resist, but which the charterless New Haven was powerless to withstand; and she decided that the former was the lesser evil. Thus, while in Massachusetts the Puritan principle prevaled and Plymouth was swallowed up by the Bay, in Connecticut the Independent principle gained the ascendancy. But there are "survivals" of each of these types to-day within the limits of our happily united commonwealth.

I am not willing to pass by another type of settlement within our limits, that namely of a military post or fort, the only true example of which was at Saybrook. Theological motives had much to do with the settlements at Hartford and New Haven; apart from these, I think we may say that those who founded the colony on the River had rather the political intention of establishing a state, and that those who took up their abode towards the west on the Sound entertained hopes of commercial prosperity. There was little of the theological or political or commercial that entered into the plans of those who established themselves at the mouth of the Connecticut; or rather, such ideas of these kinds as they had were partly embodied in, and partly subordinated to, the idea of a military garrison. The contract of John Winthrop the younger, made before he left England, was to build a fort within which should be houses for "men of quality," and to "reserve unto the fort, for the maintenance of it, one thousand or fifteen hundred acres at least of good land, as near adjoining thereto as may be." He brought with him that practical soldier and engineer, Lion Gardiner, who had been in the service of the Prince of Orange, and who was to build the spacious fortifications that were proposed and to lay out a city in the immediate neighborhood. Because it was a military post, it could have a chaplain, and after three or four years young Master Higginson came to it in that capacity; but until it was more than a military post there was no church organized in Saybrook; and Lady Alice Fenwick went to Hartford to be admitted a member of the Church there, that her daughter Elizabeth, born not long after her arrival at the fort, might be baptized by Mr.

Hooker. The independence of this sturdy little colony lasted but about ten years. In December, 1644, an agreement was made between Mr. Fenwick, as governor of the Saybrook fort, and the General Court at Hartford, by which the former yielded or released to the Connecticut colony such rights of jurisdiction as he had or claimed.

We may see, I think, that this variety of type among the settlements now merged in the good State of Connecticut has a survival in the topographical plans which were adopted by the several companies of settlers. Those who came to the Connecticut Newtown from the Massachusetts Newton, to Hartford on the Great River from Cambridge near Boston, came with a fully constituted Church, that they might have place for carrying out their principles in a state which they desired to found. They came under their own chosen leaders with plans in part matured and in part ready to crystallize into form, glad to leave their brethren with whom they did not find themselves quite in accord, and the more glad that they were leaving them before they had come to an open breach. It was practically an independent settlement of those who were to found an independent state, a community which was almost never to acknowledge any ruler not chosen by itself or any law which it did not itself originate and enforce. And in theory, church and state were to be distinct and mutually independent there. The settlers could not but have had expectations of prosperous ventures in trade and successful labor in agriculture; but they came to found a practical, working, growing state. I think that we may see this illustrated in the lay-out of the new settlement--something practical, sufficient for the present, but allowing for the possibility of growth. At the crest of a ridge, the slope of which rose not very steeply from the river, and under the protection of another ridge which ran nearly at a right angle to this, they selected a place for the centre of their settlement, taking room near the intersection for the common-house, to serve as meeting-house both for Lord's-day and for week-day assemblies, for a burial place, and I suppose also a whipping post. Thence they drew a street in a direction parallel to that of the general course of the river, and another which led to the river itself; and the town was laid out with its square and its King Street and Queen Street. From this simple plan it grew, as need required or opportunity was offered. King Street is now Main Street, and from it the land slopes both to the east and to the west; Queen Street has become State Street, which still leads down to the principal landing on the river. As one walks down this or Grove Street or Ferry Street on the one side, and Church Street or Asylum Street or the now passible Gold Street on the other, one can yet realize, if one thinks of it, how true it is that the oldest part of the principal street of Hartford is on the ridge of a hill; or one can now see at a glance how high the Centre Church stands above the Little River which is but a few rods away. The other hill, which sheltered the first square where the two streets met, does not appear now, except as traces of it are seen in the rear of the United States Hotel. This building was erected rather against and into the sides of a hill, and the general appearance of the "lay of the land" has greatly changed within the memory of some persons who are now living. The square where stood the first meeting-house and where the first of Hartford's dead were laid to rest has been encroached upon by streets, but the City Hall (long the State House) and the Post Office stand on it.

The nature of the growth of Hartford can be seen by any one who studies its map or walks along Main Street. There was no special order or method about it. One road led north to Centinel Hill and thence to the common meadows; another led southwest to the common uplands and the hanging place; while another found its way across the fields and over the mountain to Farmington, after some of the inhabitants had removed to the fair valley of the Tunxis. But the development of each side of the settlement was determined by practical considerations; and how different these were on the east and on the west can be seen by the fact that no street crosses Main Street, and that in almost no case does a street which reaches it on one side find exact correspondence with a street on the other side. All testifies to a practical, or would-be practical, community, attempting to satisfy its needs as they arose, and to have a convenient place in which to live. In the simple first outline, and then the irregular growth, of the town of Hartford, we seem to see an embodiment of Mr. Hooker's idea of a new state, practically holding to a few principles and fitted to adapt itself to the needs of the people.

On the other hand, Mr. Davenport's theocratic purposes, and the mercantile character of his community, found some expression in the plan of New Haven, when it was founded, a few years after the settlement of Hartford. At first some of the people found shelter in cabins, or as they called them "cellars," probably built into the sides of low hills or mounds; and from these cellars it was found difficult to dislodge some of the "mixed multitude" that had found a place among the "chosen people." But as soon as possible, the settlers began to build on the level ground, where they laid out a four-square city, like that described in the Apocalypse, of which the length and the breadth (though for obvious reasons not the height) were equal. What is now called George Street was laid out about half a mile in length, and on it a square was constructed, the other boundaries being the modern York, Grove, and State Streets. Then this square was divided into nine equal squares by two streets parallel to George Street and two at right angles to it; and the central square was reserved for the meeting-house, the whipping post, the burial-ground, and other public uses. In the other eight squares the planters were assigned their home-lots; and we are told that they "seem to have grouped themselves, to some extent, according to personal acquaintance and friendship in the old country." Of course, there were the common lands in the suburbs, and to these irregular lanes or roads led; but the outline of the original town itself was entirely symmetrical; and the symmetry of that part of New Haven is still well preserved. It has been almost impossible in all these years to encroach upon the central public square; and thus the Green of the city, in unshorn proportions and surrounded by ancient mansions and modern structures and academic piles, testifies to the thought of those who laid it out. It gives an impression of dignity and solidity and conscious completeness which is lacking elsewhere; it tells of a people with a lofty religious theory and a strong element of worldly responsibility. One does not wonder that they objected to being incorporated into, or rather swallowed up by, the older and more practical and more democratic colony to the north.

I speak with hesitation as to the topography of Middletown, as I have not that acquaintance with its local history which I hope in good time to acquire. We are told that the committee who came here in 1650 to explore the country reported that there might be subsistence obtained in Mattabesett for fifteen families, but that within four years there were twice that number of families here. The surface evidence points to a union of agriculture and commercial purpose in the settlement. There was the long street parallel to the river, not on a ridge, for there was no ridge sufficiently near, but on a space approximately level; from one end of the street a road branched off for Hartford, and from the other end a road could lead away from the swamp in the direction of New Haven. The three principal streets in the cross direction did actually cross the Main Street and lead to the river; the northernmost one may have taken the place of the path which Sowheag must have had from his landing-place to his castle, for he would certainly have gone down by the easiest way; the others were arranged to serve with it the convenience of the farmers who would bring their supplies from the rich fields to the west, that they might be sent by boats up and down the river, and later by sailing vessels to the coast ports and the West Indies. It appears that for some hundred years--the warehouses, of course, keeping near the water--the mansions of the merchants and the residences of other well-to-do people were on Main Street or not far from it; and thus Middletown became the most populous town in Connecticut, a port of entry, and a typical river town.

It remains to speak of two other places which have been mentioned historically, and to show briefly the type of settlement which they represent. While every town has its idiosyncrasies, I think that all in this commonwealth can be found to have some resemblance to one or other of the typical cases.

Guilford was practically, if not actually, the first of the settlements of farmers, of which there were many in Connecticut; and thus it differed from the community of well-to-do merchants and traders further west, to which in theory of government it was closely allied. It too had its central green, and its houses about it; but there were no surrounding squares to protect this enclosure (if, indeed, it was enclosed), and fields for tilling and grazing must have come close to the homesteads of all the settlers.

Saybrook, which antedates New Haven by several years and Hartford by a short time, and which is a rival of Windsor for the first place on the roll of Connecticut settlements, was before all else, as has been said, a military post. Lion Gardiner's design was to build first a fort at some convenient spot to guard the mouth of the river; and the extremity of a point of land actually within the river's mouth was selected for that purpose. Then the neck of this point was protected by a stockade, and places were marked out for the persons of quality who were expected to arrive from England, and who were to live as in a small city. There was no square or green for public purposes; the first interment was within the walls, and the church was organized in the great hall of the fort--the first fort stood further back from the river than that which some

of us remember--and then a burial-lot was laid out by the water's edge to the south, near the place where private generosity later provided a site for the College. The meeting-house stood on a street which was perhaps considered the most aristocratic in the place, where there was room for but a small lot around it. There is very little to remind one now of the original purpose and plan of the settlement.

Thus in the early settlements within the limits of that which since 1662 has been the one colony or state of Connecticut, we find different ideas, differently maintained, and expressing themselves in different ways; I venture to think that it is not uninstructive, and to hope that it is not unpleasant, to note how these ideas have prevailed, how the expression of them has continued, and how they have supplemented each other and have been brought into harmony as the years have passed on.

SOME HISTORIC DIFFERENCES BETWEEN
[2] MASSACHUSETTS AND CONNECTICUT

[For this paper, Dr. Hart abbreviated the first part of the preceding address on "Types of Colonial Settlements," skipping the entire latter portion on topography. One paragraph of the earlier paper was expanded to read as follows: "But at Guilford, which confederated with New Haven (there was a confederation in the Sound colony, though not, as has been said, here on the River) they went further yet and allowed only members of their particular church to be burgesses; while yet they showed their puritan convictions by not requiring Mr. Whitefield, their pastor, who had received holy orders in the Church of England, to receive any new ordination. This, by the way, was in conformity to what had been done in Boston, when, in some cases at least, though hands were laid on the pastors, it was expressly stated that it was not by way of reordaining those who had been ordained in England, but by way of setting them apart to special work in a special place. (I do not find any record that Davenport was ordained at New Haven.)" The end of the new address follows:]

The differing principles which thus illustrated themselves in our early history in rather the theological way were otherwise exemplified as history ran on. Massachusetts was conscious, apparently, that her charter was not what she wished it to be and what she pretended that it was; and by divers devices she fought off and warded off the day when she should be forced to surrender it. But at last law prevailed; Randolph's complaints, running, as has been said, through the whole range of the Colony's acts, from the coining of money to the prohibition of the observance of Christmas, were heard; the Charter was lost, and replaced by one which made Massachusetts a royal colony and introduced the new amusement of baiting royal governors.

But Connecticut, which had gone on quietly in her own way and had waited her time, obtained from the same King with whom Massachusetts had such sharp contentions her very remarkable charter, with no restrictions upon the powers of her government except the very indefinite one that its laws were not to be "contrary to those of England."

I suppose that we shall never know just how to distribute the credit for obtaining this charter; how much was due to the younger Winthrop's persuasiveness, how much to his interest in the Royal Society, how much to the money which he carried with him and from accounting for which the General Assembly released him; or how much again to the fact that the Colony was not Massachusetts, and that the authorities in England were not averse to having a "buffer state," in the words of modern diplomacy, between Massachusetts and New York, a state which could, in good conscience comply, as practically it had always complied, with the demands of the royal commissioners. And when troubles came in due course of law, as they did come under Andros, Connecticut saw the wisdom of submission, surrendering her seal, having her officials take out commissions under the new authority, and biding her time--she did not have to wait long--till she could resume her charter government without objection from anybody. Thus while Connecticut guarded her own rights, she was not unmindful of her loyalty to the mother country, and she resisted only when under this pretense of loyalty her citizens were asked to forego the rights and duties of British subjects; and she did not forget sisterly obligations to the other colonies.

In the days of the old New England confederation, when Massachusetts had 30 towns, and the three other colonies but 18 in all, Massachusetts would not aid the others except in so far as she could rule them; but all along, in French and Indian wars, and again in the struggle for independence, Connecticut, though she had not as much at stake as the northern colonies, did far more than her share. She has never had full credit for all this; but, as a member of this club once suggested in this connection, it is one thing to make history and another to write it.

The ecclesiastical development of the two colonies, based on the principles of which I spoke at first, really made the great and lasting historical difference between Connecticut and Massachusetts. This is true at least until we come to the last sixty years, in which the varying industrial conditions and the growth of manufacturing interests have given a different cast to the character and the life of the two States. The early controversy in the church in this town [Hartford], which led to the formation of a second church, the story of which has been so well told and interpreted by the two historians of those venerable organizations, illustrates it all. The controversy was between the independent-way, the pure Congregationalism for which the withdrawers stood, and the "Parish-way," with an element of Presbyterianism in it, which Mr. Haynes represented. Connecticut, I think, owes a great deal to Governor Saltonstall and to the Saybrook Platform for doing all that could be done to harmonize the two elements and thus to bring in something a little flexible into the ecclesiastical order. It was not approved of in New Haven, as one might expect, or in Norwich, I cannot tell why; but it made the religious establishment of Connecticut liberal towards sober dissenters, even if it was severe towards its own unruly members. Gov. Saltonstall, their pastor in New London, had given the use of his meeting-house to Keith and Talbot when these first missionaries of the S. P. G. began their journeys; and as Governor he moderated the discussion which ensued when Rector Cutler and Tutor

Brown declared for episcopacy; neither of which things could have happened in Massachusetts. The Episcopal Church in Connecticut practically dates from 1722, and very soon the General Assembly passed a very fair act for the relief of sober dissenters, an act which was repealed or modified for a time when the great awakening of 1740 had called out the enthusiasts, but the privileges of which were not taken from those for whom it was intended; so that, even at the revolution, though there were cases of severe treatment of individuals, on the whole the Episcopalians had little of which to complain.

No doubt this was due in great part to the different ways in which the Church of England presented itself to the people of the two colonies. In Massachusetts it was the State Church of the hated royal governors, which had forced itself into the Old South and stood for a tyranny; in Connecticut it sprang up among the people, it was not accompanied by any imposition of authority, and, indeed, with but one exception (if I remember) all its ministers were born and bred on this soil, and many of them belonged in every way to the community in which they lived. Thus there was no very widespread feeling of bitterness even in troublous times. Bishop Seabury, a loyal citizen of the State and of the U. S. after independence had been effected, was not thought the less of for having been a chaplain in the royal army and still drawing a pension on this account; and the foremost jurist of the State, Dr. William Samuel Johnson, was placed and kept in positions of honor and responsibility though he had not earnestly advocated seeking liberty by the sword.

Thus Connecticut grew up in a different way and under the influence of different principles from those which directed and shaped the course of Massachusetts. It seems to me that I find this more true conservatism and this more true progress in this commonwealth, though in many ways, for divers reasons, it has been the less famous and has perhaps had the less influence. It is not unfair, where so much depends upon ecclesiastical differences, to take one more example of that kind. There is the key to a great deal of history in the fact that when the great break-up of New England Calvinism came, many of the old churches of the ecclesiocracy of Massachusetts were sent into Unitarianism, while the shock was so little felt in constitutional Connecticut that but one church, if indeed one, was moved.

I have had it in mind but to call attention to some of the historic differences which have given to each of these two States, beginning though they did in ways that seemed much alike, its own manner and form of growth. Had time allowed, something might perhaps have been said as to the influence of all this upon the character, the tone and the temper of the people of these States; but it must suffice to have brought together these suggestions in the form of notes of historical circumstances and events.

THE CONVOCATION AND COLLEGE OF DOCTORS OF THE EPISCOPAL CHURCH IN CONNECTICUT

[3]

The Episcopal Church in Connecticut may be said to have had its origin at the Commencement of Yale College in 1722; it dates its complete organization from the

consecration of its first Bishop in 1784 and his return from Scotland in 1785; but it has not yet held the centenary of its Convention of Bishop, Clergy and Laity, for this first met in June, 1792, and the hundredth session will be held in June of next year.

But from an early time, after there began to be a fair number of Episcopal clergymen in the Colony, there were meetings in what were called voluntary Convocations or, to use the term which was afterwards reserved for them, Convocations, to consult on matters of common interest and to take action, so far as they were competent to take it, for the common welfare. The records of these earlier meetings are lost, unless indeed, as seems probable, they are among the inaccessible papers of Bishop and Doctor Jarvis; but knowledge of some of them can be gained from other sources. The sermon preached by the Rev. John Beach at the Convocation so-called in 1760 was printed, and this gives the earliest date known for any regular meeting of the Episcopal clergy of Connecticut. In the pages of the first volume of Dr. Beardsley's history and of his Life of Bishop Seabury there are notices of other meetings gathered from various sources. From these for the most part I take the notes of meetings before 1790.

On the eighth day of October, 1766, a Convocation was held at Stratford, eleven Connecticut clergymen and Dr. Auchmuty of New York being present; and they prepared and signed a formal address to the Bishop of London "bitterly lamenting" the fact that the government would not send a bishop to the Colonies. A similar plea was sent to the same prelate from a Convocation held on the 29th of May, 1771; and at a meeting held on the 8th of September, 1773, a petition was sent to the Venerable S. P. G. in regard to the support of the minister at Middletown. In 1776, the clergy met at New Haven on the 23rd of July, and resolved, in view of the disturbed state of public affairs, to "suspend the public exercise of their ministerial functions." On the 25th of March, 1783, ten of the fourteen Episcopal clergymen left in Connecticut at the close of the war of Revolution met at Woodbury, selected the Rev. Jeremiah Leaming as their first choice for the episcopate and the Rev. Dr. Samuel Seabury as his substitute, instructed the one who should accept the office to seek consecration in England or, failing there, in Scotland, and wrote a letter to Dr. White of Philadelphia in earnest protest against his recently published pamphlet entitled "The Case of the Episcopal Churches Considered." In the following year the clergy met at Wallingford and appointed a committee of three to consult with leading members of the General Assembly, then sitting at New Haven, as to certain of the difficulties which Dr. Seabury had met in England in his attempts to secure episcopal consecration, based on a supposed unwillingness on the part of the civil authorities of the new State to allow a Bishop to live or to minister among them. The minutes of the meeting of the next year, 1785, have been preserved, having been inserted by the Rev. Dr. S. F. Jarvis in a memoir of his father, Bishop Jarvis, which he wrote for the third volume of the Evergreen magazine. The clergy assembled at Middletown on the 2d of August to meet their Bishop. On the following day they formally acknowledged him, and he held his first ordination; on the next day, the Bishop delivered his first charge,

and a conference was held with the Rev. Mr. Parker, of Massachusetts; and on the 5th of August, the Rev. Messrs. Bowden and Jarvis of Connecticut and the Rev. Mr. Parker of Massachusetts, were appointed "a committee to consider of and make with the Bishop some alterations in the Liturgy needful for the present use of the Church." The few alterations made necessary by the changes in the form of civil government were published by the Bishop in a broadside dated at New London on the 12th day of April; and it is to be noted, as against certain historians, that though in the form of an official Injunction it was set forth after consultation with the clergy and with the advice and cooperation of a committee appointed for that purpose. The Convocation met again by adjournment in New Haven at Commencement-time on the 14th of September, when it had been expected that the matter of making other changes in the Prayer Book would be considered; but it was judged best, under the then present circumstances, to undertake no general revision at that time. In 1786, the Convocation met at Derby on the 22d of September, when Bishop Seabury delivered his second charge and set forth and "recommended to the Episcopal congregations in Connecticut" a Communion-Office nearly identical with that used by the Scottish Episcopalians, and new prayers were also ordered for the civil authority. From a letter of the Rev. Roger Viets, of Simsbury, to the Rev. Mr. Parker, of Boston, I find that the Convocation met at Wallingford on the 27th of February, 1787, and took steps towards setting out a Connecticut edition of the Prayer Book. At this Convocation also it was decided to elect a coadjutor for the Bishop; and after Mr. Leaming and Mr. Mansfield had both declined to undertake the burden of the duty, the Rev. Abraham Jarvis was chosen. The plan for his consecration was soon made unnecessary by the union of the Episcopal Church in New England with that in what were then called the Southern States. The Convocation met again in 1787 at Stamford on the Thursday after Whitsunday, May 31st. In October, 1788, it met at North Haven, and on the 15th of September, 1789, at Stratfield (Bridgeport). After this time we have the written records, the minute-book, now in my custody as Registrar of the Diocese, beginning with a meeting held at Litchfield on the 2nd of June, 1790, when fifteen clergymen were present besides the Bishop, and "by particular desire," as it is entered, they "attended divine service at the Presbyterian meeting-house," and the Bishop held an ordination. I shall revert to this meeting of the Convocation further on, taking the opportunity to trace here the brief history of the College of Doctors which was instituted at the next session.

On the third day of the Convocation at Newtown in 1790, the 2nd day of October, it was "Resolved, by a Vote of the Convocation, that a College of Doctors of Divinity be established, by the Bishop & Clergy of Connecticut: And that the College of Doctors shall be considered as the Bishop's Council, --to be consulted on any emergency that may arise:--and that the Rev. Messrs. Dibble, Mansfield, Hubbard, & Jarvis, be the first four Doctors."

In the following year (1791), at the Convocation held at Watertown on the 5th of October, the following votes were passed: "Voted: That the College of Doctors shall consist of a limited number: Which number shall never be less than four; (allowing six months to supply a vacancy

which may be caused by death or removal)--& shall never exceed six, unless by the consent of the Convocation. Voted; That the instalment of the Doctors shall be by Diploma from the College of Doctors, which shall be announced by the Bishop in public, at the next Convocation. Voted; That the Acts of this Convocation relative to the College of Doctors, shall be published in the Connecticut-Journal."

Also, a committee appointed in June, 1790, "to propose Canons for the internal government of the Church in this State" having made a report, it was "Voted: That the Canons reported by said committee, be revised & completed by the Bishop, & the College of Doctors; & laid before the next Convocation." This Committee consisted of the Rev. Dr. Leaming, and the Rev. Messrs. Jarvis, Mansfield, and Hubbard, the last three of whom were also members of the College of Doctors. It does not appear that the contemplated report was ever made; and there is in the records of Convocation no further allusion to the College of Doctors.

From these facts has grown the legend, which is repeated once in a while, that Bishop Seabury looked upon himself as a Metropolitan and claimed, among other things, the privilege which the Archbishop of Canterbury possesses of being a University sole and having the power of conferring ex mero motu degrees in any faculty. But the records already quoted show that the Convocation elected the members of the first College, and it appears that the College was expected to be a self-perpetuating body--though perhaps Convocation was expected to elect new members--and that the College itself was to give diplomas for the instalment of Doctors, of which the Bishop was simply to make public announcement. There are reasons of which I shall speak presently for the speedy and rather sudden termination of this council of advice to the Bishop; at present I am concerned only with the question as to the four members of the College of Doctors and to the position or title which the Bishop and their brethren supposed to be given them by their election into that body.

The Rev. Ebenezer Dibblee (or Dibble) was born in Danbury in 1715 and graduated at Yale College in 1734. He was ordained in England in 1747, ministered in Stamford and vicinity from 1748 to 1799, and died at Stamford in the last-mentioned year. Columbia College gave him the degree of Doctor in Divinity in 1793.

The Rev. Richard Mansfield was born in New Haven in 1723 and graduated at Yale College in 1741. He received holy orders in England in 1748, and was rector at Derby for seventy-two years, from 1748 till his death in 1820. Yale College made him a Doctor of Divinity in 1792.

The Rev. Bela Hubbard was born in Guilford in 1739 and graduated at Yale College in 1758. He was ordained in England in 1764, and died in New Haven, where he had ministered for about forty-five years, in 1812. He received a Doctorate in Divinity from his alma mater in 1804.

The Rev. Abraham Jarvis was born in Norwalk in 1739 and graduated at Yale College in 1761. He was ordained at the same time with Mr. Hubbard and ministered in Middletown until in 1797 he was chosen Bishop of Connecticut in

succession to Bishop Seabury; he died at New Haven in 1813. Yale College gave him a Doctor's degree in Divinity in the year of his election to the Episcopate.

As to the position which these men filled, it may help to determine the meaning which the Bishop and the Clergy of Connecticut attached to membership in the College of Doctors, if we observe the titles which are given to them in the official records. An examination of the minutes of Convocation shows that the members of the College were not customarily called Doctors until they had received the degree from Yale or Columbia College. In the list of members present at the several meetings, I find Mr. Hubbard and Mr. Jarvis called Doctors twice in 1794, and Mr. Hubbard once in 1799; but in every other case they, with Mr. Dibblee, are included under the general title of Messrs. until their honorary degrees have been regularly conferred, and are designated as Doctors after the colleges had thus honored them. In the minutes of October, 1791, we read of the Reverend Doctors Mansfield and Hubbard as appointed "a committee with the Bishop to confer and concur with Jonⁿ Ingersoll Esqr in drawing a memorial to be presented to the [General] Assembly in behalf of this Convocation," "praying for a repeal of the certificate or conscience act passed at their last session in May." But in October, 1792, we find a Committee appointed of the Rev'd Mr. Bowden, Rev'd Dr. Mansfield (this was after his degree from Yale), Rev'd Messrs. Hubbard and Jarvis. The same distinction as to the last three is observed in another vote at the same meeting. In June, 1797, the Bishop-elect is called in the minutes of Convocation the Rev. Mr. Jarvis, as indeed he is also called in the records of the Convocation which elected him.

It is interesting also to note Bishop Seabury's own way of entering the names of the members of the College of Doctors. His record of all his ordinations, written with his own hand, the property of the Diocese, is unusually full, containing in many cases the names of those who recommended or presented the candidates, as well as other matters of interest. In this record, Mr. Dibblee is not mentioned; Mr. Mansfield's name is once entered with the Doctor's title, but it was after his Yale degree; and Mr. Hubbard is mentioned three times and Mr. Jarvis twice, and in every case, though not as yet doctorated by Yale, the Bishop enters them as Doctor. It would appear then that in formal records Bishop Seabury recognized the title as belonging to the members of the College constituted in 1790, but that the title was not customarily given by the other clergy even in official lists and minutes. It may be added that Bishop Jarvis, in his records of ordinations, calls the Rev. Bela Hubbard "Mr." before the dates of his doctorate from his alma mater, and "Dr." after that time.

One reason why the College of Doctors, established "as the Bishop's council, to be consulted on any emergency that might arise," ceased to be heard of after the second year is, doubtless, to be found in the institution of a Convention of Bishop, Clergy and Laity in the Diocese of Connecticut and in the annual election of a Standing Committee of that Convention to perform certain duties imposed by the General Convention.

On the second day of October, 1789, at Philadelphia, Bishop Seabury, the Rev. Messrs. Abraham Jarvis and Bela

Hubbard, of Connecticut, and the Rev. Dr. Samuel Parker, of Massachusetts, signified in writing their agreement to the Constitution of the Protestant Episcopal Church in the United States of America, and by this act effected the union of the several branches of that Church--perhaps they should be called State Churches--throughout the land. That constitution provided for a General Convocation in 1792 and triennially thereafter, and that the church in each State should be entitled to--not required to send--a representation of both clergy and the laity, to be chosen by the convention of the same. And in the sixth Canon adopted at Philadelphia in 1789 it was required that every candidate for Holy Orders should be recommended by a Standing Committee of the Convention of the State wherein he resided. The clergy of Connecticut met at Litchfield, as has been already noted, on the 2d day of June, 1790, and on the following day "the Constitution and Canons formed by the late General Convention at Philadelphia" were read and "after a short examination were deferred for further consideration" at an adjourned meeting. The adjourned meeting was held at Newtown on the last day of September, on which day the Constitution and Canons were again read; on the following day a motion was made that they be adopted; but in the afternoon, after the alterations in the Book of Common Prayer made by the General Convention had also been read and considered, a motion was made in such a form as to cover both Constitution and Canons and Prayer Book, and we read: "The question was put in these words, 'Whether we confirm the doings of our Proctors in the General Convention at Philadelphia on the 2d day of Octobr. 1789'; which passed in the affirmative by the votes of every member present, the Rev. Mr. Sayre excepted; who then entered the following protest against the aforesaid vote and proceedings of the Convention." The protest is valuable as showing, the minutes of the meeting of 1789 having been lost, that Mr. Jarvis and Mr. Hubbard had been chosen by ballot to meet the Episcopal Clergy at a General Convention to be held at Philadelphia, and to treat with them upon terms of union, but with the restriction to the effect "that their proceedings in the said treaty should not be deemed conclusive till they should be considered and approved by this body of the clergy their constituents." On the following day Mr. Sayre withdrew from the Convention. He was minister of Christ Church, Stratford, and presently coming under ecclesiastical censure, removed to Woodbury and took charge of the parish there; "actual insanity" terminated his life in 1798.

It became necessary, therefore, for the Diocese of Connecticut to have a Standing Committee, and to arrange for representation in following General Conventions. No action looking to either of these ends was taken in 1790, though, as we have seen, the College of Doctors was instituted then; but in the following year, at Watertown on the 5th day of October, it was "Voted, That a Standing Committee be appointed, as required by the 6th Canon agreed on by the Genl. Conventn. at Philadelphia in Octr. 1789, and that the Committee consist of the Rev'd Messrs. Mansfield, Hubbard, Shelton, Ives, and P. Perry. The two first named were members of the College of Doctors; Philo Shelton was a native of Ripton (Huntington), the first person ordained by Bishop Seabury at his first ordination in 1785, and died in 1825; Reuben Ives was born in Cheshire, ordained by Bishop Seabury in 1786, and died in 1836; and Philo Perry was a native of Woodbury, ordained at the same time as Mr. Ives, and died in 1798. In 1792, the Convocation "Voted, That the same persons who were appointed a Standing Committee at the last Convocation be continued to the next." No further record of the appointment of a Standing Committee appears on the records of Convocation; but in June, 1796, the Convention, which, as will be noted presently included lay deputies from the parishes, elected a Standing Committee of three clergymen--the Rev. Messrs. John Bowden, Philo Shelton, and Ashbel Baldwin. From this time to the present the Convention has elected its Standing Committee, and all its members have been clergymen except in the year 1818-1819, Bishop Hobart being in charge of the Diocese, when the Hon. Samuel M. [sic] Johnson and the Hon. Jonathan Ingersoll were elected. There have been many changes of membership, but the Rev. Dr. Harry Croswell was elected thirty-one times consecutively from 1821 to 1852, and the Rev. Dr. William Cooper Mead thirty-three times consecutively from 1840 to 1873, and the Rev. Dr. E. Edwards Beardsley has now been elected each year since 1859, that is, for thirty-two times. So the College of Doctors was almost at once displaced by the Standing Committee of the Diocese.

The summoning of a Convention of Bishop, Clergy and Laity was left until the time appointed when it would be necessary to choose deputies to the General Convention of 1792. In October, 1791, the Convocation "Voted, That each clergyman recommend it to the people of his cure to choose one or more persons to represent them at a Convocation [sic] to be holden at the Church in New Haven on the 30th of May next at 10 o'clock a.m., which representations are to be considered as a Commttee of conference, to confer with the Convocation at that time and place on all matters that respect the temporal interest of the Church." The Convocation met again on the 15th of February, 1792, and among other things "proposed as Lay-Delegates to the Genl. Convention at New York in Septr. next, Messrs. Jonn. Ingersoll, Esqr, Thomas Belden, Esqr, Philip Nichols, Esqr, John Wooster, Esqr, Mark Prindle, Esqr and Ebenezar Baldwin. On the 6th of June, the Convocation met again, in Trinity Church, New Haven, and at the same time the first "Convention of the Bishop, Clergy, and Laity of the Protestant Episcopal Church in Connecticut" was held. There were present at the latter the Bishop, seventeen presbyters, three deacons, and lay-deputies from four parishes in Middlesex County, seven in New Haven County, five in Fairfield County, and five in Litchfield County. A constitution was adopted, which was referred to the Episcopal Societies in the State for their approbation. One article in this Constitution provided that the laity in the Convention should elect the lay deputies to the General Convention; and the laity thereupon chose Thomas Belden, Esq., Philip Nichols, Esq., Mr. Ebenezer Baldwin, and Samuel Marsh, Esq.--three of the six nominated by the clergy in February, and one not so nominated--the clergy choosing the Rev. Ebenezer Dibble, Rev. Dr. Richard Mansfield, Rev. John Bowden, & Rev. Abraham Jarvis. Since 1792 the Convocation has met regularly each year; only in the year 1833, on account of a steamboat accident, there was no quorum at the Convocation in Norwich. There has been no special Convention called since that which

elected Bishop Brownell in October, 1819. But the Convocation of the clergy still continued to meet, and as a rule twice in each year, once at the time of the annual Convention and once in the fall. The business transacted was rather that of a conference or council of clergymen than of a legislative body. In fact, Convocation had no legal existence and its opinions and decisions could carry but a moral weight. Still some of the matters considered were of decided importance, and the beginnings of some most useful institutions were laid by the deliberations of this body. Action was taken from time to time which looked towards the pacification of parish troubles; the notorious Ammi Rogers took up a great deal of time and of patience; the Episcopal Academy of Connecticut, now nearly a century old, had its beginning here with much continued interest, as did also the fund for the relief of aged and infirm clergymen; divers plans were made for the maintenance of that excellent publication the Churchman's Magazine; and agreement was reached as to some points in the manner of "performing divine service," as the phrase ran at that day. Thus the Convocation of this Diocese of Connecticut for many years, both before and after the complete organization of the Diocese and the summoning of its formal Convention, did a work which is worthy of mention in the annals of our Commonwealth. It is to be hoped that at some future day its records may be published and its history written.*

*Publications of the Convocation: Mr. Beach's Sermon, Induction Office, Broadside concerning Ammi Rogers.

Tuesday Dec. 16, 1890

My Dear Dr Hart:

It occurred to me after you had gone that there was another meeting of laymen from the parishes held in Wallingford May 7th 1788--"to ratify or amend the doings of the former Convention at Waterbury." I have found no trace of any subsequent gathering on the subject and this I found in the records of Trinity Parish, New Haven, some years ago and made note of at the time. Dr Saml Nesbitt, then a practising physician and a Warden was appointed to attend as he had been at Waterbury. Trinity Parish did not treat the subject very generously and voted to raise its tax of one half penny on the pound by "quarterly collections in the Church, and that if a sufficient amount should not be obtained by that method, the defic[i]ency should be made up from the Treasury." On the 17th of September 1787--the Vestry voted that ten pounds lawful money be paid to Bishop Seabury--but accompanied the vote with a "proviso that this donation should not be considered as a precedent for any future claims upon the Church by the Bishop." I think the movement of the laymen was to bring about a recognition of the right of the Bishop to some support from the Diocese other than charity.

I intended to speak to you about the Copies of the Seabury Centenary remaining with the Printers in Hartford. If you will reserve to yourself as many as you wish of this Second Edition, the rest may be expressed to me. I have disposed, in one way and another, of about half the copies which came from Southport. Clapp, then of Norwalk, and a Rector in Norwich asked for ten copies each, but they were never paid for.

Very truly yours
E. E. Beardsley

[4] HISTORIANS OF CONNECTICUT

I ought not to venture, Madam and Ladies, to entitle my paper "The Historians of Connecticut." If I called it by that name, prefixing the definite article, I should be led into a controversy, or at least an argument, as to who have been our historians, and I should use a great deal of time in the attempt to make a complete list of them. I should be obliged to begin with the skilful and intrepid Lion Gardiner, and his "Relation of the Pequot Warres," written in 1660, now at our hands through the good offices of the Acorn Club, in an edition printed from the original manuscript; and I should not allow myself to stop until I had traced out the last address or pamphlet which tells the story of any person or event connected with our State. Or I should enter upon a "longsome" disquisition, as good John Eliot would have called it, as to the amount of time or space which must be covered by a book in order that it may be called a history of the State; and I should involve myself in complications, such as those which Horace smiled at, as I attempted to fix a limit to which I should go and beyond which I should not pass. And I should promise myself a delightful hour or two or three while I might describe to you the many excellencies--or at least attractions--of that famous work of Samuel Peters which has never allowed itself to be forgotten, and by reading copious extracts ask you to decide whether it is history or fiction, humorous or sarcastic, a work of imagination or of research; or, still more delightful, ask you to apply to it the principles of both lower and higher criticism, and to resolve it into its constituent parts, attributing it, as you might, to authors of very different degrees of training or information, or accuracy or veracity. But all this, for some reasons which are obvious and for some which I may not disclose, is quite impossible; my title must be anarthrous, as the Greek Grammar says; and I must talk in prosaic strain of "Historians of Connecticut," reminding you of what you already know of the work of a few men who have undertaken to write, in full detail or with extended scope, of the important events which belong to the annals of our good State. You will be patient with me, I hope, if I tell you in advance that the moral which I hope to draw is this: that we need a new History of Connecticut, and that we are, and ought to be, making preparation for it.

Every student of the history of our State is under great obligations to Dr. Benjamin Trumbull--grandfather, by the way, of Senator Lyman Trumbull--for his diligent and careful work. He was born in Hebron, but does not appear to have come under the influence of Dr. Samuel Peters in matters either theological or historical. In 1760 he was ordained in North Haven, and for sixty years, until his death, he continued in that charge. In 1797, when he was 62 years old, he published the first volume of his History of Connecticut, extending to the year 1713; and in 1818, at the age of 83, he published the second volume, continuing the history down to his own early manhood in 1764, and also brought out a new edition of the first volume. In the original preface, he gives a general account of his labors in gathering the

material for his work and in its composition, and tells how he had employed in it "all the leisure hours which he could possibly redeem, by early rising and an indefatigable attention to business, from the stated labors of his office" as pastor and preacher. He examined the original records of Connecticut, New Haven, and the United Colonies, and those in Mr. Prince's collection in Boston; he travelled all over the State in search for material; Governor Trumbull furnished him with documents, Secretary Wyllys rendered him assistance, and the General Assembly gave him access to all the archives of the State. Judging, as he says, that authentic history, "while it instructs, affords an exalted pleasure," and that not only to the "man of genius and curiosity," but also to the "pious man" who "views a divine hand conducting the whole," he thought it wise, in writing this first history of the colony, to make it "full and particular." And doing this, "he wished to assist future historians, and that nothing useful or important, respecting church or state, might be lost." Looking upon himself as a compiler, he "judged his time too precious, and the field of usefulness before him too extensive, to busy himself in rounding periods and guarding against every little matter which might afford business for the critic," while, nevertheless, he "arrived at authenticity, propriety, and perspicuity." The result of this kind of work, as might indeed be expected, is that Dr. Trumbull's history is a work of permanent value and of great interest. There is not reason whatever to question his accuracy or his diligence; he had access to many most valuable papers, some of which are not known to be extant today; and, like other good historians, he knew by a kind of instinct what it was that later generations would want to know. And he did not dwell in any exaggerated way on strictly ecclesiastical matters. Two chapters in the first volume, comprising 80 pages out of 520, suffice for a view of the Churches, while in the second volume the theological chapters fill about a third of the space, a part not at all disproportionate to what was then considered the importance of the subject; and these chapters are by no means the least interesting. Even one who does not feel greatly excited as he approaches the "Wallingford case" can read forty-five pages on the subject and rather enjoy it.

Our State is specially fortunate in having had its early annals written by such a man as Dr. Trumbull. He was, as has indeed been more than suggested already, profoundly interested in the subject which he took in hand, and he was so situated that he was enabled to examine into it in all its details. The first half of the first volume is devoted to events before the union of the two colonies in 1665. The narrative may be corrected in some of its statements, and may be retold in a different style, and the philosophy of the history may be more explicitly brought out; but I doubt if the story will ever be better told or if it will ever be put in better perspective. To illustrate his general conclusions, and to refresh your memory as to his style, let me quote his words as to the prevalence and results of education in Connecticut in the early days: "By these means knowledge at an early period, was generally diffused among people of all ranks. This abundant public and private instruction and constant attention to the morals, industry, and good conduct of the inhabitants, has been the means of that general illumination which has always been observable among the

people of this colony; and of that high degree of civil, ecclesiastical, and domestic peace and order, which for so long a period have rendered them eminent among their neighbors. This has made it feasible to govern them by that free constitution and mild system of laws, by which they have ever been distinguished. To this are owing the wisdom and steadiness of their elections and the integrity and firmness of their public administrations. In this way they have been formed not only to virtue, but to industry, economy, and enterprise. Indeed they have been rendered one of the happiest people upon the earth."

Another extract will serve to show how this judicious author treated matters of controversy, and how well he understood the character and temper of the people of Connecticut. It had been ordered by the General Assembly of this Colony in 1666, after the union with New Haven, that a synod of elders and ministers should be called, in order to "consider of some way or means to bring those ecclesiastical matters, that are of difference in the several plantations, to an issue, by stating some suitable accommodation and expedient thereunto"; that the matters should be "publicly disputed" in the synod, and that it should have power, "being met and constituted, to order the methodize the disputation, so as may most conduce, in their apprehension, to attain a regular issue of their debates." But "the ministers," says Dr. Trumbull, "had objections to meeting in synod, and to the order of the Assembly vesting them with synodical powers," being jealous of their liberties in the premises. The General Assembly thereupon "judged it expedient to alter the name of the council, and to call it an assembly of the ministers of Connecticut, called together by the General Court, for the discussion of the questions stated according to their former order." Not to go into the details of the history, it must suffice to say here that the ministers met, voted that they would not discuss publicly the questions referred to them, adjourned, and, in spite of several attempts to secure another meeting, did not assemble again. The historian thus sums up the matter: "Whether the Assembly really wished to have a general council, or whether this was only a matter of policy to prevent a determination of the questions contrary to their wishes, is not certain. No general council, however, was called, nor does it appear that any motion was made afterwards for that purpose. Indeed, the legislators seem to have fallen under the conviction, that the clergy and churches would not give up their private opinions, in faith and practice, to the decisions of councils, that honest men would think differently, and that they could not be convinced and made of one mind by disputing. No further attempts were made by them to bring these points to a public discussion."

And, if I may be pardoned for making special reference to ecclesiastical matters, as Dr. Trumbull himself does, though it is in no unfair way, let me give the words in which he closes his account of the Wallingford case and at the same time, his second volume: "Mr. Dana was a young man at this time of his ordination, and had little acquaintance with the colony, and doubtless took his measures wholly from the ordaining council. Whatever his sentiments were at the time of his ordination, he doubtless considerably changed them upon further improvement and more

mature consideration. He made no secret of it, that he committed numbers of his first sermons to the flames. It is but just to observe, that he was a scholar and a gentleman, and a man of very general information, of hospitality, and irreproachable morals. The gentlemen of the ordination council never reconciled themselves to their brethren, but died in a state of exclusion from associational and consociational communion.... This was the unhappy issue of the ordination in Wallingford; it divided the town, alienated brethren, effected divisions in the commonwealth and churches, and, after all the arts and struggles of the gentlemen who performed it to exculpate themselves, criminate and cast reproach on others, brought dishonor and evil upon themselves. So it often eventually proves that with that measure men mete it is measured to them again."

Dr. Trumbull also made plans for a general history of the United States from 1492 to 1792, or--to quote his second title--"Sketches of the Divine Agency in their Settlement, Growth, and Protection, and especially in the late Memorable Revolution." He devoted to it what he was pleased to call his "leisure moments" for ten years, and published one volume bringing the history down to 1765. A part of the manuscript of the later volumes--for there were to be three--sent to Dr. Abiel Holmes for his editorship is still preserved.

Dr. Trumbull was a man of strong conviction, but faithful in his search for truth and honest in his statement of what he discovered; he did a great work, a large part of which will not need to be done again, and all of which will be of permanent value to posterity. The History of Connecticut has been somewhat recently republished.

The first formal history of Connecticut after Dr. Trumbull's was that written by Gideon Hiram Hollister, a native of Washington in this State. He was graduated at Yale College in 1840 at the age of twenty-three, and then studied law in Litchfield, which after a short time became his home. He engaged in political and public life, studied enthusiastically the English classics, wrote poems, including a tragedy, and an historical romance, and published in 1855 in two fairly large volumes his History of Connecticut. This extends from the first settlement of the Colony till the time of the adoption of the present Constitution in 1818, but includes some biographical sketches and notes which come to a later date. It is, or was, in a very true sense a popular history. It was written by a man who was in the habit of paying much attention to literary style and with the intention of commending to a later generation, which was in danger of getting out of touch with the past, the virtues and the exploits of their ancestors. For these reasons, it is far more rhetorical than any other history of the State which we have or are likely to have. The author allows free play to his imagination in picturing scenes in the primitive days and adorns the story with suggestions of the thoughts and impressions which must have come to the minds of the actors in it. But he seems withal to have taken much pains in the investigation of facts; he had diligent search made in the ancient records, and inquiries as to events and persons in different parts of the State where they were remembered or where some account of them could be found, and caused it all to be digested for his use.

Thus he labored, as he said, "to present in a lively way the incidents connected with the progress of our people, from the earliest existence of our government. Sketches of individual character," he continues, "of domestic life, victims of 'the age of home-spun,' of the privations and the struggles which could tame the wild lands, wild men, and wild beasts of a new country, and sow the fallow ground with the seeds of civil and religious liberty, can alone 'hold the mirror up to nature' and show us the very body and soul of our past." For this reason Mr. Hollister has rather given us extended descriptions of important scenes, sketches of the progress of events in England, and observations as to their influence upon events on this side of the ocean, than general outlines of political and social progress or philosophical reflections upon the meaning of it. Two hundred octavo pages in rather small type are given to the time before the charter, and thirty-five pages to King Philip's War; and the first volume, ending its narrative with the siege of Louisbourg, adds full chapters on early manners and customs and on the established religion in the colony. These contain much that is interesting, though adorned with "flowers of imagination and flights of fancy." Thus, speaking of the good descent of many of the early planters, he says: "It turns out upon investigation, that many a tomb that holds the dust of some pioneer whose memory is now cherished by a numerous posterity, yet cannot be distinguished from the surrounding earth, simply because no monument was placed above it to mark the spot, was entitled from the birth of its tenant to be garnished with a coat of arms among the most honorable of those that swell the volumes of heraldry with devices to modern republican eyes so quaint and strange. But what had they, who had spent their lives in waging war with the formularies of the past time that appear so irksome to them--what had men who made it a part of their education to discard the factitious distinctions of the world--to do with the gauntleted hand, the helmeted brow, the griffins, the lions, the strawberries, and the storks of the herald's college? The very fact that most of these symbols suggested to the mind the myths of paganism and idolatry would of itself make these objects of suspicion to many." This rhetorical, general statement is followed by an interesting collection of facts as to the families of early governors, what they endured and to what they trained their families; and in fact the whole chapter, though not as exhaustive or based on as thorough exploration of instances, is like one of those with which McMaster enlivens his History of the People of the United States.

The second volume, I am inclined to think, goes less into personal details, but it treats the narrative with great fulness; and the author had the advantage of a pretty full search for information of various kinds made by an antiquarian friend. In treating of the pre-Revolutionary and Revolutionary periods, special care was taken to show how full a part Connecticut took in bearing the burdens of pecuniary and personal responsibility, and how large a share of the credit for the success of expeditions belonged to her. To repeat what has been already said: While Mr. Hollister's history will not be studied as a primary source of information, it will serve to picture before us the deeds of our ancestors and to quicken our respect for them and our emulation of their virtues.

A few words must suffice for the <u>Historical Collections of Connecticut</u> of John Warner Barber. It is, as you well know and as the title-page of the book describes it, a "General Collection of interesting facts, traditions, biographical sketches, anecdotes, &c., relating to the history and antiquities of every town in Connecticut, with geographical descriptions." Mr. Barber was a native of Windsor, born in 1798; the first edition of the volume with which we have now to do appeared in 1836, and another with some additions about 1854; at the time of his death in 1885, at the somewhat advanced age of 87, it was said that he was engaged upon an entirely new edition, to be adorned with many new pictures engraved as the former ones had been, by himself. These engravings are by no means the least interesting or valuable things in the book. They stand out before the memory of those who in childhood looked at them again and again; we recall the villages which had certainly a family resemblance, with houses and meeting-houses, occasionally a courthouse and once in a while a jail, of the same quiet and simple type, just about homely enough to be attractive. The author speaks of them in his preface, deprecating hasty judgment: "The numerous engravings interspersed throughout this work were (with five or six exceptions) executed from drawings made on the spot, by the author of this work. Before deciding upon the correctness of these representations, he wishes his readers to consider that the appearance of any place will vary considerably as it is viewed from different points; thus, a north view will appear quite different from one taken at the south. A person not being used to see a place from the point from which the drawing is taken, it may not at first sight be readily recognized. Before any view is condemned as being incorrect, it will be necessary, in order to form a correct judgment, to stand on the place from whence the drawing was made."

The gentle deprecation of criticism is not unreasonable; and I am sure that most of us would rather trust Mr. Barber's engravings than our own memories for a representation to our minds of the appearance of our rural towns and villages. And where else than to his pages can we turn for an outline of the history of each town? He tells us when it was settled, and whence the settlers came; he gives us brief information as to the important events which have happened in it, the distinguished men to whom it has given birth, the trade or manufactures which have made it noted; he has collected from old newspapers items of varying interest, and copied from tombstones inscriptions in honor of the dead; he has, in short, played the part of the antiquarian who has assumed--and not unreasonably--that his readers will be interested in what has interested him: "It may be thought, perhaps, by some"--thus he writes--"that an apology ought to be made for inserting many things contained in this book; some things may be thought too trivial, others too marvellous, to be recorded. With regard to the first, it ought to be borne in mind, that many things which at the first sight may appear to us to be of little moment, may hereafter be deemed of much importance. With regard to the latter objection, it may be observed that the history of any people may be considered as erroneous which does not give an account of their religious beliefs and opinions &c. however erroneous. Although in this age most of us may smile at what we consider the

superstitions and weaknesses of our forefathers, yet it may be well to reflect that Sir Matthew Hale, Dr. Johnson, men of the greatest intellect the world ever produced, lie under the same imputations. Compared with these men, many of those who affect to smile at their opinions are but mere children in understanding." Good Mr. Barber's book may not be exactly history--it never claimed to be--but it is interesting and will help many for a long time to come to answer historical questions.

These three works give us examples of three ways of writing history, or at least of making contributions to it--the serious, the humorous, and the illustrative. Each of them has its use, if it is not taken for more than it really is. The collector of local lore, like Mr. Barber, the writer of grim satire, like Dr. Peters, the student of facts and principles, like Dr. Trumbull--each leaves to posterity what posterity, if it is wise, will use in drawing its picture and making its judgment of times that are past. A constant example of each can be found in the public records, the political pamphlets, the weekly or daily journals of each epoch; and all must be consulted and studied, as well the sarcastic as the serious, as well the local and petty as that which seems more general and more important. It is by such use of what has been left to us in writing that we are getting histories of peoples and of communities; and we may well believe that the men of a century hence will understand us better than we understand ourselves, and far better than we understand our ancestors of a century ago.

Professor Alexander Johnston's volume in the American Commonwealths series--<u>Connecticut, a Study of a Commonwealth-Democracy</u>--marked an advance in the study of our history and turned the thoughts of many students in the right direction. New methods had begun to prevail in the examination of original sources, in careful investigation of social and political tendencies, in the preparation and use of monographs on important men or events, and in generalizations from the facts which had been carefully brought together. Professor Johnston gave to us Connecticut people a better view of the history of the State and of its meaning than we had ever had before. In his comparatively small volume he set in perspective the important events of our annals, told us of principles that ran through them all and of the application of those principles, and made a most interesting panorama of pictures which had often seemed to lack distinctness and definite color. It was easy, and for that matter necessary, to find fault with the book--to say that the author viewed the history of our State rather from without than from within, and that he had not always followed the best authorities; that he had listened to men of Massachusetts who had never understood Connecticut; and that he went to New Haven for information about the river colonies; and that he did not rightly understand the meaning of some things which he rightly described. Then also it was a bit trying to read on the third page that there was no spot within the borders of the State a thousand feet above the sea-level; and the suspicious reader began to wonder whether he could trust like statements when he had no information at hand to prove or disprove them. Leaving out of the question any difference of opinion as to the authority of the first Constitution of 1639, whether, that is to say, it was a grant of power from three existing municipalities or

was the act of the freemen of one community consulting as to the common welfare, Professor Johnston understood the difference between the Plymouth and Connecticut polity on the one hand and the Massachusetts and New Haven polity on the other, in that the latter made Church membership a condition for admission to the suffrage and the former did not. What then did he mean by saying that "the ecclesiastical excrescence upon" the Constitution (or Fundamental Orders), "probably inevitable at the time, but absolutely contrary to the spirit of the whole instrument, was to remain and trouble the commonwealth until the political system came fully up to its own original standard in 1818"? The words are rather strong to use of the one ecclesiastical provision, "that the Governor be always a member of some approved congregation"; it is hardly possible to see in this an "excrescence," or to imagine how it troubled the commonwealth till 1818; the ecclesiastical question which did clamor for a solution and received it in that year was one that had to do with taxation and with the right of a citizen to live apart from connection with any ecclesiastical society. Later on in the history, the description of the act of 1727, which gave to Episcopalians, statedly attending worship according to their own forms, relief under certain conditions from paying for the maintenance of the minister of the standing order, is not as accurate as it should be; and it is rather an exaggeration to say that it "cut the tie that had so long bound town and church together." Nor does the author seem to understand how severe was the treatment meted out to the separatist Congregational societies, the "new lights," who were not reckoned "sober disserters" as Episcopalians and Baptists (and perhaps Quakers) were. Or, to come to another minor matter, but one in which we have a right to look for accuracy, while it is true that the city of Hartford now covers the whole township--though township is not a Connecticut word--yet it is not true, as is implied, that it covers the whole of the area of the old town, only one-tenth of which was included in the city limits of 1784.

In fact, the volume is one which contains many inaccuracies in matters of detail, such as irritate the reader and show some misunderstanding of fundamental matters, as in treating of the origin of the government of the river towns. But, on the other hand, it is very interesting; it brings out the leading characteristics of the people of this colony and state, and shows how these found their expression in history, and how there has been growth and progress in them. I doubt if many readers who had come in one way or another across stories of men or events of colonial or revolutionary times had seen in them the working of principles and the operation and forming of a type of character until Professor Johnston guided them to see it. Massachusetts, as he says, "posed as the pronounced champion of colonial liberties," feeling it "incumbent upon her to assume a more or less decided public attitude, and equally incumbent upon her strongest neighbor, Connecticut, to support her by a similar course." "The consistent policy of Connecticut, on the other hand, was to avoid notoriety and public attitudes; to secure her privileges without attracting needless notice; to act as intensely and vigorously as possible when action seemed necessary and promising; but to say as little as possible, yield as little as possible, and evade as much as possible when open re-

sistence was evident folly." "And its success was remarkable; it is safe to say that the diplomatic skill, forethought, and self-control showed by the men who governed the course of Connecticut during this period have seldom been equalled on the larger fields of the world's history." An example is seen in the treatment of the regicides and of those who were searching for them, so different from the conduct of the more Massachusetts-like colony of New Haven in the same matter. "The authorities of Connecticut," so writes the historian, "were as anxious as those of New Haven that no harm should come to the regicides, and the fugitives found as frequent and as secure refuge in Hartford as anywhere else. When the regicides were really not within their jurisdiction, the Connecticut authorities always seized the opportunity to make their zeal in the king's service evident. They overwhelmed the royal commissioners with warrants, letters of authority, and proclamations; the colony was in a ferment because of their haste to lay hands on the criminals; they were his majesty's most faithful servants. Under the like circumstances, the New Haven authorities showed a decorous satisfaction in saying No to the commissioners, which went far to discount the sincerity of their denials when the fugitives were suspected to be concealed within their jurisdiction with their privity." Yet, that it may not seem that he gives moral commendation to the more canny course and denies it to that which was more outspoken, it is well to read, two or three pages further on, the contrast which he draws between the "simple and manly terms," as he calls them, in which New Haven, albeit tardily and unwillingly, acknowledged Charles the Second "to be our sovereign lord and king," and "the servility of the style which the habit of the times at court seems to have extorted from Connecticut." Professor Johnston, also, as he passed on, showed the influence and the strength of the town system, and how on occasions of emergency the people could fall back upon its powers--call them "reserved" or "inherent" or what not--in order to carry them safely and with due formality over an emergency. In this way, as I was saying, he gave us a history full of life and interest, accurate in the general effect of the picture which it presented, even if there was some inaccuracy or carelessness in its details; and a beginning was made towards that full history of our colony and state which is so truly a desideratum. The author died not very long after the volume was published, before it was possible to arrange for a second edition; but not before he had expressed himself as grateful for the reception accorded his work here, appreciative of the kind tone--so he was good enough to put it--in which corrections and criticisms had been offered, and anxious to do all that he could, within the limits of his work, to bring it to perfection. We shall long regret that he was not able to do what he hoped to do with the encouragement that was offered him.

During these later years, material for the history of Connecticut has been accumulating. Researches have been making among the original sources; men with good opportunities and good judgment have been collecting materials; monographs have been written on important periods, prominent men, and principles of government; papers of permanent value have been prepared for historical societies; and thus a vast deal of work has been done which need never be repeated. It has been a time in which much has been

accomplished in the way of writing what the French call "Mémoires pour servir à l'histoire." Such investigations as those which Professor Charles M. Andrews has made concerning the River Towns; such papers as Judge Baldwin has prepared with great patience and attention to detail; such publications as those of the Acorn Club; such work as has been undertaken by your society and societies of kindred purposes; centenary, bi-centenary, and quarter-millennial commemorations of the foundation of towns and churches, calling for much careful study of our origins and our progress; all these have made and are making contributions to our knowledge of the history of Connecticut. And all this is bringing nearer the time when a complete history of Connecticut can be written, in that full and exact and interesting way in which we expect to have history written now. It ought to be the work of a master student and master writer; it ought to--it will--vindicate for our state the position which it holds among States and governments; it will, from the very importance of that of which it treats, become a necessary part of the working library of every student of history; it will find its way prepared by the diligent labors and skilful pens of many men and women; it will be welcomed by all who already know the importance of the subject of which it treats, and many others will soon learn its value. If we are in any way contributing to such a result as this, our Societies and Associations will more than justify their existence; and we shall best show our appreciation of the labors of former historians by making it possible for the future historian to supersede their work.

THE COMMON SCHOOLS OF CONNECTICUT

[5]

Almost immediately after the settlement of the three river towns in 1635 and the foundation of New Haven in 1638, the inhabitants began to make provision for the establishment of schools. The earliest records now extant which relate to this matter in the two most important towns--the date in Hartford is 1643, and in New Haven 1640--shows that free schools were already in existence there, and there is no doubt that other towns were making like provision. The first code of laws of the Connecticut colony was adopted in 1650; it provided, "That the Selectmen of every Towne, in the several precincts and quarters where they dwell, shall have a vigilant eye over theire brethren and neighbors, to see first, that none of them shall suffer so much Barbarisme in any of theire familyes as not to endeavor to teach by themselves or others theire children and apprentices so much Learning as may inable them perfectly to read the Inglish tongue and knowledge of the Capitall Lawes"; and it further ordered "That every Towneshipp within this Jurissdiction, after the Lord hath increased them to the number of fifty houshoulders, shall then forthwith, appoint one within theire Towne to teach all such children as shall resorte to him, to write and read, whose wages shall bee paid either by the parents or masters of such children, or by the Inhabitants in generall by way of supplye, as the major parte of those who order the prudentialls of the Towne shall appointe; provided that those who send theire children bee not oppressed by more than they can have them taught for in other Townes"; and "That when any Towne shall increase to the number of one hundred families or housholders, they shall sett up a Grammer Schoole, the masters thereof being able to instruct youths so farr as they may be fitted for the University." The first code of New Haven colony, completed in 1655, required that all children and apprentices should, "through God's blessing, attain at least so much as to be able duly to read the Scriptures and other good and profitable printed Books in the English tongue, being their native language"; but the parents or masters might do this "either by their own ability and labour, or by improving such Schoolmaster, or helps and means as the Plantation doth afford, or the family may conveniently provide." In 1665 the colony of New Haven was merged in that of Connecticut, and the laws of the river colony were extended over New Haven and the towns which had been confederated with it.

The second code of Connecticut, that of 1672, instead of requiring that there should be a Grammar school in every town of one hundred families (a requirement which probably had not been enforced), ordered that in each county town there should be set up and kept a grammar school for the use of the county. At this time there were four counties in the colony, bearing the names of their county towns: Hartford, New Haven, New London, and Fairfield. In 1677 the length of a school year was defined to be at least nine months; in the following year it was provided that every town of thirty families should "mayntaine a schoole"; while in 1690 the required time was reduced to six months in a year. It is quite certain that these laws, good as they were in their intention, were not always obeyed; and probably there were some cases in which it would have been impossible to enforce them. In the year last mentioned a law was passed, making it the duty of the Grand Jurors of the several towns to "sattisfy themselves wither all children under age and servants can read well the English tongue, or be in a good procedure to learn the same," and to report the names of delinquent parents or masters to the county court; the preamble to the law declaring that "notwithstanding the former orders made the education of children and servants, there are many persons unable to read the English tongue, and thereby uncapable to read the holy word of God or the good laws of the colony." As to the grammar schools, New Haven jurisdiction had actually opened one in 1660; but it was closed in 1662 on account of the political "distractions of the times". But the generous provisions of the will of Governor Edward Hopkins, who died in 1658 (though the estate was not distributed until 1664, or a final settlement made till 1712), led to the establishment of the Hopkins Grammar Schools in Hartford and New Haven. The former was for a century an ordinary free school for all the children of the town, and it was not really made a grammar school til 1798; but in New Haven the school has, ever since its foundation in 1664, been conducted in accordance with the wishes of its founder. The legacy of Robert Bartlett of New London, in 1673, enabled that town to establish a public Latin school about 1700. It does not appear that Fairfield complied with the duty laid upon it as a county town till about the same time; and its grammar school, whatever it was, having no endowment, has left no history. For the assistance of these four schools the General Assembly made grants of land and of money. In 1690 an order was made, with evident reference to the two existing Hopkins schools, that there should be "two free schools kept and maynetayned

in this Colony, for the teaching of all such children as can com there, after they can first read the psalter, to teach such reading, writeing, arithmetick, the Lattin and Greek tongues, the one at Hartford the other at New Haven."

The "code of regulations" of the New Haven Grammar School, made in 1684, shows where it began the instruction of youth. It provided, that "noe boyes be admitted in the said schoole for the learning of English books but such as have been before taught to spell their letters well and begin to Read, thereby to perfect theire right Spelling and Reading, or to learn to write and cypher for numeracion, and addicion, and noe further; and all others either two young and not instructed in letters and spelling and all Girles be excluded as improper and inconsistent with such a grammar school as the law enjoines, and is the Designe of this Settlement." It may be added that once admitted, the boys were expected to study diligently, for there is no mention of holidays or vacations; and it is directed "that the Master and Schollars duly attend the schoole hours, Viz., from 6 in the morning to 11 a Clock in the forenoon, and from 1 a Clock in the afternoone to 5 a Clock in the afternoone in Summer and 4 in Winter."

It will be seen from what has been said, that even had the intention of the laws been carried out, the youth of the country towns would have had but a limited education. Still, a constant effort was made to enforce what could be enforced, and to improve upon it as far as was possible; a good number of Connecticut youths were sent to the College at Cambridge for a higher education than this colony could afford, and offerings of produce were received and transmitted by public authority for the assistance of students there. The very fact of the establishment of the Collegiate School at Saybrook at the beginning of the new century testifies to the appreciation on the part of Connecticut of the value of as good an education as could be offered, for all who could enjoy it. The whole population of the Colony in 1700, it should be remembered, numbered little more than fifteen thousand.

The year which saw the establishment of the institution destined to become famous as Yale College and University, was also marked by a revision of the laws and the introduction of important changes in the system of public schools. It was now required that every town having at least seventy householders should provide "constantly" (and this was presently defined to mean for eleven months in each year) "a sufficient schoolmaster to teach children and youth to read and write," while every smaller town should have a like "sufficient School Master" for half of the year. Another change was with regard to maintenance of the schools. Heretofore the towns had paid their schoolmasters from the funds which they raised by taxation, unless indeed any town should devise some other means of payment. Now the school tax was made uniform throughout the colony, and fixed at the rate of forty shillings on every thousand pounds (or, as we should reckon it, two mills on a dollar); and if the amount thus raised did not suffice, "and there is not any estate given by any charitable persons, or not sufficient together with the levie," then half of the deficiency must be made up by the town, and half by the parents or masters of

children that should go to the school, unless any town should make other arrangements. If any town did not provide a teacher, the constables were to collect the school tax of the town, and pay it into the county treasury. When school parishes or societies and school districts were established, the principle of this law, which remained in force for nearly one hundred and twenty years, was extended to them, so that each division of the town received for school purposes that portion of the two-mill tax which was raised within its limits. During a time of great political and financial depression, beginning in 1754, the rate of this tax was for a time diminished; but in 1767 it was restored to the former rate.

Another change, which was made in 1712, substituted the parish for the town as a school unit. The parishes had grown up naturally under the Standing Order or Congregational establishment of the early days, when the inhabitants of remote parts of towns became able to support ministers of their own, and obtained permission from the General Assembly to organize a separate ecclesiastical society of parishes with definite metes and bounds. Occasionally a theological controversy and separation was terminated, as in Hartford and Guilford, by allowing two societies to exist with the same territorial limits; but the parishes which were taken in 1712 for school societies had each its own limits: often, where there had been no reason for a separate ecclesiastical organization, the parish was coterminous with the town; sometimes a town was divided into parishes; and sometimes a parish was made up of parts of two or more towns. At first the school law treated these parishes as districts of the towns; but after a while all school affairs were administered by them, and not by the towns. The extent of the change thus introduced may be seen when it is stated that, at the time of the breaking out of the Revolutionary War, there were in the seventy-three towns of Connecticut, no fewer than one hundred and ninety parishes "in the capacity of school societies," as the law of 1795 first designated them. These latter had the entire charge of school matters from 1798 to 1856. Another innovation, introduced in Windsor as early as 1723, and later made lawful for any town, was the division of towns and societies into districts. Before 1800 these came to have certain corporate powers and could lay taxes for building or repairing school houses, and in 1836 when they had become greatly multiplied in number, they were made bodies corporate. Of their later history notice will be made further on.

We turn now to consider the school funds, local or general, as distinguished from the taxes laid by the towns for the support of schools. A few private benefactions, designated for schools of a higher grade or grammar schools, have been already noted. For a long time there were few funds, the interest of which could be applied to the common schools, except those which came from what was known in Connecticut as the Western Lands. These were not in the remote west, but in the northwest corner of the colony itself, included within its charter boundaries, but not before 1687 laid out as towns or granted to individual proprietors. In that year, on account of apprehensions as to the claims which it was feared would be made by Sir Edmund Andros, in his capacity as Governor of New England, including Connecticut, a special session of the General Court was held. At this session grants were made

of all the land of which the title was still held by the colony, in order that Governor Andros might not be able to claim any part of it for the Crown. The largest grant, including more than half of the present Litchfield County, was made to the towns of Hartford and Windsor, nominally that they might "make a plantation of villages thereon." The immediate purpose of the grant was accomplished; but at the end of Sir Edmund Andros's administration, when the government of the colony was resumed under the old charter, a violent controversy arose as to the ownership of these western lands. It was asserted on the one hand, that it had been distinctly understood that the towns of Hartford and Windsor should but hold the title to these lands until the "usurpation," as it was termed, should come to an end, and that, as there had been no consideration for the grant, there could be no just claim advanced to ownership against the colony. On the other hand, the towns argued that by the explicit act of the General Assembly they had acquired a title to the lands in question; and they proceeded to lay them out and to offer them for sale. Against this action, the General Assembly forbade all surveyors to bound or lay out any of the land without special order. Finally, in 1726, the General Assembly proposed a compromise, which was accepted by the towns. Leaving out Litchfield, where a settlement had been already made, and some smaller tracts, the debatable land was divided into two equal parts, the eastern half (where the names of New Hartford, Hartland, Harwinton, and Winchester still testify to this part of the history) being assigned to the towns, and the western half being retained as the property of the colony. This western half was divided into seven towns; and in five of these (the other two, as it would appear, having special treatment), after three hundred acres had been reserved for Yale College, the land was divided into fifty-three rights: one for the first minister that should be settled there, one for the support of the ministry of the town, one for the support of the local school, and fifty to be sold for the endowment of the schools in the fifty towns of the colony, the proceeds to be divided among these fifty towns according to their respective grand lists of taxable property and to be held by the towns as permanent funds. If a town had more than one parish, the fund was to be divided among the parishes. Owing to the loss of old records, it cannot now be ascertained how much was received from the sale of this land. It was accomplished about 1740; and the money distributed under the law, together with certain excise money, became the funds, part of which at least is now held or accounted for by the towns, either as always theirs or as received back from the school societies or parishes.

When, in 1889, a careful inquiry was made by the State Board of Education into the origin and condition of local school funds, only twenty towns reported funds which were known or believed or which might be presumed to have been derived from the sale of lands in Litchfield county or in the "west." It is gratifying to record, however, that one hundred and nineteen of the one hundred and sixty-eight towns in the state had at that time local school funds amounting in the aggregate to over two hundred and eighty-two thousand dollars ($282,000); that about $175,000 of this sum was given before 1800; that they appear to have been wisely managed as separate funds, even where they are represented by town notes; and that considerably more than half of the income is applied to secondary education. A study of the tables as given in the report for 1890 is very interesting. In many cases the funds have come from legacies; the towns of Saybrook and Old Saybrook still enjoy the benefits of a sum left by will in 1689, the gift being next in age, as it would appear, to the gifts of Governor Hopkins to New Haven and Hartford and that of Robert Bartlett to New London; while many other towns profit by the income of like pious gifts made at a later day. West Hartford has a fund of $500 supposed to be the proceeds of the sale of old common lands; Farmington has nearly $9,500 at interest which came from the sale of surplus highway lands. In this latter case the original proprietors left wide strips of land for highways, where highways were never needed. In 1723 the town began to sell this unused public land, and in 1784 it was voted that the money arising from these sales should be invested and the interest used for the support of the schools. Of some special gifts it may be possible to speak later.

The school fund of the state of Connecticut, created by act of the General Assembly in 1795, has a remarkable history. Its source was the sale of land in the state of Ohio, known as the Western Reserve, which was owned by Connecticut under the provisions of the charter granted by King Charles II in 1662. By that charter there was conveyed to the "Governour and Company of the English Collony of Connecticut in New England in America" all that part of the country "bounded on the east by Norrogancet River, commonly called Norrogancett Bay, where the said river falleth into the Sea, and on the North by the line of the Massachusetts Plantation, and on the South by the Sea, and in longitude as the lyne of the Massachusetts colony, running from east to west, that is to say from the said Norrogancett Bay on the east to the south Sea on the West part." The territory thus defined was therefore a strip of land, lying between 41° and 42° 2' north latitude, and extending from the Rhode Island line to the Pacific Ocean. Connecticut and Rhode Island after a while came to an agreement that Norrogancett Bay meant Pawcatuck River, and the terminus a quo was thus defined. The parts of New York and New Jersey included in the strip of land had already been covered by other grants, and Connecticut could lay no claim to them. But to the west of the Delaware River all the land on the continent between the lines of latitude already noted were included by the royal charter within the bounds of Connecticut; and this inclusion, it should be remembered, carried the claim to ownership of the land as well as to jurisdiction. The charter of Pennsylvania, granted in 1681, covered a part of the territory which nineteen years before had been given to Connecticut: and a controversy ensued as soon as the disputed territory was found to be of value to settlers. Connecticut gave title to the first settlers on the Susquehanna, divided the land into towns, established schools and appointed officers there; and the inhabitants were from 1774 to 1782 represented in the Connecticut General Assembly. Pennsylvania also asserted her claim, and disputes arose which actually assumed the form of a war. Finally, in 1782, a court of commissioners appointed by Congress decided the controversy in favor of the later charter, and Connecticut was obliged to abandon its claim to any land within the boundaries of the state of Pennsylvania.

But her claim to the land within the specified lines of latitude west of Pennsylvania was not disputed; and in November, 1783, Governor Trumbull issued a proclamation, at the request of the General Assembly, warning all persons against settling upon it without the consent of Connecticut. Less than three years later, the General Assembly, recognizing the impossibility of holding the whole of the long strip of land to which it had a nominal title, and yielding to the suggestions of Congress, authorized the conveyance to the United States of all its territory west of the line drawn parallel to the western boundary of Pennsylvania and one hundred and twenty miles distant from it. The cession was at once accepted by Congress, and it left Connecticut the owner and ruler of about three million acres of land, which came to be known as the Western Reserve, or New Connecticut, the northern part of the present state of Ohio. In the year 1800 Congress relinquished all claim on the part of the United States to the soil of the Western Reserve, and Connecticut ceded to the United States all jurisdictional claim over the territory.

In 1792 the ownership of the state was limited by the grant of half a million acres at the western end of the Reserve, as a compensation to the inhabitants of towns on the shore of Long Island Sound for the losses which they had suffered during the Revolution. The tract was known as the "Fire Lands." The territory which remained was seen to be of great prospective value; and it must be confessed that other motives than those of pure patriotism, or love of education, weighed with the men who formed what would now be called a syndicate for its purchase. Connecticut had already in a way put the land into open market, but none of it had been sold. Presently, however, Connecticut capitalists were beginning to agitate for the purchase of the Western Reserve, seeing in it the opportunity of a successful investment, and stimulated by the enormous profits that had come from the appreciation of government stocks. To make sure of the support of an influential part of the community for their proposition to buy these lands from the State, they proposed that the proceeds of the sale should be devoted to public or quasi-public uses. The first bid was for the influence of the "Standing Order of Christians," the Congregationalists (often called Presbyterians), who had been the establishment, practically from the first, and formally from the date of the Saybrook platform in 1708. A bill was introduced in the General Assembly in 1791, appropriating the avails of the sale of the Reserve lands among the established ecclesiastical societies, that they might be relieved from taxation for the support of their ministers. The bill was continued to the next session and was never enacted. Two years later, a committee having been appointed to sell the lands and give deeds to the purchasers, a bill was introduced providing that the interest of the funds to be created by the sale of the Reserve should be "appropriated to the use and benefit of the several ecclesiastical societies, churches, or congregations of all denominations in this state, to be by them applied to the support of their respective ministers or preachers of the gospel and schools of education, under such rules and regulations as shall be adopted by this or some future session of the General Assembly." This bill, so worded as to gain the favor of all religious bodies, passed the lower house by a majority of thirteen and the upper house by a nearly unanimous vote. It led to very warm discussion throughout the state, in the

pulpit and in the press, among politicians and all citizens. At the next session, six months later, the lower house passed a bill for its repeal by a nearly two-thirds vote, while the upper house, more susceptible to the influence of the capitalists, defeated it; but both houses passed a resolution suspending the sale of lands. In October the upper house passed a new proposition, which it was thought would appeal to all citizens and avoid ecclesiastical and anti-ecclesiastical objections, to the effect that the money to be received from the Reserve lands should be divided among the school societies or parishes according to their lists of polls and taxable estate, and that the interest should be expended either for the maintenance of schools or for the support of the ministry, as the voters of each society should annually prescribe. The lower house would not pass this bill, but continued it to the next session. The controversy then broke out anew. The debate in the General Assembly on the former bill had been reported at length and published in nearly all the newspapers of the state; and now preachers and journalists, and in fact everybody, pressed the arguments on one side or the other. President Dwight's Thanksgiving-day sermon on the subject was published, by continuation, in three numbers of the Connecticut Courant. Town meetings took up the matter for formal discussion and vote; the town of Cheshire, for instance, disapproved "of the contemplated appropriation of the monies to be raised by the sale of our western lands," giving as one reason that it believed "the same appropriation to be an introductory step towards establishing a certain and permanent civil provision for a certain and permanent sacerdotal order; a provision which, in other ages and nations, has gone forward and proclaimed that the downfall of liberty and true religion was hastening after, and of course a provision against which the experience of ages admonished us to guard with a jealous eye." The town added the quite unnecessary vote, "That we esteem it the indispensable duty of the inhabitants of this state, and especially of the several towns in their corporate capacities, to express their sentiments upon the subject of the preceding votes." Hartford, Wethersfield, Killingworth, and other towns adopted resolutions in favor of the proposed appropriations. The whole subject was certainly well ventilated.

At last, at the May session of the General Assembly in 1795, a new bill was introduced and passed. It provided, that the principal sum to be received from the sale of the lands belonging to the state, lying west of Pennsylvania, should be and remain a perpetual fund, the interest of which should be appropriated to the support of the schools in the several school societies, to be paid to said societies according to the list of polls and rateable estate. If, however, any society at a legal meeting, warned for that purpose only, two-thirds of the legal voters present concurring, should "apply to the General Assembly requesting liberty to improve their proportion of said interest, or any part thereof, for the support of the Christian ministry or the public worship of God," the General Assembly was given "full power to grant such request during their pleasure." In this latter case, the money was to be distributed among the religious societies, churches, or congregations of all denominations of Christians within the society, according to the taxable lists of their respective members. This permission, as might have been expected, was in no case asked, and the whole fund was kept for the use of the schools. The bill was passed by a vote of 94 to 52 in the lower

house, and it probably met with no serious opposition in the upper house. A committee was at once appointed to negotiate for the lands; all the contracts, if there should be more than one, were to be consummated together, the purchasers to hold their respective parts in common and not in severalty; and the committee was instructed to make no sale for less than $1,000,000, present value in specie. At the October session the committee reported that they had effected a sale of the Western Reserve for $1,200,000, payable in five years, with interest after two years. The land was taken by thirty five people, as in thirty-six shares of quite unequal value. They were at once organized into the "Connecticut Land Company," the history of which lies beyond the limit of this paper.

Thus was founded the Connecticut School Fund, the first dividend of which to the school societies was made in March, 1799. It was managed until 1810 by a committee appointed by the General Assembly, and paid dividends amounting in all to nearly $457,000. By this time, the thirty-six original bonds on personal security had become nearly five hundred bonds, mostly secured by mortgages on real estate. Many of the securities were of doubtful value, and much interest was overdue. The accounts were in woeful confusion, and it seemed quite probable that the fund was seriously impaired. It was decided to put the whole matter into the charge of one man, to be called the commissioner of the school fund; and the Hon. James Hillhouse left the seat in the Senate of the United States which he had held for sixteen years to accept the new office. The admirable manner in which he discharged it is an honorable page in the history of Connecticut. "Without a single litigated suit," we are told, "or a dollar paid for counsel, he reduced the disordered management to an efficient system, disentangled its affairs from loose and embarrassed connections with personal securities and indebted estates, rendered it productive of a large, regular, and increasing dividend, and converted its doubtful claims into well-secured and solid capital." At the end of fifteen years, in which the annual dividends to the schools had averaged $52,000, he left the fund with a principal of nearly $1,720,000. To this principal sum he himself contributed over $10,000, which had been personal gifts to himself from three individuals in recognition of the services rendered to them while settling the accounts of the fund--a sum which, with its interest to the time of his retirement, amounted to more than the whole salary that he received from the State.

In 1825 Mr. Hillhouse was succeeded by the Hon. Seth P. Beers, who held the office of commissioner for almost a quarter of a century. He left it with a principal of nearly $2,050,000, and an annual income of about $133,400, the average during his term having been nearly $98,000. Since 1820 the dividends of the school societies had been apportioned, not according to their grand lists, but according to the number of children between the ages of four and sixteen--a principle of division which has been retained ever since. The dividend in 1826 was eighty-five cents for each child; it reached its maximum in 1849 and 1850, when it became $1.50; then, with an increased population, and later with diminished rates of interest as well, it fell off. For several years after 1859 it was $1.00, with a recovery in 1875 to $1.10. In the last-mentioned year the income was

about $148,000; in 1885 it was nearly $121,000; and in 1895 it was about $124,000. In 1894, after the dividend had remained for some time at seventy-five cents for each enumerated child, it fell to a lower amount; then, in accordance with a provision of a law passed in the preceding year, a small sum was drawn from the treasury and added to the income of the fund, that the dividend might remain at seventy-five cents. The last reported principal of the fund is a little over $2,000,000, of which about five-eighths is loaned on bond and mortgage in Connecticut. It may be added here, though it is by way of anticipation, that for some years, the state has paid to the schools from its treasury, in addition to the grant for the school fund, a dollar and a half towards the education of each enrolled child.

The position of the school fund was made especially secure by a section of the Constitution of the state adopted in 1818. It is in these words, "The fund, called the School Fund, shall remain a perpetual fund, the interest of which shall be inviolably appropriated to the support and encouragement of the public or common schools throughout the state, and for the equal benefit of all the people thereof. The value and amount of said fund shall, as soon as practicable, be ascertained in such manner as the General Assembly may prescribe, published, and recorded in the Comptroller's office; and no law shall ever be made authorizing said fund to be diverted to any other use than the encouragement and support of public of common schools, among the several school societies, as justice and equity shall require." While this fund has not been in every way an advantage to the educational interests of Connecticut--for, as will be noted, it relieved the citizens and the towns for a long time from any financial concern in them--it has been, and may long be, of great value for the maintenance of the common schools of the state and as bearing testimony to their importance.

Another fund, or series of funds, intended for the benefit of the schools in the state, is known as the Town Deposit Fund. Its source is the sum of money received by the state from the United States in 1837, when the surplus money in the federal treasury, amounting to about $35,000,000, was deposited with the several states, in proportion to their representation in Congress, for safe-keeping and repayment if demanded. The General Assembly of Connecticut, having voted to accept the deposit of the amount assigned to the state, which was $736,662, passed an act in 1836, provided that the money should be deposited with the several towns, if they should vote to receive it, in proportion to their population, the several deposits to be held in trust for the state, and the interest to be applied annually, "at least one-half thereof for the promotion of education in the common schools of each town, in such manner and proportions as the town shall direct, and the remainder for the purpose of defraying the ordinary expenses of such town"; and it was also provided that the towns should make good any deficiency which should occur through mismanagement or any other cause. In 1855 an act provided that the whole income of the town deposit funds should be devoted to the common schools. The report of the secretary of the Board of Education published in 1888 contains the result of a thorough examination into the condition of these

funds, showing how each town then accounted for its share. The nominal total was $753,326, only some $10,000 less than the amount deposited fifty years before; but of this sum more than two-thirds (say $528,000) was invested in town securities, including "a large sum upon which towns do not make any pretense of paying interest, other considerable sums which the town officers never heard of, and other sums invested in town farms, public buildings, etc. "Of the notes secured by mortgage ($145,000)," continues the report, "a large part, not accurately ascertained, are worthless. In fine, five-sevenths of this fund devoted by the state and received in trust by the towns, if not dead, is in a profound and very unhealthy sleep. The interest is not a substantial sum of money which can be devoted to schools, but a fiction, legal or illegal, which appears on the books or not, as the town desires." In 1896 the principal was reported as unchanged, and the income was reckoned as $33,288, a very large part of which was probably but a transfer from one account to another on the books of the several towns. It seemed most convenient to bring together some account of the several school funds. We return now to consider certain points in the history of the schools themselves.

There appears to have been very little change in the character of education in Connecticut during the eighteenth century. The studies pursued were reading, writing, and the simple rudiments of arithmetic. "The foundations were firmly laid, but the superstructure was not carried to a great height." The revised statutes of 1750 contained four new provisions as to schools. The civil authority and selectmen were constituted inspectors or visitors, and directed to visit and inspect all schools at least once a quarter, "and inquire particularly into the qualifications of the masters, the proficiency of the pupils, and give such directions as they shall judge needful to render such schools most serviceable for the increase of knowledge, religion, and good manners." In 1766 a law was passed authorizing the towns to divide themselves into proper and necessary districts for keeping their schools, which districts should have their proportions of the public money, according to their several grant lists. "By the practical operation of this act," says Dr. Barnard, "the school system of Connecticut, instead of embracing schools of different grades, was gradually narrowed down to a single district school, taught by one teacher in the summer and a different teacher in the winter, for children of all ages and in every variety of study residing in their several territorial limits." By an act of 1798 certain important changes were made. In the first place, the town entirely gave place to the school society, the representative of the ancient parish, and each society was required to appoint not more than nine persons "of competent skill and letters," to be visitors, with power to examine, to approve, and to displace schoolmasters, "to appoint public exercises for the youth, and to give honorary marks of distinction to such as are found to excel." In the second place, the old provision for county grammar schools was withdrawn, and any society was authorized to institute a school of higher order for the common benefit of all the inhabitants, "the object of which shall be to perfect the youth admitted thereto in reading and penmanship, to instruct them in the rudiments of the English grammar, in composition, in arithmetic and geography, or, on particular de-

sire, in Latin and Greek languages, also in the first principles of religion and morality, and in general to form them for usefulness and happiness in the various relations of social life." Very few Society High Schools were ever instituted; that in Hartford was established under the provisions of this law, but not until 1847. It may be that the law was suggested, and at the same time rendered practically nugatory, by the establishment of academies, which for a long time held a prominent and influential position. The first appear to have been the Staples School, now in the town of Easton, founded in 1781, and the Plainfield Academy, founded in 1783; the Episcopal Academy of Connecticut, at Cheshire, was established in 1794 and chartered in 1796. Many acts of incorporation were passed at different dates, until in 1838 general provision was made for the incorporation of academies.

The only act passed in restriction of schools seems to be that of 1742, which was to continue in force but four years, and the occasion for which was, almost certainly, the excitement attending the Great Awakening, the preaching of Whitefield, and the New Light movement. It was directed as well against an unlearned ministry as against unlicensed teaching and provided for severe penalties against unlawful schools, their tutors and instructors, and also their scholars and those who should harbor them, who were to be dealt with "according to the laws of this colony respecting transient persons or inmates residing in any town without the approbation of the selectmen." The law was not continued or re-enacted.

As has already been suggested, the growth of the school-society and school-district system, and the fact of the support of the common schools from the income of the school fund, did not increase the efficiency of the schools, or the interest of the intelligent part of the community in them. There were many excellent teachers, but they owed their success to their character, their self-denial, and their love for their work, rather than to their literary qualifications and to the system under which they served for a mere pittance. Those who wished a reasonably good education for their children sent them to academies or private schools; and in 1837 it was estimated that between one-seventh and one-eighth of the children of the state, belonging to well-to-do families, were instructed elsewhere than in the common schools, at an expense greater than was appropriated for the education of all, and that about one-twelfth of the children of proper age (say 6,000) were growing up in absolute ignorance. Before this, however, attention had been called to the serious condition of things. In 1825 Governor Wolcott, expressing his opinion that "the schools at present established in our cities and villages, including the select schools of the opulent, are insufficient for the proper education of all the children, and those of the poor and improvident are in the greatest danger of being neglected," suggested the introduction of the Lancasterian system and the establishment of public schools of an intermediate grade between the common school and the college. Connecticut did not fail to share in the effort which was made in various parts of the country, about this time, to improve the common schools. In 1827 a society for this purpose was formed in Hartford, perhaps the first of the kind in the country, of which the

Hon. Roger M. Sherman was president; and three years later, a convention of teachers and their friends of education was held in the same city, under the presidency of Dr. Noah Webster, which exerted a great influence. In 1834 a committee was appointed by the General Assembly to inquire what changes were necessary in the laws of the state to raise the character of the common schools and increase their usefulness; but their report was never acted upon by the standing committee of the next General Assembly to which it was referred. At last, in 1837, in consequence of a report, certain of the figures from which have already been given, a bill was passed by a unanimous vote in the Senate, and with but one dissenting voice in the House of Representatives, "for the better supervision of public schools." It provided for the appointment of eight persons, one from each county, who, with the governor and the commissioner of the school funds, should be the Board of Commissioners of Public Schools. From the organization of this board, of which the secretary was Henry Barnard, who here began his extended and efficient labors in the cause of education, dates a new era in the history of schools in Connecticut, which, though by no means an era of unfailing and steadily advancing prosperity, has yet made it possible to attain great advance and to open the way for still greater prosperity. The board of commissioners was abolished after five years, and in its place, from 1845 to 1849, the commissioner of the School Fund was appointed superintendent of common schools. Then for some time the principal of the State Normal School at New Britain was made the superintendent; and finally, in 1865, the present State Board of Education was established, consisting of the governor and the lieutenant governor and four other members, one from each congressional district, each holding office for four years. The board elects its own secretary, who is practically a state superintendent of public instruction. The secretary since 1883 has been Charles D. Hine, to whom the state owes more than it can ever repay. His reports on the schools and on matters connected with them are of the greatest value, and his personal influence on behalf of sound and wise education is and will be widely felt.

The power of school districts was greatly enlarged when in 1839 they were made bodies corporate and empowered to elect their own committees, employ teachers, and lay taxes upon the property within their limits, for school purposes. The school societies were abolished in 1856, and the towns returned to their ancient place in the school system. This change, however, was to a large extent greater in appearance than in reality; for many of the ancient towns had been so divided as to make the boundaries of towns practically, if not identically, the same as those of the societies.

From 1821, when the income of the school fund was held sufficient to make the tax for schools unnecessary, until 1854, there was practically no town or society school tax in the state. Rate or tuition bills were made out in varying ways against those whose children went to school, the town assuming the bills of those who were unable to pay them. The school tax was restored in 1854, when each town was required to lay a tax of at least three-tenths of a mill for this purpose; this was later changed so as to re-quire the town to raise enough to ensure the proper keeping of a school for the number of weeks required by law. Rate bills were abolished in 1868. In 1871 an appropriation from the state treasury of fifty cents for each child of school age was made by law, the amount to be paid to the towns with the dividend from the school fund. In the following year this amount was increased to a dollar and fifty cents.

In his annual report as secretary of the Board of Education presented in 1866, Daniel C. Gilman, well known in New Haven and late the honored president of the John Hopkins University, called special attention to the great number of school districts as a serious obstacle to the progress of education. At that time there were in the one hundred and sixty-two towns in the state no fewer than 1623 school districts, the number in the several towns varying from two to twenty-two. "These little republics," as he said, were "each independent in some respects of all others, each capable of opposing progress and thwarting by neglect, if not by literal violations, the enactments of the state." "If," he argued, "the people of the town can be brought together, or at any rate if the people of a common central village can be brought together for discussion and deliberation, there is some hope of accomplishing good results; but to go over and over again the same subject in ten to twenty places within the same township requires more energy, more time and more pay than our board of school visitors are expected to command. If all the districts were composed chiefly of intelligent and thinking men, the evil would be lessened; but it is well known that many of them are so destitute of life that it is almost impossible to get a suitable person to manage the public business.... Sometimes no one can be found competent and at leisure to assume the duties. This is especially true in some of the thinly-peopled districts of the country." His plea, based on this statement of facts, was for the town management of schools, and the consolidation of districts, not necessarily involving the abolition of school houses. And a useful example was at hand in the case of New Haven, where a few years before all the districts within the city limits had been united into one school district, having one high school, six large graded schools, and several smaller schools. In consequence of the arguments contained in this report, the General Assembly passed an act giving to the towns the jurisdiction over school matters which had been in the hands of the several districts, providing for non-partisan boards of management, and giving power to any town to maintain as many schools as there were districts, or more or less as might be found best, making the whole a system adapted to the special wants of the community. Within a year six towns sought to organize their schools under the new law; and since that time there has been a growing tendency, which the Board of Education has done much to encourage, to consolidate the districts in the several towns, and to organize the schools as departments of one school system. This has enabled towns to grade their schools and to give equal advantages to all their residents of school age. And when to this there has been added the full or partial endowment of schools by the gifts of generous benefactors, the advantages are both more extended and more apparent. A good example is in the town of Clinton where in consequence

of a large legacy of the late Charles Morgan the town is provided with a high school of excellent grade and with good facilities for preliminary and primary work, while the town tax for schools has become merely nominal.

The number of districts in the one hundred and sixty-eight towns of the state has now been reduced to one thousand two hundred and sixty-three, twenty three towns having consolidated their districts; and of these twenty-eight all but two (in which other provision is made) maintain high schools, or at least high school departments of their school system. Besides these, it may be added that there are eleven towns having high schools managed by town high-school committees, and in twenty-four towns there are thirty-four district high schools. To this there might well be added, as in reality a part of the system of public education, some notice of the normal-schools at New Britain for a long time the only one in the state--Willimantic, and New Haven. But it must suffice, within the limits of this paper, to mention them, and to suggest the existence of other departments of educational work in teachers institutes, grammar schools, night schools, kindergartens, libraries, etc.

The thorough examination of the schools in certain parts of the state which the Board of Education is undertaking, has already shown that a great deal yet remains to be done in the interests of good work in the elementary schools of Connecticut. The Board, presenting in 1896 a special report on the schools in one county, mostly agricultural and of a scattered population, used the following very serious words: "There was a time when the people of Connecticut could contentedly compare their schools with the public schools of other countries. Since that time, however, great progress has been made elsewhere in the development of public education, while the people of Connecticut, flattered by the praise of De Tocqueville and others, have been so certain of the superior quality of their schools as to relax their efforts for improvement. To-day in the opinion of competent judges, the schools of Connecticut, although on the average as good as those of other parts of the United States, are not as good as the schools of several countries of Northern Europe. We can see no escape from the conclusion that, while there are many good schools here and there throughout the state, the average quality of the teaching in our public schools is unnecessarily bad. It is disagreeable to us to say this; but we feel constrained to express our opinion unreservedly, because there can be no reasonable expectation of improvement until the self-satisfaction felt by our people is exchanged for a just and critical estimate of the actual condition of their schools."

To this work the board, with the aid (it would be better to say under the guidance) of its indefatigable secretary, is addressing itself. The problem has changed very greatly within the last quarter of a century; and the prosperity of generations to come depends upon the accuracy with which it is stated now, and the way we go about to solve it. This at any rate may be said, that the people of Connecticut will not begrudge the labor and expense necessary to secure for all their children that education which is necessary to fit them to bear their parts as citizens of their historic commonwealth.

CHURCHMEN AND PURITANS IN COLONIAL NEW ENGLAND

[6]   When we speak of Churchmen and Puritans, we need to remember that the words were not at first mutually exclusive. At the date of the first permanent English settlements on this coast, only four years after the end of the glorious reign of Queen Elizabeth, there was a strong Puritan element, and at least the beginning of a strong Puritan party, in the Church of England; but the Puritans had not separated from the Church and the Church had not cast them out. Rather they were attempting, as they professed, to complete a work of reformation which had begun some seventy years before and had been arrested in its course. They did not object, they declared, to the Reformation settlement of Church and State; they wished the ancient parishes and the ancient rights of parishioners, in matters both spiritual and temporal, to continue; and even those who were minded to exchange the episcopal organization for one that acknowledged but a parity of ministers, were seeking for the change in what lawyers would call a constitutional way. They were, to phrase the distinction in a single word, non-conformists and not separatists.

But as the years went on, great changes of principle and of action were rapidly made. The condition of affairs and of parties was not the same in 1620, near the end of the reign of James I, as in 1607, when he had been but a short time on the throne; and before 1662, when the New England colonies had practically assumed a permanent form, James's unfortunate son Charles I. had lost his throne and his life, the use of the Prayer Book had been proscribed, a presbyterian organization had been substituted for the ancient establishment, England had made trial of a commonwealth, and tired of her brief experiment she had welcomed both Church and King to their own again. When this storm was over, the Puritans had become separatists, and their history must be read thenceforth as outside that of the Church of England. The separatists or Independents of the earlier days were not, and did not call themselves, Puritans. They had, under a strong conviction of duty, come out from the Church of England as from Babylon, abhorring her prelacy and her ceremonial, her union with the state, her parish ways, and her willingness to minister the ordinances to others than those who thought themselves the elect. They had removed to Holland, that they might there carry out their principles without restraint of law, civil or ecclesiastical; and when they crossed the ocean, it was to make the ocean, as a physical barrier, a mark of the separation which had already been made in conviction and in will.

There were, then, three classes of early English settlers in New England. The professed Churchmen came first. They made a settlement in 1607 at Pemaquid near the mouth of the Kennebec in Maine, holding their first service on land only two months and a half after the first service in which good Master Hunt officiated at Jamestown--a settlement which, by the way, was never quite broken up, and which stood for a witness farthest east of all sites occupied by Englishmen. They made a further settlement in New Hampshire in 1623, and fifteen years later a church and a parsonage had been built at Portsmouth. There were remnants of the "old planters" to be found in the region of Massachusetts

Bay when the new settlers came; Thomas Morton of Mount Wollaston, and Samuel Maverick, said to be "strong for the lordly prelatical power," and William Blaxton (or Blackstone), who claimed to be the sole owner of the tri-mountain peninsula of Boston, a Church of England clergyman, who had crossed the ocean, "because he did not like the Lords Bishops," and had to remove with his "Canonicall Coate" to Rhode Island "because he would not be under the Lords Brethren." And a few came with other emigrants, but were not suffered to remain, as the two brothers Browne, who gathered a company together at Salem and read the Book of Common Prayer, until Governor Endicott "told them that New England was no place for such as they, and sent them back for England."

The Independents or Separatists came next--we usually call them the Pilgrims. They were the <u>Mayflower</u> company and those who followed them, under the leadership of Elder William Brewster, and they established themselves at Plymouth. They had no chartered rights, though at a later day they gained the privilege of a royal patent. They recognized no union of Church and State, but kept the two apart from each other, and imposed no religious test either for admission to the rights of citizenship or for election to civil office. They had utterly broken with the Church of England and were strict congregationalists; their government was not a theocracy or even an ecclesiocracy, but a democracy. Roger Williams, when he could not endure the tyranny of the Puritans in Salem, first sought shelter "under the more tolerant jurisdiction of Plymouth"; and there he was allowed to denounce the ministers of Boston for not making public profession of repentence that they had once lived in communion with the apostate Church of England.

The Puritans came a little later, and settled Salem in 1626 and Boston in 1630. They brought with them a charter which had been given for a trading company, intended to transact its business in London and to send ships to Massachusetts Bay for the exchange of commodities; and under color of this they set up a commonwealth, transferring to it the establishment of their Puritanical Church, the reformation of which they intended to complete. As their first company was sailing past Land's End, Mr. Higginson, their minister, gathered his children and others about him, and spoke words which have been preserved for us. "We will not say, as the separatists are wont to say on their leaving England, Farewell Babylon! Farewell Rome! But we will say, Farewell dear England! Farewell the Church of God in England, and all the Christian friends there! We do not go to New England as separatists from the Church of England, though we cannot but separate from the corruptions in it; but we go to practise the positive part of church reformation and propagate the Gospel in America." No doubt among the corruptions from which they felt obliged to purge themselves, they presently considered episcopacy one of the most serious; and in fact, they as really broke communion with the historic Church as did the separatists; but they maintained strict religious tests, allowing no person to become a new member of the corporation and thus to gain a vote unless he had been first admitted a member of the local congregation, having satisfied the minister and elders of his conversion; and they retained something of the "parish way" in their organization, so that their unit of government was not the town but the congregation. There were no real presbyterians among the settlers of New England; but, though the external polity of the Puritans soon conformed to that of the separatists, the later comers had more of the presbyterian tone. The others were a democracy; these became an oligarchy, and that of the most objectionable kind, an ecclesiastical oligarchy. Soon, under the pressure of circumstances, the weaker colony of Plymouth became practically dependent on the stronger colony of Massachusetts Bay. And when, the old charter having been declared forfeit, a new charter was given as to a royal colony, the older settlement was united with the later under one government. Their governor was now sent to them from England; he was a member of the established Church, and the Church had in Massachusetts some of the rights--even if it was not allowed the power--of an establishment.

In what is now Connecticut there were also two colonies, representing the two classes of non-conformists and separatists; but for a long time we read of no professed Churchmen there. The settlers of Hartford and the adjacent towns on the River came in and about 1635 from the neighborhood of Boston, having been led to emigrate to the west by reason of dissatisfaction which they did not clearly express but which was certainly due to a lack of harmony with the principles of the Bay colony. Mr. Thomas Hooker, the minister, and Mr. Ludlow, the lawyer, who led them, were nominally Puritans, but in fact independents; they presently organized a pure democracy under the first written constitution in the history of the world; and they admitted all respectable and responsible members of the community to the privileges of the franchise, imposing no religious test except that the governor should be a church-member. They had neither patent nor charter from England, and they asked for none; and they did not make their ministers and elders supreme in matters of administration; and in consequence of this the advice of the ministers was sober and rational and of great practical value. Though in some ways very different from Plymouth, Connecticut illustrated the same principles as did that original colony.

New Haven, on the other hand, while it was a settlement largely directed by wealthy merchants, was fundamentally a theocracy, and in theory more strictly so than was even Massachusetts Bay. Its founders came from England, only stopping for a short time at Boston; and their fundamental law was that revealed in the Old Testament, with such additional millenial light as might be granted to them. (The so-called "Blue Laws," by the way, belong to New Haven and not to Connecticut colony.) As a consequence they treated Church and State as one; all civil authority was put into the hands of the seven pillars designated for that purpose as by divine appointment; and they admitted no one to a share in it who was not a member of the local church. Like independence marked the other communities which came to be confederated with it. New Haven did unite with the other three colonies--none of them would have united with Rhode Island--for defence against the Dutch and the Indians; but it was hard put to it when it was crowded between latitudinarian Connecticut on the northeast and popish New York on the southwest.

Soon after the restoration of the monarchy, Connecticut, which in a very tactful way had kept on good terms with the authorities at home, applied for and obtained from the King a remarkable charter, still the wonder of students of history, which constituted it a really independent government, with full power to choose its own governor, make its own laws without reference to parliament, and administer affairs in its own way; and its boundaries were so defined as to include the New Haven jurisdiction. Unwillingly, but with some conviction that it was for the best, New Haven yielded to the inevitable; and united Connecticut remained a true democracy under her charter through all the troubles of the Revolution and for forty years later, having no constitution until the year 1818. Here then the principles of independency or separation prevailed; and, as will presently appear, the Church of England practically made no entrance into Connecticut from without. Its polity was congregational, but with at least the beginning of something like a presbyterian element. Thus having before us the outline history of Puritan and independent New England, with the two colonies of Massachusetts and Connecticut (as they came to be), the one actively opposed to the Church of England and the other quite cut off from any relations with it, we come to the interesting question as to the manner of the Church's entry into these colonies and the manner of its growth in them.

That, even in the times of seemingly entire separation from the mother Church, there was some memory of her and some longing for her ways, cannot well be doubted. It is easy to make too much of the fact that, with scarce an exception, the ministers who led the early bands of emigrants and were settled over the newly organized Churches, as they were called, had been trained in the English universities for the ministry of the Church of England, and had been actually ordained by her bishops. Many of them were non-conformists from their youth, who had refused to follow the laws of ceremonies and to use the Book of Common Prayer; it is no strange thing that their writings fail to show familiarity with the phrases of that book or their sermons any general acceptance of its tone of theology. But after all, they were Englishmen and English Churchmen by rights; and their memory must have gone back at times to their ordination and their early ministrations and their responsibility for the care of souls within their parishes. Most of them did indeed accept a new ordination on this side of the water; some from the strictly independent theory that ordination was only to the charge of a particular congregation, and some declaring that the laying-on of hands here was but a recognition of an authority which had been given before, while in one case at least a clergyman who had come with a good part of his flock protested that he would continue to minister to them in virtue of his ordination by a bishop at home. We cannot but be moved by the thought that for one whole generation the Word and the Sacraments were ministered in New England by those who had been ordained to Holy Orders by bishops of the English Church and who, even if they had been silenced, had not been deposed. It may also be remembered that neither the Puritans nor the independents were at variance with the Church as to the fundamental doctrines of Christianity. They held the Catholic faith as to the Holy Trinity and the Incarnation; and their statements of belief in the Atonement, the Inspiration of Scripture, the divine institu-

tion of the Church, and the efficacy of the Sacraments, would not be diverse from those which would be made by accepted divines of the English Church. Perhaps, however, on the points of difference they felt and expressed their disagreement the more strongly for this very reason.

But, whatever was the feeling of the ministers, there is no doubt that many of the lay folk resented the hard terms on which alone they were allowed admission to the sacraments for themselves and their children, and claimed the rights which belonged to them in England and would still have been allowed them there. This is the meaning of the petitions which were addressed to the legislatures of the colonies by men who complained that they were "detained from the seals of the covenant" and that unlawful conditions were required of them before they were allowed to receive the Holy Communion themselves or to present their children for baptism. The petitioners were not Episcopalians; if they described themselves as members of the Church of England it was either in the Puritan sense or (between 1645 and 1660) as acknowledging the presbyterian establishment; but they felt that the home requirements for the full enjoyment of Church privileges were the scriptural requirements, and that if they professed the Christian faith and undertook the Christian obedience to the moral law, they had a right to the use of the Christian ordinances. The first settlers of New England came as baptized persons, and most of those of mature years were communicants, or (to use their own phraseology) churchmembers; and their children born on this side of the ocean were admitted to baptism on the faith of their parents; but when these children grew up, few of them could satisfy the tests of regeneration and conversion imposed by the ministers and elders, and few therefore became members of the local churches; and their children, the second generation born in this country, could not be baptized, for the Puritans baptized only professed believers and their seed, until such time as they should have the religious experience which was demanded of them. The result of this was an enforced neglect of Christian ordinances and non-religious if not utterly irreligious lives; it led to the condition of things, spiritual pride and conceit on the one side and "wretchlessness and desperation" on the other, which called for the "Great Awakening" of about 1740; and the protest against it, preparing a way for the Church of England to claim her people again, led at a very early day to the adoption of what was curiously called the Half-way Covenant. This, which is still denounced by some theologians and historians as a weakening of religious obligations and a concession to the world and worldly men, was in reality a partial or half-way return to the methods and requirements which had been left behind. It allowed men and women who professed the faith of the Gospel and led upright lives but who could not satisfy the experimental conditions for full Church membership, to put themselves under the guardianship and direction of the Church, and though not becoming communicants themselves to present their children for baptism; and at the same time they were asked to look forward to the other sacrament as a privilege for themselves whenever it should please God to make them worthy and the Church to approve their worthiness. This half-way covenant was not everywhere adopted; in fact, it was in some places bitterly opposed, and it led to some divisions which were

long in healing. But it was a concession to the "parish way" of Churchmen, and for that matter of presbyterians as well; it did save in some places whole generations of Christian children from being brought up without the covenant and told that they had no place in the Church of Christ until it should please God to convert them; and it did, as I said, prepare the way of the Church as satisfying the religious convictions of those who were seeking the paths of faith and obedience.

To this should be added, as a matter turning the minds of thoughtful men towards the Church, the difficulty which was found in justifying the lay ordinations which were somewhat frequent in the early days and were really a part of the congregational theory of Church authority. Ministers seem to have been for a good while quite satisfied if they could trace back their ordination through other ministers to the English bishops, confident that a presbyterian succession was sufficient; but when they found that one or more of those who had laid hands on them had themselves received no ordination except from the brethren, they began to question whether they had authority to preach the word and minister the sacraments. And in Connecticut the fact that the legal establishment, after the date of the Saybrook platform in 1708, had a strong element of presbyterianism, the churches no longer continuing to act independently, but consulting by councils and governing by consociations, made it not difficult to see the possible advantage of a central authority such as independency had rejected and Puritanism had reformed away. To this must be added, in the latter part of the colonial period, the revulsion against the vagaries of word and action which marked the fanatics, whom in those days they called enthusiasts. Any one who could speak, to the excited minds of men doubtful of themselves and of God's dealings with them, the Church's simple message of forgiveness and strength, exerted a great influence for good and satisfied in the Lord's own way the cravings of their souls.

Such were in outline some of the underlying causes which predisposed thoughtful and religious men to return to the polity and methods of the Church of England, apart from the fact that the soul has always a true instinct which draws it to the way and ordinances of God's own appointment. But the question recurs as to the special occasion of the introduction of the Church into the New England colonies. It came into Massachusetts as the Church of the royal governors and of men of politics and of business who were in one way or another connected with them. The law which for thirty years had forbidden the "observing of any such day as Christmas or the like, either by forbearing labour, feasting, or any other way," had been five years repealed, when in 1686 Joseph Dudley came as Governor with the Rev. Robert Ratcliffe as his chaplain, and began church services on Sundays in the Town-house of Boston. Soon the parish of the King's Chapel was organized; and after Andros had for a while required the use of the Old South Church for services, the building of King's Chapel was occupied in 1689. Christ Church was not organized until 1722 and Trinity Church dates from 1735. The venerable Society for the Propagation of the Gospel--it was called venerable even when it was young--rendered assistance to other parishes in less favored places than Boston, in spite of the protests of the Puritans that its charter did not allow it to go to set-

tled towns and villages; and before the Revolution Massachusetts, which had fully 300 congregational societies, had also 15 parishes of the Church, in which ministered some Englishmen and some who had crossed the ocean for ordination and had returned. With these parishes might also be reckoned the two or three in New Hampshire; and the few Churchmen in the District of Maine really belonged also to Massachusetts. The position of these clergymen and their people showed a temper and character which was, as Bishop Lawrence says, "its own, clear, strong, and persistent." When after the Revolution there were but four clergymen left in the colony--two in Boston, one in Newburyport, and one in Salem--with one more in Rhode Island who acted with them, the teachings and plans of their leaders, Dr. Bass and Dr. Parker, were entirely in accord with those of the Connecticut clergy as to the absolute necessity of the episcopate, required as well for the organization and discipline of the Church as for the ordaining and mission of her ministers. As to the matter of lay representation in ecclesiastical councils, they were not in accord with the first Bishop of Connecticut, and from the beginning they planned for a representative body of the two orders; perhaps as a result of this, they were prepared to agree to more radical changes in the prayer book than were their brethren a little further to the south. From these beginnings grew the great and strong dioceses in the ancient colonies and the more recent Commonwealth of Massachusetts.

In Connecticut there were practically no professing Churchmen and few copies of the Book of Common Prayer at the beginning of the eighteenth century. In 1702 the first two missionaries of the Society for the Propagation of the Gospel, Mr. Keith and Mr. Talbot, travelling from Boston where they had landed, spent a Sunday in New London and by invitation of the Congregational pastor preached in the meetinghouse; but they almost certainly did not read the Prayer Book services. In the same year a body of Churchmen in Stratford petitioned the Bishop of London to send them a clergyman, or in the phrase of the day, a missionary. Four years later, the Rev. Mr. Muirson, missionary of the Society at Rye in New York jurisdiction, accompanied by the staunch layman Colonel Heathcote "fully armed," travelled some way along the shore of the Sound, looking for Churchmen and holding services; it was the only really missionary visit from without ever made in Connecticut, and the only time that Episcopacy in that Colony ever had the aid of the secular arm. No organization followed at once upon this visit. In 1707 the Stratford churchmen formed themselves into a parish and elected wardens and vestrymen. So it happens that the tercentenary year of the permanent establishment of the Church on these shores is the bicentenary year of the formal beginning of the Church in our Diocese, which later became the first to complete its organization by securing the consecration of a bishop. The Old Narraganset Church in Rhode Island is of the same date as Christ Church in Stratford; and outside of Maryland and Virginia, I know of but five older Church parishes: St. Philip's in Charleston, the King's Chapel in Boston, Christ Church in Philadelphia, Trinity Church in New York, and Trinity Church in Newport. (St. Mary's Church in Burlington was a year later.)

The Church in Connecticut dates back indeed to 1707; but its great influx of life was from the events of 1722. It is an oft-told story, but it is always wonderful and always inspiring. On the day after the Commencement in that year at the Collegiate School of the Colony (later named Yale College), the two officers of instruction, Rector Cutler and Tutor Brown, with a former tutor of high scholarship, Mr. Johnson, and four other young ministers of good reputation for learning and character, presented to the "fathers and brethren" assembled in the library a written statement to the effect that some of them were convinced of the invalidity of presbyterian ordination and the rest had serious doubts as to its validity. Mr. Johnson had come across a Prayer Book in the home of his childhood, and had studied and used it; and he and the others had been in the habit of meeting in the College library and reading the volumes of English theology which were to be found there. They were not disappointed Congregationalists; nor, for that matter, were the men who followed them in the next fifty years; they were among the best scholars and the most respected men of the community; and they were led towards the Church by their convictions, especially on the subject of holy orders--the authority to minister in the Word and Sacraments. Three of the first seven were persuaded to remain in their former connection; Rector Cutler, Tutor Brown, and Samuel Johnson went at once to England to ask from the Archbishop of Canterbury and to receive Episcopal ordination; of these Mr. Brown died in England of the small-pox, Dr. Cutler came back to be the first rector of Christ Church in Boston, and Dr. Johnson to stand for a while at the head of the clergy of Connecticut, to become a close friend of Dean (afterwards Bishop) Berkeley, who lived in Rhode Island from 1729 to 1731 and profoundly affected the Church in the Northern Colonies, and to be the first President of King's College, later Columbia College and University, in New York. Mr. Wetmore followed them the next year, and returned after ordination to minister diligently in his native Colony. In their steps went a succession of Connecticut men, making before the Revolution the full number of forty-three, every one a college graduate, all men of high character and courage, well-reported of by their neighbors before they went abroad and after they came back, and minister-ing often for their whole lives in the vicinity of their birth. They were strong and faithful men, and they educated Church-wise a strong and faithful people. And though, as might be expected, they met with opposition and some of them were harshly treated, the authorities of the Colony dealt with them generously, according to the standards of the times. Very soon after 1722, the legislature passed a law in favor of adherents of the Church of England, "soberly dissenting" from the Standing Order, allowing them in cases where they actually attended a place of worship of that Church to contribute towards its maintenance the portion of taxes which they would have else been required to pay for the support of the establishment. There was trouble, of course, in the time of the Revolution; but while there was more toryism with us than with you, it did not lead to very serious results; our leading layman, Dr. William Samuel Johnson, strongly suspected and watched in time of war, was an influential member of the Federal Constitutional Convention and the first United States Senator from Connecticut. We still have forty two parishes in our Diocese which were organized before the Revolution (only one of colonial date has become extinct), and it was estimated that in 1760 one-fourteenth part of the population was attached to the Church. When the war was seen to be practically at an end, yet eight months before the evacuation of New York, ten of the fourteen remaining clergy met, elected a Bishop who was to go to England to seek consecration, and failing to receive it there to ask for it in Scotland; and they also prepared a strong letter to be sent to the Churchmen of Pennsylvania, arguing for the necessity of the episcopate before any other plans should be made for continuing or extending the Church's work. Dr. Samuel Seabury, our first Bishop, was of Connecticut birth, though all of his earlier ministry was passed elsewhere; he, as well as his father, had been ordained in England, but he had spent a year in Edinburgh before his ordination and was acquainted with the "Catholic remainder of the ancient Church of Scotland"; and he came back from Scotland bringing to America two priceless boons; "a true, valid, and purely ecclesiastical episcopacy," and a liturgy with explicit Oblation and Invocation after the models of primitive antiquity, as was recognized by your Convention in Maryland.

Into the details of his work, his service as Bishop of Connecticut and Rhode Island, his cooperation with Dr. Parker, afterwards Bishop of Massachusetts, his earnest deliberations with Bishop White when the Church in the States became one and furnished a model for the union of the States under a constitution, his uniting with the other bishops in the consecration of Dr. Claggett for Maryland, I may not now enter.

It must suffice that I have attempted to set before you--I trust not in too many words or with too great attention to detail--the outline of the history of the New England colonies, as far as it shows the mutual relations of the Church of England and of those whom we know as the Puritans and the independents. We are near enough to the events of those years to study them with a lively interest, and far enough removed from them to look at men and their actions without too great a prejudice on either side. And as we stand on the eve of the great tercentenary of the Church in this land, and we of New England are reminding ourselves (if I had not better have said are learning) of the important history which your ancestors wrought out here where the Colonial Church had the advantages and the disadvantages of an establishment, we may hope that you will bear with us patiently if we tell how our forefathers in the faith found their way to the Church of their forefathers, and held to its teachings and handed its blessings on to us.

THE PLACE OF HEBRON IN THE COLONY--
THE BICENTENNIAL, AUG. 20, 1908

[7]

The year 1708 is memorable in the annals of the Colony of Connecticut. It in four towns were added to the goodly number of those which in more than 70 years had been incorporated within the well-established charter limits. They were Newtown, on the northwestern frontier, where an outpost settlement had been made two years earlier; Ridge-field, on the west boundary, not far back from the Sound, in

a tract of land purchased from Indian proprietors; Killingly, near the Massachusetts line, and not far from the northeast corner of the colony; and this town, much nearer the center than any of the others, yet at some distance from the great river, and having from the first an idiosyncrasy of position, as it was destined to have a history peculiarly its own. Hebron, also, like one of the other towns which keeps its bi-centennial this year, gained its land directly from the In-dians; yet not by conquest, nor by purchase, but by gift, and that a legacy. The story will presently be told you, how Joshua Uncas, son of the great chieftain, otherwise called Attawanhood, who asked that he might be buried at Saybrook after the manner of the English, left to Thomas Buckingham (son of the minister), Thomas Shipman, and others, known as "the Saybrook legatees," a large tract of land here; and a Saybrook man feels that he is in the inheritance of his fathers when he reads that John Pratt, Robert Chapman, John Clark and Stephen Post were the committee which brought before the General Assembly the matter of settlement already be-gun and of organization desired. Thus it was that there came settlers to this place from the old settlements at the mouths of the Connecticut and the Tunxis, from the Long Island to the south, and the midst of the Massachusetts colony to the north. It was a time of prospecting and of establishing new homes. Though the war with the French was making heavy demands on the men of Connecticut for personal service and for taxes, and the not far distant fron-tier needed defence, the life of the colony was vigorous. The collegiate school, established but seven years before, was maintaining its position and graduating such men as Jared Eliot, Jonathan Dickinson and Samuel Johnson; and at the seat of the college a synod was about to meet, summoned by the civil authority, at the instance of Governor Saltonstall, to frame the Saybrook platform. The two generations of Englishmen who had lived and labored in the ancient settle-ments and in their daughter towns, had so well served the commonwealth that its character had become fixed in mat-ters both material and moral, and with great variety, due to diversity of place and circumstance, their successors were exercising a like influence.

But it is not my purpose to trace out the history of this town, nor, indeed, am I furnished for the undertaking, as are those who will presently bring it before you in its many interesting details. I had in mind but to say a word of greeting and to indicate the place into which this town came two centuries ago. I should like, however, to speak briefly of the name of the town, and to bear testimony to its contributions to the written history of Connecticut.

It seems strange that after seventy years and with more than forty town names, there had been in 1706 in this puritan and independent commonwealth but one example of a name taken from the Bible, that of Lebanon, which was given in 1695. And the Lebanon of Holy Scripture is, it need not be said, the name of a mountain, the "white" moun-tain of Palestine, and not of a city. Hebron is the first city-name taken from the Bible for a Connecticut town. It was proposed by the legatees; but why it was given, or who first selected it, does not appear. It may have been chosen by some one of the ministers who, from his knowledge of Hebrew (and I take it they all knew Hebrew then), recalling that the word means a confederacy, thought it apt for a settlement of people who came from diverse directions; at

any rate, we are assured that it was no suggestion in the General Assembly, such as that which eighty years later imposed the name of Bozrah on a place which asked to be called Bath, and it gave you an historical and dignified name. The Hebron from which you borrowed it vies with Damascus for the honor of being the oldest city in the world; it was old in Abraham's day; we read that it "was built seven years before Zoan in Egypt," and scholars tell us that these words tell of a rebuilding or a fortifying, and that the real founda-tion was still further back in time. The mention of the name recalls great men and wonderful events; today the city bears the title by which the Arabs speak of the patriarch who is buried there, "The Friend"; and it is one of the sacred places of the world. Of the eight Biblical town names with-in our borders, yours is among the most famous and the most inspiring.

And if your very name tells of history, we may not forget that two men who in very different ways wrote the history of Connecticut were natives of this town, and were indeed born in the same year, 1735, and within a month of each other. Dr. Benjamin Trumbull, after his graduation at Yale college, was ordained in 1760 over the church of the standing order in North Haven, continuing its pastor for sixty years until his death at the age of eighty-five, the work of his study and his pulpit being uninterrupted except by his service as soldier and chaplain in the revolutionary army. His two volumes of the History of Connecticut, pub-lished with an interval of twenty-one years, are a monu-ment to his diligence and a mine of information to all subse-quent students. Only, as he tells us, by employing "all the leisure hours which he could possibly redeem, by early rising and an indefatigable attention to business," did he find time for that work of research, the fruits of which we enjoy today. Judging--again to use his own words, though in a condensed form--that authentic history, while it in-structs, affords also an exalted pleasure, and that not only to the man of genius and curiosity but also to the pious man who views a divine hand conducting the whole, he thought it wise to make this, the first history of the colony, full and particular, that nothing useful or important respecting church or state might be lost. The result, we gladly ac-knowledge, was worthy of the plan; he "aimed at authenti-city, propriety, and perspicuity"; and while he attained these excellent qualities, he added to them that by the greatest endowment of a historian, he had the instinct to tell what later generations would want to know, and thus made his pages interesting even when he devoted nearly half a hundred of them to the Wallingford controversy. It is no little honor for Hebron that it gave to Connecticut its great historian, Benjamin Trumbull.

The name of his townsman and contemporary, Samuel Peters, may call forth a smile or a frown; but he, too, wrote a history and he, too, has added to your fame, his connection with Hebron being more generally known than that of Dr. Trumbull. He, too, was graduated at Yale col-lege, but two years before the other; he, too, was ordained, but in England by a bishop; he, too, continued long in the ministry--it was for sixty-six years--but he lived here and in England and later in Vermont, and in the very far west of those days, and then in loneliness and poverty in the city

of New York; he, too, was interrupted by the war of the revolution; but it was because he was a Tory and an outspoken one; and he, too, but with scarcely veiled anonymity wrote a History of Connecticut. Of this volume it may be truly said that it is not of the same type as that of Dr. Trumbull, while it should not be denied the name of history. Full of anecdote, pointed in its sarcasm, and defying the attempts of either lower or higher criticism to trace its constituent parts to their sources; written with a grim view of humor at a time when that kind of humor was not understood, and read then and today by men without this power of appreciating it; the work of one who drew lines straight or crooked on his canvas, not caring whether they corresponded or not to what was actually before him, if they only helped the interpretation of his picture, a very impressionist in words; it may be truly said that the volume does help us to know men and things as they presented themselves to an eccentric but discerning mind; and it certainly has added to the world's too scanty supply of humor. Some day, when the sores which he rubbed harshly have quite healed over, we shall all laugh at it and admire its ingenuity and find out its real contribution to the history of our colony and state. While I have been writing, there have fallen under my eyes proofs that a new generation is giving Samuel Peters his due. In almost the latest published part of the new Oxford English dictionary, he is quoted as the authority for "Pope, a name given in New England to the whippoor-will, by reason of its darting with great swiftness from the clouds almost to the ground and bawling out Pope!"; and also for "Pow-wow" as "an ancient religious rite, annually celebrated by the Indians." What treasures are reserved for the later letters of the alphabet, we may not know as yet. But, in all seriousness, when the whole story of the life of Dr. Peters comes to be written, you of Hebron will, even more than now, be glad that his name is on the roll of her sons.

I leave it to your historians of today to read the record of what has been done here. But I will not close without a greeting from the Historical Society of the State, and an exhortation to you to guard your history and its annals, and to make it and them known "to the children of the generations to come."

[In a revision of the foregoing address for another occasion, Hart added the following paragraphs:]

The name of Dr. Trumbull's townsman and contemporary, Samuel Peters, may call forth a smile or a frown; but he, too, wrote a history. He claimed descent from Hugh Peters, who suffered with the regicides or (if you prefer) the Judges. After graduation from Yale College, two years later than Benjamin Trumbull, he studied theology, and then went to England and received episcopal ordination. He continued in the ministry for the long space of 66 years, living in Connecticut and in England, and later in Vermont and in the very far West of those days, and then in loneliness and poverty in the city of New York. The Church of England people in Hebron had been hard put to it to secure a minister. The first candidate whom they sent across the ocean was lost at sea on his return passage; the second died before reaching home; the third was captured by the French and died in prison. The fourth was Mr. Peters, and he narrowly escaped death

from the small-pox while he was in England. Like Dr. Trumbull, his pastoral work was disturbed by the Revolutionary War; but it was because he was a tory and an outspoken one. He escaped from two mobs without serious personal injury, avoided a third, and fled to Boston and thence to England, where he petitioned for and was granted a pension. While in England, in 1781, he wrote and published A General History of Connecticut by a Gentleman of the Province. He also announced himself a candidate for the bishopric of Nova Scotia; and after the close of the Revolution, he secured a sort of election to the Bishopric of Vermont; but the authorities of the Episcopal Church in this country would not confirm this election, and the Archbishop of Canterbury, to whom he appealed, declined to interfere. In connection with others he obtained some kind of a title to a tract of land, 100 miles square, at the falls of St. Anthony on the Mississippi River, now at or near the site of Minneapolis; and when William Pitt struck his name from the list of British pensioners, he came back to this country, spent several years in petitioning Congress to confirm his title, and lived on the proceeds of sales of township rights to his friends. At the age of 86, he went as far west as Prairie du Chien in search of his alleged property, but accomplished little. Five years longer he lived in poverty and obscurity, positively refusing to go back to Hebron. He was, however, buried there, but in a different burial ground from that in which his three wives lie. The second, by the way, only seventeen years old, died but twenty days after her marriage; and her tombstone says:

"A wedding turned to lamentation,
The greatest grief in all creation."

On Dr. Peter's own tombstone are Dr. Jarvis's words, which I think he cannot have perused without some little twinge of conscience: "His life was full of adventures, adversities, and trials, which he bore with fortitude, patience, and serenity." He is said to have been a tall man, of commanding appearance, large and muscular, with an active mind and an iron will. "He loved Kings, admired the British government, and revered the hierarchy."

Of his history of Connecticut it may be truly said that, though it is not of the same type as that of Dr. Trumbull, it should not be altogether denied the name of history. It is partly burlesque, and yet not as entirely burlesque as is Knickerbocker's History of New York; it was without doubt written that he might come out even with the Revolutionists and the Puritans, but even in its highest flights of fancy it has enough truth in it to make some of their descendants squirm. It gives the Blue Laws of New Haven--they are not credited, as is ordinarily believed, to Connecticut--in their first collected form, but these are not all by any means fictitious. To reverse the well-known words about the toad and the harrow, he knew just where the toads were and he drew his harrow so that the points should be seen to hit them....

In all seriousness, it may be said that when the whole story of the life of Dr. Peters shall be written or his extant correspondence published, it will be seen that he was recognized by his contemporaries as more than an ordinary man; and that, without weakening our criticism of his faults and foibles, we can give him credit as a close observer of men and things, and can search beneath his words for important facts of history and for their connection with one another.

34

SESQUICENTENNIAL OF CHRIST CHURCH, HARTFORD, MAY 24, 1912

[8]

...The history of our Church in Hartford seems to have a beginning in that often quoted but constantly misunderstood petition presented to the General Assembly at the early date of 1664 by William Pitkin and six other men, two of them being from Hartford and four from Windsor. They declared that they were members of the Church of England and complained that they were deprived of their rights because the ministers of the colony would not admit them to communion or baptize their children. This did not mean, as it seems to mean, that they were (to use the term which best expresses the thought) episcopalians, whom congregationalists would not acknowledge as members of their Churches. The Church of England, as by law established, had been presbyterian for the fifteen years from 1645 to 1660, and in 1664 the phrase had not become restricted to those who accepted the policies of the restoration. The petitioners doubtless had repudiated episcopacy; but they represented that small but increasingly influential minority among the colonists who wished to continue the parish way rather than the congregational way; and they demanded here the same rights from the separatist ministers which they could have had in England at the hands of the priests of the restored episcopal establishment, namely, that being parsons of respectable lives they should have for themselves and their children the privileges of access to the sacraments. Their ministers required other conditions with assurance of conversion and formal admission to their new organizations; and they probably paid no attention to the suggestion of the Assembly--they certainly did not change their action in consequence of it--that they should "consider whether it be not their duty to entertain all such persons, who are of an honest and godly conversation, having a competency of knowledge in the principles of religion." It was a passing testimony to the fact, which underlies a good deal of the troubled ecclesiastical history of this town in its early days, keeping all New England in a state of anxious excitement, that there were among the settlers many who preferred old ways of old England to new ways of New England; and that there was already a preparation making for the change which came when some of the very best of the ministers and laymen of the colony sought from the home of their fathers and grandfathers the ministry which those men had abandoned. But almost a century was to pass before we read of adherents of the Church of England in Hartford.

This seems a strange thing, when we recall that in 1707 a parish of that Church had been founded in Stratford; that in the ever-memorable year of 1722 there had begun in the person of Samuel Johnson and his associates that line of travellers across the sea, Connecticut's best men, sure that they were called of God to the ministry of the Christian Church, but sure also they could not minister in the word and sacraments without authority directly received from a bishop; and that in Hebron to the east there had been an organized Church of England parish from 1735, in Simsbury to the west from 1740, and in Middletown to the south from about 1750. But we must also remember that Hartford, although the seat of government, was not then a large or a busy place or on much frequented lines of travel; that in

fact it was in population but the twelfth town in the colony, the total number of inhabitants within the present limits being about 2,000, and it was uncongenial soil for the Church. Eighteen years after the first organization of a parish here, it was stated that while in Newtown one half of the inhabitants were churchmen, in Simsbury one-fourth, and in New Haven approximately one-seventh, here the churchmen were but one forty-fourth part of the people. And at the beginning, there was but one man of whom we know that he was a churchman by inheritance. This was Captain John Keith, son of a Scottish Episcopal clergyman who lies buried in Old Machar cemetery in Aberdeen, and brother of a priest of English ordination, who ministered in South Carolina and is buried in Trinity churchyard, Newport; his own burial was in the Mortimer vault in Middletown.

There must have been others who had been more or less prepared to take part in the organization of a Church of England parish here. Among them I am inclined to think that too little has been said as to Abraham Beach and his influence. From the fact that on a map of Hartford noting the buildings as they stood about the time of the Revolution we find the house on Main street at the south corner of Sheldon street marked "Dr. Bull and Rev. Abm. Beach, Episc. minister," it has been inferred that this was his dwelling after his ordination. But such is not the case; the map was written up from the memory of old inhabitants, and a title was given to Mr. Beach which did not belong to him while he lived here. His home had been here since 1742, when his mother, a rich widow under twenty years of age, married Dr. Jonathan Bull; he was graduated at Yale College at the age of seventeen "with a reputation for remarkable scholarship," and then returned to Dr. Bull's home. He went to the French war, opened a store here, wrote the prospectus of the Connecticut Courant (as is believed) in 1764, and having become a churchman studied theology and was ordained in England in 1768. His ministerial life was passed in New Jersey and New York, where he attained eminence; and he is said to have drafted the earliest plan for the organizing of the Church in the United States as one body. Here we are told he had a notable influence for a young man; and no wonder, for a Churchward influence came upon him and through him from two of the strongest Church clergymen of his time--his uncle John Beach of Newtown, vigorous as pastor and writer, who carried his parish through the revolution without intermitting the prayers for the King, and the husband of the widow of another uncle, the great Samuel Johnson of Stratford, father of the Church in Connecticut, scholar and teacher and philosopher, friend and correspondent of Berkeley, afterwards first president of King's College in New York and invited to be first president of the University of Pennsylvania.

But the earliest service known to have been held in Hartford in accordance with the Book of Common Prayer of the Church of England was in the first quarter of the year of which this is the sesquicentennial; and the officiating clergyman was a young man, Abraham Beach's college junior by one year, the Rev. Thomas Davies of Litchfield County, who in 1763 began Church ministrations in Great Barrington to the north of his home and in Hartford well off to the east. He was an active and faithful man, whose career

of earthly service was cut short by death; from a younger brother of his bearing the same name have descended the late Bishop of Michigan and the present Bishop of Western Massachusetts. After his visit, it was decided at once that a church should be built, and the readiness of the decision shows that there must have been the hope of a fairly large body of conformists here; Dr. Johnson, writing to Archbishop Secker in April, told him of the plan, saying that Hartford was the chief town in Connecticut--evidently as being the seat of government--and that it was expected that there would be "a considerable congregation and several people of note."

On the 6th day of the following October Charles Caldwell, for a consideration of 80 pounds conveyed by a lease for 999 years to John Keith, William Tiley, William Jepson, Hezekiah Marsh, and Thomas Burr, "as a committee of the brethren of the Episcopal Church in the town of Hartford," a half acre of land on the west side of Main street, along the south line of which Church street was after a few years laid out; it included the northeast corner of the present church lot, so that a part of this site of the first church--not built it must be remembered for thirty years--must now be in the street which (as in so many other cases) took its name from it. The legal form of the organization, which was certainly the beginning of the present parish, does not appear; nor can we tell the exact date on which it was formed. Its history for some years was certainly not one of progress; for although Dr. Johnson wrote to the Society for the Propagation of the Gospel in December, 1762, that the Church has so increased at Hartford, not by means of any parties or contentions but by the still voice of reason and benevolence, that they are like to have a flourishing church, consisting of a number of good families, many by accession; he wrote five months later to say "Hartford does not get forward as was expected when I wrote." This may have been partly because they were disappointed in their hopes of securing the services of the Rev. Edward Winslow, missionary at Stratford, for whose support indeed they had not the means, and partly because the disturbed state of the colonies led the society in England to hesitate about giving help for newly established parishes or missions here. At any rate, we find that at the close of the year 1763, the clergy were thinking "to take turns" at Hartford "once a month, so that they might not be quite discouraged." The nearest clergymen then were the Rev. Roger Viets of Simsbury, and the Rev. Samuel Peters of Hebron; presently the Rev. Abraham Jarvis came back from England and took charge of Middletown, from which place he was able to give help. Mr. Viets, son of a wealthy Dutch physician who having crossed the ocean had undertaken to work the copper mines at Simsbury and great-uncle of Bishop Griswold of Massachusetts and the rest of the eastern diocese, began the record of baptisms and marriages here in 1764 and that of burials in 1766; and the first ministration of the Holy Communion of which we find note was in the court house on the 2d day of March 1766, there being six communicants. Mr. Peters, whose eccentricities quickened his zeal for the church, visited Hartford as well as other stations which he was able to reach from his home. And presently Mr. Jarvis, who afterwards became the second bishop of Connecticut, began to serve the churchmen here with his ministrations.

But the plan for building a church lay in abeyance, no more being done than to bring the stone from its foundation. Part of the site was alienated, and Samuel Talcott, Jr., under color of the deed of one portion, carried away the stone which lay on another. Suits for trespass followed, and the churchmen recovered damages and costs, but no more work was done. In 1770, the Rev. Mr. Dibblee of Stamford preached in Hartford on Trinity Sunday; he wrote of having a numerous congregation, of good attention and behavior, but mostly dissenters; and he expressed the opinion that the recent troubles were due to "a wicked design of a powerful family, so to demolish the Church that it might never rise"; moreover, if we understand him aright, he found that a new and better foundation for the building had already been laid. If so, nothing more was done until the year 1786, nearly a quarter of a century from the date of the purchase of the land; indeed, we do not know that during the period of the Revolution and the years immediately preceding and following any Church services were held here or that the organization was maintained. But within a day of the second anniversary of Bishop Seabury's consecration, on the thirteenth of November in the year 1786, under the new toleration act of the General Assembly of the State, churchmen of Hartford effected the formal organization of "the Episcopal Society of the City of Hartford," which now continues under the title of the Parish of Christ Church. Fifteen men signed the article of association; of them William Imlay and John Morgan were chosen wardens, William Adams clerk, and Samuel Cutler, John Thomas, Jacob Ogden, and John Jeffrey vestrymen. A week later it was voted to prepare a subscription-paper for "money, labor, or any specific articles" to be used in the erection of a church. There were in all 37 subscribers. John Morgan made the largest subscription, 36 pounds (about $100) in materials, John Caldwell promised 10 pounds, in pure spirit, John Chenevard a hogshead of 110 gallons of "molasses," and Noah Webster, Jr., seven dozen of his spelling-books. The work of building was not begun till 1792, the corner stone being put in place by Prince Brewster, the mason, with a formula which does not need to be quoted here, and nine gallons of rum being used at the raising of the frame. Three years later a new subscription of $575 was made by twenty-two people for finishing the building, and a part of the original lot was sold to provide for the funds. In July 1795, Calvin Whiting, a recent graduate of Harvard College, a school teacher and student in divinity, was engaged as a lay-reader; but he was taken ill after three months and died in October; a stone marks his grave in the ancient burying-ground. Perhaps the church was used for service before this time; it it was not even then completed.

We do not know whether Bishop Seabury in his episcopate of twelve years visited Hartford; there was probably no occasion for any official act on his part, as he died before the Church was ready for consecration. But in a letter of his, dated 9 October 1793 and never quoted as yet (I think) in historical sketches of this parish, he speaks of three new congregations as having arisen in the State since he came into it as bishop. They were all on the banks of the Connecticut River and were approximately 15, 30, and 45 miles from its mouth. At East Haddam, where he said

there had been no churchman four years before, an elegant church had been built and there was a resident clergyman. At Chatham (now Portland) and at Hartford, he continues, "new congregations are engaged in building larger and elegant churches, i. e. for this country. Hartford"--I am still quoting the Bishop's words--"is the principal town in the state, the seat of their government, and the fortress of presbyterianism; and though a small number of Church people have been long in it, not more than six families, their efforts to build a church have for these forty years been baffled by the acts and violence of the presbyterians. Their influence there is now over, and the congregation in Hartford will probably become equal to any in the country."

The first clergyman called to the rectorship of the newly organized parish was the Rev. Ashbel Baldwin of Stratford, in 1797; but he did not think that he could support his family on five hundred dollars. Two years later, the parish, probably by the intervention of Bishop Jarvis, was spared the disgrace of having Ammi Rogers, "a man possessed of enough of talent to do a great deal of mischief," for its first rector. Finally, in August, 1801, only a little more than century and a decade ago, the Rev. Menzies Rayner entered upon the rectorship; and on the 11th day of November, in a heavy rain, the church was consecrated by Bishop Jarvis. It was the handsomest building in the city, with arched windows, a steeple having four urns at the corners, a spire, and an organ--the only one in this part of the State. It had eight square pews on each side, one with a canopy intended for the governor, if an episcopalian should ever attain to that dignity, and twenty-six slips. Several years later a bell was procured, and Christ Church bell was for many years the noon-day bell of the community. In connection with the consecration of the Church, Mr. Rayner was instituted as rector according to the form of the newly framed office for that purpose; this was not, however, the first occasion of its use, but may have been the second.

Mr. Rayner was a little over thirty years old when he came here, and had been a Methodist preacher. He was, says Dr. Hoadly, "an active man, an able controversialist, and in many respects a good pastor." He found the work here hard, and in a letter, not yet published, addressed to Bishop Hobart of New York in 1805, introducing to him Colonel James Ward, and asking him to give Mr. Ward an opportunity to lay the needs of Christ Church before some influential people in the city, he wrote:

"He thinks, and I believe with good reason, that unless from some quarter or other the Church here can obtain some assistance, it must inevitably sink. Much opposition has been experienced in its establishment, and a succession of misfortunes has attended its progress till now, more than half of its best supporters have either died, removed, or failed in business since I came here, the burthen of all the expenses is defrayed, and has been for two or three years past, by five or six persons. Still the congregation is respectable. It will average one Sunday with another 300 persons, but in the present situation of its resources they will not join, so as to be liable to pay their proportion of the expenses. The other congregations in this town have ample funds, we have none; under these circumstances can it be expected the Church should increase?

Indeed I am astonished (and it is owing to the unparalleled zeal of a few, with God's blessing) that it has succeeded as well as it has, and been supported till this time. The prosperity of the Church in Hartford is, I am persuaded, of great importance to the Church in this State, and especially the eastern part of it, in which several new congregations are forming."

After ten years, Mr. Rayner resigned to take charge of St. Paul's Church, Ripton (now Huntington); and after spending about sixteen years there, having embraced the tenets of the Universalists, he resigned from the Episcopal ministry, with the assurance of the personal esteem of the bishop and others of our communion. He was Universalist pastor in this city for a few years; his death occurred in 1850. While he was rector here, the number of communicants increased from six to thirty-four; there were two confirmations by Bishop Jarvis, one of 58 candidates in 1808, the other of 62 in 1811. The families under his care increased in number to about 80, of whom twelve or fourteen lived in Windsor and East Windsor; and under his care St. John's Church, Warehouse Point, in the last named town, had its beginning in 1802, being the oldest daughter of Christ Church.

Approaching now the time of the great rectors of this parish, I cannot but feel that there is a great deal that might well be said concerning them and their work, while I am conscious that I must not exceed a reasonable limit of time on such an occasion as this. To mention the names of Philander Chase, Jonathan Mayhew Wainwright, Thomas Church Brownell, Nathaniel Sheldon Wheaton, Hugh Smith, George Burgess, Peter Schermerhorn Chauncey, Thomas March Clark, and Richard M. Abercombie, all of whom were rectors here within a period of fifty years, is to suggest a careful study of this parish and the community in whose life it has taken so prominent and helpful a part, and also a wide survey of the history of the Church in this land. Of the rectors mentioned, one was the third bishop of Connecticut and held the rectorship but incidentally; but among the others there stands the lion-hearted pioneer of church work who was the Church's first bishop in Ohio and Illinois, one who was called to the charge of the great diocese of New York in troublous days and whose short term of work was crowned with the blessing of the peacemaker, the scholarly man who was chosen to be the first bishop of Maine, and the eloquent orator who continued long in the episcopate of Rhode Island, and became, as did Bishop Chase before him, Presiding Bishop of the Church in the United States. Of the rectors of later days, it may be added here that one is the Bishop of California, while an assistant minister of his in this parish is now his neighbor as Bishop of Sacramento. The whole story of the men cannot be told today; nor is it possible to put into compendium the mass of material which Dr. Russell so well collected and arranged; I may perhaps be pardoned for suggesting to some of the younger members of the parish and congregation that full material for the study of the parish's history, with careful and discriminating sketches of the work and character of the clergymen and the laymen who have taken any considerable part in it, is ready at their hand.

37

But who can fail to say something of Philander Chase, who stayed here six years and raised the number of communicants from barely thirty to nearly one hundred and ten; who left, not because of any disagreement with his people, but because matters in the diocese had taken a turn which persuaded him that he could be more useful and more happy elsewhere; who preached his farewell sermon on a snowy winter's day, and went forth the next morning with the faith of a patriarch, scarce knowing whither he went; who looked back to Hartford from the changes and chances of his life-- and he had many of them--as to the place of its sunniest days; and whose extraordinary career, possible only to an extraordinary character, sheds a lustre upon the place of his sojourn, while his influence, especially here the influence of a good pastor, abides and is felt today. It may be noted here, in passing, that soon after his coming here, Mr. Chase organized St. James's Church, Greenfield, which may thus be reckoned as this parish's second daughter.

As to his immediate successor, I cannot but quote the words of Bishop Clark in his sermon preached here a generation ago, with its kindly but keen characterization of the two men. "Much as the congregation had occasion to revere their late rector for what he had done in their behalf, and also to love him for his essentially kind and noble qualities, it was probably in some respects a relief to receive in his place a young man of twenty-five, the bland and courteous gentleman, who was careful to give no offence in anything, that his ministry be not blamed; in contrast with the fiery utterances of his predecessor his words must have seemed to "distil as the dew." Such was Mr. Wainwright; and such he continued to be.

No one can minister or worship in this building, with any consciousness of its history, and fail to think of Dr. Wheaton, rector of the parish for the ten years beginning in 1821. The congregation, after twenty years or more, needed a larger church. Church people were sharing in the prosperity of the community; a college was about to be established here, the professors and students of which would add to the number of worshippers and furnish an intellectual stimulus to the preacher; the parish was gaining consciousness of its needs and its obligations; and its new rector was not only a man of great earnestness and unselfishness, but also endowed with good taste and something of an artist's skill. Taking leave of absence from his parochial duties to solicit abroad gifts of books and scientific apparatus for the college, of which he was an original trustee, he also studied the ecclesiastical architecture of the mother country; and he came back fitted to be a wise counsellor in the building of a new Christ Church. After the present site had been secured in 1827--and it was a fortunate escape from the first choice of a site bounded by Temple, Market, and Kingsley streets--plans submitted by Ithiel Towne of New Haven were accepted, and work on the church was begun. Mr. Towne may have drawn the plans and made the specifications, but there is no doubt that more than their outline was due to Dr. Wheaton. Every detail of the work came under his personal supervision, and the building is indebted, as Dr. Hoadly says, "not only to his fine taste, but to the skill of his hands, for he fashioned some of the models for the ornaments (of the interior) and some of the stone faces on the east end were cut by him." The result was the finest church building in the United States, almost if not quite the first example of real gothic, far surpassing that of Trinity Church, New Haven, ten years its senior. It had in its windows, especially those of the tower--the erection of which was, however, delayed until 1839--outlines taken from York Minster; its buttresses, the first in the country, were the delight of visitors; and the wide roof resting only on the side-walls was a marvel of construction. Yet the full beauty of the plan was not seen in actual effect, even after the tower had been finished, until a very few years ago when the pinnacles were placed above the buttresses and the battlement or "balustrade" was carried along the edge of the front gable and the sides--a gift provided for by the generosity of one whose name has been already mentioned, Dr. Charles Jeremy Hoadly, under the careful direction of his brother. I wonder if Christ Church people and Hartford people in general sufficiently appreciate and admire the stateliness and beauty of this building or know that they have in its exterior even today, one of the best examples of ecclesiastical architecture in the country. It was consecrated the 23rd of December 1829 by Bishop Hobart of New York, Bishop Brownell being absent on a missionary journey in what was then the southwest. Dr. Wheaton presented a transparency, representing the Transfiguration after Raphael, to cover the great window over the pulpit, "the admiration of the parishioners and the astonishment of many who were not accustomed to the sight of pictures in churches." After many years, it was damaged by a ladder and taken down; and the window was filled with stained glass, "never much commended," and of which it is not well to speak in general or in detail. The present chancel window in memory of Dr. Wheaton shows in rich and beautiful form the subject of the painting which he presented. He resigned in 1821, to succeed Bishop Brownell in the presidency of Trinity College, of which he was to the end a constant friend and benefactor. The old church was sold to the Roman Catholics and, with spire removed, stood on Talcott street, known as Trinity Church, until it was destroyed by fire in 1853.

The rectorship of the Rev. Hugh Smith was short. To him succeeded in 1834, Dr. George Burgess, a "Holy-Ghost-man," to use the words in which he was described by the old colored janitor of the college, to begin a notable rectorship. I may quote again from Bishop Clark: "His time was divided between his study, his Church, and the houses of his parishioners, and no one knew that he ever passed an idle hour. There are few clergymen who study as much and write as much as he did, and there are few who visit their flocks as frequently. His whole public and private character was both subdued and intensified by the habit of habitual and sincere devotion. He lived in daily and hourly communion with God, and was ready to do whatever his Master demanded of him." The benediction of his thirteen years' work here still remains, and many know of him from the testimony of those who felt his immediate influence. In his rectorship, as already noted, the tower was completed, and a brick chapel or "conference house" was also built on the lot in the rear. With his approval and that of the congregation there was founded in 1841 the second Church parish in Hartford, that of St. John's Church.

38

Its first rector, Dr. Arthur Cleveland Coxe, is known to the Church as its poet bishop, sharing the poetic inspiration in a "strife of brothers" with Dr. Burgess; and his successors have included the present Bishop of Albany, also a poet, one of the great philosophical preachers of our Church, and a professor in the University of Oxford. Dr. Burgess's consecration to be Bishop of Maine took place here on the 31st of October 1847, Bishop Chase officiating as Presiding Bishop.

Dr. Chauncey's ministry here was short, though his withdrawal was regretted by the people. He came to this parish from a fourteen years' rectorship in Rye, New York, and went hence to St. James' Church in New York City, where he ministered for sixteen years until his death. At this time the number of communicants here had increased to more than 400, St. John's Church having besides nearly 250. I have been told by Mr. Chauncey's son-in-law, who came to a rectorship in Hartford from the parish in Newtown--once, as was noted, the strongest in Connecticut--that Mr. Chauncey declined an election to that parish while he was here, on the ground that he was not able to meet the demands upon his health and strength which he might encounter there. As to what he did here, I am permitted to quote from a letter addressed to him by the Church clergymen in this city, at the time of his leaving this parish; it is in the handwriting of Bishop Williams, then President of the college:

"Suffer us to bear witness to your unwearied diligence in the pastoral work; to your persuasive, earnest, and sound teaching as a preacher; to your sacrifice of health and strength in the labors of a populous parish; and to your uniform devotion to the manifold details of a most laborious round of duty, especially in visiting the sick and ministering to the bodies and the souls of the poor and needy." Near the end of Mr. Chauncey's rectorship, the Episcopal City Mission was established, for which after a while St. Paul's Church was built on Market street.

Dr. Thomas March Clark's rectorate covered but four years; but he made a great impression on the community as a powerful and eloquent preacher. Once a month the second service on Sunday was in the evening instead of the afternoon; and on those occasions the pews and galleries were filled and seats were placed in the aisles; and there was serious talk of enlarging the church by bringing out the whole front to the east line of the tower. He spoke in his anniversary sermon of the same "strange fatality in a given direction" befalling him which had met others of the rectors of the parish; for he was called hence in 1855 by an election to the episcopate of Rhode Island. He adds that "everything outwardly was peaceful and prosperous, and the congregation uniformly large and most intelligent and respectable in quality. The music"--he could afford to say this-- "was probably to many more attractive than the pulpit, and a more harmonious, charitably disposed, and affectionate people could hardly be found anywhere within the pale of Christendom. The long row of students that lined the gallery, the sprinkling of college professors and clergymen of various grades, the eminent physicians and lawyers, the thriving and enterprising men of affairs, the cultivated women whose names were a household word throughout the

land, combined to give reputation to this parish, and made it no easy thing for a modest man to stand in his place as their instructor and spiritual guide."

I must barely mention the names of the rectors who have followed: Mr. Abercombie, in whose time the parish of Trinity Church was organized, to which this parish willingly gave some of its oldest and most valued members; Dr. George Henry Clark, brother of the Bishop, who survived until a few years ago; Mr. Meech, now resident in Allegheny; Mr. Nichols, who went hence to Philadelphia, and is now Bishop of California; Mr. Tompkins, now of Philadelphia; Mr. Saltonstall, who died in this city while visiting a former parishioner. Note should also be made that for three years after Mr. Meech's withdrawal the Rev. John T. Huntington officiated regularly for the congregation. It was in Mr. Nichols's rectorship, on the fiftieth anniversary of the consecration of the church building, that the new chancel was consecrated and the parish house with its chapel was dedicated. These structural additions, I do not need to remind you, were a memorial, and bear the name of a family which has been and still is most bountiful in its provision for the house of God and for the offices thereof, and which has given you your present rector--whom God preserve! These changes led to a modification of the musical part of the services, as was indeed expected. In the present rectorship the Chapel of the Incarnation has been provided within the church, this also a beautiful and serviceable memorial.

Few parish churches have been the appointed place of as many ordinations as have been held here; they include those of 80 deacons and 42 priests. The largest number at one time was when ten deacons were ordained, on the 29th of June 1845, all of them being graduates of the General Theological Seminary sent here for ordination on account of the disturbed condition of ecclesiastical matters in New York; between 1855 and 1870 there was but one ordination, there was none between 1886 and 1895, and there have been but three in the past twenty-six years. The diocesan convention first met in Christ Church in 1812, one hundred years ago; the convention of this year will be the twenty-fourth to assemble in the former building or in this. If it shall be the lot of this Church to be assigned for distinctively diocesan use, it will not be found to be without some special preparation therefor. Though out of place, I may note here that for thirty years after its consecration, Christ Church was the scene of the annual commencements of Trinity College.

I can never prepare a memorial address of this kind without being conscious of the fact of many imperfections and the possibility of many more; and there is no imperfection which I so much regret as that it is impossible to enumerate the working and representative laymen of a parish as one can enumerate its rectors and other ministers. It is a special cause of regret today, because the list of helpful men in Christ Church contains so many names of those who were honored in the community and whose work endures as benefiting both the city and the Church. If I name some of those whom I saw in Church every Sunday when as a college student I sat with the bereaved mother of a classmate, they may serve as examples of those who at other times,

some earlier and some later, have filled their or the like places. Good Dr. Russell's pew was on the north side of the Chancel; Bishop Brownell's son-in-law, Mr. Holland, sat on the other side; Mr. Zephaniah Preston, with memories of the Sunday School, was just behind us; and in the center aisle I saw Governor Toucey and Mr. George Beach, Captain Ebenezer Flower, and Major James Goodwin, Chester Adams and Charles H. Northam, Charles Bouton and Flavius A. Brown, while further back were Mr. Librarian Hoadly and members of the family of George Brinley; and of course there were many whom I did not know. Henry Wilson brought wonderful music from the fine old organ and from the trained voices of his choir; but what pleased me most was to hear him on Communion Sundays begin the Gloria in Excelsis in the seat to which he had come for the rest of the sacramental service after the choir had sung the hymn and gone away. Of some of those who have passed hence, there are memorials upon these walls or within these courts or elsewhere; and none of the others are forgotten before God. We wonder at all that records and structures tell; but that is more wonderful of which these are imperfect figures and symbols--the working of grace in the souls of men, their instruction in truth and discipline in righteousness, their progress from the font to the altar, from regeneration to sanctification, from the earthly to the heavenly.

CENTENARY OF THE CONSECRATION OF BISHOP CROES-- NOV. 19, 1915

[9]

It seems strange that New Jersey should have waited so long for her first bishop. Thirty years had passed since the organization of the diocese; Connecticut was looking for her third bishop, New York had her third caring for all the work of that large diocese; Massachusetts was sharing the services of her third bishop with the three other states which were united with her in the so-called Eastern Diocese; Virginia and South Carolina had each a second bishop; and the first bishop of Maryland, whose years of life were approaching their end, had the assistance of a suffragan. Bishop White of Pennsylvania, in the twenty-ninth year of his episcopate and with twenty-one years of active service before him, alone survived of the four who had been consecrated for our Church in lands across the seas; of the six consecrated in this country before 1811 two survived, but neither of them was able to undertake any episcopal or other public duty. The great crisis of that memorable year had passed, and now there were five able-bodied bishops, but only five, in a Church which had had a full national organization for a quarter of a century. To the first bishop of New Jersey the commission of the episcopate was transmitted directly from Bishop White and two of those later bishops and indirectly from each of the other three.

The critical period of American political history, as we are often reminded, was included in the years between the recognition of the independence of the thirteen States and the adoption of the federal constitution. Our Church passed through a like critical period between the time when the revolution severed its external connection with the Church of England and the time when bishops and

deputies from New England and the Middle States met in the first truly General Convention. But, as I have already said, the year 1811 marks another real crisis in its history. Two men had been elected to the episcopate, one to be the bishop of four states and one province in New England, and one to be second assistant bishop of New York with in fact the sole charge of the Episcopal Church in that great State. They were strong men and, as the event showed, able and ready to do, each in his way, a great service for the Church in this land. But it appeared for a time impossible to secure the attendance of three bishops to consecrate them; and the question was seriously considered whether it would not be necessary to send them to England in order to secure the number of consecrators required by the ancient canons. Bishop White of Pennsylvania and Bishop Jarvis of Connecticut were in good health, and they had been in attendance at the General Convention which met at New Haven in May of that year. Four other American bishops were living: of them, Bishop Claggett of Maryland had started for the Convention, but was taken with a severe illness and obliged to return home; Bishop Madison of Virginia, who was President of William and Mary College and (it may be added) near the end of his life, declared that he could not be absent from the institution in term-time; Bishop Provoost of New York had for some ten years withdrawn from all exercise of the ministry and from public life; and Bishop Benjamin Moore, assistant in charge of that diocese, had been stricken with paralysis and could not leave his room. Finally, however, Bishop Provoost was persuaded to attend with Bishops White and Jarvis in Trinity Church, New York, on the 29th day of May, and the two bishops elect were consecrated. It was a signal, and a true signal, for new life in the Church; and action had been taken none too soon; for before the time of the consecration of your first bishop, Bishops Provoost, Madison and Jarvis had died; and Bishops Claggett and Moore did not survive the next year.

It was into this new life, guided indeed by the patriarchal Bishop White, but largely led by Hobart and Griswold in the north, by Richard Channing Moore and others in the south, and presently by Philander Chase in the west, that John Croes was called to take his place as a leader. Connecticut indeed first invited him to her vacant episcopate; but while he had this election under consideration, the people among whom he was happily serving as priest and rector called him to be their chief pastor; and the result was that a century ago this very day he was by Bishops White and Hobart and Kemp--the senior and the junior member of the college of bishops and the reviver of the episcopate, as he may be fairly called--consecrated Bishop of New Jersey.

But, as was said at the beginning, it would certainly seem that your forefathers in the faith and order of the Church, should have had a bishop long before that time. George Keith and John Talbot, the first missionaries of the Society for the Propagation of the Gospel to cross the ocean, had come to this colony, in which there were at the time perhaps two hundred communicants of the Church of England, and Mr. Talbot had become rector of St. Mary's Church, Burlington. In that town, on the second

day of November 1705, fourteen missionaries of the Society who had entered on work in New York, New Jersey, and Pennsylvania, met and framed an earnest petition to the authorities at home that they would provide for "the presence and assistance of a Suffragan Bishop." Four years later, the Society, "looking out for the best and most commodious place, as near the centre as possible of the colonies" in which they had or hoped soon to have missionaries, to fix the seat of a bishop, and having been informed that at Burlington in New Jersey, "there was a spacious and convenient house, with some land belonging to it, to be disposed of upon good terms," empowered the honorable Colonel Hunter, her majesty's governor of New York and the Jerseys, to treat with the owner for the purchase thereof"; and the property was secured and long held for the intended purpose. Later, the plan of the Society and of the friends of the adherents of the Church of England in the colonies seems to have been to establish four episcopal sees in America, one bishop to have his residence in Burlington, one in Williamsburg, the capital of Virginia, and the other two to be stationed on the islands. As we all know, nothing further came of these plans; and whether Mr. Talbot for the last few years of his life was or was not a "Bishop by non-juring consecration," he certainly did not openly act as a bishop or advance the project for a recognized episcopate in America.

In 1754 there came to New Brunswick as the first station in which he was to serve after his ordination, the Rev. Samuel Seabury, Jr., destined thirty years later to be the first Bishop on these shores and to exercise a strong and lasting influence on the Church of this great republic. There followed him, though not immediately, another Connecticut man, Abraham Beach, himself a man of strong character and wide influence. He it was who when the war of independence was over, though more than a year after the clergy of Connecticut had elected Seabury to be their bishop and sent him to England and (if need should be) to Scotland to ask for consecration, took what Bishop White called "the first step towards the forming of a collective body of the Episcopal Church in the United States." A few clergymen of this State and of the States adjacent to it on the north and the south were invited by him to meet, primarily for the perpetuation of a benevolent society which had been in existence before the Revolution, but also to consider principles and plans for concerted action on the part of the representatives of the members of the Episcopal Church, formerly the Church of England, in these States. The conference led to a larger meeting in New York, and finally to the complete union and organization of the Church in the United States; and you may well remember that in an important way the beginning of all that good work was here. There came to New Brunswick as rector in 1791 the Rev. Henry Van Dyke, one of the four admitted to the diaconate by Bishop Seabury at his first ordination, and as minister for one year in 1799 the Rev. John Henry Hobart later (as has been already noted) Bishop of New York, the strong advocate of "evangelical truth and apostolic order." His immediate successor was the Rev. John Croes, who at the age of a little more than two score entered on a rectorate of about thirty years, the last seventeen of which were also the period of his episcopate.

The Diocese of New Jersey had been organized, as far as this could be done without a diocesan bishop, in 1785. After thirteen years the Convention, by the unanimous vote of its six clerical members and the vote of seventeen out of the twenty-one congregations represented, chose the Rev. Uzal Ogden to be bishop; but the election failed to receive the confirmation of the house of deputies in the next General Convention and later of the standing committees of the dioceses. The matter was then dropped, quite certainly to the ultimate satisfaction of those who had made the election; for in 1805, as the result of a serious controversy, and of adverse action on the part of the Convention, Mr. Ogden made a declaration of withdrawal from the Protestant Episcopal Church, declaring however that he should continue to officiate as a minister of the Church of England and in virtue of a licence from the Bishop of London. It is perhaps but an act of fairness to add that Bishop White, in his guarded way, tells us that the real objection in the case was "that the gentleman elected was considered by his brethren generally as being more attached to the doctrines and the practices obtaining in some other churches than to those of his own." "What rendered the management of the case more difficult," he adds, "was his being brought forward by some gentlemen who had always professed the strongest disapprobation of the least deviation from the institutions of the Church; [but] no doubt they thought they perceived some counterbalancing advantages." In fact, he did presently join the presbyterians; but he held no pastoral charge among them.

Probably the diocese became rather discouraged. It was not very strong, and it could look either to its northern or its southern neighbor for assistance in cases of necessity. At any rate it waited again for ten years, when perhaps (may I venture to say it?) roused by the action of the Connecticut Convention which on the 8th day of June had elected the Rev. John Croes of New Brunswick in the State of New Jersey to be bishop of that diocese, and by the knowledge that he had the acceptance of the election under serious consideration, the convention of the diocese of New Jersey on the 30th day of August elected the New Brunswick rector to be its bishop. The relative strength of the two dioceses at the time may be seen from the fact that twenty-seven clergymen and delegates from thirty-six parishes took part in the election in Connecticut, while in the New Jersey convention seven clergymen and representatives of sixteen parishes were present. We are told also that the compensation offered by the other diocese (which certainly was not very large) was "considerably greater than that offered by New Jersey"; yet, because he felt that his services were more needed in the poorer and feebler diocese, and that there he could better serve God and the Church, moved also by the affectionate solicitations of the people of his parish, with whom he could remain as their rector, he decided to accept the election which had come to him from his own people. He was therefore consecrated to the office and work of a bishop in the Church of God (as has been already said) in St. Peter's Church, Philadelphia, by Bishop White, assisted by Bishop Hobart and Bishop Kemp.

The first Bishop of New Jersey was of Polish parentage, religiously brought up, and he served in the

revolutionary army before he was able to enter on the classical and the theological studies to which he wished to devote himself. Like many another good and useful scholar, most of his study was done by him as it was needed for teaching; Dr. McWhorte the presbyterian divine called him "a man of the first abilities, prudence, and discretion; a man of sense and reading, but a certain veil of modesty sheds an obscurity over his abilities and accomplishments; bred an Episcopalian, he has uniformly, without superstition or bigotry, adhered to the peculiarities of his own religion." His work as a bishop, we are assured, was laborious, but was well and faithfully done. To adopt the words of one who had followed out its results, he breathed new life into expiring parishes, imparted strength and encouragement to those that were weak, and incited those that were comparatively strong to increased effort and zeal. New missions were established in remote parts of the diocese; long-closed church doors were opened; old churches were enlarged and new ones were built; the clergy and communicants increased in number and in activity; and all this was due to his patient, persistent, and indefatigable labors. He was tall, grave, and dignified, old-fashioned in his dress and frugal in his habits, a skilful gardener, in a day of good gardeners, and turning the results of his manual labor into benefit for himself and his neighbors and parishioners; and he failed not to gain the respectful approbation of fellow prelates, his clergy, and his people. His death occurred on the 30th of July 1832.

To his immediate successor, Bishop George Washington Doane, consecrated with three others in the memorable service in Trinity Church, New York, on the last day of October of that same year 1832, Bishop Croes transmitted the episcopate through the two Bishops Onderdonk; and to Bishop Odenheimer through Bishop Meade of Virginia. Bishop Odenheimer laid hands in consecration on Bishop Stevens of Pennsylvania, and he on your Bishop Scarborough, the 111th in the American succession; Bishop Scarborough laid hands on Bishop Starkey and (a hundred and three consecrations having taken place since his own) on Bishop Lines; and Bishop Lines has but lately laid hands on Bishop Matthews and Bishop Stearley. There are but five names in the succession between Bishop Croes and the present bishop of Newark; and but six between the first Bishop of New Jersey and the present bishop of that diocese with the suffragan bishop of Newark; and this latter is 282nd on the roll of our House of Bishops, as Bishop Croes was the sixteenth.

Rev. Samuel Hart, D. D., D. C. L.,
Middletown, Conn.

206 Broad Street
Elizabeth N.J.
November 15, 1915.

Dear Dr. Hart;

Understanding that you are to read an historical paper in connection with the celebration of the centenary of Bishop Croes' consecration, it occurred to me that the following fact would be of interest to you though, of course, it may be that you already know of it. In the old parish register of St. John's Church, this city, under baptisms there is an entry under June 20, 1762 "John son of Jacob Croes pr me T. B. Chandler." Some one has written over

this "the present Bishop of New Jersey." Attention is also called to the fact that under the date of May 31, 1761, there is a similar entry so that it would seem that there was an older child of the same name who must have died before the Bishop was baptized. It seems to me a curious coincidence that the first Bishop of the Diocese should have been baptized by the Rev. Doctor Chandler who was himself offered the first American bishopric (Nova Scotia).

Hoping to have the pleasure of hearing you on Friday,

Very truly yours,

Warren R. Dix

I

THE CHURCH OF THE GOOD SHEPHERD IN HARTFORD

[10]   In the beautiful city of Hartford there are no two more beautiful buildings than the Church of the Good Shepherd and its Memorial Parish House. They stand together in a park-like portion of what is known as the south meadows, not far from the Connecticut River. The names of the streets in this part of Hartford bear witness to the fact that in former years the Indians had their homes there and that the Dutch made an early settlement near that very spot; while of the streets which lead to it from the main avenue of the city, one bears the name of an early governor of the English Colony of Connecticut and one testifies to the sturdy spirit and practical independence of the colonists. [The Church stands on Hendrixsen Avenue, not far from Sequassen Street, and is approached by Wyllys Street and Charter Oak Avenue.]

The massive dyke which protects these buildings from the annual overflow of the river protects also a great manufactory where many men are kept busy with hand and brain for six days of the week, and the homes in which some of them live. The armory, the dyke, the enclosed meadow, bear witness to the inventive genius, the practical skill, the wonderful success, and the still wider plans of one of the great inventors of this age. Colonel Samuel Colt, when his too short life came to an end on the tenth of January, 1862, in the very meridian of his powers, had in his mind great schemes for the advantage of the whole community, and particularly of those who were, in one way or other, busied in the work of his armory. Some of these, from the very nature of the case, could not be carried out without his guiding hand and brain; and though the armory itself has risen from the ashes of one most disastrous conflagration and another which threatened as serious harm, and is still a place of busy activity, yet one's thoughts go back to those earlier times to imagine the full beauty and prosperity which might have had their centre in this corner of the city of Hartford.

But, while there is much of this sort to remind us of what Colonel Colt did and what he hoped to do, the special memorial to him and to three lovely children who were taken in infancy into the land of eternal rest, is the Church of the Good Shepherd. It stands for the glory of God and for the service of men, especially (so far as may

be) of those who carry on the work begun in this place by
him whom it chiefly commemorates, and witnessing to the
undying affection of a wife and mother. Of pleasing proportions and presenting from every side a picture of
beauty, it also repays careful study and tells in every detail of design or work the story of Divine and of human
love. The Church was consecrated on the twenty-eighth
day of January, 1869; its architect was Mr. Edward
Tuckerman Potter, of New York.

In general plan the building is of an early style of
Gothic architecture, comprising a nave with clerestory and
aisles, separated by a high arch from a choir flanked on
the one side by a baptistry and on the other by an organ-
chamber and ending in a semi-circular apse; while on the
north is a large transept serving for a chapel. A semi-
detached tower, carrying a chime of bells and surmounted
by a lofty and graceful spire, stands at the northwest corner,
and provides in its lower story the principal entrance to the
nave; while at the southwest corner is the armourer's porch.
The material is Portland freestone, plentifully trimmed with
light sandstone from Ohio. The extreme length is 114 feet,
the width of the nave 47 feet, and its height 65 feet.

The special memorial in this structure is the great
west window. It is in fact two pointed windows enclosed in
a massive setting of stone and surmounted by a circular
(or rather multifoil) window within the same pointed frame.
On the exterior it stands beneath the great cross at the peak
of the roof, on which are the sacred letters I. H. S. and beneath them the words "Dei Gloriae, while on the kneeling-
stones on either side may be read, in letters and figures in-
tertwined with carved foliage, the date, "A.D. 1868." From
the interior the window is seen to contain on the one side the
figure of Joseph in Egypt distributing food, with the legend,
"And God blessed him and made all that he did to prosper,"
while beneath is the Colt coat of arms with its noble motto,
Vincit qui patitur." On the other side or division of the
window is the figure of the Good Shepherd, with the little
ones of the flock, having the legend, "He shall gather the
lambs with His arm," and beneath is the same coat of arms
united with that of the Jarvis family. The dedicatory inscription in the lowest section of the window reads thus:

IN MEMORY OF MY HUSBAND
SAMUEL COLT
BORN 19TH JULY, 1814
DIED 10TH JANUARY, 1862

AND OF OUR INFANT CHILDREN
SAMUEL JARVIS COLT
ELIZABETH JARVIS COLT
HENRIETTA SELDEN COLT

The multifoil window above contains a representation
of the Angel of Peace bearing three children in his arms or
clinging to his robes. The whole is surrounded by a painted
border containing this verse from the Apocalypse: "The
Lamb which is in the midst of the throne shall feed them,
and shall lead them unto living fountains of waters, and God
shall wipe away all tears from their eyes"; and above are
the simple words, so full of suggestion as to the meaning of
it all, "God is our hope." At the end of the aisles, on either

side of the great window, are windows with copies of two of
Fra Angelico's angels, the special gifts to the church of
the brother and brother-in-law of Mrs. Colt, Mr. Richard
W. H. Jarvis and Mr. C. Nichols Beach.

As one turns from the west end and looks up the nave,
along the lines of graceful columns surmounted by arches and
spandrels filled with carved leaves, past the massive arch
of stone which rises above the steps of the choir, he catches
glimpses of great columns of polished granite with capitals
of Ohio stone representing water-flowers, and sees at the
extreme east the thirteen windows of the apse, that in the
middle being slightly higher than the others. This contains
a representation of our Lord, while six Apostles stand on
either side, St. Paul taking the place of the traitor. The
figures are taken from Overbeck's paintings, and beneath
each is the appropriate symbol; above all are the words in
red and gold, "King of kings and Lord of lords." On the
exterior the apse is very beautiful. The windows are
separated by columns of Scotch granite, alternately red
and blue, and display in their capitals the symbols of the
twelve Apostles entwined in foliage. Above, there rises
the chancel cross in gilt; above this may be seen the Latin
cross in a circle which marks the end of the nave; and on
the kneelers are the words "Lex," "Rex," "Lux," "Dux,"
which tell of Christ as our Law, our King, our Light, and
our Leader. Returning along the south side, one passes
the arched projection of the baptistry with its hooded entrance and the three triple windows of the aisle, and ar-
rives at the armourer's porch, where the signs of the
armourer's work are carved among sacred symbols, and
where the eye catches the words, "Whatsoever thou doest,
do all to the glory of God;" and over the inner door, "Enter into His gates with thanksgiving." Then passing by the
tower with its entrance doors and looking up along the
graceful spire to the gilded cross lifted high in the air, one
notes the triplet windows of the north side of the nave, and
the single lancets of the transept chapel, the entrance to
which tells of its special use as a room for the Sunday-
school, having above it carved in stone the Agnus Dei with
the legend, "Feed my lambs," and on the corbels the
shepherd's crook. At the end of the transept is a wonderfully beautiful group of five pointed windows of equal height
and width, above which is a window in the shape of a spherical triangle. The roof is surmounted by a double triangle
in stone, while the apex-stone exhibits the crown of thorns,
and the kneelers show the other instruments of the Pas-
sion--the nails, the pincers, the spear, and the sponge.
Beyond the chapel is the entrance to the robing-room.

Returning now to the interior, we can notice the
details of the carving in stone and in wood which adorn
nave, choir, and chancel, the line of small but bright clerestory windows with a like line extending around the apse,
and the massive screen of plate glass, adorned with the
carvings of its frame, which divides the chapel from the
nave, while opposite is a mural tablet of brass, in memory
of the parents of Mrs. Colt, the Rev. William Jarvis and
Mrs. Elizabeth Miller Jarvis, his wife, and another of the
same design, in memory of Mrs. Jarvis's sister, Miss
Hetty Buckingham Hart. We shall not fail to observe the
font of purest white marble, which represents three children holding a large shell for the baptismal water, in

special memory of the three little ones whose names are repeated on its base, and the gift of Mrs. Colt's sister, Mrs. C. Nichols Beach. The baptistry in which it stands is separated from the aisle by an open screen, perhaps the finest piece of wood carving in the church. Near it on the choir steps stands the lectern of brass, adorned with carbuncles, and opposite is the pulpit bearing in its panels the shepherd's crook, the I.H.S., and the mitre, and having the carved inscription, "He shall feed His flock like a shepherd." Then, between the organ-pipes and choir-stalls on the north side and the clergy-stalls and baptistry-arches on the south, looking up we see the great corona of brass which lights the choir and the sanctuary, and further on in the apse the altar of carved wood with its altar-shelf and cross and vases, having on its front the words, "Lord, evermore give us this bread," with appropriate symbols beneath. The credence and the bishop's chair stand to the north, and the sedilia of the clergy to the south, within the rail. Inscriptions, in ornamental letters on an arabesque pattern, run along the nave walls under the cornice: "I the Lord am thy Saviour and thy Redeemer, the Mighty One of Jacob"; "When the chief Shepherd shall appear, ye shall receive a crown of glory that fadeth not away"; and over the arches on either side of the choir we read, "Blessing and honor and glory and power be unto Him that sitteth upon the throne, and unto the Lamb, for ever and ever."

The chapel is entered through doors in the great glass screen which reaches to the very peak of the inner roof, reflecting the beauties of choir and nave, and at the same time enabling the eye to study the details of this transept, for such in reality it is, framed in delicate branches of wood carving.

The decorations and appointments show the special design of the chapel for the use of the Sunday School. On diagonal bars in the glass of the windows are instructive texts of Scripture, and in the five windows at the north end are symbols of the Lord and the Evangelists, with a representation of the Christ Child holding His hand in benediction; the window above shows the dove, as the symbol of the Holy Spirit.

The vessels of the Communion Service were made chiefly from articles of silver which had been gifts to the infant children. They bear the inscription: "The Church of the Good Shepherd. In memory of precious ones whom the Good Shepherd has folded in His blessed arms."

Such is the memorial which has now for well-nigh thirty years testified to undying affection, ministered to the highest needs of man, and set forth the glory of God. As the poet-bishop of the American Church said in the sermon which he preached at its consecration: "The Christian lady who has built this Church of the Good Shepherd has been made His own instrumentality for representing here anew, and after eighteen centuries, the same compassions which moved Him then. Here the poor man shall find his spiritual home; here he is refreshed with the same blessings which are furnished to the affluent; here the 'rich and poor shall meet together, because the Lord is maker of them all.' The passenger upon the neighboring river shall often see

its illuminated windows 'in the night when a holy solemnity is kept,' or descry its spire by the starlight or its topmost cross by the moon; and so by night as by day it shall ever bear testimony to Him was 'draws all men unto Him' because He was 'lifted up.' 'His compassions fail not,' they are as fresh to-day as they were when the text was recorded; and lo! they too are 'scattered abroad' wherever wandering sheep are to be found, even to the ends of the earth."

The marvels which Colonel Colt wrought in his life-work, though they awoke admiration at the time, have been better appreciated as the years have passed on. "Contemporaries," says one who is well qualified to judge, "saw with wonder the swift expansion of his trade, the sudden evolution from small beginnings, the inflow of almost fabulous wealth, and the extraordinary impulse thus given to the growth of the city. They felt, too, the force of a personality that no difficulties could daunt, and before which obstacles on every side seemed to vanish away. But they did not see that he was setting up ideals of mechanical excellence, and training men in habits of thoroughness, that were destined to give a distinctive character to many industries." But with all this, who can tell of the influences upon character and life, the inspiration for the service of God and men, the manifold blessings which have flowed and shall flow, please God, to the end of time from this sacred memorial to husband and children, the Church of the Good Shepherd!

II
THE CALDWELL HART COLT MEMORIAL PARISH HOUSE

Very near the Church of the Good Shepherd, on a slight eminence to the southwest, stands the Caldwell Hart Colt Memorial House, which was formally opened on the tenth day of September, 1896. While the Church, as has been said, commemorates Colonel Samuel Colt and three infant children, this stately and graceful building is a Mother's memorial to the only child who arrived at mature years, whose lamented death occurred when he seemed to be in the very vigor of manhood and after he had begun to succeed in some part to his Father's place. Of this character and his life more will presently be said in the words of one who knew him well; it must suffice for the present, in order that the symbolism of the memorial building may be the better understood, to say that from his early years he was filled with a love of travel and adventure, that he had taken extensive journeys as a huntsman in the far West, and that his greatest happiness had been found on the sea. It was as a yachtsman, the master of the Dauntless, that he was best known. He entered into this life with great enthusiasm, navigating and commanding the Dauntless himself, always ready to meet any craft with which he could enter into honorable contest. He had held the position of Vice-Commodore of the New York Yacht Club, and at the time of the death was Commodore of the Larchmont Club by re-election.

It was seemly, then, that the building erected as a memorial to Commodore Colt, while adapted to the various purposes of a Parish House and supplementing the provision which the beautiful Church had made for worship and sacred

instruction, should not only recall the man himself but also indicate the matters in which he was especially interested, suggesting the sea and the wonders of both animate and inanimate nature. The skill of the architect, the same who had designed the Church, carrying out such suggestions as these, has produced most wonderful effects, both in the general design and in innumerable matters of detail. Keeping the same general style of architecture, that variety of Gothic known as Early English, and giving it what would be called a secular cast as distinguished from that belonging to a strictly ecclesiastical building, every part of the edifice tells of the active life and the trained eye and hand of one who knew all parts of the world and all manner of creatures that live upon it, but whose special delight, as has been said, was to be moving about on the great and restless deep. It seems as if wonders of sea and land had been brought together here by some great composite vessel; and that then all had been, by some magician's wand, turned into stone and transformed for the use, as well as the delight, of those whose duties keep them at home.

The building is in its general form a parallelogram with apsidal ends. The roof is broken and pierced with small windows like portholes and surmounted by a bridge running from end to end and leading to a fleche or spirelet of metal, which carries a cross at a height of 110 feet from the ground. The entrances to the main floor are on either side of a projecting balcony, the corners being occupied by porches supported by great circular columns of Scotch granite ten feet high and two feet in diameter. The capital of the east side is carved to represent life on the sea, with shells and compass and blocks and tackle; that on the west side shows the wild life of the land, heads of the buffalo, deer, bull, and mountain sheep. The four massive lintels of Ohio stone have the inscription:

ERECTED A. D. MDCCCXCV.
IN MEMORY OF CALDWELL H. COLT
BY HIS MOTHER.

The lintels of the doors beneath the porches bear the word "Welcome"; and the supporting columns of Quincy granite represent in their capitals, on the east side agriculture and physical training, and on the west side literature and the drama. The carvings near the windows between these porches and the ends of the building are emblems of the four seasons, representing fruits and flowers, with birds mating, nesting and migrating. The balcony between these two entrances, with the windows above it, is one of the most elaborate and pleasing features of the edifice. Upon its front is carved in stone a fine representation of the yacht Dauntless under full sail, while great tarpon swim in the water below and sea-horses lift their heads on either side, and Neptune with his trident controls them all. The windows above show the position of the grand staircase, with an arcade of twenty-one columns of Scotch granite, alternately red and gray, the cream-colored capitals being carved to represent a variety of flowers and foliage from trees of the northern States. The great window above, running up into a semi-detached gable of Gothic shape, is very effective on the exterior, but will be better described when we speak of it from the interior. Looking at the upper part of the build-

ing, one sees, wherever the ingenuity of the architect could place devices in the nature of gargoyles, the prows of ships projecting, in various styles of naval architecture, ancient and modern, denoting vessels for war or commerce or pleasure; and above all on the high gables is the symbol of redemption in crosses of various designs, some of stone and some of metal, the compound cross denoting both help and instruction. On the south front, where the ground falls away and access and light are thus provided for the lowest story of the building, the middle windows are crowned with the tablets of the tribune, to be described later, and above is a superb piece of work in glass mosaic, showing the Colt-Jarvis coat of arms, with its motto, "Vincit qui patitur"; while tablets on either side bear the inscriptions:

MAN CONQUERS LIFE BY LABOR
GOD CONQUERS MAN BY LOVE

The kneeling-stones and the cap-stone of the great east gable have, in interwoven foliage, the names in Greek of the three theological virtues, Faith, Hope, and Charity; those of the west gable have been left unlettered.

Entering the building by the doors which open upon the grand staircase, one knows not whether to admire most the skill of the builder shown in the solid stonework beneath the feet and on every side; or the ingenuity and gracefulness of the sculptor exhibited in carvings of great beauty and appropriateness. Each step of the ascent is one great stone, dressed alike on its four sides, which indeed are all seen as one passes above and below. A great lantern of brass hangs from above to light the stairs; on the left one looks out upon the balcony and the lawn, and on the right a large window of leaded glass gives a view of the library. On either side of this window is a beautiful column of unique Norway spar, with capitals carved in Ohio stone, one representing the palette and brushes of the artist and the mariner's quadrant among foliage and fruit, and the other representing a capstan with shells and corals. A seat of carved stone fills the space below the window. The external window is set in a frame of stone, which rests upon a landing in the stairs, the blocks of the frame being alternately of the brown Portland stone and the cream-colored Ohio stone, along all which is carved a vine of English ivy, showing the fruitage as well as the leaves; and over its arch is the verse in antique letters, "They that go down to the sea in ships, these men see the works of the Lord and His wonders in the deep." Small windows of dainty design light the upper landing, from which one passes into the great hall; first, however, looking back to see the national coat of arms in stone conspicuously placed over the entrance to the staircase.

This hall, in size 68 by 36 feet, is comfortably seated for three hundred persons, and can be made to accommodate a hundred more. The stage is at the east end, with a minstrel gallery above, and convenient dressing-rooms at the side; at the west end is another gallery, with a fireplace beneath, and the entrance to the rector's study. In this west gallery hangs the bell of the Dauntless. Wherever the eye turns, it catches some trace of beautiful symbolism. The inner roof is painted a delicate blue, and

under the peak there runs the whole length of the hall a "bridge," like that of an ocean vessel, reached by a circular stairway from one of the galleries, and itself giving access to the external bridge and the central spire.

On the middle of the south side is the tribune, raised a step above the floor of the hall and separated from it by a bronze grille. The recess of the tribune, the special memorial in the building, is the most striking feature of the whole structure. It contains a full-length portrait of Commodore Colt, by Eastman Johnson; he is represented as standing on the deck of the Dauntless, in yachting costume, with a sailor at the wheel. Around the portrait the stone setting is carved in leaves of bay (the laurel of the ancients); and on either side, making a sort of apse, are two tablets of pure white Egyptian onyx, on which inscriptions are cut with such delicacy that the letters are translucent. The first tablet to the left of the visitor reads:

TO THE
DEAR MEMORY
OF
CALDWELL HART COLT
THE BELOVED SON OF
COLONEL SAMUEL COLT,
AND
ELIZABETH HART JARVIS
HIS WIFE;
BORN IN HARTFORD, CONNECTICUT,
24 NOVEMBER 1858,
DIED IN PUNTA GORDA, FLORIDA,
21 JANUARY 1894

The first tablet to the right bears these verses:

"Sunset and evening star,
    And one clear call for me;
And may there be no moaning of the bar,
    When I put out to sea."

"Then all the more because thou canst not hear
    Poor human words of blessing, will I pray,
O true brave heart! God bless thee wheresoe'er
    In His great universe thou art to-day."

The tablets on either side of the portrait have respectively these inscriptions:

"He carried his flag with credit to himself and honor to his country in many seas. The master of his own vessel, he never feared to face danger. Always mindful of the comfort and pleasure of others, he won and kept the affectionate regard of the many friends who mourn his early loss."

"He was a true and loyal friend, strong in his affections, honest in his dealings, courageous by nature, considerate of those under his command, never giving an order which he himself would not dare to execute, liberal in his gifts, noble in his hospitality, courteous in his attentions, tenderly devoted to his Mother."

The name "Caldwell Hart Colt" appears beneath the cornice of the tribune, each letter in a trefoil of translucent marble. Carved in stone on the inner face of the entrance to the tribune are representations of the Dauntless, to the left as starting out for a voyage under full sail, while to the right the yacht is shown with sails furled, the anchor down, the voyage ended, but the light streaming over the water from the lighthouse on shore symbolizes the peaceful rest of the heavenly haven. The springers of the arch give in adorned lettering the dates of the Commodore's birth and death, having on either side his private yacht-signal crossed with the signals of the Larchmont and the New York Clubs, while the keystone shows his initials interwoven with graceful foliage; and over it is the inscription from the Canticles, "Many waters cannot quench love." Above the tribune is a window of delicately colored stained glass, divided by mullions into five parts; it shows in the centre the Colt-Jarvis coat of arms. On the one side of the arch of the window, which, it must be remembered, looks toward the south, are carved representations of the pineapple and the alligator, while the other side shows the cactus and the tiger.

Turning about and facing the north, one sees the inner side of the window which separates the hall from the upper part of the staircase, divided by ten shafts of Mexican onyx of various colors, English alabaster, and different varieties of marble, with capitals representing flowers. These shafts with their arches are grouped in pairs, five being within and five without the window, which is of leaded glass. The upper window, which admits light from the north, is of opalescent glass, and the carvings on either side represent the peacock and the turkey, in rich foliage. Below are representations of the flags of the Biscayne Bay and the Eastern Yacht Clubs crossed with the private signal which has been seen before.

At the ends of the hall, over the galleries, are verses from the 127th Psalm: "Except the Lord build the house, their labour is but lost that build it"; "Except the Lord keep the city, the watchman waketh but in vain." The springers of these arches are carved with the prows of ships of various designs, and each bears a symbolic head and other figures representing one of the quarters of the world. That which depicts Asia shows the elephant and the tiger with palms; Africa is indicated by the camel and the lion; America shows the eagle with the leaves of maize and tobacco; while the calm face of the European is surrounded by emblems of royalty and of chivalry. The inscriptions over the doors on the north side should be noted: "To do justly, and to love mercy, and to walk humbly before God"; "The grass withereth, the flower fadeth, but the Word of our God shall stand for ever."

Over the mantel-piece at the west end hangs a full-length portrait of Mrs. Colt, from the pencil of Charles Noel Flagg, presented to her by the parishioners of the Church of the Good Shepherd on the day of the dedication of the building, with the request that it might have a prominent place in this hall.

The rector's study is fitted for its purpose with a simple elegance; above it are the janitor's apartments.

46

The lower main floor of the building is entered by the two doors already described, bearing the inscription "Welcome"; that to the west leads to the rooms specially designated for the work of the women's societies and guilds, with the kitchen beyond; and that to the east leads to the rooms of the men's guilds and to the attractive room for the kindergarten and the infant class of the Sunday School. The middle section of this floor, opening into both the other sections, is the library and reading-room, furnished with books and newspapers and adorned with engravings and other works of art, among which will be noticed pictures of the Dauntless and other vessels in relief, made of silk with wonderful delicacy and skill. The iron framework of the building is shown above in all these rooms; but below it is cased in mahogany, which also is the material of the doors and their frames. The upper portion of the party-walls is replaced with glass, giving a bright and cheerful appearance to all. The lintels of the three main doorways have carved upon them, with appropriate symbols, the Latin words, "Mente," "Robore," "Mores," teaching that character comes from the combination of mental vigor and physical strength.

The lowest floor, on the side of the main entrance a basement, but on the other side looking out upon the south lawn and entered from it, is devoted to physical exercise, being provided with bowling alley, billiard tables, dumb-bells, etc., with bath-rooms and other accessories. The whole building is heated by steam and lighted by both gas and electricity.

When this building, so noble in its purpose, so elaborate in its execution, was dedicated, it was formally presented to the Parish of the Good Shepherd in the following letter from Mrs. Colt:

To the Rector, Wardens, and Vestry of the Church of the Good Shepherd, Hartford, Connecticut. GREETING:

To-day I commit to your care and keeping, in sacred trust, for the use of the parish of the Good Shepherd, this House erected in memory of a dearly beloved son, Caldwell Hart Colt. As it was always his greatest happiness to give to others, it seemed most fitting that a memorial of him, while intended to facilitate the practical charities and mission work of the parish, and to instruct and elevate the minds of the young, as also to afford a retreat for those in whose homes there is little opportunity for quiet reading, should combine with these recreation and healthful amusement. To insure this result, those to whom the building of the memorial was intrusted have worked with a loyal fidelity and unity of purpose, which is beyond all praise; and to-day even the stones tell the story of sunshine and shadow, of life and love and death, and of eternal hope, the anchor which never fails amid storm and tempest, till we come to "the land where no enemy ever enters, and from which no friend departs" where the weary and the tempest-tossed shall find rest in the quiet haven.

May this Memorial House be an incentive to all connected with it, to do a far better, nobler, and more self-sacrificing work in the Master's service than ever before.

And may He without whom our labor is in vain have it in His holy keeping, making it an increasing blessing to those for whose use it is intended, and to their children's children, that thus may be fulfilled the heartfelt prayer of their and your friend,

ELIZABETH HART JARVIS COLT.
Armsmear, September 10th, 1896.

III
ARMSMEAR IN HARTFORD

This sketch would be incomplete without some mention of the home which Colonel Colt built for himself and his family. It is still the home of his wife, and a memorial of both a husband and a son in a feature of their character which could not, from the nature of the case, be known to all. Near the street, which is the continuation of Main Street to the south, not far from a small park whence roads diverge in different directions, Colonel Colt chose the place for his home in a large tract of land on a plateau overlooking the armory and practically within the same enclosure, the whole estate being about two-thirds of a mile long and one-third of a mile wide. The ground presently slopes down towards the river which winds along between meadows, green and dotted with trees; then on the other side is the range of granite hills which marks the eastern limit of the valley of the Connecticut. To-day the visitor sees the beautiful park, diversified with lakes and ornamental shrubbery and forest trees artistically arranged; beyond, he sees the dome of the Armory, and has at least a suggestion of the busy life of the artizans there, blessed and helped by the work of the Church and the Parish House which lift up the Cross, symbol of forgiveness and of service; the river on which steamers and sailing vessels pass tells him of the ventures of commerce; then he sees the meadows to the east, which yield such plentiful returns to the farmer; the country road, on higher ground, shows the pleasant homes of busy men and women; and the wooded hills, in almost their natural condition, display a beauty of their own, as they complete the picture.

To this place, which had been beautified by the device of architect and landscape gardener, Colonel Colt removed with his wife in the year 1857. The name given to it, Armsmear, "the meadow of arms," suggests the outlook from the site with all its natural beauty and the practical purpose to which a part of it was devoted. Here four children were born, and hence three were early called to rest in the bosom of the Good Shepherd, two before the father's death and one following him soon, when after some five years of domestic happiness he was called away from the busy scenes of his earthly toil and honor. Few who knew Colonel Colt only as an energetic man of business, and not all who were acquainted with him in his home, knew the depth of his affection for these little ones. She who knew him best wrote of him thus: "His unflinching courage and resolution, his perseverance, his belief in himself and in his power to conquer obstacles that would have deterred and conquered a spirit less strong and firm, were seen and felt by all. But few, comparatively, knew him as he was at home, when the active, untiring man of business was laid aside, and he became only the kind, thoughtful friend, the wise adviser, the loving, devoted father and husband; or that with his gigantic strength of will was joined a heart

most gentle and affectionate to those whom he loved and trusted; or how, with his impulsive, passionate temperament, he yet bore wrongs that would have made the meekest unforgiving, without one word of unkindness or reproach.... There was no undertaking so vast as to deter him from attempting; there was nothing that might give pleasure or comfort to others, too small for him to remember to perform.... His taste was refined and elegant, his judgment correct and critical. The laying out and beautifying of the grounds about his house, bringing order and harmony out of confusion and roughness, was a source of continual delight to him. Each year he made enlargements and improvements of the area devoted to cultivation, and the outlay was repaid a hundred fold in his own enjoyment of it, and in the thought that he was making the dear home more attractive to those most beloved."

And those who best knew Caldwell Colt spoke in a like way of his home life at Armsmear. "A strongly marked characteristic" of that life "was the genuine courtesy and warm hospitality with which he welcomed his mother's guests; and while all felt his pleasure in greeting them and his wish to render them any service in his power, he took special pains to pay most considerate attention to those who were in any way feeble or infirm. Many of these remember the thoughtfulness and cordiality with which this active young man devoted himself to advance their happiness and comfort; and among their recollections of his home they will ever retain pleasant and grateful thoughts of him. He received his own guests with true, manly heartiness, and left nothing undone that might help them to enjoy the pleasures to which he welcomed them."

It would be out of place to speak here of the influence that still is felt within and from this home, "the benevolence that, through organized charity and private channels, has carried comfort to many, and the profusion of refined hospitality that has imparted a richer coloring to the social development of the city." To attempt to tell what the very name of Armsmear means to many would be to draw the veil from scenes of happiness, of sympathy, and of considerate gentleness, which may not be disclosed.

The house itself has been "built, unbuilt, and remodeled at different times and with dissimilar aims." Yet it does not lack unity, and all that has been lavished upon it has but added to its homelikeness. Its drawing-rooms and library and picture gallery and cabinet of memorials, all belong to it as a home. The enclosed conservatory and the open piazza with its wealth of wistaria foliage make it still more attractive; and in all seasons of the year, but especially when the lawns are in velvet, the lakes reflect the foliage of the trees, and the deer in their park add the joy of animal life to the picture, the whole is seen to be designed for both beauty and delight. Copies of the Uffizi dogs in marble guard the porte-cochère; and elsewhere, suitably placed, are reproductions of famous works of art in marble or in bronze. "And still the eye contracts its gaze to dwell with ever new delight upon the artistic cultivation of the estate, the velvet carpet of the lawn, the admirable grouping of the trees, the lake's glittering repose, the sweep of the broad avenues, the sculpture, the fountains, the flowers, until it falls with loving reverence upon what

seems the heart of this great system, when that which was mortal of the man to whom his city and his country owe so much, was for a time laid away to sleep." His body, with his children beside him, rests now in the beautiful cemetery on the hillside overlooking all this valley, beneath the shelter of a great column upon which stands the figure of the Angel of the Resurrection awaiting the summons to sound his trumpet and call the dead from their graves to stand before God; but what has been described in this little volume will long be memorials of himself and his son, telling of activity and of affection, the busy Armory, the Church, the Parish House, the Home.

SESQUICENTENARY OF HORSENECK CHAPEL, GREENWICH, JUNE 18, 1899

[11]

...But I must not dwell too long on the general interpretation or the general application of my text [Mark 4:28], interesting though the one or the other might perhaps be. I must hasten to ask you to see how it has a special illustration in the events which are brought before our minds at this anniversary. For the wonderful vitality of the truth of God, as it has been revealed in and through His holy Church, is to be nowhere seen, I venture to say, more remarkably illustrated than in the history of the Church in the towns and villages of the Colony of Connecticut. Its beginning was but as that of a seed, at one time placed in the ground by a husbandman, at another time, as men say, accidentally dropped upon the earth; its early growth was as unobserved as that of the seed beneath the surface, or that of the little sprout by the wayside; even those who cared for it had to let it alone, while it grew up, they knew not how. For here, as we look back over the history, even more than in some other places, it is evident that the earth has been bringing forth fruit of herself; that is to day, God's truth has been living and growing under the guidance of God's good providence. The progress of the historic Church in the communities of Connecticut has been that of the seed growing secretly. Men, acting under Divine commission and by Divine guidance, have fostered the life and strengthened the growth; but the work has been so evidently that of God Himself that we may well apply to it the words of the proverb-like parable to which I have been calling your attention. A two-fold influence worked upon this Colony in the last century, to attract sober-minded men and women towards the Church of England. To the parts which lay along the Sound and near the borders of New York, there came an influence from a few earnest Church people, clergymen and laymen, who felt that there was here a spiritual destitution which the Church could supply; and so it was that such men as the Rev. George Muirson and Colonel Caleb Heathcote, of whom I shall soon speak, came here to cast a seed into the ground. This influence was felt directly but for a short time, though it was certainly not without its effect. One more potent and more continued, though more insignificant in its beginning, began some fifteen years later, and may be traced to a copy of the Book of Common Prayer, which belonged to Samuel Smithson of Guilford and fell into the hands of his neighbor, Samuel Johnson. The perusal of this book, "the best missionary that the Church of England ever had among us," led to the study of Anglican theology by Mr. Johnson and others in the library of the College at New Haven, and this

brought four of these Connecticut ministers to the conviction that they could not longer minister in sacred things without a commission from a bishop, which they must seek from England. These four men were followed by others who, after obtaining ordination, came back to teach and minister to their old neighbors and friends and to persuade them to adopt and to follow the ways of the Church. Thus the good seed was quietly placed in the ground during the fifty years which followed the memorable Commencement of 1722.

And the soil was found to be ready for it. Time enough had elapsed since the settlement of the colonies of Connecticut and New Haven to show some of the defects, as well as the excellencies, of the system of religion which the settlers, and many whom they left behind in England, thought would be better than the ways of the reformed Church of that land. Those settlers were led in large part by men who had been ordained priests in the English Church and nearly all of them would have described themselves as members--though, as long as Episcopacy was established, non-conforming members--of that Church; they maintained the Christian ordinances and brought their children--the first generation born in this country--to baptism. But few of these children, when they grew up, could satisfy the requirements of their fathers for full "Church membership," as they defined it; and for that reason their children--the second generation born in this country--grew up unbaptized, and their proper Christian nurture was neglected. At the opening of the last century matters had not become as bad as they were forty years later, when the "great awakening" came to rouse, and to rouse even unwholesomely, the religious life of a large part of the Colony; but the knowledge of their condition moved the sympathy of a few earnest men and in particular, as effecting your local history, of Colonel Heathcote, lord of the manor of Scarsdale, a man of considerable wealth, great liberality, and earnest churchmanship; so that, after he had regulated the "rude and heathenish country," as he called it, which was under his charge, he felt constrained to try to do something for the people "in the westernmost towns in Connecticut Colony"; for, as he wrote in 1705, it seemed to him that there was "no part of this Province, or even America, that it would be of greater use or service to have the Church thoroughly settled in." And of the whole Colony he wrote: "I dare aver, there is not a much greater necessity of having the Christian religion, in its true light, preached anywhere than amongst them; many, if not the greatest part of them, having never been baptized or admitted to the Communion."

Mr. George Muirson, who was a Scotchman by birth, and had been a teacher in New York, had gone to England for ordination, and on his return had been appointed by the Governor to the charge of the Parish of Rye. From 1705 to 1708, when his work was ended by death, he ministered there and did itinerary work, as he was able, in this Colony; "being well fitted," as was said, "for the position in which he was placed, and admirably calculated to introduce the Church into the benighted government of Connecticut." There was an element of romance and grim humor in the journeys made by this good clergyman, as he crossed the border to Greenwich and passed on to Stamford and beyond, as far as Stratford; for Colonel Heathcote went with him, and while the parson preached and baptized and distributed prayer-books, his attendant, riding with him on horseback, was careful to show that he was fully armed and prepared to resist any attempt at violence; so that the opposition went no further than threats against both preacher and listeners.

There is no doubt that the favorable reception of Mr. Muirson's teaching was due in great part to his willingness to baptize children and to receive adults to the Holy Communion on Scriptural terms of admission to the Sacraments, and that the desire which earnest people had for the means of God's grace was a chief reason why the seed of truth which was sown in these parts brought forth fruit of itself. I have already suggested another reason, which became operative a little later and the effect of which was seen here; how some of the most influential ministers of the Colony, men of unquestioned learning and of the highest character, had been led to doubt the validity of the Congregational or Presbyterian ordination which they had received; and studying the question of the orders of the Church of England, from which indeed they were not many steps removed, they had come to accept, very willingly and very heartily, the whole of the theology of that Church. Of the four who first went to England to ask for authority to minister in the Word and Sacraments, one, Mr. Daniel Browne, died in that country; one, the learned Dr. Cutler, rector of Yale College, was assigned to work as a priest in Boston; a third, the eminent Dr. Samuel Johnson, was settled at Stratford; and the fourth, the Rev. James Wetmore, was put in charge of the parish of Rye. For some little time the few Church people in Greenwich had had occasional ministrations from the Rev. Henry Caner, the fifth candidate from Connecticut; his parish was in Fairfield, which was the nearest church to the east. But he appears to have been brought up a Churchman, and the influence of which I am speaking cannot have come so much from him as from Mr. Wetmore, who continued at Rye for the greater part of his ministry of 37 years. Of the details of his work in this parish and its neighborhood we have little account; but we may be sure as to the nature of his teaching, and the readiness and fidelity with which it was received and held. We have a note that in 1739 he officiated in Greenwich once a month, and it appears that people from this place attended service at Rye; for in a letter to the venerable Society for the Propagation of the Gospel, signed by seven clergymen in the same year, we are told of "sundry people, to the number of fifty families, in the westernmost parts of this Colony, chiefly belonging to Horseneck and Stamford, living so near to the parish church of Rye, as that they can and do attend upon the ministrations of the Rev. Mr. Wetmore, who also does frequently officiate among them, to which he was requested by their joint application to him." These families claimed that, under the law of the Colony, which had been passed for the relief of Episcopalians in their capacity as "sober dissenters," they might pay their minister's rates to Mr. Wetmore; but this was not allowed, the law granting this relief only "if it so happens that there be a society of the Church of England, where there is a person in orders, according to the canons of the Church of England, settled and abiding among them, and performing divine service so near to any person that hath

declared himself of the Church of England, that he can conveniently and doth attend the worship there." In this case Mr. Wetmore was not "settled and abiding" here, but lived within the limits of another Colony; and it would appear that it was held that, though Churchmen might attend his ministrations, they did not "conveniently" do so. A petition to the General Assembly, asking for special relief in this case, led to no results; and the Churchmen of this neighborhood were still taxed for the support of the ministers of the standing order. They had some hopes of securing a resident clergyman; but these were for a time doomed to disappointment. When Mr. Isaac Browne went abroad for ordination in 1733, they contributed towards his expenses, desiring that he might be sent to "Stamford, Greenwich, and Horse Neck," but duty was assigned him in New York; and eleven years later they had an earnest desire for the services of Mr. Richardson Miner, but he, after having been captured by the French and released, died in England.

In 1747, the Churchwardens of Stamford, writing "with the unanimous concurrence and in behalf of all the professors of the Church of England in the towns of Stamford and Greenwich," stated that they had "applied themselves to Mr. Ebenezer Dibble" (or Dibblee, as it was more usually spelled), who had "read prayers and sermons among them to their great satisfaction for near a year and a half", and they prayed that he might be ordained and sent as their missionary. Mr. Dibblee was ordained by the Archbishop of Canterbury, and appointed missionary at Stamford and Greenwich; and, arriving at his station on the 26th day of October, 1748, he "began to do duty the Sunday following." "So"--I am using the words of his successor in your neighboring parish, the late Dr. Tatlock--"his half century of work began. His immediate charge included Greenwich, and what are now in part the towns of Bedford on the north, and New Canaan and Darien on the east, and the present town of Stamford. He was a genuine missionary, however, and his frequent excursions took him to Rye, White Plains, Peekskill, North Castle, and Salem in the New York Colony, and to Ridgefield, Danbury, Norwalk, Redding, Newtown, and as far north as Litchfield, Sharon, and Salisbury in Connecticut, and to Huntington in Long Island, in all which places he preached the Gospel and administered the Sacraments."

An immediate result of Mr. Dibblee's taking charge of his care was the erection of a church building for this part of his people. Under date of September 29th, 1749, he wrote to the Secretary of the Venerable Society: "I preach at Horse Neck the second Sunday in each month, about six miles from Stamford; have had some converts to the Church there, and the people have zealously exerted themselves to build a small chapel, of about 36 feet in length and 25 feet in breadth, to accommodate our assembly at these times, which they have enclosed and glazed; and if they should be favored with a Bible and Common Prayer Book for that church, it would be a very welcome present."

This is the event, the 150th anniversary of which we are commemorating at this time. It marked an important point in the growth of the seed which had been sown and begun to grow, men knowing not how; for the soil which had been quietly prepared for it was, as the parable says, "bringing forth fruit of herself." It was but a humble structure which was built on the brow of the hill, soon to be made famous by the exploit of a brave patriot, looking towards old Greenwich and along the postroad to the east; but it told of the persuasive and continuing power of God's truth, and witnessed to the need which men felt for the sober ways of the Church of England, with her firm hold on essential truth, her ministry of undisputed validity, her willingness to minister to God's people on the conditions and in the methods prescribed by God Himself. Here Mr. Dibblee officiated, and with his congregation worshipped, according to the principles and forms of the Church of England, while the building was often much crowded with those who came to unite in the worship, or at least to listen to what was said.

Soon followed the troublous times of the War of the Revolution, which found most of the clergymen loyal to the King and the mother country, and which made them often sore perplexed as to their duty and the way in which it was possible to fulfill it. Mr. Dibblee appears to have remained at his post, probably ministering as he could, while two of his sons were in the British provinces and one was on the side of the Revolution. When the war was over, and the support of the English society was withdrawn from its former stations in these colonies, his old parishes undertook his maintenance, it being arranged that Greenwich was to have one-third or one-fourth of his time.

In the year 1799, a century ago, when the chapel here was half a century old, full of labors and good works, honored and esteemed, his ministry closed with his life. It seems almost certain that in his later years his ministrations here were infrequent and there were few to attend upon them. After his death we are told that the notorious Ammi Rogers, a man who had some strange power of making friends, though he was a very "troubler of Israel," while he officiated in Stamford, held some services in the Horseneck Church; but the building was neglected, and at last, in two gales in the year 1821, or perhaps 1823, it was unroofed and demolished. From that time until the building of the new church in 1832, and the organization of the parish of Christ Church, there were few, if any, public services of the Church held in the town of Greenwich. The history of the new building and this its fair successor, and of the parish and congregation connected with it, will be sketched by your rector.

But even if we had not the story of renewed life to read, and even if its results were not before our eyes today, we should have no occasion to say that the old Horseneck Chapel had an unworthy history. "Except a grain of wheat fall into the ground and die, it abideth alone; but if it die it bringeth forth much fruit." "The seed doth spring and grow up, the sower knoweth not how; for the earth bringeth forth fruit of herself." It was a witness to unchanging truth, and it stood, while it did stand, for the maintenance of the truth; and when it fell, it not only left a site marked with the graves of those who had died in God's faith and fear and in the full communion of the Catholic Church, but it left an indestructible influence. "Its seed remained" and lived; God alone, who guards such life and preserves its records in the book of His

remembrance, knows exactly how it lived; but it had done a work, and "brought forth a fruit"; and from it was to come still further fruit, with the opportunity and the need of further work. We date, and rightly, the full life of this parish from the event of three jubilee-periods ago; and from it a true and strong inspiration comes to the men and women of this generation.

Thus, my brothers, in compliance with the kind invitation of your rector, I have attempted to trace in outline before you the earlier history of the Church in this community. Unfamiliar with the details of the history, I have asked you to let me remind you of the principles that were at work in it and are illustrated by it, and to see how they are suggested by the Lord's words in His parable of the secretly growing seed. But you will not forget that a proverb-parable presents but one side of truth; as in this case we cannot but see how much we owe to the enthusiasm of Colonel Heathcote, the learning and fidelity to truth of Dr. Johnson and his associates, the practical perseverance of Dr. Dibblee, and the true and self-denying lives of the Churchmen and Churchwomen who, in the days when churchmanship was far from fashionable or popular, held to the life and worship which they had learned from the historic Church.

A TRIBUTE TO THE REV. WILLIAM WATSON ANDREWS
    [Died in Wethersfield in 1897. He was the father
    of the Rev. William Given Andrews, to whom Dr.
    Hart wrote another tribute.]

[12]   "The Children," says St. Paul, "ought not to lay up for the parents, but the parents for the children." I come today, in answer to one of those calls which fill men with sorrow and which yet they may not neglect, with much of a child's hesitation and a child's affection to bear testimony that a father has indeed in a long and blessed life laid up and provided for others. As a child in years compared with his, I learned to respect the age which had every title to respect; as a child in study, I listened to the words which commended themselves for sound judgment and clear argument; as a child in character, I saw a pattern of gentleness and purity which reflected the life of the Master. For a long time, several of the ministers of the neighborhood, who had (it is true) been brought up in different ways of looking at God's truth and who had differing convictions as to some parts of that truth, were in the habit of meeting regularly, at first to study the book of Revelation and then to inquire into various questions more or less closely connected with the great subject of divine worship. There was great difference in our interpretation of God's Word contained in the closing book of Holy Scripture, and there was almost equal difference of judgment as to the meaning or the importance of some matters connected with worship or even as to the principles involved in it; we who were young in study and younger in experience must have tried the patience of those who had long pondered upon these things and seen them as part of a great system of faith and practice; and I am sure that we sometimes grieved them when we did not accept their conclusions. He to whom I am permitted now to bear this humble tribute was our Nestor, our Porson, our St. John; he was the man of greatest experience, of deepest study, of most lofty thought, and withal of most true love to the Master; he taught us without knowing that he was our teacher, while we too thought that he was but a fellow-student. He gave more than due weight to all that we said or suggested; he seemed almost to think that he must be in the wrong when we had come to a conclusion adverse to his; he found no fault when we held tenaciously to what he confidently believed to be false. And thus we read lessons of what was of even more value than the interpretation of some vexed passage of Scripture or the determination of the meaning of some fact of sacred history: we could see that combination of wisdom and gentleness, of conviction and patience, of goodness and consideration, which marks the man of God. He was a father laying up for the children.

Of course, I do not mean to speak as if these noble qualities of mind and heart were shown in this great and good man at no other time than when others talked with him about "the things pertaining to the Kingdom of God." I marked them at other times, and I know that family and friends and neighbors marked them wherever he was and whatever he did. The life, as I came to know it, was a quiet life; but its purity and its wisdom and its persuasiveness were known. It was said of a great scholar who had been prominent in the life of a university that even after the infirmities of age kept him within doors so that few ever saw him, his influence was still very great; for men knew that there was a man living in the corner of the quadrangle who was competent to pass a judgment upon the great and troublesome questions of the day, and that he was sure that they could be answered from his standpoint of religious truth. I think that it has been largely so with this community and this neighborhood. We have known that there was one among us who was not afraid to look at any hard question that might be asked, who was not daunted by insinuations that his beliefs were ill-grounded or out of date, who was glad to give an intelligent reason at any time for the faith that was in him. And we were wont to see in the public press, over the well-known initials of his name, articles, sometimes in defense of fundamental verities, sometimes as to his convictions of the meaning of present events and his hopes of the future. His words were as strong as they were gentle; and in that beautiful simplicity and clearness of style in which he excelled, he at least took care that men might "know we have not loosely through silence permitted things to pass away as in a dream." I verily believe that many men and women owe to these his pointed words a reconsideration of their position, a strengthening of their faith in God and in His orderings, a hope that can only be fulfilled by the accomplishing of His great purposes. We all knew that his words were well weighed; we knew that there was truth in them; we were all helped by them.

And if there was any impatience in his heart, I think it was that holy impatience which longs to have God's kingdom come and God's will be done. I remember well how, as we came out together some years ago from the service at the funeral of a good man who had been a teacher of sacred truth, he said to me that every such service filled him with grief, and I think he said with anger, because it showed that the hand of death, God's great enemy, was still

prevailing against His saints and that the time of victory was still deferred. If ever man lived a life of happy service of God, I think it was he; none could, I am sure, have known better the blessedness of life here in the knowledge of God's truth; but the happiness of which he thought the most was the happiness to which he looked forward. He did not, as he hoped he might, and as I think the Apostle taught us all that we ought to hope for ourselves, "remain unto the coming of the Lord"; but in the Church expectant--a far larger body, we must needs remember, than the Church militant in which our lot is still cast--he awaits the resurrection of the dead and the life of the world to come. We joy in the knowledge of the light and the rest of Paradise; we look forward to the day when the saints, forgiven and sanctified, shall have the unveiled vision of eternal truth and glory.

SAYBROOK, CONNECTICUT

[13]

Saybrook, a town and a post-office village in Middlesex County, Connecticut, at the mouth and on the west of the Connecticut River. The ancient town included also (until 1665) a part of what is now Lyme, Old Lyme, and East Lyme on the east of the river. The town on the west has been divided into five by the incorporation of Chester in 1836, Westbrook in 1840, Old Saybrook in 1852, and Essex in 1854; the town retaining the name of Saybrook has the post-office of Deep River. The total population in 1800 was 3,363; in 1900 it was 7,807. The site of the original settlement is in the town of Old Saybrook (pop. 1900, 1,431), bounded by the river and Long Island Sound, where the village and the post-office keep the name of Saybrook. Its railroad station is at the junction of the Shore Line branch of the N.Y., N.H. and Hartford Railroad with its Valley branch, and is 104 miles east northeast from New York and 44 south southeast from Hartford. Two light houses stand at the mouth of the river, one on Lynde's Point and the other on a jetty built to improve the facilities for navigation, which had been much hindered by the bar, under Federal projects of 1870 and 1887. West of the lighthouse is the little borough of Fenwick (pop. 1900, 23), where are a hotel and summer homes. The point above this, known as Saybrook Point, is the site of the original settlement of 1635. Three years before this, the Earl of Warwick, holding under the Plymouth Company a claim to the land, had transferred his right to a company which included in its membership Viscount Say and Seale, Lord Brooke, Sir Richard Saltonstall, John Pym, and John Hampden. They commissioned John Winthrop the younger, son of the Governor of Massachusetts, to be governor of the new settlement for a year; and he led a band of settlers from Boston, who arrived on the 24th of November, just in time to forestall the Dutch who were seeking the same place for settlement. With the governor came Lion Gardiner, an engineer who had served in Holland; he built a fort, placed a palisade across the narrowest part of the neck towards the mainland, constructed a windmill, and laid out the body of the point in land-plots and streets for the use of the proprietors and other "persons of quality" who were expected to arrive. The first fort was burned in 1647, and was replaced by another, the earthworks of which remained until 1870; the stones of the mill

are still to be seen in situ. The name Say-brook first appears in a letter written by Gardiner 6 November 1636; it was given in honor of the two leading proprietors, and is the oldest town-name in the State. On Winthrop's departure, Gardiner remained in charge until 1639, when he removed to his manor on the island which bears his name. His place was taken by George Fenwick, who came to the settlement for the second time in the year last named, bringing his wife Alice Apsley, formerly the wife of Sir John Boteler, called by courtesy Lady Fenwick. She died in 1646 and was buried within the fort; her husband returned to England and died there in 1657. In 1644, he sold the jurisdictional rights of the proprietors, as to the exact form of which there is difference of opinion, to the colony of Connecticut, and this took for its seal that which Saybrook had used, now in a modified form the seal of the State. In 1646, after delay caused by the uncertain nature of the settlement, a church was organized in the great hall of the fort; and a place of worship was built in the next year on the middle street, to be replaced by another in 1681. In 1659, the first settled minister, Rev. James Fitch, with a considerable part of his congregation, removed and settled Norwich on the Thames River. In 1701, Saybrook was chosen as the location of the Collegiate School of Connecticut, later Yale College; and there fourteen commencements were held, at which fifty-five young men received degrees, before its removal to New Haven in 1716; but some of the classes received instruction in other towns where the rector and teachers resided. The site of the college building was marked by a boulder in 1901. In September, 1708, a synod of sixteen members, representing the Congregational church of the Colony and summoned by the General Assembly, met in Saybrook; it reaffirmed the Savoy Confession of Faith and accepted the Heads of Agreement adopted by Presbyterians and Congregationalists in England in 1691, and also set forth the Saybrook Platform of discipline in fifteen articles, organizing the ministers and the churches of the Colony into associations and consociations, the latter to be tribunals with appellate and final jurisdiction. This platform was approved by the General Assembly (or colonial legislature) and the churches organized under it were declared to be established by law; the establishment continued in full force until 1784 and in some sense until 1818. In 1777 the first submarine torpedo was made in Saybrook by David Bushnell; he called it the American Turtle. The industries of Saybrook have been chiefly agricultural, with fisheries and (for a considerable time) ship-building. There have been and are some good old buildings in the place, perhaps the most famous being the house of Captain Elisha Hart, two of whose seven daughters married Commodore Isaac Hull and his nephew Commodore Joseph Bartine Hull. Among the names which have remained in the village and its outlying districts from the beginning nearly or quite to the present time are those of Blague, Chapman, Clark, Lord, Lynde, Whittlesey, and Willard. The names of the ministers who followed Mr. Fitch--Buckingham, Mather, Hart and Hotchkiss--are also held in honor. The Congregational Church, being the fourth building, now stands in the village near the old post-road, with an Episcopal Church of stone in the neighborhood; the Acton Library, having with its predecessors a somewhat long history, is not far from them.

52

GRACE CHURCH, OLD SAYBROOK

[14]

Saybrook, August 4, 1866.

Reverend Sir,

Our Rector handed me some time since your circular of inquiry in regard to the history of our Parish, thinking that, as I had previously studied the records with some diligence, I could answer it as correctly as himself and more readily. Absence from home and other duties have prevented my giving earlier attention to the matter.

I would premise that this village has always been and still is known by the name of Saybrook; and although when the town was divided in 1852 our part received the civil name of Old Saybrook, the village and the post-office are still called by the good old name of Saybrook.

The original site of Yale College, which in those days was to be sure only a "gymnasium Saybrookense," and the place which gave name to the famous Platform, offered no very congenial soil to the Church. So far as I have been able to discover, the first service of our Church held here was in April, 1815, when Dr. S. F. Jarvis buried his mother-in-law, Mrs. Jennette, wife of Elisha Hart. The next was Dec. 22, 1825, when Bp. Brownell married the Revd. Wm. Jarvis to Elizabeth M., daughter of Richard W. Hart and granddaughter of Gen. William Hart. Elisha & William were sons of Rev. William Hart, pastor of the Congregational Church in Saybrook from 1736 to 1784; and he was a son of Rev. John Hart of East Guilford of "1722" fame. It is noticeable that of the ten communicants here before the Church was consecrated, six were his descendants or their wives. The other clergymen who officiated here before the Rev. Mr. Steele were the Rev. Peter G. Clarke of Essex and the Rev. Mr. Judd of New London.

On the 22nd of September, 1833, the Rev. F. W. Hotchkiss preached a half-century sermon in the Congregational Church here. I quote from him a succinct statement of the organization of our Parish, which will also show the light in which he regarded it. "Now we turn the leaf, and see a page altogether different;--a page blotted by disunion and the rendings of deforming schism. As early as the beginning of February [1830], the month anterior to the great accession to this church, and in the midst of a full flow of revival feelings and the all-thrilling sympathies of religious excitement, some of our opulent citizens invited an Episcopal clergyman to officiate in private dwellings and hold a weekly evening service. These meetings continued week by week, either in those mansions or the school house, till, on April 9th, they observed a public day of worship, on Good Friday. On May 31st, as I understood, they organized their church, and elected their Wardens and Vestrymen. On the 9th of August, 1830, the corner stone of the Episcopal church was laid; and, on the next year, Aug. 16th, 1831, the church was consecrated. Public worship has been sustained by them to the present time; and we have now two houses of worship within our local boundaries. All this constitutes a new era in my ministry and in the religious history of Saybrook." [pp. 13, 14.]

1. "The subscribers for building an Episcopal Church in the first Society in the Town of Saybrook" met in April, 1830, and appointed a Committee to receive proposals for building the Church. May 31, 1830, the organization was effected under the name of Grace Church. Sixteen names are subscribed to the articles of association. At the same time Samuel Hart and William Clark were chosen Wardens, and William Lynde, Richard W. Hart, William Willard, Richard Chalker, Ira Bushnell, Nathaniel Clark, Richard E. Pratt, and William H. Lynde, Vestrymen.

2. At the annual meeting, March 21, 1866, John S. Dickinson and Henry Hart were chosen Wardens, and Albert E. Chalker, William Kirtland, and Edward Ingraham were chosen Vestrymen.

3. The Rev. Mr. Steele divided his time between this parish and that in Essex from the organization of the Church till April 22, 1832. To him succeeded the Rev. John M. Guion from July 25, 1832 to March 17, 1836; the Rev. G. C. V. Eastman from April 24, 1836 to March 27, 1837; the Rev. William Warland from May 1, 1837 to June , 1842; the Rev. Harvey Stanley from July 17, 1842 to April 16, 1843; the Rev. William G. French from July 2, 1843 to April , 1844; the Rev. Junius M. Willey from May 19, 1844 to March 28, 1847; the Rev. John M. Guion from April , 1847 to 1849; the Rev. Charles R. Fisher from April 8, 1849 to January 6, 1850; the Rev. Gilbert B. Hayden from January 6, 1850 to March 31, 1850; the Rev. Samuel J. Evans from April , 1850 to April , 1854; the Rev. Jonathan Godfrey, Jr., from April , 1854 to April 2, 1855; the Rev. Peter L. Shepard from June 5, 1855.

Several of the above were never called to the Rectorship, and the exact dates are not to be found on the Parish Records. Most of the above are from memoranda in the Parish Register.

4. No historical Discourse has ever been printed, or, so far as I can learn, delivered.

5. The present Church edifice is the one of which the corner-stone was laid Aug. 9, 1830, & which was consecrated by Bp. Brownell Aug. 16, 1831. It is of wood and in the Norman style of architecture as much as in any. It has never been enlarged, and will seat, including the organ-loft, about 225 persons.

6. The Organ now in use was given by Mr. Richard W. Hart in 1831.

7. We have a commodious Parsonage, purchased by the Parish in 1851.

8. Our Parish has never received aid from any Society. Its funds are as follow;

Donation of Richard W. Hart, Aug. 16, 1831, $3,000;
Donation of Elisha Hart, Aug. 6, 1831, 310;
Donation of James A. Pratt, Dec. 22, 1858, 500;
Legacy of Mrs. Mercy Hart, who died May 8, 1847, 500;
Legacy of Miss J. M. M. Hart, who died Aug. 26, 1861, 300.

9. No particular opposition.

53

10. The parish has grown but slowly till within the last ten years. During this time, its increase has been more rapid, and more Church accommodation is sadly needed. I affix the number of confirmations in the several years. In 1831, 4; 1832, 10; 1833, 9; 1834, 4; 1835, 2; 1836, 1; 1837, 1; 1839, 2; 1842, 8; 1844, 6; 1848, 3; 1850, 4; 1852, 4; 1853, 2; 1854 or 1855, 2; 1856, 6; 1857, 3; 1860, 10; 1862, 3; 1866, 2.

11. None

12. The Sunday School was first organized in 1832 by the Revd. Mr. Guion.

There has been for many years a boarding and day School in the Parish, and it is now a Rectory School under the charge of the Rector of the Parish; but we have never had a Parish School properly so called.

In our quiet little village very little occurs of general interest. Any other information which it is in my power to obtain I will most gladly furnish you.

Very respectfully,

Samuel Hart.

To the Revd. Dr. Beardsley.

A Century of Church Life in Connecticut

[15]

1851-1897

"I beg that no one will compare my annals with the writings of those who have recorded the more ancient history of our people." So wrote a great historian of old, despairing of being able to give to the events of his own day, or those which immediately preceded them, the interest which attached to the conflicts and excitements and victories of the earlier times. "*Nobis in arto et inglorius labor.*"* It was not that Tacitus failed to recognize the importance of what had passed in Rome within the last century, a time which was in fact most fruitful in its issues and in its influence upon the history of the world, though even he could not see it in its true perspective; but he felt that what he had undertaken was a task within narrow lines and one which lacked the splendor of antiquity. So I, though far enough from venturing to compare myself with the great man whose deprecating words I have quoted, may well crave your indulgence while I undertake to trace before your minds the leading events in the history of this Diocese during the past half century, or, to speak more accurately, during the past six and forty years. I

* Tacitus, *Annals*, iv. 32.

cannot tell of the heroes who recalled the days of our "origins," who had lived through the changes of the revolution and laid the foundation of our fully organized diocesan life; I can tell of no one man who made himself notorious and everybody else uncomfortable through a long period of years; I can describe no such war of pamphlets as that which treated of Bishop's bonus and the civil rights of Episcopalians and the need of a constitution for the State of Connecticut; I cannot even suggest the effects for good or for evil which came to the Church from a bloodless but hotly contested revolution in the State. It is modern history with which I have to deal; and modern history, unless it is very exciting—and this certainly is not—is very uninteresting. All know the facts; no one is quite ready to have them criticised; praise is impertinent, and censure (if possibly it seems to be needed) is ill-advised; the writer as well as the reader or listener needs to stand a long way off before he can rightly see the picture or tell what it means.

Therefore, in attempting to do something which may serve as an apology for the discharge of the duty laid upon me, I must crave your indulgence if the record has all the faults of annals and none of the virtues of history. And may I venture, by way of laying a little emphasis upon the chronology of the time, to speak for a few minutes in a way which, but for such a reason, would be too personal? When as a youth I first came to know of the work of the Church in Connecticut outside of the little parish at my home, the Bishop in active work and practically in charge of the Diocese was the comparatively youthful Assistant. I never saw Bishop Brownell, except on the morning of three Commencement days when the procession on its way from the College to the city halted for a few moments before his door and waited, with all heads bared, for the benediction of his presence. The first Convention at which I attended to listen to any of the business transacted, was the memorable Convention of the year after that in which the venerable Bishop had died. I entered the Berkeley Divinity School twelve years after the time of its full establishment, so that for about one-fourth of its history I am entirely dependent upon the testimony of others. There is, after all, in the half century, some ancient history even for one whose place is rapidly coming to be among the elderly clergy of the Diocese.

So much may perhaps be pardoned by way, as the saying is, of orientation. If I may insert a few statistics here, you shall not be troubled with them later. In 1850 the population of the State was about 371,000, and the number of communicants of the Church in 110 parishes was about 9,500; the present population of the State, according to the latest published estimate, is about 817,000, and the number of communicants registered in 157 parishes and missions is over 30,000. That is to say, the number of communicants has increased three-fold, while the population has been multiplied by less than two and

a quarter. Bishop Williams, in thirteen years as assistant and thirty-three years as sole Bishop, has admitted about 265 young men to the diaconate, and has laid hands in Confirmation upon about 48,000 persons, more than half as many again as the present number of communicants. For the last ten years our Bishop has been the Presiding Bishop of this Church, and for several years the senior Bishop by consecration in the whole Anglican communion.

"This is a glorious day in Hartford!" wrote the aged Bishop Philander Chase in Illinois, on the "Wednesday succeeding the nineteenth Sunday after Trinity, A. D. 1851"; "our Assistant Bishop is consecrated by Bishop Brownell in that blessed city. What a contrast," he adds, "between this august assembly and the few who crept along the sidewalks, unnoticed, to the humble door of Christ Church, Hartford, A. D. 1811! The one an overflowing tide covering the banks with fertility all around; the other a little spring or rivulet giving freshness to a few humble flowers. O Lord God of grace and strength! do I yet survive to see the glory of Thy primitive Zion reflected from the waters of that beautiful river, on whose banks I first drew my breath?"* The Consecration of the youthful Assistant to the already venerable Bishop of Connecticut was indeed a memorable event. Bishop Brownell himself presided, and all the other Bishops of New England Dioceses and Bishop DeLancey of Western New York united with him in the act of Consecration, while the sermon was preached by the saintly Bishop of Maine. Eighty-six Clergymen attended the services, most of them, we are told—for it was a novelty then—wearing surplices. Dr. Williams was already well known in Connecticut, a Diocese, he said in the letter in which he accepted his election, "in which I was confirmed, and received both my Orders; in whose principles I was educated; to which I am warmly attached; and whose spotless history I reverence and love." The two Bishops immediately began a visitation, the senior Bishop administering Confirmation and the Assistant preaching the sermons and making the addresses. A new inspiration was thus given to the work of the Diocese; and when, as was soon the case, its care practically devolved upon the junior Bishop, he began that long-extended and long-continued series of visitations which were for many years so prominent and so pleasing a feature of the Church work of Connecticut. The Diocese has testified, by a unanimous vote of the last Convention, that Bishop Williams's "noble qualities of head and heart have been freely exercised for forty-six years in behalf of the Diocese. His Diocese has been his first and highest interest;

* The Motto, vol. 2, no. 5, pages 131, 143.

and while he has been willing to contribute from his abundant ability to the general interests of the Church, he has never failed to bear in mind his duty to the humblest parish in his charge. To every Clergyman and to every Layman he has been not only the Bishop but the friend, sympathizing in their joys and sorrows, and ready to hear and to counsel when his attention and wisdom were needed." To speak in any attempt at detail of that work, to make any estimate of its results, to describe the place which our Bishop gained in the affection of the Churchmen of this Diocese and of the citizens of this commonwealth, is beyond the purpose of this paper. The second generation has half run its course since that October day in 1851; the aged Prelate who had already sat for thirty-two years in the chair of Seabury and of Jarvis, nobly sustained by his son in the Lord now become his brother in the highest office of the Church, full of years and of honors, has fallen asleep, leaving the memory of kindly service and gentle guidance as a perpetual blessing to his people; the Clergymen who were forty-six years ago the chosen representatives of the Convention and the counsellors of the Bishops, Doctors Harry Croswell and William Cooper Mead and Robert Alexander Hallam and Jacob Lyman Clark and Thomas Winthrop Coit—typical men as leaders and legislators and pastors and missionaries and scholars, men whose influence will last though their names may not be familiar—have completed the service which they so well rendered to their generation by the will of God; and with them there rests from his labors one whose name is closely associated with theirs, and who was chosen to the Standing Committee before Bishop Brownell's death, Dr. Eben Edwards Beardsley, to be remembered not only for his extended rectorship but also for the lasting services rendered to the Diocese by his ready pen and for the honors which he gained in the councils of the whole Church in this land. A few may be thus mentioned by name, because they held office long and worthily,* but there are many more of those whose names were on our roll in 1851,† or have since been added to it, who have served the great Head of the Church in this portion of His great harvest-field and have left it for us to enter into their labors even as they entered into the labors of those who had preceded them. And

* Dr. Croswell was a member of the Standing Committee thirty-one years; Dr. Mead, thirty-three years; Dr. Hallam, twenty-seven years; Dr. Clark, twenty-three years; Dr. Beardsley, thirty-two years.
† There are three survivors of the Clergy of 1851, besides Bishop Williams, now canonically resident, all of whom signed his testimonials: the Rev. Messrs. Collis I. Potter, now of Stratford; James L. Scott, now of Wallingford; and Benjamin M. Yarrington, now Rector Emeritus, as he had then been twelve years Rector, of Christ Church, Greenwich. There were but eight Clergymen entitled to seats who were absent from the Convention of 1851.

of the faithful laity, who have come to be in these days the permanent part, and in a very true sense the responsible part, of our parishes, how many are there whose good lives and faithful services and liberal benefactions have advanced the work of the Church among us, staying up the hands and aiding the counsels of those who were set to serve them in the Lord, and whose works do now follow them even in the rest into which they have entered! I may read the names of a few who signed the testimonials of the Bishop-elect in 1851, that we may remember the kind of men that they were: Hezekiah Huntington, Samuel H. Huntington, James M. Goodwin, and William T. Lee, of Hartford; Beriah Bradley, Elihu L. Mix, John B. Robertson, and Pliny A. Jewett, of New Haven; Jonathan Starr and Francis Allyn, of New London; Jedediah Huntington, of Norwich; George R. Curtis, of Meriden; David Russell, of Portland; Samuel Church and Seth P. Beers, of Litchfield; J. M. L. Scovill and S. M. Buckingham, of Waterbury; Holbrook Curtis and John Buckingham, of Watertown; James R. Coe, of Winsted; John Ferguson, of Stamford; William Nash, of Stratford. The lives of such men are a great part of the history of this Diocese during the past half-century; men honored in town and in state, respected for the integrity of their lives, helpers of their neighbors, examples to the rising generation, righteous men who "shall be had in everlasting remembrance." "With their seed shall continually remain a good inheritance, and their children are within the covenant. Their seed standeth fast, and their glory shall not be blotted out. Their bodies are buried in peace; but their name liveth for evermore."*

Bishop Williams was at the time of his election and Consecration to the Episcopate President of Trinity College, and then as now the most highly honored of all the sons of his *alma mater.* He retained the presidency for two years, when it became evident that the condition of Bishop Brownell's health required that he should undertake all the active duties of the episcopal office within the Diocese. But a born teacher will always be a teacher; and Bishop Williams was a born teacher. Removing to Middletown, he organized the theological classes, which had been in an informal way under his charge at the College, into the Berkeley Divinity School. With the story of its life we are all, to some extent at least, familiar. Some will remember, if not the beginnings, at least the early days, when all lived under the same roof, offered their daily worship in the little oratory, and were guided in their studies by the great master of theology, ably assisted by men who even then were extraordinary men. More there are who can look back to their

* Ecclesiasticus xliv. 11–14.

life and studies in the enlarged and more fully appointed home of sacred learning; while a very large number, both of the Clergy and of the Laity, know how important a part of the history of these years has had its inspiration within those walls. Changes there have been, indeed, adapting the work of the School to changed circumstances or to new needs, in accordance with the principles of a healthy growth; the memorial Chapel and quite recently the Library have given an added dignity and assurance of permanence, as well as supplied pressing needs; but the principles maintained have been the same, and the School has taught the lessons of Divine truth from the lips of men who believed that Divine truth must be taught and accepted, and that the Church is the authorized teacher of Divine truth.

The educational equipment of the Diocese has been completed within these years by the establishment of St. Margaret's School for girls. The venerable Episcopal Academy at Cheshire, celebrating in 1894 its centennial anniversary, has taken on new life and awakened a new interest. And I may be pardoned for adding that Trinity College, which has its local habitation within the limits of Connecticut, though it is not a diocesan institution, and which owes much to the pious labors and generous gifts of Connecticut Churchmen, has, under the guidance of wise and learned men who have succeeded our Bishop in its Presidency, done much towards fulfilling the noble hopes and purposes of its founders.

The financial and benevolent organizations of the Diocese have received much care in this half century; their efficiency has been augmented and they have multiplied in number. One of the first matters of importance in the records of the Convention after the Consecration of Bishop Williams, is that relating to amendments of the charter of the trustees of the Bishop's Fund, providing for an annual report to the Convention and for the filling of vacancies in the board by vote of the Convention itself. These changes were really of great importance, and led to an increase of interest in a matter which concerned the whole Diocese. About ten years ago a project for a considerable increase of the Fund, and for the release of the parishes from annual assessments for it, was brought to a successful conclusion in consequence of Dr. Beardsley's untiring labors on this behalf; and a plan for a further increase of the fund is now before the Diocese. In 1855, the Aged and Infirm Clergy and Widows' Fund, which had for some years been in existence by canonical provision, received a charter; and its important and beneficent work has been carried on with great care for its safe administration and great consideration for both the needs and the feelings of those who have thus received practical sympathy and

help. To this was added two years ago, in accordance with a carefully prepared plan, a Clergyman's Retiring Fund, from the working of which we may expect before long to see most satisfactory results. The corporation of the Trustees of Donations and Bequests, organized at the instance of Bishop Williams in 1863, completes the list of diocesan organizations; it has abundantly justified its existence and commended itself to both parishes and individuals.

In speaking of the history of the past half century, we may not pass by the faithful work done in Diocesan Missions by way both of Church sustentation and of Church extension. The problems of each kind which are before us to-day are in many respects widely different from those of the year 1851. The population of the State is not as nearly homogeneous now as it was then; it is not as evenly distributed; we cannot assume that in every country town there is a preponderance of people of Anglo-Saxon stock, or of people to some extent attached to the soil; we cannot look for a somewhat even grade of rural happiness and of thrifty prosperity. In some ways we have not advanced beyond the plan of 1828 for arranging the parishes of the Diocese into cures, or that of 1843 for extending parochial supervision to all parts of the Diocese; our list of towns occupied and unoccupied partly fails to show our strength, and partly (it may be) exaggerates it; the memoranda which have been collected as to extinct parishes bear witness to some lost labor and some misdirected zeal; and there is much left for us to do before we can claim, as at the very least we ought to claim, that this Church is trying to take the pastoral care of every person in Connecticut who has not chosen to give his spiritual allegiance to some other religious organization. I do not think that most of us begin to know how many there are, at present beyond the actual and even the possible reach of our services, who are unconsciously waiting for us. But, with all this, there have been many good attempts made to learn and to do the duty which lies upon this Church in this State, and many good results have followed upon them. There are parishes and missions now doing a noble, though it may be patient and quiet, work in places where a half century ago almost no one knew or cared to know of the Church's ways, and among communities which have sprung into life as a result of modern activities; and often calling forth latent opposition and meeting with unexpected difficulties, they yet uphold the light of God's truth for some who otherwise would be utterly without its guidance. The institution of Archdeaconries, now a score of years ago, each with its responsible presiding officer (and what a list of worthy men we have had to grace

the office!), has given form and strength and counsel to the whole work of our Diocesan Missions; and, for the rather meagre amount of information which our people have in regard to this work and the rather meagre amount of their offerings to it, we are reaching fairly satisfactory results. In fact, the problems before us are but shaping themselves now, the changes are but manifesting themselves, the possibility of making mistakes with the very best of intentions has not passed away; we may in a short time, if God will and if we will, perceive and know better than ever before what things in this matter we ought to do, and also may have grace and power faithfully to fulfil the same. If we could have Church maps of Connecticut for the beginning and the end of the period now under consideration, the contrast between them would be, on the whole, such as to awaken great thankfulness and great encouragement; but when we think what such a map ought to show in 1925 or 1950, we should rouse ourselves to the determination that, while we will not abate one whit from our interest in the work of the Church in other parts of God's great harvest, we will not be guilty of neglecting that which He gives us to do here. For the future of this whole State depends, in more ways almost than we dare to think, upon the way in which this Church of ours shall hold fast what it has and shall reach forth unto the things that are before it. This is no mere flight of imagination or boast of rhetoric; either would be out of place at this time; it is but the confidence that what has been done in the past can be done in the future, only more wisely and more effectually, because the future can learn from the past and profit by the knowledge of its failure and its success.

One of the most important events in our Diocesan history in these years has been the adoption by the Convention, and the ratification by the General Assembly of the State, of a plan for the churchly organization of our parishes as parishes, instead of their congregational organization as ecclesiastical societies. This had been proposed more than once; but there had not been entire agreement as to the details; some had been loath to break with forms and phrases to which they had been accustomed; some had dreaded the possible awakening of opposition; and some perhaps were unwilling to have churchly principles made a subject of statute law. At last, however, in 1876, the draft of a proposed Act was approved by the Convention; it was received by the General Assembly with that consideration which, as a rule, the Church in Connecticut has received from the constituted authorities of the commonwealth; and in the following year the Act of the civil legislature was accepted

"as the charter of the Church in this Diocese." Besides giving a better tone to the organization and the secular work of our parishes, this has educated our people in a better phraseology and better ways, has added to our rightful self-respect, and has greatly advanced the welfare of the Diocese.

It remains to speak of two matters which in the course of the last half century have awakened special interest and shown decided difference of opinion in the Diocese. The one is the question of the division of the Diocese, brought before the Convention by the Bishop in 1865; the other was a somewhat curious episode which occurred in 1871.

At the first Convention which Bishop Williams addressed as Bishop of Connecticut, the first, that is to say, after the death of Bishop Brownell, he spoke in very solemn words of the duty of "looking forward to the erection of a new See within this present Diocese." "I do not say," continued the Bishop, "that we ought to take up [the matter] to-day, it may be not even next year. But I do trust that we may keep it in our minds as a thing to be harmoniously and considerately accomplished at no very distant day. . . . . It is because of the great responsibilities which rest on all of us; it is because of the awful responsibilities of the Episcopate which rest on me; it is because I see work growing up before me which I shall be unable to do, and yet for which I fear I am accountable; it is because of souls that will be perishing, that I ask you to think of this. . . . . _Liberavi animam meam._" This part of the Bishop's address was referred to a committee of four Clergymen and five Laymen, the Rev. Dr. Mead and Judge Samuel H. Huntington being the first named in each order respectively, to report at some later Convention. This committee presented a partial report in 1866, declaring that they thought it "wise to present the important subject of a division of the Diocese to the consideration of Clergy and Laity, as a matter which may happen at no distant day, that each may be excited to a timely examination of such a momentous event in the history of the Church in Connecticut, so as to be amply prepared to act whenever the time for action may have fully come." Then, after suggesting that the endowment of the Berkeley Divinity School would enable the Bishop to undertake more extended labors in the Diocese, and speaking of the canonical steps necessary for a division, the report ended with these words—there must be present others besides myself who remember how they rang from Dr. Mead's lips: "Every Churchman in our land who admires whatsoever is pure or honest or lovely or of good report will cheerfully exclaim with us: 'Diocese of Connecticut, _Nomen praeclarum, esto perpetuum !_'"

At the Convention of 1867 the committee presented its final report, calling attention to the fact that "no attempt at combined effort to initiate such a measure" for division had "taken place," intimating that it seemed that most of those interested had been "led to the conclusion that our need of division does not require action now," and asking to be "discharged from the further consideration of the resolutions submitted to them." Their request was granted; and, except in 1872 when a resolution looking to "the increase of the Episcopate in this Diocese" was promptly laid on the table, it does not appear that the matter has again excited much interest. An article in the _Church Review_ about 1866, circulated in pamphlet form, and acknowledged to be from the pen of one of the keenest controversialists and most persistent advocates of diocesan division in the Church, under the title "Shall Connecticut be our First Province?" urged in the strongest possible way that this Diocese should be forthwith divided into five, and showed how the common interests could be maintained under a provincial system, the province being coterminous with the State. The article was interesting, as well in the principles which it ably advocated as in its showing of the strength of the proposed dioceses of Hartford (this was to be Metropolitical), New Haven, Bridgeport, Litchfield, and Norwich, and in particular that if St. Michael's Church could be made the cathedral of Litchfield, it would have an endowment for the Episcopate second only to that of the Diocese of New York. But all this does not seem to have been taken very seriously; and I venture to think that he would be a bold man who should renew the proposal for a division of Connecticut in the immediate future.

The other matter to which I alluded would deserve notice if it were only for the fact that it was the occasion of two votes in the Convention by Orders, the only votes by Orders which have been demanded since 1850, and besides those of 1850 the only ones in our entire history.* The resolution proposed, after a preamble of several clauses, was this: "_Resolved_, That, in the judgment of this Convention, it is not expedient to send as Deputies to the General Convention more than two members of the Standing Committee of the Diocese." A motion to lay the whole matter on the table was defeated, on a vote by Orders, twelve Clergymen and six Laymen voting for it; and on the second day, the preamble having been first stricken out, the resolution was adopted, on a vote by Orders, by a large majority of both Clergymen and Lay delegates. The result was, that whereas three years

* Since this was written, I have learned that there has been one other vote by Orders, although, through some inadvertence, it was not entered in the Journal.

before all of the Clerical Deputies to the General Convention had been members of the Standing Committee, Drs. Mead and Beardsley were the only ones now honored with this double election. Thus passed away one episode which at the time was somewhat irritating to some people, and the air was cleared, as the saying is, in a wholesome manner.

There are many more matters to which one would like to allude, and of which it would be necessary to speak if one were writing a history of these years. The troubles in the country called for well-considered words from the Bishop before the outbreak of the civil war; and the prayers which were for so long a time read in our churches, for the unity of the people of this land and for the divine care of our brethren who had gone forth in our defence, will ever remain in the memory of those who lived through those anxious times. The tendencies of theological thought and ecclesiastical observance known by the not very accurate term "ritualism," led to other weighty words from the Bishop, which received the hearty approval of the Convention. The question of Christian unity has been more recently treated in the Bishop's address; and the matter of divorce, especially in its relation to the statute law of this State, has been in like manner brought before the Convention more than once. The observance of the Seabury centenaries, with the visit of the Bishop and others to Aberdeen, has given a new impulse to the study of the history of the Diocese.

Sed haec olim fuere. The records of the past, for good or for evil, close themselves; and while there remain the results of what has been said or done, the words and the deeds themselves are soon forgotten. The retrospect of these hundred years is of little interest, I suppose, to most of us, when we would rather be looking forward to the future. And as, at the close of a century from the Consecration of our second Bishop, the apostolic commission is to be given to one of strong hands and devoted heart, to carry on the good work of the Diocese of Connecticut, now under the counsel and guidance of our great fourth Bishop, and at last (if God shall so will it) with full responsibility, our prayer for him shall be that he may be guided and blessed even as they have been guided and blessed who have preceded him in this holy office; our prayer for ourselves shall be, that the God before whom our fathers did walk, the God who hath led us unto this day, would still be with us, our God and our Portion for ever.

Ωι ἡ δόξα· ἀμήν.

A MEMORIAL
OF

MRS. ELIZABETH MILLER JARVIS,

WIDOW OF THE REV. WILLIAM JARVIS,

[16] At Rest

JUNE 18, 1881.

FROM THE CHURCHMAN OF JULY 2d, 1881.

Entered into rest on the morning of Saturday, June 18th, Mrs. Elizabeth Miller Jarvis, widow of the Rev. William Jarvis of Hartford, and daughter of the late Richard William Hart of Saybrook, Connecticut, at the close of her eighty-third year.

These words record the close of a life blessed in itself, and full of blessing to others. It was not a life exempt from sorrow or from suffering; but, by Divine grace, each trial and each pain brought with it a deeper faith, a firmer hope, a stronger love, and thus an increase in holiness. With a cheerfulness which scarce showed the patience that was its source, with a deep affection for kindred on whom in declining years she leaned with implicit trust, with increasing kindness toward all her many friends, with unshaken faith in God, she lived among those who felt her presence to be a sacred benediction; and now that she has peacefully fallen asleep in Jesus, she has left a memory which will make their lives better and happier. Her body was laid to rest with the Church's words of earnest prayer and joyful assurance, "looking for the resurrection of the dead and the life of the world to come."

"Blessed are the pure in heart, for they shall see God."

REV. WILLIAM JARVIS

Was born at Norwalk, Connecticut, on the twenty-ninth of February, 1796, and was the youngest and thirteenth child of Hezekiah Jarvis. His birth-day being on the twenty-ninth of February, and the odd day not being necessary to complete the century,

59

Mr. Jarvis was eight years old before he had one of these natal days, and had but seventeen in all. He died on the third of October, 1871, aged seventy-five years and seven months.

His mother's maiden name was Sarah Whitney, a daughter of Mr. Whitney of Darien, who lived to be one hundred years, three months and three days old. His wife was over ninety at the time of her death. The mother of Mr. Jarvis was, at the time of her marriage with his father, a widow, Mrs. Nash, and he was a widower with several children.

There are some interesting facts in regard to Mrs. Whitney, the mother of Mrs. Jarvis, which are related by her only surviving grandchild.

After she had passed her eightieth year, her eyesight returned to her as clear and bright as in the days of her youth. She became an Episcopalian from her own reading and research, and was devoted to the doctrines of the Church. The Rev. Mr. Mather, the Congregational clergyman, treated her with the greatest kindness and respect, often loaning her his horse to ride to Stamford, a distance of five miles, to enjoy the Church service. Her husband, not being in sympathy with the doctrines of the Episcopal Church, sometimes refused to let her have *his* horse, when the energetic old lady would declare her intention to walk, saying, where duty dictated, the Lord would provide a way; and so it often proved, for she would hardly get started before some neighbor or friendly traveler would assist her to the place in which her soul delighted.

Bishop Jarvis and Mr. Hezekiah Jarvis were brothers, and the Bishop's son, the Rev. Dr. Samuel Farmar Jarvis, offered to fit his young cousin, William, for college, and he was thus for some time an inmate of the Doctor's family.

Mr. Jarvis was graduated at Union College, and afterwards pursued his theological studies at New Haven, Conn. In August, 1822, he was ordained deacon at Norwalk by the late Bishop Brownell, and,

on the fifth of November of the following year, was ordained priest, also by him, at East Haddam, at which place, and Hebron, he ministered for some time.

While at Hebron he won the affection and friendship of Dr. Peters, who was also Governor of the State, and this friendship continued unabated until death separated them.

Mr. Jarvis was married by the Rt. Rev. Bishop Brownell in December, 1825, to Miss Elizabeth Miller Hart, eldest daughter of Major Richard William and Mrs. Elizabeth Hart of Saybrook, Conn., a marriage which resulted in great and life-long happiness, though together they shared many sore bereavements. Of those saddened days, as well as of the later hours when life was drawing to a close, the accompanying obituary speaks most touchingly.

NOTE—An aged, honored, and saintly lady, who has "finished her course in faith, and now rests from her labors," made provision for the gift of a brass lectern, to be placed in the new Trinity Church now building at Portland, as a memorial of the efficient and faithful service of her never-forgotten Pastor, the Rev. William Jarvis. Her devoted daughters, in carrying out this sacred trust, intend to make it also a memorial of his beloved wife, so recently reunited to him by death; that thus the names, which have been treasured for long years in the affections of their parishioners, may together live in the thought of generations yet to come.

OBITUARY.

Died, on Tuesday, October 3, 1871, at the residence of his daughter, Mrs. Samuel Colt of Hartford, the Rev. William Jarvis, in the seventy-sixth year of his age.

Mr. Jarvis was one of the few remaining clergymen who connect the present generation with the founders of the Church in America. He was born at Norwalk, Conn., on the twenty-ninth of February, 1796, the youngest of thirteen children. He leaves behind him three sisters, aged Christian women, whose lives have been full of good works. He was the nephew of Bishop Jarvis. He resolved early in life to devote himself to the ministry, and with that view was fitted

for college by his older cousin, the late Rev. Dr. Samuel Farmar Jarvis, in whose family he for some time resided. Thus natural affection was deepened, and the kind interest shown him early in life, was more than requited in the love, sympathy, and aid which he gave to the Doctor in after years, under great sorrow and embarrassment. This affection grew with years, and is left, with the memories of holy lives, and of public and private devotion to the service of Christ, as a precious legacy to the descendants of both.

Mr. Jarvis was made Deacon in August, 1822, at Norwalk, by the late Bishop Brownell, and ordained Priest in East Haddam November 5, 1823. He ministered for a time in East Haddam and Hebron. In the latter place he built a church, which was then considered one of the handsomest rural churches in the diocese. This church has, only the last spring, been put in excellent repair, and Mr. Jarvis was much pleased to show his old parishioners that his affection for them remained unchanged during the many years of separation, by presenting them with a font of Ohio stone commemorative of his rectorship from 1821 to 1826.

In 1825 he married Miss Elizabeth M. Hart, daughter of the late Major Richard W. Hart of Saybrook, who survives him. From Hebron he removed to Chatham, now Portland, where he officiated as rector of Trinity Church until disabled by bronchitis. He persisted in his ministerial labors in the chancel and pulpit until his voice failed entirely. Unwilling to give up, and hoping for recovery, he obtained the assistance of the Rev. Samuel Emery, into whose worthy hands he soon afterward surrendered the parish. For months he could only speak in a whisper; and, even after recovering the use of his voice in conversation, it broke down upon every attempt to use it in reading aloud. The writer of this was several times present at his family devotion, and was painfully observant

of the difficulty with which he fulfilled this duty. Mr. Jarvis continued to reside in Portland, which was the scene of many mingled joys and sorrows. He had nine children, several of whom died there in tender years. Within eight months he lost three of the youngest, two of whom were buried in the same week. The loss of a fourth in 1843, and the dangerous illness of a fifth, deepened to many hearts the solemnities of Ash-Wednesday.

In 1852 the family residence was sold, and Mr. Jarvis removed to Middletown. After the marriage of his daughter Elizabeth to Colonel Samuel Colt of Hartford, he made that city his home.

As a preacher, Mr. Jarvis was full of fervor and impressiveness. His delivery was remarkably good, and his voice powerful. As a pastor he was distinguished for fidelity and devotion. But for thirty and five years his voice ceased to be heard in the pulpit. It pleased God to appoint that thus long he should set forth His true and lively Word only by his life. It also pleased God to try his faith and patience to the last. He became a great sufferer, yet bore his physical agony with unyielding constancy and submission to the will of his Heavenly Father. Fully conscious that the release he longed for was near, he bade kindred and friends farewell, commending them to the care of the Saviour he had trusted with a faith triumphant through untold suffering, even unto death. It was a touching sight to the writer of this as his eye left gazing upon features so calm in the exquisite repose of the Christian's death, to perceive in his folded hands a bunch of wheat. He was, indeed, full ripe unto the harvest; but the sight instantly recalled to mind the 126th Psalm in connection with his long-interrupted ministry: "He that now goeth on his way weeping, and beareth good seed, shall doubtless come again with joy, bringing his sheaves with him."

This extract from Bishop Williams' annual address, and the minutes adopted at a quarterly meeting of the parish of the Good Shepherd, show the estimate in which his life's work was held:

"The Rev. William Jarvis had been long precluded, by loss of voice, from performing the public duties of the ministry. Those, however, who remember him before infirmity came upon him, will remember what faithful and successful parochial work he accomplished, the fruits of which are living still. And those who knew him after he was removed from scenes of pastoral labor will never forget the true and living interest evinced by generous benefactions, which he took in the Church's work, the kind words and deeds with which he cheered many a brother's heart, nor the unmurmuring patience and resignation with which he bore the suffering God sent upon him while he was waiting for his summons to depart."

At a quarterly meeting of the parish of the Good Shepherd, the following minutes were adopted, to be entered on the records of the parish, and published in the papers:

The members of the parish of the Good Shepherd, sensible of the loss they have sustained in the removal from among them of the Rev. William Jarvis, desire to record herein their estimation of the privilege afforded them in witnessing his blameless life, his gentleness, his cheerful and devout demeanor, during the time he worshipped with them; and while they will not forget his former active ministry, neither would they fail to acknowledge that of his later years, wherein by patience, and in quietness, he declared his faith, and by constant and loving attendance on all the offices of religion, pointed others to its true and only source.

MAJOR RICHARD WILLIAM HART

Was the only child of General William Hart and his wife Esther Buckingham. He was born at Saybrook, Connecticut, on the fifteenth of January, 1768.

He was married on the twenty-ninth of October, 1795, to Miss Elizabeth Bull, only daughter of Mr. Nathan Bull and his wife Anna Perry of Newport, Rhode Island. Mr. Bull died early in life, and left one son named James, besides the little daughter. She was adopted by his sister, Mrs. Elizabeth Bull Miller, for whom the child had been named. She was born on the seventeenth of September, 1772, and was a child of much beauty and grace. She became a great favorite of Count Rochambeau, the commander of the French forces in the Revolutionary War, and afterwards when she grew to womanhood was a much admired belle in the cultivated society of Newport, for which it was famed, even in those early days.

Mr. John Hart of Saybrook, a brother of General William Hart, married after the death of Mr. Bull, his widow, Mrs. Anna Perry Bull; so that after the marriage of Major R. W. Hart to Miss Bull, Mrs. John Hart became by marriage the aunt of her own daughter.

Major Hart inherited from his father a large fortune, which much increased by the rise in value of the land purchased by General Hart in the Western Reserve, and he left at his death in 1837 an estate valued at half a million, which was divided between his widow and two daughters. He was much esteemed and respected in his native State, and used his means liberally for the good of those about him.

His wife was an earnest and devout Churchwoman, and owing to her influence Major Hart gave a plot of ground for a Church building in his north garden, and the larger part of the money necessary for erecting the Church. Mrs. Hart's health was feeble for many years, so that she was seldom able to be one of the congregation gathered within its walls for worship. But often in the summer days she sat by her window looking towards the Church, and could unite in the prayers and praises of God's people, in the quiet of her own room. Her life was passed in doing deeds of Christian love and charity. Major Hart died of apoplexy in 1837. They had

three children, one son and two daughters. The son, William Richard, died of scarlet fever when between ten and eleven years of age, on the thirtieth of January, 1807.

Elizabeth Miller, the eldest daughter, was born on the twenty-sixth of June, 1798. She was married December twenty-second, 1825, to Rev. William Jarvis. They had nine children, four of whom died in childhood. Hetty Buckingham Hart, the second daughter, did not marry. She was a very attractive woman, and was much beloved and admired. She took a warm interest in the Church which her parents had done so much to build, and for several years played the organ at all the services therein. After the death of Major Hart, his widow and Miss Hart removed to Hartford, Connecticut, where they lived, honored, beloved, and respected, and tenderly mourned when their days on earth were ended. The little Church of wood which Mrs. Hart so loved, has been removed, and a more imposing edifice of stone built on another site. Strangers are in the dear old homestead, and the last of their descendants bearing the name ennobled by this honored couple, sleeps with her fathers.

"The memory of the just is blessed."

MAJOR-GENERAL WILLIAM HART

Of Saybrook, Connecticut, was the eldest son of Rev. William Hart of the same town, and his wife Mary Blague. He was born on the twenty-fourth of June, 1746. He married Esther Buckingham, a daughter of Mr. Joseph Buckingham of Haddam, and his wife Sarah Tully. She was born on the eighth of March, 1745.

General Hart was a merchant. He was in the War of the Revolution, and became a Major-General. In 1785 he was engaged in business with one of his brothers, in Hartford, where they carried on an extensive business with the West Indies, and in which he accumulated a large property.

Owing to the destruction of a number of his vessels while engaged in this business, he, and his heirs since, have been among the claimants under the French Spoliation Bill, with little probability, however, of realizing anything from it, although years ago France paid these claims to our government.

"In 1795 the Western Reserve, so called, belonging to the State of Connecticut, was purchased by subscription by a company of wealthy citizens of the State for $1,200,000. General Hart was one of the company, his subscription being $30,462."

This investment proved a golden one to him and his heirs, some of the land still yielding an income to the family, though all but a small portion of it has been sold during the more than eighty-five years since its purchase. Mrs. Hart died on the fifteenth of March, 1811, aged sixty-six years. They had but one child, a son, Richard William Hart.

General Hart is described as a man of commanding person and presence, with a strong, handsome, manly face, a rich complexion, and fine, clear, dark eyes and hair.

He was an accomplished horseman, and often made the journey between Saybrook and Hartford on his favorite saddle horse. An old resident of the latter place, who long years ago departed this life, used to tell his great grandchildren, with much enthusiasm, what an imposing appearance he presented as he rode up to her door, and how it was ever her delight to set before him the very best entertainment the inn afforded.

The following is copied from his tombstone in the ancient burial ground on Saybrook Point:

"Sacred to the memory of Major-General William Hart, eldest son of Rev. William Hart of Saybrook, who was born June 24th, 1746, and died August 29th, 1817, in the 72nd year of his age. In youth active and enterprising, he early entered on mercantile pursuits, and sustained a character of unquestionable integrity and extensive respectability. By his talents he rose to some of the first civil and military honors of this State, and commanded unusual influence at home and abroad. He loved order, was an able counsellor, a professor of religion, a benefactor to the Church, a pillar in society, and has left a memory respected by his friends, instructive to his family, and honorable to the place in which he lived.

'One eye on death, and one full fixed on heaven, Became a mortal and immortal man.'"

61

BISHOP SEABURY'S

Communion-Office,

Reprinted in Fac-simile.

[17]

With an Historical Sketch and Notes

BY THE

REV. SAMUEL HART, M.A.

Seabury Professor in Trinity College, Hartford.

SECOND EDITION, REVISED.

NEW YORK:

T. WHITTAKER, No. 2 BIBLE HOUSE.

1883.

62

HISTORICAL SKETCH.

On the twenty-third Sunday after Trinity, November 14th, 1784, at the chapel in Bishop Skinner's house in Longacre, Aberdeen, "in the presence of a considerable number of respectable clergymen, and a great number of laity," Dr. Samuel Seabury was consecrated Bishop of Connecticut, by the Rt. Rev. Messrs. Kilgour, Petrie, and Skinner, Bishops of the Episcopal Church in Scotland. On the following day a "Concordate" between the Church in Scotland and that in Connecticut was agreed upon, and signed and sealed by the four Bishops. Of this Concordate the fifth article is in the following words:

"Art. V. As the Celebration of the holy Eucharist, or the Administration of the Sacrament of the Body and Blood of Christ, is the principal Bond of Union among Christians, as well as the most solemn Act of Worship in the Christian Church, the Bishops aforesaid agree in desiring that there may be as little Variance here as possible; and tho' the Scottish Bishops are very far from prescribing to their Brethren In this matter, they cannot help ardently wishing that Bishop Seabury would endeavour all he can, consistently with peace and prudence, to make the Celebration of this venerable Mystery conformable to the most primitive Doctrine and Practice in that respect: Which is the pattern the Church of Scotland has copied after in her Communion Office, and which it has been the Wish of some of the most eminent Divines of the Church of England, that she also had more closely followed than she seems to have done since she gave up her first reformed Liturgy, used in the Reign of King Edward VI., between which, and the form used in the Church of Scotland, there is no Difference in any point, which the primitive Church reckoned essential to the right Ministration of the holy Eucharist. In this capital Article therefore of the Eucharistic Service, in which the Scottish Bishops so earnestly wish for as much Unity as possible, Bishop Seabury also agrees to take a serious View of the Communion Office recommended by them, and if found agreeable to the genuine Standards of Antiquity, to give his Sanction to it, and by gentle Methods of Argument and Persuasion, to endeavour, as they have done, to introduce it by degrees into practice, without the Compulsion of Authority on the one side, or the prejudice of former Custom on the other."[1]

The clergy of Connecticut assembled in Convocation at Middletown, on the 2d day of August, 1785, and gave their Bishop a hearty welcome. We are told that when the Concordate, with the accompanying letter from the Scotch Bishops, was laid before the clergy, it excited in them the warmest sentiments of gratitude and esteem.[2] At this meeting the Rev. Messrs. Bowden and Jarvis of Connecticut and the Rev. Mr. Parker of Boston were appointed a committee to act with the Bishop in proposing such changes in the Prayer-Book as should be thought needful. The committee met immediately and agreed upon certain alterations. Part of these were reserved to be reported to the next meeting of Convocation, which

was to be held at New Haven in September[3]; but the changes in the state prayers were published at once by the Bishop in the following pastoral letter:

[1] Fac-simile Publications of the Historical Club, No. 13.
[2] Dr. Beardsley's History of the Church in Connecticut, i. 368.
[3] Dr. Parker's letter in Documentary History of Conn., ii. 318.

SAMUEL, by divine permission, Bishop of the Episcopal Church in the State of Connecticut, to the Clergy of the said Church, GREETING.

IT having pleased Almighty GOD, that the late *British* Colony of Connecticut should become a free, sovereign and independent State, as it now is, some alterations in the Liturgy and Offices of our Church are necessary to be made, to accommodate them to the civil Constitution of the country in which we live; for the peace, security and prosperity of which, both as good subjects and faithful Christians, it is our duty constantly to pray——WE, the Bishop aforesaid, have thought fit, by and with the advice and assistance of such of our Clergy as we have had opportunity of consulting, to issue this *Injunction*, hereby authorising and requiring You, and every one of You, the Presbyters and Deacons of the Church above mentioned, in the celebration of Divine Service, to make the following alterations in the Liturgy and Offices of our Church, viz.

I. In the suffrages after the Creed, in morning and evening Prayer, instead of *O Lord save the King*, You are to read, *O Lord save the Church*; to which the congregation are to make the accustomed response, *And mercifully hear us*, &c.

II. The prayer for the King, in the morning and evening service, to be left out; and the prayer for the Royal Family to be thus altered; *Almighty God, the fountain of all goodness, we humbly beseech thee to bless the Governor and Rulers of this State; endue them with thy Holy Spirit;*—and so on as it now stands.

III. In the Litany the 15, 16, 17, 18th petitions to be omitted, and the petition for Bishops, Priests, and Deacons, immediately to follow that for the universal Church. The 20, and 21st petitions to be thus read, *That it may please thee to endue the Governor and Rulers of this State, with grace, wisdom and understanding. That it may please thee to bless and keep the Judges and inferior Magistrates, giving them grace to execute justice and to maintain truth.* To both which the usual response---*We beseech thee to hear us, good Lord,---* is to be made by the congregation.

IV. In the prayer for the whole state of Christ's Church, the part relating to Rulers and Ministers to be thus altered--- *We beseech thee also to save and defend all Christian Kings, Princes, and Governors; and grant that they, and all that are put in authority, may truly and impartially minister justice, to the punishment of wickedness and vice, and to the maintenance of true religion and virtue. Give grace, O heavenly Father, to all Bishops, Priests, and Deacons, that they may---*and so on, as it now stands.

V. The prayers for the King that stand before the Nicene Creed in the Communion service, to be omitted.

VI. In the answer in the Catechism to the question---What is thy duty towards thy neighbour? for---*to honor and obey the King*---substitute, *to honor and obey my civil Rulers, to submit myself*, &c.

VII. That during every session of the Great and General Court, or Assembly, you do use the following collect, in its proper place, both in morning and evening prayer.

"Most gracious God, we humbly beseech thee, as for this State in general, "so especially for the great and general Court at this time assembled: That "thou wouldst be pleased to direct and prosper all their consultations to the "advancement of thy glory, the good of thy church, the safety, honor, and "welfare of thy people; that all things may be so ordered and settled by "their endeavours, upon the best and surest foundations, that peace and hap-"piness, truth and justice, religion and piety may be established among us "for all generations. These and all other necessaries for them, for us, and "thy whole church, we humbly beg in the name and mediation of Jesus "Christ our most blessed Lord and Saviour. Amen.

VIII. That you discontinue the observation of the fifth of November, the thirtieth of January, the twenty-ninth of May, and the twenty-fifth of October.

Commending you, Reverend Brethren, your congregations, and labours in

the Gospel, to the grace, protection, and blessing of Almighty God, We remain your affectionate brother and servant in Christ Jesus, our Lord.

Done at New-London,

Aug. 12th, 1785.

The Convention of Massachusetts, Rhode Island, and New Hampshire met at Boston, on the 7th of September, having before them the report of the committee appointed at Middletown in August. The changes in the state prayers were adopted, with the characteristic substitution of "Commonwealth" for "State," and recommended for immediate use. A considerable number of other alterations were also agreed to, but it was voted that their use should be postponed in order that it might be seen how far the other States would conform to them.[1] Dr. Parker, writing to Bishop Seabury on the 12th of September, says that this Convention adopted most of the changes proposed at Middletown, with a few others; the changes of any importance to which assent was not given, being expressly stated to be the

[1] Reprint of Mass. Journals, pp. 8, sqq.

omission of the second Lesson in the Morning Service, and that of the Gospel and the Exhortation in the Baptismal-Office.[1] In the lack of records of the early Convocations of Connecticut, we look to the journal of the Massachusetts Convention for an account of suggested alterations; and it is noticeable that the only changes proposed in the Communion-Office were the omission of the Lord's Prayer at the beginning, the omission of the prayers for the King, a different petition for rulers in the prayer for the Church Militant, somewhat different phraseology in the first Warning and the first Exhortation, and a permission to repeat the sentences at administration but once for all then present at the altar.[2] It is evident, therefore, that Bishop Seabury took no steps in 1785 to introduce the Scotch Liturgy. The Massachusetts Convention was kept under adjournments until July 20th, 1786, and at last it was left to the discretion of the different parishes to adopt the alterations or to retain the old liturgy.[3]

Bishop Seabury sent a copy of the substitutes for the state prayers to Dr. (afterwards Bishop) White, of Philadelphia, under date of August 19, 1785, with the words: "Should more be done, it must be a work of time and great deliberation."[4] And in fact, the clergy of Connecticut were found unwilling to agree to any other alterations in the Prayer-Book. Especially when the convention of the states to the south of New England met

[1] Doc. Hist. Conn., ii. 284.
[2] Reprint of Mass. Journals, pp. 11, 12.
[3] Doc. Hist. Conn., ii. 319.   [4] Ibid., ii. 282.

at Philadelphia, September 27th to October 7th, 1785, and prepared the book since known as the "Proposed Book," the Churchmen of Connecticut were alarmed. Mr. Parker had hoped that the meeting at Philadelphia would go no further than his own convention had gone; but he evidently felt aggrieved that the clergy of Connecticut were not willing to go so far. Bishop Seabury wrote to him, November 28th, 1785, as follows:

"Between the time of our parting at Middletown and the clerical meeting at New Haven, it was found that the Church people in Connecticut were much alarmed at the thoughts of any considerable alterations being made in the Prayer Book; and upon the whole, it was judged best that no alterations should be attempted at present, but to wait till a little time shall have cooled down the tempers and conciliated the affections of people to each other. And since the convention at Philadelphia, which, as report says, has abrogated two creeds and nineteen articles, and taken great liberties with the prayers, &c., we are more apprehensive of proceeding to any alterations."[1]

This Proposed Book was published in the spring of 1786.[2] On the 22nd of September in the same year, Bishop Seabury delivered his second charge to his clergy assembled in Convocation at Derby. In it he said:

"It is always a disagreeable task to be obliged to mention any matter with censure, or even disapprobation; and I am very happy that the measure of which I am now to take notice can call for animadversion only by way of caution. A number of Clergy and Laity in the southern States have undertaken to revise and alter the Liturgy and Offices and Government of the Church, and have exhibited a Prayer-book to the public. The time will not permit me to

[1] Ibid., ii. 287.
[2] The Prothonotary's certificate is dated April 1st, 1786.

say anything of the merit of the alterations in the Liturgy; but, I am persuaded, by an unprejudiced mind, some of them will be thought for the worse, most of them not for the better. But the authority on which they have acted is unknown in the Episcopal Church. The government of the Church by Bishops we hold to have been established by the Apostles, acting under the commission of Christ and the direction of the Holy Ghost; and therefore is not to be altered by any power on earth, nor indeed by an angel from heaven. This government they have degraded by lodging the chief authority in a Convention of clerical and lay Delegates, making their Church Episcopal in its orders, but Presbyterian in its government.

"Liturgies are left more to the prudence and judgment of the governors of the Church; and the primitive practice seems to have been that the Bishop did, with the advice no doubt of his Presbyters, provide a Liturgy for the use of his diocese. This ought to have been the case here. Bishops should first have been obtained to preside over those Churches. And to those Bishops, with the Proctors of the Clergy, should have been committed the business of compiling a Liturgy for the use of the Church throughout the states. This would have ensured unity in doctrine, worship, and discipline through the whole, which upon the present plan will

either not be obtained, or, if obtained, will not be durable. And should we ever be so happy, through the merciful providence of God, as to obtain such a meeting, great regard ought to be had to the primitive Liturgies and Forms, in compiling a book of Common-Prayer."[1]

At this Convocation, Bishop Seabury, acting on the principles which he had thus laid down, set forth the Communion-Office which is reprinted in the foregoing pages, and "recommended" it "to the Episcopal Con-

---

[1] Pages 11, 12. The Bishop passes on to speak of the value of the testimony of the early Church, of the doctrine of the Sacraments, and of the necessity, in view of present dangers and errors, of holding fast to the primitive faith.

---

gregations in Connecticut."[1] This office was taken, with certain alterations which will presently be noticed in detail, from that which was then in use in the Scotch Church. This latter is said to have been compiled by Bishops Forbes and Falconer, and was first published in 1764. Hall says that it "may be considered as the second standard edition"; the first having been Bishop Gadderer's edition of 1743, which was recognized by the canons of that year,[2] as the edition of 1764 (reprinted in 1765) was by later canons.[3]

The first Scotch Prayer-Book was that published in 1637, under the direction of King Charles I.[4] It is

---

[1] Dr. Jarvis's A Voice from Connecticut, p. 25; Dr. Beardsley's Life of Bishop Seabury, p. 263. A new State prayer was also provided. Ibid, p. 264. The manuscript records of Convocation do not begin till 1790, when the secretary was directed to procure a blank-book in which to record the minutes. Space was left at the beginning of the book as if to insert the minutes of former meetings, but this was never done. It seems, from a letter of the Rev. Roger Viets of Simsbury to the Rev. Mr. Parker of Boston, that the Convocation which met at Wallingford on the 27th of February in the next year (1787) took steps towards setting forth for the use of the Church in Connecticut a complete edition of the Prayer-Book. It was at this Convocation that a Coadjutor was elected to Bishop Seabury; but the union of the dioceses in the country made his consecration unnecessary.

[2] Fragmenta Liturgica, i., pp. liii., lv. The "Non-juring" and Scotch offices are in vol. v.

[3] Neale's Life of Torry, p. 270. The edition of 1743 differs in date only from that of 1735.

[4] His father King James (VI. of Scotland and I. of England) had taken steps for composing a Scotch liturgy as early as 1616. Sprott, Scottish Liturgies, p. xviii.

---

frequently called by the name of Archbishop Laud, who was appointed, together with Bishops Juxon and Wren, to examine and revise a draft which had been prepared in Scotland, the chief compilers being Maxwell, Bishop of Ross, and Wedderburn of Dunblane.[1] The chief variations from the English book which was then in

use (that of 1559) were in the Communion-Office. The prayer for the Church Militant and the prayer of Consecration were more nearly conformed to the first book of Edward VI. than to that of Elizabeth, the words of Institution being preceded by an Invocation and followed by an Oblation, an Intercession, and the Lord's Prayer. The words at the delivery of the elements were also the same as in 1549. The only variation in *order* between the proposed Scotch liturgy and that then in use in England, was that the prayer of Humble Access was placed after the prayer of Consecration.

The Prayer-Book of 1637, as is well known, was at once withdrawn; but the subsequent Scotch Communion-Offices were to some extent modelled upon that contained in it. Changes, however, began to be made in the order of the several parts of the service; and in 1735 Gadderer's book appeared, having the order which was contained in the book of 1764 and in Bishop Seabury's office, except that the Offertory preceded the Ex-

---

[1] Sprott, ibid., Introduction, to page lxv.; Skinner on the Scotch Communion-Office (Aberdeen, 1807), p. 25; Hall, Reliquiæ Liturgicæ, i., pp. xix, sqq.; Bright in Blunt's Annotated P. B., pp. 580, sqq. Bp. Juxon took no part in the revision; but Bp. Cosin would seem to have been concerned in it; see Sprott, lix., note i.

---

hortation, and that, in the prayer of Consecration, the Invocation preceded the words of Institution. The words of Institution, the Oblation, and the Invocation had appeared in this their primitive and true order, for the first time in any service-book in the English language, in Stephens's "Liturgy of the Ancient Christians," about the year 1700[1]; and this order is found also in the Non-Jurors' book of 1718, in Deacon's Liturgy of 1734, in Rattray's of 1744, and in a Scotch office of 1755, to which that of 1764 is in every respect in close resemblance.[2]

. . .

It may be of interest to add that the Scotch Communion-Office has remained almost without change since 1764. The edition published by the Rev. John Skinner of Forfar (son of the Bishop of Aberdeen), in 1800,[2] and reprinted by him in his "Scotch Communion-Office Illustrated," in 1807, differs from it only in the

---

[2] Hall calls it the third standard edition. It may be found in Frag. Liturg., v. 253.

---

insertion of the words "and oblations" and the name of the Sovereign in the prayer for the Church, the change of "who" into "which" in the Lord's Prayer, the addition of "meekly kneeling upon your knees" to the Invitation, the insertion of "and" before "our souls"

in the prayer of Humble Access, and the change of "soul and body" into "body and soul" in the words of administration. Bishop Torry's Prayer-Book, published in Edinburgh in 1849,[1] besides prefixing an "Ante-Communion Service" (of which more will be said presently), makes the same changes except that in the Invitation, begins a new paragraph in the Trisagion at the word "Holy," and does the same in the Prayer of Consecration at the beginning of the Invocation and of each of the two following petitions. As at present printed for use, the Scotch Communion-Office prefixes an "Ante-Communion Service," and agrees in other respects with the edition of 1800 and 1807, except that the Trisagion is printed in two paragraphs, the prayer of Consecration in nine, and the prayer for the Church in nine.

Although the old Scotch Communion-Offices begin with the Exhortation, we have the testimony of Mr. Skinner in a note to Bishop Horsley's Collation of Offices, which forms an appendix to his "Scotch Communion-Office Illustrated," that an introductory service was used; and the form which is given agrees substantially with that in the two services mentioned at the end of the last paragraph. This latter form differs from that in the

[1] The history of this book should be read in Neale's Life of Bishop Torry, chaps. vii. and viii.; in the appendix to which it is collated with the book of 1637, the Non-Jurors' office, and the received Scotch form (that of 1764).

English book in allowing our Lord's summary of the Law followed by a versicle to be read instead of the Ten Commandments with their versicles; in providing the collect for grace and strength to keep the Commandments, its use being discretionary with one of the two collects for the Sovereign; and in instructing the people to say when the Gospel is announced, "Glory be to Thee, O God," and at its end, "Thanks be to Thee, O Lord, for this Thy glorious Gospel."[1] It is probable that Bishop Seabury and his clergy used the "Ante-Communion Service" of the English Book; for in a folio English Prayer-Book which was used by the Bishop in St. James's Church, New London, after the Revolution, is our present prayer for the civil authority, written out and pasted over the prayer for the Sovereign which follows the Commandments.[2]

Bishop Seabury's Communion-Office seems to have been almost, if not quite, universally adopted by the clergy of Connecticut. We are told that they "became very much attached to it, not only from the recommend-

[1] Bishop Torry's edition, following that of 1637, directs the Priest to say, "Here endeth the Holy Gospel"; but there is no such direction in the later edition. There were two sets of

rubrics in 1637, one in the usual place, and the other before and after the Gospel for the First Sunday in Advent.
[2] Dr. Hallam's Annals of St. James's Church, p. 72. The first Church in New London was burned in 1781, and the second was not finished till 1787. There is a tradition that, while Bishop Seabury officiated in the Court-House, he celebrated the Holy Communion every Sunday after morning prayer, in the large parlor of the house in which he lived. Ibid., p. 71. He would naturally begin with the Exhortation. See below.

ation of their Bishop, but from the conviction that this order was in more exact conformity [than the English liturgy] with the earliest usage of the Christian Church."[1] Its general use probably ceased when the American Book of Common Prayer began to be used, October 1st, 1790; but, as will be noted below, it was employed by some of the clergy at a much later date.

A "General Convention" assembled at Philadelphia, July 28th, 1789. On the 5th day of August, on motion of the Rev. Dr. William Smith of Maryland, it was voted (inter alia) that "it be proposed to the churches in the New England states to meet the churches of these states, with the said three Bishops [the Rt. Rev. Drs. White, Provoost, and Seabury], in an adjourned Convention, to settle certain articles of union among all the churches."[2] The clergy of Connecticut met on the 15th of September, and on the next day they elected the Rev. Messrs. Hubbard and Jarvis their delegates to the adjourned convention. They were "empowered to confer with the General Convention on the subject of making alterations in the Book of Common Prayer; but the ratification of such alterations was expressly reserved, to rest with the Bishop and clergy of the Church."[3] The Convention assembled on the 29th of September, and it was divided into two houses on the 3d of October. One of the first votes of the House of Clerical and Lay Deputies ordered the appointment of a committee "to prepare an order for the administration of the Holy Communion." This committee reported on the 9th, one day after the House

[1] Dr. Beardsley's History, i. 388. [2] Journal, p. 14.
[3] Beardsley, i. 409, 410.

of Bishops (the Rt. Rev. Drs. Seabury and White) had "prepared their proposals" on this service. On the 13th, the lower house agreed to the report of their committee on the Communion Service; and on the 14th, the proposed service was sent to the Bishops, who at once made amendments and returned it. The lower house concurred in all the amendments except one, which was immediately withdrawn by the Bishops; and thus both houses agreed to the present American Communion-Office on the 14th day of October, 1789.[1]

66

That it was owing to Bishop Seabury that the Prayer of Consecration in that office followed the Scotch model is beyond a question. In a letter which he wrote to Bishop White, under date of June 29, 1789, after criticizing the action of the Philadelphia Convention in other matters, he had written as follows:

"That the most exceptionable part of the English book is the Communion Office may be proved by a number of very respectable names among her Clergy. The grand fault in that office is the deficiency of a more formal oblation of the elements, and of the invocation of the Holy Ghost to sanctify and bless them. The Consecration is made to consist merely in the Priest's laying his hands on the elements and pronouncing ' *This is my body*,' &c., which words are not consecration at all, nor were they addressed by Christ to the Father, but were declarative to the Apostles. This is so exactly symbolizing with the Church of Rome in an error; an error, too, on which the absurdity of Transubstantiation is built, that nothing but having fallen into the same error themselves, could have prevented the enemies of the Church from casting it in her teeth. The efficacy of Baptism, of Confirmation, of Orders, is ascribed to the Holy Ghost, and His energy is implored for that purpose; and why He

---

[1] Journal of Convention.

---

should not be invoked in the consecration of the Eucharist, especially as all the old Liturgies are full to the point, I cannot conceive. It is much easier to account for the alterations of the first Liturgy of Edward the VI., than to justify them; and as I have been told there is a vote on the minutes of your Convention, anno 1786, I believe, for the revision of this matter, I hope it will be taken up, and that God will raise up some able and worthy advocate for this primitive practice, and make you and the Convention the instruments of restoring it to His Church in America. It would do you more honor in the world, and contribute more to the union of the churches than any other alterations you can make, and would restore the Holy Eucharist to its ancient dignity and efficacy."[1]

The strength of Bishop Seabury's convictions on this subject appeared when, on the morning of Sunday, the 11th of October, during the session of the Convention, Bishop White asked him to consecrate the elements, and he twice declined, saying the second time in a pleasant manner: "To confess the truth, I hardly consider the form to be used [that of the English book] as strictly amounting to a consecration."[2]

"It may perhaps be expected," says Bishop White, "that the great change made in restoring to the consecration prayer the oblatory words and the invocation of the Holy Spirit, left out in King Edward's reign, must at least have produced an opposition. But no such thing

---

[1] Doc. Hist. Conn., ii. 331. See also Bp. Seabury's Sermon "Of the Holy Eucharist" (Sermons, Vol. i., Discourse vi.), in which reference is made to Brett's Dissertation and to [Bp. Rattray's] Liturgy of Jerusalem.

---

[2] Bp. White's Memoirs of the Church, second edition, pp. 154, 155. "These sentiments he had adopted," adds Bp. White, "in his visit to the bishops from whom he received his Episcopacy." This, though at first sight a natural supposition, is probably a mistake.

---

happened to any considerable extent; or at least, the author did not hear of any in the other house, further than a disposition to the effect in a few gentlemen, which was counteracted by some pertinent remarks of the president. In that of the bishops, it lay very near to the heart of Bishop Seabury. As for the other bishop [Bishop White himself], without conceiving with some, that the service as it stood was essentially defective, he always thought there was a beauty in those ancient forms, and can discover no superstition in them."[1] He then goes on to explain how in the first edition of the new book the words "which we now offer unto thee" were printed, as in the Scotch office, in small capitals; though in all succeeding editions[2] they were, as was intended, in the same type as the rest of the prayer.

The president of the lower house, whose pertinent remarks are said by Bishop White to have counteracted some disposition to raise objections to the change proposed, was the Rev. Dr. William Smith, who has been mentioned above. Dr. Smith was a native of Scotland, who had been ordained to the diaconate and the priesthood at the same time and place as Bishop Seabury. On grounds which need not be mentioned here, he "had

---

[1] Ibid., p. 154.

[2] This is not quite accurate. The small capitals appear in the editions of both 1790 and 1791. Rev. Frederick Gibson's Historical Essay, p. 23. In the first edition of the Prayer-Book, the words in the Apostles' Creed, "He descended into hell," are enclosed in brackets; but it is only in Evening Prayer that they are printed in italics; in Morning Prayer and the Visitation of the Sick they are in ordinary type. Bp. White's statement (Memoirs, p. 151) needs this correction.

---

been opposed to the non-juring bishops in Scotland communicating the Episcopate to Connecticut; and he had said some things not very complimentary to the candidate from this State, in his steps to reach the apostolic office."[1] But, as we have seen, he had proposed the invitation to the Bishop and Clergy of Connecticut; he entertained the Bishop during his stay in Philadelphia; and tradition has it that, when certain members of the lower house were beginning to object to the prayer of Consecration which was proposed by the Bishops, he reproved them for finding fault with something which they had not heard, and thereupon read the prayer with so impressive a tone and manner that the objections were no further urged. The form, says Dr. Jarvis, "was admitted

without opposition, and in silence if not in reverence."[2] It is, then, to Bishop Seabury and Dr. Smith that the Church in this country is indebted for its prayer of Consecration in the Communion-Office.

It was probably owing to the influence of the delegation from Maryland that the wording of the Invocation was changed from that in the Scotch office to that which we now use. Writing to the Rev. Mr. Parker of Boston, April 17th, 1786, Dr. Smith says that the Maryland Convention, having the "Proposed Book" under consideration, had decided to recommend "an addition to the Consecration Prayer, in the Holy Communion, something analogous to that of the Liturgy of Edward VI. and the Scots' Liturgy, invoking a blessing on the Elements of Bread and Wine," changing the prayer "that they may

---

[1] Beardsley, i. 377. Dr. Smith was at one time Provost of the University of Pennsylvania.

[2] A Voice from Connecticut, p. 26.

---

become the body and blood, etc." to "that we receiving the same, according to Thy Son, our Saviour Jesus Christ's holy Institution, etc." He adds: "This I think will be a proper amendment, and it perfectly satisfies such of our Clergy and people as were attached to the Scots' and other ancient Liturgies, all of which have an Invocation of a blessing on the Elements, as is, indeed, most proper."[1]

It may be worth while to note that both the Concordate quoted at the beginning of this sketch, and Bishop Seabury's letter, as well as Bishop White's words in his Memoirs, seem to imply that, in the opinion of the writers, the first Liturgy of Edward VI. and the Scotch office contained prayers of Consecration which were substantially the same; whereas in fact the Invocation in the first Book of Edward VI. stands in an anomalous place, followed as it is by the words of Institution, and that by

---

[1] Doc. Hist. Conn., i. 291. The vote of the Convention is printed in the appendix to the Journal of Maryland, 1855, p. 18. It is very interesting to note that the latter part of this form had been proposed in the draft of a Prayer-Book made in Scotland in the reign of King James (probably in 1619) and sent to London not later than 1629. Sprott, pp. xxxiv., lxx., 72. The prayer of Invocation, says this author, "is thought essential by the [Presbyterian] Church of Scotland, and to this day the want of it in the English Prayer-Book is spoken of among us as a very serious defect." Ibid., p. lxviii. Dr. Sancroft proposed a form almost identical with that adopted in 1789. Bulley's Variations, p. 191. Both phrases were used in 1637, the first having the form "that they may be unto us the body and blood of Thy most dearly beloved Son." The Rev. William Smith of Stepney Parish, Md., as appears from a letter written in 1785, was in the habit of using the Scotch office, and persisted in it in spite of the objections of Dr. William Smith.

---

the Oblation; while in the Scotch Book the order is that of the ancient Liturgies, as was noted above. Its compilers used the words of the book of 1549, but they put them in the order which they knew to have the sanction of antiquity.

Such was the great point in which Bishop Seabury's liturgy influenced the formation of the Communion-Office which is still, by God's good providence, used throughout the Church in the United States. It is thought that this influence may be traced in another matter which, though it is by no means of equal importance, is yet worthy of careful consideration.

In the first Prayer-Book of King Edward VI., it was provided that if the sermon did not contain an exhortation to the people "to the worthy receiving of the holy Sacrament of the body and blood of our Saviour Christ," the curate should give an exhortation to those that were minded to receive the same; and this exhortation, which is nearly word for word the same that is still used in the Communion Service, beginning "Dearly beloved in the Lord," was followed by the Offertory. Then, if there was no Communion, the Priest was instructed to say one or two collects and to dismiss the people with the accustomed blessing. But if there was a Communion, it was ordered that those who intended to partake of it should "tarry still in the quire or in some convenient place nigh the quire," and that all others should "depart out of the quire except the Ministers and Clerks." The prayer for the Church, it may be noted, came after the Trisagion. In 1552 the prayer for the Church was placed immediately after the Offertory, and the Minister was instructed, when there was no Communion, to say "all that is appointed at the Communion till the end of the homily, concluding with the general prayer for the whole estate of Christ's Church militant here in earth, and one or more collects." The same rubric was repeated in 1559 and in 1604; in 1662 it was made more explicit, requiring that everything should be said to the end of the general prayer, and that the Blessing should be given after the Collects. It was at this point in the service, then, that non-communicants were expected to withdraw from the Church.[1] But in the Non-jurors' Book of 1718, the Offertory is placed after the Exhortation, which is addressed to the communicants, and is closely followed, as in the later Scotch services, by the Trisagion; and at the end of the service, there is the following important rubric: "After the Sermon or Homily is ended, (or, if there be no Sermon or Homily, after the Nicene Creed is ended,) if there be no Communion, the Priest shall turn to the people, and say, *Let us pray.* And then, turning to the Altar, he shall stand before it,

and say one or more of these Collects last before rehearsed, concluding with the Blessing." The other Scotch offices which are reprinted in Hall's Fragmenta Liturgica contain no part of the service to be used before the Sermon, and give no instructions as to what shall be done when there is no Communion, it being evidently considered that all that is printed is, as is expressly said on the title-pages, the Communion-office " as far as concerneth the Ministration of that Holy Sacrament." The

---

[1] See Scudamore, Notitia Eucharistica, first edition, p. 391, and note the reference to Bp. Cosin.

---

editions of 1724 and 1743 begin with the Offertory; but that of 1755[1] and all that follow begin with the Exhortation; and on the reverse of the title-page of the edition of 1844, we find: "The Catechumens and other Non-Communicants being dismissed, the Holy Office proceedeth as here set forth." Bishop Torry's Prayer-Book has this rubric: "Then shall follow the Sermon; and when the Holy Eucharist is to be celebrated, the Minister shall dismiss the non-communicants in these or like words, *Let those who are not to communicate now depart.*" It would appear, then, as well from express directions in books which Bishop Seabury followed or which were based on those that he followed, as from the structure of the office which he set forth, that none but communicants were supposed to be present at the time of the Offertory; and if not at that time, then certainly not at the offering of the prayer for the Church, which invariably occupies a later place in the service.[2]

Now bearing these facts in mind, it certainly seems that the changes introduced in 1789 into certain of the rubrics of the English Liturgy, in adapting them to the use of the American Church, show that it was the intention of

---

[1] See the " Direction " on the reverse of the title.

[2] It ought perhaps to be noted that Bishop Drummond's service (1796) contemplates an offertory and the use of the prayer for the Church, and Bishop Torry's book (1849) an offertory, on occasions when there is no Communion. In the use of the prayer for the Church in the former service, it is curious to observe, the words " alms and " " are to be omitted, except when the offering is to be given away in charity. . . . N. B. The offerings of the people, when for the support of the clergy, are not *alms*, but *a debt*. See 1 Cor. ix. chap. from the 7. to the 15 verse."

---

the revisers that the non-communicants should withdraw from the Church after the Sermon and before the Offertory and the prayer for the Church. The English Book says: "Then shall follow the Sermon "—" Then shall the Priest return to the Lord's Table and begin the Offertory "—" And *when there is a Communion*, the

Priest shall then place upon the Table so much Bread and Wine as he shall think sufficient." But the American Book says: " Then shall follow the Sermon. After which, the Minister, *when there is a Communion*, shall return to the Lord's Table and begin the Offertory "— " And the Priest shall then place upon the Table so much Bread and Wine as he shall think sufficient." And instead of putting the break in the service at the end of the prayer for the Church, the American Book directs that when there is no Communion, there " shall be said all that is appointed at the Communion, unto the end of the Gospel, concluding with the Blessing."[1]

There can be no question as to the custom which prevailed, in Connecticut at least, until twenty or twenty-five years ago, when, in spite of tradition and the implied direction of rubrics, the English custom began to be observed. The Convocation of the clergy of Connecticut, at their meeting, September 6, 1821, resolved, " That the congregations be dismissed, previous to the Communion service, with a Collect and the shorter benediction."[2] This was done after the sermon, and the offerings were received from communicants alone. This was in accordance with primitive usage; " for in these days it was a

---

[1] See also the last rubric in the Form of Consecration of a Church.
[2] Ms. Records.

---

privilege to be allowed to make their oblations, and a sort of lesser excommunication to be debarred from it ";[1] and the great Intercession belonged to the most solemn part of the service.

Having thus used his influence successfully to secure to the Church in America a Communion-Office based on primitive models, and having more than fulfilled the requirements of the Concordate into which he had entered at the time of his consecration, Bishop Seabury returned to his Diocese. His clergy met in Convocation, June 2d, 1790, and made a " short examination " of the Constitution and Canons adopted at Philadelphia; but there is no minute on record of any action in regard to the Prayer-Book. An adjourned meeting was held at Newtown, September 30th, 1790, and on the second day of the session, October 1st, the very day on which the new book was to go into use, we find the following record made:

" The alterations in the Book of Common Prayer made by the General Convention at Philadelphia, were read and considered.

" On motion, The question was put, in these words : ' Whether we confirm the doings of our Proctors in the General Convention at Philadelphia, on the 2d day of Octobr, 1789.'

" Which passed in the affirmative by the votes of every member present, the Rev'd Mr. Sayre excepted."[2]

69

On the following day

"A motion was made, that the Convocation should determine on a mode of introducing the Constitution & Canons & Liturgy in our several parishes: When it was agreed that each of the Clergy

---

[1] Bingham, Antiq., Book xv., chap. ii., § 2; vol. v., p. 197, ed. 1829.   [2] Ms. Records.

---

should take that method that should appear to him the most eligible. Agreed also that in the use of the New-Prayer-Book, we be as uniform as possible,—& for that purpose, that we approach as near the *Old Liturgy*, as a compliance with the Rubrics of the *New* will allow."[1]

On October 5th, 1791, it was

"Voted: That, in the use of the Common Prayer Book we will use the *Nicene-Creed* on Communion Days, and the Apostle's Creed on all other days."[2]

The new Prayer-Book having been thus adopted, "Bishop Seabury's office passed at once out of *general* use."[3] "But the change from established customs is seldom easy, and whether the people loved to have it so or not, some of the clergy of that day never learned to carry out in full practice the literal meaning of the rubrical directions of the new Prayer-Book."[4] Dr. Hallam says that the Rev. Charles Seabury (the Bishop's son, and his successor at New London, 1796–1814), probably used it, but that it was never used there after he himself became a communicant.[5] When he took charge of the parish in 1835, Dr. Hallam found some half dozen copies of the pamphlet lying about in the pews of the Church,[6] and it was from one of these, and through his kindness, that this reprint was made in 1874. The writer was informed by the late Rev. Dr. Haight, that Bishop Brownell told him that when he came into the Diocese in 1819, he found some of the older clergy still using Bishop Seabury's Communion-Office, and that he had considerable difficulty in persuading them to substitute the Prayer-Book office in its place.

---

[1] Ibid.   [2] Ibid.   [3] Dr. Beardsley.   [4] Id., Hist., i. 415.
[5] Ms. Letter.   [6] Annals, p. 71.

The latest remnant of the former use of which the writer has been able to learn was at Cheshire in 1835, when the Rev. Reuben Ives, a former rector of the parish, who had been ordained by Bishop Seabury and had been his assistant at New London, being called upon by the Rev. Dr. Beardsley, then a Deacon in charge of the Parish, to officiate in the Communion Service, "invariably read what is called the prayer of Humble Access immediately after consecrating the elements and just before communicating, as it stands at present in the Scottish office."[1]

So Bishop Seabury's office passed out of use and has become almost forgotten.   . . .

THE ELECTION OF BISHOP SEABURY.

AN HISTORICAL SERMON.

---

[18]

ZECHARIAH xi. 7.
"And I took unto me two staves:
The one I called Beauty,
And the other I called Bands;
And I fed the flock."

By this symbolical act the prophet represented the present needs of his people and declared his faith that those needs would be Divinely supplied. The Jews who had returned from the land of their captivity were weak and surrounded by enemies; and, moreover, they suffered from at least the danger of division among themselves. In his capacity as a shepherd, it was made the duty of the prophet, acting under God's commission and in God's name, to offer them protection and to lead them to unity. This double duty he illustrated by taking to himself two shepherd's staves. To show the love of God, which would defend His people from their foes, he called the one by the name of Beauty, meaning by it the grace and favor in which alone they could find strength and safety; and to denote the blessing of fraternal concord, he gave to the other the name of Bands. Fed by one who bore these staves, the people might be secure and harmonious, blessed with peace and unity.

The words of the text serve, I think, brethren, to express the needs of the Church of God at many turning-points in her history; and no less clearly do they declare the blessings which her Lord always has in store for her and is always ready to bestow upon her. And therefore I think them not unfit to direct our thoughts to-day as I recall to your minds the anniversary which we, in this diocese, kept on Sunday last.

That day, the twenty-fifth of March, the festival of the Annunciation, brightened this year with the Easter sun, was the hundredth anniversary of the election of the first Bishop of Connecticut by ten clergymen who met at the house of the Rev. Mr. Marshall in Woodbury.

To understand aright the meaning of that act, I must ask you to carry your minds further back, to the memorable year from which we begin the history of the Church in this diocese. In 1722 there was but one missionary of the Church of England within the limits of the colony of Connecticut, and he had just arrived at Stratford, where a parish had been organized some years before, but where there had never been a settled clergyman. But in that year, on the day after the Commencement at Yale College, an event occurred which is almost unparalleled in the history of the Church of God. Mr. Cutler and Mr. Brown, the rector and the tutor of the college and its only officers of instruction at the time, and with them Mr. Johnson of West Haven, a former tutor and a man of deserved reputation for learning, and four others of the Congregational ministers settled in the neighborhood of New Haven, made a public declaration that "some of them doubted the validity, and the rest were more fully persuaded of the invalidity, of the Presbyterian ordination in opposition

to the Episcopal." It is hard for us to realize the bravery of this declaration, or to appreciate the excitement into which it threw the whole community. Some of the doubters were prevailed upon to overcome their scruples; but the three whom I have mentioned by name decided that they must leave the pleasant and influential positions which they held and undertake the perilous voyage across the ocean to seek for Holy Orders at the hands of a Bishop; and they were soon followed by another, Mr. Wetmore of North Haven. These ministers had been in the habit of meeting in the College Library to read books of theology and to discuss what they had read; and though, in their search for the true doctrine in regard to the ministry, they had had some conference with the missionary at Stratford, it is to them, and not to him, that the foundation of the Church in this diocese is due. That foundation was laid in the prayerful and earnest studies of able men, who became convinced that they could no longer venture to preach the Word of God and to minister His holy Sacraments without receiving Episcopal ordination, and who then courageously faced the dangers of the sea and the perils of the pestilence which was raging at that time, and asked the English Bishops to give them an authority which they could not obtain at home.

And that which was thus begun in study, in prayer, in self-denial, in faithfulness to convictions of duty, could not but prosper, even in the face of unpopularity and of persecution. One after another, men who had officiated as Congregational ministers resolved to ask for Episcopal ordination; one after another, earnest young men who felt the inward call to the ministry were persuaded that they must also have the laying-on of apostolic hands; the people were drawn to the Church which their ancestors had left by the seemliness of her worship, by the calm and earnest tone of the piety which she taught during the times of religious excitement and fanaticism which swept over the colony, and by the true and holy lives of her members; the clergy were themselves "an epistle known and read of all men"; and in twenty years no less than seven hundred families in the colony were adherents of the Church; while in 1774 the Episcopalians formed about one-thirteenth part of the whole number of inhabitants.

From the very first the churchmen of Connecticut felt their need of a Bishop. It was no light thing that no one could be ordained unless he could bear the danger and the expense of the voyage across the Atlantic; it was no light thing that, of those who thus took their lives in their hands, one of every five was lost at sea or died in England*; it was no light thing that children could not be confirmed, that no one had more than a titular oversight of clergy and laity, that there was no one within three thousand miles to whom they could look as the chief pastor set over them in the Lord.

*Mr. Brown, one of the three who first crossed the ocean in 1722, died of the small-pox in England. Of the men who went abroad to be ordained for the parish in Hebron, the first was lost at sea, the second died on his passage home, the third was captured by the French and died in prison at Bayonne, and the fourth was attacked by the small-pox while he was in England, and barely escaped with his life.

Almost at once formal petitions for a Bishop began to be sent to England, to meet with postponement if not with absolute refusal. There were difficulties there arising from political complications and from the too prevalent lack of energy in the Church, the rulers of which seemed to show more regard to the acts of Parliament than to the Acts of the Apostles*; there were difficulties here arising from strong prejudices, from unpleasant memories of the past, and from the idea that, whatever might be provided by statute, a Bishop could not fail to carry with him, under the provisions of common law, magisterial rights opposed to the customs and the laws of the commonwealth. And there was no one abroad, among those in authority in Church or in State, who could, or who would, face all the difficulties and relieve churchmen in America from the reproach of being Episcopalians without a Bishop. It is hard, as one thinks of all this, not to feel at least surprise that "a request so reasonable in itself, so congruous to the nature and government of the Church, and begging for an officer so absolutely necessary in the Church of Christ as they and we believed a Bishop to be, should be refused"; it is hard not to express a doubt whether "the successors of the Apostles in the Church of England had sufficient reasons to justify themselves to the world and to God."† Yet, as we look back upon those times, and see what kind of a man would probably have been sent then, and remember how God's good Providence cared for us at the last, we may even be thankful for what must have been to our forefathers in the Church a great trial of their faith. And we may well be thankful also that, in spite of all discouragements, they remained faithful to the doctrines which they had learned from the solid divines of the Church of England and to the convictions which had been so strongly impressed upon their minds. The churchmanship of the clergy and the laity of that day was not a thing of fashion or of mere acquiescence; it was something by which to live and for which, if it were needful, to die.

*See a note to Bishop Skinner's Sermon at the Consecration of Bishop Seabury, p. 15.
†Address of the Clergy of Connecticut to Bishop Seabury, August 3, 1785, p. 5.

With this loyalty to the Church of England, there grew up among churchmen here a strong feeling of loyalty to the British crown. When the war of Independence broke out, they were in great part of the number of those who felt assured that they were more likely to secure or to retain the rights of English subjects by adhering to the royal cause than by resisting it. The time has gone by when those who had such convictions needed to be defended from charges of dishonesty or of cowardice; and, however some of us may think them to have been in the wrong, we can all give them credit for courage and for obedience to their convictions of duty. But in those days of excitement it was only natural that the Church should suffer from the adherence of so many of her clergy and laity to the unpopular cause, though no one can excuse the harsh and cruel treatment which they often received*; and it was not strange that, on the other hand, the fact that they suffered for their convictions of duty should cause them to cling to that cause even more tenaciously. We cannot doubt, however, that, as the struggle went on, wise men began to revise their theories in the light of facts and to look at things as they were shaping themselves before their eyes. Churchmen who had once thought that there could rightly be no "State without a King" came to see that independence of the royal power might not only secure to them the rights of British freemen, but also release them from the necessity of remaining a "Church without a Bishop"; and they began to hope that they might obtain a full ecclesiastical organization under a form of civil government which did not altogether agree with the ideal which

they had formerly had. We cannot doubt that the clergy of Connecticut had thought seriously of all these matters, and had talked with each other about them, so that they were ready to act as soon as the war should come to an end, in the hope that they might obtain, as a Church in a foreign country, the privileges from which they were debarred as long as they were dependent upon England. And as soon as it was possible for them to act as citizens of a free state, they gladly

*See Dr. Beardsley's History of the Church in Conn., chaps. 23, 24, 25.

accepted their independence of the British crown and used it as a new and untried argument with the English Bishops in their attempts to secure the Episcopate to which they felt that they were entitled by the ordinance of God, but which had been kept from them by the devices of men.

But the clergy of Connecticut had another reason for taking early action in electing a Bishop. In the year 1782, when there was no immediate likelihood of the close of the Revolution, a pamphlet had been published which gave them much alarm. Though anonymous, it was no secret that it was from the pen of the most influential of all the clergymen to the south of New England, the Rev. Dr. White, afterwards Bishop of Pennsylvania.* In it he argued that, as it was impossible, or at least impolitic, to secure the episcopate from England, and absurd to look elsewhere for it, the churchmen in this country should first affirm their general approbation of episcopacy and declare their intention of obtaining Bishops as soon as should be convenient, and should then proceed to choose permanent presidents from among the clergy with the general power of supervision and the right of ordination. He argued for this on the twofold ground that episcopacy, though of apostolic origin, did not rest on positive precept, and that an "exigence of necessity" had arisen, such as had been often held sufficient to justify a departure from the strict rules which are binding in ordinary times.

Now these arguments were doubtless more weighty when they were first written than they were when it was known that the war of Independence was ended. Yet there was danger that they might be acted upon and that Episcopalians in some parts of the country might come to the conclusion that after all it was not worth while to make much of an effort to secure Bishops. And the teaching which the clergy of Connecticut had received and had given was very different from this. They probably would have acknowledged that there were imaginable cases in which the action suggested by

*It has been reprinted in the third volume of Bishop Perry's edition of the Journals of the Early Conventions. Bp. White speaks of it as published in the summer of 1783; but this is a *lapsus memoriae*, as he gives the reply to it, dated March 25, 1783. Memoirs, pp. 89, 282, second edition. The title-page of the pamphlet bears the date 1782.

Dr. White's pamphlet would have been necessary and justifiable; but to adopt it without once asking any branch of the Church for the bestowal of the episcopate would have been in their eyes a gross abandonment of principle.

So then, in order to secure for the now independent Church the blessings which they believed that God had connected with the episcopal office, and to do what they could for the preservation of the unity of the Church in its ancient forms, our fathers in the faith met at once when they knew that the war was at an end, some weeks before peace was proclaimed and eight months before New York was evacuated, that they might elect a Bishop. They felt the need of the two staves

—Beauty, the favor of God, and Bands, the unity of His people in truth—and they desired that they should be put into worthy and strong and faithful hands.

Thus the meeting at Woodbury on the twenty-fifth day of March, 1783, was an act of real faith and of earnest obedience. As I think of it and of all that it meant, I am amazed at the bravery and the wisdom of the men who assembled there. One might have thought that their hopes would have been all scattered; one might have expected that they would have been sorely tempted to give over their labors "for the House of God and for the offices thereof." But no! they were quick to see their duty and no less quick to do it; an emergency had arisen, and they were ready to meet it; a shadow of an opportunity was before them, and they were glad to try to avail themselves of it.

And, indeed, they were not ordinary men. Ten of the fourteen clergymen of Connecticut formed the convocation of a century ago.* And, of the fourteen, twelve had been born

*The full list includes the Rev. Messrs. Samuel Andrews of Wallingford, Gideon Bostwick of Great Barrington (reckoned ecclesiastically as in Connecticut), Richard Samuel Clarke of New Milford, Ebenezer Dibblee of Stamford, Daniel Fogg of Brooklyn, Bela Hubbard of New Haven, Abraham Jarvis of Middletown, Richard Mansfield of Derby, John Rutgers Marshall of Woodbury, Christopher Newton of Ripton, James Nichols of Plymouth, James Scovill of Waterbury, John Tyler of Norwich, and Roger Viets of Simsbury. Mr. Fogg was born in New Hampshire, and Mr. Marshall in New York. Mr. Dibblee and Mr. Newton had been licentiates among the Congregationalists. Of the other six clergymen who were ministering in the colony at the beginning of the war, the Rev. Messrs. John Beach of Newtown and Ebenezer Kneeland of Stratford had died; the Rev. Jeremiah Leaming of Norwalk, after his church had been burned by the British troops, had withdrawn to New York; the Rev. Messrs. Matthew Graves of New London and John Sayre of Fairfield were within the British lines; and the Rev. Samuel Peters of Hebron had gone to England.

and brought up in the colony, and the other two were natives of neighboring colonies; none of them had formally exercised any other ministry than that of the Church; they had all been to England for Holy Orders; they had all experienced the trials of Church clergymen in Connecticut before and during the Revolution; they had already proved themselves both brave and wise. And they did a work, the effects of which, in blessing to this church, we, at the end of a hundred years, have but begun to see.

Look with me, brethren, at the action which those men took, and see if it does not warrant even stronger words of commendation.

First of all, influenced by the considerations of which I have already spoken, they decided that it was their duty to elect a Bishop. There was no presentation of the claims and no discussion of the merits of rival candidates. It was simply a question as to who might be asked to undertake the labor and the responsibility which their choice would involve; who could be commissioned to go abroad and ask for consecration in order that he might come back authorized to guide and govern the Church here; who would be able and willing to devote his life to the hard work of the first Bishop in the United States. Their minds turned at once to the Rev. Jeremiah Leaming, venerable by reason of his years, his learning, and his sufferings, "a tried servant of the church, who carried about with him in a degree the marks of a confessor."* He had done long and faithful service in Connecticut, "defending the church with his pen, and suffering for her cause in mind, body, and estate"; and, as was testified by one of those who made him their "first choice" for a Bishop, he "merited their affections, esteem, and confidence."† But there was reason to fear that Mr. Leaming's age and infirmities would force him to decline the burden which the clergy

72

* Original draught of letter to the Archbishop; Life of Bishop Jarvis, in the *Evergreen*, iii. 148.

† Mr. Jarvis's Sermon commemorative of Bishop Seabury, p. 19. See also Bishop Seabury's letter to the Venerable Society; Doc. Hist. Conn., ii. 257.

asked him to assume; and they therefore made another choice. The Rev. Dr. Samuel Seabury was a native of Connecticut, the son of an active rector and missionary, personally known in the State, and highly esteemed by all. It was felt that the strength and vigor of his character were such that he might be expected to succeed in securing the episcopate and in rightly exercising its powers and duties. And there was no hesitation in deciding upon him as " every way qualified for the episcopal office and for the discharge of the duties peculiar to it in those trying and dangerous times."*

The clergy desired their Secretary, himself afterwards Bishop Seabury's successor, to go to New York, where both Mr. Leaming and Dr. Seabury were, in order to consult with them; and he was directed to draw up a letter to the authorities of the English Church, testifying to the character and the abilities of the candidate who should be sent out to them and urging the petition which he should present, and also to secure letters of commendation from clergymen in New York, with some of whom they had already consulted. And I think it not amiss to say that, as the excellence of the early state papers of our republic was taken as a proof of our ability to rule ourselves in civil matters, so the dignity and the learning shown in these early ecclesiastical documents were in themselves a presage of the wisdom which was to guide the councils of our national Church.

It could not but be felt, however, that the success of a petition to the English Bishops was a matter of serious doubt. Hampered as they were by their connection with the State, it might be that they would not feel authorized to consecrate a Bishop for America without royal or parliamentary license, and this license it might be impossible to obtain. But the clergy of Connecticut knew—what some English Churchmen did not know—that there was in Scotland a Church independent of the State, having a perfectly valid episcopate and in every respect a true branch of the Church Catholic. And though, as was most natural and most becoming, they desired

* Letter to the Archbishop; Doct. Hist. Conn., ii. 215.

their candidate to seek consecration from the Mother Church, they provided for the contingency which was not unlikely to arise; and—to use the words of one of their own number—they went " so far as to instruct him, if none of the regular Bishops of the Church of England would ordain him, to go down to Scotland and receive " consecration from the Bishops there.* And thus they did all that lay in their power to accomplish this most important matter and to secure a Bishop for the diocese.

But the work of these wise and brave men was not finished when they had thus taken steps to provide for this diocese the staff called Beauty—God's protecting favor—in the full organization of the Church according to the methods of Divine appointment. They also desired to put into the hands of their Bishop-elect the staff called Bands. In the interests of that unity and concord which must be based on truth, they addressed a strong, though temperate, letter to Dr. White.† They pointed out the " dangerous consequences," as they deemed them, of some things that he had said and the fallacies of his arguments, contending that the

plea of necessity could not be urged " with any propriety till they had tried to obtain an episcopate and been rejected," and least of all in the changed condition of circumstances; and, while they did not think it prudent to say what they had done, they expressed the conviction that the present was a favorable time for making an application to the English Bishops. They added that " should the scheme be carried into execution in the southern States"—that is, those to the south of New England—" it would create divisions in the Church at a time when its whole strength depended on its unity; for," said they, " we know that it is totally abhorrent from the principles of the Church in the northern States, and are fully convinced they will never submit to it." It is but fair to say that Dr. White replied, pleading for an indulgent construction of his words and confessing that the

* Letter of the Rev. D. Fogg; Doc. Hist. Conn., ii. 213.
† It is printed in Bishop White's Memoirs, p. 282, second edition.

changed circumstances of the times had put an end to the exigence which had seemed to him to exist.*

In writing as they did, it should be noted that the clergy of this diocese laid down a principle on which they insisted very strongly afterwards and on which alone could any real unity of the Church in this land be based. They held that a Church was not in any sense complete until it had a Bishop; and that nothing could be rightly done as to setting forth or changing liturgies and forms of worship, or as to arranging for ecclesiastical discipline, until the Church was fully organized. It is to most of us now a simple principle enough; but to hold it and to maintain it meant courage and patience then; it meant waiting when every moment was precious; but that waiting was an act of true obedience, and was necessary if the Church of Christ was to do her work in the way which had been prescribed to her by her Divine Head.

Such is the simple, but important, record of that quiet meeting at Woodbury a century ago. Its results will come before us, if God will, when we commemorate the centennial anniversaries of the consecration of the first Bishop of Connecticut, his return to his diocese, and the union of the Church in this country which was effected at the General Convention of 1789. It must suffice now that I remind you how, when Mr. Leaming felt that it was impossible for him to accept the episcopate, Dr. Seabury, after advising with his friends, though he " foresaw many and great difficulties in the way," † sailed for England; how, having spent more than a year in fruitless attempts to overcome the real and the imaginary obstacles which he encountered, he went to Scotland and found the Bishops there more than ready to communicate their " free, valid, and purely ecclesiastical " episcopate to the American Church; how he was welcomed by the clergy and laity of Connecticut; how he gave his diocese a liturgy based on primitive models; how, with great prudence and wisdom, he was instrumental in bringing about the unity of the Church

* Life of Bishop Jarvis, in the *Evergreen*, iii. 148. Bishop White's later remarks on the subject are in his Memoirs, pp. 80-92.
† They are his own words; Doc. Hist. Conn., ii. 257.

in the United States, and acted in harmony with Bishop White in the revision of its liturgy and the arrangement of its constitution; how, showing himself at all times, as one has said, a " simple, grand, conciliatory, uncompromising man," * he did for us what, to all appearance, no one else could have done, feeding the flock of God with the staff of Beauty and the

73

staff of Bands. And to-day, when we think of outward prosperity, this diocese with a hundred and eighty clergymen and twenty-two thousand communicants, and with it the Church throughout the land, testifies to the wisdom with which the men of that early day laid the foundations; and when we consider the faithfulness to principle, the unity in doctrine and in worship, and the earnestness in religion, which—it is no presumption to say it—so largely characterize both our clergy and our laity, we can but believe that the hand of God has indeed blessed the work which seemed so humble when a few men met quietly, only determined to do the duty which lay ready to their hands, but which we can now see to have been of immense moment for the welfare of the Church of Christ. We may well apply to them, to Bishop Seabury, and to the Scotch Bishops who granted their request, the words of an earnest friend of our colonial Church, who wrote at a time when it was impossible to know "for whom this glorious work of establishing episcopacy in America was reserved." "Blessed are they whose hearts conceived and whose hands accomplished it. Their works done in the faith and for the love of their Master shall praise them, when that Master sits in judgment, in the gates of the New Jerusalem; and all generations arising from the dust shall call them blessed."†

May I venture to add, brethren, that this anniversary, bringing to our minds the historical facts which I have thus sketched, has lessons for us as churchmen, and especially as churchmen in this venerable diocese? As our Bishop told those of us who were assembled at Woodbury on Tuesday last, the clergy who met there in 1783 did not discuss an imaginary Church of the future and inquire how they were to

---

* Dr. Shea, in his Life of Hamilton.
† Bishop Horne, quoted in note at the end of Bishop Skinner's Consecration Sermon.

---

modify the ancient faith in order to adapt it to the so-called needs of the day. They had a present problem to resolve, and they undertook its answer; they found a present duty before them, and they bravely did it; they thought that they might do something to preserve the ancient faith and order of the Church of Christ, and no fear of danger or of disappointment kept them from fidelity to the one and the other. Such is also our duty; to take up the responsibility which is laid upon us, to do the task which God makes ready to our hand, to "work our work betimes," knowing that "in His time He will give us our reward."

And, besides, it seems to me that, though the Church and the Church's ways are better understood and less assailed now than they were a century ago, it is to be regretted that we do not always know as much about them as we ought, and are not as ready to defend them as we might be. Our parents and grandparents read more and better church reading and studied more carefully the reasons for their belief and practice than most of us do; and I sometimes think that there is danger lest some sudden trial of our faith might find us unprepared to meet it. Will it not be well if, as our thoughts revert to the early history of the Church in this land, we review the ground on which we stand, ask why our ancestors were churchmen in the days when to be a churchman was by no means a popular thing, and what are the arguments by which we could defend our position if at any time we should be called to do so? Thus, knowing our reasons for allegiance to the historic Church, with her apostolic doctrine, her apostolic ministry, and her apostolic worship,

and determined to do for her the work which the good Lord makes ready to our hands, we shall best honor those to whose faithfulness we owe our privileges and whose example is our encouragement to do all that is in our power to preserve them.

And the Lord will never fail those who faithfully obey Him. The Church will always find her defence and protection in the Beauty of God's favor and her intrinsic strength in the Bands of unity; and thus she will be always fed by Him Who is the Good Shepherd, in Whose unending resurrection-life is our sole confidence and help, the witness to Whom, as to-day's Epistle testifies, is such as never fails, and Whose words, as the Gospel reminds us, are words of power as well as words of comfort and of peace.

"Now therefore bless ye the God of all, Which only doeth wondrous things everywhere, Which exalteth our days and dealeth with us according to His mercy. He grant us joyfulness of heart, and that peace may be in our days in Israel forever! Blessed is he that shall be exercised in these things; and he that layeth them up in his heart shall become wise. For if he do them, he shall be strong to all things; for the light of the Lord leadeth him, Who giveth wisdom to the godly. Blessed be the Lord for ever. Amen, Amen."

THE CONSECRATION OF BISHOP SEABURY.

AN HISTORICAL SERMON.

[19]

PSALM XC. 13–17
(Prayer-Book Version).

"Turn thee again, O LORD, at the last:
And be gracious unto thy servants.
O satisfy us with thy mercy, and that soon:
So shall we rejoice and be glad all the days of our life.
Comfort us again now after the time that thou hast plagued us:
And for the years wherein we have suffered adversity.
Show thy servants thy work:
And their children thy glory.
And the glorious Majesty of the LORD our God be upon us:
Prosper thou the work of our hands upon us;
O prosper thou our handy-work."

A hundred years ago, on the twenty-third Sunday after Trinity, November 14, 1784, these words, in an old metrical version, were sung as a part of a most important religious service. Often as they have been taken on the lips of devout men since the day when Moses first spoke them under the mighty shadows of Sinai, often as they have served as the expression of devout hope and the utterance of earnest prayer, I doubt if they were ever more appropriately used than on that solemn occasion. In a chapel within a house in a narrow street of Aberdeen, three of the four bishops of the Episcopal Church of Scotland were assembled with a considerable number of their clergy and people. After morning prayer, the youngest, himself but a little more than two years a bishop, had preached a remarkably courageous and powerful sermon; and then it was that the words of the great prophet and lawgiver of old were taken up in prayer and —we may say it now—in prophecy, before the more solemn part of the service was begun. The Psalm ended, the three bishops—may their names ever be held in honor! they were Bishops Kilgour of Aberdeen, Petrie of Ross and Moray, and Skinner of Aberdeen (Coadjutor)*—proceeded, "with all becoming solemnity," to consecrate one who stood before them, and whom, although none of them had seen him till

nine days before, they held in high esteem. I do not need to say that the person upon whom they laid their hands rose from his knees endowed with the sacred office of a bishop, and commissioned to exercise that office in the State—by this act fully organized as the diocese—of Connecticut; and I do not need to remind you that he thus became not only the first bishop of this diocese, but also the first bishop of our Church in the United States, standing at the head of a roll which already numbers more than a hundred and thirty, of whom every one that has been consecrated in America traces back one line of his spiritual descent to the Scotch Church. "*Novi orbis Apostoli sit nomen perenne!*" †

It cannot well be without feelings of devout thankfulness that we carry our minds back over the history of a century to the day of Bishop Seabury's consecration. And I am confident that it will increase our gratitude to God and our appreciation of the noble character of those who took part in the service at Aberdeen, if we look a little more carefully at some of the events which led to it and which followed upon it.

It was on the 25th day of March, 1783, that the clergy of Connecticut, acting at the earliest possible moment after it was known that the issue of the War of Independence was determined, met to elect a Bishop; and on the 7th day of July following, the Rev. Dr. Samuel Seabury, furnished with credentials of his election and with official and personal testimonials, arrived in London to seek Episcopal consecration at the hands of the bishops of the English Church, or, failing in his request, to ask the Scotch bishops to confer their sacred office upon him. The story of his fourteen months' waiting

---

*Bishop Rose of Dunblane gave his assent to the action of the other bishops, but infirmity prevented his attendance.

†Inscription beneath Bishop Seabury's mitre in the Library of Trinity College.

---

in England has been often repeated; but, please God! it will never become an old story. One cannot read the record, so faithfully and simply told in Dr. Seabury's letters, without strangely mingled emotions. He was received courteously enough by the Archbishops and others, who really seemed to wish to do for him everything in their power; but they raised objection after objection, until at one time he seemed to think that there was very little use in answering them. The more important and weighty objections were two; and though they had reference to the condition of affairs on opposite sides of the ocean, they were both of a political nature. In the first place, the Ordinal of the Church of England, like the Prayer-Book to which it is appended, is a part of an act of Parliament; and its form of consecrating a bishop contained an oath of allegiance to the sovereign which a citizen of a foreign country could not take, and to omit which would be in direct violation of law. Now the clergy of Connecticut, and Dr. Seabury as representing them, appealed to the English bishops to act simply as bishops; and, as that which they were desired to do could have no possible reference to any part of the British dominions, they were asked to fall back upon the spiritual commission which they had received from the Head of the Church and to exercise their power in a case in which they could be held responsible to Him alone. Or, if they did not venture to do this, it was argued that the King, either by his own prerogative or with the consent of his council,

could give the Archbishop authority to dispense with the imposition of the oath of allegiance. It is to be feared—I do not think that it is uncharitable to say it—that the English bishops of that day could not see the full force of the former part of the argument or understand how they could exercise their Episcopal functions apart from the enabling power of an act of Parliament, much less in direct disobedience to it; and one who studies the history of that day will perhaps not be unwilling to own that there was some excuse for them. And, as to the dispensing with the oath, I do not doubt that, whatever the theory of the English constitution might be, the King would not have dared to exercise it, nor would his counsellors have advised him to do so. It was not a century since one dynasty had been displaced and another had been seated on the English throne, chiefly because the sovereign had claimed the dispensing power; and it may be questioned whether the rulers of the Hanoverian line had yet gained any very firm place in the affections of their people. Whether the ministry would have been willing to advise the use of this power, even if they had dared to do so, is another question, the answer to which we may perhaps best infer from seeing what was the other important objection to consecrating a bishop for Connecticut.

It was claimed, then, that a bishop would not be allowed in Connecticut, and that the English authorities ought not to act in the matter until they were requested to do so by the civil rulers of the new State. It seems strange to us that the objection was still urged after Dr. Seabury had produced the act of the General Assembly "for securing the rights of conscience in matters of religion," with equal legal prerogatives, "to Christians of every denomination," and after the opinion of leading members of the Assembly had been obtained to the effect that no further permission was needed for the residence of a bishop within the State and that the proposed measure seemed to them to be necessary, proper, and prudent, so that the English bishops would in this matter "meet the generous wishes of the Legislature and do a thing for which they would have their applause." * But we must in all fairness remember that letters of another kind came to the rulers in England; and that a person of high civil rank and another who held high ecclesiastical dignity † had written to oppose the petition of their Episcopal

---

*See the collection of letters and papers in Hawks and Perry's *Documentary History of the Church in Connecticut*, vol. ii., pp. 219, sqq. As to the reasons for the attitude of the Legislature, see p. 242; but for *seventy* Episcopal congregations, read *forty*. An abstract of the testimonials is in the record of the Scotch Synod on pp. 247, sqq., and also in Dr. Beardsley's *Life of Bishop Seabury*, pp. 146, sqq.

†Governor Jonathan Trumbull and President Stiles of Yale College. See *Life of Bishop Jarvis* in *The Evergreen*, iii. 151.

---

neighbors. Besides, it doubtless was necessary for the British government to do nothing to irritate the States whose independence they had but lately acknowledged; and they knew well how bitterly the introduction of the Church of England into some of the colonies had been resisted, and perhaps how there had been an organized opposition to its further spread, * while they did not know how far the feelings and the acts of opposition had been modified by the change of political relations. And if it was useless to appeal to bishops on exclusively churchly grounds as to their office and duties, there could be no hope that the members of the Cabinet would look at the question otherwise than as politicians. We must,

75

I say, bear all this in mind, and remember that in a large part of the argument the churchmen of Connecticut occupied a position which was almost incomprehensible to churchmen in England; and probably it was in a moment of weariness that Dr. Seabury wrote, "I have been amused, I think deceived." Yet, after all, there is so much to be said on the other side that it is hard to keep altogether patient; it is hard to allow much real weight to all these excuses and to persuade one's self that the prelates of England should not have braved any danger rather than condemn a Church to which they had heretofore given a merely nominal episcopate—by placing it under the charge of the Bishop of London—to remain indefinitely without any episcopate at all; and one hardly wonders that the clergy of Connecticut could solemnly say, "We hope that the successors of the Apostles in the Church of England have sufficient reasons to justify themselves to the world and to God; we, however, know of none such, nor can our imagination frame any";† even if one remembers, as Bishop Seabury suggested in reply, that "the first characters in the Church for station and merit may find their good dispositions rendered ineffectual by the intervention of the civil authority."‡

At any rate, our Bishop-elect was not easily turned from

* See *Minutes of the Convention of Delegates*, 1766–1775.
† *Address of Clergy to Bishop Seabury*, etc., p. 5.
‡ Ibid., p. 7.

his purpose. But at last, when he learned that the authorities were encouraging churchmen in the States to remove to the Provinces which remained under the British crown and learned that some of the clergy who had elected him were leaving Connecticut, when the act which was passed through Parliament empowering the Bishop of London to ordain priests and deacons for Churches in foreign lands gave no permission for the consecration of bishops, and when he found that he could get no other reply than a "*non possumus*," he determined to obey his original instructions, reënforced as they had been by later letters from home, and to turn his face towards Scotland. *

The Episcopal Church of Scotland has had a strange and eventful history. Its original line of bishops, reaching back through many centuries, came to an end after the struggles of the Reformation in 1603. A new succession was introduced from England seven years later, and it too became nearly extinct in troublous times.† But again in 1661, four English bishops consecrated an equal number for Scotch dioceses, and during the next year these increased the number to thirteen.‡ After the Revolution and the accession of William the Third in 1688, the Episcopal Church of Scotland was disestablished for political reasons, and the Presbyterian Kirk was established in its place.§ The Episcopalians were, for the most part, loyal to the Stuart family, and the whole

* See note A at the end.
† One Bishop, Sydserf of Orkney, survived till the Restoration, but he took no part in establishing the new succession.
‡ Perceval on *Apostolical Succession*, Appendix L.
§ The former disestablishment in 1638 had been by vote of the General Assembly of the Church, which declared Episcopacy to be unlawful and deposed the bishops, the sentence being ratified by the King and Parliament. In 1689 there was no pretence of ecclesiastical action; the Parliament abolished Prelacy and withdrew from the Episcopal Church its temporal endowments and their civil advantages, without claiming to remove

spiritual authority; and Presbyterianism was established, not on the ground that it was in accordance with the Word of God, but "as being most agreeable to the inclinations of the people." See quotation from a sermon of the Primus (Bp. Eden) in *Seabury Centenary Hand-book*, pp. 38, 39.

body, laity as well as clergy, fell under the ban of severe laws, the most stringent of which were passed in 1746 and 1748. We may not here judge of the necessity of such laws as directed against political offenders; but when we think of the disabilities and penalties which were imposed upon Episcopalians simply because they were Episcopalians, it is hard to call them by any other name than persecution. Into their details this is not the time to enter.* They reduced "the Catholic remainder of the ancient Church of Scotland" to a state of great suffering and distress, and its worship was often conducted in the most secret manner and in the most obscure places.

The purpose of those who secured the passage of those laws was not accomplished; the Scotch Church was not destroyed "root and branch"; but it was weakened and to a great extent forgotten. Although in the lapse of years the authorities failed to enforce the laws or allowed them to be evaded, the Church continued to be sadly depressed. Still it kept steadfast to its principles in doctrine, discipline, and worship; thirty-eight congregations remained faithful, and there were many of the laity besides who secretly were firm in their attachment to the Church;† its forty-two presbyters—for so few there were one hundred years ago—were presided over by four bishops, enough to have the canonical number for a new consecration in case of the death of any one;‡ and they had already done something towards the great work of Church unity on Catholic principles by following the English Nonjurors in adopting from ancient Liturgies a formal Oblation and Invocation in the consecration of the Holy

* An account of them will be found in note B at the end; their effect is summed up in Skinner's *Annals*, pp. 520, 521
† See *Scottish Church Review*, September, 1884, pp. 586, 587.
‡ At one time Bishop Rose had only one clergyman in his diocese; and Bishop Jolly had but three. From 1688 to 1727, the Scotch Bishops were not consecrated with diocesan titles, but as members of an Episcopal College. In 1682 there had been fourteen bishops (two of them archbishops) and over one thousand clergy. In Queen Anne's reign there were about three hundred clergy; the present number is about two hundred and sixty.

Communion, such as has been always in use in the East, but never in the Church of England.

> "'Cast down, but not destroyed,' thou still wert left,
>   Shrine of the saintly past!
> Changeless in creed, although of power bereft
>   By persecution's blast,
> And time-worn prayer-books by their tear-marks tell
> The hearts they solaced learned to love them well." *

We have seen that Dr. Seabury was not unprepared for an appeal to the Scotch bishops; and they were not unprepared to receive from him an application for consecration.

The Church in this land had had a strong friend in Dr. Berkeley, afterwards the virtuous Bishop of Cloyne, who spent some time at Newport and gave an impulse to learning as well as to churchmanship; and his son, the second Rev. Dr. George Berkeley, inherited the father's interest. In the autumn of 1782, while he was residing at St. Andrews in Scotland, Dr. Berkeley, apparently convinced that the war in America was practically at an end, wrote to Bishop

76

Skinner † to propose that the Scotch bishops should at once send out a bishop to America, in the confidence that he would be gladly received and welcomed there. But the fact that it was not yet known that the independence of the States had been acknowledged, the conviction that it was at least well to wait till some one across the ocean should ask for a bishop, and certain personal considerations besides, prevented the plan from being carried out.‡ All this, it should be remembered, was before Dr. Seabury had been elected by the clergy of Connecticut.

* R. Montgomery, quoted in Blatch's *Memoir of Bishop Low*, p. 10.

† Mr. Skinner had been consecrated September 25, 1782, but Dr. Berkeley, writing to him in October, did not know of his consecration. In fact, he did not hear of it till the beginning of December; so long did it take Church news in those days to travel from Aberdeen to St. Andrews! Dr. Berkeley, it is interesting to note, was an intimate friend of Archbishop Secker.

‡ Part of the letters relating to this and the following events are in the *Documentary History of Connecticut*, ii. 235, sqq.; others of great interest have been first published in the *Scottish Church Review* for January and February, 1884.

Dr. Berkeley did not hear of Dr. Seabury's arrival in England till late in November, 1783. He wrote at once to Bishop Skinner, and learned from him that the question had already been addressed to the Scotch bishops, whether they would consecrate a bishop for Connecticut (this had been done by the son of a Scotch clergyman who, it appears, had met Dr. Seabury in London); and soon after he was informed that they "heartily concurred in the proposal," though they were at a loss to see why consecration should have been refused in England unless there had been some personal objection to the candidate. We know that the objections were of a totally different kind; but Dr. Seabury's patient waiting in England was not yet at an end, and it was some months before he turned his face towards Scotland.

At last, on the 31st day of August, 1784, Dr. Seabury wrote to his old friend, Dr. Myles Cooper, once President of King's College in New York but then resident in Edinburgh, to ask him to present his case to the Scotch bishops. It is not necessary to speak at length of the kind and Christian way in which his petition was received; of the pains which were taken to remove the false impressions suggested by Dr. Seabury's repulse in England and by his delay in making his application to Scotland; or of the opposition which came at the last from an ambitious American clergyman who had an idea that Dr. Seabury's consecration would stand in the way of his own advancement.* But it would not be right to omit an acknowledgment of what is due to Bishop Skinner, who seems to have been the only one of the Scotch bishops possessed of the necessary vigor to take charge of the affair,

* Dr. William Smith of Maryland (it can do no harm to mention the name now, especially in connection with what will immediately follow in this note) was a native of Scotland and had been ordained deacon and priest at the same time and place as Dr. Seabury. His feeling of opposition did not continue long. It was on his motion that Bishop Seabury and his clergy were invited to the convention at Philadelphia in 1789; he himself entertained the Bishop at the time; and it is said to be owing to his influence that the Prayer of Consecration in the Communion-Office was adopted by the Lower House in the form in which it was sent down by the Bishops.

and who was ably assisted and encouraged by his father, the remarkable John Skinner of Linsart.* They saw the greatness and the importance of the act in which they were called

to take a part, and the only hesitation which they or those who were associated with them showed was the hesitation of a wise prudence, which was soon ended by the profound conviction that they owed a duty to God and to His Church, and that it must be discharged.

Thus it was that with glad heart and ready mind they celebrated the solemn service of a hundred years ago, and not only gave to Connecticut her first Bishop, but also introduced a new epoch into the history of the reformed Church.†

For, as it seems to me, it is not well to leave the study of this consecration without asking what were the consequences which followed upon it. We, in this diocese, may not forget the meeting of the newly consecrated bishop with his consecrators on the day after the service, when they drew up and signed and sealed " a Concordate, or Bond of Union, between the Catholic remainder of the ancient Church of Scotland and the now rising Church in the State of Connecticut," binding themselves to a unity of faith and a recognition and inter-communion of the Churches with one another, and Bishop Seabury promising moreover to consider the Scotch Liturgy and, if he should approve it, to commend it to his people; and when, besides, the Scotch bishops gave to Bishop Seabury a letter to the Church in Connecticut, solemnly recording what they had done for it and begging its clergy and people to "further and carry on the good work

* See the *Life* of the latter by the Rev. William Walker and, especially as to his part in this work and in the removal of disabilities, his grandson's *Annals of Scottish Episcopacy*, pp. 522, 523. "He readily outargued the argumentative, outwitted the tribe of witlings, and failed not to outstrip those in the knowledge of ecclesiastical antiquity who buckled on the armor of the primitive fathers, whether for the purposes of assault or defense."

† Bishop Skinner's house in Long Acre, in the chapel of which the consecration took place, was destroyed in 1795. On its site a building was erected for a church, which was sold to the Wesleyans in 1817 and is now employed for mercantile purposes.

which they had happily begun." These documents, with Bishop Seabury's letters of consecration, mark the beginning of the fully organized Church in this country. They lead on our thoughts to all that he was enabled to do, not only for his diocese, but also for the Church throughout our land. They suggest to us how his unflinching bravery in matters of principle and his patient conciliation in matters of opinion really brought together what threatened to be discordant elements and made one Church in these United States. They speak of a new pattern of the Episcopal office, diligent and faithful, "not to be ministered unto, but to minister," setting an example to the generations following. They lead us to be especially thankful to God that our Church has used for well-nigh a century, and that she is almost certain to use to the end of time, a form of consecration in the service of the Holy Communion which represents in its fulness the belief and the teaching of the undivided Church, which bears witness at once against the errors of Rome and those of Switzerland, which links us closely with the great Orthodox Church of the East and thus forms a possible basis for Christian unity, and which enables us to offer to God a worship which (I venture to say) the Apostles, should they return to earth, would recognize as most like that which they were once accustomed to offer.*

And if our diocese and our national Church owe so much to Bishop Seabury and to the act of those who consecrated

him, shall we be surprised to see that they who gave were blessed as well as they who received? That brave and faithful act was a turning-point in the history of the Scotch Church. Bishop Skinner's sermon, in which the bravery and faithfulness found utterance, was published, though anonymously, in Scotland and in England. It helped to call the attention of churchmen in England to the fact that there was

* The English Communion-Office is now of primary authority in the Scotch Church. The Canons order it to be used at all consecrations, ordinations, and synods, and in all new congregations unless a majority of the applicants prefer the Scotch Office. See notes to *Bishop Seabury's Communion-Office*, p. 53.

a Church in Scotland, a Church with as real and as valid an episcopate as their own, nay derived directly from their own but a little more than a century before, and differing from it only in being poor and liable to persecution by the State. The preacher said some sharp things about the English prelates, such that it was feared that they might injure the cause which he was so stoutly maintaining.* But in reality these words were signs of life which demanded and arrested attention. The penal laws were already falling into disuse, as was seen in the fact that Bishop Skinner was allowed to have a considerable congregation worshipping regularly in a chapel within his house. The attachment of the Scotch churchmen to the banished royal family was also becoming a matter of sentiment rather than of "practical politics"; and thus preparation was making on both sides for the removal of the public disabilities of the Scotch Church. Prince Charles Edward died in 1788; and the congregations having soon after been enjoined by the Synod to pray for George the Third by name, the English friends of the Scotch Church could exert themselves in their behalf; in a little less than four years the British Parliament repealed the penal laws.†

* One of the notes, in which it was suggested that the English bishops showed more regard to the acts of the British Parliament than to the Acts of the Apostles, has been quoted more than once of late. Again (p. 38, Scotch edition), the preacher said, with reference to the duty of the successors of the Apostles to assist in forming Churches throughout the world upon the most pure and primitive model: "No fear of worldly censure ought to keep them back from so good a work; no connection with any State, nor dependence on any government whatever, should tie up their hands from communicating the blessings of that kingdom which is not of this world, and diffusing the means of salvation by a valid and regular ministry, wherever they may be wanted." Bishop Lowth's strictures will be found in a letter printed in Dr. Neale's *Life of Bishop Torry*, p. 8, and in Dr. Beardsley's *Life of Bishop Seabury*, p. 183. The sermon led to a discussion between L. L. and Mr. (afterwards Bishop) Gleig in the *Gentleman's Magazine*, which lasted from March, 1785, to September, 1786, and seems to have aroused much interest.

† The Cardinal of York claimed to succeed, as Henry IX., upon the death of Charles Edward, January 31, 1788; but his own medals bore the legend: "*Gratia Dei, non voluntate hominum.*" The Synod voted, April 24th, that on the 18th of May notice should be given "that upon the following Lord's Day nominal prayers for the King are to be authoritatively introduced, and afterwards to continue in the religious assemblies of this Episcopal Church." The royal assent to the bill repealing the penal act was given June 15, 1792. See Dr. Neale's *Life of Bishop Torry*, chap. i. The repeal of the penal acts did not mean the removal of all disabilities; see note B at the end.

Still disestablished, but not oppressed by the state or ignored by her powerful neighbor Church, the Episcopal Church of Scotland has enjoyed and continues to enjoy the blessing of God. We cannot fail to see in her prosperity a part of the reward for her faithfulness and her kindness to us; we venture to bless her as a man might invoke blessings on

the mother who gave him life; "and wherever the American Episcopal Church shall be mentioned in the world, may this good deed which her bishops did for us be spoken of as a memorial of them!"*

Nor was the English Church without a share of the blessing. We are told that many—in fact that nearly all—of her bishops were ready secretly to rejoice at Dr. Seabury's consecration; and we can well believe that they were really glad that others could act while their own hands were tied. It was doubtless a revelation to some of her rulers and to many of her members when they found that a Church could exist without support from the civil arm, and that the Church of God had rights and prerogatives and duties which were not conferred or defined or limited by acts of Parliament. Bishop Seabury's consecration in Scotland opened the way for that of Bishops White, Provoost, and Madison in England, and besides this, to the marvellous extension of the English episcopate, both colonial and missionary.† It gave new ideas, or I had better said it taught old truths anew, and it helped men to see that there is always a way, a right way, of doing God's work. ‡

In such a manner and with such results were the blessings of the episcopate—I like the phrase which recurs so often in

* *Address of Connecticut Clergy to Bishop Seabury*, p. 6.

† See Bp. Charles Wordsworth's Ramsden Sermon, *Mending of the Nets*, pp. 16, sqq., ed. 1884.

‡ See Note C at the end.

the correspondence of the day, "the blessings of a free, valid, and purely ecclesiastical episcopacy"—communicated to our forefathers in the faith and through them to us. The Secretary of the Venerable Society might quietly ignore the important part of Bishop Seabury's manly letter to him, and omit the title which was now his; * and it might be authoritatively said in Chancery in 1785 that "there is no bishop in America nor the least likelihood of there ever being one"; † but in rightfulness of election, in validity of consecration, in readiness and heartiness of reception, and in faithfulness of work and "full proof of the ministry," there was never a more true bishop than he who knelt in the chapel at Aberdeen to receive his lofty commission from the bishops of Scotland. To-day and ever we thank God for him and for them. By the act which we are commemorating, He did indeed comfort both their Church and ours for the years wherein they and we had suffered adversity. The "prayer of Moses the man of God" which they took upon their lips has indeed been answered; God has showed His servants His work and their children His glory. And with our hymns of praise we echo back once more that prayer for ourselves and for those who shall come after us:

"And the glorious Majesty of the Lord our God be upon us:
Prosper Thou the work of our hands upon us;
O prosper Thou our handy-work."

ΔΟΞΑ ΤΩΙ ΘΕΩΙ.

* See the correspondence in *Doc. Hist. Conn.*, ii. 256, sqq.

† *Atty. Genl. vs. Bp. of Chester*; Brown's *Chancery Reports*, i. 444. The *dictum* is Mr. Mansfield's.

NOTE A.

THE APPLICATION TO THE SCOTCH BISHOPS.

Two stories in regard to Bishop Seabury's consecration have been often told and often proved to be untrue. As they persistently reappear, it may be well to speak of them in this place.

78

The first story is, in the words of Dr. Neale, in his *Life of Bishop Torry* (p. 7), that Dr. Seabury "was at one time, through pure ignorance, about to seek a pseudo-episcopacy from the tulchan bishops of Denmark." It is repeated in a scarcely anonymous article on *Martin Routh* in the *Quarterly Review* for July, 1878. But nowhere in all the correspondence covering the whole time of Dr. Seabury's absence is there the slightest evidence that either he or his friends had any idea of resorting to Denmark for the consecration which could not be had in England; and the assumption that he was ignorant of the invalidity of Danish orders is entirely gratuitous. The facts which gave rise to the story are given in full in Bishop White's *Memoirs of the Church*, pp. 21, 22, and Appendix 1, second edition; see also *Doc. Hist. Conn.*, ii. 230. After peace had been declared and before permission had been given to the Bishop of London to ordain priests and deacons for the United States, "a few young gentlemen to the southward" —in those days the words meant to the south of New York—arrived in England asking for ordination, which they could not then obtain there. A suggestion was made that they might secure ordination in Denmark, and an inquiry was courteously made on their behalf by Mr. John Adams, our Minister to England, to which a favorable reply was returned. But it had no reference to the Episcopate or to Bishop Seabury; and, it may be added, it led to no action on the part of any candidate for the ministry from this country.

The second story is that the idea of seeking consecration from the Scotch bishops was first suggested to Dr. Seabury by Mr. Martin Routh, then a young man, but afterwards the venerable President of Magdalen College, Oxford, and a staunch friend of the Scotch Church. It may be found in the article in the *Quarterly Review* to which reference was just made, and in the *Scottish Church Review* for February, 1884, p. 119 (where also the Danish story is told again). The reply to it is to be found in the letter of the Rev. Daniel Fogg, one of the ten clergymen who elected Dr. Seabury to be their Bishop, written to the Rev. Samuel Parker of Boston, July 14, 1783, in which are these plain words: "We clergy have even gone so far as to instruct Dr. Seabury, if none of the regular bishops of the Church of England will ordain him, to go down to Scotland and receive ordination from a nonjuring bishop." (*Documentary History of the Church in Connecticut*, ii. 213.) In his old age Dr. Routh seems to have told the story in different ways, some of them involving patent anachronisms. We need not deny that he thought of the possibility of an application to Scotland, or even that he ventured to suggest it to Dr. Seabury; but we can affirm most positively that it was not from him that the idea or suggestion first came.

To complete the history, it may be well to note that, without Dr. Seabury's knowledge, an application was made to Mr. Cartwright, a nonjuring bishop of irregular succession living at Shrewsbury, on his behalf, and that an offer of consecration was made from Bishop Cartwright and his colleague, Bishop Price. Fortunately Dr. Seabury had already entered into negotiations with the Scotch bishops, and was not obliged to take this offer into consideration. (See Dr. Beardsley's *Life of Bishop Seabury*, pp. 134, 135.)

NOTE B.

PENAL LAWS AND DISABILITIES.

The disestablishment of 1689 (see note on page 8) surrendered the parish churches and their parsonages to the Presbyterians; it was followed by a law which forbade all ministers who had not conformed to the new establishment to exercise any part of their office. But some who had taken the oath of allegiance officiated in meeting-houses, though they were liable to prosecution; and others—including all the bishops and a majority of the clergy—who were avowed nonjurors, held services in private houses, but at the risk of being apprehended and punished both as nonjurors and as nonconformists. In 1712, the tenth year of Queen Anne, an act of toleration was passed by the Parliament of Great Britain, declaring the lawfulness of Episcopal worship in Scotland and protecting the congregations from disturbance, but requiring the ministers (as also those of the establishment) to pray in express words for the Queen, the Princess Sophia, and the royal family, and to take the oaths of allegiance and abjuration. This act "indirectly tended to protect the whole Episcopal body from the arbitrary prosecutions to which they had been subjected," though few of the nonjurors complied with its requirements. The rising of 1715, which followed soon after the accession of George I., led to a stricter enforcement of the provisions of the act of toleration; and in 1719 an act was passed forbidding any person to officiate in an Episcopal meeting-house or congregation where nine or more persons were present besides the household, unless he should take the oath of abjuration and pray expressly for the King and the royal family, the penalty being the imprisonment of the minister and the closing of the meeting-house for six months. This statute, however, was only enforced in the case of a few of the clergy while there was fear of another rising against the government. The second rising of the Jacobites, under Prince Charles Edward, was in 1745; and its suppression was followed by laws which were evidently aimed, not against disloyalty to the Crown, but against the religious belief of Episcopalians. In 1746, an act of Parliament forbade any Episcopal minister, who should not take the oaths and pray expressly for the King and the royal family, to officiate in the presence of five or more persons (or, if in a dwelling-house, in the presence of five or more persons besides the family), under the penalty of imprisonment for six months for the first offense, and transportation to the plantations in America for the second offense, the return to Great Britain after this sentence being punished by imprisonment for life; and transportation to the plantations meant, we are told, the being sold to the planters as a slave. After the first of September, 1746, no clergyman in Scotch orders was to be allowed to qualify under the act; and the clause containing this provision might be construed as imposing the penalties of the act after that date upon all in Scotch orders, whether they qualified or not. The same act for the first time imposed penalties on the Episcopal laity. Any person attending the prohibited services became liable to a fine of five pounds for the first offense, and to imprisonment for two years for the second or any subsequent offense, besides being disqualified for office, civil or military, for a year, and becoming incapable to vote or to be voted for in any election. Only five of the clergy qualified under the act; most of the rest yielded a passive obedience to the law, taking care to officiate in the presence of no more than four persons besides a family, but some suffered imprisonment for their disobedience. In 1748 another act was passed by the British parliament, though all the bishops present in the House of Lords resisted it, to remove the ambiguity in the act of 1746; and this it did most effectually. It provided that no letters of orders except those granted by some bishop of the Church of England or of Ireland, should after the next Michaelmas be sufficient to qualify any minister of an Episcopal congregation in Scotland, whether he had conformed with the requirements of the previous act or not; and it further enacted that any person performing divine service or preaching in Scotland in a house or family of which he was not the master, should be deemed to be a chaplain, and come under the provisions of the law which required all chaplains to take the oaths. The meaning of this law was that clergymen in Scotch orders were forbidden, under the most severe penalties, whether they were loyal to the House of Hanover or not, to officiate except in their own houses, or even there in the presence of more than four persons besides their own families. The clergy, as a rule, kept within the letter of the law; but after a while, when the law was found to be so cruel that it could not be strictly enforced, they held services where only four persons were present in the room, while others in other rooms or out of doors could hear; and sometimes worship was held in concealed places on the mountains. Neither clergy nor people made any resistance to the execution of the law. Among those who suffered under it was John Skinner, the father of one of Bishop Seabury's consecrators, who, though he had complied with the act of 1746 and prayed for King George by name, was imprisoned for being in Scotch orders and officiating in the presence of more persons than the law allowed. Soon after Bishop Seabury's consecration, he wrote to Mr. (afterwards Bishop) Jolly: "I depend for the accomplishment of my wishes on the wisdom of that invisible Director Who, through so many varieties, has preserved me to have a son assisting in sending a bishop to that very country to which the execution of my office has for these thirty years past exposed me to the risk of being banished as a felon! What may I not live to see after this?" These penal laws succeeded in making the Episcopal Church in Scotland, to use Sir Walter Scott's phrase, "the shadow of a shade"; but in the lapse of years they ceased to be enforced, churchmen being tacitly allowed to worship in private houses, where the regular congregations were, in some cases, by no means small. The penal acts were repealed, and their stain taken from the British statute-book, in 1792. (Professor Grub's *Ecclesiastical History of Scotland*, chaps. lxxiii.—lxxv., lxxix., lxxxii.; Skinner's *Annals of Scottish Episcopacy*, pp. 101, sqq.; *Scottish Church Review*, September, 1884, p. 597; Dean Ranken's *Sketches of the History of the Church of Scotland*, pp. 19, sqq.)

The repeal of the penal acts operated the entire relief of the Church laity of Scotland from civil penalties, provided they did not attend meetings—if there were any such—in which the King was not prayed for by name; but it did not mean the removal of all disabilities from the clergy; it operated for them only upon condition that they should subscribe the Thirty-nine Articles (this subscription not being required at that time by the Scotch Church) and should take oaths of abjuration and of allegiance. The oath of abjuration was retrospective, and few of the Scotch clergy could conscientiously take it (the bishop and clergy of the

diocese of Aberdeen declared in Synod that they could not do so); but the penalties imposed by the new law were much milder than before, being a fine of twenty pounds for the first offense and prohibition from officiating for three years for the second, the same as were provided by the act of toleration in the reign of Queen Anne. But it seems to have been understood that these penalties were not to be enforced; and it does not appear that any inconvenience was experienced from them, the principle of toleration being recognized as established. Even then, however, clergymen in Scotch orders, though they made the required subscription and took all the required oaths, were prohibited by law from officiating in England—not in Ireland; this prohibition was removed in 1840 so far as to allow any English bishop to give permission to a Scotch bishop or priest to officiate for two days in any church within his diocese, and to renew the permission from time to time; but the same law forbade officiating in Ireland except under the same restrictions. At last, in 1864, parliamentary permission to hold livings in England was granted to clergymen in Scotch orders, and they stand now on a legal equality with those ordained by English bishops. (Grub's *History*, vol. iv., p. 244; Skinner's *Annals*, pp. 250–260; Blatch's *Memoir of Bishop Low*, chap. xiii.; *Seabury Centenary Hand-book*, p. 48.)

The act of Parliament which gave permission (in 1786) for the consecration of bishops for America contained a clause prohibiting such bishops and all persons deriving orders from them, from officiating within his Majesty's dominions. The privileges and restrictions of the act of 1840 extended to the bishops and clergy of the Church in the United States, as well as to those of the Scotch Church; and the restrictions upon the American clergy, both as to temporary officiating and as to the holding of livings in England, have not yet been entirely removed.

NOTE C.

SCOTLAND AND CONNECTICUT.

I add in this place the concluding part of a Sermon preached (from II. Cor. iii. 12–18) in St. John's Church, Aberdeen, on the Seventeenth Sunday after Trinity, October 5, 1884.

The Apostle's words have led us to see (1) that the glory of Christianity far exceeds all the glory of the older covenant because it brings to men a greater revelation of Divine truth and of human duty, and (2) that the revelation is greater because its radiance, far from being dimmed as the years roll on, is ever growing brighter and yet more bright. And we have learned that the reason of this great difference, so fraught with importance to us in all our lives of faith and of action, is that, while the lawgiver of old stood but from time to time in the Presence of God, and thus brought his people but into an interrupted communion with Him, our great Lawgiver stands ever before the eternal Father, so that His Church can ever behold the Divine glory. The heart of the children of Israel must turn to the Lord, that the veil which enshrouds it may be taken away; but we all behold with open face, though it be as in a glass, the glory of the Lord.

In short, then, this is the real unfading glory of Christianity — the constant vision of God, reflected to us, as in a perfect mirror, from the Person of our Saviour Christ. Here is the complete revelation of God as He can be known by man, and here is the complete declaration of His will. If the truth is not known, if duty is not done, either by the Church or by any of her members, it is because the Church or the individual has turned away from the glorious vision which has been disclosed or has suffered some "earth-born cloud" to hide it for the time. And on the other hand, wherever the truth of God is known and wherever duty is done, there God is seen as He is revealed in Christ; and the Church or the Christian who knows the truth and does the right, is acting in "the light of the knowledge of the glory of God in the face of Jesus Christ."

Far different, then, is the glory of the Church of God from the glory of the world; far different is the glory of the life of the Christian from that which is accounted glorious in the sight of men. Neither the one nor the other needs the opportunity of display or the proof of what is called success; in humble retirement or (if need be) in suffering and undeserved disgrace there often is the brighter vision of God and the more constant abiding in His Presence; and thus they who are unknown or despised by the world know more of God's truth and of their duty, both seeing and reflecting more of the brightness of the Face of the Almighty, than do they who are better known and more highly esteemed. At some times and in some places a branch of the Church has stood forth resplendent with external beauty and decked with all that the homage of man could bring, and yet it has not held the truth and done the work which has been bravely held and faithfully done by some other branch of the Church in its lowly poverty, unobserved of men. And in like manner the deepest insight into sacred mysteries and the fullest obedience to the law of God has been often found, not among those best known and most highly honored, but among the simple believers who in deep humility have stood, as do the bright archangels, ever in the Presence of God; not among the wise and prudent, but among the babes to whom the most marvellous revelations are given by the Almighty Father. And the reason is that in each and every case the Apostle's words are true: for the Church or the soul which turns to the Lord, the veil is taken away and truth is learned and duty is done in the very sight of Him to know Whom is to have eternal life and to follow Whom is to walk in perfect light.

It would not be seemly for me, my brethren, to attempt to anticipate any of the words which are to be spoken this week, if God will, in the commemoration which especially brings together at this time the thoughts and the prayers of the Church in Scotland and the Church in the United States. But I may be allowed to suggest to you that the teaching of the great Apostle in the words of my text finds most wonderful illustration in those events the memory of which is present now to all our minds. In all that I know of Church history since the very earliest days, I can think of nothing which shows greater fidelity to the truth of God and more faithful following in the path of duty—nothing, therefore, which is a brighter reflection of God's great glory—than is to be seen in the history of "the Catholic remainder of the ancient Church of Scotland" during the time of her suffering, and in that of the Church in Connecticut while it was yet a British Colony. As I see how, in the midst of discouragements and trials, your spiritual forefathers and mine kept the faith of the ancient Creeds; as I remember how, forgotten or neglected by stronger and more powerful branches of the Church, they maintained the Ministry in the Orders which the Lord had ordained and the Apostles had handed on; as I think that not only the Apostles' doctrine and their fellowship were thus maintained, but that also the breaking of the Bread and the prayers witnessed in Scotland and in my home to the faith and the obedience of those who were derided of men for continuing in them; as I think of the young men of the Scotch Church devoting themselves to the ministry and willingly entering upon a path of poverty and suffering and worldly disgrace, and those of the early American Church in like manner incurring the dangers of the sea, of sickness, and of the violence of enemies that they might receive a true ministerial commission, though but four out of every five could expect to return to execute it; as I recall the bravery of the three bishops who held the consecration in this city a hundred years ago and of his bravery who knelt to receive the Apostolic office from their hands, and of all the benefit which has flowed from that act as well to your Church as to mine; I need no argument to prove to me that they who acted thus patiently and bravely, stood in the very sight of God and that they indeed saw God's great glory; I am persuaded that they, believing what they believed and doing what they did, were surrounded with a radiance more bright and more lasting than that which shone from the face of the great Lawgiver when he came down from the mount or forth from the tabernacle; and I am sure that it would have mattered little whether the issue of all this had been worldly prosperity or still greater suffering. God be thanked for the blessings which He has so amply given to you and to us! But let us remember that the test of faithfulness is, after all, the only test which ought ever to be applied to action or to character, and that the brightness of God's glory is the only radiance in the light of which the Church or the Christian soul can safely walk. And let the commemoration of these solemn days teach us to set a true estimate on right belief and right action, and help us to remember that in them alone is to be found the true unfading glory of Christianity, the pledge, as it is the foretaste, of the glory which is yet to be revealed.

THE EPISCOPATE OF BISHOP SEABURY.

AN HISTORICAL SERMON.

REVELATION iii. 10.

"Because thou hast kept the word of My patience, I also will keep thee from the hour of temptation which shall come upon all the world, to try them that dwell upon the earth."

The Epistles to the Seven Churches are full of instruction for the Church of God in all the ages of her warfare on earth. The words of warning and of encouragement, the threats and

the promises, which were sent to those who were specially favored with the personal ministry of the beloved disciple, have come to clergy and people in far-off parts of the world and after the lapse of many years, with an application as direct and as forcible as if the message had been sent to them alone. The marvellous power of the words of the risen Lord is thus seen at all times and in all places, as they sound forth the summons to do service for His sake, or call to repentance for neglect of duty, or hold forth the promise of the crown of life as the reward of faithfulness. Thus we may read the application in past history and in our own time of the epistle which was sent to the Church in Asian Philadelphia, a part of which I have taken as my text: there has always been, there is to-day, a door set open before the Church of Christ which no man can shut; the Church in every age has needed and has had the promise that, because she has kept the word of Christ's patience, He also will keep her from the hour of temptation which is coming upon all the world; and that encouragement and that promise are none the less really ours. In their strength work can be undertaken for the Lord and duty can be done for His sake; the angels of the Church to-day and those over whose souls they have charge, remembering that the great King and Judge is coming quickly, can strive with unfailing patience to hold fast that they have, that no man take their crown.

But it may be that this Epistle has a special application to us at this time of the Church's history. It has been a prevalent opinion among thoughtful students of the book of the Revelation, that the early chapters are as really, though perhaps not as exclusively, prophetical as any of those which follow.* While they have not failed to read in all the epistles to the churches lessons of great importance to the Christians of every age, they have been of the opinion that these epistles were also intended to set forth in order the special trials and dangers of the Church as she should pass through the several stages of her history, and the special encouragements which she should need for her help. If we accept this interpretation of the opening chapters of the Apocalypse — and certainly it ought not to be lightly rejected — we shall see an additional reason for thinking that the words of the text have a lesson for ourselves; for we seem to be living in that later age of the Church's history of which the message to Philadelphia was in some sense a prophecy. Whichever way we turn, there is in these present centuries an open door — the opportunity of obedience and of service — set before God's people, as an encouragement to those who keep the Word of Christ and do not deny His Name; while from every side there comes the warning: "Hold fast that thou hast, that no man take thy crown." Thus, as we feel the assaults of enemies of the truth and see the gathering storms which threaten to break upon the Church, as we shrink from the hour of trial and dread the danger which seems sure to come, we hear the Lord's voice of encouragement: "Because thou hast kept the word of My patience, I also will keep thee from the hour of temptation which shall come upon all the world, to try them that dwell upon the earth."

And this I verily believe, brethren, is what we of this day need especially to learn and to do — to "keep the word of

* See Archbishop Trench's *Excursus* at the end of his *Commentary on the Epistles to the Seven Churches.*

Christ's patience." The Christian virtue of patience or endurance * has a wide scope, but it may be summed up, as it seems to me, under the two heads of patient waiting to learn God's will and to receive His blessing, and of consistent and brave obedience to that will as it has been made known. Thus patience has an active as well as a passive side, and tells of faithful service as well as of humble submission. And if the Church of Christ has learned to keep the word of the patience which He teaches and of which He is the great Example, who can doubt that she will be well furnished for the hour of trial and of struggle? who can doubt that, when that hour comes, she will find a Divine strength to carry her through it so that she shall not suffer from its power? who can doubt, in fine, that the faithful and consistent waiting and doing which Christian patience implies, shall have their full reward?

An example of this patience and of God's blessing upon it comes before our minds at this time. A hundred years ago, on the second day of August, 1785, the brave and patient man who had been chosen more than sixteen months before to be the first Bishop of Connecticut, met his clergy at Middletown to tell them how he had accomplished the task which they had laid upon him and to begin the exercise of his new duties among them.† He came back from Scotland, having received

* As to the meaning of ὑπομονή, see Bishop Ellicott on I. Thess. i. 3.

† For a full account of the meetings and services of these days, see Note at the end.

The list of the clergy of Connecticut when Bishop Seabury was elected, March 25, 1783, included fourteen names. During his absence abroad the Rev. Messrs. Samuel Andrews of Wallingford, Richard Samuel Clarke of New Milford, and James Scovill of Waterbury had removed to the British Provinces; the Rev. Jeremiah Leaming had returned from New York, and the Rev. John Bowden had also come from that city to Norwalk. The list of the clergy in August, 1785, seems to have been as follows: the Rev. Messrs. John Bowden of Norwalk, Gideon Bostwick of Great Barrington (Massachusetts), Ebenezer Dibblee of Stamford, Daniel Fogg of Brooklyn, Bela Hubbard of New Haven, Abraham Jarvis of Middletown, Jeremiah Leaming of Stratford, Richard Mansfield of Derby, John Rutgers Marshall of Woodbury, Christopher Newton of Ripton, James Nichols of Plymouth, John Tyler of Norwich, and Roger Viets of Simsbury. The address to Bishop Seabury was signed by Messrs. Leaming, Mansfield, Jarvis, Hubbard, Marshall, "and others."

from the bishops of the poor, persecuted remnant of the ancient Church of that land, "out of the abundance of their poverty," a spiritual gift for the scarcely less poor Church in this new world. For many weary years the Churchmen of this colony had "kept the word of Christ's patience," while, surrounded by unpopularity and opposition, they had held fast to what they were convinced was the true teaching in regard to the organization of the Church, the worship of God, and the principles and rules of the Christian life; and they failed not in this patience when the Church of England, trammelled by the State, obliged their candidates for Holy Orders to cross the ocean and to run no small risk of losing their lives if they desired ordination at the hands of a bishop. They showed patience in bearing the trial which they could not but feel to be unnecessary and undeserved; they showed patience as well in doing their work for God with unfailing bravery in spite of all the obstacles that were put in their way. And, because they were thus patient, God kept them from the temptation to despair of the truth and to abandon it; they maintained, and they maintained successfully, the ancient discipline and doctrine and worship of the Church:

and when the opportunity came to bear witness to their faith and to make new ventures of patience, they were found ready. It was an act of Christian faithfulness and patience when the clergy of this State elected Dr. Seabury to be their Bishop; faithfulness and patience mark all that time of his prolonged sojourn in England * while he hoped against hope that the great Church of that land would give to an independent country that which she had felt herself unable to give to a colony; faithfulness and patience brighten that upper room in Aberdeen in which Scottish Bishops, "not counting their lives dear unto themselves so that they might fulfil the ministry which they had received of the Lord Jesus," bestowed the Episcopate

* See the *Sermon* of the Archbishop of Canterbury in St. Paul's Cathedral, November 14, 1884, p. 9.

upon one who might bring it to "the American strand." A glory, unseen by human eye, filled that humble chapel; the benediction of the great Head of the Church waited upon the service of that day and upon those who took part in it; and then and there, I venture to think, He repeated His gracious promise: "Because thou hast kept the word of My patience, I also will keep thee."

Brethren, all this is a familiar story, and the anniversaries of the past two years have brought its details so fully before us that I hesitate to remind you of them again. And yet I cannot think it amiss to speak at this time, in few words, of the return of Bishop Seabury and of what he did for the Church in this diocese and this land. And I am specially glad to do so in this ancient parish, the organization of which, during the very days which intervened between the election of our first Bishop and his return to Connecticut, was at once an instance of that patient consistency of which I have spoken, and an earnest of its fruits.* "That which we have heard and known, and that which our fathers have told us, we will not hide it from the children of the generations to come; but to show the honour of the Lord, His mighty and wonderful works that He hath done."

When Bishop Seabury returned to this country and summoned his clergy to meet him at Middletown just a hundred years ago, he brought with him three important documents. The good bishops who had consecrated him had given him formal letters of consecration as a testimonial of the fact that they had rightly and duly admitted him to the office of a Bishop in the Church of God. They had also put into his hands a letter to the Connecticut clergy, telling them in a less formal manner of what they had done at their request, and charging them to receive and to honor him as the spiritual head of their diocese. And Bishop Seabury had

* There had apparently been earlier organizations of the Churchmen in Branford and in Middle Haddam; but the present organization of Trinity Church, Branford, dates from June 2, 1784, and that of Christ Church, Middle Haddam (in the town of Chatham), from St. Mark's Day, 1785.

also brought from Aberdeen one of the duplicate copies of a Concordate which he had made with his consecrators, in which they professed their common faith, bound themselves and their successors to acts of intercommunion, and pledged to each other, so far as it should be possible, uniformity in worship, especially in the service of the Holy Communion. These three most precious documents* bear witness to the fact that the Church in Scotland and the Church in Connec-

ticut were patiently "continuing stedfast in the doctrine of the Apostles, and in the fellowship, and in the breaking of the bread, and in the prayers."† Or, if we speak of these marks of the Church as including discipline and doctrine and worship, we may perhaps say that the letters of consecration witnessed to their holding fast the ancient discipline—that is to say, the organization and government—of the Church, that the letter charged upon them the duty of maintaining her doctrine, and that the Concordate was their reminder as to the necessity of accord with her ancient principles and forms of worship. Thus there came to our first bishop and to our spiritual ancestors a call to renewed fidelity and patience. Under the guidance and with the co-operation of Bishop Seabury, the clergy and the laity of Connecticut were faithful to their trust, and we to-day, to whom the duty has been handed on, find that duty easier because of the blessing which has followed upon their faithfulness.

1. On the day following that on which Bishop Seabury met his clergy, after they had welcomed and acknowledged him as their bishop, he held the first Episcopal ordination in this country, receiving into the order of Deacons three candidates from Connecticut and one from another State.‡ The

* They are all in Dr. Beardsley's *Life of Bishop Seabury*, pp. 149, sqq.
† Acts ii. 42.
‡ The names are thus entered in Bishop Seabury's register:
"Colin Ferguson, A.M., of Washington College, Maryland, recommended by Dr. Wm. Smith, Rev'd Messrs. John McPherson, Wm. Thompson, and others.
"Henry Van Dyck, A.M., } Recommended by the clergy of
Ashbel Baldwin, A.M., } Connecticut."
Philo Shelton, A.M.. }
It seems certain that the candidates were not ordained in the order in which their names were entered in the register. They were admitted to the priesthood by Bishop Seabury as follows: Mr. Ferguson, in Christ Church, Middletown, August 7, 1785; Mr. Van Dyck and Mr. Shelton in Trinity Church, New Haven, September 16, 1785; and Mr. Baldwin, in the same church, September 18, 1785.

long waiting was over; valid ordination could be had by our candidates elsewhere than on English soil; and the Church could witness by what was done here at home to her belief in the necessity of the three-fold ministry, as held for centuries in the universal Church. That first ordination was an assertion of principle and an exercise of a new power in the Church in this country. The principle had been asserted over and over again, as men had gone across the ocean to seek orders from the Bishop of London or his representative; but it was worth a great deal, if only as an evidence of what Churchmen believed, that ordinations by bishops should begin to be held here. As we think of all the ordinations which during these hundred years have been held within the borders of these United States, and of the much greater number of confirmations,* each one of which has witnessed to a belief in the divinely given authority of the Apostolic order of Bishops, we can see how the discipline and organization of the ancient Church have been constantly and ever more strongly maintained in this land. The constitution of our national Church bears witness to the strength of the conviction with which our first bishop held them, and the weight of the arguments by which he led others to share his conviction; for it was owing to his influence and that of others from this diocese that bishops were recognized as a necessary and constituent part of the General Convention, and that it was provided that the administration of ecclesiastical discipline should be in the hands of the bishops, so that no clergyman

should receive sentence of deposition except from them.† In such ways and with such results—I cannot now go into details—did Bishop Seabury, while he promoted and secured

* Bishop Seabury's first confirmation seems to have been in Christ Church, Stratford; his last, in Trinity Church, Branford.
† See note to Bishop Williams's *Convention Sermon*, 1885, pp. 16, 17.

the unity of our national Church, keep the word of Christ's patience in regard to the Church's discipline. "Not by constraint, but willingly; not for filthy lucre, but of a ready mind; neither as being a lord over God's heritage, but being an ensample to the flock," he "took the oversight" of that part of the Church which was given him in charge. And, because of this his faithfulness, in a time when faithfulness required both courage and prudence, the Lord, we may well believe, kept him stedfast, and has kept this our diocese true to the teaching and the tradition of the universal Church. When, a few years ago, a schism broke out, and a bishop separated himself from our communion because he was not satisfied with our teaching in regard to Holy Orders and other matters, though many feared that it might draw away much people after it, who believed for a moment that Connecticut Churchmen would be persuaded to leave the old communion, and to accept a new form of ecclesiastical polity? We hardly knew of the temptation which others suffered then; we hardly think at any time of the possibility of leaving the Church of the Apostolic ministry. Because we have kept the word of the Lord's patience, He also has kept us.

2. On the day following Bishop Seabury's first ordination, he delivered his first charge to his clergy. It was a fit beginning of that most admirable teaching of his in which, as a bishop, he enforced and defended the doctrine of the Church. Time fails me as I would speak of his fidelity and courage— his "patience," in the Scriptural sense of the word — as he "held forth the faithful word as he had been taught, so that he was able by sound doctrine both to exhort and to convince the gainsayers." He knew the theological needs and tendencies of this part of the world. As a youth in his father's house he had witnessed the perverse acts of foolish fanatics done under the guise of a revival of religion, and had seen how his father's quiet words and plain setting forth of the way of salvation as it was taught in Scripture had served to comfort distressed souls and to lead them to the truth.* As a student

* See the letters of the Rev. Samuel Seabury, Senior, describing the acts of Mr. James Davenport and his followers in New London in 1743; *Documentary History of the Church in Connecticut*, i. 189, 195.

in college, he had seen an extreme instance, under the highest authority, of ecclesiastical bigotry and tyranny.* He knew well, as his sermons witness, the faults, both of doctrine and of practice, into which the narrow theology of the teachers of earlier generations had led and was leading their descendants; and in particular, he had the foresight to discern that a time was at hand when the fundamental truth of the Christian religion, the doctrine of the Holy Trinity, would be denied by many. † Bishop Seabury, in these matters of faith and practice, was consistent and brave. As his published charges and sermons prove, he defended the truth; he convinced men of their duty to accept it and support it; he taught the principles of holy obedience to God's law; he trained his diocese — perhaps I had better said, he continued its training — in the ancient faith. And that faith the Churchmen

of Connecticut have, by God's blessing, maintained. They have held it free from those inventions of men which have distorted and perverted it, and which have kept thoughtful and religious persons from accepting it, even if they have not driven them to accept error in its stead. And that God has blessed this patient teaching, can be shown in at least one conspicuous instance. The Divinity of our Blessed Lord has never been denied by any large body of persons within the limits of this diocese. When, in other places, men revolted from the unscriptural ways in which the doctrine of the Holy Trinity had been taught, and, in rejecting the perversion of the truth, went on to reject the truth itself, the ancient faith was taught here with a distinctness and a plainness which "commended it to every man's conscience." And Connecticut, outside our own communion as well as within it, owes it to Dr. Johnson and Bishop Seabury, and to those who shared in and who followed their teachings, that she has almost wholly escaped the errors of so-called Unitarianism. What is so

* In 1744, two brothers, named Cleveland, were expelled from Yale College, because they had attended in vacation a separatist Congregational meeting with their parents. Dr. Trumbull's *History of Connecticut*, ii. 179, sqq.
† See in particular his *Second Charge*, pp. 8, sqq.

evidently true in this case might also, did time permit, be shown to be true in other matters of the Church's doctrine. Because our forefathers in the faith kept the word of Christ's patience, He also has kept them and us in the hour of temptation, in fidelity to Himself and to His truth.

3. On the fourth day of Bishop Seabury's meeting with his clergy, a committee was appointed to act with him in considering the changes necessary to be made in the liturgy.* This action brings to our minds the influence and work of Bishop Seabury in his faithfulness to the worship of the Church. It specially showed itself at two times: first, when he set forth, with the advice and consent of his clergy, † a Communion-Office following very closely that which was used by the bishops of Scotland, and in particular having in its Consecration-prayer a formal Oblation of the elements to God and a formal Invocation of the Holy Spirit to bless and sanctify them; and again, when in harmony with Bishop White, at the first really General Convention, ‡ he united with the house of deputies in adapting the Prayer-Book for the use of our national Church, and particularly when the hearty concurrence of all was secured in the adoption of a prayer of Consecration in the service of the Holy Communion which, having the two important parts of which I have just spoken, makes our Eucharistic worship, in all its essential features, almost identical with that of the ancient and undivided Church. The extent of the influence of these most important acts of our first bishop it is not easy to imagine; they have brought a great blessing to us, if in no other way, at least in enabling us to offer our highest worship to God in a form for which we need to make no apology and no excuse, and also

* The few alterations which were thought necessary at this time — all of them having reference to the change which had taken place in civil government — were published by Bishop Seabury in a broadside Injunction, bearing date August 12, 1785.
† This was at the Convocation in Derby, September, 1786, at which the Bishop delivered his second charge.
‡ In 1789. Bishop White bears striking testimony to the harmony between himself and Bishop Seabury; *Memoirs of the Church*, pp. 149, sqq. (second edition).

83

(I venture to think) in keeping us almost free from those bitter controversies concerning the sacrament of unity and love which have so darkened much of modern Church history; and I sincerely hope that, in adopting and using the liturgy which she has, our Church has done something towards effecting that unity of all Christians in the truth for which the Church and her great Head so earnestly pray. As we study Bishop Seabury's life, we can see with what patience he accomplished all this, and we may well thank the good Lord for the reward which, as He graciously promised, He has given to those who have " kept the word of His patience."

It is but an imperfect outline of the work of the episcopate of our first bishop which I have thus, my brethren, brought to your recollection on this anniversary. But it may help to remind you how much our whole Church, and especially the Church in this diocese, owes to Bishop Seabury; how much is due to his fidelity to the discipline, the doctrine, and the worship of the Church, "as the Lord hath commanded and as we have received the same"; and how the obligation lies on us to be patient in faithfulness to truth and in obedience to it, in the sure confidence that He who has fulfilled the promises which He made to our forefathers will also fulfil the like promises which He makes to us. Our duty to the Church will of necessity be included within the same general outlines as was that of those who went before us; but its details may be very different, and they must be observed and carried out in the study of the word of the Lord's patience. It was an especial merit of the great men of a century ago, that they could hold fast to essential principles and at the same time adapt them to the changing needs of the Church and the world; it will require all our wisdom — and all our patience, too, both of action and of suffering — so to use that with which the good Lord has entrusted us that it may be of real service to the souls of men and that we may gain a blessing for our own generation and for those that shall come after. The work and the encouragement, too, as I suggested at the beginning, seem to be especially assigned and adapted to our times; may we not read the promise which follows the text and see in it a reward of faithfulness already assured to him of whom I have been especially speaking to-day, and for some part of which we may humbly hope? "Him that overcometh will I make a pillar in the temple of My God, and he shall no more go out; and I will write upon him the Name of My God, and the name of the city of My God, which is new Jerusalem, which cometh down out of Heaven from My God; and I will write upon him My new Name."

Ὁ ἔχων οὖς ἀκουσάτω
τί τὸ Πνεῦμα λέγει ταῖς ἐκκλησίαις.

NOTE.

THE PROCEEDINGS AT MIDDLETOWN.

The following full account of the proceedings at Middletown, August 2–5, 1785, consisting for the most part of an extract from official minutes, is taken from the Memoir of Bishop Jarvis, in *The Evergreen* (Vol. iii., p. 152):

"On the 2d of August, 1785, the clergy of Connecticut assembled in Convocation at Middletown, to meet and receive their Bishop. Eleven were present, with the Rev. Benjamin Moore from New York and the Rev. Samuel Parker from Boston. Mr. Leaming was, as usual, chosen president, and Mr. Jarvis secretary. As his minutes contain the ceremonial of this first reception, an extract from them may be interesting:

"'The Rt. Rev. Dr. Samuel Seabury attended upon this Convention, and his letters of consecration being requested by the same, they were produced and read; whereby it appeared to this Convention that he hath been duly and canonically consecrated a Bishop by the Bishops of the Church of Scotland.

"'August 3, 8 o'clock A.M., the Convention met. After the address of the clergy to the Bishop had been reconsidered by the Convention and approved, the clergy repaired to the church, and appointed four of their body to return to the parsonage. Mr. Jarvis, in the name of the clergy, declared to the Bishop their confirmation of their former election of him, and they now acknowledged and received him as their Bishop. Then the Bishop returned his answer of acceptance, which two of them immediately carried back to the Convention, while the other two followed in attendance upon the Bishop, who thus proceeded to the church. Being introduced and seated in his chair at the altar, the clergy assembled at the rails. Their address to him was read by the Rev. Mr. Hubbard, after which the Bishop read his answer; and then the clergy, kneeling at the rails, received the Apostolic blessing. Then the clergy retired to their pews, and the Bishop began divine service with the Litany, according to the rubric in the office for the ordination of deacons: the four following persons, Messrs. Vandyke, Shelton, Baldwin, of Connecticut, and Mr. Ferguson, of Maryland, being present to be admitted into that order. The Litany being ended, Mr. Bowden read the first Communion Service. The Bishop then read the Service, consecrated the elements, and administered the Bread. Mr. Bowden assisted by administering the Cup. The Communion being finished, the Bishop then proceeded to the Ordination. Mr. Jarvis officiated as Archdeacon. After the Ordination a sermon was preached by the Rev. Mr. Leaming, and the congregation was dismissed by the Bishop. From the church the clergy, preceded by the Bishop, returned to the parsonage. Mr. Jarvis, by order of the Convention, gave the thanks of the same to Mr. Leaming for his sermon delivered before them, with their desire of a copy of it to be printed. The Bishop then dissolved the Convention, and directed the clergy to meet him at five o'clock in Convocation. They met accordingly; and the Convocation was adjourned to the next morning, Thursday, 9 o'clock A. M.

"'Thursday, Aug. 4. At 11 o'clock A. M., went to the church. Mr. Parker read prayers, and Mr. Moore preached a sermon; after which the Bishop delivered a charge to the clergy. P. M., Mr. Parker communicated to the Convocation the purport of his delegation from the clergy in the State of Massachusetts, viz.: to collect the sentiments of the Connecticut clergy in respect of Dr. Seabury's episcopal consecration, the regulation of his episcopal jurisdiction, and their thoughts of connecting themselves with them under his episcopal charge. The clergy of Connecticut expressed their warmest wishes for the union and concurrence of their brethren in Massachusetts under Bishop Seabury.

"'Friday, Aug. 5. After appointing Mr. Bowden, Mr. Parker, and Mr. Jarvis as a committee to consider of and to make with the Bishop some alterations in the Liturgy needful for the present use of the Church, the Convocation adjourned to meet again at New Haven in September.'"

The address of the clergy, the Bishop's reply, Mr. Leaming's sermon, and the Bishop's charge were printed in pamphlet form, both in New Haven and in Edinburgh. The pamphlets also contain "A List of the Consecration of Scots Bishops since the Revolution, 1688, under William the Third, as far as the Consecration of Bishop Seabury is concerned," authenticated by the signature, "Samuel, Bp. Epl. Ch. Connect." This list is evidently from the same source as that in the appendix to Dean Skinner's *Ecclesiastical History of Scotland* (1788); but whereas this puts into a foot-note the consecration of Dr. Hickes by three deprived English bishops, Bishop Seabury places it at the head of the list.

The addresses and the charge are reprinted in Dr. Beardsley's *Life of Bishop Seabury*, pp. 209, sqq.

History of the Early Settlement of Saybrook,

Mr. Chairman, Citizens of our Ancient Town, Ladies and Gentlemen : [21]

One does not apologize for obeying the commands of a mother. Our common mother, the venerable village of Saybrook, has not passed through her quarter of a millenium without some trials and some disturbances of her quiet; but on the whole her two hundred and fifty years have been so peaceful, the wrinkles have gathered so slowly on her brow, and so little change has found its way into either her outward circumstances or her inner life, that she did not know until

the anniversary was close upon her that she had almost reached a birthday of which she might well be especially proud, and to the observance of which she would certainly wish to invite all her sons and daughters. As I am speaking to none who do not love and respect her, perhaps you will allow me to say that when it was suggested to her that the day was approaching, she seemed to be a little hard of hearing; and then she did not, we thought, quite understand the meaning of what we said; the mention of a number, and that a pretty large one, gave her the idea that we were asking for a subscription of some kind; and like a few of her descendants, she was not willing to reply until she had given the matter careful attention. And, so long was she in thinking of it, that unless a few of her energetic daughters had taken the matter in hand, this two hundred and fiftieth birthday of our common mother would have passed without due observance. May I not express to these daughters of Saybrook the thanks of all us the rest?

Now that we have come, with scanty time for preparation, to celebrate this anniversary, it must not be, as I was saying, with words of apology. We are doing as best we can a duty which has been laid upon us by one whom we have no right to disobey. But this at least may be said, that the history of Saybrook ought to be written out by some patient and skilful pen, read at some future day in your presence, and put in permanent form for the benefit of those who are to come after us.

I am to carry you back in thought, as best I may, to the earliest times of that history, when out of a sort of mythical haze we first see events shaping themselves into figures of real life, and then, if I can, to lead the way to what others, more competent and better qualified than myself, will bring before you as the important facts in the annals of our town.

Save for the records of early combats with the natives and for the traces which we find, for the most part beneath the soil, of what they did in war and in peace, how they lived and how they were buried in some hope of immortality—save for such fragmentary records, we know next to nothing of those who occupied this plain, these meadows, and these hills before the eyes of enterprising Europeans saw the mouth of our fair and quiet river, and the hope of commerce and of resulting wealth led them to set a high value on the location of our town. And there is a very legendary air about the story of the attempted Dutch occupation, when the redoubtable settlers of the New Netherlands claimed for themselves the fields at the mouth of the river and the river itself. Doubtless, as in the case of the poetic legends in which the history of early Rome is enshrined, it will be possible for some gifted student to separate, in part at least, the true from the false, and to tell us the real story of Hans den Sluys. But we are not to-day Indians or Dutchmen; we are not dwellers in Pashbeshauke or in Kievets Hook; we will simply assume that it is true that our ancestors purchased their lands from the aboriginal inhabitants and that the States General had no jurisdiction within the limits which were covered by the deed or patent under which the English settlers took possession. Homer did not begin the history of the Trojan war by describing the egg from which Helen was born*; we begin the history of Saybrook when it began to be Saybrook two hundred and fifty years ago.

It was a troubled time in England, when a great revolution was coming to a head, and when, besides, the thoughts of a large body of men were turning eagerly and hopefully to the Virginia and the New England across the seas. Under the auspices of the Plymouth Company, settlements had been made in the Massachusetts; and that company had transferred to Robert, Earl of Warwick, its rights to a tract of land a little further south; and under date of March 19th, 1631-2, the Earl of Warwick executed a deed or grant by which he conveyed to certain persons, "their heirs and assigns and their associates forever," the said lands, forming the valley of the lower Connecticut, and described as extending from a river called Narragansett to the south sea. The grantees first mentioned in this Company are those whose names our town has perpetuated—the Right Honorable William, Viscount Say and Seale, and the Right Honorable Robert, Lord Brooke—the latter being, I suppose, the eldest son of the Earl of Warwick; and among those who were joined with them were the Right Honorable Lord Rich, also of the family of the Earl of Warwick, Sir Richard Saltonstall, John Pym, and John Hampden. There is no need to ask

*Nec gemino bellum Trojanum orditur ab ovo.—HORACE, Ars Poetica, 147.

what were their political or their religious views; it could probably be said of them all as we are told it was said of those whose names stood foremost, that when they were asked to pledge their fidelity to the King, one of them would not Say the words, the other would not Brook them. The document is called the old Patent of Connecticut, though on its face it is no more than a deed. As to its meaning and its value there may doubtless be questions; certainly it was treated as if it were in some sense the patent of a government. On the 7th of July, 1635, John Winthrop, Esq., the younger, son of the Governor of Massachusetts, was appointed by the company who then held the title (and among them was then George Fenwick, Esquire) to be "governor of the river Connecticut, and of the harbor and places adjoining, for the space of one year after his arrival there"; and Mr. Winthrop agreed to undertake the settlement, to build a fort within which should be houses for "men of quality", and to "reserve unto the fort, for the maintenance of it, one thousand or fifteen hundred acres, at least, of good ground, as near adjoining thereunto as may be." Winthrop arrived at Boston in October; and, seeing the need of haste, he sent a vessel and twenty men to the mouth of the river, where there had already been the beginning of a settlement, and where they arrived just in time to frighten the Dutch from landing. It was on the 24th of November, 1635, almost two centuries and a half ago to a day, that the vessel reached here from Boston, and formal possession was taken in the name of Lord Say and Seale, Lord Brooke, and the rest of the company who claimed the lands. Mr. Winthrop himself arrived a little later.

With Mr. Winthrop (or perhaps earlier, for we are told it was on the 28th of November), came Lion Gardiner, an English engineer who had been in the service of the Prince of Orange, and who was employed to build the spacious

fortifications which were proposed and to lay out a city. It was expected that in the next spring there would " come from England three hundred able men, whereof two hundred should attend fortification, fifty to till the ground, and fifty to build houses." Under the most favorable circumstances, little could have been done that winter except to provide for the safety and the most urgent needs of the colonists landed on Saybrook Point at the end of November, with no Europeans nearer than those in the settlements at Hartford, New York, and Massachusetts Bay. But this was an exceptionally hard winter. The Connecticut River was frozen over by the 15th of November—nine days before the first settlers came here—and the snow was so deep to the north of us that the settlers of Hartford, who were coming by land from Cambridge, were exposed to great suffering, while the storms were so severe that a company who were attempting to reach Hartford by water were wrecked and wandered ten days before they met a human being.

On the 3d or 4th of December the settlers at the fort had unexpected visitors. Seventy men, women, and children, in imminent danger of starvation, came from the settlements up the river, looking for the provisions which they were expecting from Boston. The vessels for which they looked did not come; but the Rebecca, a vessel which had been frozen in below the narrows in the river, succeeded in working her way out, and, taking them all on board, carried them back to Boston. Before she sailed, however, on the 10th of December, 1635, she ran aground upon the bar, this being the first record of a phenomenon with which we have become familiar. It seems that those who returned to Massachusetts gave a dismal account of the state of things here; for the governor of that colony ordered a general fast to be observed on account of the peril of the garrison at the mouth of the Connecticut.

It was a relief, no doubt, when the winter had passed; but, to quote Mr. Gardiner's own words, the "great expectation at the river's mouth came only to two men, Mr. Fenwick and his man, who came [from Boston] with Mr. Hugh Peters and Mr. Oldham and Thomas Stanton." He was greatly disappointed; and in 1639 he removed to the island which bears his name—he called it the Isle of Wight—where he made the first English settlement within the limits of the present State of New York. His son David was born here on the 29th of April, 1636, being the first white child born in what is now Connecticut.

The earliest instance of the use of the name Saybrook which I have found is in the date of a letter written by Lion Gardiner to the younger Winthrop bearing date "Saybroock, 6 Nov. 1636"; in another letter dated the 23d day of the following January, the name is spelled Seabrooke. As the present names of Hartford, Wethersfield, and Windsor were not given till 1637, Saybrook is the oldest town-name in the State.

Of the two other colonies which were early established within the present limits of Connecticut, one was almost contemporaneous with that at Saybrook, and the other was somewhat later. There was the beginning of a settlement at Wethersfield in 1634, a settlement at Windsor in 1635, and later in that year the founders of Hartford brought their

weary journey through the wilderness to an end. This colony —for it was really one, the three grape-vines united in one shield—antedated that at New Haven by some four years. It is doing no injustice to those who made these settlements to say that they were influenced by different and mingled motives. Political convictions, religious enthusiasm, and the hope of commercial success, all doubtless had much to do with the settlements at Saybrook, at Hartford, and at New Haven. Yet, if one may make the distinction, it would seem that the political feeling was strongest in the colony to the north of us, that the religious motive was most prominent in that to the west, while here at the mouth of the river there were the strongest hopes of success in trade and commerce. The early appearance of the three settlements must also have been very different; in fact, each has in its topography to-day the character stamped upon it by those who laid out the lands of which they took possession. Hartford was laid out along the line of a broad street, which served as the backbone of a future city, and where another principal street crossed it was the place of the meeting-house for both religious and political purposes. New Haven was laid out as a great square divided into nine squares, the centremost being reserved for the public buildings. Saybrook was first of all to have a fort, or fortified place, including residences and other necessary buildings; and then evidently there was to be a large plot of land laid out after the manner of a city but so as to be dependent upon the fort at the river's mouth. The first fort stood further back from the water than that the remains of which were razed to the ground about fifteen years ago; and, a stockade being built across the narrow neck—then narrower than now—which divides the coves near the windmill lot, the whole of the point was easily defended from attacks by land.

In the spring of 1636, as has been already said, Mr. Fenwick visited Saybrook, being the only one of the grantees or patentees who ever crossed the ocean. In the following summer or autumn he returned to England.*

In 1636, before the garrison, now amounting to about twenty men, had been many months at the fort, the Pequot war broke out. The attack on the natives was not without provocation; but it was unadvisedly and hastily undertaken, against the strong advice of Lieut. Gardiner, and it certainly seems to have been cruelly carried on at the last. The settlers at Saybrook were in great danger, and some were killed after they had been tortured by the savages. The war was ended in 1637.

Meantime we hear of the arrival of other colonists, two of

---

*He probably established a system of tolls, or protective tariff, on goods carried by the fort up the river. Among the first ships to sail past were those which carried the goods of Mr. Pynchon, the founder of Springfield.

---

whom—Robert Chapman and John Clarke—are represented here to-day, while another—Capt. John Mason—made himself a name famous in the early history of the Commonwealth. After an absence of about three years, Mr. Fenwick returned in July, 1639, bringing with him his wife, Alice Apsley, formerly the wife of Sir John Boteler, from whom she had by courtesy the title of Lady. With them, or about the

same time, came their chaplain, Master Thomas Higginson, who was afterwards pastor at Guilford and at Salem, Mass. No church, however, was organized as yet in Saybrook; Lady Fenwick was admitted a member of the church in Hartford, and her daughter Elizabeth, born not long after her arrival here, was thereupon baptized.

Mr. Fenwick, as the only one of the patentees in the colony, acted, it would seem, as *ex officio* Governor. In the midst of many discouragements, he cared for the interests of the little settlement and of the other patentees; and he also united with the representatives of the other colonies in what are now the States of Massachusetts and Connecticut, in forming the confederation of the United Colonies of New England.

The independence of our colony lasted about ten years. In December, 1644, an agreement was made between Mr. Fenwick and the General Court at Hartford, by which the former ceded to the other government the fort at Saybrook,* and in the following spring he was elected a magistrate of the Connecticut colony. His wife died, probably in 1646, soon after the birth of her daughter Dorothy; and then, disappointed and discouraged, and thinking that, if the purposes of the colony were to be carried out, there was need of some further efforts in England, he sailed back across the ocean. There he became a colonel in the Parliamentary army, and was elected a member of Cromwell's Parliament, though

---

*Whatever the value of this cession or grant at the time, its intention and effect were ratified by the charter of 1660.

---

excluded from his seat because he was not satisfactory to the Protector. He died in 1657.

The death of Lady Fenwick is the romantic event in the history of our town. For long years there was something touching in the sight of the massive tombstone standing alone in the field on the spot where the first settlers had lived, as there was something pathetic in the story of which it reminded the passer-by; and the reverent care with which, when her dust was threatened with disturbance by ruthless hands, it was laid near the graves of seven generations of those who came after her, bears witness that she will not be soon forgotten.

> "And ever this wave-washed shore
> Shall be linked with her tomb and fame,
> And blend with the wind and the billowy roar,
> The music of her name."*
>
> *From a poem by Miss F. M. Caulkins.

In 1647 the first fort, within the enclosure of which Lady Fenwick was buried, was destroyed by fire; and in the following year the new fort was built close to the river's brink. Many of us remember the earthwork, far older than anything else of the same kind in the northern part of the United States, which formed so picturesque a feature of the scenery until it had to give way to structures which may be more useful but certainly are less attractive.

It was this second fort, the surrender of which was demanded by Major Andross on the 8th of July, 1675, when Captain Robert Chapman and Captain Bull of Hartford so ingeniously defended the rights of the colony; for Major Andross did not venture to fire upon the royal standard, and

either did not dare to read his commission or could not make it heard.

But before this time Saybrook had sent out a colony to settle in the eastern part of the State, where two beautiful rivers, uniting to form the Thames, offer a site for a city than which it is not easy to imagine one more attractive. The outgoing colony was led by the Rev. James Fitch, who had succeeded the Rev. Thomas Peters in the pastorate of the church at Saybrook. With him he took a larger part of his people, attracted, we are told, by the report of the fair tract of nine miles square which the faithful Uncas had granted them in remembrance of the kindness of a Saybrook man who had relieved his people when hard pressed by siege and hunger. Thus many names which occur in the early records of Saybrook are lost from its history and appear in the annals of Norwich, its oldest and fairest daughter.

After a few years Mr. Fitch was succeeded here by the Rev. Thomas Buckingham, whose pastorate extended into the eighteenth century and covered the important period marked by the foundation of the Collegiate School and the meeting of the assembly which drew up the Saybrook Platform.

It is not easy for us to draw a picture of Saybrook at the close of the century, after sixty-five years of its history had passed. The town had spread beyond the limits of the stockade which had protected the first settlement from attacks by land. A road doubtless led along the coast—it was the old post-road to New Haven; and houses were built on this road, not only on this side of Oyster River, but also beyond it. As early as 1660 there were settlers in Pochaug, afterwards called West Saybrook and Westbrook. Another road must have led to the north, branching off on the right to the ferrying-place and on the left, skirting the great swamp and passing through the northern part of the town to Haddam and thence to Hartford. The burying-ground had been early laid out at the foot of the present cemetery; I am inclined to doubt whether it was ever an Indian burial-place. In front of it ran the road from the fort, past the house and lot which were afterwards given by Mr. Nathaniel Lynde for the use of the college; and another road, also still in use, completed the circuit of the Point. On the crossroad, not far from the site of the present school-house, stood the meeting-house, finished in 1680 or 1681, the second edifice erected for the worship of God. Two other streets ran across this from north to south, dividing the land into six city-like plots. The houses were not inhabited by the "persons of quality" who had been expected from England or by their descendants; but a census taken at that time would have contained many names which are represented in this village and in other parts of the old town to-day; a few of them we can find on the roll of civil dignitaries. The town had had its own governor for a few years; but it had furnished no governor for the colony of Connecticut after it became merged in its jurisdiction. To the House of "Assistants," the upper house of the General Assembly, elected by general vote, it had sent only George Fenwick (1644–1649) and Robert Chapman (1681–1685); the representatives elected for the town had borne the names of Chapman, Bushnell, Pratt, Parker, Lay, Dudley, Post, Lynde, Clark, and Whittlesey. When in 1704 the General Assem-

bly, for the sake of confirming the title to the real estate within the town, granted a formal charter of incorporation, the document contained the names of Buckingham, Chapman, Pratt, Clark, Parker, Lay, and Sandford. We have the names of but three Town Clerks before 1700—Messrs. Tully, Willard, and Pratt. To the north of the settlement lay the common fields—that most interesting "survival" of an ancient custom in regard to the tenure of land, for the lay-out and division of which provision was made by the town within fifteen years after its first settlement. There must have been already a settlement in Pettipaug at what we call Centre Brook, and probably one at Pattaconk or Chester. But nearly a quarter of a century was to pass before a second ecclesiastical society should be organized, and nearly a century and a half before the ancient town should be cut into pieces. The country across the river had been for a short time called East Saybrook, but its connection with the civil or eccles-iastical administration of the town can have been hardly more than nominal.

It does not fall to my lot to dwell upon the important events in the later history of the town. One best qualified to do so will speak of the early annals of the Collegiate School, in regard to which we affirm most emphatically that in Saybrook and in Saybrook alone was its legal home and the place where its degrees were conferred until it was removed to New Haven, where under an honored name it has been for many years, and will be, we trust, for many more, the home of sound learning under the always recognized guid-ance of Christian principle. I may note, however, that of the fifty-five who received their first degree here, ten were young men of Saybrook, bearing the names of Whittlesey, Chapman, Lynde, Taylor, Tousey, Blague, Buckingham, Clarke, Lord, and Willard. The history and significance of the important Synod of 1708 will be described by one who can tell us of the influence of the Saybrook Platform in moulding the ecclesiastical constitution of the Standing Order—the Estab-lished Church—of this Commonwealth, and how its influence has extended beyond our own borders.

The later history of the ecclesiastical organization within the town will not, I trust, be passed by; when under the guid-ance of Mr. Buckingham, and after him, of Mr. Mather and Mr. Hart and Mr. Hotchkiss—the pastorates of these three men extending over a hundred and thirty-four years—the people of Saybrook were instructed in the faith and fear of God. Nor ought we to forget the growth of settlements in parts of the town remote from the site of the ancient fort, and the progress of all in trade and commerce, in agriculture and fisheries, and their advance in education and religion. And, turning from the pleasant thoughts of quiet rural life and of successful labors on land and sea, we ought not to forget what Saybrook men have done for the defence of their country in the times of her need; we may be proud to remember that a Saybrook captain was with Washington at Valley Forge, and that he kept his soldiers shod by selling his land here at home, even if we are ashamed at having to confess that he received on earth no reward for his self-denial.

But it is for me to do no more than point out the way in which we may study the history of our ancient town, to preface what others will say at length, and to point out a part of what we may expect when our history shall be fully and carefully written.

"Saybrook," said "A Gentleman of the Province," writing the history of Connecticut in 1781, "is greatly fallen from its ancient grandeur; but is, notwithstanding, resorted to with great veneration, as the parent town of the whole colony." If we lost our grandeur in the first hundred and fifty years, I am afraid that a part at least of the veneration has been lost in the century which has passed since Dr. Peters wrote. But we at least, who have known Saybrook best, have never failed to hold her in reverence, to recognize how much we owe to her, and to pray in the devout words of the great king, who looked back from the splendor of the newly estab-lished kingdom and the newly finished temple to see in the earlier history of Israel the pattern on which he would have its later history framed: "The Lord our God be with us, as He was with our fathers."

BISHOP SEABURY'S COMMUNION-OFFICE.

AN HISTORICAL SERMON.

[22]

I. Cor. xi. 23-26.

"For I have received of the Lord that which also I delivered unto you, That the Lord Jesus the same night in which he was betrayed took bread;

" And when he had given thanks, he brake it, and said, Take, eat: this is my body, which is broken for you: this do in remembrance [or, for a remembrance] of me.

"After the same manner also he took the cup when he had supped, saying, This cup is the new testament in my blood: this do ye, as oft as ye drink it, in remembrance of me.

"For as often as ye eat this bread, and drink this cup, ye do shew [or, shew ye] the Lord's death till he come."

The great Apostle to the Gentiles, because he was not of the number of the Twelve, had not been present at the insti-tution of the Sacrament of the Lord's death; but, as he tells us in the text, he learned the history of that institution from the Lord Himself. And when he solemnly committed to writing that which he had taught his converts concerning this, he prefaced it with almost exactly the same words which he used a little later in recounting the fundamental facts of the Christian faith, saying: "I delivered unto you that which I also received, how that Christ died for our sins according to the Scriptures, and that He was buried, and that He rose again the third day according to the Scriptures."* There would seem to be little room for doubt that an act of our Lord concerning which He made a special revelation to St. Paul and of which St. Paul spoke as he did, was an act of the utmost importance in itself and in its relations to His people. Yet in outward form it was a simple act. As He was eating the passover-feast with His disciples on the evening which introduced the day of His death, the Lord took bread, blessed

---

* I. Cor. xv. 3, 4.

---

it with thanksgiving to God, brake it, and giving it to His disciples, bade them eat it, telling them that it was His body which was then given* for them. And when the feast was ended, He took the cup of wine, and in like manner blessed it, and gave it to them to drink, saying that it was His blood

of the New Testament which was then shed† for them and for many. He commanded them to do in remembrance — for a memorial — of Him that which He thus did; and, perhaps from His express words at the time, they understood that they and those who should come after them, obeying this command, would show forth the Lord's death until He should come again.

The act, as I said, seemed in itself a simple act. Yet it is impossible to read the few words in which it is described without feeling that it has a very profound and a very solemn meaning; even as it is impossible not to feel that those who stood or knelt ‡ in the upper room and saw what the Lord did and heard what He said, must have known that this was indeed a most momentous hour. Their Master, Who had more than once prophesied of His coming passion and death, now told them that the passion and death were present facts, that for them His body was then given and His blood poured out. Doubtless they did not then understand the full meaning of His words; but afterwards they could not have failed to know that He who thus spoke had then presented Himself before God as the great Sacrifice for the sins of the world, proved by His holy life to be the "Lamb without blemish and without spot," and voluntarily offered Himself for the death in which He was so soon to be a passive victim, suffering at the hands of wicked men. And in this proper sense of the word, it seems to me that there can be no question but that the sacrifice of Christ was offered to God in the upper

---

* The present participle is used: διδόμενον (St. Luke). The word κλώμενον in St. Paul is not read by the best editors.

‡ ἐκχυνόμενον (St. Matthew, St. Mark, St. Luke).

‡ It seems that our Lord must have stood for the blessing; if so, the disciples, in all probability, stood or knelt when they received the Sacrament.

---

room and at the time of the institution of the Eucharist.* Thus performing the greatest act of His earthly life, the Lord invoked a blessing upon the bread and the wine which He took into his hands, at the same time giving thanks to His heavenly Father; † the thanksgiving must have been, above everything else, for the great work of redemption of which He could then speak as if it were accomplished; the blessing must have been in order that the elements might be for His disciples that which He presently declared them to be as a means of spiritual grace. And then, as He gave them the bread and the wine, thus connected with the great oblation of Himself and blessed with thanksgiving, He told them that they were His body and His blood, and that the repetition of that which he had done was to be their memorial of Him. These words, one can hardly doubt, must have been spoken and understood in the light of the sacrificial act and the blessing which had preceded them. The former part of the words — and these again are interpreted by the discourse recorded by St. John in the sixth chapter of his Gospel — tells of a participation in the benefits of the Lord's sacrifice by means of eating the bread which He thus identified with His body and drinking the wine which He thus identified with His blood; and the word which we render "remembrance" or "memorial,"‡ coupled with the command that it should be often made until He should come again, tells of a memorial before God whereby the one sacrifice should be commemorated and its all-sufficient merits pleaded for all the needs of the Church and of mankind.

It is not my purpose, however, to speak especially at this time of the doctrine of the Sacrament of the Holy Communion or of the benefits which come to those who receive it according to Christ's ordinance. I wish rather, having already called to your remembrance the act of institution and the meaning of its several parts, to speak of the form of

---

* See Johnson's *Unbloody Sacrifice*, i. 60, sqq. (ed. 1714).

† εὐλογήσας, of the bread (St. Matthew, St. Mark); εὐχαριστήσας, of the bread (St. Luke, St. Paul), and of the cup (St. Matthew, St. Mark).

‡ ἀνάμνησις.

---

service in which, following the Lord's command, our Church celebrates the memorial of His death. And I think it specially proper that I should do this to-day, as it is almost exactly a hundred years ago that our forefathers in Connecticut received from their first bishop a Communion-office which furnished the Prayer of Consecration to our American Prayer-Book.

The service of the Holy Communion, looking back to our Lord's words and deeds in the upper room, from which it takes its example and its authority, contains in its most solemn and essential portion three distinct things, corresponding to the successive parts of the original institution. The bishop or the priest takes bread and wine, already set before God as an offering of the fruits of the earth and representing the first-fruits, and presents them to God as a memorial of the body broken and the blood poured out when atonement was made for sins by Christ's death, thus offering the unbloody sacrifice of the Christian Church, a memorial of the one only sacrifice that could take away sin. He next blesses them by invoking upon them the blessing of God, that they may be the means of communicating to those who receive them the benefits of the sacrifice and the death of Christ; and the form of this blessing has been from the beginning a prayer that the Holy Ghost may make the bread and the wine to faithful receivers the body and the blood of Christ.* Then the consecrated elements are distributed to the communicants and reverently eaten and drunk by them, in faith that their souls are thus made partakers of Christ, and with thanksgiving.

Thus doing, thus believing, thus teaching, the Apostles and those who have succeeded them, and with them the whole Church, have showed forth the Lord's death; and thus it shall be showed forth till He come. A memorial of the sacrifice of Christ made by the offering of bread and wine, a blessing of the elements by the invocation of the Holy Spirit,

---

* On the form of the Invocation, see Bishop Dowden's (of Edinburgh) *Historical Account of the Scottish Communion Office*, pp. 16, sqq. and Appendix B. The book is invaluable to the student of our Liturgy.

---

and an eating and drinking of the gifts and creatures thus consecrated — these, and in this order, have been the essential parts of the service wherever the practice of the ancient Church has been retained. There is some reason for thinking that at the very first the words of the Lord at instituting this Sacrament, which have been preserved by the Apostles and Evangelists, were not repeated until at the time of the distribution of the elements the bishop or priest said: "The Body of Christ," "The Blood of Christ";* but from a very early time the whole account of the institution has been solemnly rehearsed before God at the beginning of the prayer of consecration, as at once a sufficient warrant for the words and acts

which are to follow and as a designation of the bread and the wine of the first-fruits to the sacred purpose of a memorial of the sacrifice of Christ. Thus, prefacing this most solemn act by words of instruction, of profession of faith, of repentance and absolution, and of lofty praise, and following it by thanksgiving and benediction, the Church has continued her worship and her life, has presented herself before the heavenly Father, and has received from Him His greatest blessing.

This order of the essential parts of the eucharistic service, in which, after the repetition of the words of institution, an oblation is made before God, and then follows the invocation of the Holy Ghost, after which the consecrated elements are eaten and drunk, has been the rule of the Church's worship from the beginning.† It has never ceased to be the type of the worship of the great Church of the East; and it was for a considerable time followed by all the branches of the Church in the West as well.

After a while, however, the liturgy of the Church of Rome, like almost everything else which testified to her faith or her practice, became confused and lost its ancient form. And when, at the time of the Reformation in England, the service

* See Mr. Ffoulkes's *Primitive Consecration of the Eucharistic Oblation,* pp. 150, sqq.

† It must suffice to refer to Brett's *Collection of Liturgies,* and to Hammond's *Liturgies Eastern and Western,* especially chapter ii. of the *Introduction* to the latter.

of the Holy Communion was put into English, though in most noble and impressive words, it followed an order which was Roman and not primitive, praying for the blessing of the Holy Spirit not only before the words of Christ were rehearsed to set them apart for holy uses but also before the oblation by which they were made a memorial of Christ's sacrifice. After three years, partly (no doubt) owing to other influences, but partly (as it seems to me) because those who were revising the Prayer-Book saw that the form was defective in arrangement, the English prayer of consecration was put into the form in which it has now been used for nearly 335 years. It is, to say the least, a most unfortunate form, for it contains no words of oblation and no explicit invocation of the Holy Spirit. It is a cause of wonder that so learned and devout a Church has been satisfied to use through all these years so imperfect a service in her highest act of worship and to separate herself to such an extent from that which has the sanction of the best and purest days of undivided Christendom.

That we, brethren, have used here in Connecticut for a century, and throughout our land for nearly as many years, a liturgy which, in the essential points of which I have been speaking, reproduces and joins us to the worship of the very earliest days, we owe thanks, under God, to our first bishop. Before he was ordained to the diaconate and the priesthood, he had spent a little time in Edinburgh in the study of medicine;* and thirty-two years after, when he found that it was in vain for him to ask for the episcopate at the hands of the English bishops, he had gone to Scotland again to be consecrated Bishop of Connecticut. The weakened remnant of the ancient Church of Scotland, suffering from political disabilities and religious persecution and for the time (so far as man could do it) utterly cut off from the Church of England, had, before his second visit, adopted a Communion-office based upon that of the primitive and undivided Church.† Its

* He went abroad prepared for the ministry and seeking ordination; and

he stayed in Edinburgh only until his twenty-fourth birthday, that he might be ordained to the priesthood and return home at once.

† See its history in Bishop Dowden's *Historical Account.*

learned and devout scholars (for such there were, in spite of poverty and distress) shared with the learned and devout men in England who were debarred from active service in the English Church because they could not conscientiously take the oath of allegiance to William and Mary, a strong desire to study and to follow the customs of the primitive Church, especially in its liturgies; and there had been used in the small congregations of the English non-jurors since about the year 1700, and in the proscribed assemblies of the Scottish episcopalians since 1755, a liturgy containing in its prayer of consecration, after the Lord's words of institution, an oblation of the elements to God and an invocation of the Holy Spirit to bless and sanctify them; * and nowhere else in Western Christendom was such a liturgy employed. In the "Concordate" which Bishop Seabury made with his consecrators, he promised "to take a serious view of the Communion-office recommended by them, and, if found agreeable to the genuine standards of antiquity, to give his sanction to it, and by gentle methods of argument and persuasion to endeavor, as they have done, to introduce it by degrees into practice, without the compulsion of authority on the one side or the prejudice of former custom on the other."†

When Bishop Seabury met his clergy at Middletown in August, 1785, a committee was appointed to act with the bishop in proposing such changes in the Prayer-Book as should be thought needful. A few alterations, made necessary by the change of civil government, were agreed upon and published at once; others which were proposed were reserved for a meeting of the Convocation to be held at New Haven in September. But, to use the bishop's own words, "the Church people in Connecticut were much alarmed at the thought of any considerable alterations being made in the Prayer-Book"; ‡ and nothing was done at that time. And when the convention representing the Church in the States

* *Ibid.*

† Dr. Beardsley's *Life of Bishop Seabury,* p. 152.

‡ *Documentary History of the Church in Connecticut,* ii. 287.

to the south of New England, in none of which was there as yet a bishop, meeting in September and October, 1785, adopted an ecclesiastical constitution on principles different from those held by Connecticut Churchmen and prepared the book known as the "Proposed Book," * having many variations — some of them serious ones — from the Prayer-Book of the English Church, the clergy and with them the people of this diocese were unwilling to follow their example. Matters remained as they were; and when the clergy met with their bishop in Convocation at Derby, September 22, 1786, he delivered his second charge, in which, besides giving wise counsel, he spoke in strong but temperate language of the work of the southern convention, and in particular criticized its proceeding to such important acts as it had undertaken before there were any bishops to preside over and to guide its deliberations. At the same time, not (as it would appear) without the assent of his clergy,† he set forth and "recommended

* The compilers of the Proposed Book, as is evident from their preface, thought that they were not only acting on the lines of the attempted revision of the English Prayer-Book in 1689, but also actually adopting many of

the alterations then proposed. An acquaintance with this revision seems also to be assumed in the preface to our present Prayer-Book. But a comparison of the statements, as to the changes of 1689, given in a note to the preface of the Proposed Book, with the printed copy of what was actually prepared in that year, shows that these statements "are partly without foundation, partly very incorrect and misleading, and in only a few points at all trustworthy." In fact, the editors of the Proposed Book relied on Drs. Nicholls and Calamy, who wrote from memory or hearsay and knew very little of value about the details of the matter. The manuscript report of 1689 was lost from 1727 (at least) to 1854. It is quite impossible that (as suggested in the *Church Review*, September, 1886, p. 217) a copy of it should have been in the hands of our revisers in 1786 or 1789. The whole matter was discussed at length in the *Churchman* newspaper, December 20, 1873.

† Bishop Seabury was not, as is sometimes insinuated or charged, in the habit of acting without the "advice and consent" of his clergy. The statement has been lately repeated in the press that he claimed for himself the right of conferring degrees in divinity. In fact, the Connecticut "College of Doctors of Divinity" was established by a vote of the Convocation of the bishop and clergy, October 2, 1790, as "the Bishop's Council, to be consulted on any emergency that may arise"; and it was voted in 1791 that the installment of new doctors — none were ever appointed except the first four — should be by diploma from the College of Doctors. Besides, a careful examination of the manuscript records of Convocation and the printed journals of Convention shows that the members of the "College" were not, as a rule, styled "Doctor" till after they had received the degree from some college chartered by the legislature and authorized to confer degrees.

---

to the Episcopal Congregations in Connecticut" a Communion-office almost identical with that which was in use in Scotland. It was generally adopted in this diocese, and the clergy were strongly attached to it; some of them were still using it when Bishop Brownell was consecrated in 1819. And, what is much more important, when the first really General Convention met in 1789, and our Prayer-Book was put into its present shape, instead of the defective prayer of consecration from the English Book, that from Bishop Seabury's office was taken, with a single alteration, which only served to make its meaning more clear.* Bishop White, the only other member of the House of Bishops who was present, assented to it willingly; and in the other house we are told that when it had been read impressively by the President it "was admitted without opposition, and in silence if not in reverence." † And the Communion-office thus adopted has been thankfully used throughout our Church ever since.‡

---

*See Bishop Dowden, *loco citato*, pp. 16, sqq.

† See *Historical Sketch and Notes*, appended to reprint of *Bishop Seabury's Communion-Office*, pp. 41, sqq.

‡ The statement of the bishop of Ohio (Convention Address, 1886) that "the slight alterations made in our liturgy to conform to the Scotch rite became a subject of discussion and added to the difficulty in the way of the subsequent transmission of English Orders," is certainly based on a misapprehension. For the alterations were made October 14, 1789, and Bishops White and Provoost had been consecrated more than two years and a half before, February 4, 1787; and it was never heard that there was any discussion or objection in regard to the consecration of Bishop Madison in September, 1790.

Bishop Seabury's Office (following the Scottish) differs from that in our Prayer-Book in several particulars, as to two of which a word may be added here. (1) In the former the Prayer for the Church follows immediately on the Prayer of Consecration. The position of this prayer — "the Great Intercession" — is different in each of the five families of ancient liturgies, as will be seen by referring to Hammond's *Liturgies*, pp. xx., sqq. The place which it holds in our office, immediately after the Offertory, shows an historical connection with the Gallican liturgy and, through this, with the Ephesine — a connection which should be retained and highly valued. (2) In Bishop Seabury's office the Confession and Absolution with the Comfortable Words are placed immediately before the administration. But certainly the preparation of the communicants should precede the great act of worship in oblation and invocation, which is the act of the

---

whole Church and not of the priest as an individual.

The idea that the Prayer of Consecration ends with the Words of Institution, not including either the Oblation or the Invocation, seems to have met with acceptance in some quarters where this would hardly be expected. The joint committee of the General Convention appointed in 1868 "to examine the stereotype plates of the standard edition of the Prayer-Book . . . and to correct manifestly typographical errors thereof," reported in 1871, among the "alterations" which they had made, that "pronouns referring to our Blessed Lord in some special cases have been printed with capitals, *e. g.* . . . in the Prayer of Consecration." (Journal, 1871, pp. 533, sqq.) But this capitalization of pronouns (including, by the way, those relating to God the Father as well as God the Son) was carried in the corrected Standard Book only through the Words of Institution. Precisely the same thing has been done in the "Book Annexed," both as reported to the Convention of 1883 and as adopted by it. In fact, if we may judge by the printing, it would appear from each of these three editions that the Oblation and the Invocation were less important or less solemn parts of the service than the Prayer of Humble Access; for in this latter the pronouns are capitalized.

So it is that, under God, we acknowledge our obligations to our first bishop for giving to us in Connecticut a hundred years ago, and to the whole Church in this land three years later, a form of words for the highest act of our worship which recalls and represents that which our Lord said and did in the upper room "the same night in which He was betrayed," which conforms our service to that offered by the undivided Church in ancient days and by the great Church of the East in all the centuries of its history, which is confessed by all liturgical scholars to contain the essence of that which should be found in such a service, and which enables us to "show the Lord's death" in the way in which he commanded "till He come." For what has thus been done for our spiritual ancestors, for ourselves, and for those who shall come after us, we may well thank God. This liturgy is for us a bulwark of the faith; it is our shield against false teaching and unseemly controversies in regard to the sacrament of love; it furnishes a basis of unity which, let us hope and pray, in days that are not far off shall do something to knit together the severed parts of Christendom "in truth, unity, and concord."

I think, my brethren, that I can not better close this sermon than with the wise and instructive words in which, a century ago this last week, Bishop Seabury spoke to his clergy with reference to the Holy Communion. Following his teaching, and using his words of oblation and of blessing, both of which he brought to us as a part of our heritage in the Catholic Church, we shall, I believe, hold fast to the truth of revelation and offer acceptable worship and prayer, in the name of Jesus Christ, to God our heavenly Father.

"Some writers on this subject," said the Bishop,* "under the idea of making it plain to ordinary capacities, have, I fear, banished all spiritual meaning, by discarding all mystery from it, making it a mere empty remembrance of Christ's death. Others have considered it as an arbitrary command and an instance of God's sovereignty over us, requiring our obedience for wrath's sake. Others represent it simply as the renewal of our Christian covenant, expecting no particular benefits from it. The primitive Christians had very different sentiments from these concerning the Holy Communion, and so I suppose our Church has also. They considered it not as the renewal of the Christian covenant, but a privilege to which the Christian covenant, into which we had been admitted by Baptism and which had been ratified in Confirmation, entitled us. Nor [did they consider it]

as an arbitrary command of God, to show His sovereign authority over us; nor as a bare remembrance of Christ's death; but as the appointed means of keeping up that spiritual life which we received in our new birth, and of continuing that interest in the benefits and blessings of Christ's passion and death which was made over to us when we became members of His mystical body. They called and esteemed it to be the Christian sacrifice, commemorative of

Second Charge, pp. 17–19. See also his *Discourses*, Vol. i., No. vi.

the great sacrifice of atonement which Christ had made for the sins of the whole world; wherein, under the symbols of bread and the cup, the body and blood of Christ which He offered up and which were broken and shed on the Cross are figured forth; and being presented to God our heavenly Father by His priest here on earth, the merits of Christ for the remission of sins are pleaded by him and, we trust, by our great High Priest Himself in heaven; and being sanctified by prayer, thanksgiving, the words of institution, and the invocation of the Holy Spirit, are divided among the communicants as a feast upon the sacrifice. And they did believe that all who worthily partook of the consecrated elements did really and truly, though mystically and spiritually, partake of the Body and Blood of Christ. Our Church evidently teaches the same thing in her Catechism, defining 'the inward part or thing signified' by the bread and wine in the Holy Communion to be 'the Body and Blood of Christ, which are verily and indeed taken and received by the faithful in the Lord's Supper.' This doctrine seems to be founded on what our Saviour said in the sixth chapter of St. John's Gospel, concerning eating His flesh and drinking His blood, which, when compared with the institution of the blessed Eucharist as recorded by the Evangelists, will sufficiently justify the Church in her opinion and judgment. We have therefore a right to believe and say that in the Holy Communion the faithful receiver does, in a mystical and spiritual manner, eat and drink the body and blood of Christ represented by the consecrated bread and wine, and does thereby partake in the atonement made by the passion and death of Christ, having remission through Him of all past sins and eternal life assured to him."

ΤΩΙ ΠΑΝΤΟΚΡΑΤΟΡΙ ΠΑΝΤΕΛΕΗΜΟΝΙ Η ΔΟΞΑ.

The Story
of a
Hill-top Parish

[23]

St. Peter's, Plymouth, Conn.

This story of St. Peter's Church, Plymouth, Litchfield County, Connecticut, was prepared as part of a sermon (from Psalm xxxvi. 7–10) preached on the hundredth anniversary of the consecration of the present Church edifice, November 2, 1897. It was a pleasing coincidence, if the word may be rightly used, that this consecration was among the first official acts of the second Bishop of Connecticut—none is recorded as preceding it except the consecration of St. John's Church, Waterbury, a day earlier—and that among the first official acts of the Bishop who stands third after him was this service of commemoration and thanksgiving.

There is a sameness in the origin and the growth of parishes, even as there is a sameness in the beginning and the continuance of human lives. And still more, we find history repeating itself in the parishes of a neighborhood or of a commonwealth, as we find the same features and the same mental characteristics repeating themselves in the members of a family. Here in Connecticut we read over and over again, as we trace out the history of the Church in the years before the Revolution, how thoughtful people were led by the study of Holy Scripture and ancient authors to acknowledge the claims of the Church of England in matters of doctrine, of organization, and of worship; how young men of high character and good learning and noble zeal crossed the ocean that they might be ordained by a Bishop—forty-three went from this colony in the fifty-two years between 1722 and 1774; how they gave full proof of their ministry here, and how the people profited by their instructions, assisted them in their labors, and followed the good example of their lives. And yet, as each individual has his peculiarities of face and of character—his individuality, as we call it—so it is in regard to our parishes; each has its own history, its own experience, its own lessons; each illustrates some special ordering of God's providence, and may confess some special privilege and duty; each, as a member in a body, has its own work to do for itself and for the whole, its own vocation and ministry. Instead of undertaking anything like a complete history of this ancient parish, my purpose is to recall some of the circumstances in the origin and the life of the Church in this place which give it its individuality.

First, I think that there is no other town in Connecticut in which the organization of the "professors of the Church of England," as they were called, followed so closely upon the settlement of the place and its organization as a separate community. For this was not the first building in which the Churchmen of what is now Plymouth met for the worship of God. In 1737 the people of the north part of Waterbury, including the present Watertown and Plymouth, settlers from different parts of the colony, were granted "winter privileges" and released from parish taxes for three months of the year, that they might maintain "the dispensing of the Word" in a place accessible. Soon they petitioned the General Assembly of the colony to make them a separate ecclesiastical society, representing that to reach the only meeting-house in the town they had to drive seven miles or more, cross the river nine times, and take down bars or open gates at ten different places. In response to this and a similar petition, Westbury society was constituted in 1738, and another society under the name

ST. PETER'S CHURCH, PLYMOUTH, CONN.

of Northbury (now Plymouth) was set off from it in the following year. A plain building for public uses had already been erected by the subscriptions of nineteen people known as the "proprietors," on a spot which is now included in the park at Thomaston, not far from Trinity Church. There the new ecclesiastical society, and presumably the Congregational Church also, was organized, and in May, 1740, Mr. Samuel Todd was called and ordained pastor. Almost immediately a controversy arose as to the location of the meeting-house which was to be built; and the society having decided to erect it on the east side of the river, the proprietors of the building which they had been using on the other side voted, by eleven to seven, that the society might no longer use their house; and thereupon the majority, we are informed, organized an Episcopal society, under the care of the Rev. Theophilus Morris, an English clergyman and missionary of the Society for the Propagation of the Gospel. It ought to be added that tradition assures us that the majority of the proprietors made up to the minority their pecuniary loss, contributing to the cost of building a Congregational meeting-house a sum equal to the interest which those whom they had ejected had had in the old building.

So much for the remarkably early date of the organization of this congregation of Churchmen. But the causes of the organization are quite as remarkable. If I read the history aright, the question as to location of the meeting-house was not so much a cause as an occasion for it. Every reader of our early history knows the bitterness and the continuance of quarrels as to the places where public buildings should be erected; and very likely some people preferred to be Episcopalians on the west side of the Naugatuck rather than to continue conformity to the "Standing Order" and be obliged to cross the river and climb the hill, that they might attend the preaching of the Word. But there were causes at work which made this a readily accepted occasion for the breach. Some of the settlers of Northbury had come from North Haven, where there was already a church; and in one family in the community there was a copy of the Prayer Book. Now the Book of Common Prayer, as Bishop Williams has said, is the first and the best missionary that the Church of England had in Connecticut; and while we cannot trace to this copy in Plymouth as great and as direct results as we can trace to Samuel Smithson's copy, which Samuel Johnson read and studied in Guilford,* yet I cannot doubt that it had a great deal to do with the determination of those eleven men to conform, with their families, to the Church of England. We are told that two other families were in the habit of meeting with the family which owned the Prayer Book for the quiet use of its services; and it may be added, anticipating what will presently be said as to the missionary influence of this parish, that tradition has it that the same Prayer Book was afterwards taken to Pennsylvania and was the occasion of starting a parish there.

Then besides, the year 1740 was a time of great excitement—and much of it very irrational excitement—in the religious world of this part of the country. It was the time of the "Great Awakening," of the wild preaching of George Whitefield and the still wilder preaching and behavior of James Davenport, and of all that was included under the not very

*See Dr. Andrews's note in Journal of Diocese of Connecticut, 1864.

appropriate name of "enthusiasm." Sober-minded religious people were shocked at what was said and done; nervous people were thrown into great distress; and whole communities seemed to be beside themselves. The simple and devout teaching of the Church came to many at this time as a voice from heaven, recalling them to right ideas of God, of themselves, of duty, and of the way of salvation. And that this weighed with those who became Churchmen in Plymouth in 1740 or soon after, we know from a letter which they addressed in 1744 to the Venerable Society in England. "We were," said they, "prejudiced strongly against the Church of England from our cradles, until we had the advantage of books from your reverend missionaries and others; and Mr. Whitefield passing through this land, and his followers and imitators, brought in a flood of confusion amongst us; whereupon we fled to the Church of England for safety, and are daily more and more satisfied we are safe, provided the purity of our hearts and lives be conformable to her excellent doctrines." Thus we have here, not the strengthening of a Church congregation by reason of the violent words and conduct of the "enthusiasts," but actually the establishment of a parish (as we should call it) due in large part to this very cause. It was the conviction of earnest but quiet folk that they needed for their souls' welfare just the kind of earnest and quiet teaching that they found in the Book of Common Prayer and the principles of worship which were there enshrined. Thus the origin of this parish was in every way remarkable. Men and women came to it as to a well of life, that in the light which it showed they might see light; and with the doctrine and worship and teaching of the historic Church, with the plenteousness of God's house, they were satisfied; and God gave them to drink of His pleasures, of spiritual help and comfort and joy, as out of the river.*

Before the Revolution, three men of Connecticut birth, all worthy of honor and still honored among us, included this parish among their missionary cures: Richard Mansfield, the Nestor of our clergy, for seventy-two years rector of Derby, but officiating in many places in the western part of the colony; James Scovill, who, from his home in Waterbury, visited a wide neighborhood and earned a name of praise in all the churches; and James Nichols, the last Connecticut man to be ordained in England, whose work was cut short by the troubles of the times. "The Lord wrought glory by them, through His great power from the beginning. They were honored in their generations, and were the glory of their times. The people will tell of their wisdom, and the congregation will show forth their praise." *See the words of the text.

Before the close of the Revolutionary war the Church in all parts of Connecticut had been much weakened. The political changes had borne especially hard on those who felt that they owed some allegiance to the Church or the realm of England. Yet neither clergy nor people lost courage, though at last some felt obliged to avail themselves of the opportunity that was given them to withdraw to the provinces which still remained under the British crown. In March, 1783, it being understood that the war was practically at an end, though the independence of the States was not formally acknowledged as yet, ten of the fourteen clergymen of Connecticut met at Woodbury and elected a bishop, bidding him cross the ocean and ask for consecration at the hands of English or Scottish bishops. Even while Churchmen were waiting for his return—for he was not consecrated till No-

vember, 1784, and did not reach Connecticut on his return till the summer of 1785—the Church's work was bravely continued. Here a formal organization of the parish was made, and fifty-seven legal voters, adherents of the Episcopal Church, became members of the ecclesiastical society under the toleration act of the General Assembly. There had been, indeed, remarkable growth in the forty-four years which had

ST. MATTHEW'S CHURCH, EAST PLYMOUTH, CONN.

passed since eleven proprietors of the "Church house" declared for the sober ways of Episcopacy. The parish was not able to secure a settled minister at once; but services were maintained regularly and (it would appear) attended diligently. Occasionally some good priest, like Philo Shelton or Tillotson Bronson, came to minister the Word and Sacraments, and in 1788 the Rev. Chauncey Prindle began his ministry of eighteen years.

During this time St. Peter's Church, Plymouth, began to be, in a sense in which the words can be used of very few other country parishes, a mother of Churches. In 1787, the parish of St. Matthew's, East Plymouth, was organized under the name of the Second Episcopal Church in Northbury, taking a Church building which had been erected some two years before by residents of Plymouth and Harwinton, and with this was presently merged the former parish of New Cambridge, now Bristol; and in 1793, Trinity Church, Northfield, within the limits of the town of Litchfield, but taking its congregation chiefly from the Plymouth Church, was also organized. The organization was in each case due to a desire for greater convenience in attending upon divine worship; but it must have been a serious matter for the old parish to lose so many parishioners and communicants. It was also in Mr. Prindle's rectorship that, after much discussion as to the relative importance of hill and hollow, and much difference of opinion as to the best way of raising funds, the present edifice was erected, some little distance to the east of the building which had been so long used, and in another village. The first service held in it was on the 24th day of November, 1796, and on the 2d day of November in the following year it was consecrated by Bishop Jarvis; the sermon at the consecration was preached by the Rev. Philo Shelton, ordained deacon by Bishop Seabury at the first ordination which he held, and at the same time sixty persons were confirmed.

It may be noted here that in 1869, when the village of Thomaston was rapidly growing, but six years before the town of Thomaston was incorporated, a new parish was formed there under the name of Trinity Church; and thus a place in the neighborhood of the site of the old Plymouth Church has now been occupied, for nearly thirty years, by a building which

in some sense replaces it and has taken up a like work in that thriving community.

Soon after 1797, several of the families of the parish, in company (it may be assumed) with other inhabitants of the town, migrated to the part of New York then known as the Whitestown territory. And so it is that, as two parishes in the neighborhood were founded from this parish before the last century closed, and another some seventy years later, we must also give credit to it as the mother of St. Paul's Church at Paris in Oneida County, New York. Nor was this, apparently, the first migration in Mr. Prindle's time from these parts to what was then called the West. In 1795 he went to hold a farewell service, with the baptism of children, within the limits of Waterbury, but apparently for some of his own parishioners, before they should remove to their new homes; and we are told that a heavy rain had made the river too deep to be forded and had carried away the boat which was kept for the convenience of travellers, so that the faithful pastor, unwilling to disappoint his people, swam the swollen stream and thus was able to meet them at the time appointed. Thus he ministered, as did indeed so many of the faithful clergy of those dark days, when it was in many ways harder for them to do their duty than it is for us to do like duty now, as one of his successors says, "an example of faith and charity and patience to his people for many years." He resigned his rectorship in 1806, in order that St. Peter's and St. Matthew's Churches might be united in one cure. This was not formally done, I believe, until in 1810, when the diocesan convention met here, the Rev. Roger Searle was instituted rector of the two parishes; and St. Peter's began to have regular services for two-thirds of the time. I have before me, as I write, a part of Mr. Searle's diary of official acts, which show constant labor and faithful attendance on the needs of his people.*

*It is well-known that the Biblical name "Esther" was commonly pronounced in New England in the same way as the festival "Easter"; but this diary is the only place where I have seen the name of the festival written "Esther Sunday".

It ends in 1817; and at the last service of the Holy Communion which he held in St. Peter's and also at the last which he held in St. Matthew's, he enters "Gave Communion to 75," the numbers being the same in the two Churches. In the early part of this year, he was absent for four months, "by consent," as he puts it. The Western fever, which a former rector, Mr. Watson, calls "the mania for emigration," had seized the place, and the good pastor did not escape. The Western Reserve in Ohio, then known as New Connecticut, was opening for settlement, and many people hereabouts were minded to try the hazard of new fortunes there. Mr. Searle looked over the ground, and then returned to Plymouth, but soon made preparations for permanent removal. The story of his journey and his entrance upon what may fairly be called missionary work has been recently told from a contemporary record. He organized the Church in Ashtabula and several other places of New Connecticut, having with him, it is believed, some of his old parishioners; and his name, with which should be joined that of his old parish in Plymouth, will be always held in thankful remembrance.*

St. Peter's Church, Ashtabula, preserves the name of this church; and St. Matthew's Church, East Plymouth (Ohio), continued the name of the other parish as well as of its church. Another settlement, in part at least from this region—though I cannot tell at what date—settled the town of

94

Cambridge in Illinois, which was most probably named from our New Cambridge, now Bristol; and there also is a St. Matthew's Church.

I am especially glad to speak of this, because we are constantly saying that Churchmen going from our smaller country towns, where there has been little increase in population or in

* See Dr. Seymour's address at the Centenary of the Consecration of Bishop Jarvis.

the number of communicants, have yet done much to establish or build up the Church in other parts of the country; yet we have not always instances at hand in proof of our assertion. St. Peter's, Plymouth, gives us a remarkable example, how a country parish in Connecticut has sent its sons, first to establish a Church colony in Western New York, and then to be instrumental in establishing more than one such colony

ST. MATTHEW'S CHURCH, EAST PLYMOUTH, OHIO.

in Ohio and at least one in Indiana—each in its time the "Far West"; and it proves the value of the labor and the permanence of the influence which were here done and exerted. Doubtless many a churchly and religious influence in remote parts of our land, could it but be traced, would lead back to this ancient parish and to this very building. The plenteousness of grace from this house of God, the sacred pleasures which God has here given His people, have been known far beyond the sight of its walls or the sound of its bell; "How excellent is Thy mercy, O God!"

It is not my purpose to enter in any detail into the later history of this parish. The Rev. Rodney Rossiter was rector from 1819 to 1829, in which time a rectory was built; and to him succeeded after an interval, the Rev. Dr. Daniel Burhans from 1831 to 1836, leaving here at the age of 76, to continue his ministrations elsewhere for fifteen years and to die, a patriarch second only to Dr. Mansfield, in his ninety-first year. His successor, the Rev. William Watson, was instituted in October, 1837. Six years later he preached an historical sermon, to which I gratefully acknowledge that I am indebted for many of the facts which I have been recounting this afternoon; and he then made the interesting statement that during the century which had elapsed since the founding of the parish, divine services had been omitted on but two Sundays, one before and one after 1806; I am informed that since Dr. Watson wrote, there has been absolutely no omission of a Sunday service within these walls. The fact speaks volumes for fidelity to the Church's principles and the Church's ways.

Mr. Watson's rectorship brings the history of the parish to the year 1850, which is little less than a half century ago. Since that time the parish has been served by a succession of men, whose rectorships I fear have sometimes been too short

for them to do all that they were qualified to do for it, and too short for the people to show how they were minded to help them and work with them. Yet in the great day, when they are called to give their account, we may well hope that each one will have some joy from his ministry here, and that among those who are then presented perfect in Christ Jesus there will be some whose conscious Christian life was begun or furthered or brought to its earthly end under the guidance of each.

So we have closed the record of a century of worship and instruction and Christian nurture in this holy place, following upon more than half a century of the self-same worship and instruction in the house where first the Church of Northbury assembled. I have but traced the outline of the history, with the special intention of speaking about those matters which, in its inception and its progress, have made this parish somewhat different from others. But at least, as we fill in even so imperfect an outline with the thought of the round of holy services in this place, Sunday and week-day worship, baptisms and confirmations and holy communions, marriages and burials, the preaching of the Word and the teaching it to children, and of the influences for righteousness and holiness which have gone forth from hence, do we not see how the words of the psalmist have had their fulfilment here? Here the children of men have come in faith and trust; here they have found that satisfying plenteousness which can be found only in God's house, while He has given them, as well in sorrow as in joy, to drink of the river of His pleasures; here they have known by blessed experience that with Him is the well of life, and have learned in His light to see light. And as we turn to look forward from this thought of the past, our prayer for ourselves, and for all who shall worship here, and for all the Church of God shall be: "O continue forth Thy loving kindness unto them that know thee, and Thy righteousness unto them that are true of heart."

A HUMBLE MASTER

A SERMON

IN MEMORY OF

THE RT. REV. JOHN WILLIAMS D. D. LL.D.

FOURTH BISHOP OF CONNECTICUT

[24] Ἡγούμενόν σε κατέστησαν; μὴ ἐπαίρου · γίνου ἐν αὐτοῖς ὡς εἷς ἐξ αὐτῶν.

"If thou be made the master, lift not thyself up, but be among them as one of the rest."—ECCLESIASTICUS XXXII. I.

More than forty-seven years ago, the newly consecrated Assistant Bishop of Connecticut, preparing to make record of his consecration and to begin the official journal of his episcopate, wrote upon the first page of the volume these words of the wise son of Sirach. In the strict sense, as a

glance at the passage shows, they were intended as an "instruction of manners" for the ruler of a feast; but in principle they may be applied to any one set in authority, and especially to any one set in authority which is entirely or largely moral. The youthful Bishop took them for a precept of life; and to-day we can testify to the faithfulness with which he followed that precept, and to the blessing which he thereby brought to himself and to those over whom he was set, and to whom for that very reason he ministered. Though made the master, he did not lift himself up, but was among us as one of the rest.*

It is for this reason among others, my brethren, that I would fain have declined the invitation, so courteously conveyed to me through your Rector, that I should attempt to put into words some things which might serve as a memorial of the

* It may be noted that the text of the sermon preached at his consecration by Bishop George Burgess was St. Luke xxii. 26, 27.

fourth Bishop of Connecticut. For many reasons which I need not mention, and for some which I cannot mention, the task is a hard one; it would not be easy to do it anywhere in this Diocese; it is far from easy to do it here. We all knew him, and he was to us all, not merely officially but really, a reverend Father in God; and for the very reason that he did not lift himself up but was among us as one of ourselves, he had a place in our affections and seemed a member of many a household. I cannot tell you, in whose sight or in the sight of whose fathers he went out and came in for well nigh half a century, much that you do not know already; I cannot hope even to touch the chord of memory which is waiting to give its echo in your hearts; I can but ask you to let me pay such a tribute as I can, not for fear that you will forget, but that it may not seem that I was unwilling in this place and at this bidding to do what I could.

"*If thou be made the master.*" Our late Bishop was always, as we or our fathers knew him, the master; and that in the two-fold sense of the guide and ruler and the teacher. And I venture to think that we shall fail to understand both his character and his work if we do not remember this. The only son of a father who was almost past middle life when he was born, and of a mother who was always proud of her boy; graduated from college with high reputation for scholarship at a very early age; trained as a favorite pupil by one of the greatest theologians whom this Church or this country has produced, your former Rector; the friend of eminent scholars and influential men both here and abroad before he was of age to be ordained to the Priesthood; elected President of a college, and that his *alma mater*, before he was thirty-one years old; chosen by a practically unanimous ballot, three years later, to be in name the Assistant Bishop and in responsibility and labor the Bishop of the oldest Diocese in the land; called upon, in the course of another year, to take charge of many of the official duties of the Presiding Bishop; and during his whole episcopate the head and administrator of a school of divinity, in which for a long time he himself gave a large part of the

instruction; his intellectual endowments from the first, and the ordering of his life until the last, made him a master of men. And a wonderful aptitude for teaching — power of acquiring knowledge, accuracy of memory, precision in recalling, readiness in imparting, clearness in statement, aptness in fastening it in another's mind, "as nails are fastened in"* and clinched—made him in another but not a different sense a master of men.

* See Ecclesiastes xii. 11.

Bear me witness, beloved; did this intellectual or official preëminence, the gift of God recognized willingly by men, lift him up? The special temptations of those who are set in authority, and in particular of those from whose decision there is either no appeal at all or no ready appeal, the special temptations of rulers and of teachers, are to arrogance and to tyranny. Was he an arrogant man? He was sure of what he knew; he did not revise his arguments or reconsider his position whenever he heard that some one had imagined or stated an objection to the one or the other; he was impatient of false statements or false logic; but he was, as became a true scholar and especially a scholar in things divine, a modest man. In fact his modesty, his lack of arrogance and self-assertion, was so real and so natural (which means so supernatural) that we rarely noticed it and did not know how much it meant. In matters intellectual he listened to those who brought forth out of their treasures things new as well as things old, and he learned from Neale and Mozley and Browne and Moberly and Lightfoot and Salmon and Mason as well as from Laud and Andrewes and Bull and Walton and Hooker and Pearson; and what he thus learned showed itself in modifications of the form, if not the substance, of his teaching. In matters practical he did not pertinaciously stand by his own judgment; and when he was reproved, for reproved he sometimes was, he was willing to yield—and it may be too easily—to the reproof. If fault there was, it was not on the side of arrogance, though the whole experience of his life had made him a master and put him in a position from which he could not be dislodged. And was he cruel, harsh in his words, sarcastic with those who did not understand what he said, turning authority into tyranny? Perhaps one would not choose out, as his specially distinguishing trait of character, the gentleness and mildness of wisdom which so marked his predecessor and senior in the Diocese; but though other qualities seem to stand preëminent above them, these too had their place and should now be thought of all the more because those others did in part hide them from our sight. Ask those who were his pupils, beginning with no technical knowledge of the great science of which he was a doctor; who did not indeed sit at his feet, because here also he was "among them as one of the rest," but who listened to his words; ask them as to the way in which he brought them to the knowledge of the most momentous truths, and helped them to know and to apprehend them. Ask his clergy, who served not him, but with him for the Gospel,* and with whose faults and failures—often remediable faults and unnecessary failures—he was very patient; ask the people who brought to him puzzling questions

and wished him to disentangle complications which they themselves had made and could not unmake. And I think that all will agree that he was singularly free from those defects to which one is specially exposed who has not been obliged to learn painfully what is for most of us the hardest of all lessons, our duty towards our equals.

* As Timothy with St. Paul: ὡς πατρὶ τέκνον σὺν ἐμοὶ ἐδούλευσεν εἰς τὸ εὐαγγέλιον.—Phil. ii. 22.

"*Be thou among them as one of the rest.*" It is obedience to this precept which, more than any other one thing (God's special grace alone excepted), makes the true teacher. We read with delight of the schools of sacred learning in the ancient Church of the English, schools of which we are reminded by the names of Benedict Biscop and Bede; their story has for English-speaking people all the charm of "the dawn of" their "history's morning"; and especially attractive for us, as it must have been especially attractive and helpful then, is the simplicity of the common life, teacher and scholar working and praying and living together in a true *collegium*. There was a tradition of this kind in the college of which our Bishop was President; in fact the desire of this was shown in the petition for the foundation of that college; and I am sure that the words in which he spoke of the days of the first President, whose assistant in the episcopate he became, may be applied to his own. "Its gentle rule, its unvarying patience, its considerate kindness, its generous allowance for thoughtlessness so long as thoughtlessness was nothing more, its frank meeting of confidence given with equal confidence returned; who that knew these things—and what student under him did not know them—can ever lose them out of memory?"* And from the earliest days of the Divinity School here—I cannot speak of its beginning from my own experience, but know it from a bright tradition — there has been that self-same simplicity which makes the office of the teacher so very natural and helpful, as is the place of a father in his household, and the work of the scholar so very happy and profitable. I shall be led too far astray if I dwell upon the work of the school of the prophets which was under his fostering care during all the time of his residence among you. As the years go on, changes must needs come into some of its methods and some of its work; but never may it lose those marks of the true

* *Address at unveiling of the Statue of the Founder of Trinity College*, in *Memorial of the Proceedings*, page 14.

teacher and the true scholar, of "him that waketh and him that answereth,"* impressed upon it by the man who was its first master, who lifted not himself up, but was among the others as one of themselves.†

Closely allied to that aptitude for teaching of which I have spoken, and in a certain way its source, was the combination in our Bishop of the enthusiasm of the youth and the dignity of the man. I well remember hearing one who was associated with him in his early college days‡ say that he thought that the reason why he retained so much youthfulness in maturer years was that he was so much of a man when he was young;

and I am inclined to believe that, as he never quite ceased to be a boy, so he never really began to be a man. He had a true dignity of bearing in the early years of his ministry, and his words, as well as his bearing, were impressive even then. And yet we know how in all his life he made friends of men and women and children in every class of life, without any feeling on either side that he was condescending to those who might have seemed his inferiors. Always and everywhere acknowledged a master, he was as one of the rest.

I have spoken somewhat of our Bishop as a teacher of theology, a doctor of divinity, for this he was in fact and by no mere compliment; yet we cannot rightly estimate the man or his work without asking what was his view of the great science which he taught. This was in part determined, I think, by the way in which he came to accept the theology of the historic Church. It was so like the experience of his predecessor, except that he himself was a younger man, not sixteen

* Malachi ii. 12, margin.

† I should like to refer to the passage of Persius, *Satires*, v. 30-51, in which he acknowledges his obligations to his tutor, Cornutus; a passage of which our Bishop made a beautiful translation. See also the passage from St. Bernard, which I found in a note to the first of Ottley's *Bampton Lectures*, prefixed to this sermon.

‡ The Rev. Dr. George Leeds.

years old, that I may again use of him the words which he wrote of another. "While yet in his course of preparatory study, he found himself brought face to face with that question which has met so many men, and almost always, when pursued, with one result, the question as to the organization and framework of the Church of Christ."* To him, no doubt, as to the other, "it unfolded a new aspect of Christianity, and the discovery afforded him unspeakable relief."† Yet a boy who had been brought up on Sir Walter Scott and who had the convictions of a Jacobite must have been already on the way to become a Churchman, and we need not be surprised that he became a strong Churchman.‡ He was affected, as I have already said, by the strong influence of Dr. Jarvis, a man versed in English theology and in that of the Fathers, who had inherited the teaching of the first Bishop of Connecticut through the second Bishop, and who not only held the strongest kind of Anglican theology, but knew why he held it in its every part. With Dr. Jarvis, as a teacher and friend, he read theology; and having a mind well strengthened by logic and furnished by history, he read it thoroughly. I have spoken of some of the divines of earlier days who influenced him and of others whom he studied in later years of his life. I wish that I could tell how far his convictions were determined or modified by the great movement which so mightily stirred the English Church about the time of his ordination. The position and the teaching of Connecticut Churchmen had been and was so thoroughly in accord with what the early Oxford Tracts were intended to promote that there was no need of the tracts here; and men of the school of Seabury and Jarvis, when they read them, wondered that it seemed necessary in England to lay stress on such fundamental doctrines

* *Sermon in Commemoration of Bishop Brownell*, page 6.

† *Ibid.*

‡ What in those days was called, and ought to be called to-day, a High Churchman. Perhaps we may adopt Archbishop Benson's suggestion, and say, a "Deep Churchman."

as the divine institution of the Church and the apostolically derived authority of her ministry.

Yet the Connecticut Churchman, and the New York Churchman instructed by Bishop Hobart, knew that it was necessary to defend their position and felt it a duty to be aggressive; and by way of encouragement the Oxford writings did have an influence here.* And certainly when the young deacon, in the enthusiasm of his early ministry, visited England, it was not strange that, as he met the leaders at Oxford, he found them friends. He had in him that combination of the poet, the historian, and the theologian which could not but attract these men; and while, as I believe, he lacked confidence in Newman's stedfastness, he could not but know the power of his personality and feel that he and his followers and friends were then upholding the true interests of the Church in England.† Some forty-four years later, on his second visit to England, some of us were with him when he stood again in the

* See preface to second edition of Palmer's *Narrative*.

† The manuscript notes in our Bishop's copy of the *Autobiography of Isaac Williams* (written in 1851, but not published till 1892 after his death), are very instructive and interesting. In a note on page 70, written in 1859, Isaac Williams says: "A little while before Henry [Wilberforce] joined the Church of Rome, Newman said to him, 'My temptation is to scepticism'"; and Bishop Williams wrote in the margin, "I always felt sure of this." On page 47, Isaac Williams tells how Newman advised the clergy to join the Church Missionary Society, "in order that, by their numbers, they might correct that Calvinistic leaven on account of which they were opposed to it"; and Bishop Williams wrote beneath: "This is thoroughly characteristic of the twist in Newman's mind, which is what Jelf was thinking of when he said that Newman 'had a Jesuistical mind.'" Corresponding to this is a note on page 99, where Isaac Williams is speaking of "a dissenting preacher from America, with whom Newman and Pusey were much taken," and Bishop Williams—who, by the way, had at his request introduced him to Newman—wrote: "Newman advised him to 'stay where he was and influence people,' on the very strange ground that wrong things by lapse of time acquired a certain rightness!" Again, on page 79, Isaac Williams says of his friend Copeland: "He was better acquainted with our English divines than anybody I ever met with, more especially the Non-Jurors"; and Bishop Williams wrote: "He certainly was that, and it saved him from being swept away after Newman." And once more, on page 110, a note of the Bishop's characterizes Newman as "a man of facile impressions" rather than "of strong convictions."

If any one wishes to know Bishop Williams's opinion of Dr. Newman and other "perverts" as recorded at the time, reference may be made to a sermon on *Errors and their Uses*, preached in 1849, and published with a sermon of Mr. (afterwards Bishop) Coxe under the common title of *The Late Apostasies*, in which Newman is likened to Origen, and to an article in the *Church Review* for July, 1851, on *The Secessions*.

barrack-like house and the painfully plain chapel in which he had seen Newman at Littlemore; but none of us knew of what he was thinking then. I am but giving my own impressions; but it may well be that he carried to Oxford more than Oxford had to give to him. For though he was not always a Churchman, he had the stability and the balance of those to whom Churchmanship is an inheritance; and his place was with those whom the great movement made stronger in their tenure of Anglican theology, and not at all with those for whom, like Newman, it was new wine set to work in weakened bottles. Certainly he made those men acquainted with the *Athanasion* of the youth who was destined to be the poet-bishop of our Church and his own friend through the Church, and thus opened the way for the Christian Ballads which had even in England an influence for Churchly thinking and Churchly living such as the Christian Year of the poet of that land, less spontaneous and less enthusiastic, could not everywhere gain.

The fact is, I am sure, that, speaking generally, while our Bishop's theology was in harmony with that of the Oxford tractarians, he did not learn it from them; his position was rather that of the Non-Jurors and Neale and Isaac Williams and Oldknow and Hook than even of Keble and Pusey.* And his knowledge of history was too extended, and his reverence for the teaching of the Holy Scriptures as the criterion of Christian doctrine was too profound, for him to yield to the claims of Rome; in fact, even while he argued mightily with her, he was inclined so to turn his argument as to apply to her the *praescriptio haereticorum* and prove that she had forfeited the right to be heard. And therefore he did not apologize for the Anglican Church,† any more than the inheritor of an indefeasible estate apologizes for his ownership in it; he knew

* See Overton's *The Anglican Revival*, especially pages 140–143 and chapter VII.

† Unlike Newman, and partly unlike Keble; see Overton, *op. cit.* page 45 and elsewhere.

that he was right and he warned off trespassers. It may be that after his visit abroad there was a feeling in certain quarters that he had been affected by some of the so-called errors of those times; but if there was such feeling, it soon passed away; and those who criticised him found fault rather with the stiffness with which he held the old teaching of the English divines.

But it is apart from my purpose, as it is beyond my ability, to enter upon any final estimate of our Bishop as a theologian. I wish rather, having suggested the general position which he held in regard to divine truth, to remind you of what was with him most important as to the way in which it should be sought and studied. He looked upon theology as a great science, as in fact inclusive of all other sciences, the "mother and mistress of them all," and in its full definition treating of God and His works. But he did not look upon it, he could not look upon it, as a science in which every man, or any man, could at his pleasure start at the beginning, collect facts, observe phenomena, and make an induction for himself; it was no place for loose experiment or for the work of an untrained or prentice hand. Theology was for him a great body of truth, to be commended indeed to reason, but not to be discovered by reason; it was to be learned, and learned in and from that organic body which is its keeper and witness; it was for him, and he made it for his pupils, truth received and tested and proved true, but first received. He held and he taught the Nicene faith, not because he or any one else could have discovered it for himself by the reading of Scripture or fashioned it by the use of his own mental powers, but because it was held and taught by the living Church of Christ bringing her varying credentials from history and reason and revelation. These convictions led him to cast his "system of divinity" (if one must use the phrase) in a scholastic mould, and to develop it rather in the forms of logic; but his historic sense led him to illustrate it from the living witness and consciousness of the Church, and his interest in individuals led him to enforce it by reference to the teaching and the lives of

the doctors and students of former days. Thus he bade us know and remember that the truth of God was to be learned, not to be discovered, and that its truth is absolute, not depending at all on our apprehension of it; and therewithal he made us understand the force and value of what St. Paul calls the distinguishing things that differ;* so that, like the schoolmen, many of his answers to hard questions began with a *distinguo*. This solid teaching, formally imparted to his students of divinity, has powerfully affected the acceptance and the holding of the Church's doctrine and her ways, not only in this ancient Diocese where Seabury and Jarvis and Brownell carried on the traditions of Johnson and the rest and found men and women ready for it and expecting it, but in all parts of this land wherever his influence as a doctor has extended; and, please God, it shall continue to the end.

It needs not that I should say much of our fourth Bishop as an administrator, in what has come to be looked upon as distinctively episcopal work. It did not largely fall to him to lay foundations, as to our first Bishop; or to strengthen a beginning work, as to the second; or to draw the outlines and raise the frame for a graceful and spacious superstructure, as to the third. A part of that good third Bishop's work he did indeed, while he was his assistant and coadjutor; and there was no break in the work when the responsibility for all the duties came upon him. He administered the Diocese through years of increased activity in some departments of Church work; a time of the erection and enlargement and decoration of church

* τὸ δοκιμάζειν τὰ διαφέροντα. —Philippians i. 10.

edifices and of other buildings for parish purposes; a time in which much attention has been given to the appointments for worship and the accessories of divine service; a time of the strengthening of old educational institutions and the establishment of new ones; a time of quickened activity in diocesan and domestic and foreign missionary work; a time of adapting or devising forms in which the external life of the Church may be expressed and its benevolent work may be carried on; a time of historic anniversaries, and therefore of renewed interest in our origins and our principles. Look at the index of our Journals, and you will see how much of all this was due to the suggestion of our Bishop; ask in our parishes, and you will learn how constantly he gave his encouragement and help. And through all this time he was, as we have been in the habit of saying, "every inch a bishop," ruling as by the appointment of the Lord yet with a rule not despotic or exclusive, in the dignity of a hierarchy yet in a manner "the very reverse of what has too often brought reproach on that name," ruling as we are more and more coming to learn that the Apostles and the early Bishops ruled, "paternally, one might even say fraternally," * the master indeed (no one could doubt that), yet among us as one of the rest.

And here I wish to allude for a moment to the thorough way in which our Bishop, although his early life was spent in another commonwealth, entered into the tone and life of this State and made them his own, and to the still more thorough way (if that were possible) in which, although not a Churchman from the cradle, he held to the tone as well as the form of Churchmanship. He was in a very true sense a typical Connecticut man; and he was the embodiment of what, for want of a better word, I must call the ἦθος of Connecticut and American Churchmanship; he had studied it, and he held it, and he lived it.

* Bright's *Some Aspects of Early Church History.*

I have yet to speak, though it must be briefly, of the personal relation in which our late Bishop stood to us. While I cannot but believe that the effect of his work as a theologian and a teacher of theology will long remain, and that his influence as Bishop of Connecticut and Presiding Bishop of the Church in this land will long be felt, I am confident that the best work that he did will be found to be in the simple exhortations which for nearly a half-century he gave to the "young men and maidens, the old men and children," who came to receive from him God's blessing by and with the laying on of hands. The words spoken at those times of Confirmation were few and (as I was saying) simple; they told of the ordinary privileges and responsibilities of ordinary Christian lives; they were as the words of a father letting his children go from him with a blessing and an exhortation not to neglect prayer or to forget to read the Bible or to stay away from the Holy Communion; but they were so full of earnest helpfulness that they will not readily pass from the minds and the hearts of those to whom they were addressed. I do not wish to speak now of the personal friendship which many have prized, and will prize all the more now that he has gone from us; but there are many thousands of men and women who, as they remember that it was through him that the grace of Confirmation, the special blessing for their conscious Christian life, came to them, will also recall those words which expressed for them the meaning of their good resolves and taught them how they were to find and to use that further grace by which alone the duties of life could be undertaken and discharged. I do not forget the power of our Bishop's sermons or the influence that they have had and still have on many souls; but to these addresses I attribute the greater value, as they were the more personal, the more practical, and the more sure to be held in the memory as influencing the life and the conduct. Through them he still speaks to us, as did St. Paul to the Corinthians in to-day's Epistle: "We then, as workers together with Christ, beseech you also that ye receive not the grace of God in vain."*

I took my text, as I said at the beginning, from the words of the wise man of old which our Bishop prefixed as a motto to the record of the acts of his episcopate. It is not amiss that I should tell you in closing of two short prayers from the Psalms in Latin which he wrote, one just before and one just after the first entry that he made in the book, the record of his own consecration. "*Deus, in adjutorium meum intende*," "O God, make haste to help me";† such the prayer with

which he began. "*Deus misereatur*," "God be merciful";‡ such the prayer with which he ended. They tell of earnest resolve, and of the conviction that only by divine grace could it be carried out; they tell of the sense of unworthiness and imperfection, and how he felt the need of God's gracious pardon. I have not tried to-day, my beloved brethren, to draw any picture of our late Bishop's character, to speak of virtues or of faults, or even to describe in any balanced detail the work of his life; each one of you will wish some things said which have been omitted and some things more accurately or more worthily told than my pen could tell them; but at least I have attempted no eulogy—he would have forbidden me to do that—and have but asked you to recall what he did and to remember the lessons of truth and of duty which he taught you. "I ask not for the praise of men, but for the mercy of God"; in these words of another Bishop, written in the expectation of death, our Bishop would have expressed his wishes, as in the "*Deus misereatur*" of his record. We use to-day the touching phrase in which it has been customary to

---

* Or, as it may be rendered, "that it be not in vain that ye have received the grace of God."—II. Corinthians vi. 1.

† Psalms lxx. 1. ‡ Psalm lxvii. 1.

---

announce the decease of the honored of earth: "It hath pleased Almighty God to take to His mercy the soul" of our father, the fourth Bishop of Connecticut; and to that mercy we thankfully leave him, looking for the glorious Return of our Saviour Christ, the Resurection of the dead, and the Life of the world to come.

OLD SAYBROOK COMMEMORATION OF THE BICENTENNIAL OF YALE COLLEGE
[25] NOV. 11, 1901

On Nov. 11th an interesting part of the Yale Bicentennial Celebration was that at Old Saybrook of the founding of the Collegiate School, which was the germ of Yale University. On that occasion the Rev. Dr. Samuel Hart, one of the most distinguished and perhaps the most beloved son of Saybrook, delivered in the name of his townsmen the following graceful address:

It is but seemly that something should be said to-day on behalf of the good people of Saybrook. Most of my work for these many years has been done elsewhere; but this has always been my home; and I am glad to be so far reckoned a citizen of this ancient town that I need make but a brief personal apology in undertaking the duty which has been assigned me.

"Saybrook," said the eccentric but observant Dr. Peters, when he wrote his "History of Connecticut" six score years ago, "is greatly fallen from its ancient grandeur: but is, notwithstanding, resorted to with great veneration, as the parent town of the whole colony." There are settlements to the north and to the west of us, which might contest our right to the title of "the parent town;" but we still claim great veneration as our due and have not lost all memory of our ancient grandeur. We do not concede that there was any permanent settlement in the new towns before the first fort was built here for the defence of the stream and plans were made for the residences of "men of quality" and the dwellings and farms of people of the humbler sort;

and the settlers here were quite ready to assert rights of sovereignty by imposing duties on goods which were destined for those who came to live above them. And we remember that with those who crossed the ocean to make their home at the fair haven to the west were some who came to augment the company already here, including one who had made an earlier visit three years before, now bringing with him his wife, the heroine of our early annals.

Thus the first contribution of Saybrook to the history of what is now the State of Connecticut was the story of fortifications and battle away and of a fair lady. Lion Gardiner's name tells the story of warfare, of the fort and the war with the Pequots, though we also remember that it was he who, discharging more peaceful duties, laid out the streets still used in the older part of the town and built the mill where once turned stones that have now lain quiet for some two centuries. And Lady Alice Apsley Boteler, wife of George Fenwick, Lady Fenwick as we call her, has left us a story of romance which will always brighten and sadden the annals of those early days. "Master Fenwick with the Lady Boteler" and Master Higginson, their chaplain, lived in a fair house within the first fort, that fort in the great hall of which the professors of religion here were in due time "embodied into church estate." There her second daughter was born: and there she died and was buried. The fort was destroyed by fire about a year after her death; a new fort was built close to the water's edge—many who are here can remember it; it was for a long time the oldest remnant of a fortification in this part of the country—and the tomb-stone placed to guard her body stood in the open field. A supposed necessity led some years ago to the razing of the earth-works and the removal of the stone with the dust which lay beneath it to its present site, so that the outward symbols of that early history do not tell the story as plainly as they told it once; but we still think that it entitles us to veneration.

To-day we are commemorating the second event of great importance in the annals of Saybrook, its contribution to the literary and educational history of Connecticut. It was no hasty plan, that of founding a second college in New England, and of placing it—one has to use imagination in the application of the term—on the bounds of the west, on the further side of the great river, looking out into unexplored wilds, the future scene of strife with the powers of darkness and ignorance. It was no accident that led the ministers to meet and decide that they could found a college; it was part of a well matured plan that led to the application for a charter and to its grant from the General Assembly. The story has been told this afternoon by the man who had the best right to tell it, the historian of Yale University, to whom our special thanks are due for tracing out the origins of the Collegiate School with the zeal and enthusiasm of Livy and with an accuracy unknown to that brilliant historian. The trustees, or "undertakers," to use the word of that day, chose this place for their meeting of two hundred years ago, and decided then that this should be the home of the new institution. And its only home it was for fifteen years, with varied experiences, under one rector to whom his church would not give permission to discharge all the duties of his office by coming into residence, and who required some of the students to be with him eight miles from here, and another who held but a temporary appointment and lived farther away. It was a time of foundations, and the foundations were well laid here. Two Saybrook men lead the long list of benefactors; and many youth of the place find their names on the roll of the graduates of those early years; there are many here to-day feeling a just pride in the pious labors and generous gifts of ancestors who did what they could to further the cause of sound learning, or a commendable satisfaction in the knowledge that their ancestors drank here of the fountains of knowledge when first they were laid open in this new Parnassus, and learned here to be of service to both church and commonwealth. Those who honor us with their presence to-day, the representatives of a great University everywhere known and everywhere honored, coming back for the moment to that day of small things which made the present day of great things possible, will not

blame us that we rest some part of our assertion of ancient grandeur upon the contribution made by this town to learning and education. Our ancestors, we are told, were not entirely pleased when it was thought that the plant which had made so good a start here might perhaps grow better on other soil; and they did not give a willing consent to the removal. Probably they had not a sufficiently clear idea of the need of what Dr. Stiles called a "Domicilium" or "Coenobium Academicum" which might be more easily secured in New Haven than here, and they were not aware of all that a college required in order to have, as Dr. Cotton Mather phrased it, "a collegious way of living." To-day, however, we are not to revive our ancient controversy, but to accept the facts of history; and we thank those who by their presence and their words so graciously testify to the place which our town bore in the history of the institution of learning which has now entered upon the third century of its career of honor and usefulness.

Seven years hence there should be in this place a gathering to testify to the importance of another event which contributed to the reputation of this town. We look back to the life of Lady Fenwick here as illuminating our history with a bright light of romance; we find in the establishment of the college a proof that our forefathers set a right value on sound learning and desired to extend its blessings to all who could profit by them; we may see in the Saybrook platform how an influence went forth hence to strengthen the ecclesiastical organization of the day, in the confident belief that thus the cause of religion would be strengthened in the community. The three events tell something of the power for good which was shown over and over again in the first homes of our ancestors, and which went forth to guide the life of the commonwealth and the nation. We do not claim that this is the only place where the influence of home-life, of education, and of religion was exerted and made itself felt; but we find a laudable pleasure in the thought that conspicuous among the many examples that may be found are those which belong to our ancient town. The hopes of those men of early days who expected to see here merchants crowding a mart of busy commerce, students thronging a university, a place of conspicuous and abiding influence in matters political or ecclesiastical, have been, we may think, disappointed. No! They have not been disappointed! The horizon has widened; what was done here by faithful men and women undertaking the duties which lay next at hand has led to results far greater and more enduring than could have come into their minds; and we are glad that those who went before us were able to do something to cherish in the first stages of its growth an institution which is now doing a great work for God's glory and the good of men, and before which there lie unlimited possibilities of usefulness. The college, standing in practical working as it stood here and elsewhere historically, in some sense between the home and the church, taking up the work of the one and leading on to that of the other, helping and encouraging both, has long been an important factor in English and American life; it is a source of great gratification to us, the sons and daughters of Saybrook, that to-day when the University of Yale is receiving the congratulations of the learned world, she is willing to accept a humble tribute from this home of her infancy. We venerate the University; we venerate also our ancient town; and we believe that even from this place may still proceed some influence which shall strengthen the homes, the colleges, the churches of Connecticut, as in the days that are past, for the service of God and man."

[26] THE S. P. G. AND THE DIOCESE OF CONNECTICUT

IT has fallen to my lot to tell you, as best I can, a little of the outline of the history of the Society for the Propagation of the Gospel in Foreign Parts, so far as it has to do with this Diocese of Connecticut. The foundation of this Society, as you will all remember, began two hundred years ago, in 1701. But let us go back a little further, so that we may get the history of the Society a little more clearly in our minds and follow it better.

In 1635 the first settlements were made in this colony of Connecticut. And there were two kinds of settlers: some would have been called Puritans, and some would have been called Separatists. They had all been brought up in England, in the old Church, and many of them became dissatisfied with the way things were going in England; and while some wanted to change and purify the Church, others thought that they could not stay in the Church of England, but must separate themselves from it. The people who came to this colony of Connecticut, whether Puritans or Separatists, soon ceased to call themselves members of the Church of England. Among their ministers were fourteen or fifteen men who had been ordained in England; but after they came here, the people began to ordain their own ministers. Some of them even believed that they could ordain their own ministers by simply the laying on of hands by the members of the congregation. In Saybrook there were two or three instances where the people insisted on it that they had the right to ordain ministers for themselves. There was a very curious ordination in Milford, where one of the members of the congregation who was to lay on hands was a blacksmith, and he thought because he used leather mittens in his work in the blacksmith-shop, that the proper thing to do was to put on his leather mittens for the service; it was called the "leather-mitten ordination." One result of this was, that sober-minded men and women began to think that perhaps, after all, the Church of England was in the right, that it might be best to follow the example which had been prevailing in the Church for many hundreds of years, that no one should be considered to have the right to preach the word of God or minister the sacraments unless he had been ordained by a bishop.

There were other things that set people to thinking, and called up recollections of what they had learned in old England. Three or four copies, perhaps more, of the Book of Common Prayer (which Bishop Williams once said was the first and best missionary of the Church) had been brought to Connecticut. One belonged to Samuel Smithson of Guilford. It fell into the hands of a young man who was then preparing for college, or perhaps had entered college, Samuel Johnson. He read it, studied it, learned from it some things that he had not known before, and thought seriously of what he had learned. He came to the conclusion that the teachings of the Prayer Book were the teachings of the word of God; and when he became a Congregational minister, he used the prayers which he had learned and the people thought that he was peculiarly "gifted in prayer" and wondered how he could express himself so well. He became, under God's providence, the founder of the Church here in Connecticut. There was another Prayer Book in Plymouth; and this led to the establishment of two or three parishes in Connecticut, one or two in western New York, and one or two in Ohio.

But let us go back to the time of the foundation of this Society—"the Venerable Society for the Propagation of the Gospel in Foreign Parts." We may well call it venerable now because it is two hundred years old, but it was often called venerable when it was very young indeed. Its foundation was due to the Rev. Dr. Bray, who had come

to this country that he might inquire into the state of religion here. In the very next year after it was founded, a few Churchmen who were in Connecticut, at Stratford, asked the Society to send them a clergyman of the Church of England. In the self-same year, the first two missionaries came, Mr. Keith and Mr. Talbot, and they spent a Sunday in New London. The minister of the Congregational society there, who was afterwards Governor of this Colony, Mr. Saltonstall, received them very courteously; and one of them preached from his pulpit in the morning and the other in the afternoon. I do not suppose that they read the service out of the Prayer Book; but this was certainly the first time that clergymen of the Church of England officiated as such in this colony. Four years afterwards came the time when the missionary from Rye, Mr. Muirson, under protection and patronage of Col. Heathcote, preached and baptized in the towns from Greenwich to Stratford. The result was the establishment of the first parish of Connecticut in Stratford in 1722, and Mr. Pigot was settled there as its first clergyman.

Now, you should remember the year 1701 in which this Society was founded, but you should remember also the year 1722, not alone because it was the year in which there was the first settled clergyman here in Connecticut, but because the most remarkable thing in our Church history happened in that year. Seven young men, Congregational ministers of good learning, men of influence and of reputation, were in the habit of meeting in New Haven, to read the books in the college library and to talk over what they read. As they read and studied, and as Mr. Johnson, who was one of them, remembered what he had learned from the Prayer Book, they came to consider seriously whether it was right for them to undertake to minister to their congregations any longer, unless they could first be ordained by a bishop; and they united in sending a document to the "fathers and brethren" who were assembled at Yale College commencement in the year 1722. It led to much excitement and discussion; and the result was that of these seven young men, four made up their minds that they must cross the ocean and ask the Archbishop of Canterbury to ordain them. I do not suppose that a thing like that ever happened before or since. Here were some of the picked men in the community, honored for their learning and their character, going across the ocean three thousand miles in a sailing vessel, because they were satisfied that they could not any longer minister to their people without receiving ordination from a bishop. Three went in the first year, Dr. Cutler, Mr. Brown, and Mr. Johnson; and Mr. Wetmore followed a year later. Yale College at this time had a faculty of two, the Rector and the Tutor, or the President and the Professor; these were Dr. Cutler and Mr. Brown. Dr. Cutler came back to be Rector of Christ Church in Boston, Mr. Johnson to be, as I said, the real founder of the Church here in Connecticut. Mr. Wetmore also ministered here; but Mr. Brown died of the small-pox in England.

Then for about fifty years, other young men followed the example of these four. Forty-three candidates crossed the ocean before the Revolution; and of these six lost their lives in the venture. It was not an easy thing in those days to cross the ocean and to return; and besides, England was continually at war with France, and the small-pox was a terrible scourge. From Hebron they sent out four men, one after another. One pined away in a French prison, one died of the small-pox, and one was lost at sea; only the fourth was able to come back to minister to the parish which had sent him. It was in this way that the Church was founded in this colony. The War of the Revolution broke out, as you remember, in 1775; and the independence of the colonies put an end to the work here of the Society for the Propagation of the Gospel. But no sooner was the Revolution over than Dr. Seabury crossed the ocean and was consecrated the first Bishop of the Church in Connecticut—the first Bishop of the Church in this land.

I want to say but two things more; and one is this: that this history shows what it is that has made the Churchmen of Connecticut, both those of older and those of later years, so strong in their attachment to the Church into which they have been baptized and to which they have professed their allegiance, and has kept them firm in their belief in the faith and order and sacraments and scriptures which have been handed down to us from the Church of ancient times.

And lastly, as to the word "Propagation." I have been speaking of the Society for the Propagation of the Gospel. We understand, of course, that this means the spreading of the gospel, but I wonder if you have ever heard of the original meaning of the word propagation as applied to a vine. If you bend down a branch and bury a little bit of it in the ground, so that it may take root and become a new vine, this is propagation. It was very much in that way way that the gospel was first extended and is now extended. A branch was bent down and took root here in our Connecticut soil, and by and by it did not need the nursing care of the mother Church, but became itself the mother of Churches. It depends upon these boys, those who have carried the banners of their parishes, and others like them, whether there shall be the same strong, true vine of the Church of God growing here in Connecticut as long as they live and for the generations hereafter, with all the strength and power with which God has blessed it here in the past, since that venerable Society began its fostering care at the beginnings of the Church here in Connecticut.

JOHN BROCKLESBY, LL.D.

JOHN BROCKLESBY, LL.D.
FROM 1842 TO 1882 PROFESSOR AND
FROM 1882 TO 1889 PROFESSOR EMERITUS
IN TRINITY COLLEGE
BORN IN WEST BROMWICH, ENGLAND
OCTOBER 8, 1811
DIED IN HARTFORD, CONNECTICUT
JUNE 21, 1889

QUI AUTEM DOCTI FUERINT
FULGEBUNT QUASI SPLENDOR FIRMAMENTI
ET QUI AD IUSTITIAM ERUDIUNT MULTOS
QUASI STELLAE IN PERPETUAS AETERNITATES

MR. PRESIDENT AND GENTLEMEN OF THE ALUMNI:

At the Commencement of this College in 1882, Dr. John Brocklesby, after forty years of faithful and honored service, retired from active duties and received the well-earned title of Professor Emeritus. It fell to my lot, as I had for some years been his associate, to continue during the next year the work which he had left unfinished. This

102

I was not willing to do without paying some slight tribute to the character and the labors of the good and wise man who had so long had charge of such important departments of College work; and when I first met the more advanced of his classes, I spoke to them in words a part of which you will, I trust, allow me to repeat now.

"I wish to say something which shall, in its poor way, testify to our recognition of the debt which we and the whole academic body owe to the eminent Professor who has, since I met you last, retired from active duties in connection with the College. Forty years ago he came here, after a successful undergraduate course in the halls of his own *alma mater* and an experience in tutorial work there. There is but one person living of the Trustees who elected him to the Seabury Professorship made vacant by the resignation of Professor Davies; and of those who were his colleagues when he was placed in the chair of Mathematics and Natural Philosophy, not one survives. Forty successive classes have had the benefit of his instruction, extending at first through three years of the undergraduate course, and then, when he was relieved by the appointment of an assistant, confined to the important departments in which he had always been most interested. If I were asked to tell of the work which he has done and the name which he has gained for himself, I might speak of the scientific books, accurate and scholarly and clear, which have been so widely used, and of the scientific investigations the results of which have brought him deserved honor; but I would rather point you to the work which he has done within the College walls, and to the respect with which he has been and is regarded by those who, during all these years, have had the privilege of knowing him. He may well look back with pleasure upon the work of the study and the lecture-room, all that he has learned and all that he has taught; but I cannot well conceive of a deeper pleasure than that which must be his as he knows that one after another, in a long succession of generous youths, has been drawn to him with a most real affection. As Dr. Brocklesby's name stands to-day on our roll as Professor Emeritus, it forms a link between the former undergraduates and the College, there being none of his pupils, I am sure, who does not feel that he owes much to his scholarship, his kindliness, and his true Christian character."

Seven years have passed; and at the beginning of the work of a new College year the Alumni of the College have made it my duty to pay the tribute of respect and affection to the much-loved Professor who rested from all the labors of life just before our last Commencement. I little thought, when I wrote the words which I have just repeated, that I should use them again; but the thoughts which they so imperfectly expressed are the thoughts which all who knew him tried to express over his newly-made grave and would wish to express now. The feelings of affection were not first called forth by the presence of death; we did not then change our estimate of the man or our way of speaking about him; the words which then came to our lips were not the conventional words of a funeral eulogy; we spoke of him, and we speak of him now, as we had spoken of him when he was our teacher and our friend. A life is worth the living if it calls forth the esteem of so many men of varied natural dispositions and varied habits of thought; it is worth while to pass through life if so strong and true an affection can follow us beyond the grave; it is worth while to leave behind one's self a memory such as that which the ancients thought to be a sure proof that a good life does not end.

One who is Professor Brocklesby's senior on academic rolls writes me that he recalls him when he was a boy at his father's house on the Talcott mountain and studying in preparation for College at a neighboring town, "dressed in a white roundabout suit, for all the world like an English schoolboy, at his play and at his books, gentle and brave, sweet-tempered yet courageous, equally eager on the playground and in the class-room. There were many things in his character," he continues, "that could only be explained by his early home-life."

Professor Brocklesby, as we knew him, was so truly and loyally an American that we were surprised when we first learned that he was an Englishman by birth; but nevertheless he retained to the last some of the sterling qualities of the typical Englishman, even as his memory went back, with an Englishman's love, to his father's house in Oxford, opposite the walls and tower of Christ Church and not far from the Folly Bridge over the classic Isis, and to the harbor of Bristol from which he took his last view of the shores of his native country. His father, a man of strong and perhaps somewhat eccentric character, came with three motherless children to America, because he was unwilling to live longer under a monarchy; and he brought with him, as he came to this new country, a large part of the equipment for a house which still stands high up on the hills to the west of Hartford. There the father trained the son in those true principles of duty and of life which he never forgot or abandoned; there he made him familiar with the Scriptures, both canonical and apocryphal, which it was the boy's part to read daily at family prayers, interchanging them sometimes with the epistles of Seneca; there he learned from the English Bible and from other masterpieces of the language that clearness and poetry of expression which marked all that he afterwards wrote; there he learned to watch and note and study the phenomena of nature in earth and sky, in solid rock and changing cloud and living things; and there he began the preparation for his life-work.

I have said that he was so loyal an American that we did not always remember that he was an Englishman. In like manner it may be truly said that he was so loyally devoted to the interests of

this College, and his life was so closely identified with it, that we often forgot that his Alma Mater was the venerable College at New Haven. Yet he never lost his affection for Yale College, and he often thought and spoke of his classmates there, and especially of two who were highly honored and deservedly loved, Judge Sheffey and Professor Thacher.

Another classmate, whom I have asked for memoirs of his college days, says of him: "There could be no other judgment respecting his aim in entering college than that he meant to avail himself of all the opportunities afforded him. It seemed impracticable to divert his mind from the work in hand. Whatever were the exercises, he was *totus in illis*, both in the class-room and during the hours of study. . . . He was not what some would call a genius, endowed with a kind of intuitive faculty to solve difficulties at sight; he worked hard and steadily for what he acquired. But when once acquired, it was held fast in full possession; and what is more, he was able to impart his acquisitions to another in a clear and deliberate way."

Mr. Brocklesby was nearly twenty-four years old when he took his bachelor's degree in 1835; and his standing in his class was so near that of the salutatorian that his was made an honor appointment with the title of the philosophical oration; and this honor has been continued at Yale College since his day, as it had been granted once before, for the student third in rank in each graduating class. At the commencement he not only delivered the oration appropriate to his appointment, but also took part, with two or three others, in a dramatic dialogue in verse, of which he was the author.

After a year spent in teaching and two years devoted to the study of the law, Mr. Brocklesby accepted an appointment from his *alma mater* to a tutorship in the mathematics. This he held for two years, declining an offer of the professorship of Chemistry here. Then, having been admitted to the bar, he entered upon the practice of the law in Hartford; but in 1842 he laid it aside to enter upon the duties of the Seabury Professorship of Mathematics and Natural Philosophy in this College.

The title of the professorship to which he was thus chosen at the age of thirty-one includes a great deal; its duties included even more. In those days the work of the three lower classes was practically divided into three equal parts. The Greek and the Latin each occupied one-third of the time of Freshmen and Sophomores and Juniors; and the remaining third was assigned to Professor Brocklesby's department and distributed among the pure mathematics, mechanics, the divers branches of natural philosophy or physics, and astronomy. He saw at once that he must, among all the branches which he was to teach, select some to which he would specially devote himself; and so, at first, though he was very far from neglecting the mathematics and the other branches of physical study, he

pursued his own investigations more particularly in the lines of meteorology and microscopy. Soon, by careful study of what had been written by others, by painstaking collection of the results of observation, and by constant and enthusiastic watching and noting of the phenomena about him, he collected material for a manual of Meteorology; and this he published in 1848, at a time when little attention had been given to that science in this country.

The book was written in the large room next to the chapel in the old college buildings, which was afterwards used as a vestry-room, and which some of us will remember as seeming well suited for observations on dampness and frost, or rather on hygrometry and psychrometry. It was a small volume, and in later years the professor did not feel satisfied with it; but it was clear in its explanations, full in its details, and showed on every page the painstaking and enthusiastic way in which its materials had been gathered. He made many observations with special reference to this work, of which the most original and valuable was a careful study as to the influence of color upon the deposition of dew, a study which was pursued with the most diligent care and in the true scientific spirit, and the results of which accorded with those of Professor Bache's elaborate investigations as to the influence of color upon the rate of cooling and upon radiation. The volume contained many notices of usual phenomena so described and explained as to call attention to them and to teach his students to use their eyes as they walked about, and also many notices of less usual phenomena, such as extraordinary rainbows, complicated halos, St. Elmo's fire (a special example being given of its appearance on President Totten's umbrella), and natural snowballs. When we woke one winter morning not many years ago to find the ground about us covered with these natural balls or rolls of snow to the number of thousands or millions, we turned at once to Professor Brocklesby's Meteorology for an explanation of the wonder and for examples of its former occurrence. The study of meteorology has of late attracted so much attention and made such progress in this country that it is eminently fitting that a due tribute of respect should be paid to a book which thus early called the attention of students to the science and excited their interest in it. It was followed ten years later (in 1858) by a manual of Microscopy, fully illustrated and intended as a guide to amateur microscopists.

Before this, however, Professor Brocklesby had published the first edition of his Elements of Astronomy for the use of schools. This book, clear in its definitions and explanations without being unscientific, and interesting without being inaccurate, was a book of great value. As one edition after another was called for, its statements were kept abreast of the discoveries of the day, and improvements of one kind and another were introduced into it. At one time the chapter on the tides was entirely rewritten, the author being dissatisfied with the explanation ordinarily given as to the un-

equal effects of the lunar action upon the waters on different parts of the earth, and proposing what certainly seems a more satisfactory explanation and one capable of a very simple statement. And the later edition or editions — there were some twenty-five in all — were enriched with an account of the methods and the apparent results of the most recent investigations into the physical constitution of the sun. This volume illustrated particularly well the ability with which the author could teach somewhat advanced truths of science to those who could not be presumed to have had much preliminary or preparatory instruction. An astronomy for schools must confine itself in large part to the statement of facts and to simple explanations of some of them; but Professor Brocklesby was able to give to those who knew nothing of trigonometry and but little of geometry, a very clear idea of the methods by which the distance of the sun is computed and the time of its axial revolution is determined. The last book which he wrote was a Physical Geography, a valuable work, fully illustrated with maps and plates, which gives an excellent idea of this great science in all its wide extent.

But Professor Brocklesby's studies were not confined to the gathering of material for his written volumes. Apart from the constant preparation for the varied duties of the class-room, which included many experimental lectures in the different branches of natural philosophy, and in regard to which it is impossible to speak in detail, he was constantly studying and noting and writing upon matters of interest to scientific men and upon scientific matters in which all intelligent men are or ought to be interested. At meetings of the American Association (of which, by the way, he was one of the first elected Fellows) he read papers upon the periodicity of the rain-fall as compared with that of the solar spots, upon frozen wells, and upon other subjects. He contributed to the *American Journal of Science*, and in a less formal way to daily and weekly journals. Often with reference to something remarkable in sky or cloud or rain, and sometimes as putting into form the results of observations or thoughts that had for one reason or another specially attracted his attention, many articles from his pen appeared in the local papers, which were always read with interest. One of the last was one of the best, an essay on the two oceans, that of the water and that of the atmosphere, in which he pointed out, in many interesting ways, their analogies and their differences.

And besides these scientific articles which were generally known to be his and to which, for that matter, his initials were usually subscribed, he sometimes allowed himself in other fields of writing. Occasionally verses from his pen found their way into the papers. Two or three extended dramas which he wrote were never published, and an epithalamium addressed to his wife on the occasion of their silver wedding was only distributed to friends; but I recall an excellent translation of the *Dies Irae* in the metre of the original with its double rhyme in triplets, which appeared in a religious paper, and which was worthy of more than a passing notice. And as an example of the labors of lighter hours, it may suffice to refer to a list of three hundred or more possible ways of spelling the word "scissors," published *à propos* of some discussion as to phonetic spelling.

For Professor Brocklesby's interest in studies and in letters was by no means confined to those which specially concerned the work of the departments committed to his care. Besides his constant study of the English Bible and his constant use of the Prayer Book, he kept himself familiar with the writings of the best authors; he never wearied of Shakespeare and Sir Walter Scott, and he never quite gave up reading Virgil; and the lucidity and grace of his writings testifies not only to a scientific clearness and accuracy of thought, but also to a literary taste which could not be satisfied except by a careful choice of words and an almost poetical balancing of sentences.

For forty years Professor Brocklesby continued in the unremitting discharge of his duties here, though, in course of time, their burden was lessened. There are many changes in a college, not only in the ceaseless flow of the stream of undergraduate life which passes through academic walls to come forth freighted with the riches of godliness and learning and to bear their influences to other and wider fields, but also in what seems to the undergraduates the fixed body of those to whom are entrusted the duties of government and instruction, and moreover in the methods, if not the principles, of the government which they administer and the instruction which they seek to impart. After only sixteen years of service, Professor Brocklesby found himself the senior professor of the Faculty; and four times he was called upon, in the vacancy of the presidency, to assume responsible duties as acting President. But in all the changes of the College, both external and internal, he was ever the same: faithful and diligent in every duty, a kind and sympathetic friend of the students, a wise and earnest counsellor of his colleagues, an honored and esteemed citizen. It was one of the professed principles on which this College was founded, and it is one which has been constantly maintained, that it should be a home in which officers and students should live together as members of one community, having common interests and pursuing the same ends. Even if he had not found this the tradition of our College, Professor Brocklesby would have done much to establish it. Every student knew that he had in him a real friend; the gentleness and unassuming goodness which showed themselves in his face were manifest in many words and deeds of kindness, and still more manifest, if that were possible, when it was necessary to speak words of reproof. And in return the students were friends of the good Professor. There were times when some of us were thoughtless in our treatment of him; but there cannot have been many times when any one treated him with intentional discourtesy;

and I am sure that if any one ever did so, he was soon heartily ashamed of it and willing to confess that he was ashamed of it. For the Professor was a true gentleman, to know whom was to esteem and love him; he was one of those good men of whom Bishop Butler says that they "had rather be deceived than be suspicious." And thus his guilelessness and sincerity and modesty conquered where other qualities of heart and life would have provoked opposition and encouraged resistance.

The appreciation of the alumni for Professor Brocklesby's character and work was never better shown than at the Commencement-tide of 1880, when the Connecticut Beta of the Phi Beta Kappa, of which he was the founder and over which he presided for the last twenty-two years of his life, presented his portrait to the College. I need not apologize for quoting here a part of the address in which the gift was accepted by the Chancellor.

"Who," said Bishop Williams, "who that looks back over all the years that have gone since, in 1842, the then young professor took up his life in the College, but must feel that on such an occasion the silent thoughts of each man's mind are more golden than any possibilities of uttered speech? The year just named was one of the few years since I came hither as an undergraduate in which I have not been more or less directly connected with the work of our College. But I well remember the satisfaction that was widely felt and expressed when the choice of the Trustees became known; and still all that fades from our thoughts as, looking on this portrait — and, thank God, on him, too, whom it presents to us — we offer him our loving gratitude for all that he has been to and all that he has done for our Alma Mater during his most honorable period of service. How many hearts will thrill, how many eyes will moisten, as men scattered all over this broad land shall read the record of this day's doings, and, recalling many a kind word and helpful act, shall grasp in thought the hand that they cannot grasp in deed! How many in coming days, when our names shall be among the *stelligeri* of the College roll, shall pause before this picture, and listen to the story of a good and noble life!"

Then, addressing the Professor, the Bishop added:

"I cannot but look back to-day to the five years which we passed together as members of the faculty of Trinity College. The memory of them will ever be among the most cherished memories of my life. For me, those years were all too short, and I could almost envy you that you were left in the academic life from which I was taken. We have seen bright days and dark days here together. But I believe I can say with perfect certainty that not a doubt of the future of this College has ever crossed our minds. But your life and your work are inwrought into the history of the College, as those of no other professor have ever been, possibly ever will. It is wise to say this for you to-day which you would never say or even think for yourself. And I do say it out of a full heart, and knowing that I speak for all who are here, for all who are absent, for all the sons of our collegiate mother."

If I have spoken thus far, Mr. President and Gentlemen, of Professor Brocklesby as the diligent scholar, the faithful teacher, and the loved member of our academic body, I have not forgotten, nor would you have me forget, that above all he was a true Christian. Nay, he studied and taught and lived as he did because of this. There are those upon whose life religion has a very real influence, but whom after all it seems to affect from without; it was not so with him, and I may speak as I do without at the least intruding into the privacy of the hidden life. We have not the entire picture of the man until we recall him standing or kneeling in his place in the Chapel, repeating the well-known Psalter without book, or reading the Lessons, especially the words of the Prophets, with an eloquence of expression which was not inconsistent with the most true reverence. We do not know all of the spirit in which he studied Nature until we read the verse which he placed on the title-page of his Astronomy: "Lift up your eyes on high, and behold Who hath created these things, That bringeth out their host by number; He calleth them all by names, by the greatness of His might, for that He is strong in power; not one faileth." And when he saw the rainbow in the sky and thought of the wonderful laws of refraction and dispersion by which he was accustomed to explain it, his thoughts passed to the words of the son of Sirach, and one who ever heard him quote these will not easily forget how they sounded then: "Look upon the rainbow, and praise Him that made it; very beautiful it is in the brightness thereof; it compasseth the heaven about with a glorious circle, and the hands of the Most High have bended it." He taught the Natural Theology of the course as one who had learned to see God's Hand in all the works of Nature, and he accepted the teaching of Dr. Pusey's great sermon that it is "Un-science, not Science," which stands opposed to the Faith. To the faith of the historic Church he held with all the firmness and simplicity of his noble soul; and in a most real humility he trod in the footsteps of the Master. So it was that, by his example as well as (when occasion served) by well chosen words, and by a quiet influence the power of which he never himself knew, he impressed upon us the excellence, the beauty and strength, of a real Christian character. Here lay the secret of his greatest wisdom, and in this is the test by which we know that his was a truly useful life. "Many are in high places and of renown; but mysteries are revealed unto the meek."

None of you can be more sensible than I am myself of the inadequacy of the tribute which I have thus offered to the memory of one who was to me a teacher, a friend, a colleague, and almost a father. But I am sure that those who knew him will fill out the picture the outlines of which I have attempted to sketch, and will pardon the unskilled hand which has drawn them amiss. There is something peculiar in the life of an academic body; there is to be seen in it a corporate memory (if I may

venture thus to call it) joined with an individual forgetfulness. Four years make for the undergraduate an immemorial prescriptive use; but there are few undergraduates who do not leave an influence which is felt more than four years afterwards by those who perhaps never heard their names. So the character and the good deeds of our founders, of men whose names, like those of Bishop Brownell and President Wheaton, stand at the head of our academic roll, are still affecting each young man who enters these walls and receives a share in the academic life which was drawn so largely from them. And so we may be sure that no President or Professor, no graduate or undergraduate, has ever done any worthy deed of devotion or truth or self-sacrifice which could by any possibility affect the corporate life of the college, without conferring a real benefit not only upon the College, but also upon all its members. During the seven years in which Professor Brocklesby made but infrequent visits to the College, it followed as a matter of course that he was unknown to most of those who were occupied here in their daily pursuits; though he watched with unfailing interest everything that could affect the welfare of the institution to which his life had been given. But his good work for the College did not cease when his active service came to a close; as long as he lived, his kindly care for us was a perpetual benediction. And for himself the years that remained were like the time of the ripening of the shock of golden grain against the hour when it should be gathered in. The end came with the peace and quiet which one feels to belong to the death of the true Christian man; he fell asleep in Christ, as the little child, wearied with its happy labors, trustfully falls asleep on the mother's breast, to rest till the sun shall rise and usher in the day.

Dr. John Brocklesby will have an honored place among the men of science and the educators of his day; but he will also have, as he has already had for these many years, an influence for good learning, and good living too, upon many generations of students who shall yet call this College their foster-mother. And so we write his name on the roll of our benefactors, and thank God for his work and his example.

SAYBROOK IN THE EARLY DAYS

[28]   [Read January 27, 1902.]

"SAYBROOK," said the eccentric but observant Dr. Peters when he wrote the History of Connecticut six score years ago, "is greatly fallen from its ancient grandeur; but is, notwithstanding, resorted to with great veneration, as the parent town of the whole colony."

There are settlements to the north and to the west of the mouth of the Great River, which might contest the right of the place for which I venture to speak to-night to be called "the parent town"; but in Saybrook we still claim great veneration as our due and have not lost all memory of our ancient grandeur.

We do not concede that there was any permanent settlement in the river towns before the first permanent fort was built at the river's mouth for the defense of the stream and plans were made for the residences of "men of quality" and the dwellings and farms of people of the humbler sort; and we recall the fact that the settlers at Saybrook were ready to assert rights of sovereignty by levying duties on goods which were destined for the colonists further up the stream. And we remember that with the men who crossed the ocean to make their home at the "fair haven" to the west were some who came to augment the company already at the fort, including one who had made an earlier visit there three years before, now bringing with him his wife, the heroine of Saybrook's early annals.

But we have a legendary history which reaches further back. Save for the records of early combats with the natives and for the traces which we find, for the more part beneath the sod, of what they did in war and in peace, we know next to nothing of those who occupied the plain, the meadows, and the hills before the eyes of enterprising Europeans saw the mouth of the quiet river. One Obed has left his name to a rough stone which is called his altar; but he was a "survival" in the days of the Platform, and his life was affected by civilization. Perhaps Adrian Block, in his venturesome voyage in 1614 from New Amsterdam through Hell Gate to Cape Cod, was the first European to spy out the sites on the north coast of the Sound which seemed best fitted for settlement, and Saybrook Point or Lynde's Point must have been one of the places where the Dutch traders in following years landed that they might carry on their trade with the Indians. They claimed that in 1632 they bought a neck of land at the mouth of the river, a place which the Indians called Pashbeshauke and which they themselves named Kieveets Hoek from the birds (called by the English peeweets) which they saw flying about the place; and that in the following year they purchased in like manner the Dutch Point, where they built their House of Good Hope, on the south side of the little stream which flows into the great river hard by the spot where the English soon founded their New Town. This, it would seem, they fortified without attempting to establish a garrison at the river's mouth; for we read that when in 1633 a company from Plymouth sailed up the river to effect a settlement at what is now Windsor—they proposed to make it New Plymouth—they encountered opposition only as they passed by the point six miles below the place where they intended to land. The Dutch there used strong words, and at least threatened to fire off guns, which probably could have done no more harm than the words did; and the Englishmen sailed by. There is a story as to the posting of some sort of a proclamation or claim of sovereignty at Kieveets Hoek with the arms of the Dutch States General, and that it was, with at least the appearance of boldness, taken down by some one who asserted prior rights for or under the English Crown; but this does not appear to have recognition from sober historians. Doubtless the Dutch made claims of discovery and occupancy and pushed their trade wherever they could; and against them the English asserted rights based on patents and grants of title, which they presently defended either by attempting to dislodge the Dutch or by warning them to depart and then leaving them alone, thus giving the first example of that policy of Connecti-

cut which has been successfully followed in all periods of its history. At any rate, it is a satisfaction to know, on the authority of Dr. Benjamin Trumbull, that the Dutch "were always mere intruders" and "had no right to any part of the country." Certainly they neglected to prepare for a fortification at Saybrook till after the English had taken actual possession, had removed all that might be held to prove Dutch jurisdiction (if any such thing there was), and had—most important of all—mounted two guns, having a caliber of about three inches.

They who thus "providentially" made settlement in November, 1635, had come from Boston, where they had landed in the preceding month, and had taken possession in the name of the Viscount Say and Seale, the Right Honorable Robert Lord Brooke, and the rest of the company to whom the Earl of Warwick had executed a sort of deed or grant which they were minded to call a patent. Soon came John Winthrop the younger, and with him the engineer, Lion Gardiner, who was to build extensive fortifications, lay out a large town or city, and provide a mill. It is he who, writing to the governor in the next year, first uses, in any document now extant, the name "Saybrook," which is thus shown to be the oldest town-name in the State.

It was a hard winter, the first which the English spent in the fort on the bluff. The river had been frozen over in November before the settlers reached its mouth; seventy persons, in danger of starvation, came from the settlements above to look for provisions, and finally sailed for Boston in December. And their vessel, the Rebecca, has the honor to be the first of which it is recorded that she ran aground upon the bar, heading a rather inglorious list of craft of every size and name which have had a like experience. We are not told that the Dutch vessels had ever run aground; probably their navigators were in no hurry, and would not have noted it if it occurred; nor is it recorded that Mr. Pynchon's ships were thus detained as they were carrying his goods from Boston to Agawam, perhaps because they expected to pay their toll in accordance with Mr. Fenwick's protective tariff. Thus the settlement had a sad beginning, and there was further disappointment when but few more settlers came in the spring; and we do not wonder that Lion Gardiner despaired of seeing the walls of his great fort and the houses of his great town built and occupied, and retired to the quiet position of lord of the manor on his Isle of Wight. But before he left, Mr. Fenwick had arrived—the only one of the patentees who ever visited these shores—and the Pequot war, against which Gardiner had strongly advised, had been waged to a cruel end, the troops tarrying at the fort for several days, and Mr. Stone, their chaplain, giving a night to prayer. Soon came other colonists, among them Robert Chapman and John Clarke—well-known names among us to-day—and the warrior Captain John Mason.

Thus the first contribution of Saybrook to the history of what is now the State of Connecticut was the story of fortifications and battle array. But with it is joined, as indeed is most meet, the story of a fair lady. Lady Fenwick, as we call her, came in July, 1639, with her husband on his second visit to Saybrook, as has been already noted. Her courtesy-title of lady came, as you know, from her former husband, Sir John

Boteler, and she should be rightly called Lady Alice Apsley Boteler, wife of George Fenwick, Esquire. She and her husband had sailed across the ocean with Henry Whitfield, the founder of Guilford, bringing with them the infant child of John Davenport, the founder of New Haven. They sailed directly for Quinnipiack, and gave to the beautiful harbor at its mouth the name of the Fair Haven; then those who were to come to Saybrook fort or to make the new settlement midway, proceeded to their destinations, as I suppose, by land. They brought across the ocean, of course, their household goods; and Lady Fenwick had also a herd—it must have been a small herd—of red Devon cattle. She gave them, we are told, to Mr. Whitfield, perhaps because she thought that there could be no pasturage near to the fort in which she was to live; and from them have come the sturdy breed of red cattle which are still so serviceable to the farmers of southern Connecticut. About this time also there came the first chaplain of the fort, Mr. John Higginson, who going to Guilford to act as Indian interpreter presently married Mr. Whitfield's daughter and became his assistant in the ministry.

It must be largely left to imagination to fill out the history of Lady Fenwick's six or seven years in Saybrook. A daughter, Elizabeth, was born to her soon after her arrival here; and to secure baptism for the infant, because there was no church organized in the fort, and probably none could be gathered until the permanency of the settlement was assured, she went to Hartford, was admitted a member of the church there, and presented her little one for the sacrament. We read of no other journey; but in the same letter which tells of this we are told that "Master Fenwick with the Lady Boteler" and one Master Higginson, their chaplain, were living in a fair house and well fortified. And we get pleasing glimpses of their life in some letters of Mr. Fenwick to Governor Winthrop of Massachusetts: "We both desire and delight much in that primitive employment of dressing a garden; and the taste of good fruits in these parts gives us good encouragement." Again: "I have received the trees you sent me, for which I heartily thank you. I am pretty well stored with cherry and apple trees, and I did hope I had a good nursery of apples, of the apples you sent me last year, but the worms have in a manner destroyed them as they came up." And we learn from another source that the lady had pet rabbits, and a "shooting gun," "which," says a sober historian, "must have been for sport, as the Pequot war was over." Thus quietly she lived, not (we may believe) without a longing now and then for the ancestral home of the Apsleys in England, past the time when (in December, 1644) the autonomy of the settlement, such as it was, was lost by a cession of its jurisdiction to Connecticut, past the time when Master Higginson had removed to Guilford and the Rev. Thomas Peters had taken his place as chaplain, but probably not long enough to witness the assembly in the great hall of the fort when the professors of religion were "embodyed into Church Estate." On the 4th of November, 1645, her second daughter, Dorothy, was born; and soon after this, possibly before the opening of the new year, certainly before the year had far advanced, the mother died. Her husband soon went to England on public business, though it is believed that his departure was hastened by his domestic affliction; and it is a

comfort to know that the children were left in the care of women who were their father's kinsfolk, one being his sister, and one probably the widow of his brother or cousin. The good lady was buried within the enclosure of the fort; this was destroyed by fire about a year later, and in the following year the new fort was built, not on the bluff a little back from the water, but on the river's edge. The grave was thus left standing in the open field, though, we may hope, not without protection. Some years must have elapsed before the tombstone, elaborate in its construction for those days, but without inscription, was put in place; for it was not till 1679 that Matthew Griswold of Lyme received for it seven pounds sterling from Mr. Fenwick's nephew by marriage. Doubtless some of you remember, as I do, the earthworks of the old fort, as they had been restored from time to time, and the tomb on "tomb-hill" as it was called, with stone posts and iron chains about it, in a strange and almost dignified loneliness.

> "And ever this wave-washed shore
> Shall be linked with her tomb and fame,
> And blend with the wind and the billowy roar
> The music of her name."

There her body rested until the year 1870, when the supposed exigencies of public convenience led to the razing of the fort—the oldest earthwork in this part of the country, if not in the original limits of the United States—and to the removal of the tomb; careful search was made beneath it, and the skeleton which was found was reverently re-interred near the entrance to the old burying-ground, and the ancient tombstone was again placed over it to be its guard, let us hope, until the resurrection of the just.

The second fort had not stood thirty years when, on a July day in 1675, Major Andros came to demand its surrender to himself as representative of the Duke of York. He was in command of a small fleet, flying the king's colors. The fort was manned by Saybrook men in charge of Captain Robert Chapman and a company of soldiers from Hartford commanded by Captain Thomas Bull. It too flew the king's colors, and Andros did not dare to fire upon it. He decided therefore to ask that he might land, intending to read the Duke of York's patent and his own commission from him. You know the story of his interview; how Andros ordered one of his officers to read, and Bull commanded him, in his majesty's name, to forbear reading; and how, when the officer did not at once cease, Captain Bull repeated his command with such energy that he did not dare to disobey; whereupon the Captain read the protest of the General Assembly against Andros's proceedings and offered him an escort to the shore. "What's your name?" said Governor Andros. He replied, "My name is Bull, sir." "Bull," said the Governor, "it is a pity that your horns are not tipped with silver." The brave captain lies buried in Hartford, and it is recorded on his tombstone that he was in command of the fort in Saybrook when its surrender was demanded by Major Andros.

We pass on to the opening year of the eighteenth century, and we find Saybrook selected as the site for the newly-founded Collegiate School of the Colony. The trustees—they called them 'undertakers' then—met there on the 11th day of November, 1701, probably at the house of the pastor, Mr. Thomas Buckingham, on the middle street of the north point, and voted that Saybrook should be the home of the infant institution. Major John Clark is reckoned its first benefactor, giving (as is believed) a right to two thousand acres of land which had been bequeathed him by Joshua, sachem of the Mohegans; and before a year had expired, Mr. Nathaniel Lynde offered for the use of the school, so long as it should continue in Saybrook, a lot of land with a house upon it; but this property, though doubtless used immediately, was not formally passed to the corporation for six years. The site of the building is sufficiently well known; it stood near the road about midway in the recent addition to the old burying-ground; and there we have placed, in the bi-centenary year of the school which soon was called a college and now bears the name of university, a boulder with a tablet appropriately inscribed. Fifteen commencements were held in Saybrook, from 1702 to 1716 inclusive; the first, we are told, was held in Mr. Buckingham's house, and the others must have been held either there or in the meeting-house. Fifty-five young men took their bachelor's degrees there (or fifty-six if we include Mr. Chauncey of 1702); of these, nine were sons of residents of Saybrook, and one was a grandson; one became pastor of the church, and five others became tutors in the college, before the year of its removal; that is to say, nearly a fifth of the graduates were Saybrook boys, and more than a quarter of them had Saybrook at some time for their residence.

If the romance of Saybrook passed away with the burial of Lady Fenwick, her hope of becoming a great seat of learning ceased when the Collegiate School was removed to New Haven; though we may be permitted perhaps to hope that the forcible detention of a part of the library witnessed to a desire to keep at least some of the concomitants of sound learning. Probably our ancestors had not a sufficiently clear idea of the need of what President Stiles called a "Domicilium or Coenibium Academicum" which might be more easily secured in a larger place, and were not aware of all that a college required in order to have, as Dr. Cotton Mather phrased it, "a collegious way of living." But at least we may claim that Saybrook bore no unimportant part in the early history of our great institution of learning, which has now entered upon the third century of its career of honor and usefulness.

We are approaching the bicentennial of another event which has contributed to the world-wide reputaton of the ancient town of which I am speaking. While the Collegiate School was still in Saybrook, a Synod or Council—though I think that it was not formally called by either name—was convened there by the General Assembly of the Colony to prepare methods and rules for the maintenance of ecclesiastical union and the management of ecclesiastical discipline. The synod was held in 1708; and it assembled, we may presume, in Mr. Buckingham's house, where so much else of general importance had taken place, and was in part under his moderatorship. It framed the Saybrook Platform, which was not a creed or confession of faith, but a plan of organization intended to combine the Congregationalism of the major part of the people of the colony with the Presbyterianism to which some were inclined. Approved and enforced by the civil authority, the Platform, although not accepted by some of the strongest churches, notably

the First Church in New Haven and the Church in Norwich, gave a special stamp of soundness and conservatism to the religion of Connecticut, and profoundly influenced its history.

If we look back to the life of Lady Fenwick as illuminating our history with a bright light of romance, and find in the establishment of the College a proof that our forefathers set a right value on sound learning and desired to extend its blessings to all who could profit by them, we may also see how from the home of that gracious lady and the first seat of that school of learning there went forth an influence to strengthen the ecclesiastical organization of the day, in the confident belief that the cause of religion would thus be strengthened in the community. The three facts and events tell something of the power for good which was shown over and over again in our early history, and which went forth to guide the life of the commonwealth and the nation. There were many places indeed where the influence of home-life, of education, and of religion was exerted and made itself felt; but we of Saybrook find a laudable pleasure in the thought that conspicuous among the many examples that may be found are those which belong to our ancient town. And from this and other like communities may still proceed some influence which shall strengthen the homes, the colleges, the churches of Connecticut, as in the days that are past, for the service of God and man.

Address at the reopening of the Acton Library, Old Saybrook, June 30, 1904

[297]

I had hoped, Mr President, that I should be able today to go back more than half a century and sketch the history of the earliest public or circulating libraries in Saybrook. But I must content myself with an allusion to the Fenwick Library, reminding you that it filled an important place in the life of the community, and that its name is to be found in a few volumes which are still preserved. Its history closed with the dispersion of its books about the year 1840; so that there is no real connection between it and the organization which today closes one volume of its history and begins another.

The opening of the Acton Library as the Public Library of the Town of Old Saybrook falls almost exactly on the fiftieth anniversary of the organization of the Ladies' Library, which thirty-three years ago gave place to the Acton Library and was merged in it. The first suggestion of the older organization appears to have been made by Mrs Emily Starkey King, wife of our resident physician, who at a gathering of ladies proposed the formation of a reading club, the members to contribute each a small sum for the purchase of books and the books to be circulated by passing them on at fixed times, so that they all could enjoy the benefit of the whole sum contributed. The suggestion was seconded, if memory serves aright, by the wife of Captain E E Morgan, and readily approved by many others; so that when, on the third day of July 1854, a simple constitution had been adopted at a meeting held at Mrs King's house, forty of the women of Saybrook became members, and each paid a dollar to the funds, for the expenditure of which in the purchase of books a committee of four was appointed. Each member was to be given a book, which at the end of three weeks she was to pass on to another designated member; when the books of the first purchase had been "generally read and circulated," they were to find their way back to the depository, and it was designed that the sale of the volumes should increase the funds for further purchases. Of the forty original members seven still survive: Miss Amelia H Sheffield, Mrs Sumner Bull, Mrs Giles F Ward, Mrs John D Ingraham, Miss Athenia Livingston (now Mrs Peabody), Miss Susan S Pratt (now Mrs Chalker), and Mrs Henry Hart. Of the forty-seven volumes which were purchased for them half a century ago, one — "Fashion and Famine" — was suppressed, one was sold, and nearly all the rest are still on the shelves and worth reading; among them are "The Days of Bruce," Mrs Strickland's "Queens of Scotland," "Half-hours

with the Best Authors," Hugh Miller's "My Schools and Schoolmasters," Hitckcock's "Religion of Geology," "The Life of Rowland Hill," "Mrs Partington," Pascal's "Provincial Letters," Thomson's "Egypt," a volume on the Philippine Islands, and others in various departments of literature. Rather more than a year passed, and a second meeting was held at the residence of Miss Hotchkiss, when the name of "The Ladies' Circulating Library" was adopted, and it was decided not to sell the books which had been, or might have been, generally read, but to keep them under the care of a librarian. The new books were to be "punctually exchanged" on the first and fifteenth days of each month, and the books of former years were to be at the service of members who should call on the librarian on the first Thursday of any month between the hours of nine and three, or in case that day was stormy on the following day between the hours of nine and twelve. Any person not a member might on any of these days draw out a book for two weeks' reading on paying six cents. Miss Hotchkiss was chosen the first librarian, and the books were kept at her house, as I well remember. There was no president of the association and the chief executive office was that of secretary and treasurer, which from 1856 was held by Miss Amelia H Sheffield, who gave to the library constant attention and unfailing interest; and it was to her and to Miss Hetty B H Wood that the members were specially indebted for a very wise and helpful and satisfactory selection of books through a period of many years. Mrs Morgan's counsel and assistance were also of great value, and she made to the association after the first year an annual payment of five dollars. The membership did not greatly decline — it was least, I think, in 1862 — and it kept for some years above fifty, and once reached fifty-nine. There soon began to be a small income from the loan of books in the library; in 1861 it was $3, and in 1864 it amounted to $4.70.

In 1865, Miss Hotchkiss being unable longer to serve as librarian, the books were put in charge of Miss Harriet Willard and moved to her residence; and at that time we first find a payment for the printing of labels, the number of volumes at this time being about 500. It was now arranged that books might be "drawn," as the phrase was, from the library on any Thursday, and in the next year it was voted that half of the money received from the loan of the books should be given to the librarian; her first year's salary amounted to $3.35. The books remained in Miss Willard's careful custody and under her care, calling for much unrequited labor willingly given, until the change which was affected in 1871.

This change, which transferred the books belonging to the Ladies' Circulating Library, or the Ladies' Library Association, as the later entry calls it, to the Acton Library, was agreed to at a meeting held July 18, 1870. The Hon Thomas C Acton had offered to provide a home for a new library association, and the ladies were "invited to place their books in said building and unite with the Acton Library." They voted to convey to the new organization "800 volumes of miscellaneous books, present value estimated at $1,200," on certain conditions, the most important of which may well be quoted in full:

"That should the Acton library from any cause be discontinued as a public library in Saybrook, they are hereby obligated to select eight hundred volumes of miscellaneous books, similar in value and condition to this gift from the Ladies' Library, and to return them to a committee of three from this association or their successors, who shall hold them in trust for the people of Saybrook and shall call a meeting of the ladies of Saybrook and reorganize a library association on the same basis on which this has been successfully conducted for the past sixteen years." Mrs Henry Hart, Mrs Sumner Bull, and Miss Elizabeth R Whittlesey (now Mrs O H Kirtland) were appointed the committee; and it was provided that in case any vacancy should occur — and no vacancy has occurred as yet — it might be filled by a vote of the Acton Library Association.

After this there was a little delay; but early in October 1871 the books were removed from Miss Willard's home and placed in the room provided for them in the building next east of the present library. Arrangements were made to have the room opened and the books accessible on the afternoon of three days in each week, and the ladies, by serving in succession two at a time, agreed to keep the hours. But after a short time, the plan proving inadequate for the wishes of the subscribers and the public, Mrs Morgan proposed one day to Miss C Amelia Clark that she might undertake the duties of permanent librarian. Miss Clark accepted the invitation, and began those thirty years of service which were of such incalculable benefit both to the library and to the community.

The generous plan and purpose of Mr Acton, to which reference has already been made, was to secure for the people of this town, in which

he had come to make his home after active service of the commonwealth elsewhere, the benefits of a library and reading room. For this purpose he purchased the corner lot on which the library now stands and by deed of date of May 23, 1870, conveyed it to certain individuals to be used for the purpose named. These persons adopted articles of association October 31, 1871. For some reason which does not appear, a second deed of the property was executed November 8, 1872; it was made conditional on the erection of a suitable building which could be occupied on the first day of the following July. Twenty-two trustees were named in the deed: the pastor of the Congregational church and the rector of the Episcopal church — and it was provided that their successors should always be trustees — together with nine other men and eleven women, who had the power of filling vacancies in their own number. It was provided that any new member elected as trustee should as far as possible be of the status of the person whose place was to be filled. Of the original trustees twelve still survive, though, owing to removals and other causes, they are not all on the present roll. The trustees met and adopted permanent articles of association January 3, 1873, in which they declared that the purpose of the Acton Library Association, as they named it, was to "conduct the business of a public library and reading room for public use, but especially for the use of the inhabitants of the Town of Old Saybrook, forever." That it might thus benefit the whole community, it was voted that the use of the books in the library building should be free to all the inhabitants and to nonresident persons temporarily in town. Anyone wishing to take books from the library for reading at home might do so on the payment of six cents for two weeks' use; or the use of two books for a year, to be exchanged as often as desired, might be secured on payment of a dollar. Those who paid their dollars came to be known as members, but in reality were annual subscribers for the use of books at home. The first president of the association was the Rev Jesse E Heald; on his removal from town he was succeeded by Mr Edwin Ayer, who presently was followed in office by Mr George W Denison, and he by the Hon John Allen. Mr Allen, who always took a discriminating and unfailing interest in public affairs, added this to his other deeds of service to the community until his death in June 1901, and he was succeeded, as I need not say, by Mr Denison, who for the second time is the worthy incumbent of the office. The association has had but one secretary, Thomas C Acton, Jr; and my mother served as treasurer of the organization until last January, when she resigned on completing about thirty-three years of service.

Mr Acton, as was said, gave to the Library Association a plot of land centrally located, on condition that a library building should be erected upon it. Toward the erection of the building he also subscribed $500. Other subscriptions did not come in as large number or as large sums as had been hoped, and it was necessary to negotiate a loan in order to complete the payments on the building. But at last, August 9, 1877, we find a record that the debt had been fully paid, Mr Acton having generously subscribed $468 besides the $500 which he had previously given, a legacy of $200 having been received from the estate of Mrs Morgan, some $500 having been received from other individuals, and a small balance having been paid out of current funds. Thus of the whole cost of the building, $1,700, nearly $1,000 was the gift of the generous donor of the land, whose name the association and the building perpetuate. The new home of the library was occupied in 1873, and for thirty years Miss Clark kept it open on the afternoons and evenings of Tuesdays, Thursdays, and Saturdays, with few exceptions other than public holidays. The number of annual subscribers at the first was not large, most of those who wished to take books home preferring to pay the small fee each time; in 1877 the income from subscriptions was $25 and from rent of books nearly $60. Two years later the town began an annual appropriation of $100, which almost paid the salary of the librarian, and from time to time it made special appropriations: in 1883, $50 for painting; in 1888, $100 for a slate roof; in 1896, $150 for repairs; and in 1897 the annual appropriation was increased to $125. But for this aid the library could hardly have been maintained; and, as it was, the ordinary sources of income did not leave a large sum for the purchase of books after the payments for fuel, lights, insurance, and ordinary repairs. There were, however, constant donations, and assistance was given in various ways. Mrs Acton made frequent contributions towards current expenses and later for the care of the grounds; the Library Aid Association in four years raised $255; the Dramatic Club and the Village Improvement Society each rendered assistance by presenting part of the results of their labors; fairs and entertainments were held for the benefit of the Library; Mr and Mrs David W Clark from one of their handsome chrysanthemum shows made a generous addition to current funds; Mrs Potter has for many years made a gift of the delivery of coal, and Mr Walker has brought all express parcels free of charge; the librarian for twenty-five years sold stationery,

and made a personal donation of the profits; a neighbor skilled in photography has furnished views of Saybrook streets and scenery, and later the popular postal cards, to be sold for the benefit of the institution; and another neighbor long kept the cellar supplied with kindling wood. There have also been donations of books both from residents and from nonresidents, among which should be specially mentioned the books of reference given by the Hon Daniel C Spencer, while the publications sent by the general government and by the State of Connecticut have made the collection serviceable for some lines of study and investigation. For several years the library has been under special obligations to Mrs E Hayes Trowbridge of New Haven, who has made constant gifts, often amounting to some fifty volumes a year, of good books in current fiction and other literature. For this reason it has been possible to make many purchases of standard books in history, biography, travels, science, and other departments of "useful knowledge," so that the shelves of our library show a large proportion of works of permanent value. For good judgment in the choice of books special credit is due to Miss Wood and Mrs Bull; and too much cannot be said in praise of the watchful care of the librarian, who made the most of the possibilities of service in the care of each volume, kept the books in neat condition and in complete repair, and with her own hands put substantial binding on some 250 volumes which must otherwise have had a short life or have been condemned at once as waste paper. This thrifty economy, with like care to avoid expense in other ways even when it entailed additional work upon herself, made Miss Clark's administration one of benefit to the community; and the benefit, it may well be said here, was most gladly acknowledged in a substantial form when she retired from office a year ago. One special collection of books holds an honored place. In 1894 a handsome bookcase with glass doors, having fifty well-chosen volumes on its shelves, was presented by the friends of Miss Louisa Sheffield Lord in her memory; and they have made additions to its contents from time to time.

In 1890 a serviceable catalogue of the books was published in an edition of 500 copies; its cost was in large part defrayed by the fees of $25 each, paid by eight life members. These, by the way, are the only life members; and their special privilege, of drawing books without fee during the term of their natural lives, has as I suppose ceased. Four honorary members have been elected: Miss Sheffield, Miss Willard, and Mrs Armstrong (now deceased) in 1893, and the Rev P L Shepard in this present year. Ten years ago, on the application of Mr F A Curtis, the first principal of the graded school, to whose memory we all recognize a debt of respectful gratitude, permission was given to the teachers of the school to take from the library without charge such books as should be needed by the pupils in connection with their school work; this vote of the trustees serves to show how really the library was acknowledged as existing for the benefit of the public. In the same year, on the 5th day of September, the institution in a way claimed its place among the libraries of the State by welcoming to a meeting within its walls the Connecticut Library Association. It was a particularly pleasant and satisfactory gathering, and those who attended were entertained at luncheon at the hospitable mansion across the street.

There is one feature of this library which belongs to it in common with other libraries, and which I think specially important in the libraries of our smaller communities: it has from the first served as a museum or place of deposit for articles of historical interest and documents which may illustrate the history of the town. There has not been as much made of this as we might wish; but we have some ancient articles connected with the names of Lady Fenwick and others; we have the portrait of Mr Hotchkiss, who was for sixty years pastor here; we have some old records and other manuscripts; and, of special value, we have the collection of historical and genealogical notes made by the accurate and careful pen of Mrs Chesebrough, of the greatest use to any one who is looking into the ancient history of the place. With these there are minor articles of various kinds, enough for the beginning of an interesting and valuable collection, but by no means as many as we should have and may in due time expect. Let me add that, while we increase what may be called our museum exhibit, we should also endeavor to preserve any and all publications, of greater or of lesser size, which can in any way illustrate the life of the community or tell of those whose lot has been cast here.

Before passing on to speak — it must be in few words — of the change which is marked by this anniversary, mention should be made of a generous and timely gift of very recent date, which will be of continual help for the practical work of this Library. On the 20th day of July 1903, the children of Thomas C Acton and Sarah Elizabeth his wife presented $2,000 to the Library Association, with the request that only the interest be used from year to year, and that it be applied for the care of the grounds in summer and winter, for the payment of charges for insurance,

111

"and to meet such necessary expenses as may not be otherwise provided for." It is impossible to speak too highly of the thoughtfulness which inspired this gift or of the help which will come from it as time passes on, quite as really under the new order of things as it would have been under the old.

There has been much change in the position, the work, and the use of libraries in the past half century. Especially it is to be noted that they have come to be recognized as a part of the educational equipment of the community, deserving to be encouraged and in some sense directed by the State. They are now considered a necessary part of the furnishing of every self-respecting town or village, and their foundation and maintenance is looked upon as a not unimportant part of civil administration. From the first the Acton Library had been both in intention and in fact, though (it must be confessed) in a somewhat limited sense of the words, a public library for the people of Saybrook; but it began to be felt that it should be made a public library in the modern technical sense, and that it should thus become qualified to receive the assistance which the State is ready to give under certain reasonable conditions. The matter was brought before the legal voters at a town meeting, at which the plan was explained by the Secretary of the State Board of Education, Mr Hine, and also before the trustees of the Library Association. The town accepted the privilege offered it with the accompanying obligations; and the trustees on the 17th day of March last passed this resolution:

"That the Acton Library Association make its library free to the inhabitants of this Town of Old Saybrook under proper regulations to be adopted by its Trustees, and amend its by-laws to that effect; provided, that the town aforesaid do pass a Public Library by-law voting the sum of $200 to be paid annually to the treasurer of the Acton Library Association towards the maintenance of a Free Public Library."

Thus the town practically guarantees, above its former annual appropriation, an amount equivalent to that received from annual subscriptions and fees paid for the use of books, and the citizens gain the advantage of a truly public library; while the Library receives the benefit of State appropriations and the counsel of experienced administrators. In preparation for the change much has been done in the Library, especially in the rearrangement and cataloguing of the books by experienced workers and by willing assistants who have lightened the labors of the new librarian. May she have as happy and as useful years here as did her predecessor!

This Library carries over into its new position and for its possibilities of new and more extended work the visible results of fifty years' collection of books, very few worthless, very many permanently valuable; and the invisible, but no less real, results of fifty years' intelligent interest in a project which has been undertaken and carried on for the benefit of the community. The record of the past half century, not without some discouragements, has been greatly to the credit of those who have administered the trust and of those who have enjoyed its benefits; may the record of the next half century, beginning under such good omens, be acknowledged as no less creditable when judged by those who can estimate its value!

[30]
GUILFORD AMONG HER NEIGHBORS.

We who have come from other parts of the State in answer to your kind invitation, may be pardoned for asking why it is that a State Historical Museum should be established in this town. It is not the first place founded in the limits of what is now Connecticut, nor is it the capital city, nor yet at the centre of territory or of population. We cannot expect that the building will open its doors to throngs of tourists, who, after giving hours to other objects of interest on their line of travel, will turn aside here for a few minutes and come out to check off in the guide-book one more thing seen and out of the way. None of these too obvious reasons will account for our gathering here to-day. Something, indeed a great deal, might be said for the enthusiasm and energy of one who has made the history and fortunes of his adopted town his own, has taught even its own citizens to take a new interest in it, and has waited for opportunities to claim for it an honored place in the commonwealth. And again, we confess that there is no place within our borders where there is ready to hand a building like this— ancient, far beyond any other structure in the State, perhaps

beyond any other in neighboring states, and probably the oldest dwelling in the territory of the thirteen colonies (for I think that even professional skeptics would find it very hard to prove the existence of an older one), built as strong as a fort, and doubtless meant to be ready to do duty as a fort, and also as spacious as a public hall, and a public hall of meeting we know it was as it is to-day. The structure still standing after all these years in a half isolated dignity, has invited the use to which it is now dedicated. And it is a great satisfaction to us who represent historical societies and patriotic associations, who care for records and mementos of the past, to know that as far as personal pledges and official action can determine the future, the Old Stone House is forever safe from harmful decay and from no less harmful innovation, and is made of permanent service to the commonwealth.

But I am inclined to think that there is another reason, such as may be called historical or may be called mystical and perhaps is both, which makes Guilford a suitable place for the custody of some of those things which we include under the name of the antiquities of Connecticut. The place which this settlement held among its neighbors made it in some way a logical centre for them. When the first colonists came here in 1639, there were three distinct settlements of distinct characteristics within the limits of what was to be the Colony and later the State of Connecticut. On the west bank of the Great River, the Ultima Thule of that day, safely below the bounds of Massachusetts, was a new commonwealth, embodying clearly defined theories in church and in State, destined to be the model of a great republic and indeed of all modern constitutional government; it had been founded by practical men, led by a practical preacher and a practical lawyer, and it had a very practical purpose. About the same time, at the mouth of the same river and also on its western bank, another party of men had built a fort and had laid out a tract of land for the occupation of persons of quality and others who were expected soon to arrive; theirs was the military government of the day, and the men who were stationed there were on the watch not only for the protection of the interests of those whom they immediately represented, but also for the defence of their neighbors; their leaders were a soldier and an engineer. A few years later, a third company, who had come from England by way of Boston, had found a home for themselves at the fair haven made by the mouth of the Quinnipiack, and had laid out there a four-square city; they combined a spirit of theocracy and a spirit of commercial enterprise; they were led by a theologian and a wealthy merchant. Close after them came the settlers of this town, sailing directly from England, bringing with them Mr. Davenport's child, whom they left with the parents at New Haven, and Mr. Fenwick (coming for the second time) and his wife the Lady Boteler, whom they had escorted half of the way to the Saybrook fort when they reached this fair plain and laid out the common about which they were to dwell. They were distinctively a company of yeomen, as the phrase then went, and this was the typical settlement of farmers; and they were a body of young men—their leader, to be sure, was forty-six years old, but no other of the "pillars" had passed his thirtieth year. Midway between an aristocratic government and a military post, they made a civil compact in which special precautions were taken that there should be no great inequality based on wealth, and they kept here for themselves and for posterity the large-bodied, wide-horned, red cattle which the wife of the governor of Saybrook had brought to these shores. Their organization was largely based on that of the New Haven

colony, with which indeed the community soon became united, while their building was somewhat in the style of that at the mouth of the river to the east. For this, though undoubtedly the largest and the strongest, was not the only stone structure here; there were other stone houses and there was a stone meeting-house, a marvel for those times.

Mr. Davenport, it was said by one of his contemporaries, was "more fit for Zebulon's ports than for Issachar's tents;" the Guilford farmers did not seek a port, though they took up their lands not far from the sound; they were rather like the patriarch's description of Issachar, a strong beast of burden crouching down in a land which he saw to be pleasant, bowing his shoulder to bear burdens and made to labor hard at his task. And in them we may see, as I think, the combination of certain of the most distinctive features of their neighbors to the right hand and to the left.

And I believe that we can also see something which makes a connection between this settlement and the colony directly north of it in Hartford and the sister towns. There was an independence here and a practical way of making plans and putting them into operation which reminds us of Hooker and Ludlow. If the compact which was formed seemed even more locally ecclesiastical than did that made in New Haven, I am inclined to think that it was in order that it might escape the danger of interference from the stronger people to the west. There must have been here from the first some ground of sympathy with the democracy of the Connecticut colony. Those who had not the franchise were not debarred from the meetings of the burgesses, but had even the right of speaking in them; and equal social standing and equal power of public debate do not consist with exclusive political rights and theories. There were those in the New Haven confederation who submitted quite willingly when they learned that Connecticut had a charter and that the bounds of its jurisdiction extended over the settlements of the New Haven colony; among them were some, like Governor Leete, who felt strongly the need of union and were willing to make sacrifices for it, and others who, like Bray Rossiter, claimed that they were debarred from the rights of English subjects and called into question the civil authority of the jurisdiction. Thus Guilford bore her share, and more than her share, in preparation for the union and in accepting it when it was proclaimed; and as it made a link between the two colonies on the shore, so it was ready, after Saybrook had been united with Connecticut, to assist in bringing Connecticut and New Haven under one government.

We may go farther yet, and trace a connection, and almost claim a neighborhood, between our ancestors here and the Massachusetts colony. For did not John Higginson, who had taught the grammar school in Hartford, and had been chaplain of the Saybrook fort, and had come here to be colleague of Mr. Whitfield—did not John Higginson, when he had started to return to England, stop at his father's old home in Salem, accept ordination to the charge of the church there, and minister to the people of that typical Massachusetts town for eight and forty years? And if we would pursue neighborhood beyond the seas, we may well remember that the first minister here, Mr. Henry Whitfield, whose name this house will ever bear and whose memorial it will ever be, ministered to the end of his days by virtue of the authority which he had received when he accepted ordination at the hands of a bishop of England, his being the only example, as far as I know, of a minister in one of our early New England churches who had no special ordination on this side of the ocean.

So we think to-day of the way in which the little colony here, separate though it seemed to be from them all, had something which made a relationship between it and each of the three original colonies, to north, to west, and to east, had until well into the eighteenth century a living connection with Massachusetts, and did not wantonly break with the mother land of England.

The stone house standing here—if neighbors came from New Haven they might have called it a mansion; or from Saybrook, a fort; or from Hartford, a town hall. Mansion and fort and town hall it was; but we have chief pleasure in thinking of it as a home, the home of the chief man of the place, the pastor and the leader of the community. And it is well that, restored as near as may be to the pristine arrangement of its ample spaces, with walls which it will need many times the centuries that have already passed over them to bring to dust, not crowded by structures of these latter days, but standing as of old in the open fields, the State of Connecticut should maintain it as a place of historic witness, to which men may come to learn what sort of folk they were and what sort of deeds they did, who laid in these colonies such abiding foundations.

"Tantae molis erat pro nobis condere gentem."

WHAT CONNECTICUT STANDS FOR
IN THE
HISTORY OF THE NATION

[32]

THE English settlement of the territory now included in the State of Connecticut was three-fold in origin and purpose, as it was in place. Soon, however, the three streams of history and of influence were merged into one, and the annals of the colony and the State show how they were combined and what has been the strength of the resultant force in character and in action. There came to Wethersfield, Windsor, and Hartford in 1635 (following the steps of earlier emigrants from Plymouth, who made no permanent settlement) a band of men who had been given, not ungrudgingly, permission to remove from the colony of Massachusetts Bay. Their leaders were men of strong character and of strong will under the restraint of sound judgment. Thomas Hooker and Roger Ludlow, with whom we might name William Pynchon, though he never really came under the jurisdiction of the new colony, were not satisfied with the ecclesiastical and civil principles which prevailed in Boston and its neighborhood. They came with their followers to the western bank of the Great River, then the very limit of civilization, that they might found a commonwealth which should be puritanically religious on its religious side, but in which citizenship should not be dependent on church membership, and laws should have their binding force from the will of those who were to be governed by them. It was a settlement made by practical men under the guidance of a practical preacher and a practical lawyer. In the same year John Winthrop, the younger, representing a company in which the names of Lord Say and Sele and Lord Brook were prominent, sent a party to build a fort at the mouth of the Connecticut River. Lieutenant Lion Gardiner was put in command of the garrison, and the place became for a few years the seat of an independent government. Soon merged in Connecticut, it contributed to it no small part of the experience of the Pequot War, and helped at least to give an element of caution in meeting danger, combined with vigor in warding it off. Three years later, in 1638, another company came from England by way of Boston, and took up their home at the fair haven — they presently called it the New Haven — at the mouth of

the Quinnipiack. They were independents, like the pilgrims who had settled Plymouth; there was among them a strange combination of spirit of almost fanatical ecclesiasticism and a spirit of commercial adventure; they were led by the theologian, John Davenport, and the wealthy merchant, Theophilus Eaton; they expected to found a theocracy in which the saints should rule, and they hoped to increase the worldly prosperity of which some of their number already had a goodly share. With this company there were affiliated from the next year Milford and Guilford, the latter being the best example of a community of yeomen devoted to agriculture. Doubtless the religious and civil history of the future State was largely molded by the founders of the River colony, while its record for neighborliness and bravery may be traced back to Saybrook fort; and speaking generally, we look to New Haven for strong intellectual influences and for the sources of material prosperity fostered by invention and secured by trade.

Early in 1639 the freemen of the three towns in the River colony met in a general assembly and, adopting the first written constitution in history, "associated and conjoined themselves to be one public state or commonwealth." The government which they established, with no recognition of King or parliament or of any devolved authority, was a pure democracy, the example and pattern of all the democracies in this land or elsewhere; and the recognition of the three towns, each with its reserved rights, was also the example and pattern of all true federal governments. The germ of the Nation was in that assembly of citizens and in their work, and all the history of our land has been profoundly affected by it. As its immediate consequence there sprang at once into existence an absolutely independent state; its members were citizens of England, and not unwilling to be called by the name, but they could hardly be called English subjects, and their commonwealth, though a colony, was not a dependency of the crown. When, at the restoration of the monarchy in the mother country, Winthrop presented a petition for a charter and a charter was granted, it was not asked or given for the bestowal of rights or the creation of obligations; on the contrary, it contained an acknowledgment on the part of what was vaguely recognized as having a permanent authority over the land, of the existing condition of things. So liberal was it in its provisions, that one wonders how it was brought about that the sovereign and his counsellors ever gave their approval to it; and so well adapted was it to the needs of the people here that for more than forty years after the Declaration of Independence it was retained as the fundamental law of the state. In but one instance, that, namely, of Sir Edmund Andros, was Connecticut called upon to submit to a governor who was not of her own choice; she followed her own laws, and not those of the English parliament until she formally adopted them as her own; she distributed estates according to the Scripture rule which she had accepted and in defiance of the English statutes, and her action was upheld by the supreme tribunal across the sea; she even refused the writ of *habeas corpus* because her legislature had not formally incorporated it in her code. And all this she did quietly and soberly. "The consistent policy of Connecticut," says an historian — and it would be easy to prove the assertion in detail through many years — "was to avoid notoriety and public attitudes; to secure her privileges without attracting needless notice; to act as intensely and vigorously as possible when action seemed necessary and promising; but to say as little as possible, yield as little as possible, and evade as much as possible when open resistance was evident folly. Her line of public conduct was precisely the same after as before 1662 (the date of the charter). And its success was remarkable; it is safe to say that the diplomatic skill, forethought, and self-control shown by the men who guided the course of Connecticut during this period have seldom been equaled on the larger fields of the world's history. As products of democracy they were its best vindication."

An important result of the granting of the charter was the end of the separate existence of the colony of New Haven. It did not submit altogether willingly to its inclusion in the boundaries assigned to what had thus far been a neighboring jurisdiction; but its leaders saw it was better to fall into the hands of latitudinarian Connecticut than into those of the papist Duke of York, and the democratic element which had gained strength in the aristocratic colony welcomed the gift of civil rights and privileges. The union was of advantage to each of the parties which entered into it, and to the whole commonwealth; and the public interests were served by a succession of faithful men, whose names, when once they had been chosen to office, appear again and again as in the same place of responsibility until their death. It must suffice to allude to the generous and willing part taken by Connecticut in the plans and acts of defence taken by the united colonies of New England, a promise of the part she was to play in the greater struggles of which notice will be presently made.

From the very first Connecticut had carefully provided for public education. The requirement of a common school in each town of fifty householders and a grammer school in each county, led to a desire for the establishment of a collegiate school to which those could resort who found Cambridge too far away; and the first year of the eighteenth century saw the foundation of such an institution at Saybrook, which was removed fifteen years later to New Haven, and there gained its name and its fame as Yale College, and was built up by the benefactions of Dean Berkeley and others. Under its shadow in its former home there was gathered in 1708, at the call of Governor Saltonstall and the legislature, the synod which framed the Saybrook platform, an act of ecclesiastical statesmanship giving strength to the congregationalism which elsewhere lacked cohesion; and from its walls in its new home went out in 1722 Samuel Johnson and other leaders of an indigenous episcopacy which was almost immediately granted legal recognition, and never deserved the charge of being the agent of alien denomination. The ecclesiastical history of Connecticut runs, in a very interesting way, parallel to its civil history. The ministers have had a great influence, willingly recognized and almost always soberly used; to recount their names would be to suggest the whole course of progress in learning, in character, and in all that makes up true prosperity.

When called upon to render assistance in the conflicts of the English against the French on this continent, Connecticut, without saying much about it, constantly sent to the front many more than the number of men assigned to her as her quota. At Ticonderoga and Louisbourg officers and men learned lessons which they practiced later with good result, not on their own soil, for it was scarce invaded by those against whom they were called to contend, but at Bunker Hill, at Saratoga, and at Yorktown. To the cause of common liberty Connecticut, though she might have pleaded that she had less than others at stake, contributed most generously the conscientious ability of her leaders, the no less conscientious service of a large proportion of her able-bodied men, and unstinted gifts from her treasury. To the Declaration of Independence there were affixed on her behalf the names of Roger Sherman, Samuel Huntington, William Williams, and Oliver Wolcott, men whose public career, could it be sketched here, would tell the history of their times. Her governor during those momentous years was Jonathan Trumbull, friend and counsellor of General Washington, the "Brother Jonathan" of popular speech, to whose wise forethought successive campaigns owed more than was or is commonly known. Israel Putnam led her troops and directed the whole action at Bunker Hill, and was soon made major-general for further service; Thomas Knowlton, gallant and brave, fell as he turned the tide of battle at Harlem Heights; Nathan Hale gladly gave up his true young life for his country — a nobler and more helpful gift than years of service could

have been; from many homes and from the State's council of safety, always vigilant, went men and supplies to Valley Forge; William Ledyard, brave defender of the fort at Groton, was slain by his own sword in the hour of defeat; Joseph Trumbull and Jeremiah Wadsworth were commissary-generals for nearly the whole period of the war; and to help the work of the State's little navy David Bushnell invented the torpedo.

When the struggle was over and independence was acknowledged, the influence of Connecticut, the State which had had long experience in self-government, was seen even more plainly than in her quiet and efficient service during the war. Two of the signers of the great Declaration, Huntington and Wolcott, were governors during the "critical period" which soon followed; Sherman, whose name appears not only on this document, but also on the Declaration of Rights and the Articles of Confederation, had the further honor of signing the Constitution; and with him was associated in the framing of this document William Samuel Johnson, a man who (as was well known) had not favored a forcible separation from the mother country, but whom his native State honored for his integrity, his legal ability, his learning, and his active fidelity to her interests. There is no doubt that it is to these Connecticut men that the Constitution of the United States owes provisions which rendered it both practicable and acceptable at the time of its adoption, and which, moreover, have commended its wisdom in all the years that have passed. The principles of the fundamental orders of 1639, tested by experience, were thus brought into a wider application; and they were expounded by a Connecticut man who was called to be the first chief justice of the new republic, Oliver Ellsworth, conspicuous for public and private virtues. Jonathan Trumbull, the younger, presided over the House of Representatives in the second Congress. Oliver Wolcott served for a time as Secretary of the Treasury, and Roger Griswold as Secretary of War.

The political history of the State has never been greatly disturbed except when the waves of controversy and party strife, moving over the whole country, have reached the land of steady habits; for the excitement and bloodless revolution which in 1818 led to the adoption of a Constitution was political only because ecclesiastical strife had passed into the political arena and politicians had taken up ecclesiastical differences. The charter government, surviving changes of civil administration, fell because the "standing order" of congregationalism fell; and the small majority who felt that they were suffering from an ecclesiastical tyranny secured the formal equality of all citizens before the law. But a full account of this change in its inception and its accomplishment must be sought in detailed histories. And it is impossible here to do more than allude to the influence, far-reaching and long-continuing, of the colonies which Connecticut sent to the western part of New York, to New Connecticut (better known now as the Western Reserve), and to other parts of the country as soon as it was possible to open them to emigration.

The conduct of the affairs of the State, still in its theory a typical democracy, did not in quiet times depend largely upon the personal ability of those who held the office of governor; for the supreme power was in the general assembly of citizens, and the affairs of state almost, as one might say, administered themselves. And when a great crisis came and the struggle for the preservation of the Union began, the flexibility and practicability of the system still were adequate for all needs. The towns took action, as they could readily and promptly do; the governor took action as he knew that he could do with the body of citizens anticipating his plans; with unselfish devotion the State kept her quota of men more than full and sent into the service of the Union more men in all than the number which appeared on her militia roll. William A. Buckingham became the War Governor by successive election after the ancient custom. For the navy, to which in former days of trial the State had given Isaac Hull and Thomas McDonough, she now gave Gideon Welles in the Cabinet, and Andrew H. Foote, with the two Commodores Rogers and others in the service; and to the roll of the army there were added such names as those of Generals Sedgwick, Mansfield, Hawley, Tyler, Lyon, and Stedman. But on this phase of the history time does not allow us to dwell here, for two aspects of the life of the State still call for our attention; the progress of learning — never in this community divorced from religion — and the progress in invention and the industrial arts which has kept even pace with it.

Two of the Presidents of Yale College, who largely molded its course for the future, Thomas Clap and Ezra Stiles, ended their work in the first century of its history; the names of Dwight and Day and Woolsey and Porter and the second Dwight suggest growth into the university of our own time. Among the leaders of the old theological order many names stand out prominent; it is no derogation of the honorable place and work of others to mention Jonathan Edwards, Lyman Beecher, Leonard Bacon, and Horace Bushnell. The Episcopal Church gained her second strength after the Revolution; three of her five bishops, Seabury and Brownell and Williams, presided over the Church in the whole country; and the two last named were presidents of the second college in Connecticut, first called by the name of Washington and later named Trinity College. The strong purposes and confidence of the Methodists were shown when they founded a third institution of higher education, which has made great progress in its service to the community. The common school system, strengthened by its endowment from the sale of the Western Reserve, fell into a decline from which it was rescued by the labors of Henry Barnard; it was long supplemented by academies of which but few survive, and it now finds its complement in local high schools, so near together that there is scarce a boy or girl of suitable age in the State who cannot enjoy the benefits of them; at least two of these, it may be noted, have handed down the benefits of very early benefactions. While New Haven has been in a sense the intellectual center, the "wits," including the author of *McFingal*, were a coterie in Hartford, where they were followed by Percival and Brainard and Mrs. Sigourney; and Noah Webster must not be forgotten in any enumeration of literary men. To mention any names among the writers of our own day might seem invidious; but we may at least name, among scholars and writers of local history, in succession to Benjamin Trumbull of an earlier generation, Hollister and Beardsley, J. Hammond Trumbull, and Charles J. Hoadly. Still, on the whole, it seems to be true of Connecticut that she has done things rather than told of them, made history rather than written it: *caret vate sacro*.

From the first, Connecticut men busily devoted themselves to commerce, and for a long time ships from her river and seaports sought markets in the West and the East Indies, and for that matter, in all available parts of the earth, and brought in oil and other treasures of the sea. The interests in traffic of this kind have largely passed away; but the spirit of discovery and of travel has been more than replaced by the spirit of invention and of manufacture. We are told that the versatile mechanical genius of the State was first conspicuously shown by one Abel Buel; it was Eli Terry who began the manufacture of wall-clocks, Eli Whitney to whom we owe the truly epoch-making invention of the cotton-gin, and John Fitch who first propelled a vessel through water by the power of steam. The manufacture of pins — the invention of the machine cannot be credited to Connecticut — led to the setting up of brass-works; the inventor of the cotton-gin undertook the manufacture of fire-arms. In his shop Samuel Colt began to make his revolvers; and then in his own shops he began to construct those instruments of precision which have made possible the work of the skilled mechanic of these later years and have given it so great encouragement. The progress of invention and the mechanical arts in the State has been beyond the power of adequate description, and the names of those who deserve honor for their part in it are so numerous that it is

impossible to make any satisfactory selection from them. At first, wherever a fall of water could be found; then wherever coal could be procured; now in almost every place from which goods can be carried to a market, there are busy hands at work to guide the machines which embody human ingenuity, and human brains as busily occupied in devising plans for diminishing labor and increasing its product.

And in all this, from the settlements in the wilderness to the work in thriving towns and cities on the lines of the world's traffic, from the gathering of a few neighbors discussing a few simple rules for the common advantage to the assembly of the representatives of a modern State, from the study of the isolated minister to the lecture-rooms and libraries of the great university, it has been the work of faithful and good men which has been of benefit to its own time and has made ready the way for the coming ages. This is true everywhere; but probably nowhere is it more evidently true than in Connecticut that the record of the men of mark is the story of the commonwealth. *Qui transtulit sustinet.*

GURDON WADSWORTH RUSSELL M.D.. LL.D.

[32] 1815-1909

Dr. Russell's long life was spent in the city of his birth, except that for three years in term-time, while he was studying medicine, he sojourned in New Haven, and for a year after receiving his degree he practised his profession in Wethersfield. He was always interested in that which took place about him, and he remembered all in which he was interested, so that he knew the history of his native place in much detail, as to both persons and events, for some fourscore and ten years. And from time to time he wrote out the record of the past from his memory of it, as in "Up-Neck in 1825," "The Old Stone Jug" (which was the Centre District School on what is now Market Street), "Physicians in Hartford in 1820 and 1837," the notes with which he enlivened the "History of Christ Church," and many communications to the local papers which ought to be collected and published. Well known to the community and knowing it well, he was indeed a part of all that he recorded and of much besides in Hartford's history which will not be readily forgotten by those who knew him.

His paternal grandfather was John Russell, who served in the Revolutionary army at Boston, on Long Island, and at White Plains; his father, bearing the same name, was a printer, who was born in Litchfield in 1790 and came to Hartford about 1810. His first home in the city was on Church Street, a little west of Christ Church, where his son was born on the 10th of April 1815; later he removed to the "Up-Neck" region. The mother was Martha, daughter of Gurdon Wadsworth, a lineal descendant of William Wadsworth, one of the company who came with Thomas Hooker and settled Newtown, afterwards named Hartford. Gurdon Wadsworth Russell as a youth went to school in the "Stone Jug" and the Hopkins Grammar School — now merged in the Public High School — and at Manchester under the care of the Rev. Van R. Osborne. Entering Washington (now Trinity) College in 1830, at the age of fifteen, he took his bachelor's degree in 1834. Immediately after graduation he began the study of medicine with Dr. Amariah Brigham of Hartford, and then entered the Medical department of Yale College, from which he received the degree of Doctor of Medicine in 1837. A year later, after a brief professional residence in Wethersfield, he returned to his native city; there he continued in the active and successful practice of medicine, until the approach of physical infirmity obliged him to limit his labors to those of an advisory nature. His office was for many years on North Main Street, as it was called, just above the turn; in 1884, he built for himself a home at Number 207 Farmington Avenue, with which, after a quarter century's experience, he wrote that he was "perfectly satisfied."

Dr. Russell married 12 September 1838 Sarah Elizabeth, daughter of Samuel and Elizabeth (Hotchkiss) Tuttle, of Hartford, who was born 11 May 1816 and died 16 July 1871; their children were Edward, born 13 June 1839, died 17 April 1877; Elizabeth Hotchkiss, born 5 January 1853, died 15 December 1855; and Gurdon Tuttle, born 6 December 1856, died 6 May 1858. He married again 27 November 1883 Mary Isabella Beresford, daughter of Dr. Samuel Barwick and Mary (Anderson) Beresford, born 17 November 1842.

At the time of his death, on the 3d day of February 1909, Dr. Russell had been for sixty-five years a graduate of Trinity College, which conferred upon him the degree of Doctor of Laws in 1905, and for sixty-three years a graduate of Yale University, his name having stood for some little time at the head of the roll of the living alumni of those institutions. For seventy years he had been a communicant and a member of the parish of Christ Church, and for sixty-two years vestryman or warden, in all this time a wise adviser and a generous supporter of its work; the large silver alms basin was his gift, and when the recess chancel was built he presented the stone reredos above the altar. He was also, as has been already noted, the historian of the parish, devoting to the work much painstaking and affectionate labor. In his early interest in historical matters, he joined in 1840 the Connecticut Historical Society, and lived to be by twenty-four years its senior member. In 1846 he was one of the physicians who organized the Hartford Medical Society, from which, forty-one years after, he received the gift of a loving cup as a memorial of a half-century of service in professional life. In 1850 he was appointed the first medical examiner of the Ætna Life Insurance Company, becoming at a later date, and remaining until his death, its medical director. In the Connecticut State Medical Society he held the offices of secretary, vice-president, and (in 1871) of president; at its centennial meeting in 1892, he read a paper on "Early Medicine and Early Medical Men in Connecticut." In 1855 he assisted in the establishment of the Hartford Hospital, to which he rendered services of a varied and important character; when in 1902 he retired from the presidency of the corporation, which he had held for fourteen years, he was made president emeritus, being also its senior director. He was also nineteen years president of the Hartford Retreat for the Insane, to which he gave a part of his farm on Cedar Mountain, erecting buildings there for the use of its patients, and for which also he built a beautiful stone chapel in 1875, naming it the Elizabeth Chapel in memory of his wife.

Dr. Russell became a Mason in St. John's Lodge in 1853, and was a charter member of Hartford Lodge which was organized in 1859. He served for twenty-five years on the Park Board and the Park Commission of the City of Hartford; and in this capacity, as in others, he gave the city the benefit of his knowledge, his taste, and his good judgment. He was also a trustee or director of several important financial institutions. From 1855 to 1869 he was a member of the Corporation of Trinity College and for nine years its secretary. In the later years of his life he bestowed much labor on a history and

genealogy of the Russell family, which he brought nearly to its conclusion.

Dr. Russell found his recreation in the study of nature in its varied forms, the cultivation of fruit-trees and flowers, the care of his suburban cottage and farm, the reading of the varied treasures of his library, and — it is not amiss to add — in deeds of benevolence to those who were distressed " in mind, body, or estate." Bishop Nichols of California, who was for ten years his pastor, testifies to " the vital relation of his devout religious character to- his profession, and of his professional success to his promotion of the interests of his church and of philanthropy in general," so that " his own winning personality had in itself a singularly happy combination of the two thera-peutic agencies, faith and skill;" and he adds that there was a " distinct blending of his religion and his medicine in his own instance of a long and happy life."

Dr. Russell, by reason of his prominence as a venerated citizen and as the representative of public institutions, was invited to attend on many occasions of general interest, and his presence was welcomed and his continued activity and aptness of speech were noticed to the very end of his life. He attended the Commencement of Trinity College in 1908, as had long been his custom, and told at the Alumni luncheon how he had seen the academic procession marching to the Commencement dinner of 1826 or 1827, and wondered whether he should ever have the honor of attending such an occasion. When the Society of Colonial Wars unveiled the memorial which it placed to mark the site of the Charter Oak, he was present, and soon after he wrote an article on the oak, des-ignating its species, and distinguishing between some trees which were really its descendants and others for which a false claim of such descent was made. At the last graduation of nurses from the training school of the Hartford Hospital, on a cold evening in October, he spoke felicitously, prefacing his remarks with the words, " I cannot hear very well, and I cannot see very well, and you will presently think that I cannot speak very well;" and at the Bridge Celebration in the October before his death, at the request of the committee of arrangements, he took the chair on the evening of the literary exercises, and later he was present at the presenta-tion of a silver service to Senator Bulkeley, president of the Commission.

At the funeral service in Christ Church, the various in-stitutions with which Dr. Russell had been connected were represented, and there was a large assembly of friends and citizens, in fact of all that is best in the life of the community which had known him so long. The bearers represented Christ Church, Trinity College, the Hartford Medical Society, the Hartford Retreat for the Insane, the Hartford Hospital, the Connecticut Historical Society, the Ætna Life Insurance Company, the Society for Savings, the Security Company, and the Farmers and Mechanics National Bank. The ser-vice was read by the Bishop of the Diocese, the Rector and the Assistant Minister of the Parish, and the Dean of the Berkeley Divinity School, seven others of the clergy of Hartford being present in the chancel. On the coffin, with a few flowers — the family having asked that but few should be sent — was a cross of hemlock and cedar and ferns and bitter-sweet from the Cedar Mountain home, prepared at his own request. The burial was in his family lot at Cedar Hill Cemetery.

It will be seen that Dr. Russell's interests were many and varied, while yet he was professionally, before all things else, a physician. His character and his works made him not only a skilful, but also a beloved physician. And his literary work showed that he had the quick and keen insight of a man who could " rerum cognoscere causas," and put into words, with gentle and true humor, what he thus discerned. Thus as he prepared for publication the annals of Christ Church, the occurrence of a name for the first time would recall to him the living man, and the thought of the man would suggest some peculiarity from which he drew in words a picture of the man; or some event, in matters financial or of other kind, would point a moral for later times, and the moral was drawn. He will be remembered, not only for his gifts to institutions of learning and beneficence, not only for his services rendered for the relief of suffering and distress, but also for the truth and kindness which in him were so well combined, and for the good example in which he still speaks and serves a new generation.

THE 150th ANNIVERSARY OF ST. PETER'S CHURCH IN CHESHIRE
[33]
[Nov. 6, 1910]

• • •

We are commemorating the 150th anniversary—the third jubilee—of St. Peter's church in this city, recalling the time when in the early winter of 1760 an organization was effected and good Mr. Scoville, the missionary in Waterbury, dedicated a church on this very site. For forty years New Cheshire had been in law the western society of Wallingford, and such indeed it continued for twenty years longer; and the second meeting-house of the standing order had been built on the village green twenty-two years before. We know of no adherents of the Church of England among the original settlers of the place; in fact we are told that in 1723 the thirty-three families living here were "all of the congregational belief." But there is ex-tant a letter written in 1729 to the Bishop of London by the wardens and parishioners of the Church of England in Walling-ford, and among the fifteen signers is Matthew Bellamy, a New Cheshire man. The letter is interesting, as stating that then they had the service of the church only once a quarter by a min-ister, but that on every Lord's day besides they performed the service as far as was proper for laymen; and also as containing the complaint that divers of them had been imprisoned and their goods from year to year distrained from them for taxes levied for the building and supporting meeting-houses; and that when the matter had come before the governor of the colony, he has lately given the sentence "to enlarge the goal and fill it with them," that is (said they) with churchmen.

Eleven years later, on the 21st of March, 1740, the Church of England people of North Haven and Wallingford and Cheshire organized a union society and built in the Pond Hill district of Wallingford a "Union church." Of their two wardens and six vestrymen, one warden and four vestrymen were of North Ha-ven—all but one of the five, by the way, bore the name of Blakes-lee—the other warden and one vestryman were presumably of Wallingford, and the remaining vestryman was the Matthew Bellamy just mentioned. The church which they built, and a part of which remained until a somewhat recent day, was, we are told, only about twelve feet square; and yet we read under date of 1744 that twenty-five "masters of families" were wont to worship in it and to "edify themselves by reading."

117

An occasional priestly service was given them by the Rev. Theophilus Morris of Derby and perhaps others, until they came under the charge of the Rev. Ichabod Camp. A native of Durham and a graduate of Yale college, he went to England in 1751 for ordination that he might minister in Middletown and Wallingford; and of the thirteen Wallingford subscribers for him, three were residents of the Cheshire district. Early in his ministry separate services were begun here, and Mr. Joseph Moss— a name ever to be held in honor—read the Prayer book service in the house of Zachariah Ives. Mr. Moss bought the church and burying ground lots for their sacred purposes, deeding them presently to the church wardens "for the consideration of £7, 10s., and for love and good will." The green also, it should be noted, was in like manner secured by him for the community.

Meanwhile the Union church organization was dissolved (1757), each of its parts becoming able to provide a house of worship for the congregation in its neighborhood. The Cheshire church was first built, being dedicated, as we have noted, in 1760; the North Haven church was opened for service on St. John the evangelist's day in the next year; and the Wallingford church was completed a year later. We have the names of the seven men who with Joseph Moss contributed to the building of St. Peter's church, as it was named; they were Henry Brooks, sr., Zachariah Ives, Dr. Benjamin Lewis, Amos Matthews, Ebenezer Tuttle, Moses Tuttle and Isaac Tyler. The building itself was small, and it served the need of the congregation but a single decade. In the year of its erection Mr. Camp removed from Connecticut, and he was succeeded in the three-fold cure of the former Union parish by the Rev. Samuel Andrews, a native of what is now Meriden, who gave a fourth of his Sunday services to this place. Under his ministry, always faithful and always successful, the church grew in numbers and in strength. After ten years we are told that he had in this cure forty-seven families with sixty-four communicants, and that eighty-six persons had been baptized by him. In 1770 a new church was built; it was forty-two feet square with galleries, and so very high, though without a steeple, that it loomed up from a distance as if it were a cathedral, while close at hand it presented (to say the least) "an awkward appearance."

In it Mr. Andrews served, coming from his home in North Haven, in the regular ministrations of the word and sacraments, the congregation maintaining lay-services on the Sundays when he was not present; and it is doubtless true here, as in the place of his residence, that his influence "accounts for much of the religious history" of the place between the time of his ordination and the close of the Revolutionary war. "He was a man of estimable character, lovable in every respect, and an indefatigable worker." He kept the people of his cure sober in the excitement which followed upon the Wallingford controversy, and in the excitement of another kind which marked the outbreak and the progress of the Revolution. He was a loyalist, and openly declared his sympathy with the mother coutry; and for a while he was under bonds for good behavior and practically confined in his house. At the close of the war, Mr. Andrews, with his friend and neighbor, Mr. Scoville of Waterbury, removed to the British provinces; the latter was settled at Kingston in New Brunswick, while the good pastor of this region, appointed to the charge of the parish of St. Andrews in Nova Scotia, lived there until 1818. His place here was not taken, and in fact there were only occasional services, until 1788, when the Rev. Reuben Ives, son of the Zachariah Ives in whose house the churchmen of the village had first gathered, was called to be the rector, giving two-thirds of his time here and the other third in Bethany or elsewhere. His salary for both places was to be £75, which in the depreciated money of that day was equivalent to $250; and at the same time it was agreed that the parish would pay a "Proportionable part of £220 annually or more for the support of Bishop Sabre."

At this time we find the first records known to be in existence of the election of officers. Moses Moss and Ambrose Barnes were wardens (constantly spelled "wordings"); Ambrose Atwater, Thomas Atwater, and Ephraim Matthews were vestrymen; David

Badger was, and continued for a long time, clerk; and there were four or five choristers. Soon we read of repairs and additions to the church. Permission was given for building a pew in each corner, the rest to be occupied by slips; then it was voted to add eighteen feet to the length of the building, and to build a steeple as high as the (bell) deck; then to complete the steeple with a spire, and almost immediately to build a cupola instead of a spire, and then to finish the inside and to take out the side-galleries. The building must have been improved in external appearance; but as years went on it did not well stand the stress of storm and wind; of this, however, we must speak presently.

In Mr. Ives's rectorship, Bishop Seabury being still the diocesan, this parish gained a unique place in the diocese and indeed in the country, in being made the seat of a church institution of learning. It would lead me astray from my special topic, and trespass on that assigned to another, if I were dwell in the foundation and early history of the Episcopal academy; but it does concern the history of the parish that this place was selected as the seat of an academy of learning, which served partly as a school, partly as a college, and partly as a theological seminary, in the education of the young men of the church, and which in the years that have followed has in varying ways "answered well the end of its establishment." Thus Cheshire became a center of learning and of ecclesiastical administration; several diocesan conventions and ordinations were held here; and the scholarly men who were principals and assistants at the academy edified the congregation by their ministrations. First among them was Dr. John Bowden, and then Dr. William Smith, to whom with Mr. Ives—for both of them took great interest in the matter—we owe it that this parish was one of the first places in the land in which the psalms and canticles were sung and anthems were rendered; we are really here at the original home of American church music.

But, as years went on, it became evident that, to use Dr. Beardsley's words, the establishment of the academy here had proved "anything but a blessing to the parish." In 1820, Mr. Ives, after a rectorship of thirty and two years, was constrained to resign his office, a serious disagreement having arisen between him and his people. The parish, having two scholarly clergymen resident within its limits, and very possibly moved by considerations of economy, invited the Rev. Dr. Tillotson Bronson, who had then been principal of the academy for fourteen years, and the Rev. Asa Cornwall, his assistant, to take charge of the services and to do such pastoral work as they could, at a united salary of $200. Dr. Bronson continued under this arrangement for five years and Mr. Cornwall for eight years; and there seemed to have been a serious declension in the prosperity of the parish. In 1828 we find it recorded that the Rev. William Rollinson Whittingham was elected rector at a salary of $200 a year, that he expressed a willingness to accept, but that his bishop declined to give him the necessary letters dimissory. The name of so eminent a man, who became a professor in the General Theological seminary and later was for nearly forty years the honored bishop of Maryland, should be even incidentally connected with Cheshire, is worthy of note. He was but in deacon's orders when he was elected principal of the academy and rector of St. Peter's church, resigned a fellowship in the seminary at New York, and even prepared a sermon for use in his new cure, when Bishop Hobart wrote him that he did not consider his proposed removal to be "correct and expedient," and could not consent to it, adding that in this opinion he was fortified by the judgment of the young man's friends. To Mr. Whittingham this was, as he wrote, "no small disappointment," but he submitted as cheerfully as he could.

The connection of the parish with the academy, or rather the dependence of the parish on the academy, lasted until the autumn of the year 1835. At that time a young deacon, a native of Monroe, came to officiate here for a Sunday, "ready," as he said using St. Luke's words, "to depart on the morrow." He read the services and preached in the old church—it had then been standing sixty-five years—rickety as it was, and at times almost dangerous to the worshippers within its walls. He was asked to assume

the charge of the parish; and with the assistance of the venerable Mr. Ives for the celebration of the communion, in which he continued at least one of the peculiarities of Bishop Seabury's office, he entered upon its duties, becoming rector on his ordination to the priesthood, October 24, 1836. Of Dr. Beardsley's relations to St. Peter's church, his twelve years of residence here, his eight years of rectorship, his unceasing interest in the parish, and the academy, his familiarity with their history, his concern for their future prosperity it is not necessary to speak, even though almost a score of years have passed since the close of his honored life. That the historian of the diocese of Connecticut should have preached four memorial sermons here, the last more than a half century after the first, and that this should have been a home of his strong affection and pleasant memories is still no little thing for you. To him you owe it that the ancient structure was, so soon after his coming here, replaced by a well proportioned and dignified brick building, nearly the whole cost of which—some $4,000—was raised by the parishioners, the rector for two years relinquishing his salary; and to him you owe a new inspiration of life, a feeling of rightful independence, and an encouragement to take and to hold the place among Connecticut parishes which rightly belongs to you.

I may but mention the names of the rectors who followed Dr. Beardsley down to a time within the ready memory of those who will tell you of what has been undertaken and done here in the latter days. For three years the Rev. Joseph Hulbert Nichols, later a professor at Racine college, ministered to this "ancient and respectable congregation," as he called it in his letter of acceptance. To him succeeded, from 1851 to 1865, the Rev. Hilliard Bryant, in whose rectorship the number of communicants increased from seventy-two to 129—almost exactly the present number—while near its close the church was enlarged and beautiful by the addition and furnishing of a recess chancel. After him came for two years the Rev. Julius Hammond Ward, for four years the Rev. Edward Mills Pecke, and then in 1873 the Rev. William Byron Buckingham, the mention of whose name brings us within the brief limits of forty years.

Twice within this time has this building been enlarged. It had been but reopened in 1864 after the chancel was built; it was reconsecrated in 1876 when it was lengthened and a transept thrown out on either side, it was again reopened after the erection of the new tower and the provision of room for various parish uses. For ten years (1760-1770) the first church edifice stood on this site; for nearly seventy years (1770-1839), the second building, once enlarged; for more than seventy years (1840-1910), this house of God, three times enlarged, has been the spiritual home of a congregation of God's people. During at least a hundred and thirty years, we may say, this church has been in building, as successive changes have been made to adopt it to new and increasing needs.

We may not add that "yet it is not finished;" it will need care and call for expense in its structure, its fittings, its adornment; the parish is in a bad way which does not see in the near future something that will make a demand on its ability and its generosity; but we know of no reason why these walls should not for more than two generations—if, indeed, the blessed day of the Lord is so long deferred—gather within them the congregation of faithful churchmen of this community for worship and for instruction, for prayer and praise and sacrament.

And what shall we say of the growth of the congregation and of the body of communicants itself? Such a retrospect as that which we have allowed ourselves this morning naturally calls for the names of those who have statedly ministered here; and with them we have joined some honored names of the laymen of early days; but one cannot look through the written records, or read the names carven on stones in God's acre here, without the thought that much—very much of the life of St. Peter's church is due to faithful and true churchmen and churchwomen who have willingly borne the reproach and carried the burdens and found the exceeding joy of the historic and catholic church of Christ. I have named the one churchman of 1729, the man in whose house the services were first held; the first lay reader; of the same family the first recorded warden, and the first clerk afterwards succeeding to the moderator's chair; one cannot worship in this church without memory of the name of Jarvis, to be added to the builders of earlier days; and with it Dr. Beardsley, twenty years ago, joined the names of Barnes, Beach, Bronson, Brooks, Doolittle, Driggs, Hitchcock, Humiston, Ives, Moss, Potter and Welton.

You will add others as in the book of remembrance which you well know is written before God for them that fear Him and that call upon His name; I should add one venerable priest, one dignified man of high judicial position, one true teacher, at the least; the memory fills with thoughts of the past; the heart passes on to sure hopes of times to come, to the knowledge of future sons of our common mother and her daughters yet unborn; and we say of this ancient parish, as was said of the second temple, "They came of old, and built of human souls this living house of God; and since that time even until now hath it been in building, and yet it is not finished." Nor shall it be finished until He, the great Masterbuilder, shall crown His work in His great day. The witness to truth and order, to earnestness and sobriety, to connection with the life of the past and outlook for the opportunities of the days that are dawning, shall, please God, not fail. The patience and the bravery of our forefathers in the faith, shall still guide and embolden our hearts. We are the servants of the God of heaven and His Son our Redeemer and our Lord; therefore, His spirit guiding us, we shall ever be building His temple, that it may be worthy of Him!

CONSECRATION OF
REV. D. TRUMBULL HUNTINGTON
BISHOP-ELECT OF WUHU

IN TRINITY CHURCH, HARTFORD, EVE OF ANNUNCIATION, 1912
[March 24]

My thoughts go back to-night to the fifteenth day of August in the year 1895—rather more than sixteen and a half years ago—when a congregation gathered in the chapel of this church for a service of God-speed to a newly ordained deacon. It was my duty, a duty which I undertook, as I then said, with joy and hope and affection, before celebrating and ministering with him the Holy Communion, to speak words of a personal farewell on behalf of those who were present. A missionary of the English Church, who had done wonderful work as archdeacon for more than a quarter of a century in the territory of the Hudson Bay Company, had spoken of the incentives to missions in the Lord's command, the abundant opportunities, and the certainty of success; and we had in our thoughts and prayers the great and humble bishop and scholar who was to sail back across the Pacific with this young deacon that, in the land where he had served in the days of his physical strength, he might use his weakened physical powers and his unimpaired mental vigor in the completion of a version of the Scriptures into its language. Archdeacon Kirkby and Bishop Schereschewsky have finished their course in faith and rest from their labors, and their works follow them; for what they were and did we render most high praise and hearty thanks to Almighty God. To-morrow morning, as we reckon time—almost at this very hour, as time in itself is—the deacon of that service, for whom and with whom we prayed, having made full proof of his ministry in that initial office and in the priesthood, is receiving his commission as a bishop in the One Holy Catholic and

Apostolic Church of God. We have seen changes here and among ourselves in this sixth part of a century; but what are they to the changes which he has seen, and in which he has borne a greater part than he knows, in the land that lies (as the Romans would have said) transverse to us! No one can tell what the morrow's journal may record

as to the progress of political changes in the land of Sinim; but no one doubts that the results of these changes will be far-reaching, and that on this very point of the history of a great and ancient people turns the momentous record of its future. The mind and heart of the civilized world is anxious, with thought and a sense of responsibility from which it cannot escape, by reason of what has recently come to pass and what may shortly come to pass in that land—a land which, far-off though it seems, the science of to-day almost enables us to touch. And the mind and heart of Christendom is anxious, not only because the Church of Christ must always feel responsible for all humanity, but also by reason of the brotherly love which leads her to recognize as her own flesh and blood those who, though in a far-off land, are knit to us in the knots of a common faith while their hearts are beating with the inspiration of our spiritual life. And our own anxiety is greater, though our confidence in the issue is stronger, by reason of our knowledge that the thoughts and purposes and the life of that people are to no little extent guided by men earnestly professing the faith of Christ the Lord and resolutely determined to follow His example by His Spirit's aid—men to whom Christ is "the sum and substance of all things." When our brother went out to preach among the Gentiles the unsearchable riches of Christ, China (as was said at the time) was bringing the offering of her people to Him but as the flow of an imperceptibly moving tide carries to the shore the precious things of the deep; it has been his to hasten and to herald—yea, and to see—the coming of the decuman wave which is bringing the desirable things of that ancient nation, their immortal souls with all their God-given capacities and faculties, to Him of whom and through whom and for whom are all things.

To-day he takes up a burden for which he has been in God's providence long preparing, by a goodly inheritance of character, in home life, in academic and theological training, in service rendered and in experience gained—largely with the guidance and help of one who nobly employed the powers of her life for the same service and experience—in the ministerial priesthood of all these years, the toil of the trade school, the care of beggars, the instruction of the ignorant, the constant setting forth of the Master's life. And that Master, through His Church carrying out His purpose for the ages, to-day gives a reward of faithfulness by the call to higher acts of faithful service, the recognition of tasks well and humbly done by the assignment of harder tasks to be done with the same ready hand and humble mind. And we can do no less, we can hardly do more, than pray that our brother's may still be the life of obedience and of service, that the newly consecrated shepherd of souls may indeed hasten the coming of the kingdom of our Lord and of His Christ!

And with our prayers for him whom this congregation knows better than does any other, except those whom he has served in these years of his lower ministry, let us add a petition for the faithful priest and teacher who also is consecrated this day that he may do like service in the island empire of Japan, Dr. St. George Tucker, Bishop of Kyoto.

God's benison be on them and on their people, and on us all! And in the words of the blessed Virgin who as on this day first sang the Magnificat, bearing witness that the mercy of God our Saviour is on them that fear Him throughout all generations, we shall ever pray that remembering this His mercy He will help His people for ever, even as He promised to our forefathers and as He hath holpen us.

THE FUNDAMENTAL ORDERS
[35] ## AND THE CHARTER
[Read October 21, 1912.]

The government of Connecticut began with the appointment of a constable for that new plantation on the 3d day of September in the year 1635. Three companies had come, or begun

to come, from the Dorchester and Newtown and Watertown of Massachusetts Bay to found places of the same name just below the head of navigation on the further side of the great river to the west; and those who rather grudgingly gave them leave to depart still took care that they should not be quite without the form of civil administration. Presently the authorities in the Bay issued a commission to eight men, two from each of the settlements just named and two from Agawam further up the river, at the desire (we are told) of those who were removing and who judged it "inconvenient" (that is, unseemly) to go away without any frame of government. It was dated the 3d day of March, 1636—before Mr. Hooker and his immediate company had arrived—and it was to hold but for a year. The commissioners were authorized to try civil causes, to punish offenders, and to make orders for the peaceable and quiet conduct of the new plantations. How far the Massachusetts General Court held that it was granting a power to be exercised under itself, and how far the Connecticut adventurers were ready to acknowledge responsibility to the Court which issued the commission, we cannot tell. Probably all knew that the three river settlements, as they were called, were below the Massachusetts line as defined by charter, and Mr. Pynchon had hopes that he also was outside of the Bay jurisdiction; probably the Connecticut "Court"—for so it was named from the first—would have declared that it represented those who had withdrawn by permission from under the authority of the Massachusetts Court. At any rate, we have no reason to believe that any one here would have thought of carrying an appeal there, or that any one there claimed, through the commissioners or otherwise, any authority here.

The first "Court holden att Newton" (that is, Hartford), of which we have any record, was on the 26th of April, 1636. But the abrupt way in which its record begins makes it almost certain that there had been one or two meetings before that date. The business of the day was varied: it had to do with the swearing-in of three constables, trading with the Indians, the ordering of strange swine, and the organization of a church in Watertown. Six more meetings were held before the year of the appointment of the commissioners had expired, at the last of which the three plantations were given their present names. All sorts of business was transacted at these meetings, as by one sovereign government, including the defining of "the bounds of Dorchester towards the Falls and of Watertown towards the mouth of the River." Near the end of March there was another meeting, the commissioners apparently assuming that they could "hold over."

But on the first day of May, 1637, the records begin with a new heading, "Generall Corte att Harteford"; and after the names of six of the former commissioners as present, we find, with the heading "Comittees," the names of three men from each of the river plantations. We do not know how they were elected or who gave order for their election; but there had

NOTE.—The chief authorities and sources for this paper are the "Colonial Records of Connecticut"; Dr. J. Hammond Trumbull's "Historical Notes on the Constitutions of Connecticut" (Hartford, 1873); Governor Baldwin's "The Three Constitutions of Connecticut" (in Vol. V of New Haven Colony Historical Society papers; page 182 line 8, read 1645, new style); Judge William Hamersley's "Connecticut, the Origin of her Courts and Laws," in Vol. I of "The New England States" (Boston, 1897).

certainly been the introduction of a new democratic element into the government, as soon as the jurisdiction was free from all semblance of connection with the aristocratic colony of the Bay; and quite probably the feeling that a declaration of "offensive war against the Pequoitt" was impending, and that it would be necessary to make requisition upon the people of the several towns for its maintenance, suggested this provision for representation. (In April of the next year, by the way, Agawam was represented at the General Court by both magistrates and committee-men.) Dr. J. Hammond Trumbull quotes from a letter of Rev. Thomas Hooker, written in the autumn of 1638, which enables us to see how the Court was constituted. He says: "At the time of our election"—probably in March—"the committee for the town of Agawam came in with other towns, and chose their magistrates, installed them into their government, took oath of them for the execution of justice according to God, and engaged themselves to submit to their government and the execution of justice by their means and dispensed by the authority which they put upon them by choice." This falls in with the doctrine of Hooker's sermon so often quoted, and points the divergence of the principles of the Connecticut jurisdiction from that of Massachusetts; for in the latter, as Winthrop confesses, though "the people had long desired a body of laws, great reasons there were which caused most of the magistrates and some of the elders not to be very forward in the matter." On the 9th of February, 1638, the record closes with these words: "It is ordered that the General Court now in being shall be dissolved, and there is no more attendance of the members thereof to be expected except they be newly chosen in the next General Court."

There must have been an election, then, holden on or before the 8th of March, which is the date of the next record, at which eight magistrates were present and eleven committee-men; the twelfth "committee," a Wethersfield man, was fined for his absence "1s. to be forthwith paid."

This court transacted all sorts of business: it took up the case of an Indian's imprisonment at Agawam, and decided "to pass over Mr. Plummer's failings in the matter"; it made a contract with Mr. Pynchon about the price at which he would furnish corn; it gave orders as to the treatment and discipline of the Indians; it ordered 50 "costlets" to be provided for military use; it appointed Captain Mason a public officer, with power to train the military men in each plantation ten days in every year, "so it be not in June or July," and ordered that all persons above the age of sixteen years should bear arms, not tendering a sufficient excuse or being or having been commissioners or church officers, and provided also for magazines of powder and shot; and it made a rule that "whosoever doth disorderly speak privately during the sittings of court with his neighbor or two or three together shall presently pay 1s. if the courte so think meet." There was, then, evidently an organized government by a legislature and judicial court, consisting of two bodies of representatives, one chosen by the whole body of citizens within the jurisdiction, the other made up of four committees of three chosen by the citizens of the four plantations respectively; they evidently sat together, but we are not told how the vote of the court was taken.

Now all this was done, and a form of civil government was adopted—even if its permanence was not guaranteed—before the famous sermon or lecture of Rev. Thomas Hooker was preached on Thursday, the last day of May, 1638. The lecture may well have been, as Dr. J. Hammond Trumbull said, "designed to lead the way to the general recognition of the great truths which were soon to be incorporated in the Fundamental Laws" or Orders; but it is quite too much to say that it was the original inspiration of those "Orders." Mr. Hooker's "doctrine" in the discourse, as Henry Wolcott's cipher was deciphered by Dr. Trumbull, was three-fold: "1. That the choice of public magistrates belongs unto the people by God's allowance; 2. The privilege of election which belongs unto the people, therefore, must not be exercised according to their humors, but according to the blessed will and law of God; 3. They who have power to appoint officers and magistrates, it is in their power also to set the bounds of the power and place unto which they call them." The second point of this "doctrine" has to do with personal duty and its motives; it is matter of exhortation; and it cannot be brought to an external test. But the first and third, that the people may elect their own magistrates and that the same people may also set the bounds of the magistrates' power, had been acted on already; and there is not the slightest reason to think that the congregation who listened to the lecture, including the members of the General Court, needed persuasion on these points, though they probably were pleased to have an apologia for what had been done and for what it was in their minds to do. And while there can be no doubt of Mr. Hooker's influence or of the direction in which it was applied, it certainly was not needed to move the people of the jurisdiction to act on principles of government which they had already accepted. Dr. Bacon's remark that the sermon is "the earliest known suggestion of a fundamental law, enacted not by royal charter, nor by concession from any previously existing government, but the people themselves," attributes to the preacher what the people had already accepted as a principle, having learned it perhaps from the minister of Hartford, but also quite certainly from the influential lawyer of Windsor.

We may be quite sure that the Fundamental Orders of the fourteenth day of January, 1639, did little more than put definitely into writing a rather complicated form of administration already in use, and also—no little thing, indeed—provide for a head of the government in the person of a governor; and this latter may have been thought by some to be rather a weakening than a strengthening of the pure democracy which had been founded. At any rate, on the day just named, "the inhabitants and residents of Windsor, Hartford, and Wethersfield, cohabiting and dwelling in and upon the River of Connecticut and the lands thereunto adjoining"—or at least so many of them as were thought fit to form a compact with one another, for their democracy did not imply universal suffrage—meeting together as one body did associate and conjoin themselves to be as one Public State and Commonwealth. Such indeed they had been; and yet it was no little thing which they did when, with the help of a skillful mind and pen, they put their articles of agreement into writing. For, as has been so often pointed out, it was the first time in the history of the world that a body of men, recognizing no allegiance to any human authority, though they had been and might have held themselves to be

subjects of a government which had an organized colony not far from them, constituted for themselves, in a formal way and with the impressiveness of a written document, an absolutely new and independent commonwealth. The commonwealth and the general court, indeed, date from a few years further back; but the "orderly and decent government established according to God," with duties and powers and restrictions put into writing and published, dates for Connecticut and for the civilized world from this 14th of January, 1639.

This Constitution, for such it really was, contained eleven Fundamental Orders; and in them we see so much either stated or implied in the records of General Courts held before this time, that we are warranted in believing that in other matters not evidently new we have the continuation of principles already recognized and acted upon. They were the principles of a true self-regulating democracy, assuming sovereignty and providing for its own perpetuation. The more important, for our purpose, may be thus stated. Once a year the whole body of citizens were to choose a governor and at least six other magistrates from a list put in nomination at a court held not less than six months in advance; a very ingenious plan, as it continued for many years, for securing reëlection of a large part if not all of the magistrates who did not make themselves specially obnoxious; for each person nominated was voted for or against severally in the order of nomination. Also, twice a year, before each regular meeting of a General Court, the admitted inhabitants of each of the three towns—Agawam being dropped out, as belonging to Massachusetts—and of each of such other towns as might be admitted, were to meet and choose three or four deputies to be members of the court; and here at any rate there was great room for freedom of choice and the possibility of frequent change. Thus a general court of governor, magistrates, and deputies was constituted, having the supreme power of the Commonwealth. In case the governor and magistrates should neglect or refuse to call the court, the freemen might order their own constables to summon them and thus might meet together, apparently in a mass meeting, and have all the powers of the court; thus provision was made against any wilful or accidental stoppage of the wheels of government. Also—and this is an anticipation of a bicameral legislative body in a democracy, which has hardly received the attention it deserves—the deputies might meet by themselves before they went into the court with the governor and magistrates, to inquire into their own elections and to "consult of all such things as may concern the good of the public"; in fact, they might prepare business for the court and bring it in with the strong sanction of their agreement. But the sovereignty remained where it had always been, in the whole body politic of the jurisdiction. There was no recognition of any higher sovereignty; the governor—the only person, by the way, who was required to be a church member—was sworn to maintain all lawful privileges of this commonwealth, and also all wholesome laws made by lawful authority here established, and to further the execution of justice according to God's word; and the magistrates' oath was in the same tenor and almost exactly in the same words. In everything there was the calm assertion of independence, as well from Massachusetts as from England.

Thus was the practice of a few years, somewhat modified, put into writing to serve as fundamental orders or constitution for the jurisdiction of Connecticut; and under this form of government Connecticut continued for twenty-three years, undisturbed by changes which took place in the government of the Bay Colony or of England, a government by itself and for itself. Yet there were changes made in the methods of that government. Nothing had been said in the Orders, adopted (it must be remembered) by the vote of the whole community, as to any possible amendment of them; it might be assumed, one would say, that the same authority would be needed for the amending as for the first establishing of so important a document. And one change was thus made in 1660, allowing the reëlection of the governor, which had been forbidden by the first of the orders. The court of April propounded the amendment to the consideration of the freemen, and desired that proxies on the question should be sent to the May court. The proxies, in the form of written or blank votes received in the several towns and sent to Hartford at the time of the election, approved the change; and John Winthrop the younger, who had up to this time been governor in alternate years, was thenceforth elected each year continually until his death in 1676. But in another important matter a fundamental order, or as we should say a section of the Constitution, was amended by a vote of the General Court without any reference to the people. It had been required that the governor or other moderator and four others of the magistrates at least should be present, with the major part of the deputies, to make a quorum of any court. In 1665, it was "ordered and adjudged" that three magistrates besides the moderator should be the number required for a lawful court. And at the same time it was required that to make a vote of the court there should be the concurrence of the major part of the magistrates and the major part of the deputies there present, either magistrates or deputies being allowed—it is expressly said—a negative vote. Thus the court became an assembly of two bodies, debating together but voting separately, and a great change of a democratic nature was made, and that without reference to the parties who were most concerned, the whole body of freemen.

Perhaps it has not been sufficiently noticed—though Judge Hamersley called attention to it when writing on the origin of the Courts and Laws of Connecticut—that the court of those early days exercised judicial as well as legislative functions. It sat as a "general court" for the exercise of all powers and as a "particular court" for the trial of a special case. There were particular courts as early as 1639, in which the magistrates sat with the governor and the deputy governor, but without the deputies from the towns; and we find mention of a jury both before and after the date of the fundamental orders. The orders themselves say nothing as to the particular courts or the juries; it is evident that they were looked upon as a part of the former administration which had not been modified by the written law. In October, 1639, less than nine months after the orders were adopted, provision was made for the establishment of a court in each town, consisting of three, five, or seven of the chief inhabitants to be chosen annually, and to meet once in two months, with jurisdiction over parties living in the town in civil causes not exceeding 40 shillings; the right

of appeal to a higher court was guarded. The office of these men was not the same as that of the townsmen or selectmen, though doubtless the same persons might be chosen to both offices; and there is no reason to think that they had juries in their courts. (At the same session, by the way, a beginning was ordered to be made for the preservation of a record "of those passages of God's providence which have been remarkable since our first undertaking these plantations," under the direction of the General Court; this was just 200 years before the renewal of the charter of the Connecticut Historical Society and the beginning of its active existence.) We have thus a true judicial system, the administration of justice, "according to the laws here established, and for want thereof according to the rule of the word of God," acknowledged to be, rather than placed, in the hands of those called magistrates, who sometimes shared this power with the deputies but as a rule administered it by themselves, lesser cases however being disposed of (when possible) in town or neighborhood courts. It may be that facility of pleading was found to be an encouragement of litigiousness, which indeed some have called a Connecticut failing from the beginning; for we find in the records as early as 1642 an entry declaring that "it is the apprehension of the General Court that the particular courte should not be enjoined to be kept above once in a quarter of a year." Five years later an addition, in form of an interpretation, was made to the tenth of the fundamental orders, declaring that for a particular court it was not necessary to have the presence of the governor or deputy governor and four (that is, a majority) of the magistrates, which was required when they made a part of the General Court; but that two of the magistrates with the governor or the deputy governor, or three magistrates when neither of the higher officials could attend, might hold a particular court. The sessions of this court, which dealt with both civil and criminal cases, became pretty frequent; in 1646 there were six and in 1047 seven, at all of which except one a jury was empanelled. The whole matter of juries was regulated by the general court in 1644-5. After a while assistants and commissioners were appointed for newly admitted towns which had no resident magistrate; and from them came by development, Judge Hamersley tells us, the "Justices of the Peace." A grand jury of twelve persons, called as a rule year by year, was first ordered in 1643, to make presentment of any misdemeanors they knew of in the jurisdiction; and in 1660, grand jurymen were appointed for the several towns, the number of which had increased to ten. Probate matters, with allowance of wills either written or nuncupative, were regulated from 1639; intestate estates were to be taken charge of by the "orderers of the affairs of the towns" and the goods divided "to wife (if any be), children, or kindred, as in equity shall be seen meet." In all this time the population of the whole jurisdiction was less than 1,000, and the number of freemen probably did not exceed 150.

Thus, under the fundamental orders and their expansion, matters went on, until the application for a charter and its grant by the Crown of England made Connecticut in law what it had already been sometimes called, a Colony of England. In the time of the Commonwealth no change had been necessary here; but the end of the Commonwealth and the restoration of the Stuarts made it a matter of prudence and of safety that this thriving jurisdiction, situated between the stronger and wealthier jurisdictions of Massachusetts Bay and New York, and exposed to the attacks of enemies, should have the protection of the government of the mother country. And the changes which had taken place and were impending beyond the sea made it also a matter of prudence and of safety that this independent community should preserve its independence and continue to exercise the rights of self-government which it had so carefully and ingeniously secured and held. It is interesting to note that, as the practices of the years before 1639 were carried over, with some amendments for the better, into the fundamental orders, so the rules of these orders and the practices under them were carried over, likewise with some amendments, into the charter.

There is not time to speak at length of the petition for the charter, the draft of such a document which Governor Winthrop carried to England, the influence which he brought to bear upon Charles II and his ministers, and the way in which it extended the jurisdiction of Connecticut so that it included that of the New Haven confederacy. The suppliants prayed for a continuance of their former liberties, rights, authorities, and privileges; and these were all confirmed by that most remarkable document of 250 years ago, signed on St. George's day, exhibited to the commissioners of the United Colonies in Boston in September, and read in the audience of the freemen in Hartford on the 9th day of October, as to which one wonders how it ever passed the Privy Council or obtained royal approval. The people of Connecticut looked upon it as granted at their petition and accepted by themselves quite as really as their former constitution; they found in it a confirmation of their own free government, and they interpreted what they deemed "minuter parts" in the new documents in accordance with the former principles which were not contravened. It is easy to see how all this could be held and made the basis of action. The charter enacted the freemen of the Company and Society of the Colony of Connecticut into a "Body Corporate and Politick"; it ordered that there should be a governor, a deputy governor, and twelve assistants, to be chosen once a year by the freemen; and that the assistants, with the freemen or deputies of the freemen not exceeding two from each town or city, should have twice a year a general meeting or assembly; that the officers should take oath for the performance of their duty, nothing being said as to the form of what is called "the said oath" or of a promise or declaration of allegiance to any external authority; that the governor and assistants assembled in courts might "make ordain and establish all manner of wholesome and reasonable laws statutes ordinances directions and instructions not contrary to the laws of this realm of England," nothing here being said as to the necessity of any royal or other approval or as to any way of determining the fact of a conflict with the laws of the realm; Connecticut interpreted the words to mean that any law of its own could hold within its borders, with the possible exception of cases in which England had made a different law expressly for this very colony. It will be seen that the General Court, which soon began to be called the General Assembly, was continued, that judicial authority emanated from that Court, and that the authority of the governor was somewhat increased.

The charter seems to have expected that all the freemen would

meet in person before the assembling of the General Court, "then and there to advise in and about the business of the company" or corporation; and certainly it required that the governor, the deputy governor, and the assistants—these corresponding to the former magistrates and now twelve in number—should be chosen at the annual meeting of the company by the major part of the members of the company then and there present. It has seemed to some careful students, as to our present governor, that the charter intended to pass the real management of the Colony to the governor and assistants, oftener called the governor and council; and he notes that the letters from the Crown officials in England were generally addressed to the governor and council. Yet the charter did provide for the election of deputies, not exceeding two persons from each place town or city, elected by the major part of the freemen of the respective towns cities and places; and, as Governor Baldwin himself says, "Whatever the intention of its authors may have been, Winthrop's charter, when it reached Connecticut, was read as if it made the deputies of the freemen as full a part of the legislature as they had always been." And perhaps the Crown lawyers meant no more by the clauses which imply that in some cases the governor and assistants might act without the deputies from the towns, than the people here were accustomed to see in the frequent sessions of the particular court. In point of fact this part of the assembly was presently, by vote of the general assembly itself, constituted a council, "to act in emergent occasions"; and though the vote was repealed two years later, it was re-enacted in 1675.

The assembly on the 9th of October, 1662, having read the charter to the freemen and declared it to belong to them and their successors, went about its business as usual. But first it put the document into the custody of three chosen men, directed the constables to collect corn from their towns "to discharge the country's engagement for the charter," ordered that the seal of the general court be retained as the seal of the Colony, accepted the submission of certain plantations and inhabitants formerly of the New Haven confederation, and declared "all the laws and orders of this Colony to stand in full force and virtue, unless any be cross to the tenor of our charter." In fact, Connecticut maintained from the first that the charter made no real difference in her form of government, and that this document was in reality in the nature of a contract, the Crown benefiting by an increase of territory, acquired by the labor and at the cost of the colonists, and also by the allegiance of a well-placed body of subjects, and the Colony gaining an assurance of protection and of interest in the affairs of the mother country. Thus indeed the preamble reads; and thus the rights derived from the charter were declared to be "sacred and indefeasible," and the charter itself was declared "to stand upon the same basis with the grand charters and fountains of English liberty." "This construction of the charter"—I use Judge Hamersley's words—"as a confirming grant by the Crown of the form of self-government already established by the people, was maintained with unvarying persistency, marked by shrewd caution as well as stubborn courage."

And the General Assembly had no more hesitation in amending the charter than the General Court had had in amending the fundamental orders. The charter, (as has been already noted,) provided that once in the year for ever, the governor, deputy governor, and assistants of the company should be newly chosen for the year ensuing by the greater part of the said company (of freemen) being then and there present; and in this it followed what was evidently the original custom or rule, giving occasion for an ambiguity in the use of the term General Assembly, which sometimes means the personal assembling of the freemen and sometimes their assembling by their deputies or representatives with the governor and magistrates. This would serve as long as the freemen all lived within a few miles of the place of assembling; but at the date of the charter there were freemen of the Colony in towns as remote as Saybrook, New London, and Norwalk, and the number was then increased by the incorporation of the New Haven jurisdiction. Before this time the freemen of the remote plantations, as we know from the wording of a record in 1660, had been used to send their proxies, that is to say to transmit their ballots, duly cast in freemen's meetings and sealed up, to Hartford, that they might be counted with the votes of those who were assembled there. In all probability this rule or custom was continued, and the more readily because it had been a provision of the fundamental agreement at New Haven; at any rate, it was confirmed or reëstablished in 1670, and that in the very teeth of the charter, that all the freemen should or might, on the second Thursday of May yearly, attend at Hartford either in person or in proxy, and consummate the election of the general officers of the Colony. The method of proxy voting, which was held in the towns on the last Tuesday of April, was that the freemen voted first for governor, then successively for deputy governor, treasurer, and secretary, and the ballots in each case were sealed up. Then the twenty nominations made for assistants were read in order, the names taken first being those of the men already in office who were renominated or willing to accept reëlection; each freeman voted in each case, putting in a marked ballot if he wished to vote for the person named or a blank ballot if he preferred to vote against him; the ballots in the case of each candidate were sealed up; and when all were counted at Hartford, the twelve candidates who had the largest number of marked ballots were declared elected assistants for the year.* The provision as to voting by marked or blank ballots is as old as the fundamental orders, and probably can be traced further back in England. The "stand-up law" was not passed until 1801.

Another amendment of the provisions of the charter, without authority from the Crown or even from the body of the freemen, was made in 1698. After the granting of the charter, the assistants or Council and the deputies had continued to sit together in one house, probably voting separately as of old; but now the General Assembly divided itself into two houses. The governor and deputy governor with the Council met as the "upper house," the governor or his deputy presiding; and the representatives of the towns met as the "lower house," choosing their own speaker. This act, though in the line of

---

* This use of the word "proxy" is noted in the new Oxford Dictionary as peculiar to Connecticut and Rhode Island, and is marked as obsolete. Proxies, in the sense of documents authorizing one person to vote for another, have never been known in English elections or legislatures except in the House of Lords; they were discontinued there in 1868.

governmental development and (we may think) encouraged by the changes of the revolution in England which gave rise to modern parliamentary government, was in its nature revolutionary. It attached the governor to one branch of the assembly, that in which most of the judicial power was vested, and it removed him from immediate contact with the other branch, in which most of the legislation would be apt to originate. About the same time it was ordered that justices of the peace should no longer be chosen annually, but should hold office during the pleasure of the General Assembly. Both these acts, said Samuel Welles writing to Governor Fitz-John Winthrop, were expected to "strengthen the government, when they are not at the dispose of the arbitrary humors of the people, and yet subject to be called to account by the General Court." To us, the former change at least might seem in reality to strengthen the power of the democratic element. Certainly it seems to have been believed that the omnipotence of Parliament was communicated to the General Assembly of Connecticut under its charter; and it would have taken much persuasion to convince the people of Connecticut that their legislature, or General Assembly, had not sovereign powers.

And Connecticut, rather warily to be sure, but very plainly, did under the charter and before independence of the British Crown was secured exercise sovereign powers. Its legislature granted a University charter to the Collegiate school of 1701; it issued bills of credit; it divided intestate estates in violation of the law of England though in accord with the law of Deuteronomy; it framed or assumed a common law divergent from that of England. Thus it claimed and exercised the powers of a sovereign, and to those powers it set none but moral limits. John Read, the great colonial lawyer, argued from a Connecticut standpoint in 1743, when he said: "God and nature have given unto mankind, or human society, a power of assent and dissent to the laws by which they are to be governed (those only excepted which proceed from absolute sovereignty); and this is the known privilege of Englishmen, to be governed by laws to which they have, in one form or another, given their consent."

At the time of the Revolution, which issued in the recognition by Great Britain of the independence of Connecticut and twelve other States, this State did not need to frame a Constitution. In October, 1776, the General Assembly, declaring that the King of Great Britain had abdicated the government of this State, approved the Declaration of Independence, absolved the inhabitants from allegiance to the British Crown, and enacted "that the form of Civil Government in this State shall continue to be as established by charter from Charles the Second, King of England, so far as an adherence to the same will be consistent with an absolute independence of this State on the Crown of Great Britain."

In 1784, a revision and codification of the laws being made, it was solemnly declared that "The people of this State, being by the Providence of God free and independent, have the sole and exclusive right of governing themselves as a free sovereign and independent state; and having from their ancestors derived a free and excellent constitution of government, whereby the legislature depends on the free and annual election of the people, they have the best security for the preservation of their civil and religious rights and liberties."

This action and this declaration were not submitted to the people, but they were accepted by them; and it was not till 1818 that the principles of the Charter of 1662, received from the Fundamental Orders of 1639, and reaching back to the very foundation of the Colony, were embodied in a formal Constitution.

CONNECTICUT'S FIRST QUARTER-CENTURY

Read at the meeting of the CONNECTICUT HISTORICAL SOCIETY, December 5, 1912, by SAMUEL HART, *President*

Two hundred and seventy-five years ago—a quarter of a millenium and a quarter of a century—late in the summer the first English settlers came to the site of Hartford. We are told that on the 3d day of September in the year 1635, William Westwood was sworn constable for the new plantation on the Connecticut; and as a constable was the one thing absolutely necessary for the exercise of civil authority, so this possession of a constable was proof of an orderly community. What did the new settlers, thus recognized as in a true sense a body politic, find here, near the head of navigation on what the Indians called the Long River and the Dutch the Fresh River? And what were their experiences in the early years of their life here? And preliminary to an outline answer to these questions we may ask, What was the place to which they and their neighbor colonists came?

First, then, the place was in the interior of a practically unknown land and beyond its first great river. The settlement of Pilgrims at Plymouth was but fifteen years in the past, and that of Puritans on the shores of Massachusetts Bay was but five or six years old; and they had not pushed out into the wilderness which lay to the west and extended no one knew how far. Those who had sailed along the coast had seen fair shores, and rivers which to the former inhabitants of a small island were great streams; and the fame of a greater river had reached them, up which Henry Hudson had gone for miles before he found that it was not an arm of the sea or a strait through which a passage lay to China and the Indies. But to go far up a river and make a home on its further bank, or to strike across wild woodlands until it was reached and crossed, this was to make a venture of courage and faith. If Abram the Hebrew showed himself the man that he was and gained a name for himself because he trusted himself to Providence and crossed the great river, the river Euphrates, surely those who left the comparatively safe shores of Massachusetts Bay and crossed the great river of Connecticut were heroes of faith as was he. And they expected to have their faith tested. The Gog and Magog, powers of antichrist, were not for our ancestors nations of the north, pushing down upon the ancient peoples of the belt within which religion and civilization had been confined; their dark land was the west, into which they themselves were bidden to go that they might wage war against the powers of evil. And what was more natural to expect than that the last great struggle would be in the end of the world, as well in space as in time, and here on the west bank of the Connecticut?

But even if it was destined to be a spiritual battlefield, as well as a place of possible bodily conflict, it was a beautiful place to which they came and in which they awaited the coming of their more dignified brethren. Others had been here,

and had told in the Bay of the fair land, suggesting withal (we may be sure) that it lay south of the line of the Massachusetts government. In 1633, William Holmes from Plymouth had sailed up the river to the Dutch Point, and had pushed on to the mouth of the Tunxis; and in the same year John Oldham had come overland from Massachusetts Bay. The Plymouth men did no more than set up a trading post at this northernmost spot, not very far below the rapids; but soon permanent colonists came from Dorchester bringing the church which had been organized in England some years before; and some of them were certainly placed and housed before there were settled inhabitants here. Also to the south of this spot there had come in 1634 a colony of Watertown people, themselves too bringing a church organization effected in England about one year later than that of the Dorchester men. And from them had come to the Massachusetts Newtown an account of the opportunities for life and work here in a new home, not too near to the ecclesiastical colony of Boston and its neighbor towns. And who that has seen this part of the valley of the Connecticut in the early summer will wonder that the early visitors spoke well of it, and that those who followed them were glad to take up their homes in it? There must have been the wide meadows, quite open or scantily wooded, for there were heavy freshets in those days as well as now; there must have been the beauty of grass and foliage, with perhaps here and there a little patch of soil turned up by the Indians with the strange kind of corn called maize growing upon it; there must have been the attraction to hunters to look in the forest for deer and other game and to catch from the river the salmon and the shad.

Moreover, the river led by a sufficiently ample stream down to the Sound; and the control of its mouth, though claimed by the Dutch of New Amsterdam, was practically, and soon became actually, in the hands of the fellow-countrymen of those who were coming hither. And under protection of a charter right, or at least of a grant from a chartered company, with a governor and a captain and an engineer, Saybrook was fitted to be a defence and help for the men up river. To be sure, there was also the Huyshope, the House of Good Hope, on the south bank of the Little River, and the Dutch had their boat with its threatening name of *Onrust;* but the garrison was a quiet one, and taking itself quietly rather than seriously, and certainly not taken seriously by the Englishmen who sailed past it and settled down but a little way above it.

Such were the beginnings of the Connecticut Newtown, now Hartford; the large emigration here, with the church organized at the Massachusetts Newtown in 1632, did not arrive until the following year. Those who had come to face an unknown winter, after it was too late to make full provision against it, must have felt that almost any place would be better than that which had been chosen for them. Very early there set in a season of terrible cold and heavy snow. By the middle of November the river was frozen over; the settlers could not keep warm and could not get sufficient food from the Indians; and some seventy of them walked on the ice and along the river banks to the fort at the mouth of the river, to keep themselves from freezing and starvation. There they found relief, and thence they were able—at least part of them—to sail back to Boston. But this experience did not break up the colony or hinder the great emigration appointed for the following year. The Newtown people sold their houses to newcomers, who organized a new church; eight commissioners were appointed by the government which had given them tardy permission to remove, and these eight men held a "corte" at the Connecticut Newtown on the 26th of April; and the last day of May saw the emigrants on the journey, most of them on foot, a few perhaps on horses, Mistress Hooker on a litter, driving cattle and goats and swine, on a fortnight's journey through the wilderness. They went almost due west, struck the great river near the mouth of the Chicopee, followed its east bank for a ways, managed to cross it—it was very likely at freshet time—somewhere near the Dorchester settlement, naturally below the mouth of the Tunxis, and arrived at their destination in June in the year of grace 1636.

Why did so many men and women, and among them persons of influence and intellectual power, undertake this journey in search of a home, when they had as yet been less than three years in the homes for which they had crossed the ocean? We have an outline record of the arguments which were pleaded in the Massachusetts General Court for and against the proposition of removal. The petitioners made a threefold plea: first, that they had not accommodation for their cattle and that the towns were set so near each other; the said towns being Boston and Cambridge, with a wide river between them, and the back country unlimited and unclaimed; second, the fruitfulness and commodiousness of Connecticut, and the danger of having it possessed by others, Dutch or English; a good secondary reason, but hardly enough to lead to so great an undertaking at such a time; thirdly—and here is the sufficient reason, though of itself it could not be called an explanation—"the strong bent of their spirits to move thither." Yes, it was "a strong bent of their spirits" which made them so determined, and which conquered all objections. But is there no way of accounting for this bent—this more than inclination? It was but two years since Thomas Hooker and Samuel Stone and John Haynes had crossed the ocean with their friend John Cotton. Why did they want to get away from him, and from the sister church to which he with Mr. Wilson ministered, and from the government which had been set up under a royal charter in a colony of England? Why did they, incurring the reproach of lack of faith and persistence, to use the words of a contemporary writer, "highe them away to a new plantation"? The real reason doubtless was that they wished "to remove from under the power, as well as out of the bounds, of the Massachusetts." In fact, it is easy to see from what they did, as soon as they were able to do it, the reason why they went as far west as beyond the great river and as far south as to be well across the line of the chartered colony. Those who had settled at the Massachusetts Newtown certainly were not in full accord, ecclesiastically or politically, with their neighbors in Boston, and were not willing to take either their church law or their civil ordinances from them.

I doubt if it has been sufficiently noted that of the two colonies within the limits of what is now Connecticut, the River Colony stood more nearly parallel to that of Plymouth and the Quinnipiack Colony to that of the Bay. Plymouth was

a settlement of Independents, who came out from England as from Babylon and repented for their sin that they had ever communed with the established Church of England; they repudiated all connection of church and state, and for that reason had no religious test for voters or for office-holders; moreover, they were not under a charter or directly dependent upon the crown. The Bay Colony was made up of a body of Puritans, who claimed that they had not left the Church of England, but on the contrary were determined to hold fast to it and to reform it; they exercised civil authority under rights derived from the king; and they required, as soon as they could do so, that the rights of suffrage and of holding office should be restricted to men who were members of their purified and reformed churches. Presently, no doubt, they carried their reformation so far that they utterly changed the polity which they had received by inheritance; but that in no way affected their theory. Now, on our side of the line, New Haven, which looked Independent in matters civil and in matters ecclesiastical, really followed Puritan Massachusetts rather than Independent Plymouth, having an even more rigid rule as to the privileges of citizenship and the exercise of the suffrage; while the River Colony, of which Hartford was the centre, in matters of greatest importance was in agreement with Plymouth, acted on Independent principles, and imposed no ecclesiastical test, except only that the governor must be a member of the church as established. This divergence between the new settlers at Newtown and their neighbors in the slightly older settlement at Boston was almost immediately felt. Some thought that Mr. Cotton and Mr. Hooker were too great men—men of too nearly an equal greatness—to be satisfactory neighbors to each other; but quite apart from this, the seed of independency was too deeply rooted in Mr. Hooker's mind, already proving its existence (we may be sure) in his earnest and cogent sermons and conversation, and ready to bear fruit in a safe and promising place. There, certainly, is the explanation of the "strong bent of mind" of the Newtown people, that they might leave Newtown on the Charles for Newtown on the Connecticut, and the persistence with which they urged that they be let go some days' journey into the wilderness, that they might have things their own way. They did not object to the appointment of a constable for the first few months or of a commission for a year or so after that time; they felt sure that the commission would not be renewed, or that being renewed it could be protested against and displaced; and with a spirit shown over and again in their history and that of their descendants, they were willing to submit for a while in the certainty that they would soon gain all that they wished. Thus it happened that, with some formalities of a legal proceeding, there was in the four years 1633-1636 what one has called "an irruption of subjects of the King of England into an unorganized and unoccupied country." Those who came here knew pretty well what they had in mind, what they were undertaking and what they expected to do. And suddenly on land which owned none but a shadowy allegiance to any external authority there sprang up this typical democracy of the modern world, if not the typical democracy of all history.

A good many years ago, a map was made of the Hartford of 1640, based on land records and other like sources, which I suppose is still regarded as accurate, except as to some minor details; we wait a new map with illustrative matter from the skilled hand of our corresponding secretary. There must have been at this time towards a thousand inhabitants, including some three hundred grown men, in the three towns of the colony; probably more than a third were here. The town was laid out on a large scale, with so many roads that it was a long time before any others were needed. There was the meeting-house yard and market-place, at first with a very small meeting house on the south side, presently replaced by a larger building on the east side near the corner by the road to the river, which served its purpose for almost a full century; there also were the jail with the whipping-post and the stocks, and the graveyard. The main road from the Palisade to Centinel Hill passed the yard on the west, running from the little river, where it looked across to the road which led to the ox-pasture and to Wethersfield. From the nature of the case there was no ford there; to find it one must go further down the little river to a place to which a branch road came from the southern town, and from which the main travelled road led to the north. From Centinel Hill, where was the pound, one could go to the cow pasture and Windsor, or Up Neck or to soldiers' field. The mill was well up the little river, beyond the place where now are the stepping-stones; a road led to it from meeting-house yard and from it into the country west. There was a main landing on the great river near the place where the ferry-boats later put in, a Dutch landing on the little river near their fort, and an Indian landing in the South Meadow. The large lots of the chief men, Pastor Hooker and Teacher Stone and Elder Goodwin and Governor Haynes, were on the north bank of the little river, separated from it by a highway, and east of the main street; nobody lived east of what is now Front Street. The common fields lay to the north and the south and the southwest; there was no central common or green. It should be added that as early as 1636 it seems that the colonists went through the form of buying the land occupied or claimed by the town from the Indians, a former sale of part of it to the Dutch being ignored by both sellers and purchasers.

Thus the place must have looked in some respects like a rather large and compact village and in others like an incipient city, when the Connecticut colonists acting as one body, the Massachusetts commission (dated March 3, 1636) for their government having expired, took the administration of affairs into their own hands. A "Corte" of two magistrates from each of the three towns, with Mr. William Pynchon from Agawam further up the river when he was minded to attend, met from time to time, beginning on the 26th of April, 1636. On the 21st of February in the next year, it gave to each of the towns a new name in place of that which it had brought from Massachusetts. Newtown was named Hartford, from Hartford the birth-place of Mr. Stone; Dorchester was given the name of royal Windsor; and Watertown was called Wethersfield, from the place of John Tailcoat's birth. On the 1st of May, 1637, independence having been fully gained, a body of the six magistrates, with nine deputies (three from each town), met in Hartford under the name of the General Court, and quietly took the administration of affairs into its hands.

Here would be the place, did time and ability permit, to discuss the question whether the government of Connecticut thus undertaken and presently put into form by the fundamental orders, was the act of one sovereign body or the result of a federation of three bodies originally independent. Historians do not agree in their answer to the question, nor do lawyers and judges; but it is my opinion that the weight of evidence is decidedly against the federation theory, and that we are to see in the acts which constituted a government acts of sovereignty exercised by one body of Englishmen, individually perhaps subjects of the English Crown but isolated from its administration and at liberty to provide for themselves. In other words, Connecticut was from the first one commonwealth; her citizens were in three or four settlements, but they all belonged together and all met (at least by deputation) in one General Assembly for consultation and legislation and one General Court for the administration of justice. The rights of the towns as political entities were allowed from the first; but the sovereignty was, as it has always remained, in the commonwealth; and that sovereignty, assumed at the first, defined by the fundamental orders, recognized in a remarkable way by the Crown in the charter, acknowledged by the Crown after a hundred and fifty years in the treaty with the thirteen independent States, held for some forty years under the charter's provisions, and now for well nigh a century under the provisions of a constitution, is the heritage of the free and independent State of Connecticut.

It is interesting to see and to note how soon the sturdy little commonwealth assumed for herself the prerogatives of sovereignty, asking no one's permission, and went through a great variety of experiences which belong to an organized and responsible state.

Almost, if not quite, the first was with all due formality to declare and wage war. It was in 1637, when one would think that there was enough to do here in the river settlement, that it was decided by the citizens that their own safety and that of their brethren at the mouth of the river called for what they called offensive warfare against the Pequots. The war was proclaimed in a very civilized way; it was begun in a very religious way, for Mr. Stone prayed all night at Saybrook before the expedition left the harbor; but it was carried out in what we must for justice' sake call a very barbarous way, though doubtless those who took part in it justified their act to their own conscience. "One wonders," says Dr. Walker, "whether, even then, a better use might not have been made of the proprietors of the soil than shooting and burning them." Only the next year, as he reminds us, the settlements on the river were saved from what seemed a fatal famine by Indians who came from Deerfield with fifty canoe-loads of corn and sold it at reasonable rates. This led to the keeping of a thanksgiving day on the 4th of October in that year 1638.

The next special act of the new colony—the word may be used, though not quite accurately—was of an ecclesiastical character, in the third month after the slaughter of the Pequots. The church in Boston had fallen into difficulties; every church fell into difficulties rather often in those days; there was the almost incomprehensible antinomian controversy, and the very extraordinary behavior of Mistress Anne Hutchinson, who expressed quite freely her opinion of the ministers and of the necessary results of their preaching of a covenant of works. An ecclesiastical synod was called, and to it the ministers of Hartford, Mr. Hooker and Mr. Stone, were summoned; with them went, as delegates from the church, Mr. Ludlow and Mr. Pynchon, the two chief men of the former magistrate, carrying with them—a most extraordinary thing to do—the scalps which had lately been cut from the Pequots' heads, and also (if the narrative can be believed) the skins of some of those warriors. It is enough to say of the synod that it sat for twenty-two days, and condemned eighty-two distinct teachings of the antinomians as being "some blasphemous, others erroneous, and all unsafe." We shall see presently that Hartford soon enjoyed a theological controversy of her own.

In the next year, 1638, the first steps were taken towards the most momentous event in all the history of this commonwealth: a General Court was elected for the purpose of framing a permanent code of laws for the Colony. We do not know the details of the work; we can read the outline of Mr. Hooker's lecture on the last day of May, drawing out a scheme of government; we are assured of the ability of Mr. Ludlow, the only lawyer in the Colony, to frame that scheme in due form of words; we know the issue of it. On the 14th day of January in the year 1639, a general assembly of the whole colony, meeting at Hartford, adopted a series of eleven Fundamental Orders, which formed the first written constitution in the history of the human race. It was a statement of governmental power with fixed limitations, an embodiment of the idea of a democracy putting itself under restraint, such as all real constitutions adopted since that day have been. Not merely a part of a code for the regulation of affairs and the administration of justice, important enough to stand by itself and to be made a little difficult of change, this constitution was in reality a declaration of principles put into operation in an absolutely independent government. There was no recognition of a supreme authority in England, or anywhere else on earth, from which the right to establish or define a government had been received; there was no faintest recognition of an aristocracy, practically an oligarchy, such as ruled in Massachusetts or in New Haven; "Democracy," said John Cotton, "I do not consider that ever God did ordain as a fit government either for church or commonwealth." And there was no recognition of any power of the church's "elders" to act as a court of advice or revision, or of the necessity of church membership as a step for admission to the exercise of the franchise. With reverent recognition of the divine providence of Almighty God, and of the duty of a people, when they are gathered together, to have an orderly and decent government established, the inhabitants and residents of Windsor, Hartford, and Wethersfield did associate and join themselves to be as one public State or Commonwealth; they determined how magistrates, including a governor, should be elected; that there should also be deputies from the several towns, who should meet together to advise and consult of all such things as might concern the good of the public; that in the General Court should consist the supreme power, but that the election of magistrates should be done by the whole body of freemen. And nothing was said as to the possibility of amendment or change of any part of this fundamental law. It was very quietly done, this momentous

act; but it called for strong determination and great courage; it made Connecticut stand by herself in a position of her own choosing, which might have been reckoned as defiance not only of the Mother Country across the sea but also of the neighbor colonies; it was a bold experiment in matters political, or rather it was a bold declaration of principles, of which the colonists were so absolutely certain that they did not feel that they were submitting them to experiment. The republic thus constituted, says a modern historian, "silently grew until it became the strongest political structure on the continent; and its principles, adopted by the Federal Convention of 1787, shaped the constitution of the republic of the western world in its most critical and important parts." Its adoption was the beginning of American democracy, and that is the same as to say of all properly safeguarded popular government.

After four years we find another act of our colony, especially interesting as coming at that time. She had organized for herself a government which was in no true sense of the word federal, because it was the act of one body of men acting together. Now in 1643 Connecticut joined with Massachusetts, Plymouth, and New Haven, Saybrook also having some place, to form a federation under the name of "The United Colonies of New England." Concerted action was needed against the Indians, and might be needed at any time against the Dutch; and no one knew, though some could guess, what the French colonies to the north might like to do. This confederacy, into which Rhode Island was not admitted because it was not thought to have an orderly government, was of great service to New England at the time, and it taught lessons of united action which was of great use at a later time; but it was an experiment in practice for an emergency, rather than the application of principles in fixed government; its influence on the future history of the land cannot be compared for a moment with that of the assembly of freemen at Hartford which adopted a real constitution of a real democracy and put both into operation. Still that this colony entered into it, and that it was treated by its neighbors as an equal, proves the permanence and dignity of the position to which it had attained.

Another event of importance, one which both asserted and strengthened the sovereignty of our colony, occurred in December of the following year. It was no less than the cession by Colonel Fenwick, as the representative of the patentees, of the fort at Saybrook with all the rights which belonged to or were claimed by the government there established. These were rights held under the Crown by a patent, or at least a grant, from the Earl of Warwick, himself having received them from the Plymouth Company; and under them a fort had been built and a site had been laid out with special provision for the homes of persons of quality. But the persons of quality had not come; the intended city or town had not grown up; the farmers were not minded to keep within the palisades; it was impossible to carry out the proposed system of impost on goods carried up and down the river; and it seemed best to part with the barren privileges which were held, in exchange for a consideration and for the advantages of union with the healthy young colony up the river. The benefit was not altogether on the side of the ceded territory; it was worth a good deal to Connecticut to have gotten the control of the mouth of the river which was its chief highway of approach, and it was worth still more to have extinguished a claim which might prove decidedly troublesome as time went on. And besides, Connecticut inherited from Saybrook, with these rights, their outward symbol in the form of its seal, with the representation of a vineyard in fruit, and its nobly religious motto, *"Sustinet qui transtulit."* The Colony and the State have continued the seal, changing the details of its design and the order of the words in its legend, but in no way modifying its meaning or its inspiration.

We pass over six years to another historical event of importance, showing the Colony in still another light, the Treaty of Hartford in 1650. Peter Stuyvesant, governor of the New Netherlands, came in state that year to confer with the Commissioners of the United Colonies, and to press the claims of the Dutch to the whole coast from Delaware Bay to Cape Cod. A less keen observer than he could have learned after a journey through the territory of New Haven and Connecticut that such a claim could never be successfully pushed; but he did his best. He dated the document which he presented as from Hartford in New Netherland; and the commissioners refused to receive it until he wrote Connecticott. He called the non-chartered colonies "pretendant"; and they did not care. Presently he drew back the eastern limit of his claim from Cape Cod to Point Judith, and soon agreed to the decision of four arbiters—all, by the way, Englishmen, and nobody knows why—that the line between the English and the Dutch on Long Island should run across from Oyster Bay and on the main land should begin west of Greenwich and run north, keeping at least ten miles from Henry Hudson's river. This decision was accepted, and the Treaty of Hartford was formally made on the 19th day of September; when its provisions were reported, the Dutch were amazed to find that they had relinquished all claim to New England. Stuyvesant, when he went back, did not tell his council what he had done, and no certified copy of the treaty reached Holland for six years. But Connecticut had gained a substantial victory in Connecticut's way.

We are now within the period of the Commonwealth in England; but the change of government in the home land made little difference in the administration of affairs in the sturdy independent colony. The notable event in these years is an ecclesiastical quarrel at home, of a rather unpleasant kind, arising, after Mr. Hooker's death, from a divergence between Mr. Stone, the teaching elder, and Mr. Goodwin, the ruling elder, of the church; Mr. Stone having refused to allow the church to vote on the nomination of Michael Wigglesworth, who was Mr. Goodwin's candidate for the pastorate, and having also refused to administer the Lord's Supper. The trouble convulsed the Massachusetts colony as well as that immediately concerned. The General Court took a hand in it, of course, and that over and over again. Councils sat in Hartford and in Boston; and the final council declared that the withdrawers—Elder Goodwin's party—were still members of the Hartford church, but that if they could not return to communion they should be given a dismissal with the privilege of removal. They were dismissed, and presently removed to Hadley, Hartford's first colony in foreign lands.

The year 1660—only a quarter of a century after the settle-

ment—brings us to the restoration in England, and that to the story of the charter of 1662 and the inclusion of New Haven within the fully established English Colony of Connecticut. In the winter of 1662-63 is the melancholy, though brief, episode of witchcraft, with the execution of Nathaniel and Rebecca Greensmith. In 1666 we see the beginning of the controversy as to the proper subjects of baptism, leading four years later to the organization of a second church, which was to follow the more strict ways of the fathers.

But even to sketch the history of these ten years would be to extend this paper far beyond its limits. It must suffice to note that the remarkable charter, the granting of which has never yet been fully explained, was the embodiment of the principles on which Connecticut had been founded and of the fundamental orders in which those principles had been embodied, and that it really created under the sanction of a monarchy a pure democracy, the type of all modern democratic government; that the witchcraft excitement was held under restraint and soon passed away, largely by the wise advice of the ministers; and that the doctrines and practices which led to the organization of the second church showed that time and distance had not quite destroyed the convictions of men who had been brought up on England's soil and nurtured by England's Church.

What a story it is, that of the first twenty-five years of Connecticut, furnishing an example of almost every kind of the events that go to make up history! The migration from the Bay, for reasons ecclesiastical and civil and personal, and the wilderness journey; the marking out of a large town on the scale of a city; the independent organization of the threefold settlement; the formal declaration and successful waging of war; the assistance given to the Bay colony in case of ecclesiastical controversy; then, the adoption of the fundamental orders which make for the modern world the beginning of democracy under constitutional government; the entrance into the New England federation; the securing of the cession of Saybrook, with its patent rights and its seal; the making of a treaty with the Dutch, which peaceably determined the map of all this coast; the controversy which led to sending out a colony to dwell across the Massachusetts boundary; and the movement toward a charter, no less wonderful in its history than in its contents. Even in a brief and hasty glimpse we can see the importance of it all, and know that it is no little thing that so great events were brought about in so brief a time.

[36] THE BETA OF CONNECTICUT

Trinity College was founded under the name of Washington College in 1823; academic work was begun in the following year, and the first class was graduated in 1827, ten young men receiving the degree of Bachelor of Arts. The first President, Dr. Thomas Church Brownell, Bishop of Connecticut, was a graduate of Union College in the class of 1804, and had been a professor in that institution; with him was associated Dr. George Washington Doane, Union 1818, afterwards Bishop of New Jersey, Dr. Horatio Potter, Union 1826, afterwards Bishop of New York, Dr. Samuel Farmar Jarvis, Yale 1805, Dr. Hector Humphreys, Yale 1818, and, as an active member of the corporation, Dr. Nathaniel Sheldon Wheaton, Yale 1814, who succeeded to the Presidency in

1831. Among the later professors were Dr. Duncan L. Stewart, Union 1830, Dr. Silas Totten, also Union 1830, who became President in 1837, and John Brocklesby, Yale 1835. All these who have been mentioned by name were members of the Phi Beta Kappa in the Alpha of Connecticut or the Alpha of New York. In the year 1845, the constitution of the College, which had made a successful beginning of its history and had graduated 262 men, was in a certain way modified; its name was changed to Trinity College, as more marked both scholastically and religiously, the alumni were organized into a convocation, and it took a more distinctive place than ever before among the educational institutions of the country.

In the year before this, an application had been made on behalf of the College to the Alpha of Connecticut by President Totten and Professors Stewart and Brocklesby, for a charter; on the 14th day of August 1844 the Alpha voted to establish the Connecticut Beta of the Phi Beta Kappa; and on the 16th day of June 1845 the Alpha delegated and gave to their "well and truly beloved brother John Brocklesby the right and authority to organize and establish" this the first Beta of the Fraternity. An organization was effected on the 2nd day of the following July, when Mr. Thomas Ruggles Pynchon, a graduate in the class of 1841 and then Tutor in the College, was admitted to membership. On the following day five members of the class of 1843, three of the class of 1844, and four of the graduating class, and later in the month four of the class of 1846, were admitted members. The constitution adopted was "in accordance with the ancient and well established usages of the Fraternity throughout the Union;" and the charter requiring that the members should be "persons of honor, probity, and learning," it was provided that they should be elected each year from the Junior Class "with the unanimous concurrence of the members present," and that "not more than one-third of the class" should be admitted. A few members of the classes earlier than 1843, eight in all, were at different times elected to honorary membership.

Dr. Totten was the first President of the Chapter; and, when he withdrew from the College in 1848, he became Professor of Belles Lettres in William and Mary College and co-operated with the venerable William Short in re-establishing the Alpha of Virginia. Professor Brocklesby was President from 1853 to 1857 and again from 1867 until his death in 1889; Dr. Pynchon, who became Professor in the College and later its President, presided over the Chapter from 1857 to 1862 and again from 1889 until his death in 1904. The term of office of the present Secretary is the longest on the records of the Chapter, having begun in 1870.

For many years there was scarcely an exception to the custom which interpreted the rule of eligibility to mean that the first third of each class, as their rank should be determined by the Faculty in what was known as the Junior Standing, should be elected to membership; only occasionally, for personal reasons, some one was omitted. In 1889, this interpretation was made the rule of eligibility, with an allowance of one additional member for a two-thirds fraction; and as the Faculty included in one list the candidates for the degree of Bachelor of Arts and those (under the new system of courses and electives) for the degree of Bachelor of Science, two students of high rank in the scientific course were admitted to membership. About this time the local society, or resident body of student members, declared their intention of electing no one to membership whom they knew to have used dishonorable means in passing any examination; and the rejection, a few years later, of three men otherwise eligible, because they could not be counted "men of honor," was a source of strength both to the fraternity and to the college. This action was com-

mended by the chapter at its annual meeting, and has continued an unwritten but invariable rule. Soon after this it was decided to make as a test of "men of learning" the attainment of a mark of 85 per cent. in the Junior or Senior Standing; in recent years, under somewhat changed conditions, this has greatly diminished the number of men admitted, but there is no intention of lowering the requirement. Since 1897, only the first fourth of the members of each class, with an allowance of one for a fraction of three-fourths, have been eligible for membership.

As has been noted above, some of the graduates of early years were from time to time elected honorary members of the fraternity; and with them a few others who had attained eminence as scholars were admitted to the same honor. Between the years 1861 and 1896 there were but five honorary elections. In the last named year, in connection with the semi-centennial of the Chapter which was duly observed in 1895, on the recommendation of a committee, nine of the alumni of classes ranging from 1845 to 1884, who had not reached Phi Beta Kappa in their college course but had proved themselves worthy of it by faithfulness and success in the work of their lives, were enrolled in its membership; and at the completion of sixty years, seven others of classes from 1856 to 1888 were added to them.

A catalogue of officers and members was published in 1895 and another in 1905. Five orations delivered before the Chapter at anniversaries—none but the semi-centennial has been thus observed since 1873—have been published. The whole number of members admitted in sixty-eight years has been 434, of whom 382 were elected in course and 21 were chosen to alumni membership, and 31 to honorary membership. The whole number of members living on the first day of July last, is reckoned as 287.

Among the most distinguished names on the roll of the Connecticut Beta of the Phi Beta Kappa are those of Presidents Pynchon and Luther of the College, Bishops Paddock of Washington Territory, Paddock of Massachusetts, Knickerbacker of Indiana, Scarborough of New Jersey, Niles of New Hampshire, Olmsted of Central New York, Nichols of California, and Johnson of Missouri; Professors Edwin E. Johnson, John J. McCook, Henry Ferguson, John Humphrey Barbour, Charles M. Andrews, George E. Beers, Charles N. Shepard, and Frank A. McElwain; Judges William E. Curtis, William Hamersley, James D. Smyth, and Joseph Buffington; Andrew E. Douglass of the Flagstaff Observatory, Richard Burton, and Clarence G. Child.

[37]   JAMES JUNIUS GOODWIN, LL.D.

JAMES JUNIUS GOODWIN, a life member of the New England Historic Genealogical Society since 1884, for several years a member of its Committee on English Research, and Vice-President of the Society from Connecticut for the years 1902–1915, died at his home in Hartford, Conn., 23 June 1915, in the eightieth year of his age.

His descent was through James,[6] James,[5] Jonathan,[4] Ozias,[3] and Nathaniel[2] from Ozias[1] Goodwin, the head of the Connecticut family of that name and younger brother of William Goodwin, one of the company which in 1635 removed from Newtown in Massachusetts (now Cambridge) to Newtown in Connecticut (now Hartford), ruling elder of the church in Hartford, and one of the settlers of Hadley in 1659. The first mention which we have of Ozias Goodwin is as an inhabitant of Hartford in 1639, granted two parcels of land "by the town's courtesie." He died in 1683, at the age of 87. His descendants, in the line of the subject of this sketch, to use the words of one who knew their history well, "have been prominent and useful citizens of Hartford, quiet and conservative, holding firmly to their own convictions, thrifty, home-loving, and public-spirited." James,[5] the grandfather of James Junius, was captain of the First Company of the Governor's Foot Guard, and James,[6] his father, was major of the First Company of the Governor's Horse Guard, while a brother Jonathan was major in the Foot Guard. Maj. James[6] Goodwin, before he became of age, was entrusted with the general management of the stage lines running to the east of Hartford, which presently employed forty coaches and over four hundred horses, with a system of fast expresses for the transmission of important news. This business he relinquished when the Hartford and New Haven Railroad, of which he was a director, came into successful operation. Later he was one of the original corporators of the Connecticut Mutual Life Insurance Company, a director, and its president for twenty-seven years. His business career was one of great courage, energy, and firmness, united with equal wisdom and caution; and his character was marked by perfect integrity and constant usefulness to the community. Major Goodwin's wife was Lucy Morgan, daughter of Joseph and Sally (Spencer) Morgan of West Springfield (now Holyoke), Mass., and sister of Junius Spencer Morgan, who became illustrious in the world of finance. Her home was in Hartford from 1817 until her death in 1890. She was a woman whose character had wonderful beauty and strength, helpful in every good work, and of deep conviction in her religious faith, guiding the community by sweet influences and acts of benevolence.

Their oldest son, James Junius Goodwin, was born in Hartford 16 September 1835. His childhood and youth were passed in his native city, his education being for a time in private schools, and later in the Hartford High School, which he attended from its opening in 1847 until December 1851. For a few years following he was employed in a number of clerical positions, and in 1857 he went abroad for eighteen months of study and travel. In the early part of the year 1859 he returned to the United States and accepted a position in the firm of William A. Sale and Company of New York, engaged in the Chinese and East India trade. He remained with them about two years, and then became the partner of his cousin, the late John Pierpont Morgan, who had just been given the American agency of the great London banking house of George Peabody and Company, of which his father was a member. The career of the Morgan firm is too widely known to need rehearsing here, and in fact Mr. Goodwin remained a partner for only ten years, though the interests with which he was connected were always allied to Mr. Morgan's. In 1871 the firm was reconstructed under the name of Drexel, Morgan and Company, Mr. Goodwin withdrawing from it, and indeed from all active business. He inherited through his father a large portion of his ancestors' Hartford property, which with the growth of the city had become a most valuable possession, and the care of which required much watchful attention. But though he was not now engaged in active business, he did not entirely sever his connection with the financial world in which he had played so important a part. On the contrary, his interests were very large and varied, and without doubt it is due in great measure to his skill and wisdom that the institutions with which he was connected had continued prosperity. Among these may be mentioned the Connecticut Mutual Life Insurance Company, the Hartford Fire Insurance Company, the Collins Company, the Connecticut Trust and Safe Deposit Company, the Holyoke Water Power Company, and the New York, Lake Erie and Western Railroad.

But Mr. Goodwin was best known and is best remembered in the city of his birth for his activity in other departments of the city's life. There were few movements undertaken for the general welfare in which he was not a conspicuous participant, aiding with generous pecuniary gifts and also with his time and personal effort. He was proud of the beautiful city of which he and his forefathers had been residents for so many generations, and it was a pleasure for him to be active, and to be known as active, in its affairs. He was prominent in the general social life of the community and was a member of many organizations, such as the Colonel Jeremiah Wadsworth Branch of the Connecticut Society of the Sons of the American Revolution, the Connecticut Historical Society, of which he was vice-president for twenty-two years, the Society of Colonial Wars in the State of Connecticut, of which he was for two years governor, and the Hartford Club. Having a residence in New York, he was also a member of several important clubs in that city, including the Union, the City, the Century, the Metropolitan, and the Church

131

Club. He was for nearly twenty years a trustee of Trinity College, which in 1910 conferred on him the degree of Doctor of Laws. He was a communicant of the Episcopal Church, being also in Hartford a warden of Christ Church, where his father had been for many years vestryman, and in New York a vestryman and warden of Calvary Church.

Mr. Goodwin was at great pains to preserve the early traditions and records of Christ Church, and it was due to his generosity in bearing the expense of publication that the extremely valuable and handsome volumes in which the history of the parish is traced in the form of annals and its register reproduced to the end of the year 1900, by Dr. Gurdon W. Russell, were printed and distributed. He rendered a like, and even a greater, service to the town and the community in providing for the transcription, editing, and publication of the first volume of "Hartford Town Votes, 1635–1716," as volume 6 of the *Collections of the Connecticut Historical Society*, and also of the "Original Distribution of Lands in Hartford among the Settlers, 1639," with later transfers and with "Early Hartford Vital Records," as volume 14 of the same series — this latter a volume of 632 pages text and 84 pages index; the two making an almost invaluable contribution to the material available for the study of Colonial history, and that of a kind which required and received in its preparation the greatest possible pains to secure absolute accuracy. His gifts to this society were many and well chosen, the most notable being the monumental "Victoria History of the Counties of England."

He rendered like service to the New England Historic Genealogical Society. When, on the death of Colonel Chester, it seemed very desirable that Mr. Henry FitzGilbert Waters should be induced to take up his residence in England and devote his time to genealogical researches for the English pedigrees of American families, Mr. Goodwin was the largest personal contributor to the fund, and he continued his gifts for this purpose through a period of seventeen years; he was also a contributor to the Society's building fund. Among the results of Mr. Waters's work, as is well known, were the discovery of the parentage and provenance of John Harvard, the determination of certain questions in regard to the ancestry of George Washington, and the material for two large volumes of abstracts of wills and genealogical notes relating to the English origin of early American settlers.

Part of Mr. Waters's investigations assisted Mr. Goodwin in carrying out his plan of providing for a thorough study of his own ancestry in all its backward-extended ramifications. In 1891 Mr. Goodwin put through the press a large volume on "The Goodwins of Hartford, Connecticut, Descendants of William and Ozias Goodwin," to which were prefixed a paper on "The Goodwins of East Anglia" by Rev. Augustus Jessopp, D.D., and a "Report on English Investigations" by Henry F. Waters, A. M., together with a paper on "William Goodwin" (the Elder) by Rev. George Leon Walker, D.D., and one on "Ozias Goodwin" by Charles J. Hoadly, LL.D. The genealogical work was the compilation of Frank Farnsworth Starr, to whom all later volumes and fascicules published by Mr. Goodwin are indebted for thorough and precise investigation, study, and arrangement. In 1896 was printed "The Roberts Family of Simsbury, Connecticut, in the Line of Captain Lemuel Roberts, 1742–1789," Eunice Roberts his daughter being the wife of James[5] Goodwin; in the same year "The Williamson and Cobb Families, in the Lines of Caleb and Mary (Cobb) Williamson of Barnstable, Mass., and Hartford, Conn.," these being the parents of Martha Williamson who married Ozias[3] Goodwin; also "The Thomas Spencer Family of Hartford, Connecticut, in the Line of Samuel Spencer of Cromwell, Connecticut, 1744–1818," Samuel Spencer being the father of Sally Spencer who married Joseph Morgan and was the mother of Lucy wife of James[6] Goodwin. In 1898 was printed "The Newberry Family of Windsor, Connecticut, in the Line of Clarinda (Newberry) Goodwin of Hartford, Connecticut, 1634–1866," the said Clarinda Newberry being the wife of Jonathan, brother of James[5] Goodwin. In 1899 appeared "The Olcott Family of Hartford, Connecticut, in the Line of Eunice (Olcott) Goodwin, 1639–1807," Eunice Olcott being the wife of Jonathan[4] Goodwin. In 1903 there followed "The Eells Family of Dorchester, Massachusetts, in the Line of Nathaniel Eells of Middletown, Connecticut, 1633–1821," Martha Eells being the wife of Samuel Spencer above mentioned and grandmother of Lucy Morgan wife of James[6] Goodwin; and in 1904 "The Miles Morgan Family of Springfield, Massachusetts, in the Line of Joseph Morgan of Hartford, Connecticut,

1780–1847," this being the Joseph Morgan who married Sally Spencer, the fourth in descent from Miles Morgan who was a resident of Springfield in 1644. There was also a volume (dated 1895) devoted to the genealogy of the Edward Jackson family of Newton, Mass., a member of which is the wife of Mr. Goodwin's brother, the Rev. Dr. Francis Goodwin. And but a short time before Mr. Goodwin's death two volumes were printed under the title of "Various Ancestral Lines of James Goodwin and Lucy (Morgan) Goodwin of Hartford, Connecticut," one of 319 pages containing twenty-four Goodwin lines, the other of 481 pages containing twenty-nine Morgan lines. Of all these Mr. Starr was the compiler, his compilation resting on the most painstaking investigation; and it may well be doubted whether any one has undertaken and done for all the lines of his ancestry more than has here been done by Mr. James Junius Goodwin. With these belongs "The First Register of Saint Mary's Church, Bocking, Essex, England. Baptisms, 1561–1605; Marriages, 1593–1639; Burials, 1558–1628. Transcribed from the original for and privately printed [in an edition of 50 copies] by James Junius Goodwin," 1903.

Mr. Goodwin had, as witnessed by the press at the time of his death, "an enlightened interest in many subjects and a desire to facilitate their study by others; largely absorbed in business, he found time for study on his own account, and provided facilities for more minute study by special students." It may well be added, in words which the present writer used at the time, that Hartford is indebted for much of its attractive beauty to him and to those who have stood in close relation to him; and the prosperity of its literary institutions is largely due to their timely and generous gifts. There were no public legacies in his will; but in accordance with his expressed wish and from a fund which he set aside for the purpose, substantial gifts have already been made to Christ Church, the Wadsworth Atheneum, the Connecticut Historical Society, Trinity College, Berkeley Divinity School, and other institutions.

Mr. Goodwin married, 19 June 1873, Josephine Sarah Lippincott of Philadelphia, a descendant of one of the early settlers of Massachusetts who was later a patentee of the first English settlement in New Jersey. She survives her husband, with three sons, Walter Lippincott, James Lippincott, and Philip Lippincott; another son died in infancy.

[April 25, 1907]

[13]

DR. SAMUEL JOHNSON and THE BEGINNINGS of the CHURCH in CONNECTICUT

AN ADDRESS delivered in Christ Church, Stratford, on St. Mark's Day, 1907,

132

At the Bicentennial Commemoration of the founding of the first parish of the Church of England in Connecticut, it is but fitting that we should specially honor the man who is rightly called the Father of the Church in this Colony and State. He had not to do, indeed, with the organization; in 1707 he was but a youth in the home of his father, the good deacon of the Standing Order in Guilford, and Samuel Smithson's Prayer-Book had not yet come into his hands.

"All things are double, one against another," said the wise man of old; and for fifteen years a preparation was going on, of the place for the man and of the man for the place. Here, as your rector has told you, the few Churchmen, almost alone in a colony threescore and ten years old, had looked across the seas for help, had been strengthened and cheered by the visits of Mr. Muirson and Colonel Heathcote, had two hundred years ago incorporated themselves in church order, had in their very weakness become so strong that the Congregationalists of the town had provided themselves with the strongest man who could be found in New England to preach against them, and had at last secured a resident rector—or missionary, to use the phraseology of the day—when Samuel Johnson was ready to come into the place from which Mr. Pigot was to be promoted. And the youth of whom we have spoken had received an academic education at the Collegiate School in Saybrook, had at the age of twenty been appointed tutor in the institution, had retired from his office after three years, when the learned pastor of Stratford was called to be rector of the College, had been made pastor of the Congregational Society in West Haven, overcoming some scruples as to the validity of non-Episcopal ordination, had pursued studies in the college library, to which the Book of Common Prayer had given inspiration, in common with Rector Cutler, his classmate and former colleague Daniel Browne, James Wetmore, and other ministerial friends, and had after two years and a half united with them in the famous declaration which culminated in the decision of the four men named, that they could no longer preach the Word and minister the Sacraments without authority from a bishop.

Then, returning from England with the desired commission, his senior having been sent to the newly organized church parish in Boston, it was but natural that he should be assigned to the one parish in Connecticut, now fifteen years old, which was unconsciously waiting for him, as he had been unconsciously preparing for it. To this parish, or to speak perhaps more accurately, to the church in this town, which then included a large part of what is now Fair-field County, he gave thirty-one years of his life from this date, and again the last eight years before his death.

The story of the intervening years, and of much in the Stratford days which is more or less closely connected with them, belongs to the annals of King's and Columbia College and to Dr. Johnson's position as a man of letters and an educator of youth; it will be told you by one well qualified to describe it and to set a right estimate on its value. It is for me to remind you of what this man of wide learning and of ever-increasing reputation was as a pastor and a teacher of theology, a priest and a divine.

The whole history of the Diocese of Connecticut has been profoundly affected by the character and the labors of its early clergy, as well as by the circumstances which, by God's providence, led them to their work and strengthened them for it. And the influence of no man of Colonial times has been as strong as that of the father whom we especially honor in this place today. The union of strong convictions with adaptability to circumstances, of studious habits with devotion to pastoral work, of great learning with the power of influencing men and persuading them to do the duties of ordinary life—we meet with this over and over again, but nowhere more conspicuously than in Dr. Johnson. No one had better abilities or better opportunities for study than he had; but he made long journeys, visiting the members of his widely scattered flock along the shore of the Sound and on the hills to the north, and ministering to scattered Churchmen or to those who wished to learn about the Church, not only in places as near as New Haven and Norwalk and Derby, but in the remoter towns of Branford and New London, Newtown and Middletown, and even in Newport and on Long Island. It was a real pastoral instinct which inspired our early clergy throughout the Colonial period, and also our first Bishop and those who labored with him in the early days of the fully organized diocese; and it was also a real missionary instinct which showed itself in their lives, not because they were missionaries in a technical sense, deriving a modicum of their support from the honored Society for the Propagation of the Gospel, but because they were willing and anxious to extend the sphere of their labors to any place which they could reach and in which they could proclaim the Church's message.

Thus there appeared in Connecticut a new form of life for the English-speaking Church, not inspired by what the young candidates for orders had seen or heard in England, not learned from the clergy in those colonies to the south in which the Church was established, but working in willing hearts with a simple enthusiasm which reminds us of the early days of Celtic and Anglo-Saxon Christianity in the British Isles. For the result of this work—for I may not now dwell on its details—which in fifty years, under the ministrations of some thirty-five men, made fully a twelfth part of the population of Connecticut to be Churchmen or adherents of the Church, due credit should be given to all those who worked in harmony for its accomplishment; but no little part of the influence which started it, the courage which maintained it, and the guidance which directed its course, came from the parsonage in Stratford.

Dr. Johnson at no time held any official position which gave him authority even to suggest to his brethren a course of action; he was never appointed commissary, to superintend as far as a presbyter could do so the work of the Church of England in Connecticut, being with the rest nominally under the charge of Commissary Price in Boston; but all in the Colony held him in reverence as their senior and asked and followed his counsel as their superior in learning and experience. It was his sound judgment, his firm hold on principles, and his prudence in applying them, exemplified indeed in his contemporaries but gaining

their special influence from him, which gave a tone of strength and confidence to the churchmanship of Connecticut, and prepared churchmen to perform the great act of faith and obedience when it became possible to complete their organization by securing the consecration of a bishop.

Dr. Johnson's own experience especially fitted him to be the leader in the constant appeals which were made to the authorities in England for the establishment of an American Episcopate. Many layfolk were led to the Church by the fact that she offered the opportunities of the Sacraments—the Holy Communion for themselves and Baptism for their children—on the simple conditions which they believed to be all that were required by Holy Scripture; it was rather the order of the Church than its orders which drew them to it, perhaps one might say rather its catholicity than its apostolicity. With those who left their positions as accepted and acceptable pastors and teachers in settled congregations of Christian men, declaring that they dared no longer minister in Word and Sacraments until they should be ordained by a bishop, the question was more largely that of the continued orders of the Church and its authority; and while the decision of all who crossed the ocean for ordination after 1722 and before 1775 bore witness to like strong convictions and like bravery, it had not the significance of the act of those who made up their minds for the declaration of 1722, who stood firm in the memorable conference in the college library, and who, supposing themselves unheralded, presented themselves in the metropolitical see city of all England to ask for ordination. Dr. Cutler had come back to serve in another colony and under different conditions; Mr. Browne, to the grief of all who knew him, had died in England; and Mr. Wetmore gave full proof of his ministry in pastoral services in another province, not being called to be a leader. It fell to Dr. Johnson's lot to present the needs of the Colonies, and especially of this Colony and its neighbors, to those in church and state on whom rested the decision of important matters in the mother country. In the rector's study in this quiet town there was maintained a constant correspondence with English bishops and clergymen, with the officials of the Venerable Society, and with prominent laymen. Many of the letters, carefully considered and carefully worded, had to do with the special needs of the time when they were written, reporting the state of the Church here in general or in detail, answering some question or asking for some special action by the Church at home; but there was also the repeated appeal that a bishop might be provided for the increasing number of those who would acknowledge no other form of polity than the Epis-

copal and who were separated by three thousand miles of ocean from any one who bore Episcopal authority. Objections were answered, often (it must be acknowledged) to be replaced by others; to the advice for patience the argument of urgent necessity was opposed; and the lukewarmness of those who cared but to have a quiet Church as a respectable department of government was met with an enthusiasm which never failed. The Church in the colonies was not granted a Bishop; but by its persistent requests it testified to its convictions, it strengthened those convictions in the minds of its own members, it kept the matter constantly before the eyes of Englishmen against the day when for very shame their great Church should be willing to continue a succession which a feebler Church, "out of the abundance of its poverty," had granted to the new republic.

It was no little thing that we had here a man who had conversed on equal terms with Bishop Berkeley, whose advice he had sought with regard to his benefactions for the cause of sound learning, and who still was in familiar correspondence with him; a man who could give to candidates for orders letters of commendation to prelates of high distinction for influence and learning, and could introduce them to the universities; a man of wide reading, whose place was among the English-speaking scholars of the day, with idiosyncrasies indeed that made him interesting and at the same time with strength of intellect which kept him a man of sound judgment.

And it must not be forgotten that he used his pen not only to keep before others a right idea of the work of the Church in this land and of its needs, but also more distinctly as a Doctor of the Church, to teach its members and build them up in the truth entrusted to it. It was the age of controversial pamphlets; and sometimes by what he himself wrote at length, and sometimes by his introductions to the writings of others and his commendation of them, he contributed to the stock of reading which they supplied and helped his own people and others to understand and to hold the Church's position. It was not alone the judgment of affection or of narrow observation which his friend and pupil, John Beach, himself of Stratford birth and of high repute as pastor and writer, expressed when he declared that Dr. Johnson was "the most excellent scholar and most accomplished divine that this Colony had to glory in." And on this two-hundredth anniversary of the organization of the first parish in this diocese, we are glad to testify to the respect and honor in which we still hold his name, as that of the Father of the Church in Connecticut.

We may well sum up our tribute to him in words which are written on the diplomas given him by the University of Oxford. On his first visit to England to receive ordination, it granted him the degree of Master of Arts, expressing the hope "that under his ministry there should arise in America a branch of the English Church, another and yet the same." And twenty years later, when it honored him with the Doctorate in Divinity, it testified to the fact "that he had striven energetically and successfully against the teachings of fanaticism, had been an earnest defender of Episcopal polity, and had in a manner so wise and so kind, so unwearied and so strong, discharged the duties entrusted to him, that in the marvellous growth of the Church it was seen that he had not only fulfilled but even surpassed the hopes which he had inspired." We look back at his work, and in the light of two centuries we make these words our own, thanking God for the wonderful grace and virtue declared in His servant Samuel Johnson, priest and doctor, whose example and influence shall ever remain with us, and whom the Diocese of Connecticut shall never cease to honor.

the Centennial of the Incorporation of the Town of Marlborough

[39]

It is a pleasure to present today to the good people of Marlborough the greetings of the Connecticut Historical Society, and to assure them of the interest which is taken in this commemoration. The recurrent anniversaries, as they have been carefully observed of late years, are bringing before us the history of the several parts of our colony and state. The older towns, with their quartermillennials, those which followed after, with their bicentennials, and others yet, like your town, the separate organization of which dates but a century back — each in its place is helping us to understand and to appreciate the circumstances of the life of former days and to know how duty was learned and character molded in the days of our ancestors. The old towns began the state, or, as some would prefer to say, began with the state; and then one after another came new settlements, until the whole of the territory was occupied. This was the work of early days, and many a pleasant and instructive picture of it has been drawn as, one after another, the towns have grown to be two centuries or two centuries and a half old. This town was formed a hundred years ago, but the three towns, in three different counties, which contributed to it, had already seen respectively a hundred and thirteen, a hundred and two, and ninety-nine years of history. The new settlement, and others like it, witnessed to neighborliness, and to the desire for more ready attendance on the worship of God, for better school privileges, and for a reasonable independence in civil organization. But the inhabitants did not seek isolation; they were making, with the approval and by the authority of the superior government, a new unit in the body politic. The question of small towns as against large towns (with possibly smaller societies within them) was a different question then from that which causes so much anxiety to thoughtful men now; a new life came to your forefathers of a hundred years ago, and they adapted themselves to it; we live under changed circumstances, and we cannot yet tell how to adapt ourselves to an order of things which has not found its lasting shape. But it is fortunate that we may be interested in history without attempting to be prophets, or even without determining how or when history shall repeat itself. And these anniversaries are re-enacting history before our eyes and recalling it to our memories; they are reminding an older and teaching a younger generation, or rather, as in few places they are less than half a century apart, they are teaching in different ways two or three generations.

Every town and village has a real history, with a real reason for it, which is much more than a bare record of annals or of the succession of events. To the knowledge of this history many valuable contributions have been made by the repeated investigations, the discoveries and rediscoveries, the rehearsings and re-rehearsings of events and facts. But, great as is the importance of this, the cherishing of the historic spirit is of no less value. What was done in New Haven by Dr. Bacon, in Middletown by Dr. Field, in Hartford by those who wrote for Dr. Trumbull, and in Saybrook and Guilford by local historians, and what has been done in preparation for this commemoration, has added to our stores of historical information; but besides this, and as a valuable result of this, it has added to our intelligent interest in affairs, and thus to

our happiness. We may well expect far-reaching results from what is said and done here today.

But to attain good results we must make good use of the means which lie at hand. The new generation should be trained to a full acquaintance with places and boundaries, with facts and traditions, with men and women, and should be taught to search for the traces of the past and to remember them. And we must have thought for those who will look back on this anniversary as matter of history. Nothing can be of more importance in our case for those who are to come after us, in matters of this kind, than that we care for the inscriptions in our burying grounds, and that we leave records, carefully made, and written with permanent ink on imperishable paper; and if one looks for encouragement or for warning in this latter particular, they can be found in every official volume of manuscript and on every signpost. It is a most imperative duty to keep and to guard original documents; and every town or village library should make it a duty, and a willing duty, to preserve everything, however insignificant, which can in any way throw light on historical events, no matter how trivial they seem at the time, or on manners and customs which mark the life of the day. A century seems a long time when compared with the average length of human life; but a century soon passes away. We turn our thoughts to the organization of this town, and recall the men of three generations ago; it will not be long, though possibly the time may be crowded with momentous events, before we shall be objects of antiquarian interest, and those who come after us will wonder at the vestiges which we have left.

As we look back on the past, or forward to the future, in any place and any community, we cannot but recognize the great and enduring power of character. It sometimes seems that the small community feels more quickly and holds more tenaciously to this influence than does the larger community or the more crowded assemblage of men; certainly where there are but few, and each man's life is of necessity known to all his neighbors, the value of character and the influence of character cannot but make themselves felt, and therefore they impose a great responsibility.

Not to speak of other considerations, though they cannot but come to the mind of a clergyman in a place of public worship, it is the duty of every grown-up man and woman, for the sake of the community, to take an active part in the maintenance of churches and schools, to foster neighborliness, to see to it that there is, both in themselves and in younger persons whom they can influence, an intelligent acquaintance with the affairs of the world and a respect for the power of intelligence. There are great possibilities in a true country life; and may the time never cease when we can look to our rural communities for examples of high character and of usefulness to the commonwealth!

GENERAL ROBERT SEDGWICK

THE material which I have used in the preparation of this paper is not new, though it has been for myself but recently sought out. It has to do with the career of one of the martial leaders of an early generation of our New England history. He was a man of good training, and as it often seemed, of excellent opportunity; in his English home and in the

colonies of the western world he had experience of military service; he gained the friendship of the ruler of England and was commissioned by him for important duties; on this side of the ocean he had the esteem not alone of his friends and neighbors but also of strangers whom he was set to govern; if he failed sometimes to accomplish the result at which he aimed, it was because fortune snatched the opportunity from him or because matters took such a turn that no one could possibly succeed: and if he died away from home and friends, a broken-hearted man, he died trying to do his duty and to serve his generation.

Robert Sedgwick, a member of the Artillery Company in London, came to Charlestown, Massachusetts, in 1635, being not far from twenty years of age. He was successful in business, associated with the younger Winthrop in the establishment of iron works, a deputy to the Great and General Court, one of the founders of the Ancient and Honorable Artillery Company, Commander of the Castle, a member of the Council of War, and finally Major-General of the Massachusetts militia.

His neighbor, Captain Edward Johnson, in "The Wonder-Working Providence of Sion's Saviour in New England," a book which, we are told, "best epitomizes the Puritan philosophy," gives us this account of the man and of his skill:

"The first Serjeant Major chosen to order the regiment of Essex was Major Robert Sedgwick, stout and active in all feats of war, nurst up in London's Artillery garden, and furthered with fifteen years experience in New England's exact theory, besides the help of a very good head piece, being a frequent instructor of the most martial troops of our Artillery men; and although Charles Town (which is the place of his own companies residence) do not advantage such o're-topping batteries as Boston doth, yet hath he erected his to very good purpose, insomuch as all shipping that comes in, either to Boston or Charles Town, must needs face it all the time of their coming in; the cost he hath been at, in helping on the Discipline of his Regiment, hath profited much." *

In 1652, Robert Sedgwick was still in Massachusetts, holding the title of Major-General. Soon after this, however, he returned to England; and about the same time, or possibly with him, went a man whose name was for a while associated with his in affairs of war and who became his son-in-law, John Leverett, son of the ruling elder of the Boston Church, himself a Captain of the Colony's forces. Their reputation may have preceded them, and may in fact have been the reason why they crossed the ocean to the home-country; at any rate, their merit was soon discovered by Cromwell; they gained his friendship, and served as officers in the army of the Commonwealth.†

But the Protector soon had pressing duties which he

* Book ii. c. 26, quoted by Fiske, *Beginnings of New England*, p. 305.
† Palfrey, *History of New England*, ii. 284, sqq.

wished to have these men undertake in the new world, and they were sent back, charged with a special responsibility. To understand the immediate purpose of their return, its failure, and what of success followed, it will be necessary to go back a little in the history.*

By the so-called Treaty of Hartford, September 19, 1650, Peter Stuyvesant, Director of New Amsterdam, had abandoned on behalf of the Dutch all the claim which had been pretentiously put forth to New England territory. He had seen enough on his journey to satisfy him that the settlers in New Haven and Connecticut could never be dislodged; and he knew, moreover, that if they were disturbed, he would be obliged to reckon with the force which the other two of the United Colonies, Massachusetts Bay and Plymouth, were ready to send against him. So after his "bluff," as we should call it, of dating from New Netherlands a letter written in Hartford, and his consent, when a reply to the letter was refused, to write as from "Conecticott," he agreed with the English to leave the matter of the boundaries between his jurisdiction and theirs to four arbiters. As the English naturally appointed two of their own people, and Stuyvesant also most unnaturally appointed two Englishmen (though one of them, to be sure, was his own secretary), a decision was easily reached. It was agreed that on the main land the boundary line of the governments should keep ten miles away from Henry Hudson's river, coming to the Sound east of Greenwich Bay, and that on Long Island it should run across to the ocean from Oyster Bay; while in the neighborhood of

* See Fiske, *Dutch and Quaker Colonies*, i. 299, sqq.

Hartford the Dutch were to hold jurisdiction over all that they actually possessed, a phrase which could be easily interpreted to mean nothing. In the summer of 1652, less than two years after this agreement was made and perhaps after Sedgwick and Leverett had crossed the Atlantic, the first war between England and the Dutch Republic broke out. Fear was naturally felt for the safety of New Amsterdam; and the city was fortified by the palisado wall that gave name to the street on which are now controlled the financial affairs of a continent. Even with this defence, the Director was not minded to hasten an outbreak of hostilities with the colonies to the east; but there seemed to be reason for believing that he was prepared, if Manhattan should be attacked by the English, to call in the assistance of such of the Indians as he could reach and trust. And indeed he had reason to be troubled; for John Underhill, who had once been "the savior of New Netherlands," was now in revolt against him and had accepted something like letters of marque from the Providence Plantations. Under color of these he had sailed up the Connecticut river to the abandoned House of Good Hope, had claimed to confiscate it to the Connecticut government, and then selling it had appropriated the proceeds. The General Court in the next year, we may note in passing, calmly took possession of the property as belonging to the Colony; and the Dutch were left no shadow of a claim on the banks of the river or in its neighborhood. Stuyvesant had cause, as was said, to be alarmed, and fully as much were the settlements in New Haven and Connecticut colonies disturbed at the possibility of an attack from savage Indians under the guise of war; and they proposed to call out the forces of the New England Confederacy for an attack

on the Dutch. But Massachusetts, farther from New Amsterdam and in no special fear of the Indians, but rather disposed to look upon them as possible allies and defenders, perhaps at this time more impartial in its judgment of affairs, and certainly as the event showed more practically prudent, was averse to active opposition. The men of our colonies became impatient and excited; there was hard talk at New Haven and Hartford about the men of Boston, armed men assembled in Fairfield and Stamford, and there was danger that the confederacy of the Colonies would be dissolved. An appeal was sent across the ocean to Cromwell, strengthened as it would seem by a rumor of a plot for the destruction of all the English colonists; the agents of our Colonies at the court pressed their case; and on the 8th of February, 1653-4, instructions were issued to "Major Robert Sedgwicke, commander of the Blacke Raven, and Captaine John Leverett, whoe is joined with him," to take charge of a fleet of four vessels, the Black Raven, Hope, Church, and Augustine, and sail for the United Colonies with letters to the governors. They were, so read their instructions, to give "intimation to them" of their "arivall and expectation of a suddayne Answer to the contents of the said letters." The document proceeds: "If upon return from them you fynde an inclination and readinys in them to joyne in the present undertaking for vindicating the English right and extirpating the Dutch, you are without neglect of any opportunitye to address yourselfes to the worke by ordering the ships for the Manhattos, and taking care that the soldgers from the Collonyes may by a land march meet them there or be taken into the ships as by advice may be judged most advantageous. You being comed to the Manhattos, you shall by way of surprize, open force, or otherwise, as you by a counsill of war consisting of the commanders of the ships and armie shall judge most conduceing to that end, endeavour to take in that place in the name of the Lord Protector of the Commonwealth of England Scotland and Ireland for the use of the said Commonwealth. And you have power to promise and give them faire quarter in case it be rendered upon summons without hostile opposition; the like alsoe you shall do to the fort of Auranea or any other place upon Hodson's river."*

There is a state paper under date of the 11th of February which speaks of the necessity of procuring masts for the ships after they should cross the ocean; it enumerates "hose, serges, cloth, rugs, blankets, bolsters, stuffs, ironware," among the goods to be sent to New England for the account of the Commonwealth, and to be disposed of that masts might be purchased.

It was not far from the first day of June when the little fleet arrived in Boston, and some time elapsed before the soldiers were collected for the campaign. The four ships brought 200 men, Connecticut raised as many more, and New Haven two-thirds as many, to accompany them; Massachusetts would send no part of her forces, but she allowed 300 men to enlist as volunteers; while Plymouth

* *Massachusetts Historical Society Collections*, IV. ii. pp. 32, 230.

promised 50 men, but did not send them. In all there were 833 under arms on the three vessels, a small enough army, one would think, but doubtless so strong a force that had a conflict taken place the Dutch must have been overcome. But alas for dreams of heroic exploit and military glory, and the hope that these brave men might secure for the English the town and fortress at the mouth of Hudson's River! Just as the fleet was to sail from Boston, on a day late in June or early in July, 1654, tidings came from across the sea that the Lord Protector and their High Mightinesses of Holland had made peace and that there was no further justification for hostilities. New Amsterdam remained in the hands of the Dutch for ten years longer, and in 1664 was surrendered to Colonel Richard Nicholls, who had been appointed governor of the place under the claims of the Duke of York; so that the glory, such as it was, of the final transfer did not accrue to the Massachusetts Major and Captain whose fortunes we are tracing.

It appears, however, that Sedgwick and Leverett had received from the Protector other instructions than to carry out, if they could, the wishes of the southern New England Colonies in defending them against the Dutch and weakening or destroying the power of the New Netherlands. England was not then formally at war with France; but the force which seemingly and in all probability really had been prepared against New Amsterdam, now that it could not be used for that purpose, was led against the French settlements in Acadia.* La Tour, who

* Palfrey, ii. 285.

had kept up in that land a conflict with D'Aulnay, petty but not without its romantic side, after a chequered succession of loss of royal favor and return to it, which probably meant of loyalty and disloyalty to Louis XIV., had incurred anew a suspicion that he was intriguing with the English. He had indeed done something to strengthen himself by taking to wife the widow of his rival, thus quieting her claims and becoming responsible for the care of her children; but it was only the appearance of Sedgwick's fleet which saved him from being called sharply to account. England, or rather Scotland, had a standing claim to the land, which James I. had granted to Sir William Alexander as a fief of his former crown under the name of Nova Scotia; and the home authorities apparently felt at liberty to attempt the enforcement of this claim whenever they might find it convenient. Cromwell had evidently foreseen that the four ships which he had sent to New England, and the eight hundred or a thousand men whom they were expected to carry, might want for employment; and, as is quite evident, he had bidden them see, if the opportunity should be offered, what they could do in Acadia. There is a clause in the instructions which appears to have been intended to mean this; those in charge were "to proceed to the gaining in any other places from the Enemie which upon advice with a counsell of war may be judged feizable and conduceing to the settlement of the peace and saiftye of the English

plantations." And in some way the need of masts was given as a reason for the expedition; for a report to the Navy Committee, dated July 1, 1654, says that "masts not being ready, it was thought good to turn their design against the French."* In that direction, therefore, Sedgwick sailed from Boston; and the attack of his fleet upon the French settlements led to a speedy victory. St. John was soon captured; Port Royal surrendered on the 16th of August without resistance; and the country from the Gulf of St. Lawrence to the Penobscot became once more Nova Scotia, subject to the protectorate of England and Scotland.

Thus by little labor an important action was accomplished. We do not know what reward Sedgwick received for his services; Leverett presented a bill of twenty shillings a day for the two years in which he had been on duty, and was promised three-quarters of what he asked; but though he received a note or warrant under the privy seal for the amount due him in 1656 (some £4,750), there was still £4,000 due him at the Restoration.† It was not a great military campaign in which our New Englanders took the lead and for which our colonies furnished most of the men; but its result was certainly creditable to those who engaged in it, and for the welfare of the state.

It was in the next year, 1655, that Jamaica, by a sort of accident, fell into the hands of the English. Some sixty years before, in 1596, during the alliance between Queen Elizabeth and the government of the Low Countries and the consequent war with Spain, Admiral Shirley had invaded the island, but he had not attempted to occupy it. Later, under Charles I., Col. Jackson had defeated

* Hazard, ii. 150.   † Palfrey, ii. 388, note.

the inhabitants at Passage Fort, but apparently he also had not cared to take advantage of his success. Jamaica, indeed, was not at this time considered as a place of much importance. Its territory was a private estate, divided into eight districts in the nominal possession of eight noble families, and the total population was about three thousand persons, most of whom were slaves of the few proprietors. The natives had been practically exterminated; but there were some descendants of slaves called Maroons who had fled to the mountains and were still able to make trouble.*

Now Cromwell, who as we have seen had just despoiled France of a province, had determined that it was for the interests of England to make that country its friend and to strike a blow against Spain.† His action was professedly by way of reprisal for acts of hostility and rapine committed in America or its islands, and it was to be undertaken on that side of the ocean on which the offence had been committed; and practically it would be a denunciation of war. He fitted out an expedition under two admirals, Venables and Penn, and gave them a secret commission to attack and capture Cuba and San Domingo. They found themselves unable to carry out their instructions or indeed to take either of the islands; and, says an historian, in words which may partially explain what must be presently said, "the failure may be ascribed as much to treacherous behavior of the persons commissioned by Oliver in the equipment as to the injudicious choice and bad execution of the officers and men by whom it was conducted. The soldiers were for the most part the refuse

* Encyclopaedia Britannica, sub voce.
† [Edward Long,] History of Jamaica, i. 220, sqq.

of the whole army; and the forces enlisted in the West Indies were the most profligate of mankind." And again he tells us of the men collected, whether as soldiers or as settlers, at Barbados and the other small islands, that they were "chiefly servants who had worked out the terms of their indentures and had derived very little morality or decency from their education, sphere of life, or habitual practices." But the admirals were determined to be able to report that they had done something, and they fell upon the defenceless island which lay between the two that they had been bidden to attack, and readily captured it; their own men were not brave, but they were less cowardly than the few Spaniards who came out against them. The forces arrived off Port Caqua (now Port Royal) on the 9th day of May, and within two days they made themselves masters of the island, and gave to its history the only event worth recording since its discovery in 1494 and its occupation by the Spaniards in 1509. The admirals presently returned to England to report what they had done and had not done, and were promptly and properly sent to the Tower. The army, such as it was, was left behind.

But though the island had not been wanted, it was necessary, now that it had come under English sway, that it should be guarded and kept. The soldiers had demolished churches and houses and ravaged the plantations, and had made preparations for many years of want and suffering, and for this reason there was all the more need that the few respectable inhabitants should have the privileges of government and care.

For this duty and labor Robert Sedgwick, who had returned to New England after his capture of Acadia, was designated. He sailed from Plymouth in the Marmaduke on the 11th day of July.* From Barbados Road he wrote to the Navy Commissioners on the 6th day of September that God had been pleased to smile on the squadron in a very comfortable passage, and that he had arrived with all the ships, we are not told how many, some days before. When he wrote he had heard "no news from the leeward save what they heard by a dogger boat after the repulse at Hispaniola," and he was about to set sail for Jamaica by order of "General" Penn, intending to touch at St. Christopher's in order to inquire after friends. "I hope," he added, "God hath brought down our confident spirits to fill us for some more noble work. When flesh begins to glory, it is a mercy if God will stain the glory of it." Besides, he thought that what had happened might not be altogether a disciplinary providence: "Many think Jamaica a more considerable island than Hispaniola, and that it may effect more than the other." Then, noting that he

found both soldiers and seamen active and willing and not discouraged, and therefore hoped God had yet a blessing for them, and that their design was His and that He would own it, Sedgwick came down to earthly things and expressed his desire that those to whom he was writing would "thank their honest brewer for supplying such good beer," and that on account of this his good service he would "find mercy for former offences."

On the same day Captain William Godfrey wrote from Carlisle Bay, Barbados, that "Major General" Sedgwick had taken in a supply of provisions for the army, and was intending to sail that day for St. Christo-

Calendar of State Papers, Colonial Series, America and West Indies, addenda, 1574-1674, 221, etc.

pher's and, if there he should have no word of the fleet, to proceed to Jamaica. Thirteen days later he was still there but intending to sail that day for San Domingo and Jamaica according to instructions from General Penn. Something, however, must have detained him longer; for we learn from a letter of his own that he did not arrive at Jamaica with his squadron until the first day of October. He found the army which had been left there less than six months before suffering from dysentery and in lack of everything. Fortescue, who in the absence of the admirals had been in chief command, had made application for "cloathing, smiths, and carpenters, tools, bread, oatmeal, brandy, arms and ammunition, medicines, and other necessaries"; but if any of these useful things had arrived, they had not been well cared for and used.* Thus Sedgwick wrote: "For the army, I found them in as sad, deplorable, and distracted a condition as can be thought of. As to the commanders, some have quitted the islands, some have died, some are sick, and others in indifferent health; of the soldiers, many are dead; and their carcases are lying unburied every where in the highways and among the bushes. Many that are alive appear as ghosts; and as I went through the town, they lay groaning and crying out, 'Bread, for the Lord's sake!' The truth is, when I first set my foot on land, I saw nothing but symptoms of necessity and desolation. I found the shore strewed with variety of casks, hogsheads, puncheons, barrels, chests, and the like, and several dry goods belonging to the state, such as linens, shirts and drawers, shoes, stockings, hats,

Calendar, ut supra, 222, 223.

armour, arms, and nails, with many other things, lying without any shelter, exposed to all the damage that sun or rain could do to them, and to the theft or rapine of either soldiers or strangers, who without question embezzled most of them." Moreover, he found that the soldiers, evidently the tractable part of them, were most unwilling to be settled where they were, and hoped that the Protector would weary of his design and abandon the island.*

In the same month of October a regiment commanded by Col. Humphrey had arrived, having 831 young healthy able-bodied men; in less than a month fifty of their number, including five officers, had been buried;

Fortescue also had died. "Jesuits' bark" was unknown then, and the remedy applied for malaria and dysentery was bleeding, which, we are told, not much to our surprise, "seldom failed of making the complaint more obstinate, if not mortal."

On the 14th of November, Sedgwick wrote to the Commissioners of the Admiralty, first describing the desolate condition of things in words such as those just quoted, and then making this report of his action in one matter of importance: "As to the wines arrived in Capt. Crowden's ship, I have disposed of 60 butts to the army and 170 to the fleet; the fleet had no need of them, but how to dispose of them better we knew not." Then he fell to moralizing: "What God will do with us here I cannot tell. He at present seems highly displeased, and shatters and breaks us to pieces, and in destroying goes on to destroy us, but I hope will spare and pity a poor

Long, i. 244, 245.

simple people." Then he tells how the conduct of soldiers and sailors distressed him. "This kind of marooning, cruizing, West India trade of plundering and burning of towns, though it hath been long practised in these parts, yet is not honourable for a princely navy, neither was it I think the work designed, though even if it may be tolerated at present." And for himself, though he had built a house and was at work on a fort at the harbor's mouth, he begs that his recall may be hastened, his constitution, as he puts it, not agreeing well with this climate, which he fears he shall not long trouble. In another letter written the same day, he tells of the terrible sickness and loss of life by the flux, saying that since his arrival 700 men had been laid in their graves and that the greater part of those who survived were sick.*

In another communication Sedgwick tells of the ravages committed in the island by the English soldiers. They have killed, he says, 20,000 head of cattle, and destroyed all the fruit and provision that came to their hand: "nothing but ruin attends them wherever they go. The army claim all the ground about the town; so that there is great difficulty to accommodate five or six poor planters with a little land. The men desire either to be employed in arms, or sent home again; dig or plant they will not, but would rather starve than work." And we have further testimony to the same effect from the Vice-Admiral: "They will not now be persuaded to do any thing toward their bellies or their security, except to fetch provender for the magazine; so that if the magazine fails, they must

Calendar, 236.

inevitably perish. For the cattle, such of them as were left in any degree tame have all been killed; few or none are left; and some regiments have tasted no flesh for a long time, except that of horses, dogs, cats, and the like."*

Again, Sedgwick writes to Thurloe: "There are two things principally enjoined by his Highness to the army, fortification and planting. Should I give you a character of the dispositions and qualifications of our army in

general (some few particulars excepted), I profess my head would grieve to write, as it doth to think of them. I believe they are not to be paralleled in the world; a people so lazy and idle, as it cannot enter into the heart of any Englishman, that such blood should run in the veins of any born in England; so unworthy, slothful, and basely secure; and have out of a strange sort of spirit, desired rather to die than live. The commanders and officers allege that the soldiers will not plant, when it is certain they are not willing the soldiers should plant, but still stand gaping to go off the island, as after a gaol-delivery, and you may be confident there will be little done in that way by this sort of people. Such kind of spirit breathing in Englishmen I yet till now never met with!"†

Such was the condition of things with the few inhabitants left on the island, some 2,500 soldiers, who might have been effective if they could have been kept from sickness and idleness, and the small body of men who had come with the general from New England; and such was the report of affairs which reached the home authorities. "The Protector," says the somewhat cynical historian of

*Long, i. 248, 250.   †Long, i. 254, 255.

Jamaica, "rebuked the vices of the soldiers with the solemn air of a rigid divine." He was not inattentive, he confesses, to the welfare of either their souls or their bodies; but he rightly judged that immorality was a principal cause of their utter neglect of both. To attempt an improvement of their condition, seven ministers at different times were sent to live with them and labor among them, but six of these had either fallen in the common mortality or returned, discouraged and broken down, to England.

When Sedgwick came to Jamaica it does not appear that he had any other than his ordinary military authority. In process of time, however, there came from the government in England a document bearing date October 10th, 1655 (O. S.), addressed to Major-General Richard Fortescue, Vice-Admiral William Goodson, Major Robert Sedgwick, Daniel Searle, and ——— Stoakes, under the title of "Commissioners for governing our affairs in Jamaica," the tenor of which is presented in this form. They were "to secure by the best means the interests of this Commonwealth in Jamaica, to endeavor the promulgation of the Gospel of the Lord Jesus Christ and the power of true religion and holiness, and the suppression of idolatry, popery, superstition, and prophaneness, and to set apart to that purpose from what shall come into their hands upon the public account as they should find necessary. And whereas we are informed of the horrible prophaneness and wickedness of very many of the soldiers and others belonging to the army, whereby the Lord hath been justly provoked to leave us a reproval to our enemy at Hispaniola," they were "to use endeavors and to bear witness effectually against the same." It was also declared that the government had resolved to use all possible endeavors to people and plant Jamaica, and to that pur-

pose had dispatched Daniel Gookin to New England with instructions to make propositions to those who might be inclined to remove thither, and in fact to urge them to do so, and to conclude agreements with them.*

On the same day, October 10th, instructions were sent to Richard Fortescue, under the title of "Major-General of the forces in America," to fortify especially the harbor of St. Jago. He was reminded that supplies of men and provisions had been sent him at the beginning of July last with Major Robert Sedgwick, and he was bidden to use his power and instructions according to his strength and ability.

When the commission, with its solemn words and its impracticable plans, reached the island, we do not know. It must have been followed soon, apparently in the spring of 1656, by an order to Sedgwick to take "the sole and supreme command." This order from the Protector came to a man "sick of his charge, wearied out with the refractory temper of the army and the unprosperous condition of the colony, and impatient to be recalled pursuant to his repeated applications. So undesirable a preferment"—I am using the words of the historian from whom I have quoted before—"was not more welcome to him than a death warrant. In short, when he reflected on the impossibility of his fulfilling the Protector's inten-

*Calendar, 232.

tions with such miserable instruments, of whose unfitness for such a work he was fully sensible after a tedious and irksome experience, and perceived how much the Protector relied upon his single ability, he could not conquer his diffidence, and the chagrin so deeply preyed upon his spirits as to overwhelm him with melancholy."*

On the 30th of April, Captain William Godfrey wrote from the Marmaduke that he was remaining on board the vessel, "conceiving it is merely for the accommodation of Commissioner Sedgwick who hath continued always on board."† Vice-Admiral William Goodson (who was, it will be remembered, one of the Commissioners appointed in the preceding October), writing home a month later, and complaining of the badness of the bread shipped in old liquor casks, and of the great increase of vermin, and of the lack of carpenters, notes that on the 23d day of May he found Major-General Sedgwick very sick and that on the following day "by the pale hand of death, they were deprived of him"; he adds: "he truly feared God, was of singular use in his work, and was generally beloved by the soldiery." This latter statement is all the more weighty when we remember how the deceased general had been tried by the conduct of the soldiers and had opposed their indolence and their seditious designs. In fact, he had set himself against the officers as well as the men of the rank and file; for when he and the Vice-Admiral had united in an exhortation to the army, proposing an allotment of land, the officers had opposed the acceptance of the plan. But that he was truly mourned and that his

*Long, i. 257.   †Calendar, 256.

memory was honored by those whose slothfulness and neglect had broken down his courage, there can be no doubt. I quote again from the historian: "The general regret which appeared in the fleet and army in consequence of this event was a clear indication of his worth. The honesty of his heart, the mildness of his disposition, his gentleness of manners, and his competence of understanding, qualified him to have been a most amicable governor over any well settled and established colony. But he wanted that severity, firmness, and fire, which were requisite to subdue and awe the stubborn, restive, and insolent spirits that had long distracted the army in Jamaica, and which grew more intractable the less they were controlled with a vigorous discipline."*

Thus his useful life came to an end in a strange land, amidst utter discouragement and every appearance of failure in a work against which he protested, but which he attempted to discharge from a sense of duty. We do well to remember his life with its episodes of service at home and in England, against the Dutch and the French, and finally on behalf of England against some of her sons who were unworthy of her.

Robert Sedgwick's descendants of his name include Theodore Sedgwick, a native of Hartford, statesman and patriot in the time of the Revolution, Speaker of the national House of Representatives and President *pro tempore* of the Senate, and Judge of the Supreme Court of Massachusetts. One of his sons, a lawyer, secured the

* Long, i. 257, 258.

charter for a railroad across the Berkshires, and another, also learned in law, acquired fame as an author, though their sister, Maria, is probably better known to-day than either of her brothers. Theodore Sedgwick of the third generation also held an honored place in the world of jurisprudence and letters. Another descendant, John Sedgwick, who was born in Cornwall in this State in 1813 and was graduated at West Point, served his country faithfully in a campaign against the Indians in Florida, in the Mexican War, and later in the War of the Rebellion; after showing great bravery and inspiring great confidence and affection, he lost his life at Spottsylvania Court House in 1864.

John Leverett, companion and friend of Robert Sedgwick, himself later made a major-general, and Governor of Massachusetts in the time of King Philip's War, married Sarah, General Sedgwick's daughter. Their daughter Ann married John Hubbard, son of Rev. William Hubbard the historian, who was a member of the first class graduated at Harvard College; and their daughter Rebecca married Rev. John Hart, the first person educated at the Collegiate School in Saybrook, now Yale College, who received a degree from it. Thus the line of descent reaches two great Universities and two States of a great Union.

A few words may be added as to the after condition of the island where Sedgwick fell the victim of a broken heart. Cromwell tried in vain to persuade the colonists on the continent to remove to Jamaica. The New Englanders politely but firmly refused to go, giving as their excuse "the prophaneness of the soldiery, the great mortality in the islands, and the continual hazard to the lives of any peaceful settlers there from the skulking negroes and Spaniards." We read of a vote of the English Council to list a thousand girls and as many young men in Ireland to assist in peopling the colony. Then, in 1674, when by a treaty between Charles II. and the States of Holland, the English gave Surinam in exchange for New York, the English planters with their negroes, about 1,200 in all, were removed to Jamaica; twenty-five years later the Scotch settlers on the isthmus of Darien were compelled to leave that place, and a considerable part found new abodes in the same island; and to them were added some settlers from Barbados. Jamaica had a regular government with an elective council, which was established in 1661 and continued more than two centuries, until in 1866 it became a crown colony. But the history has been uneventful, and the island is best known for its place in the commercial world as a source of supply for the fruit markets of colder climes.

EDWIN POND PARKER, PASTOR OF THE SOUTH CONGREGATIONAL CHURCH, HARTFORD, CT.

[January 11, 1906]

When as a college freshman I began my residence in Hartford, "consule Planco," Dr. Parker had entered upon his ministerial work then; and one of the first theological pamphlets which I read, bearing on current controversies, was a letter from an Episcopal clergyman to a friend touching the recent ordination at the South Church. Many years have passed by; we do not reckon them few and evil, as did the patriarch, for whom they were long in passing but of little value and result when he looked back upon them; but many and good, because the then youthful pastor and preacher has found in them and put into them so much that has been happy and fruitful; many and good, because they have been years in which life has grown to full maturity; yet few, because no one can look back over a life, however active and successful, without the feeling that it covers but a small space in the world's history or in the plans of him in whose sight a thousand years are but as yesterday. As men grow older, I think that they enter into something of this divine vision without complaining or regret. And they gain also, I am sure, something of the other and New Testament side of the truth, that one day is with the Lord as a thousand years. Our days of life and of service are not short. Many a one, "being made perfect in a short time, has fulfilled a long time;" and how much that is permanent, destined to endure because it is worthy to endure, comes from any faithful growing manhood of a half century! I do not need to remind Hartford people that such has been Dr. Parker's manhood, spent among them, known and read of them all; and his kindness to myself has been such that I may ask him to suffer the word of appreciation of what his life has been worth, primarily indeed to those who have known him best, in a special sense to those to whom he has ministered in holy things, but very really to the whole community, which as it has increased in numbers and in influence has never outgrown his ready sympathy and his intelligent affection. He has added to its wisdom, its happiness, and its goodness. He cannot but know something of the esteem in which we all hold him and of the gratitude which we feel for his work and for himself; but we are glad of the excuse which a special anniversary brings that we may tell him of this without intrusion and witness to it before the community. That he has our prayers and good wishes for all that remains of his life, and for all that remains after this life, he knows, but we want to assure him of it now. And may there be more like him.

"Hoc opus hoc studium parvi properemus et ampli,
Si patriae volumus, si nobis vivere cari."

Berkeley Samuel Hart,
Divinity School.

[41]

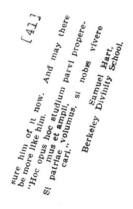

IN MEMORIAM

Elizabeth Hart Jarvis Colt

Born in Saybrook, Conn., October 5, 1826.

Died in Newport, R. I., August 23, 1905.

Sunday, October 1, 1905.

Psalm lxxi. 15, 16 (Prayer Book version). — "Thou, O God, hast taught me from my youth up until now : therefore will I tell of thy wondrous works. Forsake me not, O God, in mine old age, when I am gray-headed : until I have showed thy strength unto this generation, and thy power to all them that are yet for to come."

Three score and two years ago, on the first Sunday in September, the poet-rector of Christ Church in this city preached from this text a sermon commemorating the life and character of a parishioner who had died in the preceding week, "rich," as he testified, "in good works, in the reverence of all and the gratitude of many, and in the peaceful hope of a long-tried believer.[1]" She had been for some six years a resident here; and in that time, such had been her infirmity of body in a time of deep affliction, she had been but twice in the house of God and but once at its altar to receive the Holy Communion; "yet," said the preacher, "should we ask who, amongst all the congregation, was best and most wisely known by acts of Christian beneficence and love, I should shame none by saying, that of all who are here from Sunday to Sunday, none have a name more brightly encircled with such holy honor. It was not a burden, it was not a mere duty; it was an exceeding delight, to discharge this her stewardship. Her earthly reward is in the remembrance of the poor whom she had relieved; of the sick, whose painful beds had been softened by her kindness; of the ministers of Christ, whom in the name of their Master she had received and cherished; and of that Zion whose stones were dear to her, and whose cause never lacked her generous, ready, and anticipating aid.

Among those to whom the psalmist's words, and their application by the saintly preacher, brought comfort and instruction, there was a grandchild, to whose life and character we bear witness to-day in the words of the psalmist of old and of the preacher of two generations ago. The daughters of the venerable matron, as she then seemed, who shared with her in her good works, and whose praise is still with hers in the churches, attained a riper age than hers and followed her to the bliss of Paradise[2]; and, of the children of the elder, two well beloved brothers and a sister whose constant happiness was a benediction to family and friends also fell asleep[3], leaving one who in her turn reached a greater age than her grandmother, though we scarce thought of her as having passed the wonted years of life. And for her we take up the hymn of praise which tells of the blessed experience of the Christian soul, the psalm which fittingly described her grandparent's affliction and joy, the psalm which was read at her house before the body of her venerated father[4] was borne to this place ....

From early childhood, when in a little country church she learned lessons that confirmed the teaching of a Christian home, along all the path of life with its varied experiences, to the time when she came to worship in this church, her gift to God for His glory and for the benefit of His people, and on to the time when by her benefactions she had gained a place in many a bishop's jurisdiction and many a rector's parish as real as that which she held in this diocese and among us.

Of the memorials I hardly need speak in this place and in this presence. This sacred structure enshrines primarily and chiefly the memory of a beloved husband[5] and of children taken to be from infant days with the Good Shepherd in the Paradise of his love; and on its walls and in its pictured windows it tells of parents and brothers and sister venerated and loved, sorrowed for, but with hope, and thus constantly remembered before God. Hard by, the Memorial house for the many uses of parish work testifies to love for a son[6] who did not live to fulfil all a mother's fond hopes, but of whom she felt sure that God would "give him to her again with joy and gladness forever." And presently the home, dedicated to the comfort and help of some who otherwise would find heavy burdens in times of affliction and infirmity, shall continue the happiness and cheer, the gentle ministrations and the encouragement, which so many have found there in the years that are past.

But I am sure that you will pardon me—and the more because of my association for many years with the worship of this church—if I urge upon the members of this parish and this congregation the duty of cherishing the memorials which, destined for their use, are so largely left to their care, and of following the example of the life and work which stands out so brightly before them. It is no easy thing to make full use of all the opportunities which open before you, my brethren, here; it is no easy thing to continue the traditions, the responsibility for which has been largely felt and borne by your rectors, but which derives much of their strength and their power from one whose part is no longer with the Church militant here on earth. Each must now take an active part in the external work of the parish, each must feel a responsibility for the discharge of its duties to itself, to the community, to the work of the diocese and of the whole Church of God. And each must, if need be, learn anew the lesson of the blessedness of the Church's worship, of the strength which comes in following the Church's ways, of the brave service which is yet to be done that we, and those whom we influence or ought to influence for good, may in our day and generation bear well our part and bring forth the fruit of good works.

[1] Mrs. Elizabeth Hart, widow of Richard William Hart of Saybrook, died in Hartford, August 31, 1843; the memorial sermon was preached on Sunday, September 3, by the Rev. George Burgess, D. D., Rector of Christ Church, afterwards Bishop of Maine.

[2] Miss Hetty Buckingham Hart died August 7, 1876; Mrs. Elizabeth Miller Hart, wife of the Rev. William Jarvis, died June 18, 1881.

[3] John Samuel Jarvis died July 27, 1866; Mrs. Hetty Hart Jarvis, wife of Cyprian Nichols Beach, died October 31, 1898; Richard William Hart Jarvis died January 21, 1903.

[4] The Rev. William Jarvis died October 3, 1871.

[5] Colonel Samuel Colt died January 10, 1862.

[6] Caldwell Hart Colt died January 21, 1894.

142

Conn.

Mrs. Colt was the oldest child of the Rev. William Jarvis and Elizabeth Miller Hart, his wife, and was born in Saybrook, Conn., Oct. 5, 1826. Her father was the youngest child of Hezekiah Jarvis, of Norwalk, who was a brother of the second Bishop of Connecticut, and her mother was the elder daughter of Major Richard William Hart, of Saybrook, who was son of General William Hart and grandson of the Rev. William Hart, of that place. The Rev. William Jarvis was rector of St. Peter's Church, Hebron, and of Trinity Church, Portland. When loss of voice compelled him to retire from the active work of the ministry, he continued to reside in Portland, but after a while removed to Middletown, where his daughter, Elizabeth, was married June 5, 1856, to Colonel Samuel Colt, the eminent inventor, of Hartford. After five years and a half of married life, Colonel Colt died, Jan. 10, 1862, leaving to his wife the beautiful home at Armsmear, in Hartford, and the care of large interests, involving heavy responsibilities, which she undertook and carried out with equal courage and ability. Her life of constant activity was also a life of pressing troubles and almost constant sorrow; four beloved children died in infancy; and the one son who attained to man's estate, and on whom the mother's hopes were largely set, died early in 1894. But she never wavered in her strong faith, her constant affection, her thoughtfulness for others, or her glad devotion to good works. Her largest gifts were special memorials of her faith and her love; the beautiful Church of the Good Shepherd, built near her husband's armory, was consecrated in 1869 as a memorial of him and of their infant children; and in it she placed in later years tablets and windows in memory of others of her kindred; and the Memorial Parish House, of most elaborate design and detail, dedicated in 1896, perpetuates the name of her son; while most generous plans were made that the home and its spacious grounds should ultimately be of permanent use to the public and of special service to a class of persons for whom it is often difficult to make provision. In the specifically benevolent work of the Church and of the community, Mrs. Colt bore a ready and generous part. On the organization of the Connecticut Branch of the Woman's Auxiliary in 1880, she was appointed its president, and she discharged the duties of this office with a wise combination of prudence, gentleness, and enthusiasm; and she was anticipating with much pleasure the observance of the twenty-fifth anniversary of the branch in November next. And as to matters of local concern, there was none in which she was not asked to bear an active part and none in which she failed to do that which lay in her power. Her acts of private benevolence were so many and so quietly rendered that every one knew somewhat of them, but no one, save herself, knew their extent. In many a missionary field, in many a parish, in the homes of faithful clergymen in all parts of the land, by very many who felt the burdens of affliction or sickness or need, she will be thankfully remembered for her bounty and for the thoughtfulness and consideration with which it was bestowed. Her social duties were many, and they were always recognized by her and gracefully discharged; and the memories of her home will long abide as lessons of glad hospitality and true household life.

It is hard to write of Mrs. Colt as one would like to write in paying the tribute of deserved affection and respect. Those who knew her, and many to whom she was not personally known, while they recognize the imperfection of words, will be reminded of the reality which the words can but suggest. There will always remain the vision of a beautiful life, a life blessed in itself and full of blessing to others, a life of steadfast faith, unfailing hope, and abounding charity, for which all who came under its influence will ever give God thanks.

S. H.

ROBERT CLARKSON TONGUE

[43]

THE Rev. ROBERT CLARKSON TONGUE was born in Omaha, Nebraska, on the eighth day of February, 1869, and was given the name of the brave and honored Bishop of that Diocese; he died at Meriden, Connecticut, on the fifteenth day of December, 1904, having not quite completed thirty-six years of life.

While he was yet a youth, his father, the Rev. Thomas O. Tongue, after service in the Middle States, removed to Connecticut and took charge of St. Andrew's Church, Bloomfield. He remained there but a few years, and devoted the latter part of his life to service in the Diocese of Washington, where he made friends for himself and for the church whose commission he bore. The younger man remained near his former home, living in the family of the Rev. John B. McLean, studying in McLean Seminary, and after a while assisting in the instruction.

At this time, we are told by his teacher, "he became a leader among his schoolmates because of his intellectual gifts and still more because of his lovable comradeship. Brimful of good nature, enthusiastic, sympathetic—this is my memory of the lad. There is a demand for such men, who combine high intellectual gifts with strong common sense and Christlike manliness."

Then for a while he taught in a private school in Tolland. In 1891 he entered Trinity College, with the intention of devoting to general study as much time as it was possible to take consistently with carrying out his resolve to devote himself to the work of the holy ministry. The writer of these lines recalls the faithfulness with which he undertook his college work and the success with which he carried it on. Largely because of the way in which he had combined studying and teaching, his mind showed more maturity than most students can expect to have at the beginning of their academic course. This was shown especially by the readiness with which he wrote both in prose and verse, and by the high standard of thought and expression to which he attained. He was chosen an editor of the college literary paper and the poet of his class. On leaving college Mr. Tongue accepted a position as instructor in the English language and literature at the venerable Episcopal Academy of Connecticut at Cheshire, and after two years of successful work there he entered the Berkeley Divinity School at Middletown. While studying theology with diligence, he found time to act as a private tutor for college students, and also assisted acceptably in the work of the parish of the Holy Trinity.

Mr. Tongue was ordained to the diaconate by Bishop Williams, in the Church of the Holy Trinity, Middletown, on the third day of June, 1896, and he at once took charge of the important congregation of St. John's Church, Rockville. To it he devoted three years of diligent and acceptable service, being ordained to the priesthood in St. Paul's Church, New Haven, on the twenty-sixth day of May, 1897, by Bishop Coleman of Delaware, acting on behalf of Bishop Williams. To the regret of the church people in Rockville and of all who knew how much good work he had done among them and what promise there was of future labor and success there, Mr. Tongue felt that it was his duty to accept an election to the rectorship of All Saints' Church, Meriden, which came to him in the summer of 1899; and on the first day of September he became the second rector of that parish. Five years and more of faithful discharge of duty there proved that this parish made no mistake in asking him to become their priest and pastor, and that he had no cause to think that he decided wrongly when he accepted their call to minister to them. As in his former charge, his hearty enthusiasm, generous sympathy, willingness to labor, and anxiety to give of his best in public and private ministration, attracted his people to him and made them ready to listen and ready to do. He found a place in the esteem and affection of all the members of his congregation, both young and old, and entered readily into the relations of a pastor. As a preacher, he used diligently the abilities which were his by nature and by education and practice, and thus was able to instruct and to guide those whom his earnest words reached.

And while he gladly served those who were especially entrusted to his care, Mr. Tongue, in the comparatively

few years of his residence in Meriden, also gained for himself an honored and useful place in the life of the community, and that both as Christian minister and as citizen. He became a member of certain fraternal organizations and he was able to render service to others, and had a warm place in the hearts of the men whom he knew and who knew him. One who had intimate acquaintance with him, the rector of the mother Church in the city, said truly:

"The Church and the community could lose no laborer more diligent and self-denying; no servant honoring his Master by a more consistent Christian life; no teacher more faithful in his ministrations; no pastor whose care for his flock was more tender; no preacher who touched the hearts of his people with a more winning and eloquent message. He gave to his duties his brain, his heart, his strength, his life. In private life he was greatly beloved. There was in him a peculiar gentleness, a thoughtful regard for others, a genial heartiness of speech and manner, a bright humor, a quick appreciation, a wide intelligence, which imparted constant and varied charm to his society."

And the Ministers' Association of Meriden, after testifying to his work and his influence as man, as preacher, and as pastor, added these words:

"But Mr. Tongue's ministry has been rightly esteemed as being of far wider scope than his parish and his ecclesiastical connections. It was a ministry to the entire city; to its social life, in which he was thoroughly at home, a ready and witty speaker, a hearty comrade of men, a dispenser of enthusiasm and good cheer in every circle; to the industrial life of the city where he was held in exceptional confidence and respect; to our civic life, also, to which he brought the example as well as the advocacy of a high type of citizenship and concern for the city's culture and progress; and to our entire religious life to which he contributed his vigorous personality, his inspiring message, and his practical enthusiasm in behalf of every righteous movement."

Mr. Tongue's last ministrations were on the third Sunday in Advent, December eleventh; on the following day he was stricken with serious illness; and after a brief period of great suffering, which however was mercifully alleviated, he died on the evening of Thursday, December fifteenth. The former part of the office for the Burial of the Dead was said in All Saints' Church on the afternoon of the following Sunday; and on the next day the burial took place in Simsbury, the Bishop of the Diocese reading the committal.

Thus ended the earthly part of a true priestly life, for which those to whom in one way or another this servant of God ministered, will long give thanks—a life to which are now granted the rest and light of Paradise, and for which we expect the untold blessings which the Lord's return shall bring to all who love and fear Him.

In December, 1892, Mr. Tongue was married to Miss Minnie Wyatt of New Haven, who survives him with two children, Ruth Wyatt, aged four years, and Helen Kent, an infant.

As a memorial of the man, and as a tribute to his genius, this collection of sonnets and other poems has been made and is now published. To his friends, they carry their own commendation, as they tell of the author; and the judgment of those who have read them without having the privilege of his acquaintance, leads us to believe that they will be welcomed by others, both for their intrinsic excellence and for the thoughts which they express and inspire.

FORTIETH ANNIVERSARY OF THE CONSE-CRATION OF THE CHURCH OF THE GOOD SHEPHERD.

[Its Early History]

Sermon preached Jan. 31, 1909.

Text: Isaiah 40: 10, 11.

" Behold, the Lord God will come as a mighty one, and his arm shall rule for him;

Behold, his reward is with him, and his recompence before him.

He shall feed his flock like a shepherd; he shall gather the lambs in his arms, and carry them in his bosom. and shall gently lead those that have their young."

I. The prophet, looking forward to the time of the deliverance of his people, and bidden to make proclamation of it, describes the advent of the Lord God as a mighty King and a gentle Shepherd. He is to come a righteous avenger; with strong arm he is to do justice for His people who have been suffering, even to the double, for their sins, and to avenge them on their enemies. And He is to come also with sympathy for a flock which has been hard bested, scattered and frightened and wearied. The glory of Jehovah, God of Israel, is to be revealed; not only the glory of a victor conquering his enemies, but also that of a Shepherd caring for his sheep.

The double thought—we have all noticed it—does not belong to this passage alone. It was not only the inspiration of the great prophet, suddenly lifted up in thought to the high mountain and looking forth to visions of the Messiah who was to come; it was not merely an expectation that in the last days one should arise in whom should appear the great reconciliation of justice and goodness, of truth and mercy. Rather it had its source in the simplicity of the early days when every father was a king and every king was the father of his people. For out of fatherhood, in which as nowhere else are combined the necessity of brave defence and of gentle care, of confident courage and of unselfish affection, spring both kingship and priesthood; and a little thought will assure us that it belongs to the true king and to the true priest that they each have the character of the father. We see it in what we call patriarchal government and patriarchal priesthood; we find it not indistinctly shown in the pictures of early life preserved for us in Genesis, or again in the wonderfully parallel pages of the historian of early England; with no thought of domination or suggestion of arbitrary action, the king and the priest, in the earlier case one in person and in the latter one in sympathy, are the heads of a family, and in their position and their work there is scarce a line to sever the temporal from the spiritual. And as time passes on, and distinctions are made and duties and responsibilities are severed, the fundamental conception of duty and of service remains the same; the duty of defence springs from an obligation no less priestly than royal, the opportunity for service belongs to the king no less than to the pastor. The king must be gentle, the shepherd must be brave; each must be ready for battle, and each must do the work of peace. " The Lord is my shepherd;" so we read in the Psalm which almost seems to have suggested one of the most wonderful of our Lord's descriptions of Himself in His relations to us; but we glance at the Latin heading of the Psalm, and see that long ago

devout men thought that it would be best understood by " Dominus regit me." " The Lord is my king." And this is the connection of the thoughts expressed, as in other places, so in the verses which I have taken as my text to-day: " Behold, the Lord God will come as a Mighty One; He shall feed His flock like a shepherd: Behold, His justice is before Him; He shall gather the lambs—the little ones—in His arms, and gently lead the mothers."

And when we come to hear our Lord's words about Himself, when the "Strong Son of God" comes for battle and for victory, to claim His own in His great redemption, we need not be surprised that He takes up the other figure in the prophecies which have gone before, and calls Himself the Good Shepherd. He does not allow the words to tell of an easy task for Himself; the oriental shepherd cannot be a coward or unwatchful; no sooner does He claim the title than He tells of His very life laid down in pledge for the sheep: and presently He speaks of an obligation laid upon Him, not only to care for His own, but to find others who do not know Him and make them His own: " Them also, who are not of this fold, I must bring." The good

144

Shepherd's goodness is that of beauty of character, of bravery and of strength. And from Him the pastors of His Church, not in apostolic times alone but in all the centuries and to-day, may learn the lesson of what their pastoral work, their priestly work, their rectorial and guiding work, must be; brave yet self-denying, gentle yet strong, that of a shepherd-king and of a king-like shepherd, not to do only but to be, not to be only but to do, to work with all the might of God, yet with gentle touch to lead and guide His people on the restraint and the liberty and the progress of their true life—that they may " go in and go out and find pasture."

Thus the name which this Church bears may well lead us to ask, at this anniversary-tide, how it has maintained the principles of life and action and service which that name, in the fulness of its meaning suggests. The Church of the Good Shepherd tells of the Saviour's gentleness and care for His own, of His courage in defending them from harm, and of His wise guidance of them in their way; it tells of the knowledge which his flock have of Him, of their joyful following when He leads, of their answer to His call when He bids them draw nearer, of their ever faithful allegiance, quickened by the approach of darkness and the sense of danger. The very name recalls to many of us one side at least of the history of these forty years, abounding faith quickened by sorrow and turning sorrow even into joy; let us not forget to find in it also the other side of the history, abundant work for God and abundant and abiding fruit from it in pastors and people; the Lord God has here fed His flock as a shepherd, and here He has been revealed in strength, with work and with recompence.

CHURCH EXTENSION IN HARTFORD.

II. The year 1869, with the two months preceding it and the one following it, was notable in the annals of the Church in Hartford, as it marked external progress and the hopes of progress. In the November before the consecration of this building, Grace Chapel in Parkville had been consecrated for a congregation which had already a few years' growth, and the nave of the Chapel of the Incarnation —now St. James's Church—had been dedicated for a newly gatherede ongregation; thirteen months later that building was again opened after enlargement. Less than a year after the consecration of this building, St. John's Church in East Hartford was consecrated for a congregation which had been gathered under the same care as that which had fostered the spiritual beginnings here; and we may further note that not much later Trinity Church in Wethersfield, the inspiration of which may be traced back to the same source, was completed.

PARISH BEGINNINGS.

Ten years before this, a Sunday School had been gathered, under the care of the Rev. Dr. Washburn, rector of St. John's Church, in the building known as Charter Oak Hall, but popularly as the Flatiron building, erected by Colonel Colt as a part of his extended scheme for the moral and intellectual and social benefit of the families called into this neighborhood by the erection of his armory. The school did not continue long; but another school presently took its place, which on the first Sunday in 1864 was transferred to the care of the Rev. William Croswell Doane, who had succeeded Dr. Washburn at St. John's Church. Colonel Colt had died; but his wife was ready to make such provision as was necessary for services here in " the Meadow."

FIRST SERVICE.

In the spring the Rev. Henry Wells Nelson, Jr., a strong young friend of the rector of St. John's, was appointed his assistant; and on Trinity Sunday, May 22nd, the first service in the Flatiron building was held. If I remember aright, it was in a lodge-hall on the third floor; after a little a room on the ground floor was used, having been suitably fitted for Church worship. On this first occasion, 135 persons were present, and an address was made—it is interesting to note—by a missionary to the Indians. Within a year 37 children were baptized, 10 persons were confirmed, and $29 was contributed at the bi-weekly services.

PARISH ORGANIZED.

In the third year, 1866, Mr. Nelson began to give all his time to this congregation, and two services each Sunday were begun on the first Sunday after Trinity; on the 18th day of July a parish was organized by fourteen men, two of whom are still residents of the city, and on the 27th day of August Mr. Nelson was elected rector. Doubtless it was already known that Mrs. Colt was intending to erect a church edifice as a memorial to her husband and their three children who had died in infancy; for the parish took the name of the Church of the Good Shepherd which she desired to give to the building; and plans for it must have been soon taken in hand. The corner-stone was laid by Bishop Williams September 4, 1867; and, as you know, the Church was consecrated January 28, 1869, though it was not till a year or so later that it was completed by the erection of the spire.

THE CHURCH BEAUTIFUL.

We have become so accustomed to worshiping in this Church that, in all probability, very few of us appreciate the beauty of plan and of detail which attracted so much attention when it was new; and I wonder if many of those whose associations with the building go back but a few years have studied it within and without as many worshipers and visitors studied it then. It was well described, architecturally and symbolically, in a little pamphlet which might well be reproduced; and the help of photograpy would bring out many details which escape notice in the profusion of carving and color. The consecration was said to be "the most imposing ceremony that ever took place in any church in this State." Bishop Williams was of course the consecrator; and with him were Bishop Coxe of Western New York, the first rector of St. John's Church and while there pastor of Mrs. Colt's family, the poet of the American Church, who preached a sermon worthy of the occasion and of himself; Bishop Kerfoot of Pittsburg, recently President of Trinity College. Bishop Neely of Maine, Dr. Doane who was within a week to be consecrated Bishop of Albany, and a large body of clergymen from this and other dioceses. The feelings of parishioners and friends were so well expressed in Bishop Williams' address to the next diocesan convention that I cannot do better than quote his words:

" As to the Church of the Good Shepherd in Hartford, I hardly know how to speak in fitting terms. Seeing and knowing, as I have done, the Christian generosity of purpose and the wisdom of plan which marked the inception of the work, and being cognizant of the unsparing and willing munificence with which the work was carried on, I should be glad to say what yet I may not, because of the known wish of one whose wish must in this be law.

145

But this much I will say, that the consecration of the Church of the Good Shepherd marks a year in my episcopate to which I must ever look back with grateful joy; sets before the Church an example of unstinted giving that I am sure will kindle many hearts; offers to God's service a noble offering of faith and love; and centralizes a work for souls the value of which we cannot estimate. If, in its beauty and its sanctity, that church carries ever with itself the memories of earthly loss and sorrow, it gains for its founder a greater than the blessing promised by the wise king of Israel; for not "her children" alone, but multitudes in coming years, shall "arise up and call her blessed."

To these may be added the words of the rector in his report at the same Convention, as testifying to the purpose of the work; "A church building has been erected by a member of the parish, out of love for the Church and for men, to the glory of God and in memory of her husband and of their children now in the heavenly fold of the Good Shepherd. Throughout a labor of love, it has been blessed by a loving Father, and brought to its completion without loss or harm to any of those occupied in its construction. The church is free; its services are maintained wholly by the voluntary offerings of its people, which are amply sufficient to meet all its expenses. The congregations have been uniformly large, and the parish has been strengthened by the incoming of quite a number of families."

PAROCHIAL PROGRESS.

III. Great indeed was the comfort which the Good Shepherd brought to her who was specially concerned in the building of this church dedicated in His name, and to others to whom the structure itself, or its adornments, or the texts painted upon its walls brought a like feeling of the blessedness of those whom He guides or leads or carries in His arms. But great also was the strength which He, the King, gave here to His servants, His mighty arm stretched out for their defence and His bountiful recompense ever with Him. One shrinks from testing such spiritual power by figures; but certainly it was no little proof of the power of God exerted by His Holy Spirit and willingly accepted by men, that in four years of ministration here, there were more than two hundred baptisms—one quarter of those thus admitted into the Church being adults—and a hundred persons were confirmed, seeking the special grace of God for their lives of conscious and willing dedication and service, while the number of communicants increased from 38 to 166 and the number of children in the Sunday school from 90 to 170. The number of worshippers on Sunday evenings was large; few Church people spent a Sunday in Hartford who did not wish to see the building of which so much was said in the early days of its history, and the very hearty services, at once simple and dignified, attracted many. Men's need of the Church and its

power to meet their need were wonderfully proved under its first rector, who is followed in his present affliction of body by the affectionate remembrance of many to whom he ministered; the Church Home too, stands as his memorial. God bless him in all the years that are left to him here and in the bright vision of the world that is to be revealed!

THE SECOND RECTORATE.

It was after ten years of rectorship that Mr. Nelson resigned, less than eight years after the consecration of the church. To him succeeded in 1877 the Rev. John Henry Watson, of whose sixteen years of service, pleasant for his people and pleasant (I am sure) for himself I must speak but briefly in his presence. It was a time of quiet but active ministration; a little harder, perhaps, than it would have otherwise been, by reason of the change which necessarily came with new conditions, with the passing away of the novelty of the early years and the necessity of content with the strength that comes from quietness and confidence. The patience and faithfulness of the work of those years and the blessed results of it are in the hearts of some of those who are gathered here to-day, and the record of it is not lost. It fell to the second rector's lot to bring the comfort of the Good Shepherd to the foundress of the church as well as to others, and to minister His strength which brings joy out of sorrow and victory even from the grave.

THE THIRD RECTORATE.

Her last great affliction came early in the rectorship of the Rev. Cornelius Gardner Bristol, who followed Mr. Watson in 1893. Out of it as a memorial and—you will understand me when I say it—a thank-offering came the gift to the parish of the memorial house, which in its beauty is the counterpart of the church, and in its purpose is complementary to it. I need not tell you what it means and what it is, or how the gift came at the very time when it was needed, and provided for parish activities in many a year of history still unwritten. And I do not need to tell you how the third rector availed himself of opportunities, and how, when his ministry here of little more than eight years was cut short by death, it was seen that he had indeed a strong hold not only on his parishioners but also on the whole community. A vigorous life had been at work, the life of the mighty Son of God for the quickening of His people, the life of the gentle Son of Man for sympathetic guidance. For, of course in ways that have differed by reason of men's characters and endowments and of the changes that come with the years, there has ever been here, and there is to-day, fidelity to the great Head of the Church and to His historic Church as the means by which He applies to men His redemptive and regenerating and sanctifying grace; teaching and ministrations have ever been, as they are to-day, those which the Lord has provided for His people in His covenant of grace; and the response has been, as it still is and shall ever be

THE PRESENT AND THE FUTURE.

Of the new rectorate, if that can be called new which is about completing its seventh year, the record is about you and in your hearts, the promise is in a faithfulness which you have tested and which God has blessed. And as the years go on, and those of us who can remember the origins of the parish pass away, and presently—for it will not be long in God's eternal years, if the Church militant still remains—those who can look back to this fortieth anniversary become few in number, till He return, the glad service of souls to whom have been brought the knowledge of His grace and faith in Him and whom they have learned to follow as the Shepherd and King of their souls.

and they too fall on sleep, there shall still be here the worship of the Holy Trinity, the profession of the faith of the Church of the Apostles, the ministration of the sacraments of the Lord's institution, the teaching of Holy Scripture doubtless with added clearness of understanding. And these memorial buildings shall ever tell of personal faith and the happiness that springs out of sorrow, the joy

of unselfish service, the victory of life in Christ. He who comforted the saintly woman to whom especially our thoughts turn to-day and in whose name as the Good Shepherd—the beautiful Shepherd—she built and adorned and restored these walls and cared and made provision for them, He who spoke to this whole parish and to many outside its limits words of comfort when—it seems but as yesterday—her work on earth was done and the world by reason of this was a different world to us, will still be the Shepherd of His people, feeding their souls with heavenly food gathering the lambs in His arms and carrying them in His bosom and gently leading those who need such care.

IV. And even now, when we have passed through little more than what is called one generation of men, has there not been abundant proof in this place and in the influences which have gone forth from it, that the Son of God is indeed the Shepherd of His people? In every baptism at the font, in every benediction by the laying-on of hands, in every approach to the eucharistic feast, it is His leading, His guidance, His blessing on the strong, His pardon of the sinful, His strengthening of the weak. In every life begun, continued, and ended in the faith; at every time when the bodies of the faithful dead—our memories go back to-day to those whom we do not name, but whom we do not forget, some of them pillars of strength to this parish—have been brought here that from God's house they may be carried to their place of rest; in every word of truth spoken, in every response of conscience or of will to the truth, it has been and it is our recognition of our dependence on Him and His most gracious response. And out of it all there swells the voice of praise and the acknowledgement of the eternal strength and glory and kingship of our Good Shepherd. "Behold the Lord God doth come as a mighty one and his arm doth rule for him; behold, his reward is with him and his recompence before him." That strength is ours for life and in death; in that strength has the Lord our God been with us these forty years; in that strength God is our hope; in that strength may He be for us, as for all His servants, our Defender and our Shepherd, that when we no longer worship in these earthly courts, we may dwell in His heavenly home for ever!

Rev. Henry Wells Nelson, began services May 22, 1864; rector August 27, 1866, to September 11, 1876.

Rev. John Henry Watson, rector April 2, 1877, to June 20, 1893.

Rev. Cornelius Gardner Bristol, rector July 18, 1893 to November 30, 1901.

Rev. George Thomas Linsley, rector March 16, 1902.

YALE COLLEGE IN OLD SAYBROOK

[44] THE FIRST GRADUATING CLASS WAS A "CLASS OF ONE," RECEIVING BACHELOR'S DEGREE FROM THE INSTITUTION IN 1703

STATUE OF ABRAHAM PIERSON, FIRST RECTOR OF YALE

SAYBROOK was a town two-thirds of a century old when it was selected as the site for the Collegiate School of Connecticut. The first fort had been destroyed by fire, and the second fort had ceased to be regarded as of special military importance. The "persons of quality" who were expected from England had not arrived, and probably none of them had ever attempted to set sail, at first because the revolutionary movement in England had met with success, and later because it had proved itself a failure. The settlement had been incorporated into the river colony, and New Haven had also been obliged to submit to the force of circumstances and to become part of Connecticut. About a half of the inhabitants, with Mr. Fitch, their pastor, had removed to the head-waters of the

SAYBROOK FORT, BUILT 1648, DEMOLISHED 1870

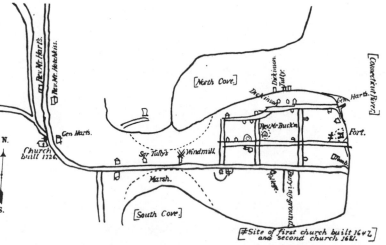

SKETCH OF SAYBROOK POINT, FROM PRESIDENT STILES'S ITINERARY, 1793. (THE FORT SHOULD HAVE BEEN PLACED TO THE SOUTH OF THE MIDDLE LANE, NOW CALLED CHURCH STREET)

147

Thames, and founded Norwich on her nine miles square of land.

Those who remained, more of them grandchildren than children of the first settlers, were living, some indeed on the squares and lots laid out on the point within the place where Lion Gardiner's mill guarded the neck of land, but some also to the west in the Oyster River district, some to the north on the Pettipaug road, and some in East Saybrook or Lyme, across the river. Mr. Thomas Buckingham who was called to take Mr. Fitch's place, had ministered four years before ordination, and now, as a thirty years ordained pastor, was at the head of the community. A new meeting-house had been built, close to the site of the former structure, more pretentious in size and style, for it was sixty feet by thirty, and had two gables, with a porch over the front door and a balustrated turret. Lady Fenwick's grave stood by itself on Tomb-hill, where she had been buried in the enclosure of the first fort ; but the bodies of the others who had died out of these two generations of men had been laid in the lot set apart for a burying ground, and still used for that sacred purpose. The life of Saybrook probably differed little from that of other towns along the coast, except that the fact that it was on a main line of travel by land and that it had easy communication with other places by river and sound and sea seemed to give the inhabitants

A REMAINING GRINDING STONE FROM LION GARDINER'S FAMOUS OLD MILL

the opportunity of a wider outlook into the neighborhood and the world.

Here, doubtless in Mr. Buckingham's house, the site of which is marked on the sketch by President Stiles, here reproduced, on the eleventh day of November, 1701, the "undertakers" named in the charter of the Collegiate School held their first meeting. Seven of the ten corporators attended, and they accepted their trust, voted that Saybrook should be the home of the institution, and elected Mr. Abraham Pierson, the pastor of the church in Killingworth, to be its head or rector. Here presently began the work of instruction with one student, to whom others soon joined themselves. And thus, at the bounds of the west, on the further side of the long river, looking back to the seats of learning in the mother country and to the Cambridge of the more ancient colony, but also looking forward to the new lands yet to be traversed and the new learning yet to be discovered and applied, the College was founded. And here it continued for fifteen years, with varied experiences, under one rector to whom his church would not give permission to discharge all the duties of his office by coming into residence and who required some of the students to be with him eight miles away, and another who held but a temporary appointment and lived at a greater distance. It was a time of foundations, but in spite of many difficulties the foundations were well laid.

The roll of benefactors of the institution was well begun by Saybrook men. Mr. Nathaniel Lynde, the wealthiest man in the place and a member of a family which had already attained honor in Massachusetts, elected first treasurer of the College, presented a fine lot with a house for the use of the institution, while it should remain in the place where it had been established. Major John Clark, descendant of one of the first settlers, transferred the right to two thousand acres of land in the Mohegan country, which had been given to him by the Chief Attawanhood (or Joshua Uncas) in grateful recognition of services rendered to him and his people. And we hear also of the gift of a large tract of land near Woodstock from Major James Fitch, of the family of the first minister. We cannot determine when the Collegiate School took possession of the home generously provided for it ; it was probably occupied soon after the work of instruction was begun, and some little time before the minute of its formal acceptance appears on the records. If tradition may be trusted, it was the home of the tutors, and also provided rooms for the library and for purposes of instruction. We are told that the windows were of oiled paper, as some of the books which had been given for the infant college had "suffered by concentration of the sun's rays through imperfect glass while they were at Mr. Russell's house in Branford." Some provision was made for the storage of philosophical apparatus, if we may accept the hints that there were provided a prism, a telescope, an orrery, and apparatus to illustrate centrifugal forces. The students were doubtless gathered each day for prayers ; but it was probably in some room designated for lectures or recitations, as we read of no separate chapel. On Sundays their college prayers were not omitted, and they probably had expositions of the Westminster Catechism at these, and later, it may be, lectures on the Saybrook platform ; and twice, without doubt, they attended in the meeting-house and listened to the ministrations of Priest Buckingham or Priest Mather—for by this sacerdotal title would they speak of their pastor—or to some one who, attracted by the atmosphere of learn-

ing, came to take Lord's Day duty there. Those of the undergraduates who were in residence lived in families in the neighborhood ; a goodly number of them, indeed, could live at their own homes, but it would appear that for the others it became more and more difficult to find accommodations, and that the food problem was a troublesome one.

Of course the young men studied Latin ; they were required to read Latin and to write Latin, and were supposed to talk Latin ; they also read the Greek Testament and some classical Greek, and very possibly they were not quite allowed to escape from Hebrew. They had

LADY FENWICK'S TOMB IN ITS PRESENT POSITION

solid instruction in solid theology, and some training, it may be presumed, in rhetoric and in moral philosophy. Such natural science as was then known was brought to their notice, and perhaps with special reference to medical skill, as most of the ministers of that day were expected to have some knowledge of the art of healing. And astronomy was taught, too, according to the Ptolemaic system; one wonders whether it is not more than a coincidence that the tutor who introduced (about the year 1715) the teaching of the Copernican system was the tutor of whom the students complained that he was not properly qualified for the duties of his position. When the three or four years' course was over, the young men were thought to be qualified for the Bachelor's degree in Arts in accordance with what would be expected at Cambridge in Massachusetts or at Oxford and Cambridge in England. The fellows, or trustees, responsible for the bestowal of the degrees, were responsible for the examinations on which they were based. And probably it was to assert an academic right and claim an academic privilege, after the manner of a university, that in 1702, although there were no students yet ready to take degrees, four bachelors' of arts of Harvard College were given their second degrees, and Nathaniel Chauncey, who had studied privately, presenting himself for examination, was adjudged worthy to be admitted master of arts. The first graduating class was a "class of one," John Hart, who had been for two years an undergraduate, receiving the first bachelor's degree from the institution in 1703; and immediately after this he was appointed the tutor, or assistant to the rector. The early commencements were probably held in the meeting-house, although there is some reason for thinking that Mr. Buckingham's study furnished the place for some of them. At any rate the meeting-house soon became the stated place for the exercises, as we know from a letter of Benjamin Lord that in his day Rector Andrew presided over them there. By that time, the number of students having increased, there were two sessions on commencement-day, as indeed was the custom long afterwards; and the candidates produced a salutatory and a valedictory, with disputations, "none in English." Probably the range of languages displayed on the stage was not as wide as in later years, but with Latin and Greek, varied occasionally by Hebrew, a sufficiently serious impression must have been made. Mr. Lord says that the rector placed a book in the hand of each candidate, but gave no diplomas. But even if not presented in public, diplomas were prepared, written in Latin upon parchment, signed by the fellows, and given to the recipients of the degrees. Some of the most ancient are still in existence, among them Mr. Chauncey's and Mr. Hart's. Mrs. Chesebrough tells us that the first commencement dinner, prepared by Mistress Buckingham, consisted of shell-fish, venison, succotash, and boiled Indian pudding.

The building presented by Mr. Lynde was occupied for scholastic purposes until the college was removed to New Haven, when, under the conditions of the gift, it reverted to the donor. We do not know how long it remained standing; Dr. Stiles in one of his journeys speaks of seeing the cellar; but the site was not forgotten, and was constantly pointed out by the older inhabitants of Saybrook. On its site, now included in an addition to the ancient burying ground, but in such a position that an open space can be reserved around it and that it can be readily seen from the street, there was placed last year a boulder from the hills above the village, bearing a handsome bronze plate suitably inscribed; and commemorative exercises on the two hundredth anniversary of the first meeting of the original corporators fitly closed the observance of the bicentenary of Yale University.

At the fifteen commencements held in Saybrook, from 1702 to 1716 inclusive, fifty-five young men took their bachelors' degrees (or fifty-six, if we include Mr. Chauncey of 1702); of these nine were sons of residents of Saybrook, and one was a grandson; one became pastor of the church there, and five others were appointed tutors in the school before the year of its removal; that is to say, nearly a fifth of the graduates were Saybrook boys, and more than a quarter of them had Saybrook at some time for their residence. The hope that the place would become a great seat of learning ceased when the Collegiate School was removed to New Haven. Into the details of the controversy as to the permanent home of the institution and of the decision which was reached, this is not the place to enter; the change was doubtless unavoidable, and history has justified it. Those who were so anxious to retain the institution in the home of its early years may have lacked a sufficiently clear idea of what President Stiles called a "Domicilium or Coenobium Academicum," which might be more easily secured in a larger place, and that they may not have been aware of all that a college required in order to have, as Dr. Colton Mather phrased it, "a collegious way of living."

Saybrook bore no unimportant part in Yale's early history.

BISHOP SEABURY AND CONNECTICUT CHURCHMANSHIP

JUNE 9TH 1896

[45]

II. The words of our Lord, on which I have been thus dwelling, seem to me, my brethren, to have an application to the subject to which I have been asked to direct your thoughts to-day. Thirteen years ago the Churchmen of this diocese commemorated the hundredth anniversary of the election of their first bishop; twelve years ago we kept the centenary of his consecration, and eleven years ago that of his return to this country, his welcome by his diocese, and the first ordination that he held. And with the Churchmen of Connecticut there were joined in these commemorations the Churchmen throughout this land, those of Scotland, and to a great extent those of England as well. The lessons which were thus brought anew to the minds of Church people in 1883 and the following years are still with us, enforced as they were by the wise and thoughtful words of our Diocesan; and thus we have before us the example of fidelity to faith and order and obedience which was conspicuous in the life and the deeds of Bishop Seabury, and by which he and the good and faithful and brave men who worked with him gave a true and indelible character to

our Connecticut Churchmanship.*

At the grave of our first bishop, "the Apostle of the new world,"† there were gathered together a few months ago bishops and clergymen and lay-people, to keep, with services of thanksgiving and words of instruction and exhortation, the hundredth anniversary of his falling on sleep after he had served his generation by the will of God.‡ And it would be seemly, were it but the right voice that should speak to-day, that this Convention of our venerable diocese should be reminded of what we

* See Reports of Seabury Commemorations in Connecticut, at Aberdeen, and in St. Paul's Cathedral.

† "*Novi orbis apostoli sit nomen perenne.*" Inscription written by Bishop Coxe to be placed beneath Bishop Seabury's mitre in Trinity College Library.

‡ Bishop Seabury died at New London, 25th February, 1796.

in Connecticut owe to our first bishop, the man in whom are summed up for us the guiding principles of those early days of faithful struggle which his episcopate crowned, and to whom also we trace back the inspiration of these later years in which his successors, ably helped by earnest clergymen and laymen, have carried out the self-same principles. Bidden to speak when all—and none more than myself—know that it needs another mind to frame the thoughts and another voice to utter the words that belong to this centenary year, it is with unfeigned hesitation that I venture to ask you to think of the application of our Lord's words in my text to the work of our first bishop in and for this his diocese, and to see how they bring admonition and encouragement to the Connecticut Churchmen of to-day. Bishop Seabury was both a reaper of the harvest that grew by reason of the sowing and the tillage of those who worked before him and with him in this colony; we are still gathering the ripened grain that has come from the good seed of which he knew hardly more than that it was good and that it had been cast into the ground, while we in our turn are sowing in the field which is our special care; God grant that they who come after us may find joy in gathering the fruits of our labors, even as we reap with happy thanksgiving that which has in due time come to maturity from the labors and cares of those who have toiled before us!

Look with me, if you will, at two or three of the aspects in which our first bishop stands prominently before us. The outline of his life and his work are with sufficient clearness in our minds; but let us consider how he was sent of God both to gather a harvest and to sow a seed; it may be that we can find a lesson as to the duty which lies before Connecticut Churchmen at the end of a century since he laid down his work.

III. It is not amiss that we should think of him as a citizen of this commonwealth. He had been born, brought up, and educated in the colony; he had had in great part the experience which made the clergy of Connecticut from 1722 to the date of the Revolution so acceptable to the people among whom they lived both before and after the time of their conforming to the Church of England. Men of blameless lives, well reported of by those who had known them from childhood, they had a place among the people of the colony, knowing its idiosyncrasies and its traditions, its needs and the way in which it would be willing to accept their supply, as those could not have known them who might have been sent from England or who might have come from neighboring colonies. In little more than fifty years thirty-seven young men from Connecticut, under strong pressure of conviction, had gone to England for ordination and returned to these shores, all but seven of them to minister in this colony; and six others, devoting their lives to the same work, had been prevented from returning by shipwreck or sickness or the violence of enemies.* As we all know, there was great prejudice against the Church of England, and some very sober men had grave apprehensions of the results which might follow upon its full establishment here; and there were cases in which individuals were treated with hardship and even with cruelty by reason of their being Churchmen or because their adherence to the Church of England made them supporters of the British Crown;† but we owe it to the civil authority of this colony and to the Standing Order of Christians established therein to confess that Churchmen in the colony of Connecticut were never under any civil disabilities, and that they were at an early date and on what were for the times easy conditions relieved from paying taxes for the ecclesiastical establishment.‡ Such men as Johnson and Leaming and Hubbard

* See Note at the end.

† Seabury himself, as will be noted presently, had been seized by a party of armed men at his own house at Westchester, carried out of the limits of the province, and kept in custody at New Haven for more than a month without a trial and in spite of a protest from the President of the Provincial Congress of New York. The Rev. Jeremiah Leaming, who was the first choice of the clergy of Connecticut for their bishop, was forced to decline by reason of his age and infirmities; he had been "taken from his bed in an inclement wintry night and lodged in the county jail as a tory, with the consequence of a severe cold, which settled in his hip and made him a cripple for the rest of his life." And these were by no means the only instances of the "sufferings of the clergy" in the revolutionary days.

‡ If there had been any Churchmen in the Colony of New Haven or in the towns confederated with it before 1665, they would have been under civil disabilities; but in Connecticut the only religious test required from the beginning was that the governor should be a member of the ecclesiastical establishment. Episcopalians were always classed among "sober dissenters" in the colony; and the first act for their relief was passed in 1727, only five years after the famous declaration of Cutler, Johnson, and others, which was practically the foundation of the Church in Connecticut; this law allowed the members of any

settled religious society to pay their ecclesiastical taxes for the support of their own services instead of those of the standing order. The greatest ecclesiastical severity in Connecticut was reserved for the Separatist Congregationalists.

and Beach commended this Church to their friends and neighbors and to good people all over the colony; and both by what they did and by what they suffered they made it easy for a bishop, at least for a bishop of the same kind, to come here after the Revolution, with an assurance, as nearly formal as it could be, that there would be no objection to him on the part of the authorities of the State.* A commonwealth which was broad-minded and wise enough to elect Dr. William Samuel Johnson to represent it in the convention that framed the Federal Constitution and to be its first senator in the Federal Congress, though some had treated him with suspicion as not favoring revolutionary methods of securing the rights of British subjects, was also broad-minded and wise enough to put no obstacles in the way of Bishop Seabury's work, and to honor him as a man if not as one having special authority in the Church, though he had a few years before been actually in confinement at New Haven as a Tory, and though he had been during a great part of the war chaplain to the royal troops in New York. And, as might have been expected, Bishop Seabury's obedience to the

* Dr. Beardsley's *Life of Bishop Seabury*, pp. 112, sqq.

authority here, "regularly and legitimately constituted," after the Revolution was not only "respectful," as the Article says it should be, but heartily loyal. Very soon after his first meeting with his clergy, he set forth certain changes to be made in the services to adapt them to the change in the civil government, prefacing them with the declaration that the Colony of Connecticut had become a "free, sovereign, and independent State";* and the next year, after the Convocation had formally agreed to similar modifications in the Prayer Book, he officially informed Governor Huntington of the same, "thinking it," he said, "my duty to lay all our transactions in which the State is in any wise concerned, before the Supreme Magistrates"; and he asked the Governor, in case he should think that anything had been done in derogation of "the freedom, sovereignty, or independence of this State," to communicate his sentiments to him.† The Episcopal Church thus continued to hold in the State by the action and the character of Bishop Seabury and his contemporaries the position which it had gained in the Colony by the character and the action of the Church people of the former generation.

* *Reprint of Bishop Seabury's Communion Office*, p. 29.

† Dr. Beardsley's *Life*, p. 266. On Bishop Seabury's relations with Governor Huntington, and the institution of the appointment of the Connecticut State-Fast on Good Friday (a custom now unbroken for a full century), see Dr. Love's *The Fast and Thanksgiving Days of New England*, Chapter XXIV. A Masonic sermon preached by the Bishop in 1795 was inscribed to President Washington "by his affectionate Brother and most devoted Servant, Samuel Seabury."

As every one knows, there have been times of excitement and bitter controversy and wars of pamphlets; and ecclesiastical and civil matters, religion and politics, have had some strange relations with each other here; but the position of this Church in this State has been a position of dignified loyalty and has been recognized as such. The early clergymen, the first bishop, and the clergymen whom he influenced, knew the historic position of the commonwealth and sympathized with the peculiarities of the people to whom they ministered; nay, they were, socially and politically and historically, members of the community and a part of the people; and as the way had in this particular been made ready for the men of a century ago, they made it ready for us; it is for us as Connecticut Churchmen to be good citizens of the State of Connecticut, to study—as so many of us are doing—its history in outline and in detail, to preserve the good qualities which it inherits, to look at the new problems that arise, and to commend the faith and order which we hold to those with whom we share the responsibility for the future of the State. And especially do we owe it to Connecticut that we uphold a high standard of honor and justice and truth, defending these under the shield of God's Commandments and with the fidelity of patriotic men.

IV. Bishop Seabury was also to us in this diocese, and to others, a pattern of what a Christian bishop and pastor should be. What he brought from Scotland to this country, to the surprise of the English-speaking world, was, in the apt phraseology of that day, "a free, valid, and purely ecclesiastical episcopacy." Such a conception of the episcopal office was practically unknown then, and such exercise of it could not have been found, except in the disestablished and persecuted Scottish Church with its four bishops and its very few clergy. Our first bishop doubtless learned his ideal in some part from them; but, under God, he himself deserves to be honored for the way in which he conceived and undertook his duty as a bishop. He could not have learned in England, at that time, that it was a bishop's office to make constant visitations of his parishes, to administer confirmation wherever there were any to be confirmed, and to be in very deed the pastor of all his people, while yet he lived in great simplicity as a rector and parson

and as a neighbor and friend. Even in Scotland, where good Bishop Jolly used to make a formal visitation of the four clergymen of his diocese once in three years, and where with high theories there was strange irregularity of practice, he did not learn what he began to do immediately on his arrival here and his recognition by clergy and people.

For our first bishop at once showed himself the pastor of all his flock, and for a while in certain ways acted as chief pastor in all these States. He visited his people; for he went diligently over his diocese again and again, confirming at first both old and young, both those who had been life-long communicants, all the time "ready and desirous to be confirmed," and those who were but just ready to be admitted to the Lord's Table, and afterwards those who were specially prepared to receive the blessing that comes with the laying-on of hands. He led and guided the worship of his people; and in particular he brought to us the ancient form of consecration in the Eucharistic service which the Scottish Church had learned from the study of the liturgies of the primitive Church; and he began in his own house, while he was obliged to hold the Lord's-day morning and evening services in the Court-house, the weekly administration of the Sacrament of the Saviour's Body and Blood. To show the constancy and thoroughness of his ministrations, it may be well to gather from a small part of his diary what he did in the fall of 1792, after he had been seven years bishop, on his way home from the General Convention. He came into the diocese about Michaelmas, and began visitations with sermons and confirmations. In about three weeks he had been to Stamford, New Canaan, Ridgefield, Danbury, Redding, Norwalk, Huntington, East Haven, North Guilford, Guilford, and Killingworth, had confirmed two hundred and sixty-five persons, and had preached twenty times. I have said that he did not learn this manner of exercising his episcopate from the bishops abroad. But in going about to minister to the people, he was in a way following the example of the Connecticut clergy from the beginning. His own father, while settled at New London, had held services in Norwich, North Groton, Windham, Hebron, Middletown, and Simsbury. And the registers kept by the clergymen of those early days tell of ministrations in every part of the colony, often at great distances from the places of their cures. It was these which made the people ready to expect such services from their bishop, and led him to expect to render them. As he went about, he was not only reaping a harvest from their labors, as he confirmed and exhorted those who had been trained by faithful pastors; the very fact of his visitations was due to what they had done. We read of no such journeys or visitations on the part of the other bishops consecrated abroad for American sees; for a while it seems as if the custom of the first bishop of Connecticut had not even passed to his successors; but the example of the first bishop and the genius of Connecticut Churchmanship again prevailed, and constant visitation became our custom here and, in fact, the custom throughout the land. Bishop Seabury was the model of the American episcopate, even more really in some ways than Bishop Wilberforce was the model of the modern English episcopate. Our fathers and we in this diocese have had great reason to be thankful for it, as we have been helped and blessed by it; and the example has reached and affected all the Church work of the diocese. I think that we may trace back nearly all that is good in our pastoral and missionary work to influences that came from the faithful men of the early times, concentrated in the example of the great man to whom our thoughts have been specially directed to-day; yet not as influences that lack the power of inspiring growth, nor as an example that is satisfied by a simple reproduction; we must needs, if we would do what they would do were they here to-day, adopt new methods and mark out our own path; but in parochial and archidiaconal and diocesan work we shall do our duty best if we enter into and appropriate and extend the labors of those who have toiled before us. We shall never act up to the ideals and the requirements of Connecticut Churchmanship if we neglect the pastoral and missionary work to which they were so earnestly devoted and which they left to us.

V. Bishop Seabury, moreover, was a bishop who taught his people plainly and persuasively, both by spoken word and from the printed page, in sermon and charge and catechism.* It is to be hoped that at least those of his sermons which have been printed may be reprinted and put into the hands of our people for study, for lay-reading in church, and for home reading. They are not antiquated either in matter or in style, and are hardly old-fashioned, except in the sense in which all re-

* His reprint of Bishop Innes's *Catechism on the Principles of the Christian Religion* ought to be better known and studied. It was published with a preface dated at New London, February 12, 1791.

ligious truth and all exhortation to duty are old-fashioned, but are scholarly and clear, thoughtful and interesting. I gather from the part of his diary which I have seen that at his confirmations he preached simple sermons on duty, such as would

be based on the text, "Having therefore these promises, dearly beloved, let us cleanse ourselves from all filthiness of the flesh and spirit, perfecting holiness in the fear of God." At ordinations he preached, most naturally, on the authority and duty of the ministry; and at other times, as his printed volumes show, he preached clearly and strongly on the Sacraments, or on some topic such as the Lord's Day, or expounded some portion of Scripture, such as a parable from the Gospels. Thus he enforced the laws of duty, while yet he did not fail to teach what I am sure our congregations are not yet tired of hearing, the doctrine of the Church as brought out in Creed and Liturgy and the round of sacred services; and thus he instructed a generation of Churchmen who could give a reason for the faith that was in them and could tell it "to the children of the generations to come."* When some fifty years ago there was a revival of Catholic teaching in England and a new appeal to the doctrine and the practice of the primitive Church, and the novelty, as it was called,

* The Bishop's First Charge (1785) is in large part eminently practical; the Second Charge (1786) touches more on doctrinal questions, but it also dwells on serious matters of religious duty. Together they give an excellent epitome of his teaching. They are reprinted in full in Dr. Beardsley's *Life*, pp. 216 sqq., 267 sqq.

awaked great excitement as well among those who accepted it as among those who did not, Connecticut Churchmen wondered at it all when they came to read the writings of the early Tractarians, because they found in them exactly what they had always been taught and had always believed.* The teaching did not originate here with Bishop Seabury. He gave it a new vigor and brought into it some ideas from the theology of the Scottish Churchmen; but his teaching was that which Cutler and Johnson and Brown had learned as they read the books of English theology in the College Library at New Haven, grafted in their case and in the case of their contemporaries upon a good inherited foundation of Churchly teaching which the sober Puritan ministers of this colony had never quite forgotten; and it was helped and strengthened by the studies of later clergymen and laymen, using among other books those which were sent to parochial libraries by the Venerable Society and by friends in England. From Bishop Seabury this teaching came to his successor and then to the learned and influential Dr. Jarvis, son of the second bishop, the power of whose learning and influence, with but one remove, is felt by so many of us to-day.

* The Rev. (afterwards Sir) William Palmer, in the preface to the second edition of his *Narrative of Events connected with the Publi-* cation of the *Tracts for the Times*, says that a larger number of copies of the first edition were circulated in America than in England. At the time of the publication there were in the Church in this country only about 1,000 clergymen and 55,000 communicants.

One cannot but fear that, as it has become less necessary for Churchmen to be ever on the defensive, we have ceased a little to study into the reasons of things and to know why we believe our Creed and follow our customs. Yet without doubt, as we still expect episcopal ministrations as Bishop Seabury gave them to the Diocese in his day, and as we use in our eucharistic worship with great thankfulness the form that he brought us, which carries us back both in principles and in words to the uses of the earliest days, so Connecticut Churchmen expect and accept the teachings of the historic Church enshrined in the Book of Common Prayer; and we are reaping part of the harvest that comes to us from the labors of our first bishop when we are taught to hold, and do hold, to the faith and the worship, the doctrine and the discipline of the undivided Church. But here also, as I said in a former case, what we need is not a blind following of a dead example without adaptation to changes of times and manners; it is a living growth as of a tree which puts forth new branches towards the light, and as it grows older adds both to the strength of its trunk and the beauty of its foliage and brings a greater delight and greater service to both God and man. We ought to be better Churchmen, at once stronger and more charitable, than those of a century ago, because we can learn more about the Scriptures and history, because we have had more experience, because our convictions have had time to grow both wider and deeper. A hundred years from now, if the Lord's Return is so long delayed, those who stand in our place ought to be able to thank us for more than that for which we to-day thank our spiritual forefathers of the last century. Are we, as we reap the harvest on which we bestowed no labor, so toiling that in due time others may enter with joy into our labors?

I ought to add that Bishop Seabury was one who taught the lessons of daily duty in the simple, quiet, charitable, effective way which marks the teaching of the Church when rightly presented and rightly accepted. "Next to a sound rule of faith," says the poet Keble, "there is nothing of so much consequence as a sober standard of feeling in matters of practical religion; and it is the peculiar happiness of the Church of England to possess in her authorized formularies an ample and secure provision for both."* The maxims of John Keble and his brother, Dean Church tells us,

"bade men to be very stiff and uncompromising in their witness and in their duties, but to make no show and expect no recognition or immediate fruit, and to be silent under misconstruction." And he goes on to say that such a man as Isaac Williams would have been "satisfied" if he could have attained and could have led others to attain "more reality, more severity and consistency, deeper habits of self-discipline on the accepted lines of English Church orthodoxy."† The words may

* Advertisement to *The Christian Year.*
† *The Oxford Movement,* p. 65.

not describe, but they indicate, the character which grew up here even in those who were forced to engage in controversy. Bishop Seabury could well remember the excitement in New London in 1743, attending the "great awakening," when Mr. James Davenport visited the place for the second time and persuaded some of the people to burn publicly Bishop Beveridge's *Thoughts on Religion* and other books of similar character, and to prepare to burn articles of clothing and other things which they imagined had been to them in the place of idols. People thronged to his father's house—he was then the missionary in New London—"some under these distresses and others surprised at the conduct of their neighbors"; and he brought them, as he himself said, "by cool reasoning and by plain expositions of the terms of reconciliation, to a just notion of the doctrines of repentance and remission of sins."* If the young man needed the lesson, these and such like things—not the least the treatment of the Cleveland brothers in college during his freshman year†—taught him, strong as he was in his convictions and brave champion as he was for the truth, to be humble and considerate, and to seek for himself and for others that type of gentle and unassuming piety which—I hope it is not presumption to say it— marks the true Churchman. All this was not

* Mr. Seabury's letter to the Venerable Society, *Connecticut Church Documents,* i. 196.
† See Prof. Dexter's *Yale Biographies and Annals,* i. 771, ii. 30, 149.

new with him; it must not be allowed to become old with us.*

VI. It is now eleven years since the third of those centenary commemorations in which there were successively brought before us Bishop Seabury's election, his consecration, and the work of his episcopate. We were then reminded of many events in his life, many things which enabled us to understand his character and his work, the part

* A few words may be inserted here as to Bishop Seabury's attitude

towards the laymen of the Church. There seems to be at times an impression that he was a man of an ecclesiastical habit of mind, in that sense of ecclesiastical which indicates a narrow kind of clericalism. I do not think that I have ever read that he was accused of this by his own people, that he ever treated the layfolk with neglect or contempt, or that he was any less their pastor and teacher and servant than he was pastor and teacher and servant of the clergy. The statement, often repeated, that he was elected by the clergy in a secret way and without the knowledge of the laity, I believe to be a mistake. The idea that ten clergymen from different parts of the State could travel over bad roads in March to meet at Woodbury, and that either the fact or the purpose of their meeting could be kept a secret, is preposterous; and I have been told by the son of a man whom Bishop Seabury ordained that his father had told him that the meeting was with the knowledge and approval of the laity. And though the Bishop did think that his official advisors should be from the clergy, yet in no way did he ignore the ancient rights of the laity or such additional privileges as they might expect under a republican form of government. There were but seven articles in the "Ecclesiastical Constitution" agreed to by the first Convention of this Diocese; and all but one of these had something to do with asserting or defending the interests of the laity, one in particular allowing a communicant who should be suspended from the Holy Communion by a Presbyter to take an appeal to the Bishop in Convocation and thence to a Council of Bishops. And the first Canons, adopted in 1799, are strict in their requirements of the clergy and really defend the interests of the laity without laying any burden upon them. There is no depreciation of the rights of the lay people in any true Connecticut Churchmanship.

which Divine Providence assigned him in the ordering of the Church in this country, and the debt which we owe him, witnessed by the organization and the canon law of this Church and the liturgical forms which it uses as it offers worship to Almighty God. The centenary of our great Bishop's death has not indeed passed by unnoticed; but it is seemly that we, the members of the Convention of his Diocese, should be in some way reminded this year of his character and his work and moved to give thanks for him and to follow in the ways which he pointed out. In undertaking this duty, I have said little on those special matters which formed the subjects of the sermons in which the fourth Bishop of Connecticut told of what the first Bishop of Connecticut had done and enforced the lessons of his life and his work; "for what can the man do that cometh after the king?" I have barely reminded you of the modest bravery with which he undertook the responsibilities laid upon him by his brethren of the clergy, and of the great influence which he had in securing the unity, the strength, and the catholicity of the Church in this country. I have rather asked you to think of what Bishop Seabury was to this his diocese in the eleven years in which he exercised his episcopate here, as a citizen, as a pastor, and as a teacher; and in all these things how he carried out principles and practices which had already marked the Churchmen in this colony and gave an inspiration to those self-same principles and practices for the Churchmen in this State; in other words, how he was and is the typical Connecticut Churchman, simple yet grand, accommodating though uncom-

promising,* with high ideas of the Church and lowly ideas of his importance in it, with wide conceptions of faith and duty, never limiting God's grace and yet sure as to the way in which he was authorized to bid men to seek it, and never teaching privilege in such way as to neglect solemn exhortation to duty or to forget that " the end of the Ministry towards the children of God, towards the Spouse and Body of Christ," is that there be no place left, not only " for error in religion," but also " for viciousness of life." I have ventured to ask you to look at all this in the light of the Lord's words which I read as the text. Bishop Seabury had not to wait for a harvest to grow and ripen; the fields were already white for him; other men had labored, and he entered into their labors. Yet it was not true that he had but the joy of the harvest; a great part of the toil and the anxiety of the sower fell also to his lot; he was both sower and reaper, the one duty overtaking and crowding upon the other. Now, at the end of a century from the time when the death for which he had prayed, sudden, yet not unprepared for, came to him who had thus reaped and sowed in a season of great happiness and great anxiety, we find our work to be largely what he and his fellow-workers

* The adjectives are those applied to him by Judge Shea, in his *Life of Alexander Hamilton*, p. 307.

made it. It is in some ways easy to serve as clergymen or laymen in a diocese where we can gather results from good and true and brave labors of our forefathers in the faith; one danger is lest we content ourselves with what others have done, another lest we forget that we stand for those who are to come in the same relation in which the men of earlier years stand for us. Had they not been faithful pastors and teachers, keeping the traditions which they had received and applying them to the new needs and the increasing knowledge of their day, we should not have had our training in the law of duty and the revelation of truth as they are taught by the Church; had they not been brave and wise, faithful and charitable, there would have been but little harvest for us to reap. Are we studying the spiritual needs of the population of this State, so greatly changed from what it was but a few years ago? are we commending the faith and order of primitive days to our neighbors at the close of this century, not of course in just the same way, but with the same effect, as the Churchmen of a hundred years ago commended them to their neighbors? are we, with labor and if need be with tears, casting into the ground, hard and cold though it often seems, precious seed, in

spite of the temptation to keep it and to use it? are we so living and so working, so holding God's truth and so teaching it, that the Connecticut Churchmanship of our day shall be really and deservedly honored and followed by the generations that are to come? Men and women of high ideals and earnest convictions are looking for the Church that has and that knows it has a history and a ministry and an appointed sacramental system, that cares for the real needs of human souls and instructs them in divine truth; and many who do not know what they want are searching, and searching anxiously, for what this Church can give them if she will. We may not as yet reap our own sheaves, but oh! let us not be content to reap that on which other men have labored! A new generation is crowding close upon us, waiting for that which shall grow from the seed that we have sown and tended; let it not be that it shall find empty furrows or blasted stalks where there should be the beauty of a joyous harvest!

And God grant that the time may not be far off when the number of His elect shall be fulfilled, when he that sowed and he that reaped shall rejoice together, when there shall be no going forth with weeping but all God's husbandmen shall come again with joy and bring their sheaves with them, when we with those who have fallen asleep in Christ shall be made perfect in joy as we look upon the vision of God and find in it eternal truth and eternal life.

$$\text{T}\hat{\omega} \ \mu\acute{o}\nu\omega \ \Theta\epsilon\hat{\omega} \ \pi\hat{a}\sigma a \ \dot{\eta} \ \delta\acute{o}\xi a \cdot \dot{a}\mu\acute{\eta}\nu.$$

ADDITIONAL NOTE—

The following list contains the names of the Connecticut men who crossed the ocean for Holy Orders before the consecration of Bishop Seabury. It will be seen that it includes nearly all the ante-revolution clergymen of the colony. Those marked * had been ordained Congregational ministers; those marked † had been licentiates.

The data for this list, it needs hardly be said, have been taken from the valuable works of Dr. Beardsley and Professor Dexter.

Date of Ordination.	Name and Graduation.
1723	*Timothy Cutler, Harvard 1701, returned to Massachusetts.
1723	Daniel Browne, Yale 1714, died in England.
1723	*Samuel Johnson, Yale 1714.
1723	*James Wetmore, Yale 1714, returned to New York.
1727	Henry Caner, Yale 1724.
1731	†Samuel Seabury, Harvard 1724.
1732	*John Beach, Yale 1721.
1733	Isaac Browne, Yale 1729, returned to N. Y.
1734	*Ebenezer Punderson, Yale 1726.
1735–6	*Jonathan Arnold, Yale 1723.
1741–2	Richard Caner, Yale 1736.
1743	Ebenezer Thompson, Yale 1733, returned to Massachusetts.
1743	†Hezekiah Watkins, Yale 1737, returned to N. Y.
1744–5	Joseph Lamson, Yale 1741, captured by French but released.
1745	Barzillai Dean, Yale 1737, lost at sea on return voyage.
1748	†Ebenezer Dibblee, Yale 1734.

1748	Jeremiah Leaming, Yale 1745.	
1748	Richard Mansfield, Yale 1741.	
1749?	John Ogilvie, Yale 1748 ; see below (1).	
1752	†Ichabod Camp, Yale 1743.	
1752	Jonathan Colton, Yale 1745, died on return voyage.	
1753	Samuel Seabury, Jr., Yale 1748 ; see below (2).	
1754	*Solomon Palmer, Yale 1729.	
1755	†Christopher Newton, Yale 1740.	
1756	William Johnson, Yale 1748, died in England ; see below (2).	
1759	Samuel Peters, Yale 1757.	
1759	James Scovill, Yale 1757.	
1761	John Beardsley, King's 1761.	
1761	Thomas Davies, Yale 1758.	
1761	Samuel Andrews, Yale 1759.	
1763	Roger Viets, Yale 1758.	
1764	Bela Hubbard, Yale 1758.	
1764	Abraham Jarvis, Yale 1761.	
1765	Ebenezer Kneeland, Yale 1761.	
1767	Richard [Samuel] Clarke, Yale 1762.	
1768	Abraham Beach, Yale 1757, returned to New Jersey.	
1768	John Tyler, Yale 1765.	
1769-70	Luke Babcock, Yale 1755, returned to New York.	
1770	Gideon Bostwick, Yale 1762 ; see below (3).	
1771	John Rutgers Marshall, King's 1770.	
1774	James Nichols, Yale 1771.	

TRINITY COLLEGE IN 1869.

* Richardson Miner, Yale 1726, went abroad for orders in 1744 with Joseph Lamson ; they were captured by the French, and released ; but on his way to London Mr. Miner died at Salisbury.

James Usher, Yale 1753, whose home was in Rhode Island, was a catechist in Hebron when he went abroad for orders. He was captured by the French and died in 1757 in the castle at Bayonne.

Thomas Bradbury Chandler, Yale 1745, Agur Treadwell, Yale 1760, and Ephraim Avery, Yale 1761, were natives of Connecticut, but they were catechists or teachers without the colony when they went abroad for orders, and returned to work without the colony.

(1) John Ogilvie is believed to have been ordained by Scottish Bishops. Perhaps he should not be reckoned as a Connecticut man ; and only the very beginning of his ministry was in this colony.

(2) William Johnson and the younger Samuel Seabury are so closely identified with Connecticut that their names are inserted in the list, although their fathers at the time of their graduation were not residents of this colony.

(3) Gideon Bostwick returned to Great Barrington, which was ecclesiastically reckoned with Connecticut.

———

The whole number of Connecticut men ordained abroad is forty-one ; of these, four died before they reached home, and seven returned to work elsewhere. Two candidates died after crossing the sea, before they could be ordained. It is noticeable that all of the forty-three were college graduates.

Of the other colonial clergy of Connecticut, William Gibbs, a native of Massachusetts, was graduated at Harvard in 1731 and Daniel Fogg, a native of New Hampshire, was graduated at the same college in 1764.

[46]

TRINITY COLLEGE, HARTFORD.

THE plan for the establishment of a second college in Connecticut was not carried into effect until after the time of the political and religious revolution which secured the adoption of a State Consti-

tution in 1818. Probably no such plan was seriously entertained till after the close of the war of Independence. The Episcopal church in Connecticut had, one may almost say, been born in the library of Yale College ; and though Episcopalians, with other dissenters from the " standing order," had been excluded from taking any part in the government or the instruction of the institution, they did not forget how much they owed to it as the place where so

T. C. Brownell

many of their clergy had received their education. In fact, when judged by the standards of that day, it would appear that they had at first little cause to complain of illiberal treatment, while on the other hand they did their best to assist the college in the important work which it had in hand. But Yale College, under the presidency of Dr. Clap, assumed a more decidedly theological character than before, and set itself decidedly in opposition to those who dissented from the Westminster Confession of Faith and the Saybrook Platform of Discipline. Besides, King's College, which had been lately founded in New York, drew away some Episcopal students from Connecticut and made others dissatisfied ; and had not the war with the mother country rudely put a stop to the growth of Episcopacy in the colony, it would seem that steps might have been soon taken for the establishment of some institution of learning, at least a school of theology, under the care of the clergy of the Church of England.

At any rate no sooner was it known that the war was ended than the churchmen of Connecticut sent the Rev. Dr. Seabury across the ocean to seek consecration as a bishop; and it was not long after his return that the diocese, now fully organized, set on foot a plan for the establishment of an institution of sound learning, and in 1795 the Episcopal Academy of Connecticut was founded at Cheshire. It was sometimes called Seabury College, and, under its learned principals, it fitted many young men for entrance upon their theological studies, and gave them part at least of their professional training. But its charter, which was granted by the General Assembly of the State in 1801, did not give it the power of conferring degrees, and the frequent petitions for an extension

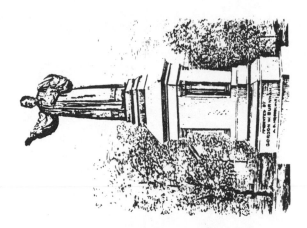

STATUE OF BISHOP BROWNELL, ON THE CAMPUS.

TRINITY COLLEGE IN 1828.

PROPOSED NEW COLLEGE BUILDINGS.

of charter rights, so as to make of the academy a collegiate institution, were refused. For a time, owing to determined opposition in the State, to the vacancy in the episcopate, and to other causes, the project was postponed. But a combination of events, social, political, and religious, led at length to the great revolution in Connecticut, in which all dissenters from the standing order united in opposition to it, and secured in 1818, though it was by a small majority, the adoption of a State Constitution containing a clause which admitted of "secession" from any ecclesiastical society and secured perfect religious equality before the law.

In the following year, while the enthusiasm of the victory was still felt, the vacant episcopate was filled by the election of the Rev. Dr. Thomas Church Brownell, who had been for ten years tutor and professor in Union College, a man of learning, profoundly interested in education, and qualified for the varied duties which lay upon him as Bishop of Connecticut. He soon availed himself of this favorable opportunity for renewing the plans for the establishment of a college. There was much strong opposition to be encountered, and the student of the pamphlet literature of the day finds much to excite his interest and his wonder in the attacks upon the proposed "Second College in Connecticut"—"Seabury College," as it was sometimes called. The whole matter was curiously complicated with discussions as to political and financial matters, the many questions between the recently disestablished order and its opponents not having been fully settled as yet. At last, on the 13th day of May, 1823, a petition for a college charter was presented to the General Assembly, and the act of incorporation of Washington College passed the lower house three days later, and soon received the assent of the senate and the approval of the governor. The name selected for the institution was not that which its friends would have preferred; but the honored name of Washington was adopted partly, as it would appear, because others than Episcopalians united in the establishment of the college, and partly that there could be no ground of opposition to it on account of its name. Among the

corporators associated with Bishop Brownell were some of the prominent clergy and laity of the diocese, such as the Rev. Drs. Harry Croswell and N. S. Wheaton, Gov. John S. Peters, the Hon. Nathan Smith, the Hon. Elijah Boardman, the Hon. Asa Chapman, Com. McDonough, and Mr. Charles Sigourney; and there were added to them representatives of the other opponents of the old establishment, among them the Rev. Samuel Merwin and the Rev. Elisha Cushman. It was expressly provided in the charter that no religious test whatever should be required of any president, professor, or other officer, and that the religious tenets of no person should be made a condition of admission to any privilege in the college. Even before the charter containing this clause was granted, it produced a most important effect; for, on the 12th day of May, 1823, — it was believed, as a last effort of opposition, — the corporation of Yale College met in Hartford, and repealed the test act which required of all its officers, even of professors in the medical school, a subscription to the Saybrook Platform.

The trustees of the new college were authorized to locate it in any town in the State as soon as $30,000 should be secured for its support; and when it was found that more than three-fourths of the sum of $50,000, which was soon subscribed, was the gift of citizens of Hartford, who thus manifested in a substantial way the interest which they had previously expressed, it was decided to establish Washington College in that city. A site of fourteen acres on an elevation, then described as about half a mile from the city, was secured for the buildings, and in June, 1824, Seabury Hall and Jarvis Hall (as they were afterwards called) were begun. They were of brown stone, following the Ionic order of architecture, well proportioned, and well adapted to the purposes for which they were designed. The former, containing rooms for the chapel, the library, the cabinet, and for recitations, was designed by Prof. S. F. B. Morse, and the latter, having lodging-rooms for nearly a hundred students, was designed by Mr. Solomon Millard, the architect of Bunker Hill Monument. The buildings were not completed when, on the 23d of September, 1824, one senior, one sophomore, six freshmen, and one partial student were admitted members of the college; and work was

Geo. Williamson Smith

TRINITY COLLEGE IN 1885.

Trinity College

JAMES WILLIAMS,
Forty Years Janitor of Trinity College; died 1878.

begun in rooms in the city. The faculty had been organized by the election of Bishop Brownell as president, the Rev. George W. Doane (afterwards Bishop of New Jersey), as professor of *belles-lettres* and oratory, Mr. Frederick Hall as professor of chemistry and mineralogy, Mr. Horatio Hickok as professor of agriculture and political economy (he was, by the way, the first professor of this latter science in this country), and Dr. Charles Sumner as professor of botany. The instruction in the ancient languages was intrusted to the Rev. Hector Humphreys, who was soon elected professor, and who left the college in 1830 to become President of St. John's College, Maryland. The chair of mathematics and natural philosophy was filled in 1828 by

the election of the Rev. Horatio Potter, now the venerable Bishop of New York. The learned Rev. Dr. S. F. Jarvis soon began his work in and for the college, under the title of Professor of Oriental Literature; and the Hon. W. W. Ellsworth was chosen professor of law. The provision which was announced in the first statement published by the trustees, that students would be allowed to enter in partial courses without becoming candidates for a degree, was a new feature in collegiate education, and a considerable number of young men were found who were glad to avail themselves of it. It is believed, also, that practical instruction in the natural sciences was given here to a larger extent than in most other colleges.

In 1826 there were fifty undergradautes. A library had been obtained which, in connection with Dr. Jarvis's, was called second in magnitude and first in value of all in the country. The professor

BISHOP SEABURY'S MITRE, IN THE LIBRARY.

of mineralogy had collected a good cabinet. There was a greenhouse and an arboretum; and, besides gifts from friends at home, the Rev. Dr. Wheaton had been successful in securing books and apparatus in England for the use of the college.

A doctor's degree was conferred in 1826 upon Bishop Jolly ("Saint Jolly" he was called), of Scotland, but the first commencement was held in 1827, when ten young men were graduated.

CHAIR OF GOV. WANTON, OF RHODE ISLAND, IN THE LIBRARY.

Of these, three died in early life, and but one, the Rev. Oliver Hopson, survives. To a member of this class, the Hon. Isaac E. Crary, the first president of the alumni, is due no small share of the credit of organizing the educational system of Michigan, which he represented both as a territory and as a State in the Federal Congress. The Athenæum Literary Society was organized in 1825, and the Parthenon, the first president of which was the poet Park Benjamin, in

1827. The Missionary Society, still in successful operation, was founded in 1831, its first president being George Benton, afterwards missionary to Greece and Crete, and from it, primarily through the efforts of Augustus F. Lyde, of the class of 1830, came the establishment of the foreign missions of the Episcopal Church of this country.

When Bishop Brownell retired from the presidency of the college in 1831, in order to devote all his time to the work of the diocese, he was succeeded by the Rev. Dr. N. S. Wheaton, an early, steadfast, and liberal friend of the institution. He secured the endowment of two professorships, and among the many good things

which he planned and did for the college should not be forgotten the taste with which he laid out and beautified its grounds. To him succeeded, in 1837, the Rev. Dr. Silas Totten, professor of mathematics. During his presidency of eleven years, additions were made to the scholarship fund, and the foundation of a library fund was laid; and in 1845 a third building, Brownell Hall, was built, corresponding in appearance to Jarvis Hall, and, like it, designed for occupation by students. In the same year, on the petition of the corporation, who acted in the matter at the desire of the alumni, the General Assembly of the State changed the name of the college to TRINITY COLLEGE. The change was intended in part to prevent the confusion which arose from the use of a name which the college had in common with other institutions, in part to attest the faith of those who had founded and who maintained the college, and in part to secure a name which (especially at Cambridge in England) had been long associated with sound learning. At the same time the alumni were organized into a convocation as a constituent part of the academic body.

In 1848 the Rev. Dr. John Williams, a graduate in the class of 1835, who, though he was less than thirty-one years of age, had given ample promise of extraordinary abilities, was chosen president, and he held the office until 1854, when the duties of assistant bishop, to which he had been consecrated in 1851, forced him to resign. He did much to increase the library funds and to develop the course of academic instruction. He also began instruction in theology, and an informal theological department grew up, which was organized in 1854 as the Berkeley Divinity School and located in Middletown. He was succeeded by the Rev. Dr. D. R. Goodwin. In 1860 Prof. Samuel Eliot was chosen president, and in 1864, the Rev. Dr. J. B. Kerfoot, who was called in 1866 to the bishopric of Pittsburgh. Under the care of these scholarly men the college maintained and strengthened its position as a seat of learning (though in the time of the civil war it suffered from depletion in numbers), additions were made to the funds, and a new professorship was founded. Among

J. B. Kerfoot

159

those whom the college gave to the war were Generals G. A. Stedman and Strong Vincent, and the "battle-laureate of America," Henry H. Brownell.

In June, 1867, the Rev. Dr. Abner Jackson, of the class of 1837, formerly professor here, then President of Hobart College, was elected president. Under his administration, in 1871–72, the number of undergraduates, for the first time, reached a hundred. In 1871 the legacy of Mr. Chester Adams, of Hartford, brought to the college some $65,000, the largest gift thus far from any individual. In 1872, after much discussion and hesitation, the trustees decided to accept the offer of the city of Hartford, which

A. Jackson

desired to purchase the college campus for a liberal sum, that it might be offered to the State as a site for the new capitol, the college reserving the right to occupy for five or six years so much of the buildings as it should not be necessary to remove. In 1873 a site of about eighty acres, on a bluff of trap-rock in the southern part of the city, commanding a magnificent view in every direction, was purchased for the college, and President Jackson secured elaborate plans for extensive ranges of buildings in great quadrangles. The work, to which he devoted much time and thought, was deferred by his death in April, 1874, but the Rev. Dr. T. R. Pynchon, of the class of 1841, who succeeded him in the

T. R. Pynchon.

presidency, entered vigorously upon the labor of providing the college with a new home. Ground was broken in 1875, and in the autumn of 1878 two blocks of buildings, each three hundred feet long, bearing the old names of Seabury and Jarvis Halls, were completed. They stand on the brow of the cliff, having a broad plateau before them on the east, and, with the central tower, erected in 1882 by the munificence of Col. C. H. Northam, they form the west side of the proposed great quadrangle. Under Dr. Pynchon's direction the former plans had been much modified, in order that this one range of buildings might suffice for the urgent needs of the college, provision being made for suitable rooms for the chapel, the library, and the cabinet, as well as for lecture-rooms and for suites of students' apartments. During his presidency the endowments were largely increased by the generous legacies of Col. and Mrs. Northam, whose gifts to the college amount to nearly a quarter of a million of dollars; large and valuable additions were made to the library and the cabinet, and the number of students was, in 1877–80, greater than ever before. By a change in the charter, made in 1883, the election of three of the trustees was put into the hands of the alumni.

In 1883 the Rev. Dr. George Williamson Smith was elected to the presidency, and was welcomed to his duties with much enthusiasm. In the following year considerable changes were made in the course of instruction, including arrangements for four distinct schemes of study, introducing elective studies into the work of the junior and senior years, and providing for practical work in the applied sciences. An observatory has been built, for which a telescope and other apparatus have been presented; and the funds have been secured for the erection of an ample gymnasium, with a theatre or lecture-hall.

Of the nearly nine hundred men who have received the bachelor's degree from Trinity College no small number have attained eminence in their respective walks in life. The class of 1829 gave a governor to Michigan and a judge to Illinois; the class of 1830, a member of Congress to Tennessee, a judge to Louisiana, and two prominent divines to Ohio; the class of 1831, a bishop to Kansas; the class of 1832, three members of Congress, one to North Carolina, one to Missouri (who has also been governor of the State), and one to New York; a distinguished clergyman to Connecticut, and a chaplain to West Point; the class of 1835, an archbishop to the Roman Catholic Church, and a chairman to the house of bishops of the American Episcopal Church; the class of 1840, a president to St. Stephen's College and a supreme-court judge to Connecticut; the class of 1846, a member of Congress to New York, another (also lieutenant-governor) to Minnesota, and a president to Norwich University; the class of 1848, a bishop to Massachusetts, a lecturer, a tutor, and three trustees to the college; and this list seems as a sample of what the college has done and is doing, in the spirit of her motto, for the

Church and the country. The bishops of Connecticut, Kansas, Georgia, New Hampshire, Massachusetts, New Jersey, Washington Territory, and Indiana are among her alumni; with them some three hundred others have entered the ministry of the Christian Church; and representatives of the college are found holding honored positions in the State, in institutions of learning, in the professions of law and medicine, and in the business of life. Her course of instruction unites the conservatism of experience with adaptation to the needs of modern scholarship, all under the acknowledged influence of religious nurture; her well-stocked library and ample museum, with her unrivalled accommodations for students, furnish her for her work, so that she is, in reality as well as in name, in the affections of her members as well as in her profession, a home of sound learning. And as her needs are supplied by the generosity of alumni and friends, she will be still better qualified for her work and will draw still closer to herself those who are entrusted to her care.

The elaborate plans for the new buildings, prepared by the eminent English architect the late Mr. Burgess, were such as to provide for all the present and prospective needs of the college. As finally arranged they included a large quadrangle six

hundred feet by three hundred, at either end of which should be a quadrangle three hundred feet square. It was not expected that all of the great pile could be built at once, and, in fact, all that has been erected as yet is the west side of the great "quad." This includes, as has been said above, two long blocks of buildings connected by a large tower some seventy feet square. The style of architecture is that known as French secular Gothic; the buildings are of brown Portland stone, liberally trimmed with white sandstone from Ohio. Jarvis Hall contains forty-four suites of rooms for the students and the junior professors, unsurpassed for beauty and convenience by students' quarters elsewhere; they are so arranged that each suite of rooms runs through the buildings, and that there is plenty of sunlight and air in every study and bedroom. The Northam tower is also fitted for students' apartments. In Seabury Hall, the plan of which was modified under Mr. Kimball, the American architect, are the spacious lecture-rooms, finished, as is all the rest of the buildings, in ash and with massive Ohio stone mantel-pieces; and also the other public rooms. The chapel is arranged choir-wise, after the English custom, and will accommodate about two hundred people; the wood-work here is particularly handsome. It is provided with a fine organ, the gift of a recent graduate. The museum contains a full set of Ward's casts of famous fossils, including the huge megatherium, a large collection of mounted skeletons, and cases filled with minerals and shells; while the galleries afford room for other collections. The library extends through three stories, and is overrunning with its twenty-six thousand books and thirteen thousand pamphlets; large and valuable additions have been made to its shelves within a few years. The erection of a separate library building, probably at the south end of the great quadrangle, will be a necessity before many years. The laboratories for practical work in physics and chemistry are at present in Seabury Hall; but there is a demand for larger accommodations. The St. John observatory is a small, but well-furnished building on the south campus. The present gymnasium is a plain structure on the north campus, between the dormitories and the president's house; but the funds have already been obtained for a handsome and spacious gymnasium, and the generous gift of Mr. J. S. Morgan, of London, has provided for the erection of an "annex," under cover of which base-ball and other games may be practised in the winter. As new buildings rise from time to time, the spacious grounds will doubtless be laid out and beautified to correspond with the lawn in front of the present buildings. Mention should also be made of the halls of the college fraternities, three of which are already erected.

Thus the college, though it needs an increase in its funds for various purposes, is well fitted for its work. In its courses of instruction it provides for those who wish to secure degrees in arts and in science, and also for special students. The prizes offered in the several departments and the honors which may be attained by excellence in the curriculum serve as work of the curriculum serve as incentives to scholarship. Nor is it least among the attractions of Trinity College that it stands in the city of Hartford.

Celebration of Its 150th Anniversary—Saturday and Sunday, October 16 and 17, 1915

Christ Church, Watertown, Conn., has the distinction of being one of the early Colonial Parishes of Connecticut, having been organized in 1765, and worship in its first Church edifice having been begun in October of the same year. It seemed fitting to commemorate both events simultaneously, on a Sunday as near as possible to that on which 150 years ago, the spiritual ancestors of the present members of Christ Church gathered for Prayer Book Worship in the little Church on Main Street, which they had built with so much perseverance, and. we may believe, self-denial.

The people of Christ Church were blessed with a warm and cloudless day for their celebration. The Parish Reception on the Saturday evening before was an enthusiastic and cordial welcoming of friends, old and new. All past Rectors now living were there renewing acquaintances unbroken by the years.

On Sunday morning, at 8 o'clock, the Bishop of the Diocese, the Rt. Rev. Chauncey B. Brewster, D. D., officiated at a Celebration of the Holy Communion, assisted by the Rev. Dr. Samuel Hart, Dean of the Berkley Divinity School, Middletown, Conn., and by the Rector of the Parish.

Morning Service was read at 10:30 by the Rector, the Rev. Dr. S. D. McConnell, the Rev. Dr. James Stoddard, the Rev. John Nichols, and the Rev. Raymond Cunningham. In the course of the Service, Bishop Brewster dedicated to the memory of the Rev. Herbert Noel Cunningham, for nearly twenty-five years rector of the parish, a marble tablet, erected by the members of Christ Church.

An address of congratulation was made by the Bishop, followed by the Historical Address delivered by the Rev. Dr. Hart.

A Children's Service was held in the Church at 3:30. There were addresses to the Sunday School by the Bishop and the Rev. Dr. Stoddard. The offering, like those at other Services during the day, went to the Emergency Fund.

The Evening Service was marked by addresses from the three Past Rectors, partly reminiscent, but all filled with inspiration and good wishes for the future of the old Parish. The Rev. Dr. Means, of St. John's Church, New Haven, and the Rev. Mr. Lewis, of St. John's, Waterbury, assisted the Rector in reading the Service. The closing prayers were said, and the Benediction pronounced, by the Rev. Dr. McConnell.

The following is a list of the rectors of Christ Church, with their terms of service:

James Scovill—1759-1783
Chauncey Prindle—1788-1804
Russell Wheeler—1805-1814
Frederick Holcomb—1814-1839
Nathaniel Richardson—1839-1845
Frederick Holcomb—1845-1849
Horace Reid—1850-1856
Benjamin Stone—1856-1859
William Lewis—1860-1874
  (The Rev. William Peck, Assistant)
Samuel McConnell—1874-1876
James Stoddard—1876-1886
Herbert N. Cunningham—1886-1890
John L. Nichols—1890-1894
Herbert N. Cunningham—1894-1912
Francis B. Whitcome—1912-

161

THE SESQUICENTENNIAL OF CHRIST
CHURCH, WATERTOWN
* * *

There are periods and events in the history of the Church of Christ to which the psalms that I have quoted, have a close application. God has wrought deliverance for His people in these latter days, comparable in their greatness and their effect to those which He wrought for Israel in the days of old. Sometimes when He has bidden His people to act courageously against the powers of darkness and moral evil, sometimes when He has called upon them to wait with patience for Him, often when, as at the Exodus, He has given the double command to "stand still and see the salvation of God" and presently to "go forward" into the waters which seemed a bar to progress, over and again God has "mightily delivered His people." But to-day I have it not in mind to speak of these great events, the turning-points of the Church's history, of which the deliverance in Hezekiah's day was an obvious type and pledge; rather I would ask you to see in an outline of the annals of this Connecticut parish the working of the same divine providence in His gracious protection and guidance of His people, and the working of the same spirit of gratitude and allegiance on the part of His people to Him. Surely in every parish of loyal Church-folk there has been in divers ways the assurance that God has been His people's hope and strength, that in their experience He has shown Himself greatly to be praised, that with confidence they may declare that He will ever be their God and pledge themselves to be ever His faithful people. And, if I mistake not, we shall be taught once more the lesson that, however much the circumstances may change which surround the Church of God, she still remains the same, having the same power for inward strength and for victory without; her principles endure, her lessons of duty and of service are unchanged, that which has been learned from the generations of old is taught with even greater confidence to the generations to come. The faith, the hope, the charity, the good works, the worship, the devotion, of the early Churchmen in this commonwealth and this community, are our heritage and our example; see we to it that those who come after shall receive from us, strengthened and beautified, all that we have received from those who have gone before!

Almost eighteen years ago, at the hundredth anniversary of the consecration of St. Peter's Church in Plymouth, the Northbury of olden times—a church from the ashes of which a new house of God is rising — we were reminded that three-score years before that church was built, the people in the northern part of the large town of Waterbury were granted "winter privileges." By these they were released from parish taxes for three months of the year, that they might maintain "the dispensing of the Word" in an accessible place during severe weather. They had represented to the General Assembly that to reach the only meeting-house in the town they had to drive seven miles or more, cross the river nine times, and take down bars or open gates at ten different places. There followed almost immediately the constitution of this Westbury

Rev. S. D. McConnell, D. D.

society (or parish) in 1738, and that of Northbury society in 1739. In Northbury, by an experience repeated in no other place in Connecticut, the first building erected for worship and other public uses came almost immediately into the hands of a society of members of the Church of England, which numbered eleven of the eighteen proprietors. Here in Westbury those who were minded to conform to the Church of England were not organized until some fifteen years later. But as early as 1742, a service of the Church of England was held here, which was very notable. It was the solemnization of a marriage, in

Rev. James Stoddard, D. D.

which the officiating clergyman was the Rev. Samuel Johnson, of Stratford, under God, if not exactly founder, yet long the leader of the Episcopal Church in Connecticut, who, twenty years before, had, with three others of the best Congregational ministers of the Colony, crossed the ocean to seek Episcopal ordination; the bridegroom was Lieut. William Scovill, the oldest Church of England resident in Waterbury; the bride, Mr. Scovill's second wife, was the daughter of James Brown, commonly known as "Bishop" Brown on account of his enthusiastic attachment to episcopacy, and of the same family as Daniel Browne, one of the three who had gone to England with Samuel Johnson for ordination; the place was a new barn on the Buckingham farm; and probably an interested attendant at the ceremony was James Scovill, the bridegroom's son by his former marriage, now nine or ten years old, destined as missionary and rector to play an important part in the Church history of this district of Connecticut and later in the British provinces. It was this William

Scovill who in legal form, twelve years later, warned "all the male inhabitants in Westbury, professing the Episcopal form of Worship and Discipline," to meet at the Sabbath-day house on the 6th day of December 1764, at 8 of the clock before noon, to organize themselves into an ecclesiastical society. They met, and chose (of course) a moderator and a clerk; then they elected wardens, a society's committee, a collector, and tything-men. The wardens were Noah Judd and Wait Smith, Eli Curtis was the Clerk, and he with Amos Belding, Abel

162

Rev. John F. Nichols

Bronson, and William and Darius Scoville, were the Society's Committee.

They soon gave attention to the building of a church, having the dimensions of 45 by 36 feet, on a parcel of land south-east of the old cemetery presented by Capt. George Nichols. The site of this church, I am glad to mention, has been suitably and permanently marked, on this special anniversary, by those who love the place where their forefathers worshipped a century and a half ago. Here the congregation assembled in the latter part of May 1765, "to give glory to Him who had put it into their hearts to build it;" a sermon was preached on

Rev. F. B. Whitcome

this occasion by the Rev. Samuel Andrews, of Wallingford.

Before this we find notes of ministration here by Theophilus Morris and James Lyon, one an English and one an Irish clergyman, whose labors on this American soil were not very successful, and by good Richard Mansfield, a man of another kind, who from his home in Derby took charge of Westbury and Northbury, later extending his care to Oxford. He lived to be the Nestor of our Church in Connecticut, and at the time of his death had held one rectorate for sexenty-two years. Seven years before the church was built, the young James Scovill of whom we have already spoken, having taken his degree at Yale College, had been ordained in England, the Waterbury Churchmen contributing £22 10s. "to carry him home," as was the touching phrase of colonial affection. When he came back, it was arranged that he should give half of his time to Waterbury, a quarter to New Cambridge (now Bristol), and a quarter to Northbury; then when the Churchmen here had a place of worship, he agreed to give them a part of the last quarter; and presently Waterbury and Westbury (which in 1780 became the town of Watertown) had the benefit of all his time. He was a strong tory in political convictions, and in the Revolution his position was not always comfortable; but he was a good and faithful man, and it is left on record that he suffered no personal indignity.

It is probable, however, that, as we are told was the case with all the principal members of his congregation, he was carefully watched by the "Sons of Liberty," and not allowed to go beyond the limits of his glebe or farm. If he and his people were permitted to assemble for worship on Sunday, the minister read nothing out of the Prayer Book—if he could not use the whole service, with prayers for the king, he would not abridge it and even the Psalms were read out of the Bible version; there were no responses, but all said the Lord's Prayer together. At the close of the War, as you know, Mr. Scovill removed to New Brunswick, as did others who wished to remain under the British crown; he was put in charge of Kingston parish, and died in 1809. A son and a grandson succeeded him in the cure, the latter ministering until his death in 1876.

It is recorded of Mr. Scovill that he was diligent and faithful in the discharge of his duties. "He comforted the aged, instructed the young, and made himself agreeable to children—no despicable qualification in a clergyman. He had a grave and becoming deportment, and he was sound in doctrine."

After the Revolution, the first settled minister here was Mr. Scovill's nephew, Chauncey Prindle, a native of this place and a graduate of Yale College in the class of 1776, for some years a lay-reader and then ordained to the dioconate and the priesthood by Bishop Seabury. A formal call came to him in 1788 from Northbury which offered £37 10s. a year and from Watertown which offered £30. (It should be remembered that at this time a pound in New England was twenty shillings of Yankee currency and of the value of three and one third dollars.) He served both parishes, dividing his time equally between them, and his labors were "earnest, judicious, and successful." Here a new church, larger and on

a more elegant plan than the first, was built and consecrated by Bishop Seabury, 18th of November 1794; in Plymouth also a new church was built three years later and consecrated by Bishop Jarvis. In 1804, Mr. Prindle resigned his duties here, in order to give more care to Plymouth, from which many families had migrated to the "western wilderness," a few miles beyond Utica. In his last sermon here he stated that in the sixteen years of his rectorship, ten church families had moved into the parish, thirty families had joined the Church, forty-one had left the place, and two

had died out; the number of his baptisms had been 381, of marriages 86, and of burials 66.

In the earlier part of Mr. Prindle's ministry, on the 5th and following days of October in the year 1791, an important meeting of the clergy of Connecticut, assembled as a Convocation, was held here. It was but two years since the first General Convention had met in Philadelphia, in which the dioceses of New England and of what was then called the South had come together under one organization and the English book of Common Prayer had been revised for use in the United States. In 1790 the Convocation had confirmed the action of their deputies—they called them "Proctors",—in accepting the Book as thus revised, the clergy agreeing that in its use they would "approach as near the Old Liturgy, as a compliance with the rubrics of the New would allow." Now in 1791 it became necessary, in accordance with the constitution of the General Convention, to choose a Standing Committee of the Diocese, and to provide for the election of deputies, lay as well as clerical, to the General Conventions. For the Standing Committee five clergymen were at once chosen, and

this has been the rule of the Diocese to this day, except for one year when it was under the provisional care of Bishop Hobart. With reference to lay representation, it was voted to desire the people of each cure to choose one or more persons to represent them, by way of conference, at a coming meeting of Convocation in regard to "all matters that respect the temporal interest of the Church." The action was indeed "guarded," as one has said; but it does not seem unreasonably so; and it led to the first "Convention of the Bishop, Clergy, and Laity of the Protestant Episcopal Church in Connecticut," which was held in New Haven in June 1792. It is a matter of no little interest and importance that here in Watertown formal action was first taken for calling the help of the laity to the service of the diocese in other than financial matters, even as in the parishes without exception they had already borne a noble share in advancing the Church's interests. That the action was well taken and with most beneficial results, no one can possibly doubt; and certainly here, where the roll of laymen is a roll of workers for the Church's service in labors abundant and abundantly blessed, its benefit, given by all and received by all, has been made evident.

In 1807, the Convocation met here again, as did also the diocesan convention for the only time in the history of the parish; and Mr. Russell Wheeler, who had been serving as a deacon for some two years, was ordained priest and "inducted" as rector. The parish had petitioned Bishop Jarvis for his early ordination, as the Churches in Waterbury, Plymouth, Northfield, Bristol, and Woodbury were all vacant, and there was great need for the services of a priest in this neighborhood. The parish had voted to pay him $400 a year, and at the end of each year to give a promissory note with interest for so much of this as had not been paid; three-fourths, however, might be offered in merchantable produce at market price if this were done before the 15th of January. The people were at first, as they recorded, "well satisfied with the public performances of Mr. Wheeler," and they provided him with a rectory; but after a while some difficulty, which would seem to have been of a financial kind, sprang up, and in 1814 he resigned the rectorship.

From the records as to the "New seating" of the church, and as to the division of the rear seats in the square body, and later as to the sale of slips, it would appear that there was in the church at this time a row of enclosed pews against the wall under the windows on each side of the building, probably put in by individuals or families for their own use, that rows of slips ran across the "square body" between the two alleys, and that seats were assigned to persons or families according to their social or religious deserts, by a process which was called "seating" or sometimes 'dignifying" the church. This was the common practice in Congregational houses of worship, until I read your records, I had not known of it in any of our old churches except that in Waterbury. (It was not till about 1816 that permission was given to put a stove in the church.)

When I mention the name of the Rev. Frederick Holcomb as the next rector, I seem to myself—unreasonably, I confess—to have

reached modern history. His death was not till three years after my own ordination, and I remember seeing his widow, some years after that, teaching a Bible class of good women who seemed themselves veritable "mothers in Israel." But he was a graduate of Williams College in the class of 1809, and was ordained by Bishop Jarvis. He had served three years in Harwinton and Northfield when he was invited to give three-fifths of his time to this parish at a salary of $365, leaving two-fifths of the time and $235 salary to Northfield. Here he lived for nearly fifty-eight years, including a rectorship of 24 years, an intermission from rectorial duties of 7 years, a second rectorship of five years, and then 22 years in which he served as he was able—and he found that he was able to do a great deal. If not the memories, certainly the results of all that patient and brave faithfulness remain. There are marks of material prosperity making provision for spiritual needs, as in the building of the academy, now your parish house; there are records which tell of pastoral services, which have much to do with the lives and characters of successive generations; there are names and deeds written in the volume of God's remem-

Stone to mark the location of the
First Episcopal Church

brance. When Dr. Holcomb's life came to an end, Bishop Williams said of him:

"Some years ago he sent me word that the time seemed to have come when he must withdraw from active duty, and I so reported to the Convention. But inaction was too irksome for endurance, and it was not long before he was at work again, telling me, when I expostulated with him, that if so God pleased he wished to die in harness.' He gave his labors cheerfully and unreservedly during his later years to those older parishes in which, under many discouragements and oftentimes with less of sympathy than is their due, a few faithful people are striving to 'strengthen the things that remain.' I count this work of our deceased brother very noble, as it was also

purely disinterested. He has left in it, as in all his life, an example of quiet and unassuming but unflinching devotion to the duties of his sacred function, which we may all of us well lay to heart and strive by God's help to imitate."

The interval between Dr. Holcomb's two rectorships was filled by that of the Rev. Dr. Nathaniel S. Richardson, whom some of us recall as the vigorous editor of the American Church Review. To Dr. Holcomb succeeded, for seven fruitful years the Rev. Horace Hall

three, besides your present rector, congratulating you in person (or by letter) on this anniversary: the first an historian of the American Episcopal Church; the second principal for a time of the venerable Episcopal Academy of Connecticut and later in other ways a man of letters; and the third, an enthusiastic parish minister and student of things human and divine. With them we recall another, twice your rector, who came from the church of the old home to which the earlier rectors had gone for ordination, and cast in his lot and

Reid, under whom the spacious new church was built; and to him for three years the Rev. Benjamin W. Stone. The next rector was the Rev. Dr. William H. Lewis, a native of Litchfield, who had served acceptably in Brooklyn before he came here for a thirteen-years' rectorate, and spent here the four years that remained after his retirement from active duty. By the use of his printed sermons for the Christian Year, lay-readers have carried his teachings into many congregations. I may but speak of those who have followed him;

that of his family with us. To him who follows them all, I bring to-day the salutation, the congratulation, and (may I add it?) the benediction of a teacher-friend.

In this historic sketch—it could be but a sketch—I must seem to have wandered from the words of the Psalm which I took as a text. But all along I have felt the power of the confidence and the thanksgiving of the poet who wrote of the now long-past deliverance. The foundation of this parish followed soon after the time of what was called the Great Awakening, a movement which was in a certain way a revival of religion, but which was marked by an extravagance of words and acts which was then called by the name of "enthusiasm." Many sober-minded religious people were shocked at what was said and done, nervous people were thrown into distress, and whole communities seemed to be beside themselves. The simple and devout teaching of the Church of England, as expressed in her Book of Common Prayer, came to many at this time throughout the Colony as a voice from heaven, recalling them to right ideas of God and of themselves, of their duty and the way of salvation. As some of them said, writing (from Plymouth) at this very time to the Society for the Propagation of the Gospel: "We have fled to the Church of England for safety, and are daily more and more satisfied that we are

Parish House

safe, provided the purity of our hearts and lives be conformable to her excellent doctrines." Simple, if stern, lessons of duty; lofty, if simple, words of praise and prayer; the ordinances of the Christian covenant offered to men and women on scriptural terms, and ministered by those who had unquestioned authority; the quietness and confidence which bring strength: these commended the historic church to our forefathers in the faith in the early days. Do I need to say that in the same way that Church is commended to-day, "by mani-

festation of the truth, to every man's conscience in the sight of God?" May I not bid you, in words of a prophet, which are echoed in the Psalms, or (it may be) echo them, to "look upon Zion, the city of our solemnities; our eyes shall see Jerusalem a quiet habitation, a tabernacle that shall not be taken down; not one of the stakes thereof shall ever be removed, neither shall any of the cords thereof be broken; for the Lord is our judge, the Lord is our lawgiver, the Lord is our king; he will save us." Great is our thankfulness, great our encouragement, great our call to well-directed and enthusiastic labor; for "the Lord of Hosts is with us; the God of Jacob is our refuge."

A note which I was reading in the exposition of these Psalms has recently turned my attention to a great passage in an old Greek historian, of which I should not else have thought in this connection. When Thucydides in his history comes to the end of the first year of the Peloponnesian War, he records, as from the mouth of Pericles, a funeral oration in honor of the Athenians who had fallen. The words are of surpassing eloquence, and they are the embodiment of piety—natural affection— in the old sense of the term and almost of religion in its more modern sense. See how, in my translation of a few phrases, they run parallel with the psalm and teach us Christians a lesson of duty to our motherland, the Church. "Thus," he says, "the dead came to be worthy of their city; and we who are left should not by words only look for strength, saying things which sound well as a defense against the enemy, but rather daily viewing the power of our city from the reality of what it does and we may do, and growing more and more in love with her; and when you see her great glory, remember that it was brought about by men who were brave and knew their duty and were shamefast in doing it; and if in any attempt they failed as individuals, they could not endure that their country should be the loser, but overpaid her with the offering of their lives." The words hardly need to be changed in their application to ourselves; they furnish matter for an oration or a poem or a sermon. They may serve to inspire us with an overpowering love of the Church, even as Christ loves it; they may remind us of the strong characters of the men of old, brave and modest and glad to do their duty; they may check the vain boasting and pretensions of words, and bid us, to translate exactly, to look with action, to admire by service. The

The Rectory

Greek orator seems indeed not to inquire into the source of the strength and virtue of the men who adorned Athens by what they were and what they did; but the Hebrew and the Christian trace the glory, the one of the earthly city, the other of the heavenly, to God, the builder and the maker of both. And we, pledging our love, our service, our very selves to the Church of God, dedicate ourselves anew to Him who is its eternal and glorious Head, in brave humanity, in patient courage. Let not the Church mean less to us that Athens meant to Pericles, that Zion meant to those who indited the imperishable Psalms; "Great is the Lord, and highly to be praised, in the city of our God, even upon His holy hill!"

THE EPISCOPAL BANK OF HARTFORD

[The Phoenix Bank, founded in 1814 to be the "Toleration"

or Episcopal Bank, greatly helped the Church to secure charters and privileges from a reluctant and Congregationalist General Assembly.]

The Phoenix Bank of Hartford has recently observed its centennial; and the observance has brought to memory the fact that the organization and chartering of the institution

was an important event in the political and ecclesiastical annals of Connecticut. The memorial volume published by the Bank and the newspaper notices of the anniversary have told us that the Phoenix Bank was at the first an Episcopal and Democratic institution, and bore part in an important revolution; while the Hartford Bank, twenty-two years its senior, stood for the standing order in religion, the federal party in politics, and (it was claimed) the "sober habits" traditional to the Commonwealth. It may not be amiss to remind Connecticut Churchmen of the condition of affairs a century ago which led our ancestors in the faith to take prominent part in a petition to the General Assembly for the charter of a second bank in Hartford.

In the year 1708, the local churches of Congregational type consociated in accordance with the Saybrook Platform into a quasi-Presbyterian order, were made by legislative act an ecclesiastical establishment for the colony. As soon as 1727, the adherents of the Church of England were recognized as "sober dissenters," and presently a like privilege was granted to Baptists and Quakers; and these, if they actually attended worship in a congregation of their own order, were allowed to turn their ecclesiastical tax to its support. As far as the law was concerned, these sober dissenters met with generous treatment, considering the habits of the day; the separatist or non-Platform Congregationalists and the few regular Presbyterians were treated more harshly. Three of our parishes, those at Fairfield, New Milford, and Brooklyn, were actually established by law; and that at Newtown would have had the same privilege, had it not been that a "not" crept into the act of the legislature by which it was intended to give it that position.

In 1784, after the close of the Revolutionary War, the whole body of the laws of the Colony, now become a State, was revised. The revision contained a declaration, in meaning the same as that adopted in October 1776, that the form of civil government in the State should continue to be that established by the Charter from King Charles II. in 1660, as far as was consistent with "an absolute independence on the Crown of Great Britain." And this revision also by implication repealed the establishment act of 1708, by putting all dissenters on an equality with each other and leaving to the old establishment only the privilege of including within its power of taxation all who did not, by a certificate filed with a clerk of the ecclesiastical society, "sign off" and declare their adherence to some other existing religious organization—a privilege by no means worthless on the one hand or devoid of irritation on the other. Out of this condition of things, combined with political controversies, came the bloodless revolution which culminated in the adoption of a

Constitution for the State in 1818; and, as we shall presently see, the establishment of the Phoenix Bank was a factor in that revolution. For, while the State was decidedly federalist in its politics, there was a minority of strong "republicans" as they called themselves or "democrats" as their opponents persisted in speaking of them; and the presidency of Thomas Jefferson had strengthened their position. They were bold in their affirmation that the State of Connecticut was without a constitution, the ratification of the charter after independence was declared and gained not having been submitted to the people; they appealed to the religious dissenters, who still felt humiliated by the requirement that they must file certificates and have the sufficiency of these passed upon, before they could enjoy their equal rights under the law; they appealed also to those—not an insignificant number—who did not wish to be forced to pay any tax for religious purposes; they objected to the repeated grants made to Yale College in addition to the privileges secured to it by its charter, which was under the exclusive direction of the standing order, and still required from all its officers of government and instruction that they should subscribe to the Saybrook Platform of the old establishment; and they specially appealed to the Episcopalians, who were asking for their Academy in Cheshire (founded in 1792) an endowment and the charter privileges of a College, and for their diocesan organization a fund which should secure the support of their bishop. In 1802, the general assembly did give permission to the academy to raise $15,000 by a lottery; and the trustees of the Bishop's fund (chartered in 1799) succeeded with difficulty in holding their charter and collecting a few thousand dollars. Moreover, the war with Great Britain, unpopular in New England, brought hard times and inspired hard feelings. We do not wonder that the federalists did not want to vote money from the State treasury for the support of a bishop or the foundation of an Episcopal college; and we do not wonder that the churchmen, and with them the other dissenters, associated themselves with the growing republican party, which began to call itself by the name of "tolerationist."

In Hartford and the region thereabout the federalist influence of the Courant (established in 1764) and of the Hartford Bank (chartered in 1792) had been strong and increasing. In opposition to the politics of the one, the Hartford Times was founded, but did not begin publication till 1817; and in opposition to what was charged to be narrowness and abuse of financial power on the part of the other, petitions were circulated in the spring of 1814 for the chartering of a new bank to be a "Toleration" or "Episcopal" bank. The petitioners, according to the custom of the day, offered to the legislature a

bonus of $60,000, "to be appropriated, if in the opinion of your honors it shall be deemed expedient, in such proportions as by your honors may be thought proper, to the use of the corporations of Yale College and of the medical institute established in the City of New Haven, and of the corporation of trustees of the fund of the bishop of the Episcopal Church in this state, or to be otherwise disposed of for the use of the state, or for any purpose whatsoever which to your honours may seem best." The petitioners evidently thought that a general assembly which should be republican enough to grant the charter would be tolerationist enough to make, from money largely subscribed by Episcopalians, an appropriation to the Bishop's fund as well as to Yale College for the use of its recently founded medical school. The lower house in the Assembly assented to the petition; the Council (corresponding to the Senate) rejected it, but sent it to a committee, and presently accepted the proposal of an act of incorporation with a capital of $1,000,000 and a bonus of $50,000 to be paid into the treasury of the State. Thereupon a bill was passed unanimously appropriating $20,000 to the medical institution of Yale College; but a bill proposing an equal gift to the Bishop's fund was rejected. Then arose, in the phraseology of the time, a great

"contestation," with charges on both sides of "intrigue and management and religious intolerance;" and the churchmen, demanding "Bishop's Bonus and Seabury College," were ready to cast in their lot more distinctly with the rising political party, though they did not very willingly break with the conservative federalists. In 1815, they petitioned twice for their "first installment" of $10,000, and found both houses hostile to them. In the next year, by way of "conciliation and compromise," the general assembly voted to appropriate the larger part of the sum of $61,500, which the federal government had paid to Connecticut on account of disbursements in the recent war, among the religious bodies of the State in proportion to their numerical strength; the Congregationalists had one-third, to divide among their societies; one-seventh ($8,785.71) was given to the trustees of the bishop's fund, "for the use and benefit of the Episcopalian denomination of Christians;" the Baptists had one-eighth, and the Methodists one-twelfth; then one-seventh was given to Yale College, and the remainder, not quite one-sixth, was left in the treasury. The act pleased nobody; the federalist Congregationalists thought that too much had been given up; the Church people complained that they ought to have their bonus and that the standing order and its college were getting nearly four times the amount which came to themselves; the "minor sects" did not think that money raised by taxation should be taken by them for religious purposes, but they finally took it. And the struggle went on, with additional complications resulting from the Hartford convention and the termination of the war with Great Britain. In 1816 the "American Toleration and Reform" party nominated for Governor Oliver Wolcott of Litchfield, an old federalist of distinguished services and high character, and for lieutenant-governor Jonathan Ingersoll, an eminent lawyer of New Haven, senior trustee of the bishop's fund. Mr. Wolcott was defeated by a small majority, and Judge Ingersoll was elected. The next year, Mr. Wolcott was elected governor by a small majority, and Judge Ingersoll, whose name was on both tickets, was re-elected without opposition. In 1818, both houses of the assembly being anti-federal, and the election sermon having been preached for the first time by a "dissenter," the Rev. Harry Croswell, rector of Trinity Church, New Haven, the revolution was assured. An act had been already passed for "securing equal rights, powers, and privileges to Christians of every denomination in this State." And this was fully assured when the Constitution framed by the Convention which assembled in August 1818 was ratified later in the year by vote of the people, albeit by a comparatively small majority. The article which really determined the adoption of the Constitution is that on

Religion. It makes these declarations: "It being the duty of all men to worship the Supreme Being, the great Creator and Preserver of the universe, and their right to render that worship in the mode most consistent with the dictates of their consciences, no person shall by law be compelled to join or support or be classed with or associated to any congregation, church, or religious association.——— And each and every society or denomination of Christians in this State shall have and enjoy the same and equal powers, rights, and privileges." And its second section provides that "if any person shall choose to separate himself from the society or denomination of Christians to which he may belong, and shall leave a written notice thereof with the clerk of such society, he shall thereupon be no longer liable for any future expenses which may be incurred by said society." The toleration party had triumphed, and religious liberty was assured in Connecticut; but the constitution conserved much that was valuable in the older form of government.

The victory did not carry with it any benefit to the Episcopal Church from the Phoenix Bank bonus; for the remainder of this had been expended by the State for general purposes. But in 1820 the trustees of the bishop's fund accepted, in lieu of their claim against the State, the grant of a lottery with liberty to raise by it a net sum of $15,000. They assigned the grant to two men, who paid to them in 1826 as profits the sum of $7,064.88. It may be a relief to the consciences of some who are interested in the fund to know that by the failure of the Eagle Bank of New Haven, at about the same time as that of the receipt of the lottery money, the Bishop's fund lost $5,500.

We may note in closing that by the election and consecration of Bishop Brownell in 1819, after a vacancy of six years in the episcopate, the diocese was much strengthened, and that his gentle but firm administration carried it well through some difficulties which came with material advantages. In 1823 the charter of Washington (now Trinity) College was granted, its preamble stating that the petitioners were "sundry inhabitants of this State of the denomination of Christians called the Protestant Episcopal Church," but several of the trustees named being non-episcopalians, and one of the articles forbidding the application of any religious test as a condition of admission to any office or privilege in the institution. On the day before the passage of this charter, the corporation of Yale College repealed their requirement, dating from 1722, that all its officers of government and instruction should subscribe to the Saybrook Platform.

For many years now, the men most prominent in the management of the Phoenix Bank have been of non-Episcopal families, and the

Hartford Bank has seemed to have more of a personal connection with the Episcopal Church than its sometime rival. The Bishop's Fund owns 70 shares of stock in the Hartford National Bank and 71 shares in the Phoenix National Bank.

Phoenix Bank of Hartford has recently given occasion for a review of the ecclesiastical side of the history of that "Episcopal" institution. And its close connection—at least in the design of some of its founders—with the corporation known in law as "The Trustees for receiving Donations for the Support of the Bishop" may be a sufficient excuse for an article on the Bishop's Fund.

It was truly said by one of the older clergy

of the diocese in a commemorative address some years ago, that the pains taken by the churchmen of Connecticut to secure a Bishop at the earliest possible moment after the establishment of diocesan independence could only be equalled by their indifference to the support of their bishop after they had one. Bishop Seabury was consecrated in 1784 and died in 1796; during that time indeed he continued as rector at New London and he had

THE BISHOP'S FUND

The centenary of the establishment of the

half-pay as a retired chaplain of the British army; but for his services to the diocese, which were constant and arduous, it is believed that he did not receive as much as the interest of the money which he expended from his own property while he was seeking for the diocese the accomplishment of its earnest desires. Bishop Jarvis, his successor, had private means, and he made no personal complaint; but at the last convention before his death in 1813, speaking the more freely (he declared) by reason of his advanced years, he said that the support of the Bishop of Connecticut had been up to that time "regarded with languor"; and he added, "little have been the aids afforded by the Church towards the support of the office since we have had the privilege of enjoying it." The length of the interval between his death and the consecration of his successor in 1819—one person who was elected having declined the office—was largely due to the fact that there was no certainty of an adequate support for a bishop. And Bishop Brownell felt constrained to reserve to himself the right, until a sufficient provision was made for the support of his family, to increase his income "from any other suitable source."

Yet the duty of supporting the Bishop had not been quite unrecognized or ignored. There was no Convention of the Bishop, Clergy, and Laity of Connecticut until 1792; the Bishop met his clergy at meetings of the Convocation. But in 1788, on the 13th of February, a meeting of lay delegates was held in Waterbury, which recommended a sort of assessment on the parishes for the support of the Bishop; and certain trustees were then or presently appointed to receive and administer what might be paid in. At the first full Convention in 1792, a committee was appointed to consider a plan of incorporation, evidently to be embodied in a petition to the General Assembly of the State, "for the promotion of religious and charitable purposes"; and in the following year, it was agreed to make the application, but specifically for the support of the Bishop. At last in 1799—three years after Bishop Seabury's death—the Assembly granted a charter to eight men as trustees, with the title which is still in use, giving them the usual powers of a corporation, but restricting the amount of the income of its property to one thousand dollars, this being the largest sum for which it was thought expedient to ask. In 1802, it was discovered that these trustees had not met for organization; and in October 1803, the General Assembly granted a special resolve, increasing the number of trustees by four, for the express purpose of making it possible to secure a quorum in or near New Haven. The Convention from time to time urged the collection by each parish of one-half penny on each pound or (later) one and a half mills on each dollar of its grand

list; and what was thus given seems to have passed through the hands of its secretary, who also acted as treasurer. In 1813, after Bishop Jarvis's death, the healing power of the General Assembly had to be invoked again, there having been no quorum on the day designated for the annual meeting of the trustees; and at this time begins the real work of the corporation.

It elected as its treasurer Charles Sigourney, Esq., a Hartford merchant, clerk of Christ Church parish (afterwards vestryman and warden), soon to be an original director and the second president of the Phoenix Bank, destined after a few years to marry Lydia Huntley, the poetess, and to become an original incorporator and the first secretary of Washington College. [Samuel Tudor, Esq., was another Christ Church officer connected with the work of the Bishop's Fund at this time, a director of the Phoenix Bank and an incorporator and the first treasurer of the new college]. The assets of the fund which came into Mr. Sigourney's hands from the estate of his predecessor consisted of two shares of stock of the New Haven Bank and $192.73 in cash.

The history of that fund for the forty years from 1813 to 1853 is told, at least in outline, in a report which was presented by Mr. Sigourney to the Convention in the last named year. The corporation was a self-perpetuating body, and it was not required by its charter to make any report either to the Convention or to the State authorities; and after 1817 no report was asked for or offered, as far as appears, except in 1820 at the beginning of Bishop Brownell's episcopate, and in 1843 when the Diocese was found to be heavily indebted to him. The newly organized board of trustees, as instructed by the Convention in 1813, proceeded to lay an assessment on the parishes, 71 in all, in the ratio of their grand levy of the preceding year, the total amount being $16,570—a sum which at six per cent. interest would yield almost exactly the $1,000 allowed by the charter. The largest sum $1,096 was assigned to Newtown, the second $1,059 to New Haven, the third $868 to Litchfield, the fourth $588 to Hartford, the fifth $571 to New Salem and Ripton (Naugatuck and Huntington), the least $36 to Washington. The total amount received from these assessments was $7,619.32, less than half of the total expected. Eleven parishes, including New Haven and Hartford, paid in full; five overpaid—may their names ever be held in honor!—Middletown sending $507 instead of $304, Marlborough and Middlebury, which were not assessed at all, contributing respectively $45 and $5, Wilton over-paying its $180 assessment by $7, and Saybrook (that is, Essex) increasing its $90 by one dollar more. Thirty-two parishes paid in part, the

whole amount being towards 43 per cent. of the assessment; and twenty-seven, including that from which the third largest sum was expected, paid nothing at all. Norwalk paid the interest on a bond given for its assessment year by year almost from the beginning, and finally liquidated the bond.

To these contributions from the parishes there was unexpectedly added in 1817 the seventh part (being the Episcopal share) of $61,500 refunded to the State by the Federal government for expenditures in the then late war with Great Britain—$8,785.71—the gift being perhaps intended to soothe the disappointment of church people for the loss of $25,000 expected from the Phoenix Bank bonus; and the trustees held, at the time of the Convention in that year, 6 shares of stock in the Hartford Bank of $400 each and 109 shares in the Phoenix Bank of $100 each. Another largess came through legislative action in 1826, when the two men to whom the trustees had sub-let the privilege of a lottery, granted by the General Assembly for the benefit of the Fund as a further commutation for the loss of the bonus, paid over as profits the sum of $7,064.88. The whole amount of the Fund therefore became nearly $23,500, of which less than a third had been contributed by the parishes. Before the payment of the lottery

money, however, the Fund lost $5,500 by the disastrous failure of the popular but irresponsible Eagle Bank of New Haven. In Mr. Sigourney's report, while this loss is mentioned, its amount is not subtracted from the total of receipts; it would seem that it must have been made up from accumulation of interest and perhaps in part by some generous donor or donors, as was done in at least one similar case in later years.

The salary of Bishop Brownell was fixed at first at $1,500; in 1831 it was increased to $1,800. As the interest of the Bishop's Fund did not provide this amount, the Convention made a call and "earnest recommendation" for annual "contributions" from the several parishes, equal in each case to two and a half per cent. of the salary of the rector, which were to be paid at the Convention to a person designated and by him (apparently) to be transmitted to the Bishop; at any rate the money did not go through the hands of the treasurer of the fund. This produced an average of about $550 a year, rather more than half the parishes paying something. The result was, to use the words of the report, "inconvenience, embarrassment, and loss to the party least able to bear it and who ought to have been saved this trouble"; and when a special inquiry was made in 1843, it was found that the Diocese was in arrears to the Bishop to the amount of nearly $4,500, his full salary having been paid in but two years previous to 1835. The trustees had begun to pay the Bishop the whole amount (apparently) of their income, instead of six per cent. on the principal, and the parish collections also increased, so that by 1853 the whole past indebtedness, with interest (nearly $3,400) was paid.

The writer was told by Bishop Williams that when he was elected and consecrated Assistant Bishop in 1851, he felt that it was necessary for the sake of the Diocese as well as for the sake of the Bishops, that a change should be made in the administration of the Bishop's Fund. The close corporation, it will be remembered, was quite independent of the Convention and was not required to render any report of its accounts; and for nearly forty years it had been practically managed by one man. The report of 1853 was the result of preliminary action taken in the preceding year, when it was also ordered that a list of parishes contributing to the support of the Bishop's Fund with the sums severally paid, and also a list of those neglecting to contribute, should be printed each year in the Journal. In the same year the General Assembly of the State, on petition of the Trustees, amended their charter, inserting a provision that a report should be made each year to the Diocesan Convention and another provision that all future vacancies should be filled by election in the Convention, and also

increasing the amount of the funds which the corporation might hold to a sum which at the rate of six per cent. per annum should amount to $5,000. A full report of the financial condition was presented in the next year and published in the Journal, as has indeed been already noted. It was shown that the fund amounted to $25,757, that the income was about $2,680, that the assessments on parishes brought in $850, and that the Bishop might be paid $1,800 and the Assistant Bishop $1,600, reserving a small amount for a sinking fund.

At the time of Bishop Brownell's death in 1865 there had been practically no increase in the Fund, and the income had been of late divided by an arrangement between the Bishops, the aged diocesan receiving $400 and the assistant $2,500. Fifteen years later in 1880, the market value of the fund was about $36,000, while its income was practically the same as in 1853, but the parish assessments brought in some $3,000, and the Bishop's salary was $5,000. In that year a movement was begun for increasing the principal of the fund by an amount not less than $50,000, that it might be possible "to meet the demands upon it from the income thereof." The Rev. Dr. Beardsley of New Haven was president of the Trustees and the Rev. Francis Goodwin was treasurer, and both took great interest in the movement; appeals were made for individual gifts, and a Sunday was designated for special offerings in the churches. In the first year $22,000 was received, $12,500 of which came from six individuals, in the next year $7,000 more, and in 1887 the fund had been increased to about $94,000. In 1894, largely through the efforts of its then treasurer, Col. Jacob L. Greene, a beginning was made of a further $100,000 addition to the fund; and in twenty years the amount received has been towards a quarter of the desired sum. The present income of the fund is about $6,000. It may be noted that in 1884 the General Assembly authorized the Trustees to receive and hold funds to the amount of $300,000. There is a special Episcopal Residence Fund of more than $5,000.

But the history of the Bishop's Fund is not complete without some notice of its ancient investments and of the "additional" or "nontransferable" stock which it held in the Episcopal bank and in some others.

When the Hartford Bank was chartered in 1792, the State reserved the right to subscribe for shares of stock in addition to those which were offered to the public; and in 1803 such subscriptions were authorized in other banks. Presently this privilege was extended; and in 1813 the Bishop's Fund put $2,400 into additional shares of the Hartford Bank. In the charter of the Phoenix Bank there was what had come to be the customary provision, that

in addition to the authorized capital stock and the investments from the State Treasury, the bank should be at all times open for subscriptions at par for additional shares of stock from the school fund of the state or from the funds of any college, ecclesiastical society, school, or corporation for charitable purposes, within the State; these shares might not be transferred, but the investment might be withdrawn on six months' notice, and the number of additional shares was never to exceed the number of those held by individuals. The new bank was in danger, it thought, of being overwhelmed with the care of funds which it was to treat as capital and on which it was to pay dividends; and in 1821 it appealed to the courts against a demand from the Asylum for the Deaf and Dumb that it should be given 200 shares of stock for $20,000 which it had on hand; but the decision was against the bank. The Bishop's Fund had secured at an early date 108 shares in the Phoenix Bank, 37 of which had been taken as non-transferable or "preference" shares, while 71 were transferable. The other non-transferable stock held at this last mentioned date was 50 shares in the Fairfield County Bank—which four years before had been transferred from the New Haven County Bank—and 120 shares of $50 each in the Farmers and Mechanics Bank. In regard to this additional or non-transferable stock of banks there were several difficult questions

brought before the courts leading to important and interesting decisions. It must suffice here to say that this stock was held to be exactly like other stock, sharing in losses like that of the Eagle Bank and benefiting in increase of value as in the case of the Phoenix Bank, which in 1868-9 paid to the Bishop's Fund $5,471.28 and expenses for its 37 shares of privileged stock, the "nationalization" of the State banks having led to the termination of the non-transferable stockholdings. In other cases an equitable adjustment of financial rights was made.

A curious example of this peculiar Connecticut provision appears in the reports of the Bishop's Fund. In 1854 the Trustees say that they "are indebted $6,000, which sum they borrowed, paying interest therefor at the rate of six per cent. per annum, and subscribed for stock at $100 per share which pays ten per cent. dividends." This was evidently the non-transferable stock of the Farmers and Mechanics Bank which was chartered in 1833 as a Democratic (and therefore not a non-Episcopal) bank. The amount borrowed was diminished from time to time and the final payment was reported in 1869.

THE SERMONS OF
PROF. EDWIN EMERSON JOHNSON [49]

PROFESSOR JOHNSON'S SERMONS.

At the time of the lamented death of the late Rev. Professor Edwin E. Johnson, the hope was expressed by many of his admirers and friends that they might have a memorial of his life and his teaching in the shape of a volume of his discourses. We regret that the fulfilment of this hope has been so long delayed; but we are glad to announce the publication of a work which demands attention for so many reasons. Professor Johnson was well known in Hartford as a most eloquent and earnest preacher, and was moreover held in high esteem on account of his excellent qualities of mind and of soul. In academic circles he took a high rank, and his acuteness of perception, subtlety of reasoning, and grace of expression were duly appreciated by the college students, in whom he inspired not only an admiration for himself, but also an enthusiasm for the work which was specially entrusted to his care. He was moreover, it need not be said, highly esteemed outside of local and collegiate circles; and his written or spoken words had a wide influence and were long remembered.

Professor Johnson was a ready and prolific writer. In the midst of other literary duties he prepared the sermons for each Sunday's services in his parish church, and at times wrote special discourses for the college chapel. Few of those who listened to his words, always graceful, always earnest, always persuasive, would have imagined that he wrote at all times rapidly and frequently under great pressure. He was a man of ready thought, easily grasping great truths, quick to see them in new lights, apt in discerning the way in which they could be forced upon the attention, and having at his command the powers of a remarkable natural rhetoric. And thus, although the cause of the Christian year suggested the topics of many of his sermons, and though others were based on familiar passages or texts of Scripture, they were seen to contain fresh thoughts, and when they illustrated and enforced the old, to do

it by means of the new. Very much the same thing may be said as to his theological views. His mind accepted the teaching of the Episcopal church in regard to fundamental doctrines and principles, because he was rationally persuaded that they were taught in Scripture and commended by right reason: and in regard to many other matters which can hardly be called fundamental his judgment led him to concur with the views commonly held in the church of which he was a clergyman. But his belief in both classes of doctrines was often supported by unexpected methods of reasoning; and not infrequently he drew from them lessons which startled his hearers by their convincing truth as well as by the way in which they were stated and defended. His mind was not one which was forgetful of what is called the "analogy of faith;" but the tenor of his thoughts and his studies led him to think and write much on the life beyond the grave and on the second coming of Christ as the event which would lead on, if it did not itself bring at once, the fulfillment of all the hopes of man and of nature; and he was convinced that in the Incarnation was found the great truth of the ages and the answer to their great problems; so that very many of his discourses had reference to these important truths.

In the preface to the volume before us, it is suggested that if Professor Johnson himself had ever been able to prepare a volume of sermons for the press, it would probably have been on one of the two great topics which have just been mentioned. We venture to question, however, whether the present is not the better memorial of his work as a parish and academic clergyman. The first sermon which the volume contains is an extended discourse on the Intermediate State, or, as the title of the book seems to call it, on "Life After Death;" it is followed by five characteristic and impressive Advent sermons, on different aspects of the Lord's coming; then are placed two Christmas sermons and four discourses which have to do with the Easter and Ascension tide, one of these being an ordination sermon and one a sermon before the diocesan convention. The eighteen other sermons are on different topics, and they have been so selected as to present examples of Professor Johnson's methods of setting forth both speculative and practical truths, and of teaching both doctrine and duty. They will be largely read, and to some or others of them almost every reader will turn more than once, attracted by the great earnestness and enthusiasm of the writer, by the readiness and power of his style, and by the fact that what he has written, even apart from the magnetism of his presence, demands attention and challenges thought. To make quotations would be to do injustice to the author and to the sermons. Those who knew Professor Johnson will not need to be told of the value of what is now put in a permanent and attractive form; and to those who did not know him the words in which we have spoken of the excellence and permanent value of his work, will, we trust, serve to commend the volume; while as to the man himself they will gain an idea from the loving words of Bishop Niles's "Memorial Preface."

The volume is published by Messrs. Brown & Gross; and it contains a photographic portrait of the author.

OBITUARY OF
THOMAS WINTHROP COIT [50]

[Died at Middletown on June 21, 1885]

THE REV. DR. T. W. COIT.

The Rev. Thomas Winthrop Coit, D. D., LL. D., died at his residence in Middletown on Sunday evening, having nearly completed his 82d year. Dr. Coit was born in New London of good New England ancestry, and was graduated at Yale college in 1821, and that in turn from Trinity college in 1821. After receiving his degree he studied medicine, but soon went to Princeton seminary to begin the study of theology. The reading of ecclesiastical history, however, persuaded him of the truth of the claims of the Episcopal church, and he became a candidate for holy orders in the diocese of Connecticut under Bishop Brownell, who ordained him to the diaconate in Trinity church, Newtown, June 7, 1826. He was soon transferred to the Eastern diocese, where he was ordained to the priesthood by Bishop Griswold, and became rector at Salem, Mass., and afterwards at Christ church, Cambridge. In 1834 he was elected president and professor of moral philosophy in Transylvania university, Kentucky, and he discharged the duties of this position for three years; and he then became rec-

received his doctorate in divinity from Columbia college in 1835. Dr. Coit is well known as a vigorous controversial writer against Puritanism, not only in his well-known book bearing that title, but also in numerous sermons, pamphlets, reviews and newspaper articles. He was no less vigorous in his attacks on the system of the church of Rome. A volume of lectures on the early church history of England has lately been republished. He was also an accurate and painstaking student of the liturgy of the Episcopal church. The standard prayer book of 1844 was edited by him with great care, and the report which accompanied it has been reprinted by order of the general convention. In 1834 Dr. Coit published an edition of the (so-called) authorized edition of the Bible, paying great attention to ty-

tor of Trinity church, New Rochelle, N. Y. In 1849, it having been decided to provide instruction in theology at Trinity college under President (now Bishop) Williams, Dr. Coit was elected professor of ecclesiastical history; and he also gave instruction to undergraduates in Butler's analogy. On the removal of the theological department of the college to Middletown, where it was organized as the Berkeley Divinity school, Dr. Coit accepted an election to the rectorship of St. Paul's church, Troy, N. Y., which he held from 1854 to 1872, delivering courses of lectures each year to the students at Middletown. In 1872, he removed to Middletown, and became resident professor of ecclesiastical history there, at the same time constantly officiating on Sundays in churches in the neighborhood. Dr. Coit

pographical accuracy and punctuation, making careful divisions into paragraphs, but noting the verses only in the margin, and printing all the poetical portions, including the greater part of the writings of the prophets, in verses as poetry. He also published the apocrypha in a paragraph arrangement.

Dr. Coit had a large library which he cherished with great care; the books were thoroughly read, and annotated in his round, clear handwriting. He was always ready to give authorities, and many of them, for his theological and historical statements. Many years ago a large number of his books were placed by him in the library of the Berkeley Divinity school, and about the time of his removal to Middletown, nearly all the rest were secured for

the same library, making a collection of no little value. It may be added, as a matter of more than local interest, that Bishop Berkeley's chair, in which the president of Trinity college sits on Commencement day, to confer degrees, was presented to the college by the kind interest of Dr. Colt.

There is no clergyman now surviving of those who were in the Diocese of Connecticut at the time of Dr. Colt's ordination, fifty-nine years ago.

PRESENTATION OF THE PORTRAIT OF EDWIN EMERSON JOHNSON TO TRINITY COLLEGE

[51]

PROF. HART'S REMARKS.

Gentlemen of the Corporation: I cannot but feel that the duty with which I am charged might easily have been entrusted to more ready and more eloquent lips. Another might better recall to the academic body to-day the memory of what it owes to the active mind which guided the ready pen lately fallen from unwearied hands and inspired the burning words the utterance of which has been silenced in death. But I may speak as a constant friend of an honored alumnus who began his brilliant career as a professor at almost the very time when I was called to assist in the work of college instruction, as one who saw much of the use which he made of the marvelous powers with which God had endowed him, and as one who feels none the less for the lapse of time the loss of a brother and a friend. And you will know that my tribute is none the less sincere because it is most unworthy of that to which it is rendered.

A college community feels and shows more quickly and more completely than any other the influence of change. In no year can more than three-fourths of its members have any personal knowledge of what was done in the year that has just passed; and a custom, to have the prescription of the jurists that "the memory of man runneth not to the contrary," need, in a college, reach back to no greater antiquity than that of four years' space; so that within academic walls we see almost the only survival in these degenerate days of the ancient time of which the satirist wrote, when

"venerabile erat praecedere quatuor annis."

A few years ago a venerated and beloved professor retired from the duties here to which he had devoted forty years of his life; and the new-comers of that very autumn had knowledge of his faithful work only as a matter of tradition. To-morrow three of the four classes who were last under the instruction of him whose memory we honor to-day, will have passed out from among us; and in one year more there will be no undergraduate here who can recall his face or cherish the memory of the words which fell from his lips as a professor, a clergyman, and a friend.

If this were all the truth, collegiate work would be the most discouraging of all kinds of work. But I speak of it to-day only that I may declare my conviction that it is not all, nor even the more important part of the truth. If personal memory soon dies away in academic halls, personal influence remains here more powerful, more distinct, and more marked—I think I may venture to say it—than in any other place. The academic body is a real body; and, though in a somewhat different sphere, it is as true of it as it is of the Lord's body, the church, that the honor or the suffering, the faithfulness or the negligence of each member tells most certainly upon all the other members. I do not need to remind you, sirs, many of whom have so truly and so well influenced our academic body during all the years in which your lives as graduates have been interwoven with its life—I do not need to remind you how true this is; for, though I can trace in not a few cases the influence of former officers and students upon our corporate life and thus upon young men to whom their very name is unknown, you can trace it in very many more.

Thus the influence of Professor Johnson is still strong in our college, and thus it will remain, affecting more and more of the minds of "heroic youth" as they

"Shall come in after days,
Fresh to the fields of glory."

Though few of those who live and work here now can remember his unflagging enthusiasm, his devotion to duty, his determination never to rest while anything remained to be done; though few of them can recall his earnest words and thus be moved by the spirit which made him so strong as a teacher of truth; yet the memories of former students who learned from him during sixteen years how to study, how to discern beauty, truth and goodness, how to live faithfully, and how to die in hope, will cherish his influence, so that they will be the wiser, the braver and the stronger because of that which

he taught them; and, besides, through all the years in which students shall come up to our Alma Mater to receive from her "light and sacred draughts of wisdom," an influence for earnest work, for faithful service, for the true life of the Christian scholar shall be felt, the source of which shall be traced back by those who know its history to the life which closed so peacefully but little more than two years ago.

Yet we are not willing that there shall be nothing done on our part to point those who shall receive the benefit to the fountain from which it came. The alumni have desired to place within the college a portrait of the instructor and friend whom they loved and whose memory they will never cease to cherish. It will serve to quicken that memory as from time to time they may look upon it; it will witness to the affectionate honor in which they hold him; it will help to teach those who shall come after us somewhat of his character and his work and of that which they themselves owe to him; may I add that it will bring encouragement to us to whom is entrusted a share of that duty in which he bore this part so well? It will fulfil its purpose, if it leads on beyond itself to the lesson traced by the master-pen of a great historian: "Men themselves pass away, and we can make no representation of their faces which shall not be perishable; but the form of the mind is immortal, and this can be held and expressed, not by the skill of others' hands, but in the life and character of those who look upon it and imitate it."

Gentlemen of the corporation, in behalf of the alumni, I ask you to accept for the college this portrait of the Reverend Professor Johnson.

[52]

BISHOP WILLIAMS'S JUBILEE.

On the second day of September, 1838,—it will be fifty years ago to-morrow,—Bishop Brownell held an ordination in Christ church, Middletown, and (to quote the words of his record) "admitted Abner Jackson, assistant professor of languages in Washington college, and John Williams, tutor in that institution, into the holy order of Deacons." The persons ordained had been college friends, one entering the freshman class and the other coming from Harvard college to the junior class in 1835; they were associated in academic work together; and the future had for them closely allied duties. Professor Jackson became president of Hobart college, and was after some years recalled by his *alma mater* to fill her vacant presidential chair; and he died in 1874, greatly lamented in the community and by his many pupils and friends elsewhere. Called to lay down his life's work at the end of the first half century of the history of Trinity college, he had shaped to no small extent the course of its progress for many years to come.

The younger of the two who were ordained that day commemorates to-morrow the jubilee of his ordination. It has been the wish of many friends that there might be some public observance of the anniversary, and some opportunity for an expression of the thankfulness and the affection which the anniversary cannot but inspire anew. We are violating no secret when we say that the only reason why there is to be no such observance is that the person principally concerned, with characteristic modesty and desire to avoid display, made an earnest request—equivalent, in this case, to a command—that the proposed arrangements for a commemorative service should be given up. But it would be most unseemly that nothing should be said at this time with reference to one who occupies the highest position in an influential religious body, and is also in a very true sense the foremost citizen of our state. For while Bishop Williams is officially at the head of the

Episcopal church in Connecticut, he is, in the respect and affection in which he is held, the bishop of all Connecticut; and he must pardon us if we feel that we cannot allow the occasion to pass without some special notice.

"Tibi nunc," dignissime praesul,
"Excutienda damus praecordia, quantaque nostrae
Pars tua sit . . . animae tibi . . . .
Ostendisse juvat; pulsa, dignoscere cautus
Quid solidum crepet et pictae tectoria linguae."

An eventful half-century has elapsed between the day when the youthful student, just one-and-twenty years old, was admitted to the lowest order of the sacred ministry, and the present day which sees him the senior bishop, in order of consecration, in the Episcopal church in this land. And he has left upon the history of these years an impress which will be long recognized, and given to the history of future years an impulse which will not soon expend itself. After a few years of parish work, most of them spent in an academic town where he specially attracted to himself the youth who were engaged in liberal studies, Dr. Williams was called, a graduate of thirteen years' standing, though not yet thirty-one years old, to undertake the duties of the presidency of Trinity college. Born to be a teacher, with a wonderful power to engage the interest and arouse the enthusiasm of the young, and with a strong conviction as to the proper methods to be used in education, he also had a deep affection for his college, an affection which has not weakened as the years have passed away. And in all the work of his life he has been preëminently a teacher. There gathered around him while he was still president of the college a company of young men, mostly graduates, who wished to pursue their theological studies under his care, and within a few years the Berkeley Divinity school was incorporated and established at Middletown. Of this theological seminary Bishop Williams (for such he was before his removal to Middletown) has been the presiding officer and also the principal instructor. He has shaped and guided the course of those who for now thirty-five years have studied there; he has always lectured on the very important subjects of doctrinal theology, the book of common prayer, and the history of the reformation, and has never omitted, we believe, to expound some portions of the scriptures to each class. His logical mind and historical instinct have enabled him to hold firmly to the good features of the scholastic methods in divinity and to teach in a strong and convincing manner the historic theology of the church of Christ.

And as Bishop Williams, in the discharge of his Episcopal duties during the past thirty-seven years, has visited again and again all sections of this state and diocese, he has been teacher of a large part of our people. With the strong convictions and the remarkable logical ability of which we have spoken, there have always been united in his discourses the powers of persuasive rhetoric and the grace of a poetic instinct. And the words of truth which have fallen from his lips and have been heard by so many at turning-points in their lives, have done a work for God and for good and exerted an influence which is beyond computation by the arithmetic of earth. Long may it be before that familiar voice of

instruction and guidance shall cease to be heard throughout the length and breadth of Connecticut! Long indeed it will be before the echoes of its utterance shall pass from the minds of men.

It was at the convention of 1851 that Dr. Williams was chosen assistant to Bishop Brownell, who had then presided over the diocese with gentle wisdom for thirty-two years. In accepting the election, the "unanimity and heartiness" of which he gratefully acknowledged, he wrote: "I am most willing to devote my life to the service of a diocese, in which I was confirmed and received both my orders, in whose principles I was educated, to which I am warmly attached, and whose spotless history I reverence and love;" and he expressed the hope that "by no fault of his the harmony and peace, which had ever made the diocese 'a city at unity in itself,' should be disturbed." There is universal testimony to-day to the faithfulness with which the pledges made then, and more solemnly repeated at the time of his consecration, have been kept. A large part of the official duties of the venerable prelate whom he was chosen to assist fell at once upon his shoulders; and for many years before Bishop Brownell's death in 1865, it was but in name that he was an assistant. How Bishop Williams has, in all his administration of "Columbia's primal see," drawn to himself the respect and the affection of his own people and in fact of the whole community, it needs not be told at this time. The ancient rite of confirmation as practised in the Episcopal church, bringing each person who is admitted to full communion to receive a personal blessing from the bishop with the laying-on of his hands, and expecting this to be done at an early day in the conscious spiritual life, knits the members of that body very closely together and helps each of them to feel that he has a special relation to the body through its chief ministers. Over thirty-seven thousand persons have been confirmed in Connecticut since 1851—some (of course) by Bishop Brownell, but by far the larger part by Bishop Williams—a number exceeding by thirteen thousand the whole number now registered in the diocese; and these figures will serve to suggest the intimate relations of the Episcopalians of this state to their bishop.

And outside of the limits of the diocese, Bishop Williams's influence has been and is widely felt. It is not only owing to the fact that the three hundred and twenty-five persons who have been ordained in Connecticut since 1851, and a large part of whom have been personally influenced by him, have been engaged in ministerial work in all parts of our great land and even beyond the seas; but from the very first he has held a prominent place in the house of bishops and in the councils of the church in the United States. While he was assistant to Bishop Brownell, who was the senior bishop in the country, a large part of the duties of the presiding bishop passed through his hands and were discharged by him; and when, after an interval of but little more than twenty years, the bishop of Connecticut was again the senior on the episcopal bench, the responsibilities and labors of the position fell upon one who was universally acknowledged to be eminently qualified for them. The Protestant Episcopal church in this country has no archbishops; its presiding bishop is a *primus inter pares;* but in this case, when he who by the accident of years stands at the head is also a born ruler of men and every way preeminent among his brethren, though he would be the last to seek an honor of this kind, it seems most natural to salute him as the primate of his church in this land, the *papa hujusce orbis.* Whatever the title may be or ought to be, his lovers in Connecticut are rightly proud that others know and honor their bishop.

In no age, and certainly not in this country, could any man have attained the position and influence which Bishop Williams holds who was not in sympathy with those about him and with all that is best in the spirit of the times. He has lived with men, keeping a real and almost enthusiastic sympathy with the youth in his college, to whom he has continued through all these years to give his historical lectures, knowing in what men of learning and of thought at home and abroad were taking special interest, and watching the development of the history of the church and of the world. His published works have been, like his lectures and his sermons, scholarly, persuasive, and of great value. The record of his life and of his work for the church and the commonwealth is one which it is a pleasure to recall at this jubilee time. And it is also a pleasure to assure him of what he must know in part, but cannot know except in part—the sincere respect and deep affection in which he is held by the people of Connecticut, for whom we do not hesitate to claim the right to speak to-day; the gladness with which we all, puritans and churchmen, claim him as our own.

Church Growth in the Hill-Country of Connecticut.

To the Editors of The Standard and The Church.

Now that the reports of the supervisors of the census have been published for nearly all the towns in Connecticut, I have been making a comparison of some of the figures which represent the population with the numbers of the communicants in the several towns as taken from advance sheets of the new Convention Journal of our Diocese. I venture to send you certain of the results, as regards the typical hill-country of the State. They are more accurate, and certainly no less satisfactory, than the approximate statistics of comparative growth which you kindly published a few weeks ago.

Litchfield county contains twenty-six towns, in nineteen of which we have twenty-five parishes. Two of these towns have a little over 6,000 inhabitants each; none of the others has quite 4,000; eight have less than 1,000 each. The population of the county in 1880 was 52,044; in 1890 it is 52,917, showing a net gain of 873, or less than two (1.7) per cent. Nearly all the gain has been in the two manufacturing towns of Torrington and Winchester; only five other towns show any gain at all, while nineteen have fewer inhabitants than they had ten years ago. In reckoning the number of communicants, I am obliged to omit two small parishes; that in Harwinton, which made no report either in 1880 or in 1890; and in East Plymouth in the town of Plymouth, making no report in 1880, but reporting twelve communicants in 1890. The other twenty-three parishes in 1880 reported 2,253 communicants, and in 1890 they report 2,768, showing an increase of 515, or twenty-three per cent. in ten years. Counting these by percentages, the increase in the number of communicants in Litchfield county has been more than thirteen times as great as the increase in the population. Or, looking at the same facts in another way, whereas in 1880 there was one communicant of our Church in Litchfield county for every twenty-three inhabitants, there is now one communicant registered for every nineteen inhabitants.

In my former letter I compared the changes in the number of inhabitants and of communicants in certain towns. With your permission, I can now give them ber of communicants in two parishes has increased from 125 to 195, making a gain of 56 per cent.; and the ratio to the population has increased from one in thirty to one in seventeen. New Milford, which has in ten years added but 16 to its former population of 3,907, has increased the ratio of the number of communicants to that of the population from one in thirteen to one in nine; and Woodbury, which has lost 345 from 2,149 inhabitants, has increased the ratio from one in sixteen to one in twelve and a half. The only agricultural town of the county in which there has been a marked growth in the population is Watertown, where it has increased from 1,897 to 2,324, or by twenty-two and a half per cent.; and there the number of communicants has increased from 231 to 322, or by over thirty-nine per cent., and now one-seventh of the inhabitants are enrolled as communicants of the Church. Such are numerical facts in regard to parishes among the hills of Litchfield county. They serve at least to

with reference to the figures of the Journal of 1890, and will include all the parishes within the limits of the towns, and not merely, as in two instances before, the mother parishes.

In Litchfield, the county-town, where for the 3,410 inhabitants of 1880 there are now but 3,092—a loss of nine per cent.—the number of communicants in the four parishes has increased from 272 to 341, showing a gain of 69 or twenty-five per cent.; ten years ago there was one communicant in twelve and a half inhabitants, and now there is one in nine. In Salisbury, the population has diminished from 3,715 to 3,253, showing a loss of about 12½ per cent.; while the num-

show that patient work in what may seem small fields of labor is not without its visible results, and that there is very much to encourage those who devote themselves to the pastoral work of our country parishes. I refrain from adding at this time statistics as to other parts of Connecticut. SAMUEL HART.

TRINITY COLLEGE, August 19th, 1890.

[53]

was followed in the established order. The rector of St. Michael's, Litchfield, says that in the records of that parish no reference to the custom is to be found. Is it possible that we had but one "dignified" church building in Connecticut?

SOCIAL DISTINCTIONS IN COLLEGES, AND DIGNIFYING CHURCHES.

[YALE AND EPISCOPAL PARISHES]

Prof. Franklin B. Dexter, of Yale College, has published a very interesting paper, "On Some Social Distinctions at Harvard and Yale before the Revolution," which he read at the last annual meeting of the American Antiquarian Association. It is well known that in the catalogues of graduates—the "Triennials," as they are still called—at Harvard College down to 1772, and at Yale College down to 1767, the names of the men in each class are arranged in an order which is not alphabetical, nor yet expresses the scholastic attainments of its members, but which was intended to indicate the social rank of the families to which they belonged. It may seem strange that such a system of ranking should ever have been adopted, and stranger yet that, when it was set aside for an alphabetical arrangement, the former order of the early classes was not changed. Yet to one in any way familiar with the early history of the Massachusetts colony, and with the academic traditions which came so directly from England to the college at Cambridge, there will readily occur a natural explanation of the fact that the young men who entered Harvard College at any one time should have been placed in an order corresponding to the order of social rank which was so well recognized in the community—an order which was retained throughout their college course, unless it was changed as a matter of discipline, and which still remained in the lists of graduates. And the Collegiate school in Connecticut, soon known as Yale College, though it was founded in a more democratic community, in which there were fewer distinctions of rank and of wealth, and after democratic influences had been at work for two generations, not unnaturally followed the example of the older college in this matter.

Prof. Dexter's is the first careful study which has been made of these early class-lists of the two oldest colleges of New England, with a view to discovering and stating the principles on which their arrangement was made. As might have been expected, the theory appears more simple and the application of it more ready in Massachusetts than in Connecticut. "In the earlier generations at Harvard, family pedigree seems to have been the paramount consideration, while the father's individual standing was distinctly secondary; but as a longer interval separated the colonists from their English home and its definite laws of precedence, the more difficult became the determination of family rank in communities as homogeneous as those of New England." "Taking the whole of the class-lists at both colleges, Winthrop is the name which is uniformly found in a higher position than any other occurring as often." But, aside from family rank, the comparative wealth and the professional or official standing of a father were regarded in determining the place of a son on the college rolls; and the memoranda of President Clap made against the names of young men at the time of their admission, "Justice of the Peace, Deacon," or "of middling estate much impoverished," show the considerations which determined important decisions. In practice, Prof. Dexter tells us, there was no simple formula of arrangement. "I do not profess to have fathomed the intricacies and perplexities of the subject, nor to be able to explain particular instances which look like the arbitrary vagaries of personal partiality or prejudice.".

The abandonment of this system is traced at New Haven, in connection with the increasing tendency on all sides to a democratic equality, to the fact that, on Dr. Clap's retiring from the presidency, the administration of the college was practically in the hands of three young tutors, "all men of exceptional ability, and hospitable therefore to new ideas and responsive to new influences," so that the modern era begins from this point. At Cambridge the immediate cause of the change, which brought to a crisis a long-felt dissatisfaction, was a complaint made by Samuel Phillips, afterward the founder of Phillip's Academy at Andover, that he had been ranked below Daniel Murray, although his father had been commissioned Justice of the Peace and of the Quorum before Murray's father. This led to a report from a committee of the overseers as to the inconveniences of the method and the recommendation that it be laid aside. But "degradation" remained on the list of college punishments at Harvard as late as 1820.

Prof. Dexter closes this valuable paper with a brief notice of "the New England and more lastingly the Connecticut habit of dignifying the meeting-house." Fairly familiar to the students of old records, the custom is quite unknown to most New Englanders of to-day, and the verb "to dignify," in this peculiar sense, is so utterly obsolete that it is not to be found in the recent American dictionaries. The meeting-house was "dignified," from time to time, by a committee who assigned to families or individuals their seats in accordance with their "age, state, and parentage." The dignifyings and re-dignifyings were matters of great importance and great delicacy, and caused many quarrels and heart-burnings; and traditions as to them linger in our country towns to this day. They were strange survivals of aristocracy in a remarkably democratic community. Prof. Dexter tells us that the custom had largely disappeared before the present century, but that it lingered a while later "in a few specially secluded or conservative congregations." In East Hartford, Conn., it continued until 1824, and in Norfolk, Conn., it was retained as a form until 1875.

The fact that so learned a scholar in all the details of our local history spoke of this custom as the "allotment of seats for congregational worship," led the present writer to call his attention to one instance in which an Episcopal church in Connecticut had been "dignified"; and Prof. Dexter replied that he had not before known of the custom extending to Episcopal churches. In the hope that, if other instances have come under the observation of custodians or students of old records, they will bring them to the notice of those who are specially interested in such matters, it will not be amiss to call attention to this case. The following extracts are from the records, in the archives of the diocese of Connecticut, of the "Society of the Second Episcopal church in Northbury" (or Watertown), now St. Matthew's church, East Plymouth, Conn. The records begin with the organization of the parish in 1791.

"Nov. 10, 1794. Voted, to dignify and seat the house. Made choice of Ens. Ozias Tiler, Mr. Noah Andruss, and Mr. Calvin to dignify the house. Made choice of Messrs. Isaac Shelton, Justice Cook, Stephen Graves, Timothy Sperry, and Moses Cole [to be] seaters to the members of this society, and make returns of their doings at this place on Monday next at half after 4 o'clock in the afternoon."

"Nov. 17. Voted, That we approve of the doings of the seaters in seating the house."

Again, nearly twenty years later:

"April 20, 1813. Voted, That a committee be appointed for the purpose of seating the church. Voted, that Messrs. . . . be a committee for the afore-mentioned purpose. "Voted, that the seaters shall proceed in seating according to age and list." As late as 1841, there is the record: "Voted, that the house be re-seated." But a change was soon made; for two years later, in 1843, it was "Voted, to rent the slips to the highest bidder."

The writer has made no attempt at a general search in the records of old Connecticut Church parishes; a few inquiries which have been made give the impression that there were not many instances like that in East Plymouth. The rector of St. John's church, Stamford, writes that in the old church there the pews seem to have been put in as money was raised for the purpose; and while there are several votes of the "Professors of the Church of England" assigning particular seats to individuals in consideration of benefactions received from them, and others permitting individuals to build pews for themselves, there seems to be no trace of any general system of "dignifying," such as

173

TO DIGNIFY THE HOUSE (CHURCH).

To the Editor of THE CHURCHMAN:

Dr. Hart's most interesting paper in your issue of Aug. 11 has most naturally sent me to examine the old records of the First Episcopal Society of Plymouth, Conn., and the results are curious. The society at Northbury was formed in 1784, and the present St. Peter's consecrated in 1797. In the new church, a committee of several members has, among other duties, "to grant seats to those persons who shall desire them," and this is all, for a few years. In 1805, at an annual meeting, it is voted that there be "a general seating throughout the church ; . . . that this house be seated according to age and list, except men sixty years old and upwards. Then "seaters" are appointed. In 1808, they resolve "to seat the church, and that $30 in the list be equal to one year of age, except persons sixty years old and upwards"; of two committees chosen, one has "to seat the house" and the other "to dignify the house." In 1814, the committee is appointed "to dignify the church"; in 1821, "to seat the church and dignify the house" and in 1825, "to dignify and seat the church." It is evident that a change is in progress, as in 1822 it is "voted that the church be seated in future according to age without any reference to list"; and in 1837 it is decided to take "measures relative to the disposal of seats in the list" and "selling the slips."

JAMES GAMMACK, LL.D.

Plymouth, Conn.

AN OLD DIOCESAN REGISTER.

[THE EASTERN DIOCESE] [54]

Dr. Charles J. Hoadly has presented to the library of Trinity College a volume of early date which is worthy of notice as being a precursor of the Church Almanacs and Church Year Books of later day. It is worth while to transcribe the title page in full:

"The Diocesan Register and New England Calendar, for the Year of our Lord and Saviour 1812, Being Bissextile or Leap Year, and Thirty Sixth of American Independence. Containing the usual Astronomical Calculations and Calendar; with an explanation of the Feasts and Fasts of the Church. The Civil, Ecclesiastical, Literary and Military Lists of the States of Massachusetts, Rhode Island, New Hampshire and Vermont. A list of the officers in the several departments of the Government of the United States. An account of the formation, constitution and regulation of the Eastern Diocese. A Sketch of the Life and character of the late Hon. *Fisher Ames.* Prepared and Edited by Gentlemen in Dedham, Massachusetts. Printed by G. Mann, Dedham."

The volume is of about 24mo size, and extends to 261 pages. It contains nearly, if not quite, everything that would be looked for in a "Register" of all the New England States except Connecticut, together with matters of special interest to Churchmen. Thus, under each state it gives full lists of civil and military officers and lists of all the clergy in the state, their denomination being designated by initial letters; and there is also a list of the clergy of the Protestant Episcopal Church in the United States, corrected, however, only to 1808, and evidently taken from the Journal of General Convention

of that year. The calendar is especially interesting. To each month two pages are assigned, on one of which are matters usually found in farmers' almanacs, not neglecting pretty safe prognostications as to the weather, while on the other is a column for the "Feasts and Fasts of the Church, etc.," and a space in which is given an "Explanation of Feasts and Fasts of the Church." The list of holy days contains, besides those found in the American Prayer Book, black-letter days from the English calendar, and also some other days, such as Shrove Tuesday, Corpus Christi, Cranmer burnt 1596 (March 20), Thomas à Becket [but with a capital A] (July 7), Assumption (August 15), Powder Plot (November 5), and the dates of conventions. The explanation of the feasts and fasts has only reached St. Matthew's Day at the bottom of the second December page, and it is continued for over two full pages further; and to it are added two pages of observations on Christian festivals.

The lists of State officials are very full; and we find also lists of banks, insurance companies, educational institutions, etc. After the colleges of Massachusetts (among which, of course, Bowdoin College has a place), the Phi Beta Kappa has its place, and is called an "ancient and very respectable literary institution," "founded at the University in Oxford." The United States Calendar is very full, and includes the names of all the officers of the army. Then, toward the end, is "An Account of the Formation, Constitution, and Government of the Eastern Diocese," telling how "the decayed, disorganized and depressed situation of the Protestant Episcopal Church in the four Eastern States" had led to it, giving its constitution and the act of incorporation of the Trustees of Donations, and "A short and humble Address" to the trustees, "by a well wisher to the institution," written in a very earnest and decided style. The brief memoir of the Hon. Fisher Ames is interesting and includes, it seems, facts not to be found elsewhere.

It is not known that this Register of the Eastern Diocese for 1812 was followed by other numbers in later years. But, for the time, it was certainly a noteworthy publication.

FAREWELL TO DANIEL TRUMBULL
HUNTINGTON
MISSIONARY TO CHINA. [55]

FAREWELL SERVICE TO THE REV. T. D. HUNTINGTON.

Interesting Occasion in Trinity Church—Personal Farewell Address by Dr. Hart.

The service of farewell and commendation for the Rev. Daniel Trumbull Huntington of this city, about to leave the country for missionary work in Central China, was held in Trinity Church yesterday morning, there being a large and interested congregation. The Rev. Storrs O. Seymour of Litchfield, formerly rector of Trinity Church, began the service, the epistle being read by the Rev. Jared Starr of Newington, and the Gospel by the Rev. F. W. Harriman of Windsor. After the hymn, "Jesus Shall Reign Where'er the Sun," an address was made by the Rev. Dr. W. W. Kirkby of Rye, N. Y., who was for twenty-seven years a missionary of the English church in the territory of the Hudson Bay Company. He spoke of the incentives to missions in the Lord's command, the abundant opportunities and the certainty of success, and he closed with an exhortation based on these words: "Finally, brethren, pray for us, that the word of the Lord may have free course and be glorified, and that we may be delivered from unreasonable men." The hymn, "O Spirit of the Living God," was then sung, and the Rev. Dr. Samuel Hart then made a personal farewell address to the new missionary. He spoke in full as follows:—

My Brother—I welcome the invitation that has come to me, to speak to you at this time the special word of farewell and of commendation to the grace of God. For though others might doubtless speak with greater authority or in more fitting words, none could speak with greater joy or with greater hope or out of a more true affection. I know, and remember with thankfulness, to-day, the special calls to duty that have come to you, to devote yourself to the service of the Master in a godly life, to undertake the blessed responsibility of the ministry of the church, to accept the grace of preaching among the Gentiles who as yet know not His name, the unsearchable riches of Christ. But I cannot say this without

thoughts of sorrow. Every true disciple of the Lord must lament the fact that there are not more young men, of the kind that we know He would have, who are willing to become laborers in His fields already whitening to the harvest; and it is a grief which one hardly dares to try to express in words, to know that the Lord's great command that His church should at least bear witness to Him among all nations, calls forth so little willing service, so little of enthusiasm, of manliness, or of energy. And we consider at what ought to be almost the most natural of things, that a young man should wish to serve in the holy ministry, or that a young clergyman should wish to have his sphere of duty in some part of the world where Christ has not been named or where His blessed name is known to few. And yet men can tell of the noble ambitions that lead so many youths along unattractive and difficult ways, that they may lay the foundations of useful and scientific life-work in professional or scientific or mercantile life. "To scorn delights and live laborious days," to give up present enjoyments and comforts, to isolate one's self for the time from home and friends, to travel to the ends of the earth and to sojourn there, all this is not reckoned too great a hardship for one who would serve his generation and make the most of himself in some of the many paths of life that call for the energy and the self-denial of faithful men; why is the

174

Lord's command unheeded and ignored, why does the church act as if she has no conviction that it is really to be obeyed, why do so many of us, both clergymen and laymen, feel sure that it has laid no special obligation on us?

But this is not a time for complaint. We are not ashamed to-day to have a special joy in that of which we confess that it ought to be no extraordinary thing, as we pray that your devotion and your obedience may bring forth fruit unto God, not only in your own life and in the lives of those whom you may bring to the knowledge of His grace and to faith in Him, but also in the example that it shall furnish and the encouragement that it shall give to others here. And for you, my brother, we joy that you have seen a heavenly vision which some of our eyes have been too dim to see, and that to that vision you are rendering an obedience which some of our hearts have been too sluggish to give. We know that you are entering upon a hard duty; but we know that the only work which is really worth the doing at all, the only work which really bears a divine stamp, is hard work; and we know that it will call for the exercise of all the good that is yours by nature, by education, and by grace; yes, and for more strength and wisdom than you have; but we know in whose strength you can do and suffer all things, and by whose wisdom you can learn all that you shall in any way need to know and do rightly all that you shall in any way need to do. "God is faithful," such is the message of this week's Epistle to you, "who will not suffer you to be tried above that you are able." The apostle, as he wrote these words, was certainly not thinking of "temptation" in any narrow sense; the words apply to that which in any way tests a man, finds out what is in him and what he is worth, and whether he has anything on which he can fall back when he feels that he is tried as to how much he can do or bear. It would be no mark of the heavenly Father's faithful love if He should not at all put you, your character and your resolutions, to the test; but you may be sure that His faithfulness and His love will be shown in so defending—I had better said, so strengthening—you, that you shall never be tested beyond that for which He will enable you. I do not doubt that the tests will be severe, often unexpected, sometimes in seeming even cruel; but I do not for a moment doubt the divine word that none shall ever come to you without the opening of a door by which the grace may enter that you may be able to bear all that God allows to come. And thus "the trying of your faith" shall, as St. James says, "work patience," not the patience of endurance alone, but the patience of action as well, and patience thus having her work perfect, you shall be "perfect and entire, wanting nothing."

You are going, my brother, to what we deem a far-off land and a strange people; and we, the moderns of this western world, are at a loss as to what their place shall be in that perfection of manhood which can only come when the Son of Man shall, in the fulfillment of His great work, have brought all nations and all men to be summed up in Himself, the one Head of all. But that He has a place for them in His Kingdom, you will not doubt; and you must not be surprised if you find that it is not exactly the same place as that which He has assigned to us. Do your best to prepare them for that which they are to be and to do in the bounds of their determined habitation; and when they from the land of Sinim come to take their citizenship and find their home in the eternal city, may many of them be your children in the faith, whom you shall, to your great joy, present on the great day perfect in Christ Jesus. Thus far they have been brought into the church of the one living and true God only as the flow of an imperceptibly moving tide brings the precious things of the deep to the shore; may it be yours to see and to herald, the coming of that decuman wave which cannot be long delayed, when the desirable things of that ancient people, their immortal souls with all their God-given faculties and capacities shall be brought to Him for whom all nations were made, "of whom and through whom and for whom are all things."

The Lord taught His people, as after His resurrection He spoke with two of the Apostles near the Sea of Galilee that there was a two-fold service of Himself, the service of obedience to which He then called St. Peter and the service of suffering, a higher service, for which He destined him. We feel to-day that as we, who tarry in the easier places, send you forth to the harder work, we dare hope for ourselves little more than that we may try to obey, while there is offered to you the crown of those who suffer for the truth's sake. But we listen again, and we learn from what the Lord said of St. John that there is a more blessed thing than either obedience or suffering. For the disciple whom He loved, He implied that it might be that He would will that he tarry till He Himself should come. In this blessedness of waiting, both obedience and suffering are brought to their perfection; and there is no better or more happy thing that either you or we can do than thus to wait for the coming of our Lord Jesus Christ. For that coming we may all look, and in some way we may all hasten it. He Himself give us all at the last the crown of righteousness laid up for all them that love his appearing.

And now, brother, we commend you to God and to the word of His grace; may He accept your service and your suffering and your waiting; may He build up both you and those to whom you minister, and give you an inheritance among all them that are sanctified; may you both save yourself and them that hear you; and with you may we both we and them find joy when we shall be called at the last to give account of our stewardship!

At the close of Dr. Hart's address he proceeded with the communion service, being assisted in the administration by the Rev. Mr. Huntington, nearly all in the congregation receiving the sacrament. The communion hymn was "All Hail the Power of Jesus's name." Before the blessing, special prayers were offered for the candidate on his journey to the missionary field and for Bishop Shereschewsky, who goes out in the same steamer to take charge of the printing and publication of his great translation of the Scriptures in the Christian language. Besides the clergymen mentioned as taking part in the service, there were present the Rev. Dr S. J. Horton of Cheshire, the Rev. George M. Stanley of Winsted and the Rev. J. D. Ewing of Middle Haddam.

The Rev. Daniel Trumbull Huntington is a son of Major Robert W. Huntington of the United States Marine Corps, and grandson of the late Judge Samuel H. Huntington of this city. He was graduated at Yale University in 1892 and at the Berkeley Divinity School this year, being ordained to the diaconate by Bishop Williams in June last. He is to sail from Vancouver for China on the 26th instant, and his field of work is to be at Hau Kow, in the province of Hupeh, under the charge of Bishop Graves. He goes out under the auspices of the Church Students' Missionary Association, being the first missionary for whom it has made provision. An offering for mission work in China was received at the service yesterday.

[ELIZA, CHARLOTTE, JULIA AND CATHERINE DRAPER]

[56]

MEMORIAL TABLET.

UNVEILED, WITH EXERCISES, AT CHRIST CHURCH.

To the Memory of the Misses Draper, Who Conducted the Famous Draper Seminary—Address by Dr. Samuel Hart.

A handsome memorial tablet to the memory of the Misses Draper, who conducted the famous Draper Seminary for Young Ladies on Trumbull street for about thirty years, was unveiled in Christ Church yesterday morning. Appropriate services were held.

The service was that appointed for All Saints' Day. The morning prayer was made by the Rev. J. P. Faucon, assistant minister of the parish, and the Rev. Francis Goodwin; then Holy Communion was celebrated by the Rev. Dr. Samuel Hart of Trinity College, the Rev. Dr. George H. Clark, formerly rector of Christ Church, reading the Gospel. After the Gospel Dr. Hart made an address, first reading the following letter from Bishop Williams to Mrs. Gurdon W. Russell:—

Middletown, Oct. 31, 1895.
My Dear Mrs. Russell:—
I very greatly regret my inability to be present with you to-morrow at the memorial service in Christ Church. My memories of the Draper family in Greenfield and of the school in Hartford go back for more than sixty years. When I came to Hartford in 1833 I found the school in full success, and doing an admirable work, such work as it continued to do as long as its founders lived. It occupied a prominent position among the girls' schools of the period, a position which I think it never lost.

I rejoice to know that a memorial to the Misses Draper is to be placed in Christ Church, where they so long worshipped, as members of a parish in whose welfare they always took a deep and generous interest. I am, very truly yours,
J. WILLIAMS.

Dr. Hart then spoke substantially as follows:—

"When I was asked to suggest a verse of Scripture to be placed on the memorial which has just been unveiled, there came at once to my mind the words which have often served a like purpose in commemorating those whose life has been devoted to teaching: 'They that be wise shall shine as the brightness of the firmament.' The phrase has had this application in great part, I suppose, because of the alternative reading which stands in the margin of our authorised version, suggesting that the wisdom spoken of is not so much that of those who have been taught as that of those who have been teachers: 'They that be teachers shall

shine as the brightness of the firmament.' Thus, too, the parallelism is exact with the words that follow: 'And they that turn many to righteousness as the stars forever and ever.' They have been words of encouragement to many who have been engaged in hard work, and words of commendation for them when they have rested from their labors. As such, they have been graven on the tablet which grateful hands have to-day placed in this house of God in memory of those who for long years did the work of teachers well.

"There is a divine contrast which is brought before us in the services for to-day, the epistle taken from the book of Revelations, describes the blessedness of the saved; the hundred and forty and four thousand 'of all the tribes of the children of Israel,' who were in the sight of man the elect of God, and with them 'the great multitude that no man could number,' gathered out of every nation, and in hymns of triumph ascribing the praise of their salvation to God and to the Lamb. Our minds are lifted up above the world, as we read of their glory and their blessedness as they serve God day and night in His temple and dwell in the brightness of His presence. But when we pass to the Gospel for the day, to learn from it who they are that are counted worthy to attain such blessedness and glory, we find the words of the Lord as He spoke the Beatitudes, describing men and women whose lives attract little attention and whose deeds do not gain the applause of their fellows. The poor in spirit and the meek, the pure in heart and the peacemakers, the meek and the persecuted for righteousness' sake—such words seem to tell more of suffering than of action. The saints of God, the heirs of eternal glory, we are reminded, are people of what would be called ordinary and inconspicuous lives, who have taken and used the disciple that has fallen to their lot, and thus have been prepared for the blessed rest of paradise, that in it they may be further prepared for the vision of God in heaven. The historic church makes no distinction between All Saints and All Souls; we commemorate to-day not only those who have been pre-eminent in holiness and good works among Christ's people, but all who have submitted to and used the discipline of life, and have grown meek and true and pure. For all of them we give thanks to-day, thinking of their blessed rest and of the glory that awaits them, in which we pray that we may have a place.

"If we would seek to embrace in one word the character of the saints as described in the Beatitudes, we should find it, I think, summed up in the great gift and quality of patience—'the patience that bears, and the patience that dares.' And this is the quality that teaches—and, I doubt not, with them parents and all who have any responsibility for others—need almost above all else. As they look back over their life's work, I think that they lament, more than any defects in study or in instruction, the fact that they have too often failed in patience, and as former pupils think of their relations to their teachers, they will most often have occasion to regret their own lack of patience and the fact that they have tried the patience of those whose work was not always very easy or very pleasant. Then we may well bring the Beatitudes into connection with the words of the prophet, and commemorate to-day the faithful and patient teachers, of whom be believe that, because of their faithfulness and patience they shall 'shine as the brightness of the firmament.'

"Each week adds to the number of those, for whom in the weekly service we give thanks, who have 'departed this life in God's faith and fear,' each year adds many to the list of those who have entered into rest, and whose example, as 'blessed saints,' we pray that we may follow. A special sorrow has but just fallen upon this parish, but it is brightened, as is every such sorrow, by our assurance of the rest that is now the portion of the saints, and the glory which awaits them. Thus we stand, trying to serve God in faithfulness and patience, but 'with love of the further shore,' 'looking for the resurrection of the dead and the life of the world to come.' "

There was a large number of communicants, all of the clergy who had officiated assisting in the administration. Before the blessing a special prayer of dedication was read with a prayer from the burial service.

Among the clergy present beside those who assisted in the beautiful and appropriate service were, the Rev. John J. McCook of Trinity College, the Rev. John T. Huntington, rector of St. James's Church, and the Rev. Dr. Finch and Mrs. Finch, the latter having been a pupil at the school.

The relatives of the Misses Draper who were present were, Judge Conant and Mrs. Conant of Greenfield, Mass., Miss White, Mrs. Jonathan Ellis of Huntington, L. I., Mrs. George Draper and Mrs. Charles N. Kent, nieces of the Misses Draper.

Among the teachers and pupils of the Draper Seminary present were the following: Mrs. G. W. Russell, Mrs. James Bolter, Mrs. J. G. Batterson, Mrs. Jacob Le Roy, Mrs. Charles N. Beach, Mrs. Charles R. Fisher, Mrs. A. B. Crowell, Mrs. William B. Clark, Miss Williams, Mrs. Finch, Mrs. S. Woodruff, Mrs. Simonds, Mrs. Mead, Miss Holbrook, Miss Rebecca Brainard, Mrs. Hale, Mrs. Morgan, Mrs. George Bulkeley, Mrs. Jared Starr, Miss Davis, Miss Foster, Miss Root, Miss Tracy, Mrs. John Tracy, Miss Gilbert, Miss Jennie Shelton, Mrs. Richards, Miss Sarah Johnson, Miss Clark. Many were accompanied by their husbands and children and their friends.

The Memorial Tablet.

The tablet is placed on the south wall of Christ Church, between the two center windows. It is of brass and is mounted on an Alp green marble slab. The tablet was made by the Gorham Manufacturing Company and cost about $400. Other expenses brought the total expense to nearly $500. The fund was contributed by about 100 pupils and former teachers of the school.

The tablet bears the following inscription:—

To the Glory of God
And in Grateful Memory of four sisters,
Eliza, Charlotte, Julia and Catherine Draper,
This memorial was here placed on
All Saints Day, 1895,
by some who have been their pupils,
1831-1863.

"They that be wise shall shine as the brightness of the firmament."

ANNALS OF CONNECTICUT CHURCH HISTORY. [57]

[CHRIST CHURCH, GUILFORD]

On the occasion of the commemoration of the 150th anniversary of the formal organization of Christ church, Guilford, Conn., an historical address was delivered by its faithful and scholarly rector, the Rev. William G. Andrews, D.D. This address, revised and somewhat enlarged, has now been printed in attractive form, including portions which were omitted in the delivery.

Guilford is fortunate, as indeed other parishes in Connecticut are, in having a rector who has entered into the life of the community in which his lot has been cast and has made himself familiar with its municipal, religious and family history. The 250th anniversary of the settlement of the town was duly commemorated a few years ago, and the occasion owed to Dr. Andrews much of its inspiration and its success. He had also been for some time furnishing himself with material for the history of his parish and the recovery of early records, not long before the ecclesiastical anniversary, made the work both easier and more interesting. Beside this, Dr. Andrews has, for a long time, made a study of various phases of Church history in this country, and he was thus specially qualified to point out the influences that were at work in Connecticut at the time, say from 1722 to 1750, when so many of the "Standing Order" conformed to the Church of England. The volume before us is thus a valuable contribution to the ecclesiastical history of New England, especially valuable for its treatment of the principles that underlay what is known as the "Half-Way Covenant," and of its practical working. This part may well be read in connection with Prof. Williston Walker's article on that subject in the New Englander for February, 1892.

Guilford was an old town of the New Haven confederation, organized on the strict New Haven model, with an independent Church and a civil organization closely dependent upon it, until its peculiarities were lost at the time of the union of Connecticut in 1662. Its first minister was Henry Whitfield, who had been a clergyman of the Church of England, and who returned to the mother country and accepted (it is said) a living in the then Puritanized Church; and its second minister was John Higginson, son and afterwards successor of Francis Higginson, of Salem, whose words of farewell on leaving England have been often quoted. These were two of the "seven pillars" of Guilford; and it is highly probable that Samuel Desborough (who, like John Higginson, was Mr. Whitfield's son-in-law) and John Hoadly (two of whose sons took Episcopal orders), two others of the pillars, "died in the communion of the Church of England," after bishops and Prayer Book had been restored." Now, as Dr. Andrews reminds us, the Puritans here claimed to be members of the fully reformed Church of England, just as the Puritan Parliament in England still legislated for the "Church of England" after it had abolished episcopacy therein. And later than 1730, Thomas Ruggles the younger, then minister of the "first church in Guilford," declared that that church "was and always had been a congregation of the Church of England." This, by the way, ought to

put writers of history on their guard against supposing that people who called themselves members of the Church of England, especially during the years when episcopacy was abolished by the civil (and professedly other) authority in England, were what we should call Episcopalians.

But there was this difference in the old England and the new. At home the Puritans, as distinguished from the Separatists, were obliged to hold to the parish system; no minister "could deprive any member of his congregation of full Christian privileges"—admission to the Lord's Table for himself, and baptism for his children—"unless he were grossly ignorant or openly wicked"; but here the Puritans had adopted Separatist ways "by requiring a 'relation of experiences' from all who desired to be communicants, while only communicants could obtain baptism for their children"; and the demand soon came, from men of blameless life and calm temperament, that they should be granted the spiritual privileges for themselves and their children which the laws would secure to them if they were in England. This demand led to the Half-way Covenant, which allowed baptized people of good conversation to "own the covenant," as the phrase was, and put themselves under the watch and care of the Church, even if they could not make the profession which was required for admission to the Lord's Table; and these covenanters were allowed to present their children for baptism. It was an attempt to satisfy a claim and right a wrong; but "the measures adopted were inadequate, and their inadequacy has much to do with the welcome afterwards given to the Anglican missionaries." There were, in nearly every community in Connecticut, excellent men, feeling the need of Christian ordinances, and asking for what they felt to be rights, which nevertheless Congregationalism denied to them.

And besides this, people began to wish for what their forefathers had had not very long before, the dignity and simplicity and fixity of liturgical worship. "The Book of Common Prayer," as our bishop has told us, "was the first and the best missionary of the Church of England in Connecticut"; and the Prayer Book which began that good work was one which Samuel Smithson, himself a Nonconformist, who came to Guilford from England about 1707, lent some seven years later to a youth just graduated at Saybrook, named Samuel Johnson. It bore fruit in the declaration made at the time of the college commencement in 1722, and in the work of Dr. Johnson and his contemporaries and successors, and when the young man, after his journey to England to receive episcopal ordination, came to his father's house in Guilford, he probably found a few who were ready or nearly ready to profess conformity.

Moreover—though Dr. Andrews says little of this—the Standing Order had had troubles of its own in Guilford. The elder Thomas Ruggles had died in 1728, after a ministry of thirty-three years; and the first church and society had called and ordained his son of the same name, "against (says Dr. Trumbull) a large and respectable minority, who had opposed him from the beginning. They alleged that he was not such a distinguishing, experimental and animating preacher as they desired; that they were not edified by him, and could not choose him as their minister." They set up separate services, renounced the Saybrook Platform, organized as sober dissenters under the law of William and Mary, while their preacher subscribed the Thirty-nine Articles, with the exception of the thirty-fourth, thirty-fifth, thirty-sixth and part of the twentieth. In their plea before the General Assembly they quoted the sermon delivered in 1717 by Bishop Hoadly, himself the son of a native of Guilford, which gave rise to the Bangorian controversy; and after five years of strife and councils, the civil authority organized the Separatists into a distinct ecclesiastical society with the same boundaries as those of the first parish.

Such were some of the causes, or at least occasions, for the establishing of a congregation in Guilford of those who were led to conform to the Church of England. Different circumstances, but involving like principles, brought about the same result in other places; but here we are specially helped by the guidance of records and a historian. For the detailed history of the parish itself until the beginning of this century, and for an outline of its history during the century, we must refer to what Dr. Andrews has written.

Yet we may well notice a fact to which, as his narrative proceeds, the author of the address calls particular attention. Although there must have seemed reason for expecting a goodly number of Conformists in Guilford, and although Dr. Samuel Johnson, with a commendable interest in his birthplace, pleaded its cause with the Society for the Propagation of the Gospel, yet that society never made the place one of its formally established missions, because it was not able to offer a due measure of support, including a glebe, to the missionary. The venerable society was far from seeking to make "proselytes" in every possible way and under all circumstances. "It was," says Dr. Andrews, "the strong and persistent pressure on the part of the colonists themselves which led this society to establish its New England missions, and it was never able fully to meet the demand. The eagerness of young men to 'go home for orders' from Connecticut had to be checked, and the sincerity and extent of the popular desire was thoroughly tested by throwing on the people not only the expense, no trifling matter, of sending the young men 'home' and of building churches, but also of paying part of the stipend, with the serious additional cost of providing a house and a glebe."

"That the Church of England steadily increased in this commonwealth was far less due to 'aggressive work' on the part of the Anglican clergy than to the fact that the Anglican Church supplied what Puritanism had taught men to value as their lives, and New England Congregationalism, with an honorable though misguided zeal for the holiness of God's house, had placed almost out of their reach. Their 'ancient mother' entered New England in response to the cry of her wandering children, and the venerable society, upon the whole, simply pursued the course defined by its title, in laboring to propagate the Gospel by the method prescribed in its charter, of providing for the wants of English subjects with 'the administration of God's Word and Sacraments.'"

So it happened that the little company of Conformists who, in 1744, organized the parish afterwards named Christ church, Guilford, had no resident clergyman until that good man, the Rev. Bela Hubbard, came back from England in 1764; and in 1767 he removed to New Haven, stipulating that he should visit his old parishioners four times a year, and then there was no resident clergyman till the Rev. James Sayre came in 1784, to stay a very short time. But, as was said, it is not possible in this notice to enter upon the details of this special history. It must suffice to say that the writer has treated them with sufficient fulness, with great accuracy, and in a most interesting manner, and has contributed not a little to the annals of neighboring parishes, as he has to the history of the Church in Connecticut.

TALES OF AN OLD MANOR. [53]

Rumored Destruction of the Hart Homestead Revives Some Stories of Love and War.

[Saybrook letter to the New York Herald.]

The residents of this usually quiet little town are greatly stirred up over the rumor that James H. Day, a former member of a large dry goods firm of New York City, who owns a fine summer residence and considerable landed property here, is to demolish the bunch of weather-beaten buildings that stand on the old Hart property, and erect in their stead a handsome public hall. Mr. Day himself is reticent on the subject and refuses to disclose for the present his intentions, but it is certain that when another summer rolls around the ancestral halls of one of the most prominent families in the early history of the State will be no more.

The old Hart homestead is located in a cluster of noble elms on the main street of the town, and is one of those big, square structures that are pointed out in nearly every New England village as a landmark of colonial days. It was erected by Captain William Hart, who was an important personage in the early portion of the present century, and who, for meritorious and patriotic services during the war of 1812, was presented with a grant of several hundred acres of the "Connecticut Western Reserve," which comprised nearly all of the present State of Ohio. The old records of the town tell of the birth of innumerable Harts beneath the roof tree of the old mansion, many of whom won high honors in the military and naval service of the United States and in the civic professions of the ministry and bar.

Sentiment and Romance.

But the most interesting fact connected with the history of the house, and one that is tinged with a degree of sentiment and romance, is that within its oaken walls two commodores of the United States Navy, a celebrated divine and a brilliant statesman wooed and wedded four sisters.

The ladies were the daughters of Captain Elisha Hart, who early in life showed proclivities for "trade and barter," and accumulated a snug fortune by the sale of West India rum and molasses. He was blessed with seven daughters, who by their wit, beauty refinement and accomplishment were known all over the country as the "Seven Graces of New England," and tradition says that among their admirers they counted many of the

prominent men of the day.

Sarah, the eldest, although a high-strung beauty, succumbed to the ardent wooing of the Rev. Dr. Samuel Jarvis of Middletown, one of the most eloquent and prominent divines of the Episcopal church, and a relative of the saintly Bishop Jarvis. But they were not congenial mates, and were finally legally separated. In after years Mrs. Jarvis embraced the Roman Catholic religion and gained much notoriety by the zeal she displayed in promulgating and advancing the claims of her new faith. When the remains of Lady Fenwick, the first white woman who died in Connecticut, were removed from their resting-place by the river side and interred in the old church yard, she had a cross cut upon a tombstone. This placing of a Catholic symbol upon the monument of one who in life had, in common with the Puritan colonists, a fanatical hatred of anything that represented popery, raised a great hubbub at the time and called down upon Mrs. Jarvis's head some rather harsh denunciations from the descendants of the settlers.

Her Conquest.

Ann, the second daughter, who was considered the fairest of them all, while at a grand ball in New York made a conquest of Commodore Isaac Hull, who at that time was the lion of the hour. Only a short time before, in the frigate Constitution, he had administered a mortifying and decisive blow to England's naval pride by his conquest of the Guerriere, and the young officer was in the height of his glory. He was smitten with Miss Hart's charms, followed her to her home in this place, and proved as zealous in love as he was in war. Soon the wedding bells were ringing, and there was a grand and fashionable marriage in the old homestead. Guests were present from New York, Philadelphia, Washington and Baltimore, and such a gathering of notables was never known before or since in the town. Up to the time of his death, in 1843, Commodore Hull spent his summers here, and many stories are related of his stately courtesy and his kind-heartedness.

Captain Joseph Hull, a nephew of the commodore, a few years later paid a visit to his uncle, and at once fell a victim to the charms of Miss Amelia, another of the galaxy of beauties. His suit lingered for a while, but he was indefatigable in pressing it, and about the time he won his rank as commodore he won his bride also.

Elizabeth, the only one of the four remaining sisters who wedded, became the wife of Herman Allen, a Vermont Representative and a brilliant statesman. His native State conferred many honors upon him, and at one time he was appointed Minister Plenipotentiary to the State of Colombia, South America.

His Request.

Captain Elisha lived along until 1842, when he peacefully passed away and was placed in the old family plot in the village graveyard. Just before his death he called his family about him and made a singular request, which was afterward carried out to the letter. It was that his body should be taken out through the front entrance, that the door should be immediately closed and securely fastened and never reopened as long as the property remained in the possession of his family. It was done, and as the last of the pall-bearers at the captain's funeral stepped out of the door two carpenters who were in waiting closed it, and bolted a heavy plank across it. For forty years, until Mr. Day purchased the place, the plank remained there undisturbed.

When the widow of Captain Elisha followed her life's partner to the grave she left a provision in her will by which one-half of the estate was bequeathed to the town for a public park, provided that the owner of the other half should do the

same. But the latter didn't do it, and the town relinquished its claim.

HART HOMESTEAD AT OLD SAYBROOK

Some Additional Facts Regarding a Noted House.

To the Editor of The Times:

The story of the "seven beautiful Miss Harts" of Saybrook has been often told, and with great variety of detail and disregard of historic accuracy. But never have I read the story in such an accurate form as in a letter copied from a New York journal into The Times of Friday last. Many of the statements may be allowed to pass as harmless romance; a few of them, in the interests of both the dead and the living, ought to be corrected.

Captain Elisha Hart was a son of the Rev. William Hart, the first of the name to reside in Saybrook. General (not Captain) William Hart was an older brother, as was also my great-grandfather. The Elisha Hart house was built by himself, and not by his brother, the General, whose mansion stood, and still stands, farther down the street. The only Harts born in the house of which the article speaks were the seven daughters.

Of these daughters, Sarah, the eldest, married the Rev. Dr. Jarvis, son (the article says "a relative") of Bishop Jarvis. She could not have caused the cross to be cut upon the tombstone of Lady Fenwick, at the time of its removal to the old cemetery, in 1870, for the reason that she herself died in 1863. In fact, the cross was cut on the stone long before the remains were removed; I have often heard of the person who caused it to be done, and it was not Mrs. Jarvis.

And the story as to the barring of the front door of Captain Hart's house, after his dead body has been carried out, is pure imagination. He died in New Haven in 1842; his body was brought to Saybrook for interment, but it was not taken to his house. It was not his wife, for she died twenty-seven years before him, but one of his daughters, who desired to have the homestead made into a park or green for the town. But legal complications as to the ownership of the property led the town to decline this gift.

Hartford, February 15. S. H.

Reprinted from The Deep River New Era November 13 and 27, 1942.

ELISHA HART HOUSE IN OLD SAYBROOK

Elder inhabitants of Old Saybrook may recall a house of the colonial type which stood about where the St. John's church property is now placed. It was the home of one of the sons of the Rev. William Hart who for 45 years was the beloved pastor of the Congregational church.

The impression of Elisha Hart which has come down is of a broad-minded, genial man, public spirited, who had won a competency by lawful commerce, and who, if like his brothers, was humorous and witty.

In front of the house stood three majestic elms, commonly called Abra-

ham, Isaac and Jacob. One by one they fell, the last being Abraham, a reverse order to that of the Old Testament.

The house and its owner were hospitable and not a few distinguished visitors were entertained there, among them Fitzgreen Halleck, the Guilford poet.

More or less has been written of "the seven beautiful Hart sisters." My own impression, from having seen their miniatures many years ago, is that their reputation was due in part to their combined effulgence, like the Pleiades — each Pleiad is lustrous — but it is their combination which renders the galaxy so notable.

They were not shy about their own distinctiveness. In unity there was strength. And they observed, even between themselves, a punctilious and meticulous etiquette which may have been derived from or at least intensified in Paris.

An amusing letter has come down describing the first appearance of Heman Allen, the U. S. minister to Chile, in the family circle, and, if I may be permitted, it was at first chilly! If Homer had been introduced to the court of Juno and her sisters he would scarcely have met more critical eyes. But Heman passed.

One sister married this Chile youth, another Commodore Joseph Hull and Ann, Commodore Isaac Hull, the hero of the battle of the Constitution and the Guerriere.

She lived on in the Elisha Hart house until her death, and used to tell the story of the courtship of young Isaac Hull, one of the most beautiful romances in American history, in which "Papa," it is evident, had no fatherly hand, pro or con.

An unwritten tradition has come down that Jeanette was for a short time engaged to be married to Simon Bolivar, the liberator of South America, and that it was broken off, owing to the opposition of her parents. If so, it was in Paris, but there are some clouds on its credibility. According to Ybarra, Simon never contemplated marriage after the death of his wife.

Miss Jeannette Hart passed her latter days in the Elisha Hart house, dignified and beautiful. Her tribute to her parents may be read on the marble monument which she placed in Cypress cemetery.

COMMODORE ISAAC HULL'S COURTSHIP

When Ann Hart, one of the daughters of Elisha Hart, was a young girl she went to visit an aunt in Philadelphia. On that visit at some social af-

fair she met a young naval officer. He seemed attracted by her, and invited her to visit the ship where he was on duty.

She did so, he showed her about the ship and in the course of their perambulations her eyes fell on a coil of tarred rope. Although her father was a sea captain, apparently she had never seen one, and her curiosity led her to ask about it. The young officer explained its use, and for that day the incident was closed.

But shortly afterward she received a necklace made of tarred rope, with a note asking her to accept it as a memento of her visit to the ship. She not only accepted it, but put it around her neck, and from that day on wore it constantly.

Some years afterward she was at another reception or ball, wearing the tarred rope necklace, and again met an officer of the navy. He observed the necklace, and asked some question about it. Miss Ann replied that years before an officer of the navy had given it to her, and that she had always worn it. He then told her that he had once met a young girl, had sent her a tarred rope necklace, and had vowed to himself that he would never marry anyone else. And so Isaac Hull and Ann Hart plighted their troth and in due time were married.

This is the story which, many years later, Mrs. Commodore Isaac Hull, then a widow, living in the Elisha Hart house in Old Saybrook, told her young niece, Elizabeth Hart, showing her the tarred rope necklace, which she had worn continually from the day when she had received it from the young man who was destined to become the ablest officer on either side in the war of 1812.

It is scarcely necessary to add that Isaac Hull distinguished himself at Haiti, and at Tunis, and won the battle with the "Guerriere" in the man-of-war "Constitution," called "Old Ironsides" from the quality of her stout oak,—a ship which was rescued from destruction by Oliver Wendell Holmes's poem.

According to tradition, Ann Hart Hull accompanied her husband on some voyages, and was so fascinating at her "teas" that the U. S. Government passed a law forbidding officers to bring their wives on board ship.

Melville K. Bailey.

ARTHUR CLEVELAND COXE.

Although forty-two years have passed since he preached his last sermon as rector of our St. John's and went away to wider fields and weightier burdens,

he was known personally to many more Hartford churchmen than remember him as a Hartford clergyman. His visits were not so frequent as his old friends could have wished, but he came back here occasionally, on one errand and another, always a most welcome visitor. One of the best-remembered of his later public appearances in Hartford was at the time the "American Congress of Churches" met here. He didn't altogether like the title of that body—"Congress of Christians" would have suited him much better—but he thoroughly liked the spirit and aim of it, and took a leading part in its discussions. If we except Professor Shields, Father (now Bishop) Grafton and Hartford's lamented Dr. Nathaniel J. Burton, perhaps no one there left as distinct an imprint of his personality in the memories of those who attended the sessions as Bishop Coxe.

Presbyterian born, he was never—even as a boy—at home and at ease in Presbyterianism. Prelacy and prayer-book claimed him for their own, and their own he became. He was what is called an old-fashioned high-churchman, all his life. He had little patience with the latter-day innovations in ritual, nor with the "Romanizers" who practice them. He was a man of positive opinions on that subject, as on all others. His pet aversion was the Jesuit; a very vigilant eye he kept upon that emissary of Rome and his doings. He read a great deal and wrote a great deal. His published works include several volumes of verse. His completed works will include not only his delightfully characteristic open letter to the Pope, but his recent series of letters to Monsignore Satolli.

He had convictions, originality, character, picturesqueness, a mind of his own, and his own way of speaking it out. The members of the house of bishops will have many a story to tell of him; the older clergy and laity of his diocese will never forget him.

THE DEAD POET-BISHOP.

ARTHUR CLEVELAND COXE.

The death of the poet-bishop of the American Episcopal church calls for more than a passing notice in this city, where was almost the beginning of his ministerial life and of his poetical work. He retained a strong affection for Hartford, and there are not a few here who remember with no less affection the youthful rector of St. John's Church and many who have felt his influence upon their convictions and their lives.

Bishop Coxe was a son of the eminent Presbyterian divine, Dr. Samuel Hanson Cox, and on his mother's side was descended from the famous Cleveland family of eastern Connecticut. He was born at Mendham, N. J., on the 10th of May, 1818, being thus less than a year the junior of Bishop Williams his life-long friend. At

the age of twenty he was graduated at the University of New York, and immediately began his studies at the General Theological Seminary. His father was a man of great learning, but withal full of humor; and at times he alluded to the fact that his son was not following in his theological footsteps in such a way as to lead some to suppose that it was to him a source of great irritation. In later years these stories were told in such a way as to cause the bishop some pain, and to oblige him to say publicly that it was not without his father's approval that he attended the services of the Episcopal church while he was an undergraduate and then decided that his work in life should be in the ministry of that church. The bishop's recollections of the years of his boyhood and youth were vivid and full of interest. Not long ago, the writer listened with delight to the story of a part of his college days, when Professor Morse, whose room was near his, was at work on his great invention, and called the youthful student into his room to tell him something of what was in his mind; and to other Hartford friends he told at a recent visit of the interest with which the arrival from England of successive parts of the "Pickwick Papers" was awaited, and repeated page after page of the story though it was many years since he had read it.

Beginning his ministrations at St. Ann's Church, Morrisania, Mr. Coxe was called at Easter, 1842, while he was yet a deacon, to the rectorship of the newly organized St. John's Church in this city; and here he was ordained to the priesthood by Bishop Brownell, the Rev. John Williams preaching the sermon. His rectorship here lasted for twelve years, while he exerted a great influence not only in his parish, but in the whole community, among the officers and students of the college, and in the diocese. The truly reverend and revered George Burgess, afterwards bishop of Maine, was at that time rector of Christ Church; and the way in which the two men, both scholars and poets, but looking at divine truth from different standpoints, maintained a strong friendship and worked in harmony, was brought out in Mr. Burgess's poem, "The Strife of Brothers." Mr. Coxe's theology was that of the Oxford school of that day, though learned in this country; and he taught and practiced it with all his natural enthusiasm and with all the earnestness of a strong conviction. The early Easter morning service, never intermitted at St. John's, and now customary throughout the country, was begun by him; and in many ways, by his writings as well as by his parochial instructions, he trained churchmen of more than one generation in the church's ways. His "Christian Ballads," part of which were first published while he was a theological student, appeared in their completed form with a preface dated from St. John's Parish, Hartford, in July, 1847; they were soon reprinted in England, and their influence in the mother church was perhaps even greater than here. To the freshness and brightness of a natural poetry they added the sense of historical continuity, of unchanging faith, and of earnest devotion; and from the minds of many of their early readers their lessons have never been displaced. To this volume was added "Thoughts on the Services," which brought out the teach-

ings of the Prayer Book for the Sundays and holy-days of the year, more clearly and more instructively than was done by the verse of Keble's "Christian Year"; and the record of his journeyings in England in 1851, reprinted from newspaper letters four years later under the title of "Impressions of England"—a book that will never lose its freshness and its interest—taught many Americans much in regard to the life of the English church and the English people. Mr. Coxe labored while here in the work of church extension; and in particular the parish of St. Gabriel's (now Grace) Church, Windsor, owes its foundation to him.

In 1854 Mr. Coxe was called from Hartford to the rectorship of Grace Church, Baltimore; and nine years later he became rector of Calvary Church, New York. In less than two years he was elected assistant bishop of Western New York, and was consecrated on the 4th day of January, 1865; and three months later, on the death of Bishop De Lancey, he became bishop of the diocese. Of his diocesan work this is not the place to speak; and it is hardly possible to do more than allude to the important position that he held in the church of which at the time of his death he had become fifth bishop in order of consecration. Well instructed in the Roman controversy and persuaded of the importance of maintaining the historic Anglican position, he labored both with pen and with voice to impress his convictions upon his fellow-churchmen and all his fellow-citizens. His sympathy with the Old Catholics of Germany and with others in different parts of the continent of Europe who desired to effect a reformation on like principles was earnest and constant and showed itself in many ways; and he endeavored to set forward in this country the great cause of Christian unity. He was the founder of the Christian Literary Company of New York, and edited for it the series of Ante-Nicene Fathers and St. Augustine on the Psalms.

Bishop Coxe was always interested in academic matters. While in Hartford, he had much to do with the work of Trinity College, and with the changes made in its organization about 1845; for eleven years he was a trustee and for nine years lecturer on English literature; and one of his most brilliant poems, "Athanasion," was delivered by appointment before its House of Convocation. In Western New York he was not only ex officio but ex animo an earnest supporter of Hobart College; he was Baldwin lecturer at Ann Arbor, Bedell lecturer at Gambier, and Paddock lecturer at the General Theological Seminary. He was made Doctor of Divinity by the College of St. James in 1856, by Trinity College in 1868, and by Durham University in 1888, and Doctor of Laws by Kenyon College in 1868.

In this notice it is not possible, did space allow, to speak of all of Bishop Coxe's literary work. But any notice would be incomplete which did not mention his last volume of collected poems, "The Paschal." It stands to the latter part of his life as did the "Christian Ballads" to its earlier part; it shows the same enthusiasm, the same conviction, the same aptitude and earnest desire to teach the lessons of Scripture as the church has received them; but, as a rule, its thoughts are more profound and it touches on great problems which force themselves upon the attention of the mature men of the day.

Yet, neither in his poetry nor in his sermons nor in his conversation, did Bishop Coxe lose the fervor of youth. Many people will remember him in many ways and for many things; but all will remember him as the enthusiastic, fearless, poet-bishop. "Multis ille bonis flebilis occidit"; nay, rather, "Vivet extentum in aevum, notus in fratres."   S. H.

THE SUCCESSION OF THE BISHOPS OF CONNECTICUT. [60]

* The figures in parenthesis indicate the numbers in the order of consecration.

The centenary of the consecration of the second Bishop of Connecticut has brought to memory some interesting facts as to the succession in the American episcopate; and the consecration of a bishop coadjutor as the fifth bishop in Connecticut has suggested an inquiry as to other matters relating to the succession in that diocese.

It is well-known that Bishop Claggett (5) * was consecrated by the four bishops who had been consecrated abroad, and that his was the only consecration in which Bishop Seabury took part. Bishop Claggett laid hands on Bishop Robert Smith (6), Bass (7), B. Moore (9), and Parker (10); and of these four, Bishops Smith and Parker took part in no consecrations of other bishops, Bishop Moore laid hands on none but Bishop Parker, and Bishop Bass laid hands on none but Bishop Jarvis (8). In the consecration of the second Bishop of Connecticut, therefore, the English and the Scottish lines of succession were united, his consecrators being Bishops White, Provoost and Bass.

Now it is a most interesting fact, in connection with this, that every bishop consecrated in this country since Bishop Parker (10) traces back his succession through Bishop Jarvis; for the latter laid hands with Bishops White and Provoost on Bishops Hobart (11) and Griswold (12) at the memorable consecration in 1811, and also with Bishops White and Hobart on Bishop Dehon (13) in 1812; and a glance at the list of consecrators will show that all who come after go back in some way or other to these.

Bishop Brownell (19) was consecrated in 1819 by Bishops White, Hobart and Griswold, and thus was but one step removed from his predecessor.

At the consecration of Bishop Williams (54) in 1851, Bishop Brownell himself presided; while of the six other bishops who laid on hands, three—Bishops Hopkins (26), DeLancey (34) and Eastburn (40)—had received the succession through Bishop Griswold, on whom Bishop Jarvis had laid hands, and four—Bishops Eastburn, Henshaw (41), Carlton Chase (42) and George Burgess (49)—had received the succession through Bishop Brownell himself. Among Bishop G. Burgess's consecrators were also Bishops Eastburn, Henshaw and C. Chase.

Ten bishops laid hands on Bishop Brewster (183), of whom the two seniors, Bishops Littlejohn (91) and Doane (92) stood on either side of the line which before this consecration divided the list of the names of the American bishops into equal parts. On these two, and also on Bishop Whitaker (94), hands had been laid at consecration by Bishop H. Potter (62), and Bishop Williams was one of his consecrators; Bishop Williams himself had laid hands on Bishops H. C. Potter (131), Nichols (154), and Lawrence (171); he had also laid hands on three of the consecrators of Bishop Walker (133), and on two of the consecrators of Bishop Worthington (138); while among the consecrators of Bishops Whitehead (128) and Paret (137) was Bishop Stevens, and among his consecrators were three on whom Bishop Williams had laid hands. At Bishop Paret's consecration, it may be further noted, Bishop A. Lee (38) presided, and among his consecrators were Bishops Griswold and Brownell. Of course, these statements do not indicate all the particulars of the succession in this particular case; but they do show that the succession is a network and almost a closely woven fabric.

The Coadjutor-Bishop of Connecticut is the one hundred and twenty-ninth bishop consecrated in the American Church since the Bishop of Connecticut. When Bishop Williams was consecrated, thirty-four of the bishops who had preceded him were living, so that in the forty-six years of his episcopate, he has already been the contemporary in office of one hundred and sixty-three bishops of this Church. He has laid hands on but twenty bishops, presiding at the consecration of six.

It may perhaps be noted that there is no doubt that Bishop Jarvis was consecrated on St. Luke's Day, Oct. 18, 1797, although the almanacs, perpetuating an ancient error, give the day as Sept. 18. The official records and contemporary accounts all agree, as does the entry in the bishop's register in Bishop Jarvis's own handwriting. How the wrong date got into the document purporting to be a copy of the letters of consecration in the General Convention Journal of 1853, will probably never be discovered.

MARLBOROUGH'S ANNIVERSARY [61]

Dr. Samuel Hart on Historical Celebrations.

Rev. Dr. Samuel Hart of Middletown,

kept on good paper with permanent ink and that an effort should be made everywhere to preserve the headstones and monuments in old burying grounds, and closed with an appeal in behalf of the foundation of character. An abstract of Dr. Hart's deeply interesting address follows:—

Dr. Hart presented the greetings of the Connecticut Historical Society and spoke with approval of the recurrent centennial, bi-centennial and quarto-millenial anniversaries as bringing history before us anew. The old towns began the state or with the state and then one after the other came new settlements, new societies and new towns. So this town of Marlborough was formed from three towns belonging to three counties, Glastonbury, then 113 years old, Colchester, 102 years old, and Hebron, 99. The new settlements witnessed to neighborliness and stood for worship, for common school privileges, for the old independence and Sunday privileges first, then for civil organization. But they guarded against isolation, by making a new unit in a body politic. The question of small towns as against small societies is different now from that of a century ago; the new life came in then and the people adapted themselves to it; we do not know yet how to adapt ourselves to circumstances which have not yet fully found shape. But those interested in history need not attempt to be prophets, or even determine how history shall repeat itself.

The anniversaries are re-enacting history before our eyes and recalling it to our memories. They are reminding an older and instructing a younger generation. Or rather, as in few places they will be less than a half century apart, they are teaching two or three generations in different ways. And a real history—more than annals—in every town and village.

He then discussed the value of the contributors to history by the repeated investigations, discoveries and re-discoveries, rehearsing and re-rehearsings of what was done, and said: And of no less value is the cherishing of the historic spirit. What was done in New Haven by Dr. Bacon in 1839, in Middletown by Dr. Field, in Hartford by those who wrote for Dr. Trumbull, in Saybrook and Guilford has added to our knowledge, but, more important, to our interest in things, and thus to our happiness.

So it is here to-day. Let the new generation grow up with a knowledge of facts, places, boundaries, men and women, and even when away feel that this is a part of their furnishing. These are days of whipping-in. And learn to save records and material for history. Good paper, good ink, careful records; encouragements and warnings for these, I doubt not, are even here. Don't let documents disappear; put them where they will be safe and be of use. Let a library watch for and keep all that can be kept.

We think a century rather a long time for human life; yet it soon goes. Wyckliffe lived only 500 years ago, at any rate, far enough back to have the interest of antiquity. And we shall have the same kind of interest for those who come after; perhaps the time will seem longer by the crowding of events.

Dr. Hart referred to the influence of character, how great it is in small communities, and spoke of the importance of keeping up churches, schools, neighborliness and acquaintance with the world and the power of intelligent young men and women. Not those only who go away, but also those who stay. He dwelt upon the power of a true country life and the possibilities from it.

CHARLES JEREMY HOADLY

DR. HOADLY DEAD.

STATE LIBRARIAN AND A WELL-KNOWN ANTIQUARIAN.

He Had Been in Feeble and Failing Health for Some Time—His Careful and Intelligent Work in Building Up the Library and in Historical Research.

Dr. Charles J. Hoadly, state librarian, died about 1 o'clock yesterday afternoon at his home on High street. He had been very feeble and in failing health for about two years, and for several months he had been able to leave the house only occasionally. Arrangements for the funeral will not be completed until his brother, James, of New York, who has been in Hartford for a week past and who was called away yesterday by the death of a friend, returns to this city. It is probable that services will be held at Christ Church Monday afternoon at 2:30 o'clock. The burial will be at Cedar Hill Cemetery.

The death of Dr. Charles J. Hoadly has taken away one of the best known and most deservedly honored of the citizens of Hartford and Connecticut. The earliest settler of that name was John Hoadly or Hoadley, a non-conforming clergyman of the Church of England, who came to Guilford in 1639 with the Rev. Henry Whitfield, but who returned after sixteen years to England, favored the restoration, and rendered substantial services to Charles II. He married Sara, daughter of Francis Bushnell, and through his son Samuel, born in Guilford, became the grandfather of John Hoadly, successively archbishop of Dublin and of Armagh, and of Benjamin Hoadly, who as Bishop of Bangor gave name to the Bangorian Controversy, which affected the London money-market and caused the suspension of Convocational action in the Church of England for a century and a half, and after holding the bishoprics of Hereford and Salisbury died bishop of Winchester. Our Dr. Hoadly traced his descent through one who is believed to have been a kinsman, and perhaps a brother, of this early settler, known as "Captain" William Hoadley or Hoadle, who was also born in England. He was a signer of the plantation covenant of Branford and later one of its patentees and represented that town at nine sessions of the General Assembly. His great great grandson, the Hon. Jeremy Hoadley, removed to Hartford about 1806, where he was a selectman of the town for some twenty years, acting mayor of the city in 1835-36, and high sheriff of the county from 1828 to 1834; he was also chairman of the whig state central committee in the presidential campaigns of 1836 and 1840. In the parish of Christ Church he was one of the early vestrymen, and the last of the "clerks" appointed to lead the responses and give out the psalms and hymns. His son, William Henry Hoadley, who was born in Guilford in 1800, married Harriet Louisa Hillyer, and their oldest son was Charles Jeremy Hoadly (the only one of later generations to omit the "e" in the spelling of the name), who was born in Hartford, August 1, 1828. The father died in 1849; but the mother reached the age of ninety-two and died in 1895. She was the daughter of Colonel Andrew Hillyer and granddaughter of Captain James Hillyer, whose wife's father married into the Grant family, while his own mother was a daughter of George Hayes, one of the first settlers of Granby and ancestor of President Hayes. Colonel Hillyer's wife, Mrs. Hoadley's mother, was Lucy Tudor, daughter of Elihu Tudor of South Windsor, who was graduated at Yale College in 1750 and became one of the best educated physicians of his day. He served as surgeon in the British army during the French war, was with Wolfe when he fell at Quebec, and was present at the fall of the Havana, as was also his son-in-law, Colonel Hillyer. He was born in 1733, and died in 1826, so that his life and that of his granddaughter covered a period of 162 years, having more than twenty years in common. He received half-pay from the British government from the date of his retirement in 1767 till his death, a period of nearly sixty years; and it is said that the treasury officials actually sent to make inquiry whether he could still be living. Although his father (Yale College, 1728) was a congregational minister, he was himself strongly attached to the Church of England; and in the time of the revolution he was closely watched and sometimes threatened. His own descent was from Owen Tudor, one of the first settlers of Windsor; and his wife, Lucretia Brewster, was a direct descendant of Elder William Brewster, the "chief of the Pilgrims."

Charles Jeremy Hoadly was prepared for college at the Hopkins Grammar School of Hartford; and entering Trinity College in 1847, he was graduated as valedictorian of his class in 1851. Among his classmates were the Rev. Dr. John Brainard, now for a long time rector of St. Peter's Church, Auburn, N. Y., George Douglass Sargeant and Dr. Charles Edward Terry, all three Hartford boys, the Hon. John Day Ferguson of Stamford, the Rev. Dr. Charles Frederick Hoffman of New York, and Charles Collins Van Zandt, governor of Rhode Island. In 1854 he received the degree of Master of Arts in course from his alma mater, delivering the master's oration. The same degree was conferred upon him, honoris causa, by Yale College in 1879, and ten years later Trinity College made him a Doctor of Laws.

Soon after his graduation he entered the office of Dr. Henry Barnard, then superintendent of public instruction, and began the study of law in the office of Welch & Shipman. In 1855 he was admitted to the bar by Judge (afterwards Chief Justice) Seymour. In 1854 he was appointed librarian of Trinity College; and though his services in that capacity covered but one year, he continued his interest in that library and his acquaintance with its condition, even in matters of detail, till the end of his life. In April, 1855, he was called to the position of librarian of the state of Connecticut, an office in which his only predecessor was the late Dr. J. Hammond Trumbull, appointed in the preceding November. His life-work was done as state librarian or in historical and legal studies connected with his duties there; and in that capacity he served the state for forty-five years, a longer time than any other official of either the colony or the state of Connecticut, with the exception of George Wyllys, who was the secretary of the colony and the state for the sixty years from 1734 to 1794. When he en-

tered upon his office, the newly established state library was but meagerly furnished. There was not a full set of any legal publication, not even of the Connecticut Reports up to that date; and not a volume of any of our own federal reports or of those of English courts. The new librarian undertook the task of collecting sets of law books for the state. The library committee appointed by the Legislature, in order, as they thought, to facilitate the gathering of a working library, gave instructions for the purchase of certain compilations and condensed series of reports. Mr. Hoadly was wiser than the committee, and was determined in every possible case to purchase only the original and full reports, though it might be at greater expense of money and of time. As a result of this policy, which guided the whole period of his administration, the Connecticut state library possesses to-day complete sets of the originals of all official American reports, practically complete sets of reports for England, Scotland and Ireland, and also of Canadian reports as far as they relate to our law.

The same policy was pursued in making collections of statutes. Mr. Hoadly's purpose, in which absolute success was practically impossible, but in accomplishing which he was eminently successful, was to procure for the library every publication of session laws and every official revision of the statutes, not only of the United States and of every state and territory, but also of England, Scotland, Ireland and Canada. Beyond this he did not wish to extend the scope of the library, except to include publications relating to the general or local history of Connecticut, the documentary histories and state papers of the other states, and the writings of eminent statesmen of the nation, together with a few especially desirable works of reference; but the collections made under these heads are of great and permanent value.

To those who asked how many volumes there were in the library and who seemed prepared to judge of its value by its size, he was wont to say that the value of a library is not determined by the number of volumes upon its shelves, but by its completeness in the departments which it undertakes to represent. Realizing this fact, Dr. Hoadly declined to purchase or to accept many volumes which some desired to see in the collection under his care, and often referred intending donors to that particular library of the city to which the volumes in question most naturally belonged. To this principle of exclusiveness on the one hand and co-operation on the other, cultivated by Dr. Barnard, Dr. Trumbull and Dr. Hoadly, is largely due the present admirable system of libraries in Hartford.

While the late librarian was a man of deep learning in law and jurisprudence, and knew many of the mysteries of both, he never argued a case in court. Nor did he seek active work as a counsellor, but followed the strong bent of his mind to proficiency in determining, recalling and applying historical facts. For this reason it was that he became most widely known, and will be specially remembered, as an antiquarian and historian. As he succeeded. Dr. Trumbull in the office of state librarian, so he took up the work which he had begun of editing the Colonial Records of Connecticut and in which he had completed the records to 1689 in three volumes. First editing the records of New Haven colony (1638 to 1665) in two volumes, he took up the records of Connecticut colony, transcribing them with his own hand, filling out lacunae

from other sources where this was possible, inserting illustrative notes, adding appendices of documents for the most part unpublished before, and preparing careful indexes. The work was slow, for it was difficult and accurately done; and the twelve volumes (in number 4 to 15) needed to contain the records of the years 1689 to 1776, occupied the time which could be given to this work until 1887. Than by special act of the General Assembly the librarian was authorized to transcribe and edit the records of the state from 1776 to 1789. Of this series two volumes have been issued, and a third volume is in manuscript lacking a few notes to make it ready for the printer. The value of these publications, sixteen large octavo volumes, is beyond calculation, and the work has been so carefully done that it is hardly possible that any part of it will need to be done again.

Of Dr. Hoadly's other publications, the best known is probably "Goodwin's Genealogical Notes," edited in 1856. They include papers prepared for historical societies, the Annals of Christ Church, Hartford, to 1828, included in Dr. Russell's history of the parish, and communications addressed to "The Courant" and other journals. The results of a large part of his investigations remain unpublished.

In his work as editor and investigator, Dr. Hoadly's attention was of necessity called to the study of ancient manuscript documents. Of these documents some, through the carelessness and liberality of official custodians, had become scattered, while others, through the greed of collectors, had been deprived of their signatures. By his efforts many of the missing autographs have been regained and replaced, while certain manuscripts, including a large number of muster and payrolls of the early wars have been either restored or definitely located. The most important volume regained is that lettered "Particular Court, Vol. II., Probate Records," discovered by him in New York in 1863; it contains 196 pages of court proceeding on all subjects of judicial controversy within the colony from 1649 to 1663 and 185 pages of wills and inventories. His familiarity with the manuscript records and archives of the several states and the federal government, and his historical acquaintance with the leading men of the age made a visit to the State Library under his direction an event not soon forgotten. In a few words, he could plainly place before the visitor the impressions he had formed concerning the leading characters of our history, impressions not always in harmony with the generally accepted traditions, but never without foundation and always strongly expressed.

Dr. Hoadly was a member of many learned bodies, especially valuing his membership in the Massachusetts Historical Society, the American Antiquarian Society, the New England Genealogical and Historical Society, and the Connecticut Historical Society, of which latter, after long service as its corresponding secretary, he was president from the year 1894 until his death, and to which he presented his portrait.

Allusion was made to Dr. Hoadly's interest in the library of Trinity College, of which he was for one year librarian and for many years a member of the library committee. As far as his influence went, he carried out here the same principle as that on which he built up the State Library, desiring to strengthen the strong collections rather than to build up strong and weak alike; and it is for this reason that the College Library is so well furnished with lexicons in various lan-

guages, English state papers, the works of eminent mathematicians, and volumes illustrating epigraphy and archaeology. His own gifts to the library were constant and valuable, among them being the new edition of Stephanus, which he brought from England on his last visit there, and the "Grande Larousse," presented a year or two ago. In fact there is no part of the library which is specially worthy of notice that does not show both his skill in selecting and his generosity in giving. All through his life he kept well acquainted with the work of the college and with the roll of its alumni. He was elected a trustee in 1865 and was secretary of the corporation from 1865 to 1876 and again from 1888 to 1896. From 1854 to 1862 he was secretary of the Connecticut Beta of the Phi Beta Kappa, and from 1862 to 1867 its president. For very many years a member of the vestry of Christ Church, at which he regularly attended, he was from 1864 to 1879 a clerk of the parish. Thus a large part of the records of the college, the society and the parish are in his admirably clear handwriting.

Dr. Hoadly had a memory of wonderful accuracy and tenacity; he not only knew where things were, even in the midst of seeming confusion, but he knew what they were. He could repeat long extracts, even from classic authors which he had not read since his college days; he remembered the dates of ancient volumes to which he had not referred for many years; and he would remind a listener of events or facts which had utterly slipped from the other's memory. And thus he was on the watch for all sorts of interesting things, "desiderata" of every kind; and his house on Ann street, which was the family home from 1833, became a storehouse of historical treasures.

Among the mass of papers in the executive correspondence of Governor Buckingham, on file in the governor's office, is a note from Charles J. Hoadly in which he offers his services to the governor to serve in any capacity in which he might be needed.

Three brothers and a sister survive him: James H. Hoadley of New York and George E., Francis A. Hoadley and Mrs. Harriet L. Corwin of this city. A sister, Mary Robins Hoadley, of this city, died in 1896, and a brother, Major Frederick W. Hoadley, of Little Rock, Ark., was killed at Vicksburg in June, 1863.

S. H.

[63]
RECORDS OF CONVOCATION.

A Volume Full of Interest for Connecticut Folks, Churchmen Especially.

At the convention of the diocese of Connecticut held in New Haven a week ago, advance copies were presented of a publication which has much interest in connection with the ecclesiastical history of the state. Beginning with 1792 there has been an annual convention of the bishop, clergy, and laity of the diocese, and the journals have been published; some years ago there was a reprint of the earlier and rarer journals, from 1792 to 1879 inclusive. But there was also in existence a volume of manuscript records of the meetings of a "convocation" of the clergy with their bishop, to which reference had been often made, and which had been consulted and used by Dr. Beardsley and others, but had never been published.

It begins with 1790, and contains the records of meetings (often two in a year)

with almost no gaps until 1830; after this there are brief notes of meetings, in 1837 to consider the matter of a church newspaper, and in 1847 and 1848 for consultation, as to which we learn more from tradition than from the minutes. We know of voluntary meetings of the Episcopal clergy of Connecticut beginning in 1739, and contemporary notices of six of these have been found in the pages of "The Courant." There were also eight convocations in which Bishop Seabury met his clergy before that of 1790, and for the record of these blank pages were left at the beginning of the book now published; but the minutes were not entered, and very probably could not be found.

Although the convocation had no legal authority in matters either ecclesiastical or civil, it had much influence and guided the councils of the diocese in important matters. Here was founded the "College of Doctors," which soon gave place to the standing committee; here plans were made for the formulation of the now venerable Episcopal Academy, and for assistance to the sons of poor clergymen studying in it; also for the relief of "decayed clergymen," for the proper examination of the qualifications of candidates for holy orders, for the publication of the "Churchman's Magazine," and for missionary work within the diocese by the organization of the Society for the Promotion of Christian Knowledge. Here we find the vote accepting the Prayer Book as it was set forth at Philadelphia in 1789, and Rev. James Sayres's protest against it; we read over and over again of the trouble made by the irrepressible Annie Rogers; and we are reminded of the visit made by Bishop Brownell, at the request of the general missionary society, to "that portion of our country which lies west and south of the Allegheny Mountains."

The volume has been carefully prepared, and the original records have been followed "verbatim literatim, et punctualium," they cover eighty-five octavo pages. To them have been prefixed some thirty pages of introduction and added some seventy-five pages of notes from the pen of the Rev. Joseph Hooper, to whom the convention expressed its gratitude for much labor bestowed upon the work. Both introduction and notes contain valuable historical matter; and in particular the notes include full biographical sketches of twenty-eight of the early clergy.

The publication of these records has been too long delayed, and it is a great satisfaction that they are now in the hands of the students of the history of Connecticut.   S. H.

---

[64]

FREDERICK DAN HUNTINGTON.

Bishop Huntington has died, as the old chroniclers would have said, full of years and of honor. He was born in Hadley on the 28th of May, 1819, more than eighty-five years ago, and in Hadley he died yesterday. It was his old home, and it never lost for him the attractiveness of home.

His father, Rev. Dan Huntington, pastor at Litchfield from 1797 to 1809 and at Middletown from 1809 to 1816 (succeeding in the latter place his father's second cousin, Enoch, whose pastorate had extended from 1762 to 1809, and who, by the way, was brother of Samuel Huntington, president of Congress), was the third in descent from Lieutenant Samuel, the first of the family to remove to Lebanon. Samuel's father was Deacon Simon Huntington of Saybrook and Norwich, who married Sarah Clark of Saybrook, and he was son of Simon, the first emigrant of the family, of whom tradition says that he died at sea a few days before his family landed on these shores. The future bishop was graduated at Amherst College in 1839 with the first honors of his class. His father had not entered again upon active ministerial work after leaving Middletown, but he conformed to the Unitarian doctrines which were then prevalent in Massachusetts, and in these the son was brought up. After a course in theology at the Harvard Divinity School, he was ordained in 1842 over the Old South Church in Boston.

From this position, in which he showed the wonderful powers of his mind both in thought and in expression, he was called in 1855 to the highly responsible and influential position of Plummer Professor of Christian Morals in Harvard College and became as such professor preacher to the university. At the time of his induction his address on formally accepting the office attracted much attention on account of its deeply spiritual and evangelical tone.

Five years later, in 1860, having accepted the teachings of the Episcopal church, he was ordained by Bishop Eastburn; and having organized the new parish of Emmanuel Church, he became its rector. In 1869, the diocese of Western New York having been divided, the new diocese of Central New York elected him to be its bishop; and he was consecrated in his own parish church on the 8th day of April. The thirty-five years which have passed have all testified in some ways even more strikingly than did the former years of his preachership and his rectorship, to his intense earnestness in matters of religion and to the power with which he has been able to enforce them from the pulpit or from the written page. His "Sermons for the People" belonged to his earlier years; the "Sermons on Christian Living and Believing" were published about the time of the great change in his life, when also for two years he was one of the editors of "The Church Monthly;" at a later time he edited "Elim, or Hymns of Holy Refreshment;" and among the most useful of the works published during his episcopate were "Helps to a Holy Lent" and "Steps to a Living Faith." His preaching, quiet and scholarly, but impressive and earnest, was such as to answer great questions and to inspire great thoughts. At the General Convention of 1883, in Philadelphia, he was chosen to write the pastoral letter on behalf of the house of bishops, and it made a strong impression on the church. Impatient, as might have been expected from the tenor of his mind, of much that awoke passing controversy and had but an ephemeral value, he seemed in the last part of his life to withdraw from the general work of the church, but to his diocese he spoke as a father in God on matters practically and vitally religious. With him has passed away a great representative of the scholarly and thoughtful type of American Christian leaders. He outlived in years all other members of the house of bishops of the Episcopal church in this country, except Bishop Watson of East Carolina who is his senior by nearly a year, while Bishop Morris of Oregon is his junior by but two days and Bishop Gillespie of Western Michigan by about half a month; and he leaves but three bishops on the roll his seniors by consecration, Bishop Tuttle of Missouri, Bishop Morris of Oregon, and Bishop Doane of Albany. He is succeeded in Central New York by the coadjutor, Dr. Charles Tyler Olmsted, consecrated in October, 1902.

Bishop Huntington was married November 21, 1842, to Miss Hannah Davis Sargent of Boston. Two sons are in the ministry of the Episcopal church, Rev. Dr. George Putnam Huntington of Hanover, N. H., and Rev. Father James Otis Sargent Huntington of the order of the Holy Cross.   S. H.

---

[65]

DEATH OF DR. PYNCHON
DIED IN NEW HAVEN AT THE AGE OF 82.

PRESIDENT OF TRINITY COLLEGE FROM 1875 TO 1883.

His Ancestry Was of the Best in New England—Graduated at Trinity in 1841 — Was Tutor and Professor for Many Years.

Thomas Ruggles Pynchon, D.D., LL.D., ex-president of Trinity College and a professor in the institution for many years, died in New Haven yesterday, at the home of his sister, Miss Sarah Pynchon, on Temple street. Dr. Pynchon had been sick for two days with a complication of heart and liver troubles and died suddenly.

The funeral will take place from Trinity Church, New Haven, at 2:30 o'clock tomorrow afternoon. President Luther and the faculty of Trinity College will attend, as will Bishop Brewster, if he can leave his engagements in Boston.

The ancestry of Dr. Pynchon was of the best in New England. He was in the direct line from the colonist William Pynchon (otherwise spelled Pinchon, Pinchin and Pincheon), who was descended from good stock of his own name in England and from a sister of the great archbishop Chichele, founder of All Souls' College, Oxford. The "worshipful" William Pynchon came to this country in 1630 with Governor John Winthrop, as one of the patentees of Massachusetts Bay, and removed in 1636 to Agawam, where he founded a settlement and named it Springfield from the place of his birth in Essex, England; and below the rapids in the Connecticut he built a storehouse for convenience of traffic, which gave name to Warehouse Point. The new settlement was for a time thought to be outside the limits of the Massachusetts

jurisdiction, and Mr. Pynchon acted with the Connecticut colonists, became a magistrate, and sat in the General Assembly at Hartford; but the claim of the Bay colony was presently acknowledged, and he accepted a commission from the government of Massachusetts. While on a visit to England in 1650 he published a volume on the atonement, entitled "The Meritorious Price of Our Redemption," which was not in accord with current New England theological teaching. Returning to this country, he found that the work had aroused great indignation, and that the general court had ordered it to be publicly burnt in Boston market-place. The author refused to appear in defense of himself; and presently, weary of what he considered abuse and ill treatment, he returned to England, where he lived until 1662, devoting himself to theological writings and dying in the communion of the national church. His son John succeeded him as councillor in the Massachusetts government and the general administration of affairs in Springfield and its neighborhood, and was in active service in King Philip's and the first French wars; like his father, he gained the confidence of the Indians, and was skillful in managing them. In 1660 he built for his home the brick house long known as the "Old Fort." His great-grandson, Joseph, was graduated at Yale College in 1757, and settled at Guilford, marrying a daughter of the younger Rev. Thomas Ruggles of that place, whose wife was the eldest daughter of Rev. John Hart of East Guilford (Yale College 1703), and sister of Rev. William Hart of Saybrook, and who traced her descent to Rev. William Hubbard, the early historian of Massachusetts; their home was for a while in the old Stone house, of famous history. (Joseph's brother Charles, it is interesting to note, was an intimate friend of Colonel Ephraim Williams, the founder of Williams College and great-uncle of Bishop Williams.)

During the Revolutionary War the Sandemanian views which Joseph Pynchon had embraced made him a non-combatant and thus exposed him to suspicion; and in 1781 he migrated with his family to Shelburne in Nova Scotia, but after the war returned to Guilford. In all succeeding generations the name Thomas Ruggles has been retained. The first of the name, the son of Joseph and grandfather of President Pynchon, was a physician in Guilford, studying at first in the hospitals of the British army in New York. His son lived on Temple street in New Haven, where the late Thomas Ruggles Pynchon was born on the 19th of January, 1823. In consequence of his father's death, he was brought up in the family of his mother's sister, who had married Dr. Hale of Boston, of the family of the "martyr spy" and connected with the Everetts and other well-known families. The mother, who survived until about 1880 and is pleasantly remembered by many persons in Hartford, was a native of Schenectady, N. Y. The young man received his early education in the Boston Public Latin School, but came to Hartford in 1836, at the age of thirteen, to enter a preliminary class at Trinity (then Washington) College, under the care of Professor John Smyth Rogers, who built the house afterwards owned by Senator Dixon. For a while he roomed with John Williams, afterwards Bishop of Connecticut, and James Roosevelt Bayley, afterwards Archbishop of Baltimore, both graduate students of theology under Dr. Samuel Farmar Jarvis. Entering the freshman class in 1837, he was graduated with the honors of the salutatory in 1841; and from

1842, before he was twenty-one years old, till 1847 he was tutor in classics and lecturer on chemistry in the college. He was ordained deacon in Trinity Church, New Haven, in 1848, and priest in Trinity Church, Boston, in 1849; and then for six years he was rector of parishes in Stockbridge and Lenox, Mass. Having been chosen professor of chemistry and natural science by his alma mater, he went abroad, and devoted a year to study, chiefly under eminent men of science at Paris, returning in 1856 to enter upon the duties of his professorship. They were of a wide scope; and under his care all the students of the college for twenty years were carried through an ample course in animal and vegetable physiology, zoology, chemistry, mineralogy, and geology. This latter he considered the crown of all the rest, and he never lost the interest with which he had studied it at a time when theories, now generally accepted, were beginning to attract attention. It was his good fortune, when once on the cliff which is now the site of Trinity College, to see the distinguished Sir Charles Lyell examine the formations there, and hear him say that a visit to the place was worth a voyage across the Atlantic. As professor he had charge of the cabinet, which was of no little value in its early days, and to which he secured valuable additions; and he was also librarian, devoting to the interests of the library much time and care. Besides these duties, he constantly assisted in the services of the chapel, and for five years had the full office and title of chaplain. On the death of President Abner Jackson in 1874, Professor Pynchon was elected to the presidency of the college, and he entered upon this office, in addition to his professorship, in January, 1875. The duties which came upon him at this time were many and arduous. The former college site had been sold, and a new site had been purchased and elaborate plans prepared for buildings. It fell to the new president's lot to determine what was necessary to be done and could be done, and to provide in a limited time and with limited means for all the needs of the college in a new situation. With much judgment and after great labor this task was accomplished, and the college entered upon its work in buildings ready for occupancy in the fall of 1878. In the year before the removal he exchanged his scientific professorship for that of political and moral philosophy, in which he labored diligently, and gave much time to the work of the class-room. Under his presidency, the college made advance in many ways; and the number of candidates for the degree of Bachelor of Arts was greater than at any other time before or since; but a decline in numbers preceded his resignation. In 1883, when he withdrew from the presidency, he was elected Brownell professor of moral philosophy, in the discharge of the duties of which office he continued until 1902.

The notice of his academic work would not be complete without a reference to his part in the religious instruction of the college, many successive classes having read with him the Epistle to the Hebrews in the original Greek.

Professor Pynchon received the degree of Doctor of Divinity from St. Stephen's College in 1865, being the first honorary degree conferred by that institution, and that of Doctor of Laws from Columbia College in 1877. He was a fellow of the American Association for the Advancement of Science and of the Geological Society of France, and at one time president of the American Metrological Society. A chapter of the

Phi Beta Kappa was founded at the college during his tutorship, and he was the first person admitted to membership in the Beta of Connecticut. From 1857 to 1862 he was its president and was again elected in 1889 and each succeeding year; and he represented it at several of the triennial meetings of the National Council. In 1869 he published a "Treatise on Chemical Physics," the second edition of which bore the title of a "Treatise on the Chemical Forces," heat, light, and electricity. It was clearly written and well received; but appearing as the new chemical nomenclature was about to displace the old, and just before the wonderful advance in the study and application of electricity, it was not as extensively used as might have been expected. And in 1889 he published a volume entitled "Bishop Butler, a Religious Philosopher for All Time," being a sketch of the great philosopher's life with an examination of the "Analogy." This was based in part on lectures given in the class-room and in part on an address delivered at the time of the presentation of a portrait of Bishop Butler to the college; and it shows his enthusiastic admiration of the man and his writings.

In the Diocese of Connecticut Dr. Pynchon was a member of the Standing Committee from 1871 to 1882; and also at the time of his death an examining chaplain and a trustee of the Episcopal Academy at Cheshire, having been appointed to the former office in 1872 and to the latter in 1875. He had also been for several years a trustee of the General Theological Seminary in New York.

Dr. Pynchon appeared to younger men, who thought him much more their senior than he really was, as an old-fashioned man. He was a student and teacher of a kind now becoming obsolete, and a gentleman of the old school. He had a dignified bearing and a somewhat precise way of speech; but he had also a true gentleness, and while he did not decline the responsibility which came to him in the discharge of the important duties to which he was called, he did not cling to honors or grieve at laying them aside. He devoted himself enthusiastically to the service of his alma mater, and took great pains to bring his students both to learn and to understand the subjects which he taught; and while they sometimes complained of the way in which they were required to study and to work, they confessed that they learned and remembered what was thus impressed upon them. All that the college owes to him in material matters very few persons can know; it was shown in his great care and anxiety in the adaptation of the first buildings erected on the new site to the imperative needs of the institution, in the erection of the Northam Towers, the gift of personal friends, and in the enrichment of the museum and the library. In many ways he showed himself a man of true chivalry, and not least when at one important crisis he took the entire responsibility for a course of action to which he had consented only at the urgent advice of others, and against his own best judgment. And when it seemed best that he should retire from the presidency, he continued his work as professor in the most natural and quiet way, without any manifestation of impatience or disappointment. His constant appearances in the chapel and the lecture-room and on the campus was an object lesson to successive generations of students.

The thought of Dr. Pynchon will recall to the memory of former students many sayings which marked for them his idiosyncrasies of thought and expression. Very few could tell whether

it was an unconscious humor which was expressed in this seemingly strange way, always effective and never to be forgotten; or whether it was a conscious humor which thus found utterance without betraying itself. But it was always kind and considerate, and always the expression of a heart controlled by the instincts of a gentleman and the training of a Christian. While in the annals of Trinity College, Dr. Pynchon's name will have an honored place, he will long be remembered by those whom he taught and guided and whom he made his friends.   S. H.

NEWTOWN BICENTENNIAL

SAMUEL HART'S ADDRESS.

Your Newtown was not the first place in the colony of Connecticut to bear its name. Seventy years before these fair hillsides and valleys were secured as a home for your ancestors, a company of earnest men and women had moved to the westward from the shore of Massachusetts bay to seek a new abode on the further side of the Connecticut. It was for them a far journey through forests and over ridges and across streams; they went along in the wilderness wherein was no way; and their passage of the great river was for them in a very real sense what the passage of the great river of the eastern world was to the fathers of all the faithful. They were warned by those whom they left behind that in the bounds of the west, where they were minded to dwell, they would meet with strange experiences, and that they must expect to contend there in the great battle with anti-Christ whose abode was in the ends of the earth. But they were sturdy men and brave women, who believed that they had a call to found a new commonwealth, and who were convinced that at a safe distance from their brethren they could put into operation certain principles of association and government which did not quite commend themselves to those whom they left behind. Turning their steps a little to the south as they went westward, they crossed the river below the line which bounded the Massachusetts patent in a fair valley of the beauty and fertility of which they had heard before. They had come from the New Town just across the river from the older town of Boston, a place which was soon to become the seat of a college and to adopt a name that should recall the seat of an ancient university in England: but when they left it, the Massachusetts Cambridge was still New Town. They went through the fields and came to the site of their new home; and there, as those who settled above them continued for a time the name of Dorchester and those who took up their abode a little below brought the name of Watertown they founded a new Newtown. In some sense indeed they might have said that theirs was the original Newtown; for the organized church of their former home came with them, and was not the church the most important part of their organization? But at any rate such was the name which they brought; and for a short time there was a Newtown in Connecticut established in the sight of the Dutch fort of slightly earlier foundations and guided in matters ecclesiastical and civil by Mr. Hooker and Mr. Stone. But soon the thoughts of the

settlers went back past their recent abode on the bay to their old home in England; and after two years they agreed that Newtown should be called Hartford—they doubtless called it Hartford—from the name of the old dwelling place of one of their ministers. The former name lapsed; but it was after a while suggested for adoption in the eastern part of the colony, and was actually renewed by those who fixed on this place as a home for themselves and their children; and at the end of two centuries we find the name perpetuated here. We may feel obliged to apologize for it, as one apologized for the name of the venerable foundation of New college at Oxford, by saying: "It was new once;" but we gladly keep the word which has almost lost the significance of its derivation, and has come to mean, for many who live here and many more who are scattered in divers parts of the country and it may well be in remote parts of the earth, all that is denoted by the name of an ancestral home or of their own home in childhood or of their only home in youth and active life and happy age. One who may venture to speak for the State Historical society which has its local abode in the capital city of the state may venture to say that he brings today a salutation from the old Newtown of 1635 to the new Newtown of the comparatively recent date of 1705, seventy years its junior.

Seventy years pass beyond the limit of the active life of man in these degenerate days, save in a few extraordinary cases, but seventy years is not a long time in the life of a family or a church or a nation. Still, it is a period which often marks the occurrence of important events, the passage of importants actions, the influence of strong men. Especially the first three score years and ten in the history of a commonwealth cannot but determine in great part its future life. The Connecticut into which the settlement which was made here two hundred years ago, was soon admitted as a town was already the Connecticut of an important history. Let me remind you—it must be briefly and almost by suggestion—of some of the events by which that history was marked and its issues determined.

The Connecticut colony had, as we may say, gained conciousness of its power and of its rights in the Pequot war; it had made declaration of its principles of government and claimed and accepted the responsibilities of a commonwealth in the adoption of the fundamental orders, the first written constitution in the world, establishing a pure and strong democracy; and it had strengthened itself by acquiring such governmental rights as were possessed by the commander of the fort at Saybrook. Meanwhile there had been growing, under the influence of an aristocratic settlement at the mouth of the Quinnipiack, a federation—for it was rather this than a commonwealth

—the principles of which were not in entire accord with those of the River colony. We may remind ourselves, by the way, that in the first sermon preached at New Haven the settlers were bidden to think of themselves as led into the wilderness to be tempted of the devil.

Soon, the days of the Commonwealth in England came and passed; the king fell and the king came to his own again; and the new king gave to the

younger Winthrop for his colony of Connecticut that wonderful charter which continued to it all that it had ever had or claimed, and in fact assured its perpetuation for all time. An immediate result of the charter was the inclusion (in 1662) of New Haven in Connecticut, not very willingly accepted by those who were thus deprived of a sort of sovereignty without their consent, but seen to be necessary for common safety and for mutual advantage; and the united colony was able to take her place among friendly neighbors and to assert her rights against her opponents. It is not amiss, perhaps to note the growth of the body politic by enumerating the towns which came under the general provisions of the charter. In Connecticut proper, besides the original towns of Wethersfield, Hartford and Windsor, there were eight; Saybrook (of equal antiquity with the three), Stratford, Farmington, Fairfield, Norwalk, Middletown, New London, Norwich. With New Haven there were four others; Milford, Guilford, Stamford and Branford. (I do not mention the towns on Long Island which were under one or other of these jurisdictions, as they did not long continue their relations to them). These fifteen towns formed on the whole a homogeneous and prosperous community. Under the spiritual care of well educated and godly ministers; with upright magistrates, who administered wisely the laws made by the representatives of the people; training their children in as well furnished schools as the times would afford and founding a collegiate school for their higher education; practicing and strengthening what came to be known as the New England conscience; the people of this commonwealth took, quietly but surely, their place as men and as Christians.

Before the time came when these lands were secured for a settlement, Connecticut had been called upon to do a good deal and to suffer a good deal for the common interests of New England and for the maintenance and defense of the rights and claims of the mother country, and in doing this she had come into a depressed financial condition and felt the needs of greater activity; but she was ever the same brave and patient commonwealth, doing her best and waiting her time.

And in all these years the colony was growing by the occupation of new territory and the organization of new towns, each a political unit, as the former towns had been, and each taking its place in the common life. In this neighborhood Derby and Woodbury had been founded before 1700, and Danbury further west became a town before the first settlers here were ready for incorporation. Such lands as we see lying about us could not be left unoccupied; it is to hear the story of their occupation and of that which followed upon it that we are assembled today. I have already kept you too long from listening to your historian; but I have tried to sketch a background on which the local record may be projected, and to suggest what sort of a body politic it was, with its 18,000 inhabitants, its churches and schools, its rising college having four students already graduated, its simple and strong form of government, its honorable history, its high ideals and aspirations, and its preparation for a noble future,

in which the settlers of this community were preparing, two hundred years ago, to form a new unit of life and administration. Let me but add that a commemoration of this kind has a value and an influence far beyond the limits of the town in which it is held. It effects the life of the state, and gives an inspiration to many who have but a remote connection—perhaps no personal connection at all—with your history. The deserved praise of "famous men and our fathers that begat us" awakens in others than their descendants an appreciation of the past and a determination to make the future worthy of it. And while we look for a result of what is said and done here today in a renewed interest in local history, a better appreciation of the value of your foundations, a clearer view of the opportunities of your town and of the duties of its citizens, a sense of the importance of records and documents, and a willingness to make plans both for the near and for the far-off future of your home, we may not forget that all this tells on the life of the state and the nation; and that as the present in its wide unfoldings is what the past, sometimes in narrow lines of work and influence, has made it, so the future is affected far beyond the possibility of our thought by our labor, our character, our unselfish devotion to the common good.

LET NEWTOWN FLOURISH!

Newtown is growing an old town now; a week from today its good people will be celebrating the two hundredth anniversary of its planting. The program includes sunrise and sunset salutes, a parade, a collation, poetry and oratory, music and fireworks.

Newtown had a rather narrow escape from having to hunt up some other name for itself. Under a power delegated to them by the General Court that sat here in Hartford May 14, 1685, the governor and secretary issued a "pattent" (February 4, 1686), to the proprietors of "Newtown or Preston," and it was confirmed by the General Assembly and Court of Election that met here May 13, 1703. But at the General Assembly that met at "Newhaven" five months later, Deputy John Richards was recorded as from Preston; and at the General Assembly of October, 1704, Deacon Caleb Fobes and Mr. Daniel Brewster were similarly recorded. So Preston it was, and remained.

That's how we come to have the Newtown over west, now busily preparing for next week's celebration. Joseph Curtis, James Judson, Samuel Hawley, John Read, John Burr and the rest of them found the name unappropriated, and they straightway appropriated it.

A STILL EARLIER ONE.

We reminded Newtown the other day of a hazard that befell it before it was born and christened. If some good colonial folk over east had not finally decided to cleave to Preston as the nicer name of the two, Newtown's first plan-

ters and proprietors would have had to draw upon their imaginations (or their memories) for some name not already appropriated.

At this anniversary season it seems safe as well as civil to assume that our Newtown friends are much too well up in their Connecticut history and antiquities not to know all about an earlier hazard of which they are (so to speak) the spared monuments. Outsiders—Massachusetts people and such—may not be so thoroughly informed; for their benefit we mention that four of the first seven Connecticut "Cortes" whose records have come down to these times were held in "New Towne" or "Newton." The eighth (February 21, 1636) made the Newtown of today possible by the first of the two decrees here following:—

It is ordered that the plantacon nowe called Newtowne shal be called & named by the name of Harteford Towne, likewise the plantacon now called Watertowne shalbe called & named Wythersfeild.

It is ordered yt the plantacon called Dorchester shalbee called Windsor.

We wish the Newtown that is skies of blue and the finest of weather for its anniversary. The phrases of diplomacy "come easy" in a summer when the land of the Yankees is the diplomatic center of the world; we avail ourselves of the opportunity to renew to Newtown the assurance of our distinguished consideration.

[67]

UNVEILING OF THE STATUE
OF COL. SAMUEL COLT

COLT STATUE UNVEILED.

Simple Ceremonies Attending the Formal Turning Over of the Memorial to Hartford.

THE REV. DR. HART'S ADDRESS.

In the presence of relatives, the board of park commissioners, its clerk, and the executors of Mrs. Elizabeth H. Colt's will, the memorial to Colonel Samuel Colt, erected by his widow, the late Mrs. Elizabeth Hart Colt, on Colt park, was unveiled Thursday afternoon. The public was not invited, owing to the desire of the late Mrs. Colt's relatives that the exercises be brief and unostentatious.

The relatives present were Colonel and Mrs. C. L. F. Robinson, Mr. and Mrs. George Watson Beach, Master Caldwell Colt Robinson, Colonel and Mrs. Samuel C. Colt and Miss Colt, Miss Fitzgerald, Miss Mary C. Fitzgerald and Mrs. John S. Jarvis. The park board met in the parlors at Armsmear at 4 o'clock. Mayor Henney, who presided, stated the purpose of the meeting, and then called on Commissioner Charles E. Gross to speak.

Mr. Gross gave some interesting history regarding the memorial that was to be unveiled. Mr. Gross said that when Barnard park was reconstructed nearly ten years ago a small knoll was

left upon it which at once suggested itself as a site for the statue of some man whom the city might care to honor. It occurred to Mr. Gross as an ideal location for a memorial to Colonel Colt, situated as it was at the very gateway to that section of the city which his energies developed. Mrs. Colt was willing. Mr. Gross found that most of the friends and old associates of Colonel Colt had passed away and for that reason he considered that it would be difficult to raise the funds necessary to build a memorial.

Two years later Mrs. Colt sent for Mr. Gross and told him that she had not given up the idea of a memorial to her husband, but that she had determined to erect it on the grounds at Armsmear. Two reasons had led to her decision as to the matter of the site, one being that she had already determined that the grounds should be given to the city for park purposes and the other being that the site she had chosen was that where her husband and three children were buried and where their bodies remained until removed to Cedar Hill cemetery. When Mrs. Colt had decided upon the matter she was eager to carry it out and interested herself in every detail of the work. J. Massey Rhind, the sculptor, studied the paintings and the bust of Colonel Colt, and Mrs. Colt did not relax her interest until all the details were arranged and the contracts drawn for the work. Then she hesitated, for she did not wish to disturb the soil where the members of her family had been buried, and it was one time her desire that the work might be deferred until after her death. When she saw, finally, that the work must go on she was anxious that it should be finished, and her will left ample provision for this work.

Remarks by the Rev. Dr. Hart.

The Rev. Dr. Samuel Hart, one of the executors of Mrs. Colt's will, said: Your Honor, and Gentlemen:

We are unveiling before you to-day a memorial of Colonel Samuel Colt, placed by his wife's munificence on these grounds which her gift has made a park of the city of Hartford. It was her wish, as you know, that here, on the plot of land which he beautified, and near the home which he built and in which he lived and died, there should stand for all time a worthy memorial of him; it has fallen to our lot to complete on her behalf that which she had carefully planned and begun, and for which she had made provision.

This indeed is not the only structure which tells of Colonel Colt and his work. On the banks of the river stands the armory, devoted to the busy activity of skilled labor, which has for these many years witnessed and still witnesses to his inventive genious, and which also reminds us of the plans which he made for the movement in both the method and the pursuit of the work of men's hands and brains. Hard by, the memorial church cherishes his name and testifies to strong faith and brave assumption of duty on the part of the wife and mother to whom was left so much responsibility, while it also silently teaches the lesson that the work of test needs to be prefaced by the Lord's day of rest and worship and the bodily skill needs the inspiration of consecrated wills and lives. Besides these, the parish house, a memorial to the son who attained manhood, while it tells the story of later sorrows and grievous disappointment, shows that the church of Christ stands ready to guide and bless every true act of his servants and to supply for them every real need.

Still, as I said, the noble woman whose whole life bore witness to an enduring affection, after she had linked her husband's name with structures which showed her sympathies with the devotion and the activities, the joys and the burdens of many-sided life, felt that there was need of a special personal memorial on these fair acres of Armsmear which she had dedicated to the service of the city in the confident hope that she might thus add to

the happiness of generations to come. This memorial, which she was not permitted to see in its completed form, we as Mrs. Colt's chosen representatives entrust to your care to-day. It bears in its design the record of powers of invention and of their successful prosecution on the part of him whose name it perpetuates; it shows the sailor-boy shaping the first model and giving form to thoughts which had come into his mind; and it shows the man, after he had perfected both model and machinery, exhibiting his work before the chosen representatives of a great nation and receiving recognition of his skill from a mighty ruler; it presents to the eye the figure of the man himself, who, working along the lines of his early imaginings, gained for himself honor and prosperity and set forward the material intents of a great community, the man who gave the example of precision of workmanship and elaboration of detail which is followed in the great workshops not of this city only but also of the country and of the world.
While under any circumstances of life the benefits of Colonel Colt's work could not but remain; it might have been that, as years rolled on, his name would be less frequently mentioned and that inventors and laborers of a future generation would fail to learn of what he did and what they owed to him; but now this memorial shall stand, to be seen by those who pass by the way, to be studied by those who enter these grounds, to be admired as a work of art, to challenge attention as it reads the lesson of success waiting on diligence, to encourage the faithful toiler in the laboratory of nation's powers, and with all this to bear the simple but touching record of an abiding affection. So may it stand here, under the reverent care of yourselves and your successors. Long shall the echo of industrious labor be heard from the armory; long shall the church bells call to worship and tell of joy in prosperity and comfort in sorrow; long shall the parish house minister to the wants of active parochial work; long shall this mansion provide a home for gentlefolk whose path adversity has crossed; and long shall this structure in enduring stone with its statues and pictures in bronze of a life of diligence and success and of the undying love which provided that it shall ever be held in grateful remembrance.

Memorial Unveiled.

Mayor Henney asked those present to go to the memorial, a short distance from the house. The grounds surrounding it had been placed in order and the figure of the sailor boy, which is in front of the main group, had been uncovered. When the guests were assembled Caldwell Colt Robinson, a grand nephew of Colonel Colt, and a son of C. L. F. and Mrs. Elizabeth Hart Jarvis Robinson, of Newport, R. I., pulled the cord and unveiled the memorial.

Corporation Counsel Arthur L. Shipman, one of the executors of Mrs. Colt's will, spoke briefly, saying that it gave him pleasure to present to the city by its executive a memorial to one who had so greatly benefitted Hartford. It would be a memorial not only to Colonel Colt, but also to the life long devotion exhibited to his memory by his widow.

Mayor Henney, in response accepted it for the city, speaking of the great impetus which Colonel Colt had given to the city's industries and accepting it as a trust for himself and his successors.

[68] **TRIBUTE TO**

DR. SAMUEL JAMES ANDREWS

TRIBUTE TO DR. ANDREWS.

By One who Received Instruction from Him at Trinity.

The writer was a member of the first class at Trinity College of instruction from the lips of the simple-hearted and wise-minded man, the news of whose death reached us yesterday. Our course in philosophy had been begun under a scholarly and thoughtful teacher, President Kerfort, who was called away to the bishopric of Pittsburg. Dr. Andrews was asked to complete the work of the year, and in particular to lead us in the study of the history of philosophy. Those of us who are left will testify, as will others of later classes, to the patience and the clearness with which he gave us to know the meaning of the thoughts of the wise men of old, and pointed out what they themselves could not have known, the tendencies and the results of their doctrines. But, with all this and in it all, he taught us to think, and oftentimes, when we would have asked him his opinion, he would, with equal modesty and wisdom, lead us to think out and to state clearly a judgment of our own, oftener suggesting that he would give it consideration than proceeding to criticise it. In the course of an academic life, one falls under the influence of many good teachers; but Dr. Andrews excelled all others whom I have known in what the great philosopher called the "maieutic" art; in fact, his mind and his method were both socratic, and he had wonderful aptitude for bringing both thought and expression into life. We owed him much for the direction in which he turned our thinking and the studies and convictions of our later lives. More than once he was called in to help in some literary or philosophical department of the college; and from 1874 to 1885 he held an appointment as an instructor.

Dr. Andrews was brought into pleasant and helpful relations with several of the ministers of Hartford—all of them, I think, his juniors in age, and certainly all of them his juniors in learning in a company which met stately at first to study the book of the Revelation and later to discuss topics connected more or less closely with the liturgy of the church. He was always the leader, though unintentionally and almost unconsciously; and by his wealth of learning, his carefulness in preparation, his readiness of adaptation, and his accuracy and attractiveness of expression, he helped all the rest to the study and the learning of truth of varied kinds.

The value of Dr. Andrews's written work is such that it will not be soon forgotten. In particular, his "Life of Our Lord Upon the Earth," first published in 1862, fully revised and rewritten and published again in 1891, has been recognized on both sides of the ocean as a most important and useful volume. Its scope, restricted (as the title page read) to the historical, chronological, and geographical relations of that life, did not allow of much use of rhetoric or much theological expression of the great truths with which it dealt; but it showed thorough scholarship, a reverent tone, great carefulness of investigation, equally great clearness of statement, entire frankness in stating the objections of others joined with entire willingness to meet them, and admirable adaptation for the needs of intelligent students of the gospel. I esteemed it a great privilege that the author asked me to read the proofs of the rewritten volume and to render a little assistance in a chronological matter; and it was a pleasure and a wonder—though not indeed a surprise—to see how as the years had passed he had read and studied what had been written by others on matters akin to those with which he was dealing, and how fresh were his knowledge and his power of expression. It was not a controversial work, but it pointed to the solution of many problems and suggested the end of some controversies.

Dr. Andrews's other published books were on subjects which give rise to discussion, but they also were not controversial, in the common acceptation of the term. They dealt with great topics, such as God's covenants with man, Christianity and that which opposes it, the Incarnation and what it means for men, the revelation of God in history and in prophecy. While he had clear convictions on other matters, and in some cases convictions which were not held by those whom he would have been glad to bring to accept his views, he did not obtrude them when writing of the generally accepted fundamentals of Christ's religion, and it was often by no more than an allusion that any attention was called to them. The hasty reader might have called him a pessimist; but he seemed such only because he looked seriously at the serious side of history and of life. If ever he was disposed to be impatient and discouraged, it was when men who ought to have been thoughtful, and even men who had a commission to be teachers of divine truth, seemed neglectful of truth or even careless as to whether there were any truth at all. He did see the dark side of certain tendencies of thought and conduct, and he feared their strength; but his soul was nevertheless full of brightness and courage, based on the assurance, not primarily at least of the restoration of man, but of the return of Christ and of the power of His might as the incarnate Son of God and the head of the church. It is a beautiful and helpful life which has thus come to its earthly end; but its influence will remain, and the Lord whose appearing His saints love, will at the last bring them with Him.

S. H.

OLIVER ELLSWORTH [69]

THE CHRISTIAN CITIZEN

OLIVER ELLSWORTH LAUDED IN WINDSOR

Honor Paid to the Third Chief Justice of the United States in the Old Palisado Church.

CENTENNIAL OF HIS DEATH.

Dr. Hart's Address.

Led by the choir, the audience sang "O God, Beneath Thy Guiding Hand." Then the Rev. Dr. Samuel Hart, dean of the Berkeley Divinity school, gave an address. His subject was "Oliver Ellsworth, the Christian Citizen." He spoke as follows:

The testimony of the elder President Dwight, no careless observer of men, as to

the dignity of Oliver Ellsworth, the honor instinctively paid him, and the sense of inferiority which he inspired in others, has just been read to you.

And almost, it would seem, as a special confirmation of this, we are told that a member of Roger Sherman's family, who in early life often saw Judge Ellsworth at her father's house and in society in New Haven, said that she "remembered that Dr. Dwight always led the conversation in any company, in which she ever saw him, unless when Judge Ellsworth was present; but then the former became a listener."

It is of a man such as this, honored by his state and his country, as we have been reminded, and entrusted with heavy responsibilities by reason of his wisdom, his integrity, and his eloquence, that you have asked me to say a few words, as he was a citizen, a Christian citizen, here at home.

We can visit few of the ancient towns of this commonwealth, and read the inscriptions on the tombstones in the burying grounds or study the local annals, without finding the names of men who had in their day, and for that matter have still, a place of deserved honor for the public services which they have rendered. "Men renowned for their power" were they, as the son of Sirach wrote long ago, "giving counsel by their understanding, leaders of the people by their counsels, and by their knowledge of learning meet for the people, wise and eloquent in their instructions, honored in their generations, and the glory of their times." In those days, to be sure, there was not the difference which there is to-day, between great cities, busy marts of manufacture and trade, and small communities in which even agriculture seems at a standstill; still there was a different life in New Haven and Hartford and New London from that of less frequently visited towns. But, as I was saying, in nearly every one of the minor towns of the colony and the state there was a succession of men of influence and position, who kept the life of the place in touch with the world without and drew the life of the outer world into the village and the hamlet. Students of theology went to live for a time in Bethlem, because Dr. Bellamy was pastor there; students of law climbed the hills to Litchfield, because Judge Reeve had his office there; men with heavy responsibilities for the welfare of an infant republic found their way to Lebanon, that they might consult with Governor Trumbull in his office, the war office of Revolutionary days. It is hard for us to realize how much this meant in the earlier time, when travel was not very easy and the established lines of travel were few, and when even the centers of population and business felt the burden of isolation. Such influence was not lost within the memory of many of us, and still to-day is it retained, but more I suppose, from a leveling upwards of the conditions of life by reason of the facilities afforded by modern civilization. So as we look back it is an interesting question for us to ask ourselves how such a man as Oliver Ellsworth, chief justice of the United States, lived in his home at Windsor, what kind of a citizen he was, and how he appeared to his fellow citizens.

They were not unused to a seemly dignity on the part of ministers and lawyers and physicians and other educated men, some of whom they had always had with them, and towards whom they ordered themselves with a corresponding respect. But they were accustomed also to see ministers and judges and governors taking up duties as members of their respective communities in a simple and natural way as they themselves did, and at church and town meeting, on the farm and in the household, engaging in ordinary work with even more carefulness, though perhaps with less apparent labor, than themselves. Nobody was surprised to find them occupied with handiwork or such household cares as fall to men's lot; and every one would have been much surprised if they had been found at any time negligent of religious and civic duties. Judge Ellsworth was a thoughtful and busy man, who did really think as well as really work. At times he sat for hours, it is said, apparently looking out of his window at a great cedar tree, that his mind might not be distracted from the important matters on which he was coming to a decision; and at times he would walk to and fro in his library and the hall of his house, working out some problem of thought. But we are also told that when his little ones came into his study, he would stop to play with them and to draw pictures for their amusement; and that fondness for children was always a prominent trait in his character, and that he found himself at home with men in every rank of life and of every age. He was a shrewd investor and careful of what came into his hands; we are told that he was the first man to build houses in Hartford to let; in the latter part of his life he opened and kept a country store, quite as much (it would seem) for profit as to start his sons in trade or to study human nature and meet his neighbors; and he concealed the amount of his wealth, which was large for those days, even from his family. But with all this he was a kind-hearted man and ready to help. In the winter after his return from Europe he offered to five young men of the town the use of his office and his library, and gave them personal instruction in history, mathematics and political philosophy. And all the "duties of neighborhood" he discharged naturally and willingly, yet always with sagacity.

We should expect of such a man in such a community that he would attend seriously to religious matters, and that in his reading and studying he would find some place for theology. In fact, we are told that in youth it was expected that Oliver Ellsworth would turn all his studies that way and become a minister of the gospel. And the influence of this early design, whether made chiefly for him or by him, seems to have remained. His library had many works of theology, which he had purchased in England, and he constantly read in them. Always, in any place in the house of worship, for the building of which he had contributed, as for the maintenance of worship in it he gave his support, he sometimes conducted the service himself and read a sermon to the congregation, if the pastor was unable to attend. Then returning home, after the two-fold Lord's day service, he read, as his custom was, one of Archbishop Tillotson's sermons to his family. Perhaps it was the tone of the archbishop's teaching which led him to write with a tone of gentle sarcasm in regard to some of the tenets of the traditional theology of New England.

Towards the latter part of his life he contributed to the Connecticut Courant, with the assistance of Dr. Webster and others, a series of agricultural papers. Into these he wove remarks moral and political and theological. Thus, writing on the use of fertilizers, he noted:

"The lowlands of Virginia, fixed as it seemed in the garden of Eden, except that there is no account of the Lord ever walking there, after cultivating Indian corn and tobacco only, till a hundred slaves can scarcely support their master, are now beginning to cowpen their fields for white clover."

And in a more striking allusion to a doctrine which he doubtless often heard from the pulpit, his topic being the protection of cattle:

"If any one doubts whether cattle feel the cold, let him look at their miserable contraction after lying out on a severe night, or listen to their piteous bellowing in a storm of hail, and hear in that moan the denunciation of heaven against him that is not 'merciful to his beast.' If cattle are doomed, as some suppose, to work and die as appendages to lapsing Adam, that is paying quite dear enough for their relation, without being cursed again to starve and freeze by the folly of his descendants."

I have not dwelt on the acknowledged strong traits of Judge Ellsworth's character which were shown in his public duties; his integrity and fearlessness, his belief in the immutability of the moral law, and the other qualities which fitted him for the high positions which he held. I may but allude—and that in the words of one intimately acquainted with his life through marriage with the daughter of his son, the governor, the late Dr. Abner Jackson, whose sketch of the chief justice I have had before me as I have written—to the fact that he had "a perfect understanding and sympathy with his state, and that she never faltered in her confidence in him. There is in it," said he, "something beautiful and scarce to be matched in our history except in the case of South Carolina to Calhoun and of Kentucky to Clay."

The reality and implicity of his affection to his family, affected in their expression by his dislike for the manual labor of writing and shown in two letters which I find quoted in full in the same manuscript. The one was written to his wife from Paris, August 15, 1800:

"Dear Mrs. Ellsworth,
"I shall leave France next month, let our business, which is yet unfinished, terminate as it may. If it please God that I see my family and friends once more, I shall certainly love them more than ever.
"Oliver Ellsworth."

The other she received after anxiously waiting to hear from him as to his return from a session of congress which seemed to have been unduly prolonged:
"One week and then—
"Oliver Ellsworth."
Such was the Christian citizen whose life on earth ended here a century ago.

THE SEMI-CENTENNIAL OF ST. JAMES'S, GLASTONBURY

[70]

ANNIVERSARY SERMON AT ST. JAMES'S CHURCH.

Rev. Dr. Hart Reviews Fifty Years of History of Glastonbury Episcopal Parish.

CHIEF EVENTS OUTLINED.

188

The semi-centennial of St. James's Protestant Episcopal church, Glastonbury, is being observed to-day with appropriate exercises. The historical sermon, preached this morning by the Rev. Dr. Samuel Hart, vice-dean of the Berkeley Divinity school, Middletown, was one of much interest. Dr. Hart preached from the text:

"And thus they returned us answer, saying, 'We are the servants of the God of heaven and earth, and build the house that was builded these many years ago.'"—[Ezra v., 11.

The sermon was as follows:

We look back, and rightly, to the history of God's people in the olden time for types and prophecies of these later days and of the Church of Christ. And we have special warrant for finding in the ancient ordinances of divine worship shadows cast before from the great realities of the worship of the church; both tabernacle and temple, alike the first temple in all its grandeur and the second in its humbler beauty, read us lessons of how we may acceptably approach God. But it cannot be without a reason that we seem to turn most naturally for such lessons, not to the temple which Solomon built at the beginning of the monarchy, when everything concurred to tell of permanence and stability, but to the tabernacle in the wilderness which the priests carried about in the years of wandering and to the temple reared by the returning captives after their sojourn in the land of their conquerors. The church on earth seems to be more fitly figured to us by that which tells of journeying and of restoration than by that which speaks of rest and of completion. And this thought is confirmed by suggestions in the Old Testament and by direct teaching in the New. Solomon's temple stands, we may say, in line with the monarchy, permitted indeed by God but not approved as His ideal for His people. His abode had been among them in a tent, while they dwelt in tents, the tent of meeting, of their meeting with Him; it was among their goodly tents spread out in encampment or in march the goodliest, but yet it was like all the rest. And in the land of promise, when a fixed capital was established in the citadel of Jerusalem, it was for the bringing in of the ark to its abode in a new tent that the welcome of song was prepared and the heads of the ancient gates were bidden to lift up their heads that the Lord of Hosts might enter. The stately palace might be needed by the earthly king, but God was content to find His abode in a home more like that of the humbler people. Thus, moreover, it was shown, as in other ways, that the covenant made under the law was transitory, and indeed a shadow of a reality yet to come; and worshipers were bidden, although unconsciously, to look past it to that which was enduring, the true temple for all nations, the universal Church of the Christ. The first temple was, one may reverently say, an exaggeration of the truth as to the acceptable manner of God's worship, as the monarchy of Solomon was an exaggerated expression of God's supreme sovereignty. And while men's use of the tabernacle was faulty, the faults were found to be even more closely attached to the temple: spiritual religion was not increased by the new surroundings of the divinely appointed worship.

We read the like lesson in the New Testament. It cannot be determined, I suppose, whether the Epistle to the Hebrews was written before or after the fall of Jerusalem and the destruction of the ornate temple which had gradually displaced the simpler structure built some centuries before on the return from the great captivity. But whether it were standing or not, we might expect the writer, in drawing the parallel between the old Covenant with its typical ordinances and the new Covenant with the great realities, to trace out the relationship between the temple on the hill of Zion and the church of the living God, the ministrations of priests in the stately structure of old and those of the Christ in the true house whose outer courts are this earth and whose holy of holies is in the heavens. But no, it is to the tabernacle, the tent, that he looks back, and in this that he finds the shadow of the good things to come. The temple, whether nearing its destruction or already razed to the ground, is entirely passed by; it is not the real type; that is seen in the tent of wilderness days and of the beginning of the possession of the promised land. Our instinct, if instinct it is, is right, the church of God is best presented to us in type by the ancient tent of meeting and the simple building which corresponded to it in after years, the temple of the returned exiles. From the one we learn lessons as to the beginnings of the church; by the latter we are instructed as to the days of her meeting with opposition and disaster and of her restoration. And in the narratives of the priestly scribe Ezra and of the lay governor Nehemiah, we find a picture of many an act of the building up and the rebuilding of the church of God in these latter days. It is more than with a sense of accommodation of words, it is as representing what was done long since as a prophecy and picture of that to which we are called now, that we may apply to ourselves the words in which the Jews, returning to their homes, gave their heathen rulers and their adversaries, an account of the undertaking in which they were engaged: "We are the servants of the God of heaven and earth, and build the house that was builded these many years ago." The church's mission is largely that of rebuilding; the rebuilding of organization, of worship, of character, of life.

We have been reminded during the past year of the beginning of a work like this in our colony of Connecticut two centuries ago. Godly men had lived and taught and learned here, who held the faith of ancient times and accepted the written word and held to the value of sacred ordinances; but they had broken with the ancient organization, under the pressure of what was deemed at the time to be necessity. The conviction came to the minds of some of the most godly and learned among them that they must build up again the spiritual house which had been built in the earliest days, which had long stood for service even if it had suffered from neglect and decay, and from which finally men had turned away. That process, the process of rebuilding on this New England soil the structure of the Catholic church, with its organization and its ministrations as the Church of England had retained them, and as it could transmit them and did transmit them to these shores, has continued and still continues, and is within our limits the history of the church in Connecticut. We commemorate to-day a contribution to this work of building, and a glance at a half-century of labor and of waiting here will be for us all a lesson of faith and encouragement.

Fifty years after these meadows and uplands had been surveyed and apportioned as a part of the ancient town of Wethersfield, a new town was organized bearing the honorable and inspiring name of Glastonbury; and presently in the year 1693, a place of worship for the standing order was built. It was more than a century later, after the colonies had gained their independence and had settled down to self-government, and after the first bishop of Connecticut had passed to his rest, that there were in this town enough churchmen to warrant the organization of a parish and the building of a church. In the year 1806 the first St. Luke's church was built, at about the middle point of the main road which runs through the town, some little distance below this spot. Most of the adherents of the church lived to the south of this building, and after a little more than thirty years it was abandoned as a place of worship, and the present St. Luke's church was built in South Glastonbury in 1838. A period of twenty years more elapsed, and then it appeared that the number of adherents of the Episcopal church in this neighborhood was sufficiently great, and their ability and the expected help of friends sufficiently large, to warrant the organization of a new parish. In September, 1857, preliminary meetings were held, and a consultation was had with the bishop; among the early petitioners were at least three representations of the families of original settlers here, and one other who has in many ways served the parish during all this half-century and whose name still remains on the list of its officers. On the 10th day of April, 1858, an organization was effected, and in the following month, now fifty years ago, land was bought for a church and a burying-acre. Before this the Rev. Dr. Chapin, editor of the Calendar, who had been rector in South Glastonbury, had held such services as his feeble health allowed, and the Rev. Mr. Kellogg, then rector of St. Luke's, had maintained Sunday evening services for a year or more, and Bishop Williams had baptized at the home of Esquire Thaddeus Welles fifteen persons, including Mr. Welles's five children. Now the charge of the congregation came into the hands of a young deacon, a native of the town next south of this, the Rev. Samuel Hall. What he did for the parish as deacon and as priest in the labors of some five years will always be testified by these walls within which we are gathered and the tower which rises from them, for it was owing to his patience and perseverance that the building was erected, and owing to his judgment that the services of a good architect were secured and his plans carried out, so that there was erected a church building with one of the most beautiful and fitting exteriors in the diocese. The records show that the people here gave according to their ability or even beyond it, some in money, some in material, some in labor; one lad, now for almost forty years a clergyman, gave ten days' work, and others helped in a like way. And I doubt if any other church in this part of the world has been helped by so many persons from without; the minister presented his requests to all whom he could reach and accepted gladly the least gifts. One is not surprised, perhaps, to find that eighty-six people in Hartford, fifty-seven in Middletown, and nineteen in South Glastonbury contributed; but it could hardly be expected that there could be found eighty-seven in Portland, thirty-three in Hebron, the same number in Litchfield, and twenty in Middle Haddam, to give something for the work. And the spirit of those who carried the responsibility of building is shown by an entry in the records, which it is well worth while to read and remember now. After note of fifteen parish meetings held within four months, at most of which no vote was taken except for adjournment, we read: "These meetings were for the purpose of mutual counsel and encouragement, in the work of preparing to build. They were opened with singing, the reading of Scripture, and prayer. May divine blessings attend the parish down to remotest generations!" How much was it worth that so many were interested, and interested in the right way, in what was doing here—in building in this New England Glastonbury the house of God which was built these many years ago in Jerusalem, and Glastonbury in the home country, and Canterbury, and Jamestown, and Stratford!

It was on the 25th of April, St. Mark's day, 1859, that the cornerstone of the building was laid, and on the 20th of the following December it was consecrated, Bishop Williams officiating on both occasions, and the Rev. Dr. Washburn preaching the consecration sermon. Mr. Hall's labors for the parish, but by no means the fruits of his labors, ended on Whitsunday, 1862. He was succeeded, though not immediately, by the Rev. Edward Goodridge, whose memory is still gratefully cherished here; he was one of the three clergymen married in this church, and one of those whose bodies await in the adjacent burial-place the resurrection of the dead. These first two rectors recorded in ten years 177 baptisms—no little proof that the church was needed here and that it had a real work to do for the community.

Thus the organization of this parish, the rebuilding of the historic church of God on this spot—for such, in the phrase of the pious Jews of old, we may well call it—began in such a way as to attract and secure the interest not only of a few large benefactors, for whose generosity we may well remember to be thankful, but also of many whose part in the work, though small, was no less real. And as we glance over the events of the half-century which has elapsed since its foundation, the forty years following those in which the first two rectors lived and labored here—and to-day it can be but a glance that we give to it—we shall see that it has gathered about it a wealth

of youthful enthusiasm and an abundance of interested memory which cannot but have an influence on its life. The circumstances of its position, readily reached from the college in Hartford and from the divinity school in Middletown, and the fact that from no fault of the parishioners it was not always possible to provide for the full support of a clergyman, make a long roll of names of rectors and ministers in charge; but they also increase the number of those who have here begun their sacred work as God's ministers and priests, and who can never forget where they first undertook the responsibilities of the ministerial and priestly life and came to a real knowledge of its difficulty and its blessedness. Some of these served the parish before their ordination as lay-readers, and to their names may well be added, as sharing to some extent in their memories, a goodly number of youth who came here on Sundays to render such help as they could in reading the service and caring for the Sunday-school. I will not now rehearse the names of those who are shown by the records to have been formally elected or to have ministered here, some are present with us to-day, from others we shall hear by letter, all (I doubt not) will be remembered by those whose memory is carrying them back to some event in their lives made memorable by a service rendered in this church or in connection with it. Two, however, call for special mention: the Rev. Douglass C. Peabody, who in his ministry here of less than three years administered the sacrament of baptism to sixty-five adults and children, and whose body was brought here to rest after faithful service elsewhere, and the last rector, whose good work for the parish earned for him the title of emeritus. But in regard to them all, it is, as I was suggesting, no little thing to know that many look back to this country church and to its parishioners, as the place where they learned and the people from whom they learned, in their early ministrations, the meaning of the work for God and His church to which they had dedicated themselves; the place of that special joy which belongs to the early worship, the early baptisms, the early eucharists, the early teachings, of the life of the dedicated and ordained man of God; the place—one need not hesitate to say it—of the mistakes and the disappointments which must mark every earnest life, and which are keenest felt at the beginning of responsibility assumed, even if recovery from them is easiest then; the place whence strong resolutions have been carried; the place to which, and not without a real power of their own, thoughts of benediction and of hope have turned back from an ever-increasing number of intercessors.

And if I do not attempt to-day to speak of the men and women of this parish, to whose pious labors and generous gifts its life and its influence have been so largely due, it is not that I forget them or think lightly of their work. Some of them within my own memory, and many more remembered by those who are gathered here to-day and by those elsewhere whose thoughts are turned to this commemoration, could tell, were it given them to speak, how great a blessing St. James's church was to them, how their lives were built up, here by worship and sacrament, by faith and self-dedication, and how their lives did in turn build up the house of God. Of some we have enduring memorials; or none has the memorial perished which lives before our God. They are, as they were, the servants of the God of heaven and earth; and, as the pious Jews of old coming back to their home, so they, reorganizing the church of Christ as their home, builded here, each according to his ability, and each in his place, the house that was builded these many years ago.

It remains to make record of a few events of special importance in the annals of this parish, one of them a great disaster followed by a speedy recovery. In 1882, owing to the efforts of the church guild, a convenient parish house was built; in 1902 a rectory was purchased; in 1904 the present organ was secured and put in place. In the last-named year, on the 14th of February, the inflammable parts of the church building were destroyed by fire. Fortunately, the walls and the tower, with its fine bell, were uninjured, and while services were continued in the parish house, the work of reconstruction was courageously undertaken and diligently carried out. In less than a year, on the 26th day of January, 1905, a bitterly cold day, when the roads were filled with snow, the new St. James's church—old, yet new—was consecrated. Its interior fittings could then be made more suitable than at the first, to the seemly dignity of the exterior; and the church now stands, as please God it may long stand, worthy of its place, for the honor of God and the service of men.

It witnesses to ancient truth; while the name of the town, almost unique (strange to say) in this land, reminds us of the earliest days of Christianity in England—"Splendor apostolicus Glastoniam irradiat"—the faith here professed, the Scriptures here read, the sacraments here ministered, the ministry here exercised, flow from a source earlier yet, even from the beginnings of the church of Christ; while the ancient communion vessels, made in England and long used in St. Peter's church, Hebron, are a visible bond of connection with colonial days and with the mother church. Its service to the community is witnessed by the 390 baptisms and the 214 confirmations on its register—no small number, indicating many more blessed by its services and brought under its influence; and its possibilities are limited only by the circumstances of time and place. To-day is a day of thankfulness and of courage. The workman, busy in the day's labor, does not know how he is helping on that which in after years shall be seen to be a temple for the abode of God and the home of the souls of men; but you, my brethren of this parish, may be helped this day to see how important it is that you do bravely and faithfully your work here and now for the house of God and for the offices thereof. And if you ask yourselves why you should thus be called to renewed courage and fidelity, if others ask you why it is worth while to do so much in the service of the church, you may answer with sure confidence, as did those who began and carried on this work: "We are the servants of the God of heaven and earth, and build the house that was builded these many years ago."

The Rectors and Ministers.

The first baptism was administered by Rev. William A. Hitchcock. Before the church was built the Rev. Alonzo B. Chapin, the Rev. Charles T. Kellogg, and the Rev. J. B. Robinson, former rector and rectors of St. Luke's church, South Glastonbury, officiated. The rectors and ministers have been:

1858—Samuel Hall.
1863—John T. Pearce.
1864—W. F. B. Jackson.
1864—Edward Goodridge.
1867—George G. Carter.
1869—Erastus Webster.
1870—Enoch Huntington.
1871—Jacob Van Linge.
1873—Charles M. Pyne.
1874—Thomas H. Gordon.
1876—Douglass C. Peabody.
1879—Beverley E. Warner.
1880—Charles W. Boylston.
1884—John R. Lambert.
1888—Samuel F. Adam.
1890—Robert Harris.
1894—Joseph P. Cameron.
1901—Joseph R. Peckham.
1902—Wilfrid H. Dean.
1908—Edward G. Reynolds.

[71]

THE REV. THOMAS BUCKINGHAM

OF SAYBROOK

(Died April 1, 1709)

MEMORIAL EXERCISES
FOR THOMAS BUCKINGHAM

Enclosure Placed About the Grave of Noted Divine at Saybrook Point.

The inscriptions on the stones of Mr. Buckingham and his wife are as follows:

> Here lies the body of the
> Rev. Mr. Thomas Buckingham
> pastor of the Church of
> Christ in Saybrook dec'd
> April ye 1st 1709 in ye
> 63 year of his age

> Mrs. Hester Buckingham
> wife to ye Rev. Mr. Thomas
> Buckingham Pastor of ye
> Church of Christ in Saybrook
> Dec'd June 3, 1702, in
> ye 56 year of her age

Rev. Dr. Hart's Address.

The address by Dr. Hart was as follows:

Two hundred years ago the third minister and second settled pastor of Saybrook had entered upon the last year of his busy and useful life. Early in April, 1709—for his death occurred on the first day of that month—his body was buried here, where lay already the dust of more than two generations, by the side of his wife, whom he had mourned for seven years. She was the daughter of Thomas Hosmer, one of the first settlers of Hartford, as he was the son of Thomas Buckingham, who had been among the first settlers of New Haven and one of the "seven pillars" of Milford. Unable to bear the expense of a college education at Cambridge, he had studied theology privately, probably in Hartford, and at the age of 18 had begun to preach in Wethersfield. Within about a year, in 1665, he was called to minister here, and took charge of a large parish, including all the original town of Saybrook, now Old Saybrook, Saybrook, Westbrook, Chester, Essex, and a large part of the old town of Lyme. The community had been weakened five or six years before by the removal of its pastor with a considerable number of the church members and other inhabitants to found the fair daughter-town of Norwich; but there was still left a great extent of territory and men and women enough to call out all the energy of the youthful minister.

A stated preacher had been in charge during the interim, but it was a relief both to himself and to the people when he turned his footsteps westward and removed to Greenwich. Mr. Buckingham was not ordained until 1670, so that for five years the people were dependent for the sacraments on the ministration of visiting pastors, probably from the up-river towns. At the ordination a council of ministers and churches assisted, but the actual laying-on of hands was lay brethren of the local church deputed for that purpose—a purely Congregational method of conferring ministerial authority. This had been practiced at the former ordination here, that of Mr. Fitch in 1646, when, though Mr. Hooker of Hartford was present, he was not allowed to lay on his hands, because he was not a member of this particular church; and it was in this manner, also, that Mr. Prudden had been ordained, under whom Mr. Buckingham had been instructed in his early years at Milford. The first meeting-house was standing, less than twenty years old, in 1665, on the north side of the middle lane, facing the central green which

separated it from the spot on which we stand, set apart for a burying ground. The minister's house built by Mr. Peck stood near it, further west than that in which Mr. Fitch had lived. In 1681 a new house of worship was erected, sixty feet by thirty on the ground and sixteen feet high; it stood "near about the place of the old one." The dwelling and the church both served the local community and the colony in events of great importance under Mr. Buckingham's ministry.

In 1666, almost immediately after the new minister had come here, the people across the river were allowed to provide for public worship by themselves, as a preliminary, doubtless well understood, to the organization of a town and a church. To it came Moses Noyes as minister; but as he was not ordained for twenty-seven years, almost certainly because his views of ordination were Presbyterian and not Congregational, the people of Lyme still brought their children here for baptism and came themselves for the Lord's Supper. We hear of no controversy and no objections on the part of Saybrook to the formal settlement and organization in Lyme, which finally took place in 1693.

Besides these matters of local interest, several events of general importance mark the forty-four years of Mr. Buckingham's life here. We must remind ourselves of them to-day, passing by with a word much that was doubtless no less important in itself, but of which, as it had to do with individual lives and with the quiet labors of a pastor and preacher, no record remains on earth. We must not, however, omit to recall the fact that the good man ministered not to his own people only, but also to the remnant of the aborigines; that Obed, whose "altar" has been often pointed out to us, was his devoted friend, and that the chieftain's daughter sat in the minister's pew; that Attawanhood, son of Uncas, made him an executor of his will and guardian of his children, directing that he himself should be buried in Saybrook after the manner of the English; and that he purchased of Joshua Uncas a tract of land within the limits of the town of Lebanon, on which some of his name settled at a later day.

It was on the morning of the 8th of July in 1675, that the fleet of Sir Edmund Andros, whose name was to these colonies what the name of Bonaparte was for a while to the Englishmen, a word of terror and threatening danger, appeared at the mouth of the river. The pastor was summoned to consult with Captain Robert Chapman, captain of the train-band; a courier was despatched to Governor Winthrop at Hartford, and all who could be reached were summoned to come to the fort under arms. The crisis, for a crisis it was, was boldly met by both the ecclesiastical and the civil authority; and Mr. Buckingham wrote an account of the affair which shows how largely the success of the resistance made near this very spot was due to him.

It was not strange that the pastor of Saybrook should be one of those who shared in the plans for the establishment of a collegiate school in this colony. Some sixty students had gone from Connecticut to Cambridge for their education since the establishment of a college there; and it was very desirable to provide opportunities for like study nearer home. Mr. Buckingham met with others at Branford to make plans; he was one

of those named as "undertakers" or trustees in the charter granted by the general assembly of the colony; and it was at his house, on the spot in plain sight of which we stand, that the first meeting of the trustees was held on the 11th of November, 1701. The institution, as you know, was established here; Mr. Nathaniel Lynde gave for its use a plot of ground with a house on this side of the green, the site of which is now marked by a simply inscribed boulder; and on the 16th of September, 1702, the first commencement was held in the minister's home, which, though "private," was attended with an expense of three pounds and four shillings.

Later commencements to the number of fourteen were probably held in the meeting house; and at these sixty young men received degrees, of whom the most eminent in after-life were Jared Eliot, Jonathan Dickinson and Samuel Johnson. In all these years the rector of the college, or president, as we should call him, was non-resident; and Mr. Buckingham was the "nursing father" of the institution and pastor of its students until his death, seven years before its removal to New Haven. His scholarly but kindly ways perhaps more than atoned for the fact that he was not actually in station and governance; and we can hardly begin to estimate the extent of the influence which he exerted in the early years of what has grown to be a great school of learning.

It remains that we should speak of the highest honor that came to the good man whose memory we recall to-day, and which marked the very end of his life. On the 9th of September, 1708—not quite two centuries ago—a council or synod assembled here, at the call of the general court of the colony, itself acting at the instance of Governor Saltonstall, to draw up a form of ecclesiastical discipline with a view to uniting the Congregationalists, who were really Independents, and those of Presbyterian tendency, if not into one body, yet under one regimen which should receive the sanction of the civil authority. There were then forty-one Congregational churches in the colony, including one across the boundary in Rye, and none of other names, except two which were but a year old, a Baptist organization in Groton and a Church of England parish in Stratford. These forty-one churches acted county-wise in the four counties in choosing delegates, sixteen in number,—twelve ministers and four messengers,—two of the latter being Robert Chapman and Deacon William Parker of this place, who met at this ecclesiastical center of Connecticut. Two men were chosen to preside over the synod as moderators; one was the Saybrook pastor, now in the sixty-second year of his age, and the forty-fourth of his ministry, who had received lay ordination but had led his church to the practice of the half-way covenant—we might call him a strict Congregationalist with moderate tendencies,—and the other, the venerable James Noyes, pastor at Stonington, of the same ministerial age as Mr. Buckingham and seven years his senior by birth, son of the teacher of the same name in Newbury, Massachusetts, who had used his influence to introduce the Presbyterian system into New England, and brother of the minister in Lyme who had waited so long for ordination—a representative of the other "school of thought" which was becoming influential and which practically prevailed in the framing of the platform. Into the details of the famous plan

which was here devised under the joint moderatorship of these two men, with its provisions for ordered councils in consociations and for associations of teaching elders or ministers, we need not enter now; nor need we discuss the principles on which it was founded or the value of the results to which they have led; this must be left to the historian and perhaps to some historian who shall stand more than two centuries from the date of the synod. But that the Saybrook platform had and still has a strong influence in this historic commonwealth cannot be doubted; and, as I was saying, we count it a special honor crowning the life of the Rev. Thomas Buckingham that he took part in presiding over the synod by which it was framed and in guiding its councils.

Mr. Buckingham has been honored in his descendants in four sons, one of whom was for thirty years pastor at Norwalk and others who settled here and whose descendants are widely scattered, none being better or more worthily known than our Governor William A. Buckingham; and in three daughters, all of whom married here, and whose descendants are traced through families bearing the names of Beeman (Beaumont), Kirtland and Doty. His grave and that of his wife, marked by simple tombstones as became the time when they lived and died, not neglected indeed, but needing as time went on, special care and protection, have now, after long years, been enclosed and as it were consecrated by the veneration and affection of a later generation; and we are assembled to witness to the provision which has been made by kinsfolk and friends, to express the gratitude of the community and of others who for various reasons are interested in what has been done, and to pledge ourselves that this good and faithful man, the first Christian minister to end his life in this ancient town, shall be had in everlasting remembrance.

REV. DR. SAMUEL HART.

Historical Address on Killingly and Its Growth.

[Delivered July 3, 1908]

Rev. Dr. Samuel Hart, dean of the Berkeley Divinity School at Middletown, made the historical address. He said:—

Two hundred years ago, when the General Assembly of the colony laid out a tract east of Woodstock, eight miles in length and six in breadth, and made it a distinct town by the name of Killingly, the colony itself had reached maturity of age. The three old river towns, the nucleus of Connecticut, had been settled for more than three-score and ten years; there had been a fort at the mouth of the Great River for the same period of time; and it was the seventieth anniversary of the settlement of New Haven. Saybrook had long been merged in Connecticut; Agawam or Springfield had seceded to Massachusetts; the union of the two colonies, so unlike in many things, but so well harmonizing into one commonwealth, had been accomplished for forty-six years; Gurdon Saltonstall was governor, and from the manor of his family in England, called Killingly near Pontefract (pronounced Pomfret) in Yorkshire, the new town was named.

All along the Sound there were thriving settlements and busy homes, partly of traders but for the great part of farmers and artisans. Back from New Haven and Fairfield, along the colony road in the one case and partly follow-

ing the Housatonic in the other, Derby and Woodbury and Waterbury, Danbury and Newtown and New Milford, had been settled, and men of enterprise and labor were pushing back into the wilderness. Litchfield was still uninhabited by Englishmen; and its site with the "western lands" about it had not yet come into the market. On this side of the great river, New London, by reason of its fine harbor and its advantageous position, had already a history of three-score years; and it lacked but one year of half a century since the time when the nine miles square of Norwich had become the home of a goodly company from the mouth of the Connecticut. In what is now Windham County, there were but three incorporated towns: the county town, dating from 1692; Plainfield, of seven years later; and Canterbury, set off from Plainfield after four years. To these we should, I suppose, add Woodstock, which was incorporated by Massachusetts in 1690, but not formally annexed to Connecticut until 1749. And Hebron, later included in the new county of Tolland, became a town at the same time as did Killingly. In all the colony there were forty-one Congregational churches for as many parishes, in nearly as many towns.

In all this time, more than two generations of the activities of Englishmen within the limits of this colony and in other colonies on the Atlantic coast, great changes had taken place. These were in part due to changes in the mother country. The flow of emigration, at first rapid, had been soon checked by the victories gained at home by the opponents of monarchy and episcopacy; it was only ten years after our first settlements that the supreme power was gained by Parliament, and within three or four years more the monarchy was abolished. Then England had had her experience of a commonwealth, and in its place had accepted the Stuart sovereigns of an unworthy generation. The glorious revolution, as they called it, had taken place, and to William and Mary had succeeded Queen Anne, interested in the colonies and generously providing for their welfare according to the best of her judgment and ability. Seven years before this town was settled, the Society for the Propagation of the Gospel in foreign parts had been founded in the Church of England; and in the very year before its settlement, the kingdom of England and that of Scotland, united for more than a century under the same sovereign, had been united into one kingdom with one parliament. It was a time of good learning and graceful literary work; and its effects in loyalty, scholarship, and culture were felt on this side of the sea.

And changes, it needs not be said, had also taken place here. The very push of the growing population away from salt water and the necessary lines of roads show this. One wonders whether it was by a kind of instinct which saw the advantage of settlements on the bank of rivers with the certainty of power that could be used for greater enterprises than they had then in hand; one wonders whether the Yankee mind was not half-consciously thinking of the use which could be made here of the waters of the Quinebaug as in the west of those of the Housatonic; but at any rate we can see the colonizing spirit of the Anglo-Saxon, pushing ever into new lands and ready ever for new undertakings. The colony was doing more, and preparing to do more, than ever before. The records of her General Assembly show how truly she was carrying out the principles of free government—pure democracy—which the river-towns had asserted for the first time in history when they framed the Fundamental Articles of 1639, and which had been secured to the united colony by the charter of 1662—that remarkable document, granted by a king to subjects dwelling in a remote part of the earth, and making them a free people, a pattern for a free nation which was to be framed and established after no very long time, to the astonishment of itself and of the world. There were statesmen in this little home of freedom, guiding its counsels and training its

generations for later responsibilities.

After the coming in of the eighteenth century, that is to say after the first settlement had been made here, and before a year had elapsed since the incorporation of this town, two events of great importance to the colony took place.

The one was the foundation of a Collegiate School, as it was then called; the other an organization of most of the churches in the colony into an establishment recognized by law. The College at Cambridge had for many years served Connecticut as well as Massachusetts in affording education of university grade to those who could carry their studies beyond the provision made for them in common and grammar schools, with the added help of the scholarly ministers to be found in nearly every town; but now the colony was strong enough and brave enough to have its own college; and on a sort of neutral ground between the two centers, in an accessible place from north and east and west, the college had been placed at Saybrook, beginning there a great work which it was soon to transfer to a new home in the New Haven of New England. Your town thus came into a commonwealth which was making full provision for the education of her people. It came also into a commonwealth in which provision was making, in a way that showed earnestness of purpose and serious intention, whether or no we agree with the details of the plan, for the unification and direction of religious organization and for giving it the sanction of the civil authority. It would be quite beyond my purpose to enter at all into a discussion of the principles involved in the Saybrook Platform, which was adopted in 1708, largely through the influence of Governor Saltonstall, or to trace out its effects as they may be read in history. It must suffice to say that it did involve important principles and that it did, in itself and through the support given to it as an establishment, profoundly affect the history of Connecticut.

Thus it was that this town of Killingly became two centuries ago a constituent part of Connecticut. Its history, the story of all its achievements, will be told by those who know it in its details. It has been for me but to sketch a background on which the record of progress may be cast, to suggest a setting which may bring out the relation of its history to that of our colony and state. Suffer me, Mr. President, while I bring to you today a greeting from the Historical Society of the state, to enter a plea to all who are interested or who in this commemoration shall become interested in the annals of your town, that you will not let the interest of these memorial days pass away with the days themselves. See to it, I pray, as I have said elsewhere, "that the whole town become a sort of historical society, for the appreciation and preservation of that which is old, for the lending of a proper prospective to that which belongs to our own day, for preparation rightly to understand and rightly to value and use that which is coming. They best do the duties of the present, they best provide for the future, who read and value the lessons of the past."

[72]

THE SAYBROOK PLATFORM.

Two hundred years ago today (if we make no allowance for change of style), on the 9th of September, 1708, an ecclesiastical synod summoned by the civil authority of the colony of Connecticut met at Saybrook. There had been a similar, but less formal and authoritative meeting, at the same place forty years before. In 1668 the Assembly had commissioned four ministers, one from each county, James Fitch of Norwich, Gershom Bulkley of Wethersfield,

Joseph Eliot of Guilford, and Samuel Wakeman of Fairfield, to meet at Saybrook, "to consider of some expedient, how far our churches and people may walk together within themselves, in the fellowship and order of the Gospel, notwithstanding some various apprehensions among them in matters of discipline." It led to a declaration by the General Assembly that "we can do no less than still approve and countenance" the present profession and practice of the churches "until better light in an orderly way doth appear." In 1703, the trustees of the newly founded collegiate school, meeting at Guilford, sent a letter to their brethren in the ministry, calling their attention to the Westminster Confession, as approved by a synod in Boston, and asking them to "manifest their concurrence with us in addressing our religious government, that they would please to recommend to our people and their posterity" the same Confession. In 1708 the government of Connecticut had become more religious than ever by the election of Rev. Gurdon Saltonstall from the pulpit to the gubernatorial chair. At his instance, it cannot be doubted, the General Assembly "ordained and required that the ministers of the several counties in this goverment shall meet together, at their respective county towns, with such messengers as the churches to which they belong shall see fit to send with them"—this last clause being an interlineation in the draft of the bill—"and shall at the same meeting appoint two or more of their number to be their delegates, who shall all meet together at Saybrook at the next commencement to be held there, where they shall draw a form of ecclesiastical discipline, which shall be offered to this court in October next, to be considered of and confirmed by them."

In consequence of this order the synod, for such it may rightly be called, met two hundred years ago. It consisted of twelve ministers, of whom eight were trustees of the college, and four lay messengers. Of the ministers, James Noyes of Stonington and Thomas Buckingham of Saybrook were chosen moderators, representing the two tendencies of opinion as to discipline which it was sought to bring together at that time: the former approximating in his views to Presbyterianism, the other a more strict Congregationalist who had had only lay ordination. With them were such men as Timothy Woodbridge of the First Church in Hartford, James Pierpont of New Haven, who is said to have written the first draft of the Platform, Samuel Andrew of Milford, acting rector of the college, Charles Chauncey of Stratfield, and John Davenport of Stamford, all of whose names suggest others in ascending and descending lines of honor and service. The lay members were John Hayes of Hartford, grandson of the first governor and son of the second pastor, Samuel Hoyt of Stamford, and Robert Chapman and Deacon William Parker of Saybrook. We do not know how long the synod sat. Its report to the General Assembly included the Confession of Faith recommended by the trustees of the college

five years before, the "heads of agreement" between Congregationalists and Presbyterians adopted in London in 1691 (under William and Mary), and largely the work of Increase Mather, and fifteen articles which are the Saybrook Platform. The objects of this Platform, to use Dr. Chesebrough's words, were: "1, The promotion of order and harmony among the ministers and churches; 2, The regular introduction of candidates into the ministry; 3, The establishment of a fixed and definite board of appeal, the County Consociation, a council by which such difficulties might be adjusted as the particular churches themselves could not settle." The Assembly, receiving the report, did at once proceed to "declare their great approbation of such a happy agreement, and ordain that all the churches within this government that are or shall be thus united in doctrine, worship, and discipline be, and for the future shall be, owned and acknowledged, established by law." A conscience clause was added for such societies or churches as might "soberly differ or dissent"; but those accepting the Platform, which combined both Congregational and Presbyterian principles, was the established church of Connecticut from 1708 until the act of establishment was silently repealed in 1784 in a revision of the statutes.

The influence of the synod of two hundred years ago was very great, and its history calls for careful study both in itself and as illustrating important principles of theory and administration. The Historical Society of the state and that of Middlesex county are to hold bi-centennial commemorations of so important an event on the last Tuesday in this month. At the meeting of the State Society in this city an historical paper is to be read by Professor Williston Walker of Yale Divinity School, and at that of the County Society, which will be held in Saybrook, the address will be given by the Rev. Dr. Lewellyn Pratt of Norwich.   S. H.

Old Saybrook, Sept. 29.

There was a large attendance at the annual meeting of the Middlesex Conference of Congregational churches which was held today in the church at Old Saybrook, the occasion being of especial note as the exercises were in commemoration of the Saybrook platform, an ordinance and constitution often referred to in doctrinal discussions. There was a large attendance and the papers read were of the highest interest. On September 9, 1708, an ecclesiastical synod, summoned by the civil authority of Connecticut, met at Saybrook, the result of which was the ordinance and constitution known in the history of the churches as "The Saybrook Platform." The morning session today was given over to the regular business of the conference. The address of welcome was made by Rev. Edward M. Chapman of Old Lyme; and then Rev. E. H. Burt of Ivoryton gave an address on "A Study in the Evolution of Fellowship Effected by the Saybrook Platform." Then Rev. Dr. Williston Walker, professor of ecclesiastical history in the Yale Divinity School made an address, and the morning's exercises closed with devotional exercises conducted by Rev. N. T. Dyer of Deep River.

At the afternoon session a joint meeting of the Middlesex Conference and the Middlesex County Historical Society was held in commemoration of the two hundredth anniversary of the Saybrook Platform. The exercises were in charge of the historical society. Rev. Dr. A. W. Hazen of Middletown, president of the society, presided.

Welcome By Rev. Dr. Hart.

The welcome was extended by Rev. Dr. Samuel Hart, president of the Connecticut Historical Society, who spoke as follows:—

We welcomed you to Saybrook, Mr. President, on one of the early days of last June, when we assembled in the old burying-ground to do honor to the memory of the third minister and second settled pastor of the place. We were reminded then that it was almost two hundred years since the close of his life, and that as he was one of the founders of the Collegiate School in this place and in a very true sense its foster father from its foundation, so he was honored as his life drew to its end, though far from being a very old man, by being chosen one of the two moderators of the synod which assembled here and framed the Saybrook Platform. It is for a commemoration of the bi-centennial of that synod that our Middlesex County Historical Society is meeting here today; and we are thankful to you that you have provided for this in addition to the more strictly ecclesiastical commemoration of the morning. The history of that important assembly and the far-reaching results of its decisions are to be told by one who is deeply interested in this ancient town and in what was done here two hundred years ago; some of us remember that he brought the event and its meaning before us when in 1886 we kept the quarter-millenial anniversary of the settlement of Saybrook. We shall be glad to hear from him again the story of the platform in the light of his recent investigations; and I will not detain you long from the special address of the afternoon.

But to the words of greeting, which I am sure are all the citizens of this ancient town will permit me to speak on their behalf to those who honor us with their presence today, I am minded to add a suggestion as to the place which the platform holds in the history of Saybrook. The early days of adventure and romance had passed, and two new generations had lived on the well laid-out squares at the Point and the promising fields along the shores of the Sound and the bank of the river; there was still a military band which could be called into service, and the fort was still serviceable for defense; but there was no garrison for an independent fort, as there had been for a few years, and Lyon Gardiner's mill was more busily kept on duty than were his well-constructed ramparts. Lady Fenwick had slept for three-score years on the mound of her burial; the church, not organized till military had given place to civil government, had made more than a beginning of its history; and it was almost half a century since good Mr. Fitch with a large part of his congregation had removed to the head of the Thames, to found the fair town of Norwich on its nine miles square of land. Parson Buckingham had come here in 1665, a youth of eighteen to minister to the community in sacred things, though his ordination by the brethren of his church did not take place till five years later; and since 1666 Moses Noyes had preached to the people in East Saybrook across the river, but he had waited twenty-seven years before accepting the ordination which was necessary to authorize him to minister the sacraments. A second house of worship had been built here near the site of the former and of the minister's dwelling, looking across the green to the place of burial; and now for a few years a college-house had stood on the south side of the green, for the place of a military post and an abode for "persons of quality" had given place to the plan of a collegiate town. Since 1701 the work of the school, as it was modestly called, had gone on with very fair success; this was becoming the center of education and learning for the now well-united colony of Connecticut; and it was the natural thing that when the General Assembly called upon the churches in the four counties to send their delegates to a synod, to consult about matters of importance, it should bid those delegates to assemble in Saybrook, where the meetings of the trustees, we are told, had already become "the most representative ecclesiastical gatherings in the colony."

Saybrook was busy in other matters than synods in 1708. It had just been colonizing again, as it had first sent out a colony in 1659. Joshua Uncas, whose brother was a close friend of Mr. Buckingham, had left his lands to certain Saybrook Legatees; and John Pratt, Robert Chapman, John Clark, and Stephen Post had secured the incorporation of a town in the interior, to be named Hebron; it was actually incorporated two hundred years ago last May. But Robert Chapman and his townsman, Deacon William Parker, turned from the thought of territorial expansion to sit as the two messengers from this county and half of the lay delegation from the whole colony, in conference with twelve chosen ministers, under the moderatorship of Mr. Buckingham and Mr. James Noyes of Stonington (brother of the minister at Lyme), in the synod of September. And in it all Saybrook must have been interested, to it indeed the thoughts of all Connecticut, and for that matter of all New England, were turned. That the occasion was momentous, no student of our ecclesiastical history can doubt. But for the exposition of the action of the assembly and for the interpretation of its results, we await the words of the wisely appointed speaker of the day.

Some time ago the learned historian of Congregationalism (we welcome him also here today), asked the question: "Why did not Massachusetts have a Saybrook Platform?" We should have answered, Mr. President, that it was because Massachusetts did not have a Saybrook; he answered that it was because that commonwealth did not have a Governor Saltonstall. But you will allow us, I am sure, to think that Saybrook did have something to do with it.

Address by Rev. Dr. Lewellyn Pratt.

The principal address was made by Rev. Dr. Lewellyn Pratt, of Norwich, who spoke in commeration of the bi-centennial of the Saybrook Platform.

Dr. Pratt in his address called attention to the fact that Saybrook was a kind of ecclesiastical center in the early history of the colony; this council in 1708 being the third convened there.

This council, although composed of only sixteen members—twelve ministers and four messengers or laymen—was a proper representative body of "picked" men worthy to act for the forty-one churches then existing. The council was called by the Legislature and its duties defined. The report of its action was made to the Legislature and approved by them at their October session in the same year. The report had two parts: a "Confession of Faith;" and "Heads of Agreement" and "Articles for the Administration of Discipline." Of these the fifteen rules for church government was the distinctive feature of the Saybrook Platform; the other two were simply reaffirmations of what was already received.

These fifteen articles were wrought out from models prepared in the four county conventions which sent the delegates, principally, it is claimed, from the one drafted by the Rev. James

193

Pierpont of New Haven. These articles did not interfere with the management of the affairs of the local church, but grouped the churches of each county into a consociation to which particular churches might refer cases too difficult for them to settle, and which should constitute a kind of standing council. They also grouped the ministers of each county into an association for mutual counsel, which should have the duty of examining and recommending the candidates for the ministry, have a watchful care of churches without pastors and see that they were supplied. Up to this time there were no regular stated meetings of ministers or groups of churches, and no regular way of introducing candidates into the ministry. The Platform was designed to bring these things into more system and order. The articles also recommended a general state association composed of one or more delegates from each of the county associations which should meet once a year. For this no duties were prescribed by the platform as this was in no sense a legislative body.

This was the Saybrook Platform—a scheme for the regular and orderly working of the churches in their fellowship with each other. The three prominent objects had in view, as stated by Dr. Leonard Bacon were: "1. The promotion of order and harmony among the ministers and churches. 2. The regular introduction of candidates into the ministry. 3. The establishment of a fixed and defined board of appeal—the consociation—a council, by which such difficulties as the particular churches themselves could not settle, might be adjusted."

Thus the work of the Saybrook synod was completed by unanimous vote, and the result was one month later presented to the Legislature for its approval at its autumnal session at New Haven. The Legislature acted at once, and after referring to the meeting at Saybrook and its unanimous agreement made this deliverance: "This Assembly doth declare their great approbation of such a happy agreement and do ordain that all the churches within this government that are, or shall be, thus united in doctrine, worship, and discipline, be, and for the future shall be established by law; provided that nothing herein shall be intended or construed to hinder or prevent any society or church, that is or shall be allowed by the laws of this government, who soberly differ or dissent from the united churches hereby established, from exercising worship or discipline in their own way according to their consciences."

So, by legislative enactment the churches united under this platform became the Established Church, or as it was known the "Standing Order," and all others were dissenters. This so continued for seventy-six years, or till 1784, when the state constitution was adopted, and the legal establishment was by omission abrogated, leaving all persons free to worship with whatever church they preferred. All, however, were still taxed for some church, the church of their own choice. In the year 1818, when a new constitution was formed, the last restriction was removed, and all the churches were left to voluntary support.

The platform was made the law for the colony before it had been submitted to the bodies whose delegates prepared it. The next year—1709—it was approved by the county conventions, and associations and consociations were formed in each of the four counties.

In May of that year when the first General Association met the Legislature ordered that the platform be revised and prepared for the press "and being revised, that the same shall be forthwith printed." Accordingly in 1710, "The Saybrook Platform" was issued—the first book ever printed in Connecticut.

All the Congregational churches existing in the colony at the time the synod met were sooner or later consociated, and so late as 1841, when there were two hundred and forty six, all but fifteen were consociated. Gradually, since the civil authority was wholly withdrawn, most of the consociations have been changed to conferences without judicial authority, and the churches have been left to select their own councils.

The union of church and state then existing here and elsewhere complicated and misapplied the work done at Saybrook. Making that into the established religion provoked opposition at the first, which increased in bitterness as the years went by. It was not, certainly at the first, opposition to the platform as an ecclesiastical system or to its doctrinal statement, but to the political use made of it. The numerous petitions and pamphlets of the time were directed against its enforcement or discrimination outside the established churches. Any other church-order enacted into law to be enforced upon all would have been resisted.

The General Court in October, 1708, cooly assumed that the platform had been "unanimously agreed to by the churches," and imposed the result by making it the religion sanctioned by the colony to the practical exclusion of others. The act ordaining that the churches united under this platform be established by law was passed before the churches had accepted it, thus imposing it even upon the churches.

Then, too, while the proviso inserted in the act of establishment made allowance for "sober dissent," the laws were enforced too often as if no such proviso were made, and the established or consociated churches were treated and legislated for as if including the whole colony. Much of the the legislation seemed designed to enforce the universal acceptance of the platform. This produced strifes and separations and did much to bring into disrepute the very system these enactments were intended to uphold.

This legal status was injurious in its effect upon the members of the favored churches. It made a favored class with special privileges; it was inconsistent with the democratic spirit of those made into an aristocracy; let to political and social ostracism; fostered that love of power which tends to tyranny, and separated those who should have lived together as brethern. It led to restlessness in the membership of the favored churches and drove many of them into the forming of other churches; for having come hither to escape state religions they could not help being restive under the inconsistency of state interference and dictation in religion, even when they constituted the state and administered the laws. "The Great Awakening" in the middle of the century, and the necessity of all uniting for common defense in the French and Indian wars and the War of the Revolution with the growth in the conception of civil liberty helped to liberate them and to prepare the way for a free church in a free state.

It may be wondered that the separation of church and state was so long delayed. It must be borne in mind that when our fathers planted churches independent under Christ all Christendom refused to tolerate them, and, on the defensive, they were jealous of their liberties and tried to protect them by law, following the general custom. It must also be remembered that practically dis-establishment in Connecticut dates from the formation of the colony into a state—more than one hundred and twenty-four years ago and in the 18th century, while even now in the 20th century it has not come in some other Christian countries.

That union of church and state left a stigma upon the scheme of church government here devised that does not belong to it taken by itself. It left also two entails from which we have not wholly emancipated ourselves—the parish system or ecclesiastical society and our independent, incorporated missionary societies. The churches came out of state connection in bondage to the ecclesiastical society; but it is more and more felt that the distinction between the secular and the spiritual in church matters does not require the dual organization, and that a single one is more safe tnd expedient. And, in like manner, it followed that if churches were incapable of conducting their pecuniary affairs, but needed a town or state and then an ecclesiastical society to transact such business, then they could not be exepected to be competent to unite and carry on vast missionary enterprises at home and abroad. Gradually the close, self-perpetuating mission boards are giving way to the representative principle: but their history shows how hard it has been to get away from dependence on outside control.

That there were grave infelicities in the platform viewed simply as rules for the churches is doubtless true. It was a compromise, and it had the possibility of double construction that usually inheres in compromises. Light is thrown upon the true interpretation by the minutes of the convention which formed the Consociation of New Haven county April 13, 1709. Doubts were expressed by the messengers or delegates whether Congregational liberty had been sufficiently guarded, whereupon Rev. Mr. Andrew of Milford and Rev. Mr. Pierpont of New Haven—both members of the Saybrook Synod and the latter the reputed author of the original draft from which the platform was formed—explained the fifteen articles separately, giving the intent of each. The articles were then adopted with the explanation, "to prevent a different interpretation hereafter." This interpretation placed at the time upon the articles "makes," as Dr. Bacon claimed in his Historical Discourses, "the platform a purely and thoroughly Congregational confederation of Congregational churches."

It is also to be observed that in the printing of the platform in 1710 it is divided into two parts, and that the "Heads of Agreement" and the "Articles of Discipline" go together, showing that the latter were always to be construed in conformity with the former.

It seems probable that, left to itself and to the free discussions that would have followed in the consociations as they were formed or as they would have developed separate from state interference, the platform would have been modified according to the original intent and made a safe and wholesome system of government. There were Presbyterian tendencies, for some of the synod were looking in that direction. These, fostered by the power of the state, became strong and in many of the records of that 18th century the consociated churches are called indiscriminately either Congregational or Presbyterian.

The Saybrook Platform was designed to remedy certain defects in the administration of the churches when working together. Although in some particulars it went too far, yet it is an interesting comment upon the foresight and wisdom of the fathers in that Saybrook synod that now, after two hundred years of centrifugal revolt, Congregationalists are drawing together and in their National Council are proposing measures that bear strong resemblances to the Saybrook plan and, though suggesting different names, are looking towards the consociation idea, and to a standing council. An instructive parallel might be drawn between the platform's fifteen articles and the eleven recommendations of the committee on polity of the National Council of 1907.

The union of church and state of two hundred years ago had a baneful effect upon Congregationalism, but the platform bore good fruits and ought to have borne a larger part in shaping our polity. As Massachusetts guarded the one principle—the independence of the local church, Connecticut emphasized its co-ordinate—the fellowship and ordered co-operation of the churches. It gave to our churches, what to this day they so sadly lack, the feeling and strength of organized life, and kept the churches of Connecticut from apostacy when so many in Massachusetts under the Cambridge platform, lapsed into error.

It would have been well if in our swing towards independency we had preserved more of what was really wholesome of the Saybrook system; and, while guarding our independence of outside control, had recognized that we need to be organized into a body, and had preserved some more system in organizing churches, in calling councils, in introducing into the ministry and dismissing from it, and some

practical and fraternal watch and care between churches of the same faith and order.

I close as I did twenty-three years ago at the two hundred and fiftieth anniversary of the settlement of Saybrook.

"Whatever fault," said Dr. Bacon in his historical address in 1859, "we may find in our ecclesiastical system, whatever erors may have been from time to time in the working of it, whatever reasons we may have to inquire whether the system needs revision and reconstruction. . . . . . our own Connecticut today, with all its imperfections, is the convincing testimony to the value of these two principles the association of pastors for professional fellowship and mutual cooperation, and the friendly confederation of the churches, which was first inaugurated and made effective by our fathers, here at Saybrook, 150 years ago."

[73]
ST. JOHN'S PARISH OF NORTH HAVEN.

CELEBRATING THE ONE HUNDRED AND FIFTIETH ANNIVERSARY OF ITS ORGANIZATION.

The Rev. Dr. Hart, Dean of Berkeley Divinity School, Makes Historical Address.

North Haven, October 30.

The one hundred and fiftieth anniversary of the organization of St. John's Episcopal parish of North Haven is being observed to-day, and the observance will be continued until Monday. The members of the parish are taking a great deal of interest in the event and those of other churches and citizens of the town generally are showing a sympathetic interest in it. the event and those of other churches and citizens of the town generally are showing a sympathetic interest in it. The entire town of New North Haven is proud of the venerable parish. People from New Haven and from other towns in the county and state are attending the exercises. On a page of the program of the exercises a condensed history of the parish is given. It reads as follows: "In 1723 the first meeting of Church of England was held at Mr. Ebenezer Blakeslee's and a temporary society was formed. In 1740, on the Monday after Easter, a union church was organized by the churchmen of Wallingford and North Haven, and a church building was erected in the Pond Hill district near where Mr. Arthur Blakeslee now lives. Of the men who assisted in organizing this, the beginning of the North Haven and also of the Wallingford parish, five out of eight were North Haven men, so that we may really be said to date our history from that date. On April 24, 1759, St. John's parish was organized, and on St. John the Evangelist day, 1761, the new building was dedicated by the Rev. Mr. Punderson on the spot where the rectory now stands. The present church building was consecrated in June, 1836, by Bishop Brownell. Twenty-five years later an addition was made to it, completing it as it is at present, the most perfect example of its style of architecture anywhere in

this vicinity." The Rev. Arthur F. Lewis, the rector of the parish, has general charge of the arrangements.

The celebration of the anniversary began in the parish church this forenoon, at 10:45, with the Litany and holy communion, at which the Right Reverend Chauncey B. Brewster, the bishop of Connecticut, was the celebrant. The sermon was preached by the Rev. Dr. Stewart Means. A luncheon was served at 1 o'clock. In the afternoon, at 3 o'clock, there was a historical service, at which the Rev. Dr. Hart made the address.

Sermon by the Rev. Dr. Hart.

The Rev. Dr. Samuel Hart, dean of the Berkeley Divinity school at Middletown, gave the historical address at the service at 3 p. m. Dr. Hart spoke as follows:

Remember the days of old,
  Consider the years of successive generations;
Ask thy father, and he will tell thee;
  Thine elders, and they will say to thee:
"When the Most High gave to the nations their inheritance,
  When he separated the sons of men,
He fixed the borders of the peoples
  According to the number of the children of Israel.
"For Jehovah's portion is his people;
Jacob is the lot of his inheritance."

Thus, we read, the great law-giver and leader of Israel turned the thoughts of his people to the past and bade them learn the lessons of history, that from these they might draw encouragement and warning for the time to come. His song was to be a witness to them, its stirring words remaining in the minds and on the lips of successive generations,

THE REV. ARTHUR F. LEWIS,
Rector St. John's Parish.

to wake them from indifference and neglect of the law, to reprove them for breach of their covenant with their God, and to strengthen them for renewed allegiance and for more faithful duty. Thus he bids his people look over the ever-lengthening vista of past generations, and ask those of the earlier days, whose experience was complete and whose work was ended, what God had done for them and with

them, and what their earlier history meant. And he adds the answer which will come from fathers and elder men, who have known the works of the Lord and who can interpret their meaning. They will, he declares, assure those who call back to them and ask for an interpretation of the days of old, that there was in the far-off time a plan and a purpose for the care and blessing of Israel. The history of the nations, they will testify, was ordered with reference to the covenant people; when the Most High assigned to each nation its place, He fixed its limits "according to the number of the children of Israel." It is a poet's way of saying that all other things were so ordered that Israel, the chosen of Jehovah, should have his place well defined and secure; that while all were under the protection of Him who was Lord of all, a special blessing should be assured to those who were called to a special covenant relation with Him as their own God. And the reason for this was that Jehovah had chosen one people to be His own portion, even the sons of Jacob to be His own inheritance. We do not need to look far to see what is not stated here but seems implied at the end of this very song and is clearly declared again and again in the words of psalmists and prophets—that "God's dealings with Israel have an interest and importance for the world at large," that God's people hold His blessing and their prerogatives in trust in order that as His ministers they may prepare others to receive those very blessings, or even something greater to which they are preliminary, and that through them they may be imparted until all the nations confess the true God and yield to Him. We must not forget this, even while we learn the application to our own times of the words written long ago, and read a lesson for ourselves as Israel was bidden to store in memory the echo of the words of their fathers.

It is certainly a part of what we call the philosophy of history that its events are ordered by a divine Providence for the fulfilment of a great moral plan; not merely as Bishop Butler has taught us, that the universe is administered in the interests of virtue, but that what we call "the changes and chances of this mortal life" work into a great plan for the advancement of God's kingdom. When we stand far enough from any period of history to enable us to study it in some sort of perspective, and can trace its causes and effects, we see that its relations to the truth of Christ's religion and to the organized body of Christ's church are among the important matters presented to our minds. One event after another, interesting perhaps in itself but seemingly of no great general importance, is seen to work into a great plan for carrying on the life of Christianity in its organized society and for establishing or increasing its influence. "God has set the bounds of the people with reference to the welfare of the children of Israel."

The annals of the diocese of Connecticut in its early years, as they come into our thoughts and hearts on successive anniversaries, afford many examples of the truth of all this. A quarter of a century has passed since we kept the centenary of the consecration of our first bishop, "apostle of

the new world;" and its lessons must be read again in the ears of a new generation; but when they are thus read, or for the older among us recalled, it will be seen that the act of faith, on the part of the clergy of Connecticut in choosing Dr. Seabury, on his part in seeking consecration from the Scottish bishops, and on their part in giving out of their deep poverty the richness of spiritual gifts, was the inspiration of new life for the church, and, that not only in our new republic and in Scotland, but also in England, even reaching out from England to her colonies. In like manner, as really if not as conspicuously, the history of our older parishes shows an influence working upon them and in them and from them which has helped and shaped the growth of the historic church of God in the colony and the state. And each has its special lesson, as each has had and still has its present work; for that lesson we must ask our fathers and they will tell us, our elders and they will show us.

The story of this parish, observing its third jubilee two years after the second centenary of the oldest, and for some fifteen years the only parish of the church of England in Connecticut, and (as was just said) twenty-five years after the first centenary of the consecration of our first bishop, suggests much which all such recurring anniversaries have in common, while yet it has its own special points of interest and brings its own special contribution to the history of the diocese. We go back for its inspiration to that memorable day in 1722, when four of the leading ministers of the established order went out from a conference with their fathers and brethren in the College library in New Haven, strengthened in their conviction that they could no longer preach the Word of God and minister the sacraments of His Church without the authority conferred by ordination from a bishop. Two of them, Mr. Cutler and Mr. Browne, came directly from academic life, and in fact were the rector and tutor, the whole teaching force of the college; a third, Mr. Johnson, had been a tutor there, and was always a scholar and a teacher; the fourth, and the only one who distinctly represented the parochial ministry, was Mr. James Wetmore, 27 years old, and a graduate of the college of four years' standing. He had come to this village to be its first minister under the Congregational order, had been ordained over its church in 1718, had ministered to its people some four years in the house of Ebenezer Blakeslee, and in 1722 had just begun to preach in the new meeting-house, when he announced that he felt it his duty to withdraw from his ministry and to seek episcopal ordination in England. We do not wonder that his people were surprised and grieved, especially as they had declared that they did "sit very easy under Mr. Wetmore's ministry," and that most of them remained in the former organization. A few, however, as we shall soon see, followed their first minister and professed their adherence to the Church of England. Mr. Wetmore crossed the ocean for ordination, and returned to spend the rest of his life as missionary and priest at Rye in the province of New York, where he died but a short time after the organization of this parish. We do not know that he ever came again to this place; but it is to his honored name that we trace the inspiration of the work for which we do this day praise God.

Dr. Ezra Stiles, of famous memory, a native of this place and son of Mr. Wetmore's successor in the Congregational ministry, tells us that two Blakeslees and Aaron Tuttle were the only men who were led by their pastor into the communion of the Church of England, that one churchman came from England eight years later, and that then for twenty-two years there were but two accessions, meaning presumably of grown-up men. They were few indeed, though their families were in several cases large; but they held faithfully to their convictions. In 1741, nineteen years after the first break was made, they met with the few men of like convictions in Wallingford and Cheshire and organized a union parish, one of the two wardens and four of the six vestrymen elected being North Haven men; and in the Pond Hill district of Wallingford they built a small church, some twelve feet square. It was not long used for worship as in each of the towns named a more spacious church was soon erected; but you may well think of it with reverence as the religious home of your ancestors in the faith in a day of small undertakings, but of strong convictions and of brave hearts. There the life was fostered under the general care of the Rev. Theophilus Morris and perhaps some one or more of the few clergymen in the colony, which presently manifested itself in the establishment of three neighboring parishes. That with which we are especially concerned, the parish of St. John's church, North Haven, was organized a hundred and fifty years ago, on the twenty-fourth day of April, 1755, being the second Tuesday after Easter. In the course of a generation a great change had taken place. For the three men who had declared themselves churchmen in 1722 or 1723, thirty-six, with twenty-four different surnames, signed an elaborate declaration of principles, professing themselves "members of the national established Church of England," and submitting themselves "to the pastoral care of the Revd. Ebenezer Punderson, the venerable society's missionary in Connecticut, but more especially in this town, hoping and trusting to be at all times intreated in his prayers and blessings and pastoral labors, so far as his extensive charge will admit of." The officers elected were Ebenezer Blakeslee and Matthew Blakeslee for wardens, Abraham Blakeslee, Zophar Blakeslee, and Gershom Barnes for vestrymen, and Oliver Blakeslee for clerk. Mr. Punderson, under whose care they placed themselves, was in charge of the church parishes in West Haven and New Haven, and now agreed to give a quarter of his time to North Haven; like others of our colonial clergy, he was a veritable general missionary, his earlier labors extending from North Groton to Hempstead on Long Island, to Hebron, and to Middletown, while from New Haven he reached Guilford and Branford, as well as this neighborhood. Services were held first in Ebenezer Blakeslee's house, which was the foster-home of this congregation, as it had been of the congregation of the standing order; but soon a church, thirty-eight feet by thirty, was erected on the northeast corner of the green, a spot conceded by the first ecclesiastical society to "those that profess to the Church of England;" and on St. John Evangelist's day, December 27, 1761, as the pleased clerk enters in the records, "St. John's church in North Haven

was dedicated by the Revd. Mr. Punderson, itinerant missionary in Connecticut." Before this time fourteen children had been baptized. The records of the "Vestry"—that is to say the body of communicants, for as yet there was no parish or society in law—began at once, and show the regular election of officers and presently of "Quiristers," and occasionally of some one "to assist in Reading;" the duty of reading the service and a sermon in the absence of an ordained minister falling ordinarily (I suppose) upon the wardens.

In 1784 a revision of the laws of the state having been made at the close of the Revolution, and "dissenters of the Episcopal church" and of other names having been empowered to form ecclesiastical societies, meetings "of the members of the Episcopal church and Congregation in the parish of North Haven" began to be held, at which a prudential committee was elected, taxes were laid, and provision was made for the maintenance of worship and for other expenses. This was probably the only place in Connecticut where annual meetings of the "Episcopal society and Congregation," known as the Second Ecclesiastical society, were "in the form of and in conjunction with the other society" in the town, and where the assistant clerk of the First or Congregational society was the clerk of the Second or Episcopal society. Such was the case here for years.

When Mr. Punderson, in 1762, was transferred to Rye, there to succeed good Mr. Wetmore, his place here and in parts adjacent was taken by the Rev. Samuel Andrews, a native of what is now the town of Meriden. He "returned from England"—so writes the clerk of the vestry—"January 23d, Anno Domini 1762, missionary for 3 parishes viz., North Haven, Wallingford and Cheshire, and delivered his first discourse February 14, at St. John's church in North Haven, to an audience of one hundred people." There had been much dissension in the standing order of this neighborhood; the "Great Awakening" had been a cause of much excitement and unrest; the "Wallingford controversy" had stirred up much hard feeling; the ministry of the Rev. Isaac Stiles had been

ended by death just as his resignation had been demanded by a considerable part of his people (his own son said that he had sinned the sin unto death in opposing the New Light and that it was imputed unto himself); and many were welcoming the sober ways of the English church. The historian of your town says truly of "Parson" Andrews that "the influence of this man accounts for much of the religious history of North Haven, Wallingford, Meriden and Cheshire between the year 1762 and the close of the Revolutionary War. He was a man of estimable character, lovable in every respect, and an indefatigable worker." And the historian of our diocese bears witness that he was a prophet who had honor in his own country. When the war came he showed himself a loyalist; but though hindered in his work elsewhere he was not molested here. After the independence of the states was assured he withdrew to New Brunswick and died there at an advanced age. When he went away there were forty-five names of men on the list of members of the parish and to these thirty-five more were added before the end of the century. He was rarely able to give to this congregation more than one-quarter of

his time, and his home was in Wallingford; but he was the pastor of this people, and his works here do still follow him.

The story which follows the Revolution is that of a quiet parish in a quiet town of scarce 1,200 inhabitants, a large part of whom were under the pastoral care of Dr. Benjamin Trumbull, honored as the only great historian of Connecticut, but honored also as the pastor of a congregation here for sixty years. The church people were faithful and well-instructed, and they occupied a respectable position in the community; but they were not able to provide for the constant services of a resident clergyman; and perhaps their very proximity to stronger parishes, while it gave them the opportunity of calling upon able men for a part of their time, made it all the harder for them to stand in this respect alone. Between the time of the building of the church and the election of the first sole rector, nearly a century passed, and in this time thirty clergymen officiated here with some regularity.

Two of them were North Haven men, Edward and Solomon Blakeslee; the names of several others bring memories of good work elsewhere, as of David Butler in Troy, Seth Hart in Hempstead, Reuben Ives and Tillotson Bronson in Cheshire, Smith Miles in Chatham, Ashbel Baldwin, last survivor of those first ordained in this land, in Stratford. In 1833, the Rev. Charles William Bradley, honored in matters civil and political as well as ecclesiastical, came here; he laid the corner-stone of this new church building on the 12th day of June in the following year, and it was consecrated by Bishop Brownell a twelvemonth later. Other names follow his on the roll, among which we note those of Alonzo B. Chapin, historian and controversialist; Charles W. Everest, poet and scholar; Seth B. Paddock, pastor and teacher, from whom have come three bishops of this church; Frederick Sill, under whose care the bell was purchased for the church tower; Alonzo G. Shears, physician and teacher, in whose day the legacy of Ebenezer Pierpont turned the tide of the parish's history towards its present prosperity; Seth Davis, first occupant of the rectory, and Joseph Scott, first in the long succession to be elected rector. To him succeeded the energetic rector of half a century ago, Cuthbert C. Barclay, under whom the chancel was built as an addition to the church, and who preached in it the centennial sermon at a special commemorative service. There are doubtless some here to-day who recall that commemoration, and who have known all who have ministered here in the past fifty years; and there are others to whom that day seems to belong to an ancient history and the names of many who have been active in it bring no personal memories. Some have fallen asleep; and the blessed memory of men of older and of later time brightens this day, while we think of their lives built into the spiritual fabric and of their influence reaching to men and women whom they never knew. There can be none, I think, who hears my voice, that does not recall with gratitude a strong and gentle life, nineteen years of which were given to unremitting pastoral work here, and eight years more to a quiet but none the less real benediction, and reckon it as a choice part of the heritage that the Lord has given to His people here. [The Rev. William Lusk died January 17, 1907.] And some remain, bringing to-day a thanksgiving and a benediction with them, and quickening the memories of their special work; one under whose care the church was again enlarged to its present spacious dimensions, adding to its suitableness for its sacred purposes and (if possible) to its seemly dignity; one under whom it was again consecrated almost forty years ago this very day by the great fourth bishop of this diocese; and others of whom I venture to say that they still seem as in a sense belonging to you. From all, living and departed, comes to your rector—long may he remain yours!—and to yourselves the word of cheer, the inspiration of the abiding past, the encouragement of the opening future.

In all that has been said of the clergymen who have officiated here, we have not forgotten, we could not forget, the faithful men and women and the children of the congregation. From those earliest days when the worshippers were few and the priestly ministrations infrequent, but when ten families furnished eighty-three persons, past the time—it was a hundred and twenty years ago—when there were elected thirteen choristers and twelve "singers on the treble," and when the close of the eighteenth century showed that there had been three hundred baptisms, down to the time rather more than a century ago when but thirty-four communicants were enrolled, of whom eleven were widows, and then passing on to the present time, when that number has been increased more than six-fold; what thoughts of fidelity on the part of wardens and vestrymen, readers and singers, teachers and learners, worshippers and suppliants, fill the mind! Some names there are which call for mention here: Samuel Pierpont, warden for nearly a whole period of fifty-nine years; Evelyn Blakeslee, warden for fifty years; Ezra Stiles, warden for thirty-two years; Joseph Pierpont, clerk for well-nigh fifty years; the names themselves tell of the working of a strong conviction which brought their holders into the historic English church with its episcopal organization; and we see the fruits of the work of these men and others like them. "There be of them that have left a name behind them, and some there be which have no memorial; but their righteous deeds have not been forgotten. With their seed shall remain continually a good inheritance, and their children are within the covenant. Their bodies are buried in peace, and their works endure to all generations."

You will perhaps think that these are but simple records, "short and simple annals," and it is hardly worth while, even at an anniversary time, to dwell much upon their details; that in part they are common to this parish with many another, and that in no way can they greatly affect us now. Is it indeed so? Does all our inspiration come from the present and from the thought of the immediate future? Nay, rather are there not lessons from your early and later history, is there not a life flowing from it of special value to you, my brethren of this now venerable yet youthful parish? And have you made no contribution to the life and the energy of this historic diocese, strong for action because she is well founded, ready to undertake new work with courage because she has already done much, firm in holding to principles and therefore trusting herself for new ventures? Your history has been divinely guided, you may well be assured, in order that you may in these days, when you enter on a fourth jubilee period, do a work for God, for His church, for the community, for yourselves, which shall have its special value and its special reward. "Remember the days of old, ask they father, and he will tell thee, thine elders and they will answer thee, that the Most High so guides the order of the world that it may further the work of His holy church; for the Lord's portion is His people, and we are the lot of His inheritance." With the hymns of thanksgiving to-day, we join solemn vows of dedication; with the memories of the past we look for bright visions of the future. The Lord our God be with us and with our children as He was with our fathers, a guide and a stay, the strength of our lives and our portion forever!

[74]
SOME GLIMPSES OF EARLY HARTFORD.
INTERESTING PAPER BY REV. DR. SAMUEL HART.
Read Before the Connecticut Historical Society.
DEALS WITH FIRST 25 YEARS IN THE COLONY.

An interesting paper on early glimpses of Hartford was read by Rev. Dr. Samuel Hart at the meeting of the Connecticut Historical Society last evening, as follows:—

Two hundred and seventy-five years ago—a quarter of a millenium and a quarter of a century—late in the summer the first English settlers came to the site of Hartford. We are told that on the 3rd day of September in the year 1635, William Westwood was sworn constable for the new plantation on the Connecticut, and as a constable was the one thing absolutely necessary for the exercise of civil authority, so the possession of a constable was proof of an orderly community. What did the new settlers, thus recognized as in a true sense a body politic, find here near the head of navigation on what the Indians called the Long River and the Dutch the Fresh River? And what were their experiences in the early years of their life here? And as preliminary to an outline answer to these questions we may ask, what was the place to which they and their neighbor colonists came?

First, then, the place was in the interior of a practically unknown land and beyond its first great river. The settlement of Pilgrims at Plymouth was but fifteen years in the past and that of Puritans on the shores of Massachusetts Bay was but five or six years old and no one had pushed far into the wilderness which lay to the west and extended no one knew how far. Those who had sailed along the coast had seen fair shores and rivers which to the former inhabitants of a small island were great streams, and the fame of a greater river had reached them, up which Henry Hudson had gone for miles before he found that it was not

an arm of the sea or a strait through which a passage lay to China and the Indies. But to go far up a river and make a home on its further bank, or to strike across wild woodlands until it was reached and crossed, this was to make a venture of courage and faith. If Abram the Hebrew showed himself the man that he was and gained a name for himself because he trusted himself to providence and crossed the great river, the river Euphrates, surely those who left the comparatively safe shores of Massachusetts Bay and crossed the great river of Connecticut were heroes of faith as was he. And they expected to have their faith tested. The Gog and Magog, powers of antichrist, were not for our ancestors nations of the north, pushing down upon the ancient peoples of the belt within which religion and civilization had been confined; their dark land was the west, into which they themselves were bidden to go that they might wage war against the powers of evil. And what was more natural to expect that the last great struggle would be in the end of the world; as well in space as in time, and here on the west bank of the Connecticut?

But, even if it was destined to be a spiritual battle-field, as well as a place of possible bodily conflict, it was a beautiful place to which they came and in which they awaited the coming of their more dignified brethren. Others had been here, and had told in the Bay of the fair land, suggesting withal (we may be sure) that it lay south of the line of the Massachusetts government. In 1633, William Holmes from Plymouth had sailed up the river to the Dutch Point, and had pushed on to the mouth of the Tunxis; and in the same year John Oldham had come overland from Massachusetts Bay. The Plymouth men did no more than set up a trading post at this northernmost spot, not very far below the rapids; but soon permanent colonists came from Dorchester, bringing the church which had been organized in England some years before; and some of them were certainly placed and housed before there were settled inhabitants here. Also to the south of this spot there had come in 1634 a colony of Watertown people, themselves too bringing a church organization effected in England but a few months later than that of the Dorchester men. And from there had come to the Massachusetts Newtown an account of the opportunities for life and work here in a new home, not too near to the ecclesiastical colony of Boston and its neighbor towns. And who that has seen this part of the valley of the Connecticut in the early summer will wonder that the early visitors spoke well of it, and that those who followed them were glad to take up their homes in it? There must have been the wide meadows, quite open or but scantily wooded, for there were heavy freshets in those days as well as now; there must have been the beauty of grass and foliage, and perhaps here and there a little patch of soil turned up by the Indians with the strange kind of corn called maize growing upon it; there must have been the attraction to hunters to look in the forest for deer and other game and to catch from the river the salmon and the shad.

Moreover, the river led by a sufficient ample stream down to the sound and the control of its mouth, though claimed by the Dutch of New Amsterdam, was practically, and soon became actually, in the hands of the fellow-countrymen of those who were coming hither. And under protection of a charter right, or at least of a grant from a chartered company, with a governor and a captain and an engineer, Saybrook was fitted to be a defence and help for the men up river. To be sure, there was also the Huyshope, the House of Good Hope, on the south bank of the Little River, and the Dutch had their boat with its threatening name of Onrush; but the garrison was a quiet one, taking itself quietly rather than seriously, and certainly not taken seriously by the Englishmen who sailed past it and settled down but a little way above it.

Such were the beginnings of the Connecticut Newtown, our Hartford; the large emigration here, with the church organized at the Massachusetts Newtown in 1632, did not arrive until the following year. Those who had come to face an unknown winter, after it was too late to make full provision against it, must have felt that almost any place would be better than that which had been chosen for them. Very early there set in a season of terrible cold and heavy snow. By the middle of November the river was frozen over; the settlers could not keep warm and could not get sufficient food from the Indians; and some seventy of them walked on the ice and along the river banks to the fort at the mouth of the river; to keep themselves from freezing and starvation. There they found relief, and thence they were able—at least part of them—to sail back to Boston. But this experience did not break up the colony or hinder the great emigration appointed for the following year. The Newtown people sold their houses to new comers who organized a new church; eight commissioners were appointed by the government which had given them tardy permission to remove, and these eight men held a "corte" at the Connecticut Newtown on the 26th of April, and the last day of May saw the emigrants on the journey, most of them on foot, a few perhaps on horses. Mistress Hooker on a litter, driving cattle and goats and swine, on a fortnight's journey through the wilderness. They went almost due west, struck the great river near the mouth of the Chicopee, followed its east bank for a ways, managed to cross it—it was very likely at freshet time—somewhere near the Dorchester settlement, naturally below the mouth of the Tunxis, and arrived at their destination sometime in June in the year of grace, 1636.

Why did so many men and women, and among them persons of influence and intellectual power, undertake this journey in search of a home, when they had as yet been less than three years in the homes for which they had crossed the ocean? We have an outline record of the arguments which were pleaded in the Massachusetts General Court for and against the proposition of removal. The petitioners made a three-fold plea: First, that they had not accomodation for their cattle and that the towns were set so near each other; the said towns being Boston and Cambridge, with a wide river between them, and the back country unlimited and unclaimed; second, the fruitfulness and commodiousness of Connecticut, and the danger of having it possessed by others, Dutch or English; a good secondary reason, but hardly enough to lead to so great an undertaking at such a time; thirdly—and here is the sufficient reason, though of itself it could not be called an explanation—"the strong bent of their spirits to move thither." Yes, it was "a strong bent of their spirits" which made them so determined, and which conquered all objections. But is there no way of accounting for this bent—this more than inclination? It was but two years since Thomas Hooker and Samuel Stone and John Haynes had crossed the ocean with their friend, John Cotton. Why did they want to get away from him and from the sister church to which he with Mr. Wilson ministered, and for the government which had been set up under a royal charter in a colony of England? Why did they, incurring the reproach of each of faith and persistence, to use the words of a contemporary writer, "highe them away to a new plantation?" The real reason doubtless was that they wished "to remove from under the power, as well as out of the bounds, of the Massachusetts." In fact, it is easy to see from what they did; as soon as they were able to do it, the reason why they went as far west as beyond the great river and as far south as to be well across the line of the chartered colony. Those who had settled at the Massachusetts Newtown certainly were not in accord, ecclesiastically or politically, with their neighbors in Boston, and were not willing to take either their church law or their civil ordinances from them.

I doubt if it has been sufficiently noted that of the two colonies within the limits of what is now Connecticut, the River colony stood more nearly parallel to that of Plymouth and the Quinnipiac Colony to that of the Bay. Plymouth was a settlement of independents, who came from England as from Babylon and repented for their sin that they had ever communed with the established Church of England; they repudiated all connections of church and state, and for that reason had no religious test for voters or for office holders; moreover, they were not under a charter or directly dependent upon the Crown. The Bay Colony was made up of a body of Puritans, who claimed that they had not left the Church of England, but on the contrary were determined to hold fast to it and to reform it; they exercised civil authority under rights derived from the king; and they required as soon as they could do so that the rights of suffrage and of holding office should be restricted to men who were members of their purified and reformed churches. Presently, no doubt, they carried their reformation so far that they utterly changed the policy which they had received by inheritance; but that in no way affected their theory. Now on our side of the line, New Haven, which looked independent in matters civil and in matters ecclesiastical, really followed Puritan Massachusetts rather than independent Plymouth, having an even more rigid rule as to the privileges of citizenship and the exercise of the suffrage; while the River Colony of which Hartford was the center, in matters of greatest importance, was in agreement with Plymouth, acted on Independent principles, and imposed no ecclesiastical test, except only that the governor must be a member of the church as established. This divergence between the new settlers at Newtown and their neighbors in the slightly older settlement at Boston was almost immediately felt. Some thought that Mr. Cotton and Mr. Hooker were too great men—men of too nearly an equal greatness—to be satisfactory neighbors to each other; but quite apart from this, the seed

of independency was too deeply rooted in Mr. Hooker's mind, already proving its existence (we may be sure) in his earnest and cogent sermons and conversations and ready to bear fruit in a safe and promising place. Here, I am sure, is the explanation of the "strong bent of mind" of the Newtown people, that they might leave Newtown on the Charles for Newtown on the Connecticut, and the persistence with which they urged that they be let go some days' journey into the wilderness, that they might have things their own way. They did not object to the appointment of a constable for the first few months or of a commission for a year or so after that time; they felt sure that the commission would not be renewed, or that being renewed it could be protested against and removed; and with a spirit shown over and again in connection with their history and that of their descendants, they were willing to submit for a while in the certainty that they would soon gain all that they wished. Thus it happened that with some formalities of a legal proceeding, there was in the few years 1633-1636 what one has called, "an irruption of subjects of the King of England in an unorganized and unoccupied country." Those who came here knew pretty well what they had in mind, what they were undertaking and what they expected to do. And suddenly, on land which which owed none but a shadowy allegience to any external authority, there sprang up this typical democracy of the modern world, if not the typical democracy of all history.

A good many years ago, a map was made of the Hartford of 1640, based on land records and other like sources, which I suppose is still regarded as accurate, except as to some minor matters; we wait a new map with illustrative matter from the skilled hand of our corresponding secretary. There must have been at this time towards a thousand inhabitants, including some three hundred grown men in the three towns of the colony; probably more than a third were here. The town was laid out on a large scale, with so many wards that it was a long time before any others were needed. There was the meeting-house yard and market-place, at first with a small meeting-house on the south side, presently replaced by a large building on the east side near the corner of the road to the river which served its purpose for almost a full century; there also was the jail with the whipping-post and the stocks, and the graveyard. The main road from the Palisade to Centinel Hill passed the yard on the west, running to the little river, which it looked across to the road which led to the Ox Pasture and to Wethersfield. From the nature of the case there was no ford there; to find it one must go further down the little river to a place to which a branch road from the southern town led, and from which the main traveled road led to the north.

From Centinel Hill, where was the pound, one could go to the cow pasture and Windsor, or Up Neck or to Soldiers' Field. The mill was well up the little river, beyond the place where now are the stepping-stones; a road led to it from meeting-house yard and from it into the country west. There was a main landing on the great river near the place where the ferry-boats later passed in, a Dutch landing at the little river near a fort, and an Indian landing in the South Meadow. The large lots of the chief men, Pastor

Hooker and Teacher Stone and Elder Goodwin and Governor Hayes were on the west bank of the little river, separated from it by a highway, and east of the main stand; nobody lived east of which is now Front street. The common fields lay to the north and the south and the southwest; there was no central common or green. It should be added that as early as 1636 it seems that the colonists went through the form of buying the land occupied or claimed by the town from the Indians, a former sale of part of it to the Dutch being ignored by both sellers and purchasers.

Thus the place must have looked, in some respects like a rather large and compact village and in others like an incipient city when the Connecticut colonists acting as one body, the Massachusetts commission for their government having expired, took the administration of affairs into their own hands. A "Corte" of two magistrates from each of the three towns, with Mr. William Pynchon from Agawam further up the river when he was minded to attend, met from time to time, beginning on the 26th of April, 1636. On the 21st of February in the next year it gave to each of the towns a new name in place of that which it had brought from Massachusetts. Newtown was named Hartford, from Hertford the birthplace of Mr. Stone; Dorchester was given the name of royal Windsor; and Watertown was called Wethersfield, from the place of John Tailcoat's birth. On the first of May, 1637, independence having been fully gained, a body of the six magistrates, with nine deputies (three from each town), met in Hartford under the name of the General Court and quietly took the administration of affairs into its hands.

Here would be the place, did time and ability permit, to discuss the question whether the government of Connecticut thus undertaken and presently put into form by the fundamental orders, was the act of one sovereign body or the result of a federation or three bodies originally independent. Historians do not agree in their answer to the question nor do lawyers and judges; but it is my opinion that the weight of evidence is decidedly against the federation theory, and that we are to see in these acts which constitute a government acts of sovereignty exercised by one body of Englishmen, individually perhaps, subjects of the English crown but isolated from its administration and at liberty to provide for themselves. In other words, Connecticut was from the first one commonwealth; her citizens were in three or four settlements, but they all belonged together and all met (at least by deputation) in one General Assembly for consultation and legislation and one General Court for the administration of justice. The rights of the towns as political entities were allowed from the first but the sovereignty was, as it always has remained, in the commonwealth; and that sovereignty, assumed at the first defined by the fundamental orders, recognized in a remarkable way by the Crown in the charter acknowledged by the crown after 150 years in the treaty with the thirteen independent though United States, held for some forty years under the charter's provisions and now for well nigh a century under the provisions of a constitution, is the heritage of the free and independent state of Connecticut.

It is interesting to see and to note how soon the sturdy little commonwealth assumed for herself the pre-

rogatives of sovereignty, asking no one's permission, and went through a great variety of experiences which belong to an organized and responsible state.

Almost, if not quite, the first was with all due formality to declare and wage war. It was in 1637, when one would think that there was enough to do here in the river settlement, that it was decided by the citizens that their own safety and that of their brethren at the mouth of the river called for what they called offensive warfare against the Pequots. The was was proclaimed in a very civilized way; it was begun in a very religious way, for Mr. Stone prayed all night at Saybrook before the expedition left the harbor, but it was carried out in what we must, for justice's sake, call a very barbarous way, though doubtless those who took part in it justified their act to their own conscience. "One wonders," says Dr. Walker, "whether, even then, a better use might not have been made of the proprietors of the soil than shooting and burning them." Only the next year, as he reminds us, the settlements on the river were saved from what seemed a fatal famine by Indians who came from Deerfield with fifty canoe loads of corn and sold it at reasonable rates. This led to the keeping of a Thanksgiving day on the 4th of October in that year, 1638.

The next special act of the new colony—the word may be used though not quite accurately—was of an ecclesiastical character, in the third month after the slaughter of the Pequots. The church in Boston had fallen into difficulties, every church fell into difficulties rather often in those days; there was the almost incomprehensible antinomian controversy, and the very extraordinary behavior of Mistress Anne Hutchinson, who expressed very freely her opinion of the ministers and of their preaching of a covenant of works. An ecclesiastical synod was called and to it the ministers of Hartford, Mr. Hooker and Mr. Stone, were summoned; with them went as delegates from the church Mr. Ludlow and Mr. Pyncheon, the two chief men of the former magistrates, carrying with them—a most extraordinary thing to do—the scalps which had lately been cut from the Pequots' heads, and also, if the narrative can be believed, the skins of some of those warriors. It is enough to say of the synod that it sat for twenty-two days, and condemned eighty-two distinct teachings of the antinomians as being "some blasphemous, others erroneous and all unsafe." We shall see presently that Hartford soon enjoyed a controversy of her own.

In the next year, 1638, the first steps were taken toward the most momentous event in the history of this commonwealth. A general court was elected for the purpose of framing a permanent code of laws for the colony. We do not know the details of the work; we can read the outlines of Mr. Hooker's lecture on the last day of May drawing up a scheme of government; we are assured of the ability of Mr. Ludlow, the only lawyer in the colony, to frame that scheme in due form of words; we know the issue of it. On the 14th day of January in the year 1639, a general assembly of the whole colony, meeting at Hartford, adopted a series of eleven fundamental orders which formed the first written constitution in the history of the human race. It was a statement of governmental power with fixed limita-

tions, an embodiment of the idea of a democracy putting itself under restraint, such as all real constitutions adopted since that time have been. Not merely a part of a code for the regulation of affairs and the administration of justice, important enough to stand by itself and to be made a little difficult of change, this constitution was in reality a declaration of principles put into operation in an absolutely independent government. There was no recognition of a supreme authority in England or anywhere else on earth from which the right to establish or define a government had been received; there was no printed recognition of an aristocracy, practically an oligarchy such as ruled in Massachusetts or in New Haven; "Democracy," said John Cotton, "I do not consider that ever God did ordain as a fit government either for church or commonwealth." And there was no recognition of any power of the "church's elders" to act as a court of advice or revision or the necessity of church membership as a step for admission to the exercise of the franchise. With reverent recognition of the divine providence of Almighty God, and of the duty of a people when they are gathered together, to have an orderly and decent government established, the inhabitants and residents of Windsor, Hartford and Wethersfield did associate and join themselves to be as one public state or commonwealth; they determined how magistrates, including a governor, should be elected, that there should also be deputies from the several towns who should meet together to advise and consult of all such things as might concern the good of the public; that in the general courts should consist the supreme powers, but that the election of magistrates should be done by the whole body of freemen. And nothing was said as to the possibility of amendment or change of any part of this fundamental law. It was very quietly done, this momentous act; but it called for strong determination and great courage; it made Connecticut stand by herself in a position of her own choosing which might have been reckoned as defiance not only of the mother country across the sea but also of the neighboring colonies; it was a bold experiment in matters political, or rather it was a bold declaration of principles of which the colonists were so absolutely certain that they did not feel that they were submitting them to experiment. "The republic thus constituted," says a modern historian, "silently grew until it became the strongest political structure on the continent;" and its principles, adopted by the Federal Convention of 1787, shaped the constitution of the republic of this Western world in its most critical and important parts. Its adoption was the beginning of American democracy, and that is the same as to say, of all properly safe-guarded popular government.

After four years, we find another act of our colony, especially interesting as coming at that time. She had organized for herself a government which was in no true sense of the word federal because it was the act of one body of men acting together. Now in 1643, Connecticut joined with Massachusetts, Plymouth and New Haven, Saybrook also having some place, to form a federation under the name of the "United Colonies of New England." Concerted action was needed against the Indians and might be needed at any time against the Dutch; and no one knew, though some could guess, what the French colonies to the North would like to do. This confederacy, into which Rhode Island was not admitted because it was not thought to have an orderly government, was of great service to New England at the time, and it taught lessons of united action which were of great use at a later time; but it was an experiment in practise for an emergency, rather than the application of principles in fixed government; its influence on the future history of the land can not be compared for a moment with that of the assembly of freemen at Hartford which adopted a real constitution of a real democracy and put both into operation. Still that this colony entered into it, and that it was treated by its neighbors as an equal, proves the permanence and dignity of the position to which it had attained.

Another event of importance, one that both asserted and strengthened the sovereignty of our colony, occurred in December of the following year. It was no less than the cession by Colonel Fenwick, as the representative of the patentees, of the Fort at Saybrook with all the rights which belonged to or were claimed by the government then established. These were rights held under the Crown by a patent, or at least a grant, from the Earl of Warwick, himself having received them from the Plymouth Company, and under them a fort had been built and a site had been laid out with special provision for the homes of persons of quality. But the persons of quality had not come; the intended city or town had not grown up; the farmers were not minded to keep within the palisades; it was impossible to carry out the proposed system of impost on goods carried up or down the river; and it seemed but to part with the barren privileges that were held in exchange for a consideration and for the advantage of union with the healthy young colony up the river. The benefit was not altogether on the side of the ceded territory; it was worth a good deal to Connecticut to have gotten the control of the mouth of the river which was its chief highway of approach and it was worth still more to have extinguished a claim which might prove decidedly troublesome as time went on. And besides, Connecticut inherited from Saybrook with these rights, their outward symbol in the form of its seal, with the representation of a vineyard in fruit, and its nobly religious motto, "Sustinet qui Transtulit." The colony and the state have continued the seal, changing the details of its design and the order of the words in its legend; but in no way modifying its meaning or its inspiration.

We pass over six years to another historical event of importance, showing the colony in still another light, the treaty of Hartford in 1650. Peter Stuyvesant, governor of the New Netherlands, came in state that year to confer with the commissioners of the United Colonies, and to press the claim of the Dutch to the whole coast from Delaware Bay to Cape Cod. A less keen observer than he would have learned after a journey through the territory of New Haven and Connecticut that such a claim could never be successfully pushed; but he did his best. He dated the document which he presented as from Hartford in New Netherland; and the commissioners refused to receive it until he wrote Connecticut. He called the non-chartered colonies "pretendant;" and they did not care. Presently he drew back the eastern limit of his claim from Cape Cod to Point Judith; and soon agreed to the decision by four arbiters—all, by the way, Englishmen, and nobody knows why—that the line between the English and the Dutch on Long Island should run across from Oyster Bay and on the main land should begin west of Greenwich and run north, keeping at least ten miles from Henry Hudson's river. This decision was accepted, and the treaty of Hartford was formally made on the 19th day of September; when its provisions were reported, the Dutch were amazed to find that they had relinquished all claim to New England. Stuyvesant, when he went back, did not tell his council what he had done, and no certified copy reached Holland for six years. But Connecticut had gained a substantial victory in Connecticut's way.

We are now within the period of the Commonwealth in England, but the change of government in the home land made little difference in the administration of affairs in the sturdy independent colony. The notable event in those years is an ecclesiastical quarrel at home, of a rather unpleasant kind, arising after Mr. Hooker's death from a divergence between Mr. Stone, the teaching elder, and Mr. Goodwin, the ruling elder, of the church, Mr. Stone having refused to allow the church to vote on the nomination of Michael Wigglesworth, who was Mr. Goodwin's candidate for the pastorate, and having also refused to administer the Lord's Supper. The trouble convulsed the Massachusetts colony as well as that immediately concerned. The general court took a hand in it, of course, and that over and over again. Councils sat in Hartford and in Boston; and the final council declared that the withdrawers—Elder Goodwin's party—were still members of the Hartford church, but that if they could not return to communion they should be given a dismissal with the privilege of removal. They were dismissed and presently removed to Hadley, Hartford's first colony in foreign lands.

The year 1660—only a quarter of a century after the settlement—brings us to the restoration in England and that to the story of the charter of 1662 and the inclusion of New Haven within the fully established English colony of Connecticut. In the winter of 1662-63 is the melancholy, though brief, episode of witchcraft, with the execution of Nathaniel and Rebecca Greensmith. In 1666 we see the beginning of the controversy as to the proper subjects of baptism, leading four years later to the organization of a second church which was to follow the more strict ways of the fathers. But even to sketch the history of these ten years would be to extend this paper far beyond its limits. It must suffice to note that the remarkable charter, the granting of which has never yet been fully explained, was the embodiment of the principles on which Connecticut had been founded and of the fundamental orders in which those principles had been embodied, and that it really created under the sanction of a monarchy a pure democracy, the type of all modern democratic government; that the witchcraft excitement was held under restraint and soon passed away, largely by the wise advice of the ministers; and that the doctrines and practices which led to the organization of the second church showed that time and distance had not quite destroyed the convictions of men who had been

brought up on England's soil and nurtured by England's church.

But what a story it is, that of the first twenty-five years of Hartford, furnishing an example of almost every kind of the events that go to make up history. The migration from the Bay, for reason ecclesiastical and civil and personal, and the wilderness journey; the marking out of a large town on the scale of a city; the independent organization of the three-fold settlement; the formal declaration and the successful waging of war; the assitance given to the Bay colony in case of ecclesiastical controversy; then, the adoption of the fundamental orders which mark for the modern world the beginning of democracy under constitutional government; the entrance into the New England federation; the securing of the cession of Saybrook with its patent rights and its seal; the making of a treaty with the Dutch, which peaceably determined the map of all this coast; the controversy which led to sending out a colony to dwell across the Massachusetts boundary; and the movement towards a charter, no less wonderful in its history than its contents. Even in a brief and hasty glimpse we can see the importance of it all, and know that it is no little thing that so great events were brought about in so brief a time.

[75]
Consecration of Old Trinity Church.
[Hartford]

To the Editor of The Times:

In the historical sketch of Trinity church which was published in THE TIMES of Monday, no notice was made of the consecration of the former church building. This took place on Tuesday, May 28, 1861. The clergy met at the house of Elisha Johnson, and entered the church repeating the twenty-fourth Psalm alternately with Bishop Williams. Mr. Johnson, as junior warden, read the request for consecration, and the bishop proceeded with the service, the Rev. Pelham Williams, rector, reading the sentence of consecration. Morning prayer was read by the Rev. David H. Short of Broad Brook, the Rev. Francis T. Russell of New Britain, and the Rev. N. J. Seeley of Bristol. In the communion service the Rev. Dr. E. M. P. Wells of Boston assisted the bishop, and the service was preached by the Rev. Dr. Frederick D. Huntington of Boston, from the text II. Corinthians, xii., 14. It was described as "an exceedingly well written and impressively delivered discourse on the doctrine of the Trinity, the hearing of which afforded great satisfaction to the congregation present." It was also a matter of peculiar interest that Dr. Huntington (who afterwards became bishop of central New York) was the preacher on this occasion, as he had in April, 1846, being then a Unitarian minister, preached at the dedication of the edifice on the corner of Asylum and Trumbull streets, which was rebuilt as Trinity church. The other clergymen present at the consecration were the Rev. R. M. Abercrombie of Christ church, the Rev. E. A. Washburn of St. John's, the Rev. C. R. Fisher of St. Paul's, the Rev. P. V. Finch of Plainville, the Rev. J. B. Robinson of South Glastonbury, the Rev. J. M. Willey of Waterbury, the Rev. Samuel Hall of Glastonbury, the Rev. R. H. Tuttle of Windsor, the Rev. Edwin

Rowland, the Rev. David H. Banks and the Rev. W. W. Niles, deacons.

On the following day, Wednesday, May 29th, Bishop Williams instituted the Rev. Pelham Williams as rector of the church, himself preaching the sermon from St. Matthew, xi., 4-5.

H.

ABLE HISTORICAL ADDRESS BY DR. HART AT AFTERNOON SERVICE AT ST. PAUL'S
Dean of Berkeley Divinity School Interests a Large Audience With Lucid Talk on Church and Departed Pastor Emeritus, Rev. C. M. Selleck.

[76] [Norwalk]

One of the most masterly offerings listened to in Norwalk in some time was the historic address by Dr. Samuel Hart Dean of Berkeley Divinity school, secretary of the House of Bishops, custodian of the prayer book and registrar of the convention, given in connection with the dedication of the Selleck memorial at St. Paul's church yesterday afternoon. The address was as follows:

Exodus xx. 24. "In all places where I record my name (cause my name to be remembered) I will come unto thee, and I will bless thee." St. John iv. 21. "The hour cometh, when ye shall neither in this mountain, nor yet at Jerusalem, worship the Father."

The verse from the Pentateuch almost seems to belong to the New Testament, and that from the gospel reads as if its place were in the older part of the Bible. That God would come to His people and bless them in many places, whenever he should cause His name to be remembered, does not accord, we might say, with the command so often expressed that God should be worshipped with the full honor of sacrifice in no other place than at the tabernacle or the temple. That Christ should forbid worship at any mountain or in any city, or should declare that it would in any place become impossible, appears to be inconsistent with the generous freedom of the revelation which He came to proclaim. It cannot be, of course, that there is any inconsistency in the two declarations, except that which belongs to the progress made in God's revelation to His people in the twelve or thirteen centuries that separates them; but how are we to read them and to find out what they mean? How ought we to understand them and their applica-

tion to us, who are gathered here in one of the innumerable "shrines" of Christendom, to mark the passage of a mile-stone in the history of congregation of believing people?

They tell us who have carefully studied the older books of the Bible, that the verses which stand at the end of the 20th chapter of Exodus, after the proclamation of the moral law in the ten Words which God spake, are a part of an ancient code of directions which had to do with matters of duty and of worship. The phrase there which implies that God will by the remembrance of His Name make many places holy, so that He may meet there with men and give them His blessing, may almost be said to come to us with the sanction of the earliest covenant. God would make easy the way of approach to Himself; and this benediction would be upon every place in which He might be worshipped and every assembly of His worshippers. The limited covenant had not yet been promulgated. The law, as it was Mosaic and national, had not begun to set aside or limit for a time and for a part of mankind the covenant as it was universal. That which came in, by way of parenthesis (as St. Paul speaks) and for transgression's sake, to hold until the promise could be fulfilled and renewed, did after a while make it necessary that God's special people should restrict their acts of highest worship to one place; but it was long before any such law was proclaimed and longer yet before it was enforced; and even then there began to be, almost as by an instinct working unbidden, places for the reading and teaching of the divine word. In fact I venture to think that the sacred writers labor to express the truth that the temple, "exceedingly magnifical" indeed and the dwelling place of the Lord of Hosts upon the earth, did not express the spirituality of true worship and was not a prepar-

ation for His Coming in whose Name all true worship should be rendered, as really and as impressively as the simple tent of the wilderness-days or that which succeeded it upon the Mount Zion. The universal covenant of the earlier days as well as universal, of the days of the Messiah who was yet to come, almost demanded that the God of all men should call upon them to celebrate His name in many places, and should in every sacred place reserve a blessing for them.

But why then did the Messiah, first revealing Himself by that name at Jacob's well to a woman of Samaria, accustomed to worship at a shrine which stood in rivalry to the temple at Jerusalem—why did He so solemnly declare to her and to the world that the time was at hand when neither Gerizim nor Zion should be an accepted place for the worship of the God whom He revealed as Father? It must have been His way, in somewhat hidden strain, of saying that the rivalry of temple and temple, of holy place, and holy place, must soon cease: that worship would soon be no longer limited to any central shrine; they who should worship at Jerusalem, or at the Samaritan sanctuary because it was believed the one place for worship, could not bring acceptable praise and homage and sacrifice. It was the return; but in the day of a brighter vision and a greater revelation, to the invitation of early times, it was the declaration that the Law, as the Law, however understood, must yield to the Gospel for which it had been a preparation. Henceforth it was a matter of indifference whether Jerusalem was bigoted or Gerizim was in error; for neither could be the only place where God's name should dwell or in which His truth should be proclaimed or His blessing given; neither could be the center to which all men must resort or look or from which a benediction should be expected; the Father would everywhere make His name to be remembered and everywhere hold out a blessing to His worshippers.

This is the sanction for Christian worship, as through all these centuries it has been celebrated in thousands and thousands of consecrated places. This is the warrant for erecting such places as dwellings of God, houses for the meeting of God with man, buildings set apart for worship and preaching and sacrament, not like every Christian home fit for prayer and the reading of the word as well as for many other duties and conveniences; but as

indeed in each case God's abode among the homes of the people, fitted for the great eucharistic worship of the redeemed church, as the one temple alone was fitted for the sacrificial oeffrings of the church which was a figure of the true. This is the sanction of our consecration of each Christian church—called indeed by the same name as is borne by the great company of believers—for all holy offices, for the very greatest, which stands parallel with the ascended Lord's worship and action in the heavens, as well as for the humblest approach in the courts above. This warrants us in calling to mind today the meaning of this holy building and of those which have preceded it upon this very spot; this bids us realize the importance of consecration for a church and of our recognition of the meaning and the purpose of such consecration.

———

The special occasion of today's commemoration is the consecration of a church which literally sprang from the ashes of its predecessor. It is a century and a quarter since the first bishop of Connecticut, for us the "Apostle of the New World," consecrated the third church offered to the service of God by the churchmen of this place. We are passing through the 175th year in the history of this parish; it is nearly 170 years since the more spacious and dignified building was begun which after five years replaced the smaller structure in which the adherents of the Church of England here met for worship, and 150 since it was completed; next July will mark the 182d anniversary of the burning of the first church by a torch which should never have been applied to it; on the eighth day of September next it will be 70 years since the building in which we are assembled was consecrated by the bishop of New York, in the enforced absence of Bishop Brownell. But the consecration of the third building was an event of no little interest in the history of our church in this land. Our first bishop returned to this country after receiving from the bishops of the Catholic remainder of the ancient Church of Scotland," that "free, valid, and purely ecclesiastical episcopacy" which they had in their power to bestow "out of the abundance of their poverty"—may their brave and pious deed be ever held in thankful remembrance!—and in August, 1785, he had met his clergy at Middletown and had held there his first ordination. Then, entering upon his busy and faithful episcopate of twelve years, he was called upon in the next year to consecrate the new church in this place, and thus to discharge for the first time in this land the sacred episcopal function of giving a special blessing and consecration to a place of worship. Of course, many such buildings had been designated and dedicated for sacred purposes in various parts of the country in the early one hundred and eighty years which had passed since the settlers at Jamestown had provided according to their means a fit place for the worship of God; and by intention and use they had been set apart from "unhallowed, worldly, and common uses," and devoted to the service of the Triune God in accordance with the rites and usages of the Church of England; but here first in all this land was a church formally consecrated. We do not know what form Bishop Seabury used in consecrating St. Paul's church, Norwalk, and the eleven other churches which he consecrated during his episcopate, or Bishop Jarvis in consecrating the three churches for which he performed a like service before the consecration office in the Prayer Book was set forth in 1799. But as Bishop Andrewes's office for the consecration of a church appears to have been customarily used in England for many years before this date, we may feel pretty confident that this from which indeed that in the Prayer Book was taken, was used here and elsewhere as occasion required. (It is interesting to note in passing that the authorized form of consecration, displacing and almost certainly growing out of that used here, and the office of institution drawn up here, were both for the first time in St. James's church, Derby in November 1799). Our special commemoration today, therefore, touches on all the history of the church in this country, and places the name of this parish at the head of the long list of those who have asked and secured the blessing of an episcopal consecration for the places of worship which they have provided.

But with this special, and at the same time in one sense general, commemoration, it is but seemly that we should glance over the full period of time in which we know that churchmen have been in Norwalk and the well-nigh one and three-quarter centuries which have passed since this parish was organized. (With the par-

ishes of Derby and Ridgefield, which have the same age in years, it increased to eleven the number of parishes in the Colony of Connecticut. The mind goes back to the summer of 1706 and to the famous ride of Colonel Caleb Heathcote escorting the Rev. George Muirson of Rye along the shore as far as Stratford. They must have passed through Norwalk, where the society of the standing order now more than half a century old was under the care of its second minister. Whether they found any professed members of the Church of England here, or attracted any of the inhabitants of the place to that church, we cannot now tell. We first read of Norwalk churchmen eighteen years later in 1724, when Samuel Johnson, the father of the church in Connecticut, found them here. Three years later Henry Caner, Jr., a young graduate of the collegiate school at New Haven, having been ordained in England, was appointed missionary of the Society for the Propagation of the Gospel in Fairfield and Norwalk, his residence being in the first named place extending his labors also to other towns in the neighborhood. After a while he went to England for his health, and his half-brother, Richard Caner, who had come to Fairfield as a teacher after his graduation, acted as lay-reader. In 1737, as has been already noted, the parish was organized and a small church was built; it stood on the northeast corner of the present church grounds. Henry Caner returned to this cure, leaving it in 1746, after nearly twenty years' service, to take charge of the King's Chapel in Boston. He was here long enough to see a new and more spacious church begun and (apparently) occupied, the first building being turned into a parsonage; and when he went away he noted that the twelve communicants whom he had found in Fairfield when he first came there had increased to 68, and that at Norwalk where there were none a score of years before he left, 115. Mr. Caner left Boston at the beginning of the Revolution, went to Halifax and London, returned to Bristol in Rhode Island, and at the age of ninety-two, six years after Bishop Seabury had consecrated a third church here, died in London. His brother Richard was ordained in 1742, and died three years later.

Nineteen years was the second church in building and furnishing; a bell being also provided. The parish, so strong under the Caner brothers,

surpassed indeed by none except perhaps the mother parish at Stratford, declined in strength, largely on account of the failures of its attempts to secure a settled clergyman; and this doubtless was a reason for the long delay in the completion of the building. The churchmen here looked for clerical services and pastoral care, as it would seem, to the Rev. Ebenezer Dibblee, missionary of the united cures of Stamford and Greenwich, the history of whose half-century of ministerial life belongs especially to Stamford. When he died, it was said of him that he had become endeared to all his people "by his unwavering devotion to their best interests, his holy life and unremitted zeal in the name of Christ and His Church." But the history of this parish was destined to be honored by the names of men who should bear a notable part in the church of the land. There had served here as lay-reader for two years after his graduation from college, a young man of promise, named Jeremiah Leaming. After his ordination abroad, he was assigned to duty as teacher and assistant at Trinity Church, Newport; and thence in 1758 he was transferred to this place, where he remained for twenty-one years. Busy and anxious years they are. In politics events were moving on towards the war of the Revolution; in church matters there came the inevitable break-up and discouragement; brave men on both sides grew braver, and needed more and more patience, and courage. Mr. Leaming entered with quick mind and ready pen into the controversies of these later colonial times. He stood as a brave champion between two adversaries, strong upholders of the Congregational policy, Noah Hobart of Fairfield and Noah Welles of Stamford, and rigorously defended the authority, doctrines, and worship of the Church of England. He wrote on behalf of the clergy of Connecticut to the bishop of London, urging as others had done and were doing, the provision of bishops for the colonies; and affirming that none opposed it on this side of the ocean except "out of malice or mere wantonness." On Mr. Beach of Newtown and Mr. Leaming, who became the senior clergyman of Conecticut when Dr. Johnson died in 1772, came a heavy responsibility, which grew heavier as time passed on, and the colonies were beginning to offer resistance to the Crown. The clergy felt themselves under the strongest obligations to hold to the oaths of allegiance which they had taken at their ordina-

tion, and many of them dared not keep silence in declaring their convictions or in urging their people to follow them. Mr. Beach, in spite of threats and actual peril of his life, read the Prayer Book services in public, with the petitions for the King, during the whole period of the war. Mr. Leaming because he was a Tory and so declared himself, was seized on a cold night, hurried off to jail, and left without bed or fire, with the result that he was lamed in his hip and made a cripple for life. This was in 1776; and three years later, in July, the British troops under the command of General Tryon, after burning Fairfield, came to Norwalk and set fire to the town, so applying the torch "as to spare neither friends nor foes, loyalists nor patriots." The church was burned, as a few days before that in Fairfield was burned, and two years later that in New London was burned; and a severe blow was negligently if not wantonly inflicted on pastors and congregations who were risking all for their allegiance to the cause of England and of England's church. Mr. Leaming, who lost everything except, as he said, the apparel which was on his back, was carried by a band of Hessian soldiers to the British commander, and taken to New York, where he remained till the end of the war. When the clergy of Connecticut met on the memorable 25th of March, 1783, and decided to elect a bishop and to send him in search of consecration to England and Scotland, their choice fell upon Mr. Leaming, and, failing him, on Samuel Seabury, son of the former missionary at New London, either of them being judged a fit man for the sacred office and duty. The former judged that his age and infirmities would not allow him to carry the burden; and as you well know, Dr. Seabury became our first bishop, while

Mr. Leaming preached when his clergy met and "recognized" him on his return. Mr. Leaming later became rector at Stratford, declining an election as coadjutor bishop of Connecticut when there was a possibility of the need of perpetuating the Scottish succession, taking an active and influential part in the organization of the church in the United States, and living to be the oldest church clergyman in the country. "A small emaciated old man, very lame, totally blind, his mind eclipsed, quiet and gentle," he died in New Haven in 1804. On his tombstone, recently restored, we may read the true words: "Well instructed, especial-

ly in his holy office; unremitting in his labors; charitable, patient, and of primitive meekness; respected, revered, and beloved in life, and lamented in death."

For some five years after "the burning," while the town was slowly recovering from the disaster which had befallen it, the churchmen here worshipped in a temporary structure which they had built before they reconstructed their own homes, and Mr. Dibblee officiated for them as he was able. In December, 1784, on the evacuation of New York by the British, the Rev. John Bowden accepted the charge of the parish at a salary of 80 pounds a year—a pound then being three and a third dollars. He had been an assistant minister of Trinity church, New York, and when his voice failed, a resident of Jamaica on Long Island. He was, we are assured, both a scholar and a man of common sense. He must have had powers of inspiring men to work and courage; for the parishioners at once made plans for building a new church on the old site, of the same size as the former, 55 feet long besides the steeple and the chancel and 36 feet wide. The timber was cut, hewn, and drawn in the winter, and before the first of April it was ready for the framing. It is probable that it was finished, and that the rector had set out the trees which still adorn the site, before Bishop Seabury arrived in Connecticut; and to it the bishop came in the following year, now a century and quarter ago, to accept the building in God's name and to consecrate it. It was not immediately pewed and furnished; but it was a comely structure within and without. Says your historian: "Its vaulted ceiling with dependent chandeliers, its chaste pulpit, and cushioned desk and neat communion-table with circular rail, are still remembered, while its projecting chancel, and west end tower, and tasteful belfry and graceful spire, with the line of Lombardy poplar rising from a carpet of living green, formed a pleasing picture." After five years Mr. Bowden resigned, to live for a short time in the West Indies, then to return to Stratford, then to become the principal of the Episcopal Academy at Cheshire, while there to decline a unanimous election to be Bishop Seabury's successor, and later to be a professor in Columbia college.

The Rev. George Ogilvie was next rector of the parish for six years, and was succeeded by the Rev. Dr. William Smith, a Scotchman by birth as Dr. Bowden had been an Irishman. He was not the Dr. William Smith—also a Scotchman—of Maryland and Pennsylvania, Provost of the University of Philadelphia and President of the House of Deputies in General Convention; but he was a man of hardly less ability and influence than his namesake. He came here from Trinity church, Newport, in the steps of Dr. Bowden, in 1797, and remained until 1800. He went hence to the important post of principal of the Academy in Cheshire, as again his predecessor had done, and devoted a large part of his life to teaching. He was a man of wide learning, of facile expression, of musical skill, all joined with the "pervidum ingenium Scotorum," but never as successful as might have been expected. While rector here he preached the sermon at the consecration of Bishop Jarvis, himself a native of Norwalk, an honor as preacher which has fallen to no other priest in our church save two—and he prepared for the Diocese an Office for the Induction of Ministers, which slightly modified, became the office for the Institution of Ministers (really rectors) inserted after some years in our Prayer Book. It was he also who introduced into the American church the practice of chanting, his belief being that the chant was the only fit and scriptural form of psalmody, and that rhyming translations and metrical rendering of the psalms or kindred writings were presumptuous and irreverent. By his writings and influence he did much to further his principles. I cannot tell how far he carried them out in St. Paul's church; but as he wrote the Office of Induction in its rectory, so he wrote his "Primitive Psalmody" while living in Norwalk as one of its parishioners. Dr. Smith resigned his rectorship here in the year 1800, the parish having at that time about a hundred communicants.

The Rev. Henry Whitlock, who came next, died while yet a young man as rector of Trinity church, New Haven; and the Rev. Bethel Judd, leader of the movement for a diocesan missionary society, had two short rectorates, and after a while became principal of the Academy of Cheshire. We must pass by with the mention of their names, the Rev. Evan M. Johnson, and the Rev. Reuben Sherwood, teacher as well as pastor, and the organizer of the Sunday school. Nor can we tarry over the illustrious names of Jackson Kemper, who was led here by the attractions of a rural pastorate after serving in large parishes in Philadelphia and Baltimore. His benignant and saintly service in this place was brought to an end in 1835, the year of the birth of true missionary spirit in our church, when he was elected and consecrated bishop of the great district known as the northwest. The story of his episcopate of thirty-five years does not in strictness belong to this day's commemoration, but the suggestion of it bring to our hearts and our lips thanksgiving for the man, his example, and his influence. And it cannot but be a satisfaction for us to remember that as a boy he studied in our venerable diocesan school and as a priest he went from one of our most ancient parishes to be a leader in "the sacramental host of God's elect," the first missionary bishop of the American church.

This brings us, after a rectorate of a few months only, to the forty-three years' rectorate of Dr. William Cooper Mead, the only long rectorate in the history of the parish, itself covering nearly one-fourth of that history. He came here a mature man, having passed full forty years of his life; he attained the age of eighty-four. He found 120 communicants here; and he left 300. The address delivered here twenty-five years ago by one whose memory is today to be especially honored well characterizes the man, and I do not hesitate to quote his words:

"Dr. Mead was a strong man; a man of energy and ability, and of clear vision and quick perception of that which was feasible and practical. He possessed singular administrative wisdom, and as concerned ecclesiastical jurisprudence was to be trusted with entire confidence. He deprecated changes, and was the apostle of the bidding of law. His views had weight in the committee-room, he graced the moderator's chair, and was a power upon the floor of the convention. He was a sage counsellor, but an acute debater as well. He was for 33 years a member of the Standing Committee of the Diocese, he represented the Diocese in 13 triennial General Conventions, and he was chairman of the committee on Canons in the House of Deputies. The church has reason to be proud of his services. Uncompromising in his allegiance to it, never swerved by policy, but ever acting from conviction, inflexible, intelligent, influential, he won the admiration of his contemporaries. And as to that which he here accomplished, everything speaks of him. Not a building, not a wall, not a

paling even is standing which stood when ne came hither. He filled and straightened and paved and smoothed; he built, first the church, then the walls, then the sheds, then the walks. He labored unweariedly; he faithfully proclaimed one topic; it was the text (in 1841) of the last sermon preached in the church of 1786; it was the theme of his life-long sermon: 'We preach Christ crucified'."

The writer of these words was in charge of the parish after the great rector's death and indeed often ministered in the church and to the church-people here. On the hundredth anniversary of the consecration of the third church, when he read the address from which the words are taken, a young and enthusiastic rector nad entered on his ministrations here; others have followed, until the present rectorship, as to whom, their memories being fresh in the minds of so many, it is not needful—it would hardly be seemly—to speak today.

Thus on this special anniversary, a matter of peculiar interest, I have sketched out most imperfectly the history of this parish as it has been illustrated by the rectors, many of them really distinguished men. I have not even mentioned the names of the laymen and women, who have here served God and done good deeds for His house and people. "There be of them that have left a name behind them, that their praises might be recorded; and some there be that have no memorial; but they were all godly men, whose righteousness shall not be forgotten. With their seed shall continue their goodness, and their inheritance unto children's children." That which they began in faithfulness and continued in patience has been blessed; ye, the rector and the people of this parish, have entered into their labors; see ye to it that your work, with its increased opportunities and facilities, be so faithfully and constantly done that they who shall reap its fruits shall bless you for beginning and furthering it!

For here has the Almighty God recorded His Name, and here from generation to generation it has been taught and worshipped; here has the God of covenant come with sacramental blessings; here has been offered the homage of redeemed souls, the service of the holy church; here has been the approach to the Father more blessed than in any temple of old; here, let us humbly pray, until the Lord shall come again, shall worship be rendered

and accepted, grace offered and received, the Father honored in the Son by the Holy Spirit, the true faith confessed, and men built up in it unto life eternal!

ST. PAUL'S, WOODBURY, SINCE 1740 [77]

DR HART'S SERMON AT WOODBURY CHURCH

INTERESTING HISTORY OF ST PAUL'S SINCE 1740.

First Connecticut Parish—Stratford Presbyterians—Earliest Woodbury Services—The Rev Mr Marshall—His Persecutions—Later Clergy of St Paul's Church.

The historical services of St Paul's, Woodbury, on Sunday opened with a celebration of Holy Communion at 8 o'clock, the bishop of the diocese, the Rt Rev Chauncey B. Brewster, being the celebrant. Morning prayer was said at 9:45 by the Rev G. B. Gilbert. At 10:45 there was a second celebration, the rector of St Paul's, the Rev Alexander Hamilton, being the celebrant, and at this time the historical sermon was preached by the Rev Samuel Hart, D. D., dean of Berkeley Divinity School, and registrar of the diocese.

Dr Hart took as his text Isaiah, ii:3, and in beginning his discourse, said: "I doubt whether there is in all history a more wonderful example of all this than is seen in the rise and progress of the Church of England in this commonwealth of Connecticut. The early settlers had been on conscientious grounds non-conforming members of that church, and they organized their polity on principles of non-conformity, which led of necessity to formal separation. Yet within a few years of the death of the first ministers, who had been ordained in England, but had begun here a non-Episcopal sucession, some of the best and most learned of their successors were crossing the sea to ask at the hands of the bishops 'at home' authority to preach the word of God and minister the sacraments."

The first parish of this "revised Church of England" in this colony was organized at Stratford, while as yet the oldest settlement within its boundaries was not 70 years old. There was a split in the old Stratford church between Congregationalists and those who believed in Presbyterian ordination, and many of the latter came to Woodbury in 1673 and were the parishioners of the Rev Zechariah Walker. In 1722, when 11 men and one widow in Newtown asked that the English Society for the Propagation of the Gospel for a "lawfully ordained minister", Thomas Wheeler of Woodbury and Moses Knapp of Chestnut Ridge added their signatures. Soon the only Church of England clergyman in Connecticut, Dr Pigot of Stratford, held services in Woodbury and about 1740 John Beach organized a parish and built a church in present Roxbury, where the Conformists who lived near the center went to worship

for seven years. Dr Hart then went on to speak of the early days of St Paul's, when Solomon Palmer, "that noble young missionary," Thomas Davies (of whom a second namesake is this week to be consecrated to the Episcopate) and Richard Samuel Clarke of New Milford officiated from time to time, and when members of the congregation probably read service in the absence of a clergyman.

In speaking of the Rev John Rutgers Marshall, Dr Hart said he was the last but one of Connecticut's 43 picked young men who "went home" across the ocean to receive ordination from the English bishops, and that "he was indeed a remarkable man. His youth and the fact that he spent all his ministry in one place have kept him from being as widely known as some others and from deserved recognition in volumes of biography; but he rendered great service, not to this parish only, but to the church in this commonwealth and to the church in the United States. For what he suffered and for what he did, for the use of his worldly goods and of his intellectual powers, for his influence as pastor and as leader, he should hold—he does indeed hold—an honored place in the records and memoirs of this particular branch of the catholic church of Christ. He was a native of New York, and a near kinsman to the first bishop of that state; his earlier studies were under Dr Bellamy at Bethlem, and his academic training under Dr Johnson at King's College; he was ordained in England by Bishop Terrick of London, and returned as the controversies which led to the Revolution were waxing hot, to make the eighteenth in the number of the Church of England clergymen in this colony, and to serve both here and in other places in this neighborhood. No other of them all suffered as much or as persistently for allegiance to the British Crown as did he; one does not care now to tell the story in detail, but it is not fair to him or to the cause which he represented to conceal the fact that there is in our history such a chapter of suffering and shame. Twice he was dragged from his pulpit and twice he was beaten and left for dead by the roadside. The strength of his congregation may be inferred from the fact that there were 70 subscribers for the purchase of a glebe on which he erected a good-sized and dignified house; in it he lived for some 14 years and in its secret passages and rooms he hid himself from his persecutors; at one time for six weeks in the daytime. Later he acquired a home of his own, and the glebe house was sold and the proceeds applied to the erection of a church."

Dr Hart then went on to tell the story of the election of Bishop Seabury, in 1783, saying: "We cannot tell why this town, not very central, was chosen for the meeting; it must have been at the cost of a long journey that some reached the place over the bad roads of the springtide; but one is inclined to think that they came here because it was at the invitation of Mr Marshall that they assembled, and that he gave the invitation because he was in touch with the condition of affairs in New York (it was not yet evacuated by the British), and knew the possibilities of the situation and the way in which they could be turned to service." Dr Hart explained the proposition that had been made by some of the clergy for temporary adoption of the Congregational, or rather Presbyterial form of polity and the protest against this which culmin-

ated in the choice of Bishop Seabury, and spoke of the meeting held in New York during Dr Seabury's absence by deputies from states outside of New England, at which Mr Marshall was present, to "consult on the existing exigency of the Church," when Mr Marshall, with Dr Samuel Parker of Massachusetts, afterward bishop of that state for a short period, maintained that the church could not be properly organized here until it had at least one bishop, and refused to consent to definite action till the result of Dr Seabury's application for orders should be known. "They spoke with authority for their brethren in the New England States; and they taught the others a lesson which they did not, indeed, learn at once, but which was presently accepted by all, that the church must not undertake her work until she is furnished for it by the organization which her Lord has provided for her; that she must build and be built upon the foundation which has been laid and in accordance with the plans made known to apostles and phophets by the Spirit. It was no little thing that this needed 'bracing' of the churchmen in the other colonies came in part from the strong city on the Massachusetts Bay and in part from the glebe-house in a quiet Connecticut village, by the words of two leaders of men, insisting on principles and destined finally to secure their triumph."

The story of the building of St Raul's was then told at some length. Then Dr Hart spoke of the successors of Mr Marshall, none of whom, unless it was the first, gave his whole time to the parish or even resided there; the Rev James Sayer, who for a while kept Woodbury out of agreement with the newly organized diocese; the Rev Seth Hart of Waterbury and later of Long Island; the Rev Reuben Ives of Cheshire, who married a daughter of Mr Marshall; the Rev Tillotson Bronson and the Rev Bethel Judd, D. D., of Cheshire Academy, with whom the parish passed into the nineteenth century. In that century 32 rectors or clergymen statedly officiating were at St Paul's; those who were there seven years or more being the Rev Joseph D. Welton, the Rev Sturgis Gilbert, a famous school-teacher; the Rev Solomon G. Hitchcock, under whom the new rectory was acquired and the famous horse sheds were built; the Rev John Purves; the Rev L. Robert Sheffield; also the Rev F. D. Harriman, during whose rectorship the church building was "altered, repaired and beautified," and the Rev Robert Nelson, D. D., who had been a missionary to China and whose rectorship was brought to a close by his death.

At the vesper service on Sunday Bishop Brewster spoke earnestly on the celebration and the things for which it stood. The Rev Mr George of Newtown was unable to be present, but the Rev Mr Beers of Bethlehem spoke in behalf of Newtown, the mother parish, in which he was brought up. Addresses were made by representatives of the Congregational and Methodist Churches of Woodbury, all expressing cordial good feeling and speaking in high terms of the friendly spirit of the present rector of St Paul's. In the evening the church was crowded to its utmost capacity, when the confirmation service was held. Three girls were confirmed and the bishop gave an impressive address on the theme of loyalty—loyalty to the vows of the Christian profession. The music at all the services was largely congregational in character. At the offertory in the morning, and at the vesper service, Miss Bishop of Branford sang solos which added greatly to the beauty and completeness of the service. The ladies of the parish kept open house at the parish hall, serving lunch on both days. Many visitors from Waterbury, Watertown, and other places were present.

All the services were very largely attended. The addresses on Saturday were of a highly interesting character, especially from a historical standpoint, that of the Rev W. D. Humphrey, rector of Christ Church, Roxbury, who gave a description of the site of the old church and its surroundings on a now disused and well-nigh forgotten road through the woods, which he had recently visited. Fragments of glass and mortar were still to be found by digging on the spot, and an old barn contains a considerable portion of the timbers that once formed part of the old church, though there is no way of identifying them positively. The old graveyard is there, where lie the mortal remains of the doughty Revolutionary soldier, Seth Warner, under a flat tombstone, which, like that which covers the remains of Rector Marshall, in the rear of St Paul's, may owe its position to a survival of the customs of the time when it was necessary thus to protect the graves from the incursions of wolves.

The senior minister of Woodbury, the Rev J. L. R. Wyckoff, read a long paper, dwelling much on the present good feeling existing among those of different forms of faith in contrast to former bitterness. The Rev E. J. Craft of Christ Church, Bridgeport, and Archdeacon Plumb of New Milford also spoke of matters of historical and churchly interest. The Rev Mr Waterbury of Waterville gave a brief account of a visit to the church which Bishop Seabury attended when a medical student in Edinburgh, and the Rev Frederick D. Buckley spoke a few words of greeting and congratulation. In the evening the Rev G. B. Gilbert of Middletown gave an address on the duty of men to the church, saying that men would work for what interested them, and their interest must be aroused before they would do their duty. Letters of congratulation were received from descendants of Bishop Seabury and from former rectors and others.

DEDICATION OF THE WALL ABOUT THE OLD ANGLICAN CEMETERY AT NEW CAMBRIDGE (BRISTOL)

DR. HART'S ADDRESS AT WALL DEDICATION [78]

Delivered Historical Sketch at Exercises Held in Bristol.

Rev. Dr. Samuel Hart delivered the historical address in connection with the dedication exercises last Friday celebrating the completion of the new wall about the ancient Episcopal Burying Ground on Federal Hill, Bristol, which was erected through the energy of the members of Katherine Gaylord Chapter, D. A. R. His address was made in the parlors of the Congregational Church and he spoke as follows:—

New Cambridge was a district in the venerable town of Farmington. An ecclesiastical society was organized here; and after strong opposition to the candidate preferred by the majority, on the ground of his strong Calvinistic views, the newly constituted church in 1747 called a minister and arranged for his ordination. When the final vote to this effect was taken and recorded, the clerk made this entry: "And here it must be added that at the same meeting Caleb Mathews, Stephen Brooks, John Hikox, Caleb Abernathy, Abner Mathews, Abel Royce, Dannell Roe and Simon Tuttel publikly declared themselves of the Church of England and under the bishop of London." Nehemiah Royce added himself to their number in a few weeks. They were all men of importance in the community, and some of them held prominent places in the ecclesiastical society. Before the year ended, the Rev. William Gibbs, Missionary at Simsbury to the Society for the Propagation of the Gospel, began to minister to them and to those who met with them for worship. It was forty years since the establishment at Stratford of the first congregation of English churchmen in Connecticut, and twenty-five years since the memorable day when, at the college commencement in New Haven, Cutler and Johnson and Brown and Wetmore took their stand for episcopacy, and made the church at once a power in the community. Churchmen were considered as "sober dissenters" and were granted toleration under an old enactment; and as early as 1727 the General Assembly of the colony passed a law allowing any person who had declared himself of the Church of England, and who lived so near to the place where a clergyman of that church ministered that he could convenietly and did attend services there, to have the tax collected from him for the support of the ministry paid to such clergymen; and the clergyman was given power to receive the tax.

Many devout and earnest persons were persuaded of the truth of the teachings of the Church of England and were drawn to her by her willingness to minister the sacraments under simple Scriptural conditions and also by the dignity and serviceableness of her forms of worship. It was a time of declension in the "standing order," as it was called, of congregationalism, and the church was of great spiritual benefit to the descendants in the third and fourth generation of those who had come to these shores in large part because they were dissatisfied with her ways. Then had come the "great awakening" of 1740, causing much excitement in the colony, and some of it very irrational excitement. The more sober of the members of the standing order were put on their defence under the wild preaching of George Whitefield and the still wilder preaching and behavior of James Davenport and all that was included under the name (one is sorry to say) of "enthusiasm." While some good doubtless was done by those who called for greater earnestness in religious matters, great harm followed from the unwise words and deeds of others who sowed the seeds of bitter feelings and divisions in families and neighborhoods and set up new religious organizations, differing from the old in little except the claim that they were composed of truly converted men and that they were the true successors of the founders of a century agone.

The same influences, we may be sure, were working in those who three years later declared themselves churchmen here in New Cambridge. But all the circumstances, and in particular certain events of which I must speak in a few minutes, cannot be understood if we fail to remember that every declaration of conformity to the church by a taxpayer, if he came under the conditions named in the act, brought a pecuniary loss to the established society within the limits of which his property was situated. There was, therefore, reason for suspecting that some of those who about this time declared for episcopacy, were really discontented congregationalists, who wished to escape taxation for the support of societies with which they did not agree; and it was not strange that some of the civil officers

were not minded to give to the rather vague provisions of the law a very liberal interpretation.

Now the nine churchmen here had put themselves under the care of Rev. Mr. Gibbs, who lived in Simsbury, that part of the old town of Simsbury which is now called North Bloomfield; and it was a question whether they could conveniently and did attend his administrations. And—the suggestion is not my own; and I do not need to apologize for it—Mr. Gibbs was a Massachusetts man, and did not quite understand how to get along with Connecticut people; and it may be that already his judgment, through no fault of his own, was not of the best. However that may be, we find that before July, 1749, some of the churchmen here had refused to pay their tax for the support of the pastor of the established order (Mr. Gibbs called him "the dissenting minister") and for their refusal had been committed to Hartford jail; that they had then paid their tax to the collector, and that Mr. Gibbs had thereupon demanded it of him, and had been refused for the reason that his mission did not extend to New Cambridge. The trouble did not end here; for on the 28th day of the following December we find Mr. Gibbs writing a letter to the venerable society in England dated from "Hartford Gaol," in which he says that he had brought a suit against the collector for the amount which he believed his due, had "been cast" in the suit, and then refusing to pay the costs had been taken and brought to the jail.

Soon after this his mind began to weaken, and he fell into a condition of what his sister called melancholy; and one cannot read without emotion the inscription on his tomb-stone in the churchyard of old St. Andrew's Church, which tells us that he "died March 22, 1777, in the 63rd year of his age and thirty-third of his mission and twenty-third of his illness."

In 1773 another young man from Waterbury was ready to go to England for ordination, Mr. Nichols, the last of the noble company of forty-three men from this colony who crossed the ocean to seek ordination to the diaconate and the priesthood. The churchmen here voted on the 2nd of April, 1773, "that they would have Mr. Nichols for their minister," and later in the month that they would "give Mr. Nichols forty pounds lawful money yearly for our part of his stated salary," and further that they "would raise 26 pound to carry him home"—that meant to England, and the use of the word at so late a day is touching—"to be raised upon our list at two pence half-penny upon the pound."

It was on the 8th day of the following May that he officiated here for the first time, and here he took up his abode; he was the only resident clergyman of the old church. He found here, as appears from Mr. Scovil's report of 1772, about thirty-three church families and forty-seven communicants.

The business of the old society was brought to an end on the 21st of May, 1792, when a committe was appointed to dispose of the old church house in New Cambridge to the best advantage and return the affect to the committee that was chosen and appointed to carry on and affect the new church in Northbury; and it was also ordered that the church land shall be fenced and inclosed.

Thus the history of the old New Cambridge parish passes into that of the East Church, as it was long called or St. Matthew's Church, East Plymouth. There the deed of a church lot was passed on the 25th day of April, 1792; a church was soon built, and a key-keeper and a gravedigger were appointed in the following December; in 1794 the building was finished and before the end of the year provision was made that it should be dignified. In the next year on the 21st day of October it was consecrated by Bishop Seabury.

It needs but a word to tell the fate of the old "Church House." It was sold, removed, and used for a barn; its arched windows, or part of them, were built into a gambel-roofed house which stood near the site of the pres-

ent house of worship of the Swedish Lutherans. Both barn and house have been destroyed. A boulder marks the site of the church, and the church-yard, which lay too long neglected, has been cleaned and the gravestones put in order, while a careful copy of the inscriptions on them, which includes the names of five of the founders of the old parish, is preserved against the day when they shall crumble into dust.

DEDICATION OF [79] ARMSMEAR CHAPEL

BISHOP C. B. BREWSTER CONDUCTS CEREMONY.

Rev. Samuel Hart and Rev. George T. Linsley Speak.

St. Elizabeth's Chapel at Armsmear was dedicated at 4 o'clock Saturday afternoon. The chapel is named for St. Elizabeth of Hungary, a saint of the early Christian era. It is at the north of the old main entrance, and occupies the room used by Mrs. Samuel Colt as a drawing room. It is on the west side of the house. Saturday was the church day of the Feast of the Epiphany. Bishop Chauncey B. Brewster conducted the dedicatory ceremonies. Others with the bishop within the chancel were Rev. Dr. Samuel Hart of Middletown, dean of the Berkeley Divinity School, Rev. Dr. Francis Goodwin, and Rev. George T. Linsley, rector of the Church of the Good Shepherd and warden of Armsmear.

At the opening, Miss Helen A. Seymour, soprano in the choir of the Church of the Good Shepherd, led the singing of "Christ Is Made the Sure Foundation." Clifton C. Brainerd, organist and choirmaster of the Church of the Good Shepherd, was at the organ. After the invocation, collects, the creed, and special prayers, the bishop pronounced the sentence of dedication. "Call Jehovah Thy Foundation" was sung. Bishop Brewster, in part said:—

'This chapel is the heart of Armsmear. Armsmear is devoted to womanhood in accordance with the will and purpose of one who herself illustrated a noble type of womanhood in its simplicity and strength. This place is devoted to God. A supreme need of womanhood in God." The bishop pointed out that woman's life needed God for consolation, for elevation, for enlargement, for peace, for strength.

Rev. Dr. Samuel Hart said:—

The dedication of this church that is in the house of Armsmear has a special interest, not only for the few who can be gathered in it but for the whole community. We read that in ancient times families, or gatherings of two or three families, had synagogues of their own in the holy land, almost five hundred being established in the city of Jerusalem. At a much later day, but one still far removed from our own, there were in the city of London at least as many churches as there were considerable estates, the boundaries of the parishes

still showing their closeness to one another and the limited number of persons for which each made provision; while the cathedral and the collegiate buildings and suburban churches were open for other congregations. This house, when it was one home, was a place of family worship.

Here for many years the gracious woman whose memory will always be its benediction, sometimes with family and kindred about her, often with guests, and not infrequently with but one or two from her own household, maintained the daily offering of prayer which sanctified the duties, often arduous, and lightened the burdens, often very heavy, of the hours that were to follow. In the very words which had guided her devotions as a child, and from the very book out of which her good father, a priest of the church, had so often read, she daily committed herself to the care of a loving God, and prayed for blessing through the intercession of a gracious Redeemer. This home told of domestic happiness and of domestic sorrow; from it came many pleasures to neighbors and friends, and to it came the sympathy of friends and neighbors in oft-recurring seasons of affliction; it welcomed men and women of honored place in the life of the world and the church, and it stretched out a helping hand to those who needed encouragement and assistance; and all was the more cheerfully done and endured because it was a home of true and simple and strong religion.

Now, by the gracious act of her whose home it so long was, and in accordance with her wishes, entrusted as a sacred confidence to friends, this building, modified and enlarged, indeed, but still the same, has become a collection of homes and a neighborhood—a neighborhood of religious homes in its destined purpose and (we doubt not) in the experience of the few months of its already accomplished history. And it is but seemly that they who dwell thus neighborly in this place should have the opportunity of sharing in one act of neighborhood, that namely of common worship. The one home should have within it a place set apart for prayer; the several homes should have among them a place apart from the several abodes, yet belonging to each and to all, as God's place among those in which His people dwell. As on the village street, where are the abodes of families, some large and some small, some with undiminished numbers and some with sadly broken ranks, yet the homes of men and women, there stands the house of God, with its provision for the one great common need of worship and the gifts of grace, so here, not far from busy streets and places where men labor and toil and jostle one another, this quiet company of neighbors is now to have, as the one thing which indicates that the neighborhood is in its way a community, this seemly chapel as the place where severally or together its members may meet with God, may seek His blessing, may present their petitions and offer their praises to Him.

Here at all times, I trust, will be a place for quiet, private devotion; here on suitable occasions will be an assembly for common worship; to this place others may come who shall find cause for thankfulness that, at times when they cannot conveniently reach their parish churches, they can find opportunity for prayer and sacrament. And thus I see a benediction from this home (for such it was of old), from these homes (for such they are

now), to a wider neighborhood, to the whole community, and especially to the worshipping church of God in this fair city. Thus I see from this place a continual manifestation of Him whose Epiphany we commemorate today. Thus I see that this place shall tell the lesson of the grace and truth, the beauty and the reality, which He ever shows forth to those who can behold His glory. Here may that glory ever be known, that beauty seen, that truth recognized and followed; for here the Lord will surely command His blessing, even life for evermore.

150th ANNIVERSARY OF ST. JAMES'S CHURCH, DANBURY.

HISTORICAL ADDRESS.

Interesting Anniversary Sermon by Rev. Dr. Hart.

Dr. Hart took for his text, Acts 16:10, "And when Paul had seen the vision, immediately we sought to go forth into Macedonia, assuredly gathering that God had called us to preach the gospel unto them." [80]

He said:

"Such was the decision of the band of Christian missionaries led by St. Paul, that they should cross the head of the archipelago and carry the gospel into Europe. It was nearly twenty years since the ascension of the Lord and the birthday of the Church of Christ; much had been done, much learned, and much determined in that time. By direct inspiration and by the lessons of experience the Apostles and those who had followed them had been taught in large part the meaning of the responsibility which lay upon them and the wide extent of its application. The ministry of grace and truth, the grace and truth which had come by Jesus Christ, was proving itself, was demanding that it be accepted, as a service needed by mankind and destined for all. Jerusalem, in the mind of the earliest followers of the glorified Lord, soon widened out into all Judaea, Judaea sent a message and a gift of grace to Samaria; the truth and the blessing could not be kept from the Jews of the dispersion, and from those whom we are wont to call Grecians, Greek-speaking Jews; St. Peter learned and proclaimed that those in any nation who did the right because they feared God were eligible to all the blessings of the new covenant; and presently one who had set himself, as no one else (we may say) would or could have done, in opposition to the faith in Christ destined for all mankind, had been made to see not only the truth of that against which he had contended, but also its illimitable power and scope and destiny. He had preached the gospel to the Gentiles as Gentiles; he had met at Jerusalem those who were determined to stop him in his progress; he had conferred with James and Peter and John; he had argued in the council of apostles and elders, and with the written evidence of the approval of those who had a right to speak for the church, he had passed over districts beyond his

former journeys, testifying to both Jews and Gentiles the gospel which he had accepted for himself and which he knew was meant for all who could be made to hear its message. And as he and his companions went on their journey, they were conscious of a divine direction. Coming near to a fairly large and very important district, the Holy Spirit hindered them from speaking the word in it, when they thought of moving in a direction nearly opposite, the Spirit of Jesus did not give them permission to do so. Whether the Spirit spoke by the mouth of inspired prophets, whether He directed the minds of St. Paul and the others as they thought and deliberated, or whether circumstances showed that their plans were not possible, we cannot tell. All we know is that they found themselves by the site of ancient Troy, pushed on (as it were) from the inland, forbidden to go either north or south, looking westward toward the sea, as Israel of old was shut in on the shore, forced to move on and able to move only towards the watery barrier which separated them from another land. It would seem that they had talked the matter over, wondering what God meant them to do next, and had gone to sleep, leaving the decision until the morning. When the morning came, their leader told them that he had had a vivid dream which he was sure had been sent by God. Across the water, in another region of the world, was Macedonia, a country of Europe; and not far from the coast was a Roman military outpost or colony. St. Paul had dreamed, he said, that he could see the coast, and that on it there stood a man, and that the man called to him, 'Come over and help us.' The others agreed that it was plainly shown to be God's will that they should sail across the head of the sea to the new land—new probably to them all as a land on which their foot might tread, new certainly to them all as a land to which they might carry the Christian grace and truth. And the modest historian, who has not let us know when he became of St. Paul's company is so moved by the enthusiasm of the journey that he says 'we'; 'When Paul had seen the vision, immediately we made plans to go to the land from which the call had come, for we could not but decide that God had sent word to us that we were to take the good message to those who dwelt there.' Thus, the gospel came into Europe, a new quarter of the world, to pass from Phillipi to Corinth, to Rome, to Spain, to Gaul, to Britain, and in the fullness of time to follow the course of empire westward across the great ocean.

"There has not always been a distinct call to the church from the lands into which it has not entered, men have not been seen at all times standing on the shore and shouting over the water for help. Often the gospel has halted at the doors of barred nations, waiting for an opportunity of entrance; often have its messengers asked for a hearing or almost demanded a hearing from those who had no sense of need of the truth and the grace

which they wished to offer. There have been and there are various degrees of preparation; thank God, there is always some preparation for the gospel and for the church to which that gospel is given in trust; and it is a part of the church's wisdom, be it in our own or in apostolic days, to recognize that preparation, and to know with greater or less confidence that she has in each case been called to carry her message to some new part of the earth and to adapt it to some hitherto unknown need.

"The recurrent commemorations of our church's work in Connecticut are for the most part striking examples of events of the same kind as that which befell St. Paul with St. Luke and others at Troas. Men stood and called to their mother church, the historic church of English-speaking people, 'Come over and help us.' Those who called were not, indeed, as in the case which we have thus far had specially in mind, men ignorant of the fundamental truths of the gospel; they were not careless as to Christian faith or Christian practice; but they were not satisfied with what they had, believing that it lacked completeness. This feeling in some ways went back nearly to the time of the first settlements in this colony; and in the memorable year of 1722, forty years before the event which we specially commemorate to-day, that memorable year in which four of the leading ministers of Connecticut decided that they must seek and receive episcopal ordination before they could undertake longer to preach the Word of God and minister the Sacraments of His Church, it found its first distinct expression. From that time on, the call was heard constantly and distinctly. The quaint seal of the Society for Propagation of the Gospel in Foreign Parts, whose first missionaries had passed through the colony twenty years before our 'annus mirabilis,' shows a ship under full sail drawing near to the land, a clergyman in canonical attire standing on the deck with an open book in his hand, while on the shore is a company of people, evidently heathen natives, crying out in the words of Macedonia, 'Transiens adjuva nos.' 'Come over and help us.' The cry which was actually heard from this part of the new world was not from the natives but from the descendants of the earlier colonists. They were coming to the consciousness that their forefathers, godly men and seeking the truth, had lost some things of great importance and had taken heavy burdens in their place, when they had parted from the order of the Church of England; they called to that church for help; and that help came through the action of the venerable society 'to which our church is indebted, under God, for her first foundation and a long continuance of nursing care and protection,' venerable from the first in dignity, venerable now by reason of her age and her record of good works. Yet the petition was not that men might be sent hither to teach again the old ways; it was that able and good men here, well furnished for the work

and already had in reputation, might receive the authority of which they felt the need; it was that the 'recognized leaders of the people in sacred things might be lawfully empowered to minister the grace and the truth of the gospel. This is the meaning of the wonderful history of the ante-revolution Church of England in Connecticut; this is the key to the history of the church in this diocese and state. It was not necessary that men should come from the mother-land; the mother-land was asked to empower our own best men and to give them such moral and material help as should be needed that they might do their work lawfully and well.

"This town had had three-quarters of a century of history, when two disturbing elements came into its ecclesiastical affairs. Whether it was more than a coincidence that Episcopacy and Sandemanianism began orgnized life here about the same time, we cannot tell; certainly the former had individual followers at an earlier date than the latter as might be expected from the fact that the first settlers came from Norwalk and Stratford. John Reed, surnamed 'the Lawyer,' was an early inhabitant here; he had been Congregational minister in Stratford, though apparently not ordained, in the interval of pastorates there which preceded the arrival of Timothy Cutler; and when the Rev. Mr. Muirson and Col. Heathcote made their famous ride along the coast in the summer of 1706, Mr. Reed, we are told, 'manifested a friendship for the doctrines and worship of the Church of England' and expressed a desire if matters could be rightly arranged to receive holy orders from her. He was, in the language of the day, an 'ingenious man' of decided ability and great talents but with some eccentricities. He presently devoted himself to the law, leaving the study of theology, and was one of the first men in the colony admitted as attorneys; and he became, it may be noted, after removing to Boston, the most eminent lawyer in New England, 'the pride of the bar, the light of the law, and the chief among the wise.' Probably his influence churchwards was not very strong, though he deserves to be held in honor among us; others must have been ready to guide the minds of members of the Standing Order towards the Church of England.

"The first clergyman to gather the Danbury churchmen together was the Rev. Henry Caner, an Englishman and a churchman by birth, but a graduate of Yale an da pupil of Dr. Samuel Johnson. He was ordained across the ocean in 1727, and returned to minister in Fairfield, his former residence, and in the places which he could reach, such as Norwalk and Redding, with Ridgefield and Danbury, finding here a few families who desired his ministrations. He was a popular preacher, and was called home in 1746 to the charge of the King's chapel, in Boston. Thence he went, at the breaking out of the Revolution, to Nova Scotia, and thence to England, where he died at the age of ninety-two. His name also should always be held in honor here.

"The Sandemanian influence had begun as the result of reading and correspondence, and it prevailed especially in this neighborhood, in a very extraordinary way, affecting ministers and people and even, in a serious way, the teaching staff of the college at New Haven. It was quickened by the arrival of Mr. Sandeman himself, who lived here from 1764 until his death, seven years later. We may well believe that, as in the eastern part of the colony the discords of the 'great awakening' had sent many to seek rest for their souls in the quiet ways of the church, so here the controversy of the ancient establishment and the breach in the religious order of the community prepared the way for the organization of those who were ready to declare their adherence to the principles and practices of episcopacy. Such an organization was effected a century and a half ago, and in the following year a church building was erected in a church-yard; it had a 'decent steeple' and was of ample size; it was opened with a service by the Rev. Ebenezer Dibble, of Stamford, a native of Danbury, ordained five years earlier. We are told that those who assisted in the cost of the building were, John McLean, who paid for the steeple, and St. George Talbot, an energetic and loyal churchman of the province of New York. Tho first building escaped fire at the time when the British soldiers burned the town; and it was consecrated by Bishop Jarvis in 1802, and was used until 1844; the second church, enlarged after fifteen years, served for a full generation; the present structure dates from 1867, though it was not completed until 1872.

"Before the church was built the church people here had occasional services from the good priests of the neighborhood, Dr. Johnson, of Stamford; Mr. Read, of Newtown; Mr. Leaming, of Norwalk; Mr. Lamson, of Fairfield, and Mr. Dibble already mentioned. Even after the church was occupied, it seems to have been nearly twenty-five years before services were held regularly. These were indeed troublous times, including the whole period of the Revolution and the years which led up to and followed it. The patronage of the Propogation Society in England was diminished and then withdrawn; the adherents of the English church were looked upon with suspicion at the very least, and many of them met with severe treatment; and here, when the Sandemanians were either adherents of the royal cause or non-combatants, the position of the churchmen was especially difficult. Even later, the settled pastors until well within the last century were settled over a two-fold or three-fold cure, Ridgefield and sometimes Redding being included; one of them by reason of ill health withdrew from the ministry before ordination to the priesthood, and another, having been admonished by his brethren, resigned both his charge and 'the exercise of the ecclesiastical function'. The first report of parochial statistics which we find is of date 1809, and has a note of about sixty families and twenty-two communicants here. St. James' church, Dan-

bury, and Christ church, Redding, were still united during the thirteen years' rectorship of the Rev. Lemuel Beach Hull, a grandson of John Beach of worthy memory; near the end of that time, a chapel bearing the name of St. Thomas was built in the 'flourishing village' of Bethel. The parish then reported forty-nine communicants. Mr. Hull, it may be noted, was rector at Wallingford for a time after leaving here, and went thence to Wisconsin, being the first clergyman of our church to settle in that state. In 1839, for the first time, we find Danbury a cure by itself, the church and the chapel being under the charge of the Rev. David H. Short; in six years, under his care, the number of communicants increased from forty-six to 108. In the next rectorship, that of the Rev. Thomas T. Guion, Bethel at Easter, 1846, became a separate parish, leaving in St. James' church about 75 families and 65 communicants. To Mr. Guion succeeded the Rev. William White Bronson in a rectorship of equal length—seven years; to him Israel Leander Townsend for ten years, including the centennial of the parish, when there were some 187 communicants on the roll, nearly three times as many as were reported sixteen years before. Next came Dr. Hawley's rectorship of eleven years, which brings us down to a date well within the memory of many who are now living, so that I may spare you the recital of dates and figures, only asking you yourselves to remember and to bid the new generation remember those who here have ministered the grace and spoken the word; whose faith follow, considering the issue of their lives. And because Jesus Christ, whose is both the grace and the truth, is the same yesterday and to-day and for ever, I exhort you to hold to Him as did your fathers in the faith, and to be not carried about with teachings that are diverse or strange.

"To many of those in whose hearing I recount these gleanings from your annals, the story of three half centuries ago as it comes down to the year which is but one-half century behind us is indeed the story of small things. The little band gathered here, asking for spiritual help from hard working and faithful clergymen in stations but little stronger, confessing the faith and the worship of the Church of England at a time when the political bond which united the colonies to the mother country was weakening; the small company of churchmen who were found here after the Revolution, and whose strength was shown in little except faithfulness; even the fairly strong country parish of fifty years ago—any and all of these are scarce to be reckoned in comparison with the great body of church men and women and children whose spiritual home is to-day in this house of God. True, there has been great increase in the community itself, business and prosperity have pushed everything forward; still, it is no little thing that the church which scarce had a name to live has now so wide a scope for work and so ready an entrance as is now granted to this parish in its varied opportunities of worship, of labor, and of help.

209

"Yet the present has grown out of the past; the seed sown by the fathers is yielding a harvest for those who have come after; it is because Johnson and Cutler and Brown, and those who followed them, were faithful to their convictions; that the historic church of the English speaking people, that the faith of that church and its organization are believed and maintained in Connecticut now; it is because England gave to these men apostolic authority to minister and to teach, that our church has to-day the position and opportunity which it holds in this state and in this land, and the responsibility which it is permitted to carry; it is because of the fidelity of those to whom the few things were entrusted, that we dare to undertake the charge of the many things—many, at least, in our estimate and in outward appearance—which appeal to our hearts and our hands. Then 'Come over and help us,' which was the inspiration of the work of the Venerable Society in England, heard and answered, is the reason for our being gathered here to-day for this service of thanksgiving; the response to a like cry, sent forth in the days of weakness and discouragement, has shown its results in the maintenance of the faith and the orders and the worship which have come down in the church from the earliest ages. Their names may well be held in everlasting remembrance, the record of whose work of faith and labor of love and patience of hope is rehearsed in our ears on our diocesan or parochial anniversaries; for then we render most high praise and hearty thanks to Almighty God.

"But do we value as we ought that which meant so much to them but which we can so readily take for granted? It is not a very hard thing for us, here to-day, to profess the faith and join in the worship and follow in the ways of the ancient church. If they have not come to us with our very life, if their influence has not been operating upon us from our earliest consciousness, yet at least it has not cost us much that we acknowledge and follow them. Do we all set upon these privileges their full value? Do we all study their meaning, as is but seemly for so great an inheritance? Do we, most of all, begin to know about the church what they were forced to know who confessed her in the days of her beginning in this commonwealth? Believe me, we must do this if we are to fulfill our duty to ourselves and to others. We need an intelligent understanding of our position and our duties, why we are and why we must be in this place in which we find ourselves or are found; and men and women are waiting that we may tell them what it is that satisfies our minds and quickens our emotions and instructs our souls, making us brave and patient, wise and religious; they are wondering—though they may not know it—why the blessing which has come to us has not passed beyond us to them.

"For it is not alone from Macedonia in apostolic days, not alone from New England in the former part of the eighteenth century, that a vision has been seen and a cry heard. In our strength, in our enthusiasm, in our settled estate, we see men, not of our own people, not all of our own race, standing and crying, 'Come over and help us.' And God has so wakened us that we cannot but hear, and so shut up our path that we cannot turn to the right hand or to the left, much less go back. From less fortunate parts of our own diocese, did we but know it; from the newer or poorer or less favored regions of this our great land, and we do know it; from the islands in the seas and the continents beyond them, and may God give us the vision which will make us know it; yes, even more clearly, sometimes more hopefully and sometimes more warningly, the cry is sent across the narrower or the wider barriers which we must pass to carry the answer, to do the answer, 'Come over and help us.' Each anniversary opens our ears to this call, and turns our eyes to the source whence it comes. If our reply shall be at all, when compared with our obligation and our ability the equivalent of that which our forefathers in the faith received from those to whom they called, there will be no need that our brethren, or those whom God would have to become our brethren, should need to repeat or to emphasize their appeal. The missions of the church are the missions of the church; so St. Paul with St. Luke and his other companions learned when they were bidden to sail for Troy to Macedonia; so they learned who crossed from the continent to Britain when it was but Britain, to England when it had become England; so the true heart of England's church turned to the colonies on these Atlantic shores, giving us the priesthood and the prayer book; so, when England's faith failed, the 'Catholic remainder of the Church in Scotland,' 'out of the abundance of its poverty,' gave us the episcopate; so our first bishop, and those who followed him and felt his inspiration, went up and down in this diocese and turned the hearts of the children to their fathers; so our church in this land has striven to carry her message of truth and grace over its wide expanse; so we have been trying to learn, and, God helping us, have learned in part, that we have a duty to the regions beyond, even to those from which a call can reach us but faintly—a duty which is a lofty privilege and the understanding of which is itself a blessing. When Paul had seen his vision, immediately we sought to go forth, assuredly gathering that God had called us to preach the gospel unto the men across the sea.' If the apostle had not been thinking of such things, he would not have had the vision; if he had not told the vision, the others would not have given counsel for the journey; if they had not thought it worth the while, 'we should have been but here then in our day.' In like manner, if Johnson and Caner and Leaming and Seabury had not known that the essentials of faith and order and worship were so essential that they cannot be omitted or exchanged, the history of this diocese would never have been written, the wondrous opportunities which open before it would not be possible, the appeal for wider sympathies and wider help could not be made with the confidence with which it is made to-day.

"God, before whom our fathers did walk, the God who hath led us even unto this day, He who hath defended us from evil and inspired us for good, bless us for all that remains; and may His Name be named upon us for blessing evermore."

ADDENDA FROM THE PRESS ACCOUNTS

PARISH OF ST. JAMES'.

An Honored Institution for a Century and a Half.

The building in which the St. James' Episcopal church of Danbury started its existence was the second ecclesiastical structure to be built in Danbury, the first having been that of the First Congregational society, which was built in 1696. The St. James' structure was built in 1763, on South street, the year after the parish was incorporated. For thirty-five years previous to this, Episcopal services had been held in Danbury by clergymen settled at Fairfield, Newtown and Stamford, who were missionaries to the parishes within riding distance.

The graveyard on South street was the churchyard of the Episcopal building, as first built. This building was moved, when the second church edifice was built, to the west corner of Main and South streets, where it was modernized and converted into a tenement house. At this time it is interesting to note the Baptist church was on Deer Hill avenue, and the Universalist church was on Main street, opposite the present Court house.

A historical sketch of St. James' Episcopal church in the "History of Danbury" says: "In 1728 Rev. Henry Caner, a Yale graduate, who had been to England for holy orders and had become, on his return, a missionary to Fairfield, paid visits to Danbury and Ridgefield, and stated in his first report that 'there were in these places ten or fifteen families professing the doctrine of the Church of England.'"

The first Episcopal church building was opened by Rev. Ebenezer Dibble, a native of Danbury, who was then a missionary in Stamford and Greenwich. He was born in Danbury, a son of Wakefield Dibble. Rev. Mr. Leaming and Rev. John Beach, of Newtown, held occasional services in the building. We are told that the Newtown missionary spoke of the Danbury church building in 1769 as having "a decent steeple" and being "large enough to accommodate from 400 to 500 people;" that the steeple in question "was given to the church by John McLean, a notable citizen of old Danbury." John McLean was the grandfather of Mrs. Horace Marshall, whose husband was a prominent warden of St. James' church for many years.

and the father of the late Mrs. Caroline Marshall Wheelock.

When Danbury was burned, in 1777, General Tryon's men took the military stores out of the church building and burned them, but did not harm the church edifice.

Rev. David Perry, of Ridgefield, was in charge of the Danbury parish, together with the parishes of Ridgefield and Redding, for a few years, but resigned in 1794, to be succeeded by Rev. David Butler, who in turn was succeeded by Rev. Elijah G. Plum, who was rector of the Danbury church from 1808 until 1812. Bishop Jarvis consecrated the Danbury church October 6, 1802. In the year 1809, seventy families and twenty-two communicants were reported. In 1816 there were 41 communicants and in 1824 forty-nine communicants.

Rev. Reuben Hubbard was rector from the year 1812 to 1819. He was succeeded by Rev. Ambrose S. Todd, who was rector until 1823. Rev. Lemuel Beach Hull was rector from 1823 to 1836. Mr. Hull was the grandson of Rev. John Beach, of Newtown. Mrs. Anthony M. Rundle, of this city, is of this line. Rev. David H. Short was rector from 1836 to 1840, and he was followed by Rev. Thomas T. Guion, who was in charge of the church until 1847.

The "History" says: "In 1836, there were only five families and forty communicants remaining of the original churchmen. Up to this date the parish had clerical services once in three or four weeks, and from 1808 had been associated with Christ church, Redding, and for a part of the time with Ridgefield. After the chapel (now St. Thomas' church, Bethel,) was built in 1835, the services were divided between the two alternately once in four weeks. In 1836 the parish of St. James' church and St. Thomas' chapel attempted to have the services of a clergyman the whole time, but failed. There were not enough clergymen to 'go around' in those days, and the church which had a rector 'all to itself' was fortunate indeed. From Easter in 1838 to Easter of 1839, Dr. Short divided his time equally between Danbury and Brookfield, and the Christian Knowledge society aided in the payment of his salary."

The original church building was abandoned in 1844, and a new church building was built on West street, near Main street. The site of the new church was bought from the estate of the late Captain Elijah Gregory. It was called "the store porperty." Rev. Henry Olmstead and Rev. John Purves were associated with the rector, Mr. Guion, living in Bethel and being in charge of the chapel there. In 1847 Rev. William White Bronson succeeded Rev. Mr. Guion as rector; and remained in charge of the church until 1854, when he was followed by Rev. I. Leander Townsend. Rev. Mr. Townsend was rector for a decade, being succeeded, in 1864, by Rev. Dr. Fletcher J. Hawley. The church was enlarged and improved by the addition of a chancel and new furniture in 1859.

Rev. Fletcher J. Hawley, D. D.

Dr. Hawley, who was rector of St. James' church for a decade, from 1864, was born in Arlington, Vt., November 22, 1813. He was graduated from Union college, Schenectady, N. Y., in 1840, and from the General Theological seminary, in New York city, in 1843.

His first parish was St. John's church at Christiansted, Santa Cruz. It was under the supervision of the bishop of Antigua, and was largely composed of wealthy planters. Mr. Hawley was the architect of a stone church which his parish built, seating 1,200. He worked out the models with his own hands, for the native workers in the building to go by.

The king of Denmark honored him, during his stay in Santa Cruz, by appointing him to head the Colonial council, and also by making him special adviser to the governor general. In an insurrection in Santa Cruz Mr. Hawley lost all his property. He and a Catholic priest held the insurrection in check for three days, by going about together in white robes, admonishing the natives.

Soon after returning to the United States, in 1859, Rev. Mr. Hawley went to New Orleans, where he became rector of Trinity church. He went south reluctantly, finally consenting to take the new charge only after many urgent requests had been made. He worked zealously in New Orleans, as everywhere. For months he worked without pay, as the Civil war was impending, and the church was poor. He finally had practically nothing left and came to New York, arriving there December 25, 1862.

Ministering in Danbury from 1864 to 1875 he went from here to Stafford Springs, where he went energetically to work and raised money and built a handsome new church. From Stafford Springs he went to Brainerd, Minn., where he was rector of St. Paul's church. He died in May, 1891.

Rev. Fletcher J. Hawley was the architect of the present church and labored zealously for its completion. It stands a monument to his untiring devotion and self denying sacrifice.

The chapel, the chancel, and the first bay of the nave of the present church edifice, on West street, were built in 1867. In 1872 the nave and tower were completed, "all save the stone spire." This last phrase is of particular interest at this time, as the uncompleted tower of the church has just been finished off with attractive stone work, and topped with a copper roof, giving the church building a much improved appearance.

Rev. Arthur Sloane became rector of the church in May, 1875. He was succeeded in September, 1880, by Rev. Byron J. Hall, who was rector of the church for fourteen years.

Rev. Byron J. Hall.

Rev. Byron J. Hall was born in North Adams, Mass. He was graduated from Williams college. He came to St. James' church in September, 1880, from Lansingburgh, N. Y.

The building of the church had been a large work for a parish of no greater means to undertake, and when Rev. Mr. Hall became rector, there was a debt. He made the reduction of this debt his first important work, and early in 1881 the church was free from indebtedness.

Rev. Mr. Hall resigned in 1894, his health having become impaired. He was the only rector of St. James church who died in the parish. He was the grandfather of Martin H. Griffing, Jr., of this city. He was dearly beloved by his parishioners, and the church thrived under his guirance.

Rev. John D. Skene.

Rev. John Dolby Skene succeeded Rev. Mr. Hall, beginning his pastorate here November 1, 1894. He was called to St. James' parish from St. Paul's, Brooklyn, N. Y. He is the only living ex-rector of the Danbury parish. He is now the rector of St. Andrew's Episcopal church, in Stamford.

Mr. Skene began his ministry thirty-six years ago, in the diocese of Albany. He was ordained to the diaconate and advanced to the priesthood by Bishop Doane, while being an assistant to Rev. Dr. Nichols, rector of St. Mark's church, Hoosick Falls, N. Y., where he served about six years.

He was the rector of St. Augustin's parish, in Ilion, N. Y., from 1882 to 1885, when, on account of the serious illness of one of his children, he removed to New Jersey, where he was rector of Trinity parish, in Asbury park, until called to the Brooklyn parish, in 1889.

Mr. Skene, who is attending the celebration, is held in affectionate esteem by hundreds of Danburians. During his rectorate in Danbury he was very successful in his work and was rewarded for his untiring efforts by seeing his parish prosper. A man of sterling qualities, he won to him all with whom he came into contact, and on every trip to Danbury he is greeted cordially by his many friends and admirers, with whom he enjoys talking over incidents of his residence in this city.

Rev. George W. Davenport.

Rev. George W. Davenport, the present rector, came to the Danbury parish in the fall of 1902, succeeding Mr. Skene. He came here from Astoria, Long Island. Concerning the fruits of his work here during the decade of his rectorship, it would be superfluous to say much, as they are so obvious. The scope of the church has practically been doubled under his leadership. Under his capable guidance the church has prospered as never before, both spiritually and materially, and now stands as one of the most powerful agents of good in the community.

The Rectories.

The earliest known rectory was a house on Main street, near South street. During the rectorate of Rev. William White Bronson, the church bought a rectory on Deer Hill avenue. This was sometime between 1847 and 1854. Dr. I. Leander Townsend, who was rector from 1854 to 1864, conducted an Episcopal military school, on the northwest corner of Deer Hill avenue and West Wooster street, on the William P. See-

211

RECTORS OF ST. JAMES'S
DANBURY

lev estate, and made one of the buildings of the school his rectory. For a few years after Dr. Townsend's resignation the rectory continued to be in the same place.

The rectory was the house on Delay street formerly owned by Dr. William C. Wile for some time. When Rev. Byron J. Hall became rector the house on Deer Hill avenue now occupied by Dr. Paul U. Sunderland was rented as a rectory.

When Rev. Mr. Skene became rector the house on West street, now used as a parish house, was purchased and fitted up as a rectory. Mr. Skene and family lived at the Turner house for a time after his arrival here, until the new rectory was ready for his occupancy. Rev. Mr. Davenport occupied the same rectory until a few years ago, when it aws decided to build a new rectory on Terrace place, and use the old one, remodeled, as a parish house. Mr. Davenport and family lived in the Horace Peck house on Farview avenue, while the present rectory was being built.

For many of the interesting facts contained in this historical sketch of the St. James' parish, the News is indebted to Mrs. Chester H. Brush, of Stony Hill, who generously assisted with data collected by her in preparation for the publication of a history of the local parish, which will be made soon.

RECTORS OF ST. JAMES'S
DANBURY

...1794—REV. DAVID PERRY
1794-1808—REV. DAVID BUTLER
1808-1812—REV. ELIJAH G. PLUM
1812-1819—REV. REUBEN HUBBARD
1819-1823—REV. AMBROSE S. TODD
1823-1836—REV. LEMUEL BEACH HULL
1836-1840—REV. DAVID H. SHORT
1840-1847—REV. THOMAS T. GUION
1847-1854—REV. WILLIAM WHITE BRONSON
1854-1864—REV. I. LEANDER TOWNSEND
1864-1875—REV. FLETCHER J. HAWLEY
1875-1880—REV. ARTHUR SLOANE
1880-1894—REV. BYRON J. HALL
1894-1902—REV. JOHN D. SKENE
1902-   REV. GEORGE W. DAVENPORT

[81]
MIDDLETOWN—PAST AND FUTURE

Dr. Hart's Address.

Rev. Dr. Samuel Hart's address follows:—

A little more than twelve years ago, Middletown celebrated her 250th anniversary. We recalled then that it was the fifth settlement in the old river colony and the tenth in the united colony under the charter; and that varied in character as the others had been, this had an individuality of its own, a special place at the time, and a special destiny for the future. The settlement at Mattabeseck, as I said at the time, marked in a way the completion of the fundamental plan of the colony, which needed a center to which men could look from the river-towns above, from the fort at the mouth of the river, and from the republic further up the Sound with its daughters on either side, whence also the colonists could look forth into the forests and fertile lands of East and West.

It was more than the beauty or even the convenience of the locality that attracted the first settlers and those who presently cast in their lot with them. The sloping hillside on the west bank of the great river, with the narrows like a gorge below, must have appealed to those who looked up from their boats as they made their way down the stream, or who looked down from the heights of the Indian fort to which they doubtless climbed. They saw that the land was good and pleasant, and they had a vision of homes and cultivated fields and pasture lands, and also of access to the sea and thus to older colonies on the one side and the other, to the islands of the West Indies, and to the western country. Would they have been disappointed if they had come back a century or two centuries and a half later? Would they be disappointed if they were to come back today?

A hundred years after the settlement, in 1750, they would have found intimations that the colonial period was drawing to its close; but with a little prophetic vision they would have seen how, here as elsewhere, a good foundation had been laid and progress had been made in building on it. With the steadiness of an agricultural community, on this spot and on favoring lands hard by, there was already the outlook of a trading community sending its products to other places and receiving for them what they had to give in exchange. It was in the center of the colony, and probably already the first in population among the nearly equal towns of the jurisdiction; and here as elsewhere had developed, on the firm foundations of religion and education and self-government, a strength and breadth of character which was not only serviceable for the time then present but also a preparation for the changes that were close at hand. By doing duties and using opportunities the fathers did well the work that lay before them, as individuals and as members of the community; and thus they handed on a store of influence for faithfulness and bravery to those who were to follow them. The first settlers would not have had cause for disappointment if they could have looked forward a hundred years, nor have we cause to be ashamed when we look back a century and a half to the time of the turning-point in the history of the republic and ask what such a community as this had done and was doing to serve that republic.

In 1900, when we observed the quarter-millennial of Middletown, we could not but contrast the city of that day with the town of 1750 and the settlement of a century earlier. Even the methods of agriculture had largely changed, while manufactures and commerce and transportation had come to be carried on along new lines and by the application of newly discovered forces, and education was seen to be extending to fresh fields of knowledge and to have wonderfully varied applications. All this was recognized in words and represented to the eye and the mind by the addresses and the pageants of the celebration of that year. They showed not only what had been accomplished but also the reason why and the manner in which the changes had been wrought and accepted and used. As to the facts, they were, as I said, before our eyes, and most of us were astonished as we saw them brought together and vividly presented to us; they would have much more surprised those who came here as the first settlers of the place. But the reason for the changes in life and work did not lie among things mysterious, for it belongs always to the guiding laws of nature and of the human soul. Nature with her forces comes into better knowledge of the mind of man; the mind by experiment and experience—how nearly the two words mean the same thing!—applies those forces better in their separate action and in their correlation; and we come to the progress which is so sure a mark of the material side of civilization. The real reason for all such progress is faithfulness in vision, the watching for opportunities which often seems as if it created them, and the using of them in the confidence that they were meant for us to use. The forefathers would have seen, I think, that their successors had not lost the ideals which they themselves brought here; they could not indeed have improved upon those ideals, for they were the very highest in personal and civic and religious character; but they would have noted applications of them unfamiliar and even startling; but after a while they would certainly have commended all that in those applications was well grounded and of true service; they would have seen that the new life had sprung out of the old and was guided by it; they would not have been ashamed of their descendants and successors;—but I am sure that they would have trembled at the responsibilities which had fallen upon those descendants and successors and at the lightness of heart with which they seemed to be undertaking them.

In the life of such a community as this one could not venture to draw any special lesson from its history in the eighth part of a century, unless indeed that short time had brought some extraordinary moral or political crisis and made special demands on strength of character. No such extraordinary crisis has fallen upon us in the past twelve years; yet it has seemed to some of those most deeply interested in the welfare of the community that there might well be a consultation as to present opportunities and duty, in the firm conviction that he serves himself best who serves his neighbor and his neighborhood best. The hopes and prophecies of the founders, real even if not expressed, have been more than fulfilled; and if we study our present duty and look forward to the future, it is in the firm assurance that the moral and religious character of this community, its civil life, its position as a home of learning, its devotion to high standards of patriotism, its advance in that true prosperity which comes from the use of opportunities for the work of hand and brain, shall be more than worthy of its history in the years that are past, while yet they grow out of it in accordance with every true principle of progress.

We may well be thankful that we are committed to sound principles, to principles of duty, honor, and unselfishness, and that, though these met with opposition, they will be strengthened by every conflict and be victorious in the end.

[82]
THE FIRST FORT AT SAYBROOK
1635-1647

(Special to The Courant.)
Saybrook Point, May 27.

Notwithstanding the unpleasant weather of this afternoon about 150 people gathered at Saybrook Point to attend the dedication of the monument erected by the Connecticut Society of the Colonial Dames of America as a memorial of the old fort at

this place. The women came by auto directly from their annual meeting at Old Lyme.

The president of the society, Mrs. Williston Walker of New Haven, read the preamble of the constitution of the society and then introduced Dr. Samuel Hart of Middletown, to tell why they had decided to mark the site of the old fort. After his speech Mrs. Walker presented the monument to the town in a few words. It was accepted by Selectman Calvin C. Fairbank in behalf of his town.

"The First Fort at Saybrook, 1635-1647."

Rev. Dr. Samuel Hart of the Berkeley Divinity School, Middletown, told of "The First Fort at Saybrook, 1635-1647," saying:—

As the English settlers, more than 275 years ago, sailed slowly along the coasts of this new world, they must have wondered at their natural beauty of land and water, at the possibilities of advantage to be gained, and at the importance of securing possession of them. The broad rivers must have had a special attraction for them, leading back, as they did, into the unoccupied country. Sailing to the west up Long Island Sound, they found three fair streams, and they soon took possession of the mouths of the Thames (as they presently named it), and the Long River or the Connecticut, and the Quinnipiack, and at the head of the Sound they came upon a great arm of the ocean, of which they conjectured that it gave access to the South Sea.

It would seem that they believed this site on which we stand to have a special value for defence against the Dutch of New Amsterdam and the Indians of the neighborhood and also for the establishment of trading posts in the interior. The Dutch had, in a quiet way, seen its importance as an approach to their House of Hope some fifty miles above; but their occupation or claim had no real influence on history. Soon the English from the Massachusetts Newtown made a settlement close to that house, not much disturbing it, or disturbed by it; and, almost at the same time, there came here a band of twenty men, representing Lord Say and Sele, Lord Brooke, and their company, under authority of a patent or deed of lands, prepared to assert possession, to build houses, and to construct a strong military defense or fort, and later to cut off the whole point of land by a palisade, to build houses for "men of quality" who were expected and a windmill for the use of tillers of the fields. The first landing of this body of settlers, or garrison, was on the 24th day of November, old style, in the year 1635; and work on the enclosure of the fort must have begun at once, to be completed under the competent direction of Lion Gardiner, and thus the Indian Pashbeshauke and Dutch Kievets Hooke were displaced by the English Saybrooke.

This first fort was the center and almost the circumference of the life of the settlement for about twelve years. It occupied a mound of land near the site of the stone which we are placing today as its memorial, a mound which later came to be known as Fort Hill, commanding a view of the mouth of the river; and its enclosure was large enough to provide for a "great hall," houses for residences, and an orchard and garden. Hither came John Winthrop, the younger, with supreme authority for a year, which he administered in residence for no more than three months; Lion Gardiner, who served as surveyor and builder, and also as lieutenant in charge for four years; Colonel George Fenwick, a patentee, who on his second visit, assumed charge of fort and plantation, and in 1644 ceded all territorial and governmental rights of the settlement to the colony of Connecticut, of which Saybrook thereupon

became a town; and with him, at his second visit, giving a touch of romance and beauty to this history, his wife, Lady Alice Apsley Boteler, who was buried within the fort in 1646, and whose name and memory shall remain as long as her home is mentioned; also, John Higginson, appointed chaplain when he was but 20 years old, who married Sarah Whitfield, daughter of the founder of Guilford, and became one of the nobles of New England; and Thomas Peters, his successor in the chaplaincy and a practitioner of medicine, who remained here but a short time. Here in the Great Hall, after the military garrison had become a town, a church was organized on the principles and according to the usages of Congregational Puritanism; and thereupon the church chose a "famous young gentleman," James Fitch by name, to be its pastor, and he was solemnly set apart and commissioned for his office by the laying-on of the hands of designated members of the newly organized body. About the same time Captain John Mason came from Windsor to instruct and guide the garrison; and in other ways than this he brought strength and encouragement to the community.

Thus, in the course of a few years, and under the shelter of the old fort, the civil government of a small but important company was administered until it was merged in that of a formally organized colony; buildings and defenses were erected; the mouth of the river was held against enemies and the place was kept safe against possible attack from the Indians; men who would have been distinguished anywhere cast in their lot with those who had come at the first; a gracious lady brought the amenities of family life, with the service of domestic cattle and pets, of flowers and fruits, and then fell asleep in Christ, leaving behind her a blessing and a word of patience and encouragement to all generations; and a congregation of elect souls was gathered and placed under the care of a Christian pastor, to hand on the word and ministry of grace to those who should come after. It makes an important chapter of history, involving both wholesome growth and wholesome change.

But the days of the fort were numbered. Its structure was of wood; and one day it caught fire, and all that was within the enclosure, with some buildings that were without, was speedily destroyed. A new fort, more like a fort than the former, took its place; it stood close to the river's bank, and its form was that of an earthwork fitted for attack and defence, rather than to be a place of residence. The affection of Colonel Fenwick placed a seemly monument over his wife's grave, unmarked with name or date; and this grave, with its monument, enclosed after a long while by a simple protection, was all that remained to tell simply, but touchingly, the story of the early settlement and the early days. There are those who remember the earthwork of the second fort, far older than anything else of the same kind in the northern part of the United States, which formed an instructive and picturesque feature of the scenery until it gave way to structures which may be more useful but are certainly less attractive; and the solitary tombstone, with that which remained of the body that had been buried beneath it, was removed to an honored place in the burying ground hard by. Today you, madam and ladies, have honored this place by your presence and by the erection which suggests the annals of the first fort at Saybrook; today and for all time to come you invite the passer-by to know that fort's history and its influence on all the latter days.

MARKER FOR OLD FORT AT SAYBROOK

COLONIAL DAMES TO MARK SITE OF FIRST FORTIFICATION IN COLONY.

Lion Gardiner Colonel Fenwick and John Mason Were Historic Tenants.

INDIANS BESEIGED IT FOR AN ENTIRE WINTER

The Connecticut Society of Colonial Dames will this afternoon dedicate a marker in Old Saybrook, designed to mark the site of the first fort in that settlement, said to be the first fort in Connecticut, built in 1635 and burned, or "destroyed by fire," as the Dames, with a disregard for brevity, put it on the marker, in 1647. Deep as the contractors may place the foundation of the granite marker it will reach down to the hopes which the founders of the colony once cherished, for they said in their hearts, while on English soil, that they were to found a great city, and yet now, almost 280 years later, Old Saybrook remains a little country town, not as large as its once next-door neighbor, Guilford, some four years younger and precious near 100 times smaller than its once saintly old friend, New Haven, while its rival, Hartford has also become a great city, all of which would mightily surprise the settlers of Saybrook could they but know it, because they made haste to work at the fort when they found that the Hartford colony had taken form.

It was to be an aristocratic settlement, the only one north of Virginia with Lords Say and Seal, Brook and Rich in it and with Hampden and Oliver Cromwell seriously considering a removal of it. But it is more than 250 years since these hopes met a killing frost. The Earl of Warwick gave the lords above mentioned a liberal but vague grant of land, "of all that territory which lies west of Narragansett River 120 miles on the sea coast, and from thence in latitude and breadth aforesaid, to the South Sea." That was in 1631 and it was four years later. So unhurried were people in those days before John Winthrop, the son of the Massachusetts governor, being at that time in England, was commissioned agent of the lords to build a fort at Connecticut River to erect houses for the accommodation of himself and men," and for the reception of persons of quality, and they made him governor of Connecticut River and the places adjoining, for the space of one year. The fact that he had nothing but a wilderness to govern had nothing to do with the honor.

Winthrop came to America by way of Boston and when he arrived there he found that some of the colonists had already come on to the territory granted to the lords and that it was time he got busy with his fort and the erection of houses for himself and the persons of quality. He went to Saybrook (it became Old Saybrook years later) and laid out the site for a settlement on the point with parallel streets, intersecting streets, a fort and back of it a great square on which houses were to be built for the persons of quality who never came.

The fort was built as soon as possible but, for reasons which appeared shortly after, the houses for the persons of quality were not erected then

or later. Before the work was completed Winthrop's commission had run out and he turned the job over to Lieutenant Lion Gardiner, a man well calculated for the task. He was of a warlike disposition and had fought in the low countries before he came to Boston in November, 1635, with his wife, being then 36 years old. He was the man Winthrop wanted, but he asked about the Indians and was informed by the truthful Puritans that they were negligible and that their bows and arrows could not harm an Englishman who wore a stout leather jacket.

How they contrived to tell this story to Gardiner still passes understanding, for, only a year before Winthrop began his fort, the Indians had captured a sloop at the mouth of the river and killed Stone and Norton, the two white men aboard, looted the boat and then burned her to the water's edge. Winthrop made a treaty with the Indians, which was not worth the trouble, because, in October 1635, when five men left the fort to gather hay on the Lyme shore, the Indians surprised them and caught one, "a godly young man named Butterfield," and tortured him to death.

That gave Gardiner an idea, but more were to follow. Within a week Joseph Tilley came to anchor with a bark opposite Calves Island and, taking a man with him, went on shore, hunting. Indians waited until he had discharged his musket and then they caught him and the man with him. They killed the latter, but Tilley they tortured for three days before he died. A house two miles away had been erected as a sort of outpost and Gardiner had sent six men to keep it, with strict orders not to straggle. Three of them went out hunting and the Indians attacked them, capturing two, the other escaping with two wounds.

During the winter the fort under Gardiner was practically in a state of siege and the Indians burned or carried away everything of value that was near it. In March Gardiner went out with a dozen men to burn the dry grass on the marshes, when he was attacked by the Indians, who killed three men and wounded a fourth, so that he died the next day. By this time Gardiner was thoroughly aroused. The man who was wounded and who died the next day was shot through the body by an arrow which lodged in a rib on the opposite side. Gardiner cut out a section of the rib containing the arrow and sent it to Boston with a grim comment as to the effectiveness of the weapons of the Indians. A day or so later the Indians captured three mariners and ripped them open and hung their mutilated bodies on trees in sight of the fort as a cheerful sight for Gardiner's men.

About this time Captain John Mason was sent with twenty men to reinforce the fort and was probably welcomed, but he was soon relieved by Captain John Underhill, both men prominent in early colonial history. While this was going on the Indians made the raid at Wethersfield, which started the settlements on the river on the desperate project of the Pequot War, and the task accomplished by them at Porter's Rocks was so effectual as to bring peace to the men in the fort. Gardiner remained there until some doubtful period between 1639 and 1641, when he took possession of Gardiner's Island, where his descendants welcomed and entertained Captain Kidd, and which has remained in the Gardiner name unto this time. It is interesting to note

that he wrote a very graphic account of his stay at Saybrook, which remains among the most interesting of Connecticut documents.

In 1639, after the trouble with the Indians, Colonel George Fenwick came to the fort. He and his wife, Lady Alice Fenwick, came over with the the Guilford colony and Lady Fenwick was the only branch of the nobility to reach Saybrook. She, then a young woman though a widow when Colonel Fenwick married her, spent the rest of her life in Saybrook, not a long one. She was buried there but her resting place was moved when the Valley railroad was built. Fenwick went back, probably early in 1648, taking with him three daughters born of the marriage; Elizabeth, Dorothy and Mary. He died in 1657. An interesting tradition has it that, on the boat which brought them from England to Guilford, Lady Fenwick and her husband brought some Devon cattle and made a gift of one or two heads to Parson Whitfield of the Guilford colony. Some of the descendants of these cattle can still be found in Lyme and Saybrook, and, until a generation ago, they might have been seen in Guilford.

In July, 1639, Davenport of the New Haven colony wrote to Lady Vere: "By the good hand of God upon us, my dear child is safely arrived with sundry desirable friends, as Mr. Fenwick, his lady, Mr. Whitfield, &c., to our great comfort. Their passage was so ordered, as it appeared that prayers were accepted. For they had no sickness in the ship except a little sea sickness; not one died but they brought to the shore one more than was known to be in the vessel at their coming forth, for a woman was safely delivered of a child and both were alive and well. They attained to the haven where they would be in seven weeks."

The old fort lost much of its importance with the successful close of the Pequot War. After that event Captain John Mason came back to the settlement and remained there until, with sundry others, he left to form the new settlement at Norwich. The fort was erected at a very power point and was mightily useful in its day. During the winter of 1647 it was burned and a new one was begun in the spring a little further to the north and on what is known as New Fort Hill. Before it was finished the Dutch attempted to send a boat up the river but two guns were manned and landing was prevented. In 1675 it was able to prevent the surrender of the town to Major Andross. By the time of the Revolutionary War it had lost its importance and, though needed, it had "passed away" by the time of the War of 1812-14. The address of the day will be made by Saybrook's distinguished son, Rev. Dr. Samuel Hart, and the presentation to the town will be by Mrs. Williston Walker and the acceptance by First Selectman C. C. Fairbanks. The inscription on the marker follows.—

Say Brooke Fort
Commanded by
Colonel George Fenwick
At the Mouth of the Great River
Near This Place Stood the First
English Fort in the Colony of
Connecticut, Built in 1635.
It was Destroyed by Fire in
1647. Beyond it, on the Bank
Of the River, Stood the Second
Fort, built in 1648. Its Earthworks were demolished in 1870.

This Memorial is Erected by
The Connecticut Society of the
Colonial Dames of America
in 1913.

VETERAN RECTOR
OF GUILFORD DEAD

**Rev. Dr. William G. Andrews Was
Prominent in Episcopal Church.**
(Special to The Courant.)
Guilford, Dec. 23.

Rev. Dr. William G. Andrews died at his home here at 9 o'clock this morning. He had been in poor health for six years but his condition was serious for the last three weeks. The funeral will be held in Christ Church, at 2 o'clock, Thursday afternoon.

William Given Andrews was a son of Rev. William Watson Andrews, who spent the latter part of his life in Wethersfield and died there in 1897.

Rev. Dr. William G. Andrews.

and half-brother of Professor Charles McLean Andrews of Yale University. He was born in Kent, this state, October 8, 1835, and was graduated at Marietta College, in Ohio, in 1855. After teaching for a while, he studied for two years at Princeton Theological Seminary and then served for a year as tutor at Marietta. He was ordained by Bishop Oxenheimer of New Jersey, September 26, 1862, and officiated in Princeton and its neighborhood until 1866, when he accepted a position in the Rectory School at Hamden. From 1868 to 1879 he was rector of the Church of the Ascension in New Haven; and in the spring of 1881 he accepted the rectorship of the venerable parish of Christ Church, Guilford, from which Rev. Dr. L. T. Bennett was retiring after an incumbency of forty years, and in this parish he continued for the rest of his life; but he signified to the parish that at Easter, 1906, at the close of twenty-five years' service, he should ask to be relieved from pastor duty. This was done and he was made rector emeritus.

Dr. Andrews received his honorary degree in divinity from his alma mater in 1885, when he delivered an address at the semi-centennial of the institution, on "Culture and Government in America." While living in New Haven he was for seven years (1873-1880) secretary of the New Haven County Historical Society. He also became a member of the American Historical Society and of the Society

of Colonial Wars. In 1899, at the time of Bishop Williams's illness and death, he served as instructor in doctrinal theology in the Berkeley Divinity School.

Dr. Andrews was profoundly interested in historical study, and gave special attention to the early religious history of this country and to local history. The successful observance of the two hundred and fiftieth anniversary of the settlement of Guilford, in 1889, was in very large part due to his plans and labors and to the enthusiasm with which he inspired his fellow-townsmen. It led to the restoration of the old Henry Whitefield House and its acceptance as a state historical museum under the care of a board of trustees, of which he was deservedly elected president. The building was formally opened and dedicated to its new purpose in September, 1905. In 1894, the one-hundred and fiftieth anniversary of the foundation of his parish, he prepared a discourse giving a full account of its early history based on careful study and research, which was published in the following year. Some of his other historical papers, on early Moravian missions and other subjects, have also been printed.

In the diocese of Connecticut Dr. Andrews held an honored and responsible place. From 1893 until the diocesan convocation of 1905, he was a trustee of the fund for the relief of aged and infirm clergy, and also from the time of its organization in 1899 of the clergyman's retiring fund, in the work of both of which organizations he was much interested. He had also been a member of the standing committee of the diocese by successive annual elections since 1896, and an examining chaplain by appointment of the bishops since 1899. In 1895 he married Miss Caroline Caldwell, daughter of the late Rear Admiral Jenkins. U. S. N., who survives him.

Dr. Andrews was an accurate scholar and careful student, having command of a clear and impressive style in writing, of generous sympathies while following clear convictions. He made himself a good and useful citizen of the community in which his life was cast, and devoted himself earnestly to everything which he felt to be for its interests. He will be greatly missed by a large body of friends.

[84]

Bishop Niles.

To the notice of the life of the late Bishop William Woodruff Niles, which appeared in yesterday's "Courant," may be added a few words by way of appreciation by the man and his work. He began in early life to be a teacher, his first experience being in the Hartford High School, where also his future wife was engaged in like duties; and a tutorship at his alma mater commended him for the professorship upon which he entered three years after his ordination and from which he was elected to the bishopric of New Hampshire. In that diocese there was already the famous St. Paul's School, almost the first example or pattern of the boys' schools which have given New England so influential a place in the secondary education of the country; and to it the new bishop gave his interest and his care. But he saw that the community in which his lot had been cast needed also schools of a

high grade for the boys and girls who had been born and might be expected to spend their lives in it; and to this conviction was due the establishment and successful growth of the Holderness School for boys and St. Mary's School for girls in Concord.

Succeeding as a fairly young man to the venerable Bishop Carlton Chase, Bishop Niles brought into his episcopal work an element of enthusiasm and (if the word may be allowed) of neighborliness. The number of clergymen whom he found in New Hampshire was not large; it was augmented by young men whom he had influenced in college and others, and the bishop was the personal friend of each, watching all good work sympathetically and assisting in it, and opening new fields of labor. The bishop coadjutor, Dr. Edward M. Parker, called eight years ago to be his assistant, has both furthered and extended their plans. The results can be partly measured by the increase of the twenty-two parishes in 1870, with one missionary station, to seventy-two parishes and places of stated worship in 1914, and by the increase of the number of communicants in the same time from 3,500 to 6,000.

Bishop Niles rendered service to the whole Episcopal Church in this country, serving on several commissions, which had to do with the prayerbook and the translation of the Bible. He maintained his interest in the institutions in this state in which he had received his education. A trustee of Trinity College for the whole period of his episcopate, he was constant in attendance on public occasions and at business meetings; his two sons were graduated here in 1887 and 1883, and a grandson is a member of the class of 1916. He was the first graduate of the Berkeley Divinity School to be called to the office of a bishop; and he was the president of the alumni of the school until Bishop Brewster's election in 1898. It was seventeen years before Berkeley had another bishop among its graduates; and this time it was a classmate of Bishop Niles, Dr. Elisha S. Thomas, chosen assistant bishop of Kansas. Since that time the number has been largely and rapidly increased.

Bishop Niles lived to attain the second place on this roll of the house of bishops, being next to the presiding bishop. His death, coming close upon that of Bishop Scarborough of New Jersey, will be widely felt.

S. H.

JAMES J. GOODWIN DIES AFTER LONG ILLNESS.

Long and Prominently Identified With Business Interests of His Native City.

[85]

OF COLONIAL ANCESTRY.

James Junius Goodwin, long identified with the civic and business interests of Hartford, a liberal supporter of the Connecticut Historical society, recently the giver of the bishop's residence at No. 93 Woodland street, to the Protestant Episcopal diocese of Connecticut, and interested in everything that ad-

JAMES J. GOODWIN.

vanced his native city, died at his home, No. 83 Woodland street, this morning at 2:30, at the age of 79 years, 9 months and 7 days.

Mr. Goodwin had been failing for a long time, and at different periods had been very ill. His naturally strong constitution enabled him to rally. He retained his intellectual vigor to the very last.

Of Colonial Ancestry.

James Junius Goodwin was born in Hartford, September 16, 1835. He was a son of Major James Goodwin and Lucy Morgan Goodwin. The latter was a daughter of Joseph and Sally (Spencer) Morgan. Mr. Goodwin was a descendant of Ozias Goodwin, who either accompanied the emigrants, or came soon after the emigrants, who sailed from England on the ship Lion, which arrived in Boston, September 12, 1632. The line of descent follows: Ozias, Nathaniel, Ozias second, Jonathan, James, Major James.

Nathaniel Goodwin was admitted a freeman by the general court of Connecticut in October, 1662, and was one of the "townsmen" of Hartford in 1669-73-82. Ozias Goodwin, second, inherited from his father the homestead on Village street, which remained in his possession until 1764. He was a selectman two terms and grand juror several terms. He was a deacon of the First church, January 1, 1756, to his death, January 26, 1776.

Jonathan Goodwin was a corporal in the Hartford train band, which for a time did escort duty for the governor. He owned a tract of land on the north side of the Albany road, about one mile and a quarter from City Hall, still the property of his descendants.

James Goodwin, his son, (father of Major James Goodwin), inherited from his father the land on the Albany road and spent his entire life after 1783 (when his father moved to it) on the homestead. He was a first lieutenant in the First company, Governor's Foot Guard,

in 1807, and became captain in 1809.

His Father.

Major James Goodwin was born in the house of his father, James Goodwin, known for many years as Goodwin's tavern, and which was a stopping place for the western stages. When a young man Major Goodwin was employed in Morgan's tavern on State street by Joseph Morgan, father of Junius S. Morgan, the well known London banker. He became familiar with the express and stage business, and had many mail contracts. He was active in many leading Hartford corporations and was president of the Connecticut Mutual Life Insurance company at two different periods. He was vice-president of the Hartford hospital and a large owner of Hartford real estate. He was a vestryman of Christ church and a commandant of the First company, Governor's Foot Guard.

Business Career.

James Junius Goodwin was educated in private schools and in the Hartford High school. Clerical work occupied a large part of his time, succeeding his school days, until 1857, when he went abroad and spent the next year and a half in study and travel.

From 1859 to 1861 he was with William A. Sale & Co., East India and China shipping merchants in Boston. In September, 1861, he became a partner with his cousin, the late J. Pierpont Morgan, who in 1860 had become the American agent for George Peabody & Co., of London, of which his father, Junius S. Morgan, was a member.

Mr. Goodwin continued in the succeeding firm of Dabney, Morgan & Co., and until the last named firm was dissolved and the business merged into a new firm, Drexel, Morgan & Co., in 1871.

Since 1871 Mr. Goodwin had not engaged in active business. Following the death of his father, in 1878, he had, with his brother, the Rev. Dr. Francis Goodwin, been in charge of the extensive real estate holdings of the family in this city.

Mr. Goodwin's business connections were widespread. He was the senior director in the Connecticut Mutual Life Insurance company, the Hartford Fire Insurance company, the Collins company and the Connecticut Trust & Safe Deposit company, and a director in the Holyoke Water Power company, the Erie railroad and the Susquehanna railroad. He was a former director of the New York, Lake Erie & Western railroad, his service beginning with its reorganization in 1878.

Religious and Social.

Mr. Goodwin was a communicant of Christ church and junior warden of the parish. He was a vestryman in Calvary church in New York for several years, and later senior warden.

He was a member of the Colonel Jeremiah Wadsworth branch of the Connecticut society, Sons of the American Revolution; the General Society of Colonial Wars in the state of Connecticut, and the Hartford club. His membership in New York clubs comprised the Union, Century, Metropolitan, City and Church clubs.

Mr. Goodwin married June 19, 1873, Josephine Sarah Lippincott of Philadelphia, a descendant of Richard Lippincott, a resident of Massachusetts in 1640, and in 1665 one of the patentees of the first English settlement in New Jersey.

Besides his wife he leaves three sons, Senator Walter L. Goodwin, James L. Goodwin and Philip L. Goodwin, and one brother, the Rev. Dr. Francis Goodwin. There are four grandsons, Walter L., jr., Henry S., Granville Parker, and John, children of Senator and Mrs. Goodwin.

Funeral Friday.

The funeral will be held at Christ church Friday afternoon at 3 o'clock the Rev. Dr. James Goodwin, rector of the church, a nephew of the deceased, officiating. Burial will be in the family lot in Cedar Hill cemetery.

Interest in Historical Matters.

Of Mr. Goodwin's deep interest in all that pertained to the early days of Hartford, an appreciation by the Rev. Dr. Samuel Hart of Middletown, president of the Connecticut Historical society, is appended.

In addition to the gifts mentioned by Dr. Hart, Mr. Goodwin had in preparation a map showing the present property lines and the original lines of property as distributed in 1639. It will be, if published, the first map of Hartford of such nature ever printed.

Mr. Goodwin gave to the society many early English parish registers, one being a copy of the register of St. Mary's church, Bocking, England, which Mr. Goodwin published in a private edition of fifty copies, on a splendid quality of paper. It is interesting to note that the register of St. Mary's church contained records of many of the early Hartford families, including the family of Mr. Goodwin. Other gifts were sets of "Visitations of England and Wales," and "Visitations of Ireland," large books containing the pedigrees of many prominent English, Welsh and Irish families; two volumes of the "Genealogies of Hertfordshire and Northamptonshire," a copy of the first edition of "Connecticut Laws" printed in 1673, and of which less than twelve copies are known to be extant; and a more recent gift of a valuable series of early Connecticut newspapers.

Dr. Hart's Appreciation.

The words which would pay tribute to Mr. James Junius Goodwin as an honored friend fail at such a time as this; and others can better estimate the value of his life and his services to the city which was his home. To look on such a man in the strong simplicity of his character, fulfilling duties which affected the life and happiness of many whom he might never see, was to read a lesson of fidelity and integrity and beneficence. The quietness of his best acts kept us from knowing all that entered into the development and the happiness of his heart and character.

His interest in Hartford and in the careful study of its history has in more ways than one benefited the community. Its present beauty owes much to him and to those who stood in close relation to him; and the prosperity of its literary institutions is largely due to their timely and generous gifts. As a communicant and a member and officer of the parish of Christ church he did much to preserve its records and to put within ready access most important facts which they contain. The handsome volume, filling more than 750 pages, in which the history of the parish is traced in the form of annals to the year 1895 is a memorial to Dr. Gurdon W. Russell as its compiler and editor and to Mr. Goodwin as having with no less interest and carefulness provided for its publication. The second volume—or rather, as it is called on the title page, the volume of additional contributions—with very carefully, corrected and extended records of baptisms, confirmations, communicants, marriages and burials, covering over 300 pages of text and 180 pages of index, owed its publication to the same generous hand.

A like service, and it is not invidious to say, a service of greater and more extended value, was rendered by Mr. Goodwin in his provision for the publication of two volumes of the collections of the Connecticut Historical society. For nearly thirty years he was a member of that society, and for a considerable part of that time his name stood at the head of its list of vice-presidents. He knew the value of the society's work and of the service which it renders and might more fully render to those who are led, for one reason or another, to investigate the early history of the town and the colony. In 1897 he provided for the transcription, editing, and publication of the Town Notes of Hartford from 1635 to 1716—a work of skilled labor for those who prepared it for the press, and requiring in every way the greatest possible pains. It filled some 340 pages and called for a full index; and it has put at the disposal of students of our early history a large amount of original matter in clear type though with unrevised spelling. The whole edition was presented to the society to be Volume VI. of its Collections. Fifteen years later, Mr. Goodwin provided another volume of collections numbered XIV., containing, in much more than twice the amount of printed matter of the former, the records of the original distribution of the land in Hartford among the settlers, begun and in large part entered in 1639.

Accuracy of transcription, and of editing, and of proof-reading is absolutely necessary in such work; and the gift of this volume to the society was with the ample generosity which provided all the care that could be desired; it is a possession for all time. It may be added now that the promise or offer to provide for transcription and publication of this important volume was made after a very brief and simple statement as to its value and the need of it.

This is not the time to enumerate Mr. Goodwin's valuable gifts to the Historical society's library; but mention should be made of the greatest of them all, the Victoria History of the Counties of England, not yet completed, a library in itself. With this have been many like additions to the collections of historical and genealogical works. A generous gift

of money has for several years past kept the treasurer's account from showing a deficit, and there have been other gifts which have not appeared on the treasurer's books.

I have written somewhat fully in regard to these matters, because I feel that we may well be reminded of them at this time. They testify to an intelligent appreciation of history and of the present value of its study, and to a true sense of what is due to the men of old and especially to their public acts, if we would rightly connect the present with the past and wisely provide for the generation to come. They help us to understand and to be thankful for the man to whom we owe so much and whom we shall so greatly miss.

SAMUEL HART.

[86]

75th ANNIVERSARY OF
ST. JOHN'S CHURCH, HARTFORD

[NOW WEST HARTFORD]

75 YEARS' WORK IS COMPLETED BY ST. JOHN'S PARISH

Missionary Hymn, Written By Bishop Coxe In Old Vestry Is Sung.

The seventy-fifth anniversary of the foundation of St. John's Parish was observed at the morning services yesterday, and a large congregation filled the handsome edifice on Farmington avenue. Rt. Rev. Chauncey B. Brewster, Bishop of Connecticut, was present, and the preacher was Rev. Dr. Samuel Hart, dean of the Berkeley Divinity School at Middletown. At the conclusion of the sermon, the Holy Eucharist was celebrated, the celebrant being Bishop Brewster, assisted by Dr. Hart, Rev. Dr. James Goodwin and Rev. James W. Bradin:

Bishop Brewster spoke briefly from the chancel preceding the sermon, congratulating the congregation on the attainment of seventy-five years of Christian work and the minister on his success. He reminded them, however, that the work of the parish lay not in the past but in the present and future. A feature of the service was the singing of the missionary hymn written by Bishop Coxe when he was rector of the parish. The hymn, "Saviour Sprinkle Many Nations," was written one Good Friday evening in the vestry room of the old church on Main street.

Mr. Bradin, in a short address to the congregation, reminded them of the labor of those no longer living which had gone to help build up the parish, and said that the exercises should be considered chiefly as a cele-

bration of the fruition of their efforts. "Churches, like men, have periods of trial and of prosperity," he said. "When I came to this parish, it was undergoing its period of trial. That it has learned well the lessons taught by those days when we did not know whether or not we could continue to maintain the parish, is shown by our present prosperity. Let us not forget the lessons that those days of adversity taught us."

Dr. Hart's sermon was preached from the text in Second Corinthians, VI, 16: "Ye are the people of the living God, as God hath said: I will dwell in them and walk in them, and I will be their God, and they shall be my people." He said, in part:—

The churchmen of New Haven have but lately kept the centennial anniversary of the consecration of the present Trinity Church, the second house of worship of our communion in that city. The former edifice, a building of respectable size, had served the worshippers for more than sixty years; but a century ago they had so increased in numbers and in strength that they could need, and built a church which with its galleries would provide room for some 1,500 people. New Haven was at that time a town of about 7,500 inhabitants; but at almost the same time, during the war with Great Britain, when the churchmen built Trinity Church, the Congregationalists built two large houses of worship, so large that well nigh, if not quite, half of the population could have been accommodated in them and the new Episcopal church. Within fourteen years the number of churchmen in New Haven had so largely increased that a "chapel of ease" was built, itself a large church, for the overflow of the congregation; this overflow was organized in 1845 as the parish of St. Paul's Church. This was the first instance of the erection of a second Episcopal church in any city of Connecticut; though as we shall presently note, there was a second parish in Hartford before the second parochial organization was effected in New Haven. (I said, "in any city"; for in the town of Plymouth there had been from colonial days two congregations of the church, each with its own place of worship, the west church or St. Peter's and the east church or St. Matthew's.)

Interesting Parallel.

Here in Hartford, although the beginning had been later, there was an interesting parallel to the church history of the sister city. The dates of the new buildings here were for the first church of the Standing Order 1807 and for the second 1827; and in 1829 a new church edifice for the parish of Christ Church was consecrated, almost as large, and quite as stately as the new Trinity Church in the other city, and more beautiful in the details of its architecture; so that on the west side of Main street here, as on the west side of Temple street where it crosses New Haven Green, there were three large churches which would hold nearly half of the inhabitants, the entire population of the town of Hartford being less than 10,000. The new parish of St. John's Church was organized on March 18, 1841, seventy-five years ago yesterday, four years before St. Paul's in New Haven; and the church edifice, a large building for 800 worshippers, was consecrated by Bishop Brownell on April 20, 1842. While we are speaking of historical parallels, it may be well to remind ourselves that Hartford was the first town in Connecticut to have two societies each with its meeting-house, the one coming here in 1635 or 1636 in the persons of the first settlers of the place, and the second having been allowed to organize itself in 1669 after a controversy of more than ten years, the occasion of which seems to have been forgotten before it was ended.

Separation Harmonious.

It was no controversy that led to the

organization of this parish of St. John's Church. Thirty-six men and one woman, all from Christ Church, organized the new parish, and forty-two men were warned to attend its first meeting. Their names would, with scarce an exception, be familiar to any one who from personal memory or from tradition knows the family history of Hartford; I myself, who began to attend St. John's Church as a student twenty years after the church was built, could tell something of nearly all of them. As they left their old parochial connection they declared that "though they now separated from the parish of Christ Church, they felt a lively interest in its prosperity and harmony, and cherished the most affectionate attachment and respect for its faithful and beloved rector," Rev. George Burgess. That rector preached the sermon at the consecration of the new church from the text, "And so were the churches established in the faith, and increased in number daily." In it, with other serious words he said: "All the institutions of the church bind us together; requiring that we be united in those truths of faith which belong to the very existence of the Gospel, and in that common worship which answers to all our common necessities; leaving in doubtful opinions and in private practice a peaceful liberty. Thus have we hitherto lived in signal harmony; thus without any breach of that harmony we have parted, when a wider border was needful; and thus may we still, with one heart and with one mouth, maintain the truth, the unity, and the order which are our spiritual inheritance." And in his report to the bishop of diocesan convention, the last report, as he said, "which will have embraced the whole body of members of the Episcopal Church in Hartford," he bore testimony to "the devout zeal and liberality of the very valuable men who are chief in the undertaking, the entire purity and benevolence of purpose in which it has been begun, and the harmonious union of both parishes in seeking its success." One hundred and six communicants went from Christ Church to St. John's, leaving 326 in the old parish; and that in a town in which seventy years before, out of the entire population of 4,881, only 111 persons were counted as attached to the Church of England.

A Poetic Rector.

The first rector of the new parish, it needs not be said, was the youthful Arthur Cleveland Coxe, called to its charge as a deacon a little before he was of canonical age for the priesthood. He brought to it an enthusiasm, quickened by the revival of life which marked in England the Oxford movement and was recognized here as the carrying out of principles that had marked Connecticut from the beginning, principles which had perhaps been called to the memory of the mother church by influences from this "primal see" of the West. It was an enthusiasm for the church in her doctrine and discipline and worship; and working in a poetical mind it found expression in the use and the conduct of the services of the book of Common Prayer and in teaching based upon those services and upon "the rites, liturgies, history, and creed of the Catholic Church." Mr. Burgess was but ten years the new rector's senior, and he too was a poet; but he seemed older and (to use an abused word) more conservative; and by the two men whose differences were as those of true brothers or differing ages and somewhat differing literary taste and historical judgment, good provision was made for the then present and the then prospective churchmen of Hartford.

Services Attractive.

It is no disrespect to the scholarship and the attractiveness—certainly not to the godliness—of the rector of Christ Church, in a few years to be called to the bishopric of Maine, if we say that the beginnings of St. John's Church were made specially attractive by the devout buoyancy and poetical scholarship of its first rector, with his Christian ballads and his "Thoughts on the Services"—would that their influence might return or at least be passed on by some channel inspired in like

manner as were they! In a way they succeeded to the poetry of the elder Bishop Doane, when he was professor of belles lettres in the newly founded college, and of William Croswell, whom he assisted in editing the "Episcopal Watchman"; they were seconded by the active mind, at once logical and poetical, of one who before long became president of the college, and after a little the fourth bishop of Connecticut, whose little volume of translations from "Ancient Hymns of Holy Church" was dedicated to Mr. Coxe, "in memory of many conversations on the sacred ritual of the Church of God"; and they passed on after a generation to the third rector of this parish, son of the professor, disciple of the president, born to be a poet, a teacher, and a leader, later the first bishop of Albany. It is worth noting here, that in the volume of forty poems, published in 1851 for the third jubilee of the Society for the Propagation of the Gospel, were two which have a special interest for us: "Saviour Sprinkle Many Nations," which Mr. Coxe began in the vestry room of the old St. John's, after reading in evening prayer on Good Friday the fifty-third chapter of Isaiah, and "Fling Out the Banner, Let It Float," from the pen of the elder Bishop Doane; and that for the fourth jubilee of the same venerable society, the younger Bishop Doane wrote the one hymn contributed by an American to the publication of 1901, "O Risen and Ascended Lord."

The College Church.

It is hardly strange that St. John's Church became, in a way, the college church of Hartford; five of the professors of the college were among the original corporators; President Williams had a strong personal attraction to it and to its first rector, and chose it as the place of his consecration to the episcopate, presently calling upon its second rector to assist him in the instruction of candidates for orders in his school in Middletown; and each of the first three rectors, so scholarly was their knowledge of letters, served as lecturer on English literature at the college. One of the first acts of the new parish, before a rector was chosen, was to vote that the seats in the south gallery of the church be appropriated to the use of the students of the college, free of charge, with the judicious addition, "provided one of the officers of the college will sit with them." And the literary and academic tone did not by any means cease with the first three rectors; Bishop Doane's successor became a professor in a very learned department of the University of Oxford; and his successor was elected to a professorship in our Divinity School at Philadelphia. To Dr. Washburn, the parish's second rector, the church in this land owes much, even more (it sometimes seems) than it recognizes or knows. His earnest mind, generous in its acceptance of new aspects of truth, his strong presentation of the claims of righteousness, his unceasing desire to extend the influence of the kingdom of God, left their mark on his generation and are not now devoid of power.

Twenty-five Years Ago.

But on such an occasion as this, one should not rehearse formal annals nor point the moral of a detailed history; much less should there be an attempt to measure by any artificial or worldly standards, the progress of a spiritual work. Even the influence reaching back to those early days of frequent worship and the observance of special occasions, and then of scholarly and earnest preaching, of the call to duty and to good works or again the summons for adaptation to new forms of service and to changed conditions in the community, the opportunity for growth by sending out colonies into unoccupied fields or to anticipate forseen wants, or even the removing of the visible center of parochial work—these, which come into the minds of us all, and especially of those whose memories reach farthest back, need but to be suggested now. I may but remind you how, twenty-four years ago, on Easter Day, which was almost exactly the fiftieth anniversary of the consecration of the church, the present rector marked the close of his first decade of ministry here by a service which among other things recorded the extinguishment of a long harassing debt; seventeen more years of his rectorship led to the consecration of the present church; and now that he reckons thirty-four years, he can tell of ampler provision for corporate life and for service in the recently dedicated parish house.

A Lesson for the Future.

Bidden by the bishop and by your rector—we were all close together in divinity school days—to preach at the consecration of this sacred house, I took my text from the epistle for the service, as speaking of the spiritual house which is built up from the souls of faithful men, and of the consecration of the building as calling for a consecration of those who should worship therein, both as a body and severally. Today I have read for my text further words from the same passage, in which the Apostle went back to the book of the Old Covenant to illustrate and confirm what he had so earnestly written, "Ye are the temple of the living God; as God hath said, I will be their God, and they shall be my people." Yet the former part of this discourse serve as in a way an amplification of the text of seven years ago; it has been in large part a record of God's gracious dealing with this fold within His great flock, and has suggested to us somewhat of a fulfilment and somewhat of a renewal of the promises of earlier days. Let me venture to draw a lesson of instruction and inspiration for the future, from the quotation which St. Paul makes in this connection from the Law and the Prophets.

For the words are not all from one book or from one part of the Old Testament. The Pentateuch and earlier prophets and later contribute to emphasize the apostle's admonition and exhortation; the declaration that God's people are His temple. His shrine, belongs to all revelation of earlier and of later time; the living God ever makes Himself known as dwelling in living men. The truth is based on a promise; the promise came with redemption and is fulfilled in its fulfillment. But—and here I find the special lesson for today, the moral of the years which are past and the inspiration of the years that are yet to come—the words pass beyond the figure of a shrine, of the abode of a God who might be thought to find all His life in the adoring worship of those who should come to bow before Him. "I will dwell in them"—this might be by having His home among the homes of His people, as the temple stood crowning the height above the dwellings of Jerusalem, as the churches in our villages and towns and cities are God's houses among the homes of men and women and children; or it might be by finding Himself acknowledged and honored as a guest in the souls of men who have accepted Him. The promise, however, is greater and includes much more: "I will walk in them"; originally, perhaps—for the phrase is taken from Leviticus—with reference to the journey in the wilderness, when the manifest indication of divine presence went before them in the pillar of a cloud by day and of fire by night, taken not away from leading them wheresoever and whensoever they journeyed; but most certainly referring also to the daily life, the going out and the coming in of God's people and of every one among them; God in the activities of those who, passing to and fro on their varied occasions, seek to have Him ever with them. "I will walk in them"; so speaks a God who does not dwell aloof from His worshippers, asking of them only that they come to Him and bring Him offerings, but who also comes forth and is with them when they sit in their own houses or when they walk in the road, when they lie down, and when they rise up; a God who is concerned in the undertakings of His people and seeks their good and their happiness in their adventures for themselves and for Him. Dwelling in them and with them, He is their God; walking in them and with them, He makes them His people. For each the power, the promise, the inspiration comes from our becoming and being His temple; each reaches us normally and naturally through the holy church, in which, incorporated into His Son and growing with the life of His Spirit, we are in Him and He is in us; and the place where, above all other places, the power is received, the promise is effectually made, the inspiration is offered, is in the house of God, the abode of worship, of prayer and praise and sacrament. It is no little thing for our welfare that at least on the Lord's day we may enter into His gates with thanksgiving and into His courts with praise and may bow before Him in prayer and intercession; it is no little thing for our weakness that we do not find ourselves on His day or at other times in His house. For as He whose home is in the highest heaven and abides in the all-holy place dwells also here below with the man who is of a meek and lowly spirit, so He to whom we consecrate the best of earthly abodes, that He may dwell in the midst of the assembly of the saints upon the earth, goes forth hence to bless our way upon which in His name we enter and to prosper our right undertakings. In the narrowing definition, which yet includes all things, He dwells among us; in its far-reaching application, which yet has its full power everywhere, He walks in us.

See to it, I pray you, my brethren of this parish, how this church building which is for you the house of God, the church organization in this city, this diocese, this land, yea the Church Catholic throughout the world, which is for you the true though mystical body of Christ, calls upon you for worship here, constant and faithful and ever deepening in devotion and in meaning, and also leads you out into the varied paths of life, to which indeed you are ever led, that in ways known and in ways yet unknown you may make this—God through you may make this—the source of great power for helpfulness, for righteousness, for salvation.

ARCHIVISTS*
OF THE
DIOCESE OF CONNECTICUT

EBEN EDWARDS BEARDSLEY
(1866-1874)

SAMUEL HART
(1874-1917)

WILLIAM AGUR BEARDSLEY
(1917-1946)

ARTHUR ADAMS
(1946-1951)

KENNETH WALTER CAMERON
(1951-   )

---

* Originally called
"Registrars.

218

150th ANNIVERSARY OF THE CHURCH IN NEW CAMBRIDGE [BRISTOL] --1904

[87]

This year brings, as you have been reminded, the 150th anniversary of the building of a church in New Cambridge for the use of conformists to the Church of England, the 120th anniversary of the organization of a legal society of their successors, now adherents of the Church in the United States, and the 70th anniversary of the forming of a new parish in the town which soon after the Revolution had been incorporated under the name of Bristol.

New Cambridge was a district in the venerable town of Farmington; and it was not until 1742 that those who resided here were granted "winter privileges," that is to say, permission to assemble for worship at some place near their homes during the winter half of the year under the care of "an Authordox and suitably Quallifyed person" instead of taking each Lord's day the journey of eight miles to the meeting-house in the center. Presently, the needed authority having been obtained, an ecclesiastical society was organized here; and after strong opposition to the candidate preferred by the majority on the ground (as it appears) of his strong Calvinistic views, the newly constituted church in 1747 called a minister and arranged for his ordination. When the final vote to this effect was taken and recorded, the clerk made this entry: "And here it must be added that at the same meeting Caleb mathews Stephen Brooks John hikox Caleb Abernathy Abner mathews Abel Royce danell Roe & simon tuttel publikly declared themselves of the Church of England and under the bishop of london." Nehemiah Royce added himself to their number in a few weeks. They were all men of importance in the community, and some of them held prominent places in the ecclesiastical society. Before the year ended, the Rev. William Gibbs, missionary at Simsbury of the Society for the Propagation of the Gospel, began to minister to them and to those who met with them for worship. It was forty years since the establishment at Stratford of the first congregation of English Churchmen in Connecticut, and twenty-five years since the memorable day when, at the College Commencement in New Haven, Cutler and Johnson and Brown and Wetmore took their stand for episcopacy and made the Church at once a power in the community. These years had brought great changes in matters ecclesiastical, and in some ways their influence in this part of Connecticut had been specially marked. Churchmen were considered as "sober dissenters" and were granted toleration under an old enactment; and as early as 1727 the General Assembly of the colony passed a law allowing any person who had declared himself of the Church of England, and who lived so near to the place where a clergyman of that Church ministered that he could conveniently and did attend service there, to have the tax collected from him for the support of the ministry paid to such clergyman; and the clergyman was given power to receive and recover the tax. Many devout and earnest persons were persuaded of the truth of the teachings of the Church of England and were drawn to her by her willingness to minister the sacraments under simple Scriptural conditions and also by the dignity and serviceableness of her forms of worship. It was a time of declension in the "standing order," as it was called, of Congregationalism, and the Church was of great spiritual benefit to the descendants in the third and fourth generations of those who had come to these shores in large part because they were dissatisfied with her ways. Then had come the "great awakening" of 1740, causing much excitement in the colony, and some of it very irrational excitement. The more sober of the members of the standing order were put on their defence under the wild preaching of George Whitefield and the still wilder preaching and behavior of James Davenport and all that was included under the name (one is sorry to say) of "enthusiasm." While some good, doubtless, was done by those who called for greater earnestness in religious matters, great harm followed from the unwise words and deeds of others, who sowed the seeds of bitter feelings and divisions in families and neighborhoods and set up new religious organizations, differing from the old in little except the claim that they were composed of truly converted men and that they were the true successors of the founders of a century agone.

How this turned seriously minded religious people to the Church of England we know from many things that may be read in the records of those times; it will suffice to quote here the words of a letter written in 1744 by Churchmen in your neighboring town of Plymouth (it was Northbury then) to the venerable Society in England for the propagation of the gospel: "We were," said they, "prejudiced strongly against the Church of England from our cradles, until we had the advantage of books from your reverend missionaries and others; and Mr. Whitefield passing through this land, and his followers and imitators, brought in a flood of confusion amongst us; whereupon we fled to the Church of England for safety, and are daily more and more satisfied we are safe, provided the purity of our hearts and lives be conformable to her excellent doctrines."

The same influences, we may be sure, were working in those who three years later declared themselves Churchmen here in New Cambridge. But all the circumstances, and in particular certain events of which I must speak in a few minutes, cannot be understood if we fail to remember that every declaration of conformity to the Church by a tax-payer, if he came under the conditions named in the act, brought a pecuniary loss to the established society within the limits of which his property was situated. The separate societies of Congregationalists, which had been tolerated by the act of conformity in 1708, had lost their position as recognized dissenters by a repeal of this toleration clause in 1743; but Episcopalians and Baptists and (strange to say) Quakers still had the rights of sober dissenters. There was, therefore, reason for suspecting that some of those who about this time declared for episcopacy were really discontented congregationalists who wished to escape taxation for the support of societies with which they did not agree; and it was not strange that some of the civil officers were not minded to give to the rather vague provisions of the law a very liberal interpretation. Nor was it strange, on the

other hand, that the few Church clergymen, ministering to small and scattered flocks and living on small stipends, should feel that it was their right and, for that matter, their duty to receive from their people all that belonged to them by law and by the wish of those to whom they ministered.

Now the nine Churchmen here had put themselves under the care of the Rev. Mr. Gibbs, who lived in Simsbury--that part of the old town of Simsbury which is now called North Bloomfield--and it was a question whether they could conveniently and did attend his ministrations. And--the suggestion is not my own, and I do not need to apologize for it--Mr. Gibbs was a Massachusetts man and did not quite understand how to get along with Connecticut people; and it may be that already his judgment, through no fault of his own, was not of the best. However that may be, we find that before July, 1749, some of the Churchmen here had refused to pay their tax for the support of the pastor of the established order (Mr. Gibbs called him "the dissenting minister") and for their refusal had been committed to Hartford jail; that they had then paid their tax to the collector, and that Mr. Gibbs had thereupon demanded it of him and had been refused for the reason that his mission did not extend to New Cambridge. The trouble did not end here; for on the 28th day of the following December we find Mr. Gibbs writing a letter to the venerable society in England, dated from "Hartford Gaol," in which he says that he had brought a suit against the collector for the amount which he believed his due, had "been cast" in the suit, and then refusing to pay the costs had been taken and brought to the jail, "where," says he, "I now am; thus presumptuous and bold are these men in these parts." It is easy for us to see that the good man, who believed that he was contending for a principle, was unwise in the manner of his contention; it is not easy for us to excuse the treatment which he received from the exasperated authorities. A jail in the dead of winter was no easy place to stay in for even a few days; Mr. Jeremiah Leaming, the man who was the first choice of the Connecticut clergy for their bishop, was lamed for life after such an exposure; but there seems no reason to doubt the story that the Simsbury clergyman was subjected to greater indignity and sufferings──── being carried to Hartford strapped to a horse with hands and feet tied together under the animal's belly. Soon after this his mind began to weaken, and he fell into a condition of what his sister called melancholy; and one cannot read without emotion the inscription on his tombstone in the churchyard of old St. Andrew's Church, which tells us that he "died March 22, 1777, in the 63rd year of his age and 33d of his mission and 23d of his illness." One is glad that he was able to write a little more than a year after his imprisonment that there appeared in the dissenters "a relaxation and respite"; and matters, doubtless, grew quieter when, very probably at the judicious advice of the Rev. Samuel Johnson of Stratford, the Churchmen here were put into the cure of Waterbury, which was nearer than Simsbury and was in charge of good Mr. Richard Mansfield and (as he wrote) the matter was accommodated.[1]

It is not pleasant to tell of such quarrels among neighbors, but it would not be honest to omit the mention of them; and one is glad to find on record, as the historian of the Congregational society tells us, that though as late as 1749 the society instructed its collector "to collect the Rates of them that call themselves of the Church of england among us and we will defend them," yet peaceful counsels came to prevail, and in 1774 and thereafter the society, in the meetings of which episcopal members were still permitted to vote on certain subjects, appointed two collectors, one for the standing order and one for the Churchmen. But we must go back and trace briefly the internal life of the congregation.

The ancient pages which have preserved for us the few items of business transacted by the Churchmen of New Cambridge at their meetings, which in those days were called "vestries," contain also the register of baptisms, beginning with that of a "daughter of daniel wormer" on the 11th of July, 1747; thirty baptisms are recorded before the date of the first service in the church building. The register was well kept, apparently by the clerks of the vestry, in a book on the first page of which a child had written out the copy, "Fear God and honour the King," but with a spelling which is extraordinary even for those times. No name of an officiating clergyman is given until in 1753 we find that of the Rev. Ichabod Camp, not long before a candidate for the congregational pulpit here, who had been ordained in England in the preceding year; he was in charge of the Churchmen at Middletown, Wallingford, and Cheshire, residing at the first-mentioned place, and he can not have come here very often in the six years in which his name appears on the records; perhaps he served in this work as a substitute for the Rev. Richard Mansfield, whose charge included Derby, West Haven, Waterbury, and Northfield, and whose rectorship at Derby covered a period of seventy-two years.

In 1754, a hundred and fifty years ago, on the 26th day of April, the first vestry was held; "Abel roys Stephen brooks chosen church wardens, Caleb mathews chosen clerk"; and a church was speedily built, which was opened for service on the 10th day of June; at the next annual vestry a sexton was appointed. The Church was but a small building and stood on the other side of the street from the meeting-house, on land now occupied by the north wing of the schoolhouse. The records of baptisms do not show that Mr. Mansfield officiated in it till 1756; and in the three following years we find that a large number of children were baptized by the Rev. Christopher Newton, who had also been a candidate for the congregational pulpit when it was vacant, but was then the Church of England clergyman at Ripton (now called Huntington). The congregation was gaining in strength and evidently wished to do more for itself; at the vestry held in March, 1758, a committee was appointed "to hire six days' preachings for the year ensuing," with the evident intention of having a celebration of the Holy Communion once in two months; but soon they became more bold and in the following July "voted

that they would have Mr scovel to be their minister one quarter part of the time" and "would pay one quarter part of the forty five pounds [of] Mr scovels salary." The Rev. James Scovill was a native of Waterbury, and this call and pledge were made before he was ordained. He returned from England the next year and began his ministrations, giving half of his time to Waterbury, a quarter to New Cambridge, and a quarter to Westbury (now called Watertown). He officiated here constantly for twelve years and occasionally, I think, after that time, and baptized very many--the number in 1760 was thirteen. In 1762, it was voted that he should "oficiate in farmington in the old society two sundays one in the winter and one in the sumer this year." Three years later they increased his salary, voting him "fifteen pounds for the year ensuing and that we migt have the liberty of paing it in pork and grain at the market price." These were peaceful and prosperous days for the Church.

In 1773, another young man from Waterbury was ready to go to England for ordination--Mr. James Nichols, the last of the noble company of forty-three men from this colony who crossed the ocean to seek ordination to the diaconate and priesthood. The Churchmen here voted on the 2nd of April 1773 "that they wold have mr nicols for their minister," and later in the month that they would "give mr nickcols forty pounds lawfull money yearly for our part of his stated salary," and further that they "would raise 25 pound to carry him home" that meant to England, and the use of the word at so late a day is touching--"to be rased upon our list at to pence half penny upon the pound."

It was on the 8th day of the following May that he officiated here for the first time, and here he took up his abode; he was the only resident clergyman of the old Church. He found here, as appears from Mr. Scovill's report of 1772, about thirty-three Church families and forty-seven communicants--the latter number being the same as that reported twelve years earlier. [It may be noted here, as a matter of interest, that we have, apparently of an earlier date than this, the following list "of vessels belonging to the Church in New cambridge": "one beacker given by lieut john rew one platter given by nehemiah roys one bason boght with the churches mony one tankart bought with the churches mony a cution given by caleb mathews Mr. Abel roys nehemiah roys one beackcer given by simon tuttle."]

Soon came troublous times for those of the colonists who were minded to maintain the cause of the English crown, and many of the adherents of the Church of England were of that number. The clergy were bound, as they thought, by their ordination vows as well as by their convictions, to remain loyal to the home government; and they were not willing to minister--they did not think it right to minister--unless they could use the whole of the Prayer Book service including the petitions for the King. This was done in Newtown, where Mr. Beach read the service publicly throughout the Revolution, in spite of threats and worse than threats; but most of the churches were closed, though in some cases the clergy gathered

their people together on Sundays to hear instruction. Mr. Scovill in Waterbury, as others also in their cures, lived quietly and unmolested, though their political sentiments were well known. But Mr. Nichols was not one of this kind; he was, we learn, "an ardent loyalist, and his people almost unanimously followed him. Chippin's Hill, where most of them lived"--I am using the words of the accomplished historian of your town--"became a rendezvous for tory gatherings from all over the State, where soldiers were enlisted for King George, officers appointed, and information gathered to be sent to New York. Not far from there was the famous 'tory den,' where a few loyalists, whose lives were not safe abroad, lay in concealment, their wives bringing them food by night."

It is not strange, then, that even in 1776 and three times later in the course of the war we find men bold enough to make profession that they were of the Church of England; and perhaps not strange that vigorous action was taken against the offending tories. Mr. Nichols, it is said, was tarred and feathered; and Joel Tuttle was seized by a vigilance committee of patriots, given a summary trial, hanged near the whipping-post, and left for dead until a traveller passing by, or, according to another version, one of the patriots returning, cut him down and saved his life. At the session of the Superior Court in Hartford in January, 1777, only six months after the Declaration of Independence, the Rev. Roger Viets of Simsbury was convicted of giving food to captured British soldiers and assisting them to escape, and was lodged in jail; at the same Court Mr. Nichols was tried on a charge of treason but acquitted; while one of his parishioners, Moses Dunbar, who had accepted a captain's commission under General Howe and had enlisted men for the British army on Long Island, was also tried for treason and being found guilty was executed by hanging on the 19th of March at Gallows Hill in Hartford where the College buildings now stand--the only execution for treason ever inflicted by the civil authority in Connecticut. In his last statement he declared that he died "in the profession and communion of the Church of England," and in his parting letter to his children he wrote, "I charge you all never to leave the Church." He refused to go to the meeting-house to hear a sermon from its pastor, Dr. Nathan Strong, before his execution, and was not required to go against his will; and the Rev. Abraham Jarvis, afterwards Bishop, was summoned from Middletown to preach to him in the prison. He was, doubtless, justly convicted and punished; yet, as your historian says, he was "a man high-minded, devout and heroic."

We are told that there were at this time other convictions for treason, though no other persons suffered the extreme penalty. Whether they were arrested at the same time as Dunbar or not we cannot tell; but at the time of the May session of the General Assembly in the same year, 1777, seventeen men from the town of Farmington, fifteen at least of whom were connected with the Episcopal Church in New Cambridge, were confined in Hartford jail "on suspicion of their being inimical

to America." They petitioned the General Assembly for relief, claiming that they "were ready and willing to join with their country and to do their utmost for its defence." A committee was appointed to labor with them and hear what they had to say; and it reported "that they had been much under the influence of one Nichols, a designing church clergyman, who had instilled into them principles opposite to the good of the States," and "that under the influence of such principles they had pursued a course of conduct highly displeasing to those who are friends to the freedom and independence of the United States"; but that as they had committed no particular positive act and had been grossly ignorant of the true grounds of the present war with Great Britain, and were now convinced of their error and ready to take an oath of fidelity to the State and to defend the country against the British army, they might well be liberated on paying the costs of their imprisonment; and this was accordingly done.

Mr. Nichols fled to his former home in Salisbury; and in 1780 he became rector at Litchfield, still however receiving some stipend from parishioners here, and apparently for a while ministering one third of the time at "west briton," which is now Burlington. [It is but fair, I think, to say here that Mr. Nichols's toryism did not blind the Churchmen of Connecticut to faults which later appeared in his conduct; in 1779 the Bishop and Clergy of this Diocese sent a communication to the Convention of the Church in Vermont, where he then lived, expressing formal disapproval of his conduct. He renounced the ministry in 1819 and died in Western New York ten years later.]

There is no doubt that public church services were discontinued here during at least the latter part of the Revolution; the church building suffered from neglect and probably did not escape wanton injury. Its location was not very convenient for the majority of those who attended it, and suggestions were made that they might unite with the Churchmen in East Plymouth and Harwinton in building a new church in which they could all worship. In 1783, it was voted "that it is the mind of the vestry to make further trial to agree upon a place to build a Church for the convenance of cambridge and west britton to meet together," and a committee was appointed "to Pitch upon a place & Draw a subscription and Git an assignment for the same purpos." But for a while other counsels prevailed. Taking advantage of an act of the General Assembly passed in 1784, the "professors of the Episcopal Church" met after due summons on the 17th day of November of that year (three days, as it happened, after Bishop Seabury was consecrated in Scotland) and organized as an ecclesiastical society. The first Society's Committee elected were Captain Zebulon Frisbie, Nehemiah Royce, and Captain Abel Matthews. At that time there were twenty-nine legal voters on the enrolment; to these sixteen were added before the end of the next year, and twenty-five more before 1792, making seventy adult men who became members of the parish. "At the same meeting," the record says, "voted that we were willing to meet again in the church which had lain Desolate for some time on account of the persecution of

the times, and voted that we would Repair the Church house." But the new parish had no settled clergyman. The Rev. Samuel Andrews of Wallingford was here early in 1785 and baptized thirteen children at the house of Joel Tuttle, and in the summer Mr. Scovill of Waterbury baptized nine more. In October of that year the name of the Rev. Ashbel Baldwin, of Litchfield, one of the four ordained by Bishop Seabury at his first ordination in the preceding August, appears on the record; he baptized eighteen in 1788 and twenty-four in 1791, besides smaller numbers in other years. In the autumn of 1787, Bishop Seabury made his visitation of Litchfield County "with great applause to himself and much pleasure to the Church people," as Mr. Baldwin phrased it. We get an idea of the strength of the parishes from the number of those whom he confirmed, which probably included all the communicants or intending communicants who could get to church; there were 56 here in [New] Cambridge, 103 in Northbury, 40 in Harwinton, 165 in Litchfield, and about 200 in Simsbury. (He confirmed 99 more in Litchfield in 1795.) Meanwhile, a plan had been entertained for joining with Waterbury and Salem (that is, Naugatuck) "in settling a minister a quarter of the time or less"; but this did not succeed, and it was decided that it was best to unite with the east part of Northbury (that is, Plymouth) and the south part of Harwinton in organizing a new parish. The decisive action was taken on the 3rd day of March 1791, when the society voted that they were "willing to keep up and frequent the Episcopal Society as has been proposed on the East part of Northbery" and adjourned to meet on the 4th day of April at Ensign Ozias Tyler's new house in Northbury, at which time and place the first vestry meeting and the first society's meeting of the "Second Episcopal Church in Northbury" were held, and the new organization was practically complete. The business of the old society was brought to an end on the 21st of May 1792, when a Committee was appointed to "Dispose of the old Church house in Newcambridge to the best Advantage and Return the affect to the Committee that was Chosen and appointed to Cary on and Affect the new Church in Northbury": and it was also ordered "that the Churches Land shall be fenced and inclosed."

Thus the history of the old New Cambridge parish passes into that of the East Church, as it was long called, or St. Matthew's Church, East Plymouth. There the deed of a church lot was passed on the 25th of April 1792; a church was soon built, and a key-keeper and a grave-digger were appointed in the following December; in 1794, the building was finished with "pews below and seats in gallery," and before the end of the year provision was made that it should be "dignified"; in the next year on the 21st day of October it was consecrated by Bishop Seabury, who also held at the same time what proved to be his last ordination, advancing to the priesthood the Rev. Alexander Viets Griswold, nephew of the Rev. Roger Viets and afterwards Bishop of the Eastern Diocese. The records of baptisms by Mr. Griswold for 1795 to 1799, contained in the old book, evidently belong to this parish, which Bishop Seabury calls "Plymouth, formerly Cambridge, in Connecticut."

222

It needs but a word to tell the fate of the old "church house." It was sold, removed, and used for a barn; its arched windows, or part of them, were built into a gambrel-roofed store-house which stood near the site of the present house of worship of the Swedish Lutherans. Both barn and store-house have been destroyed. A boulder marks the site of the church, and the churchyard (which lay too long neglected) has been cleaned and the gravestones put in order, while a careful copy of the inscriptions on them, which include the names of five of the founders of the old parish, is preserved against the day when they shall crumble into dust.

[In 1897, at the time of the celebration of the 150th anniversary of the Congregational society, Mr. George Dudley Seymour provided for cleaning up the old cemetery and for placing on the site of the church a boulder of pinkish quartzite brought from Chippens Hill, its primitive home having been, as the geologists say, in the vicinity of the Massachusetts Cheshire. It is now his purpose to provide a foundation for the boulder and to place in the foundation a memorial box. Two years ago the same generous benefactor began a movement for the erection of a stone wall around what remains of the burying-ground, a work the completion of which we are privileged to note and record today. Most of the work, he tells me, has been done by his sister, Mrs. Miles Lewis Peck, whose husband is a grandson of the Abel Lewis who bought the old church after the close of the Revolutionary War. For what has been so well planned and done we may well be most thankful.][2]

It is but a bare recital of events separated from our day by more than a century--their beginning by more than a century and a half--which I have been able to make today. Yet I believe that it reads for us and for those who shall come after us lessons of high principle, true courage, earnest devotion, and glad service for the house of God and for the offices thereof. "And if I have done well, and as is fitting the story, it is that which I desired; but if slenderly and meanly, it is that which I could attain unto. And here shall be an end."[3]

1 [Inserted in the MS. at this point:] Churchmen at New Cambridge received under care of Rev. Richard Mansfield, October 4, 1749:

Capt⁰ Caleb Matthews	Mr. Benjamin Brooks
Mr. John Hickok	Mr. Nehemiah Rice
Mr. Abel Rice	Mr. Edmund Matthews
Mr. Stephen Brooks	[Mr.] Simon Tuttle
Mr. Caleb Abernatha	Mr. Joseph Gaylord
Mr. Daniel Row	Mr. Thomas Lory

2 This bracketed portion was a later insertion in the MS.
3 Hart exchanged letters with Judge Epaphroditus Peck, of Bristol, before giving his address and, doubtless, drew upon an historical address Peck had made on Oct. 12, 1897, on the 150th anniversary of the First Congregational Church in Bristol. The following paragraphs are reprinted from pages 35-40 of the published Programme and Addresses for that occasion:

The nine men who seceded from the church before Mr. Newell's ordination, with their families, and some others who followed them later, formed the pre-Revolutionary Epis-

copal church whose history is so tragic and interesting, and so closely connected with the history of this church, that I will ask your indulgence in a digression of a few minutes to sketch it. The Episcopal church had at that time no American bishop, and but very few settled clergymen in New England. The church maintained a feeble existence by the labors of traveling missionaries and clergymen, who performed sacred offices in several parishes in rotation. Such offices were now obtained by the New Cambridge "churchmen;" a regular record of baptisms, beginning in 1747, is still in existence. The first of these officiating clergymen, who came here from Simsbury for several years, was Rev. William Gibbs.* Afterward, as has been said, Messrs. Camp and Newton, who had been candidates for the Congregational pastorate, served them, then Rev. Richard Mansfield occasionally from 1756 to 1759, Rev. James Scovel for about fourteen years, and, from 1774 until church services were suspended. Rev. James Nichols. In 1754 they completed and opened for service a little church standing across the highway from the Congregational meeting-house where the north wing of the schoolhouse now stands. In 1758 they voted to have six days' preaching for the year ensuing, probably a bi-monthly communion; at other times they paid a quarter or a sixth of the salary of a clergyman, who gave them corresponding service.

For several years the society refused to release them from its ecclesiastical taxation; they evidently refused payment, and the society, in 1749, instructed its collector "to collect the Rates of them that call themselves of the Church of england among us and we will defend them." This instruction was evidently acted on, for, a year later, the collectors presented a bill of charges for collecting the rates of "those that call themselves Churchmen," and it was allowed.

Later, more peaceful counsels prevailed, and the churchmen were released from the "minester Rates as long as they do bring a Recept from their minester provided they will al of them Quit their Right in the meeting-house;" they had already been released from the tremendous meeting-house rate. Thereafter, the relations between the two churches were friendly, the churchmen still acting in society meeting and holding office on non-ecclesiastical subjects; in 1774 and afterward it even appears that the society appointed collectors for each body of believers, the churchmen's payments going to their rector and that of the Congregationalists to Mr. Newell; so that the society seems to have really acted as the legal ecclesiastical organization serving both churches.

But with the outbreak of the Revolution all this changed. The natural sympathies of the churchmen, who deemed themselves under oppression in the Congregational colony, and looked to the established church of England as their mother and protector, were with the crown. Mr. Nichols

* For the tragic history of his later years see "Historical Papers Concerning the Early Episcopal Church of New Cambridge," by Rev. X. A. Welton, Ms., Bristol Public Library.

WELTON, X. A., ed. Records concerning the pre-Revolutionary Episcopal Church of Bristol: Record of meetings, 1754-1800; Record of baptisms, 1747-1800, with lists of rectors, etc.; License from the Bishop of London to Rev. William Gibbs, the first Episcopal clergyman, also his commission from the Society for the Propagation of the Gospel in Foreign Parts, assigning him to "Cymsbury" in New England; Deed from Stephen Brooks to the church; Deed of land to St. Matthews, Plymouth; Original roll of membership of St. Matthews Church, Plymouth, with signatures; and a list of sacred vessels and other sundries.

WELTON, X. A. Historical sketch of the Episcopal Church in New Cambridge (Bristol) and East Plymouth, to which is appended a copy of the petition to the General Assembly, October, 1790, for the establishment of the church at East Plymouth, and a copy of the resolution of the General Assembly, May, 1777, releasing from the Hartford jail seventeen Episcopalians of Bristol.

was an ardent loyalist, and his people almost unanimously followed him. Chippin's Hill, where most of them lived, became a rendezvous for Tory gatherings from all over the state, where soldiers were enlisted for King George, officers appointed, and information gathered to be sent to New York. Not far from there was the famous "Tory den," where a few loyalists whose lives were not safe abroad, lay in concealment, their wives bringing them food at night.*

The Congregationalists, on the contrary, with Parson Newell at their head, were stout patriots.† Naturally, the flames of hostility raged against the church that was deemed the hotbed of toryism..

Let me read an extract from the printed state records of 1777, vol. 1, page 259: "On report of the committee appointed by this Assembly to take into consideration the subject matter of the memorial of Nathl Jones, Simon Tuttle, Joel Tuttle, Nathaniel Matthews, John Matthews, Riverus Carrington, Lemuel Carrington, Zerubbabel Jerom junr, Chauncey Jerom, Ezra Dormer, Nehemiah Royce, Abel Royce, George Beckwith, Abel Frisbee, Levi Frisbey, Jared Peck, and Abraham Waters, all of Farmington, showing that they are imprisoned on suspicion of being inimical to America; that they are ready and willing to join with their country and to do their utmost for its defence; and praying to be examined and set at liberty, as per said memorial on file, reporting that the said committee caused the authority, &c. of Farmington to be duly notifyed, that they convened the memorialists before them at the house of Mr. David Bull on the 22d of instant May and examined them separately touching their unfriendliness to the American States, and heard the evidences produced by the parties; that they found said persons were committed for being highly inimical to the United States, and for refusing to act in defence of their country; that on examination it appeared that they had been much under the influence of one Nichols, a designing church clergyman who had instilled into them principles opposite to the good of the States, that under the influence of such principles they had pursued a course of conduct tending to the ruin of the country and highly displeasing to those who are friends to the freedom and independence of the United States; that under various pretenses they had refused to go in the expedition to Danbury; that said Nathaniel Jones and Simon Tuttle have as they suppose each of them a son gone over to the enemy; that there was, however, no particular positive fact that sufficiently appeared to have been committed by them of an atrocious nature against the States, and that they were indeed grossly ignorant of the true grounds of the present war with Great Britain; that they appeared to be penitent of their former conduct, professed themselves convinced since the Danbury alarm that there was no such thing as remaining neuters; that the destruction made there by the tories was matter of conviction to them; that since their imprisonment upon serious reflexion they are convinced that the States are right in their claim, and that it is their duty to submit to their authority, and that they will to the utmost of their power defend the country against the British army; and that the said committee think it advisable that the said persons be liberated from their imprisonment on taking an

oath of fidelity to the United States:—Resolved by this Assembly, that the said persons be liberated from their imprisonment on their taking an oath of fidelity to this State and paying costs, taxed at £22 7 10; and the keeper of the goal in Hartford is hereby directed to liberate said persons accordingly."

Of these seventeen names I can identify thirteen names as members of the Episcopal church of New Cambridge, and two others as having had children baptized there; and Mr. Nichols, the "designing church clergyman," was the rector. But imprisonment was not the worst of their suffering. The Joel Tuttle there mentioned was seized by a band of overzealous patriots, and hanged on the green east of this building, near the whipping-post; one of the party, seized by remorse or fear, returned and cut him down, and he revived; Chauncey Jerome narrowly escaped whipping; Mr. Nichols is said to have been tarred and feathered,* and was indicted for treason before the Superior Court at Hartford in January, 1777, but escaped conviction;† and Moses Dunbar, who was tried and convicted, and hanged for treason in March of the same year, was a brother-in-law of the two Jeromes, and four of his children were baptized in the New Cambridge church. Dunbar had been a resident of Waterbury; after his marriage to Phebe Jerome he lived in a house north of the South Chippen's Hill schoolhouse, east of the highway. He was the only tory hanged in Connecticut for treason. His dying statement and last message to his children, printed in the recent history of Waterbury, show him to have been a man of character, conscientious in his loyalist views, tender to his family, and of Christian spirit.‡

Church services were entirely discontinued here, and we may well believe the little church to have been the target of many bitter curses, and of more material missiles. After the storm of the war was over the little parish gathered itself together again, but the church appears to have been unfit for use. Occasional meetings were held in private houses for a time. In 1784 they voted, "that we are willing to meet again in the church which hath lain desolate for some time on account of the persecution of the times, and voted that we would repair the church house." But the load was too great for the weakened company to carry. In 1792 they united with the Episcopalians of Harwinton and Plymouth to establish the little church, midway between the three towns, which is now known as East Church; and Episcopacy ceased to exist here until Trinity Church was organized in 1834.

The record of this early Episcopal church was some twenty years ago in existence in East Plymouth, bearing on the cover the significant motto, "Fear God and Honor the King," but it has since disappeared. By good fortune an authentic copy is in existence, and has just come into the possession of the Bristol Public Library. The church building was sold to Abel Lewis, who used it many years as a barn; and the arched windows were until a few years ago in the gambrel-roofed house which stood near the site of the Swedish Lutheran church. The churchyard, in the rear of the schoolhouse, had long lain neglected, until by the public

---

* See "Historical Papers" above cited; also, "Moses Dunbar, Loyalist," by Epaphroditus Peck, Ms., Bristol Public Library.
† See his patriotic letter in the Connecticut Courant, Jan. 2, 1775, Conn. Hist. Soc. Library.

* "Historical Papers," as cited before.
† Conn. Courant, Jan. 27, 1777.
‡ For a full account of him, see "Moses Dunbar, Loyalist," above cited.

spirit of one of my auditors,* it has very lately been cleared of weeds and rubbish, and the gravestones put in order. A boulder has also been set to mark the site of the church building, on which an inscription is shortly to be cut. Five of the nine original seceders from the Congregational church lie buried in that yard; and three of them are among those whose imprisonment I have spoken of.

---

* Mr. George Dudley Seymour.

CENTENNIAL ANNIVERSARY OF THE EPISCOPAL ACADEMY OF CONNECTICUT
[Cheshire, June 21, 1894]

[88]

The establishment of the Episcopal Academy of Connecticut a hundred years ago was due to the concurrent operation of several causes. To begin with, it was a time when many academies were founding both in this state and in Massachusetts. It had been the theory in these two colonies at the very first that every considerable town should maintain a grammar school in which boys might be taught at least the rudiments of Greek and Latin by competent masters and thus be prepared to enter the collegiate school in which more advanced instruction was given. (In the sister colony there were both a larger population and greater wealth; and as late as 1789 two hundred and thirty towns in Massachusetts were under legal obligation to maintain each its grammar school.) The ancient law of Connecticut dating from 1650 required that when any town should increase to the number of one hundred families or householders, they should set up a grammar school, "the master thereof being able to instruct youths so far as they may be fitted for the University." This was a brave act for a colony the whole population of which did not exceed 2,500 souls. In 1672, the law was made more practical by requiring every county town to have its grammar school. Governor Hopkins's benefactions had established the grammar schools that bore his name in New Haven and Hartford, and substantial help for their schools was before long given to the two other county towns of New London and Fairfield. The show was far less than in Massachusetts, but a law finally passed in the northern state in 1824 probably discloses about what the facts of the case were there; by it one hundred and sixty-five towns were freed from the statutory obligation of employing a master who could teach Greek and Latin, and but seven were left as grammar-school towns. The system had been, as I said, bravely devised; but it did not work, and, indeed, one wonders whether anybody really expected that it would work.

Now into the place assigned to these public grammar schools academies were coming to give instruction of a higher grade to those who wished to prepare for collegiate work. The first of which we read was the Phillips Academy at Andover, Massachusetts, founded in 1777 and taking its honored name in 1780, though the Dummer School at Newbury, opened in 1762 and in-corporated as an academy in 1782, should, perhaps, precede it. Our ancestors in Connecticut were not far behind. The Staples Free School, now in the town of Easton, founded in 1781, seems to have been the first academy in Connecticut, and the Plainfield Academy was founded two years later. The years, then, which led on towards the close of the last century marked a change in the system of public education in New England. The collegiate schools, doing university work as best they knew how, were well established; the district schools were a necessity, and they also probably did their proper work as well as they knew how; but into the place of the largely theoretical and mythical grammar school was coming the academy.[1] This latter owed its existence to private enterprise or private benevolence or both combined; it could have in each case a special purpose and set before itself certain definite ends, though in every case it was meant to provide the secondary education, as we call it, and fit the district schoolboy for the college. It is no wonder, therefore, that Bishop Seabury, who had in his earlier ministerial life been the master of a private school and who knew the importance of education, should have moved at the earliest possible moment for the establishment of an Episcopal Academy in Connecticut. It was all that could be done at the time for Church education here; and it was a wise provision for the needs of that time and of the future that led to the undertaking.

But there was another reason for the establishment of this academy--more closely connected with Christian education as Bishop Seabury and his faithful company of clergymen and laymen looked at it. The collegiate school of the colony, the college of the state, had been rightly and of necessity under the control of the Standing Order. To the library of that institution and to the events connected with the Commencement of 1722 the Churchmen of Connecticut looked back with special interest. So far as I know, they never claimed any rights in the management of the institution on the ground that both members of its teaching body had conformed to the Church of England, and they never complained of the passage of the test act which debarred such conformists from holding positions of honor and trust in the college. They quietly accepted their disabilities as dissenters and were grateful for the liberal treatment which was granted to them by the civil authority as "sober dissenters." They gave a generous support to the College, and they gladly availed themselves of its advantages as a home of sound learning, most of their clergy holding academic degrees from it. But under Rector Clap's administration, which began in 1740, the College assumed a more distinctively theological character; The "enthusiasts," as they were called--that is to say the New Light Congregationalists--received very harsh treatment; and even sober dissenters such as Episcopalians were not regarded with very great favor. In the very year in which Bishop Seabury entered the College (1744), the two Cleveland brothers had been expelled because they had attended in vacation a separatist meeting with their parents and would not publicly profess repentance for so heinous an act. Moreover, Dr. Samuel Johnson, a learned man and once a light in the College who had become a Churchman at the same time as Rector Cutler and Tutor

225

Brown, was now the President of King's College in New York; and it has seemed to me that, had it not been for the breaking out of the War of Independence, steps might have been taken at an early day for the establishment of a school of theology--possibly connected in some way with King's College--under the care of the learned and respected clergymen who were in charge of the rapidly increasing parishes of the Church of England in Connecticut.[2]

At any rate, when the war was ended and the Church in the State of Connecticut had been able to complete its organization, and when urgent matters of ecclesiastical importance had been determined and the Church in the United States had become one, using the same Book of Common Prayer and uniting for purposes of general consultation and legislation in one Convention, Bishop Seabury and his clergy and people felt that they could no longer delay the establishment of a school of sound learning under the direction of Church principles; and to it I suppose that they meant to join at least the distinctively theological part of the training of the Church's candidates for Holy Orders. The plan or scheme for the Academy, as contained in the Memorial presented to the General Assembly of the State, apparently proposed that provision should be made here for full collegiate instruction, though there was no petition at the time for the power to confer degrees; but in point of fact the studies pursued seem to have been those that properly belonged to the academies, which, as has already been said, were growing up into the place that grammar schools had in theory occupied; and at the same time arrangements were made for the "reading" of theology, as the old phrase was, on the part of college graduates or others who were far enough advanced to undertake it. The library which was gathered here--some of its ponderous tomes now weigh heavily on the college shelves in Hartford--seems to have been adapted to the latter class of students. We hear, indeed, of young men studying for the ministry, receiving their full education here; but I doubt if after the foundation of the Academy there was any diminution of the ratio of college graduates among those who were ordained by the bishops of Connecticut. This was rather a place for preliminary studies and also for graduate work in special preparation for the ministry, which latter, it must be remembered, was in those days much less formal and more personal than at present. In this way a most important work was begun and carried on for Christian education, as our Church understands it, though there was no real interference with the position of Yale College in the community or with the way in which Churchmen in general availed themselves of its facilities for liberal study. And it should not be forgotten, though I may not dwell on it here, that the early principals, Dr. Bowden and Dr. Smith and Dr. Bronson, were all competent to guide and direct the studies of theological students.

But though the Churchmen of Connecticut were minded thus to set in order the things that were wanting and to meet a special emergency, it was in no narrow conception of the meaning of Christian education that they founded and maintained this academy. It would have been contrary to all the traditions and all the convictions of the Anglican Church if they had attempted to educate by themselves, apart from contact with other youths and thus in an important sense apart from contact with the world, boys and young men of whom it was thought or hoped that they had a vocation for the ministry. Of course, when the candidate for orders has finished his general preparation and is entering upon special study in theology, he must devote himself specially to this; and it is generally well that he should study theology with other theological students and in a distinctively theological atmosphere. But no religious organization can make a greater mistake--I had almost said that none can experience a greater curse--than when it puts into seminaries by themselves the youth whom it is hoping by and by to lead to the study of theology. The decree of the Council of Trent on seminaries, we are told by a wise and learned theologian, "was perhaps the gravest practical error committed by the Council," and its provision for the separate education of youth destined for the ministry from the age of twelve years has produced, he says, "the most disastrous results," substituting as it does, for the liberal education of public schools and universities, "a course whose hyper-professional narrowness and shallowness is matter of frequent animadversion" on the part of intelligent men who hold to the general position of the Roman Church.[3]

This academy would not have been founded a century ago had it not been for the strong ecclesiastical convictions; but it would have accomplished little, if anything, of value if the educational ideas of its founders had not been broad and liberal. It is gratifying, as it is instructive, to see how they felt that they could best promote the cause of Christian education. They proposed to have pupils instructed in "the English Language, Philosophy, Mathematics, History, and every other science usually taught at Colleges; likewise the Dead Languages, such as Greek and Latin"; they looked forward to having "an instructor in the French Language," and purchasing "a Library and Philosophical Apparatus"; and they meant to provide instruction "in Logic, Rhetoric, Geography, Philosophy, etc." (Perhaps it may be noted that in the preliminary Constitution it was added, in not very felicitous phraseology, that "French education may be attended to under this Institution, by such instructors, and under such regulations, as the Trustees shall direct"; though it does not appear that any advantage was taken of this permission.)[4] There was no idea in anyone's mind that it would be to the advantage of the Episcopal Church in Connecticut to give to the young men of Church families an education less wide or less liberal than was given elsewhere; it was but desired that the education should be given to them under the influence of that Church which had moulded the minds of so many generations of scholars and statesmen, men of influence and men of affairs, in England, the Church of English literature and of English freedom. The work was thus well undertaken; that it was well carried on must be left to others to tell. It can only be said here that in 1819, after about twenty-five years of work, it was reported that ninety of the pupils had been prepared for college and twenty-eight had received Holy Orders. The numbers

are not large; they serve to show, however, that there was no undue theological bias here; and they also show, indirectly, since we are sure that there was a large number of pupils who did not enter college, that the advantages of a liberal education, at least in its beginnings, for those who could not carry their studies into opening manhood had reached a considerable number of the youth of the State, most of whom must have belonged to Church families.

I have dwelt at length on this earlier phase of the work of the Academy, and I have, I am afraid, trespassed on the themes specially assigned to others, because I have wished to show the high and broad conception of Christian education which was in the minds of the founder, the early supporters, and the first principals of the institution. It made an impress on the life of the Diocese and of the State; its results were to be seen in many ways then, and they have not even yet disappeared.

We have been reminded of the failure to secure a collegiate charter for this academy and how, after the long vacancy in the episcopate, one of Bishop Brownell's first acts was to move for the establishment of a Church college in Connecticut--though not for Connecticut alone--on an entirely new foundation. That this was done in this way was doubtless wise, but I suppose that there were some who thought that when the college at Hartford had been put in operation and good Dr. Bronson had been called to his rest, the Academy had ended its work. There was certainly a time of discouragement, but it was only because it was necessary somewhat to modify the methods of instruction and the general plans of work by reason of changes in times and circumstances. The grammar-school idea had been lost; the collegiate wants-- always supplied scholastically at New Haven--were now supplied both scholastically and in other ways at Hartford; strictly theological study was provided for at the General Seminary, which had been founded at New Haven and removed to New York. The work of the Academy for some seventy-five years was to be based on that of its first quarter of a century, but it was to be in some respects different from it. Under Mr. Morgan and Dr. Beardsley--I cannot mention his name without the feeling that this anniversary needs his voice to express and interpret its meaning--and Mr. Paddock, the school life was organized and carried on, and under them and their successors to our own day this academy has contributed in no little degree to the advancement of the interests of Christian education. The name "academy" has, indeed, been retained as a part of the corporate name of the institution, but in ordinary thought and in ordinary talk the word, which might have reminded of Plato (though rather presumptuously) or might have carried the mind back to the dissenters' schools in England (though very unhistorically), has been replaced by the simpler word which we apply to every place of the lower or secondary education. The school at Cheshire, under the care of wise and learned men, apt to teach and patient, has not perhaps stood forth before the public as specially demanding popular attention, but it has been an integral part of the form in which the work of a strong and in-

fluential diocese has been cast and carried on, and no inconsiderable number of young men have here received a training such as they could not have received elsewhere and have carried hence a power and an influence which have been of incalculable good. For many it has been the early home of liberal study which, continued at college, has fitted them for entrance upon professional life, shaping them to be leaders among men and to do good to others in their day and generation; to many more it has given the opportunity for acquiring enough of a liberal culture to fit them to be useful and happy members of society and to take a position of respect and influence in the communities in which their lot has been cast; to none has there failed to come something of that inspiration, that quickening of faculties both spiritual and mental, which the Church's methods and the Church's training can give in so much better a way than can anything that has ever been devised by the thought of even the wisest of men. We cannot begin to measure all this. Even if we could place before us the full roll of all the pupils of this academy and could estimate the value of the work done for the Fatherland and for the Church of God by those who have here been taught their duty and have been furnished to undertake it and to carry it on, even if we could trace back here the many threads of influence which have come from faithful instructors and from noble companions, we could not know, still less could we tell, all that these things have meant. But this at least we may say: that the Episcopal Academy of Connecticut has ever borne witness to the fact that healthy religion has a part in the life of a healthy boy and in the character of a healthy and true man; that the Church does care to lay the foundations of sound scholarship on principles that have met with the approbation of the ages, and to build upon that foundation according to the wisdom that experience brings and according to the special opportunities that are found from time to time; and that in the life of a Christian family, the home of a Christian minister, should be found the varied influences that train the character imperceptibly, but nonetheless surely, for goodness and truth. Thank God, we live in a commonwealth in which these lofty truths have never been denied by those who have had the shaping of her destinies, and in which a Christian school has never needed to apologize for its existence or to defend its place. Thank God, too, that our own Church in Connecticut has not looked to this historic academy as the only place where youth might be trained in the learning of books and for the duties of life on the basis of those principles which it specially belongs to her to maintain. But all of us who care for the good work of Christian education in this state and diocese--a work not limited by territorial bounds--will thank God for the good work--nonetheless good that it has often been very quiet, of the Episcopal Academy of Connecticut.

I have spoken of the change which came over the nature and scope of the work done here at the end of the first quarter of that century, the record of which we are to close today. Such changes are rarely seen at the time except by very wise men, and those who see them rarely understand them, though if they be wise men they shape their conduct by them. It cannot be doubted, how-

ever, that as the real Academy grew into the place of the somewhat theoretical grammar school, so the high school of these days is growing into the place of both. There are wise men who have the interests of this academy at heart and who are charged with the duty of caring for them and maintaining them. It is for them to consider what is to be for some years to come the place of such an academy as this in the scheme of Christian education to which as Churchmen we are committed. That it has a place no one can question; that it has a most important work before it for the benefit of this generation and of generations to come none of us shall be willing to doubt;

that it can be fitted for such work is certain; that it will be furnished for it is left for us to decide. If we have the faith and the faithfulness, the sense of responsibility and the willingness to meet it, that marked our first bishop and those who gathered around him a hundred years ago, we shall decide aright.

-----

1 For Massachusetts, see "The District School and the Academy in Massachusetts" in New England Mag., Dec., 1893; for Connecticut, see "Public Education in Connecticut" in Report of State Board of Education.
2 See my article in the University Magazine, March, 1891.
3 Littledale, History of the Council of Trent, p. 103.
4 The original documents are printed at the close of Dr. Beardsley's half-century address, whence also much other information has been taken.

BIOGRAPHICAL SKETCHES

Samuel Hart
[89] Class of 1866.

Samuel Hart was born at Saybrook, Connecticut, June 4, 1845, the son of Henry Hart and his mother Mary Ann Witter. Henry Hart was a farmer, banker, and Judge of the Probate Court in Saybrook, and a distinguished and useful citizen. Dr. Hart included among his ancestors many persons of note in the history of Connecticut and New England, being descended from Deacon Stephen Hart, an early settler of Farmington, and the Rev. John Hart, the first student to receive a degree from Yale. Dr. Hart's interest in historical subjects naturally led to a study of his ancestry, though his interests were always historical rather than genealogical. He was an original member of the Society of Colonial Wars in the State of Connecticut, and always took a deep interest in its affairs.

Dr. Hart received his preparation for College in the Episcopal Academy at Cheshire, Connecticut, and entered Trinity College in September, 1862, with the Class of 1866. In College his career was most distinguished. He was awarded the Freshman Greek Prize, the Latin Prize in his Junior Year for the best examination on all the Latin of the College Course, and the Senior Prize. He was Valedictorian of his Class, and was graduated A.B., with the title of Optimus—the first to be so honored. Perhaps no student in the history of the College has received more honors for scholarship and doubtless no one deserved them more. He was elected a member of Phi Beta Kappa in his Junior Year. In 1870 he was elected Secretary of the Connecticut Beta of Phi Beta Kappa, and held the office until his death, the longest record of service as Secretary in the annals of the Fraternity. In 1892 he was elected a Senator to the United Chapters of Phi Beta Kappa, and in 1917 was made a Senator for life, he being then Senior Senator. His interest in the Fraternity was keen, and his faithfulness and devotion to its interests unfailing.

Dr. Hart was a member of the Beta Beta Chapter of Psi Upsilon, and no more loyal, enthusiastic, and useful member ever adorned a college fraternity. He was constant in at-

tendance, wise in counsel, and devoted in friendship to the members of the Society for more than fifty years, and his memory is a precious possession of all whose privilege it was to be associated with him in this connection as in so many others.

Dr. Hart entered the Berkeley Divinity School, graduating in 1869. In 1868 he was elected a Tutor in Trinity College, and for the next three years was now and again called on to teach whenever any member of the Faculty was in any way disabled, perhaps giving more instruction in Greek than in any other department.

He was ordained Deacon in Middletown, June 2, 1869, and Priest in 1870 by Bishop John Williams.

In 1870 he was made Adjunct Professor of Mathematics, in 1873 Professor of Mathematics, and in 1882 was made Seabury Professor of Mathematics and Astronomy. This Professorship he resigned in 1883 to become Professor of the Latin Language and Literature. He was long Secretary of the Faculty, editor of the Catalogue, and from 1889 to 1899 acted as Librarian. In 1899 he resigned his place in the College to become Professor of Doctrinal Theology and of the Prayer Book, and Vice-Dean in the Berkeley Divinity School. In 1908 he became Dean of the School, and so remained till his death February 25, 1917.

The value of Dr. Hart's services to the College cannot be over-estimated. He was a profound scholar in several rather diversified fields. He was as good a mathematician as he was a Classical Scholar, and above all he was a Theologian and faithful Priest and Teacher. He was elected a Trustee of Trinity College in 1913, and his intimate familiarity with the College, together with his sound judgment, at once won for him recognition as one of the most useful members of that body.

Dr. Hart's services to the Diocese and the Church at large were most valuable. He was Registrar of the Diocese from 1874 to his death. For more than thirty years he was a member of the Standing Committee of the Diocese. He was long Chairman of the Committee on Constitution and Canons of the Diocesan Convention, and brought to the work of the Committee an unusual knowledge of Canon Law. In 1886 he was made Custodian of the Standard Book of Common Prayer; in 1892 he was elected Secretary of the House of Bishops; and in 1898 he was elected Historiographer and Registrar of the General Convention. He served on the Commission appointed by the General Convention on Prayer Book revision, and had much to do with the revision of 1892. He was also proving himself a most valuable member of the Commission at present engaged in the work of revision. Dr. Hart certainly was one of the most learned Liturgists of the American Church, and his taste in liturgical matters was not inferior to his learning. In this very important field, the Church is his debtor as in many others.

Though never technically in parish work, Dr. Hart was most faithful in the work of his ministry. For forty years he missed hardly a Sunday in his visits to the Hartford Hospital. There is hardly a small parish in the Diocese within his reach to which he did not give freely of his services. Though he never had charge of a parish, yet many are stronger and better because of his ministry.

Dr. Hart's historical attainments made him in constant demand for anniversary sermons, historical discourses, and the like. He always responded cheerfully and produced many most valuable studies. It is hardly too much to say that if his papers of this sort were collected, we should have a valuable source for a diocesan history on a generous scale.

Nor were his historical interests confined to the Church. He was deeply learned in the whole history of Connecticut, and his election to the office of President of the Connecticut Historical Society in 1900 in succession to Charles J. Hoadley was a simple recognition that he was the person best fitted to continue the labors of that distinguished student of the history of the State. This office Dr. Hart held worthily and with pardonable pride as long as he lived.

Naturally Dr. Hart was a member of many learned societies and received many academic honors in recognition of his attainments and contributions to knowledge. He received the M. A. degree in 1869, delivering the "Master's Oration" on the topic "The Age of Synthesis". This oration at the time received much favorable comment. From Trinity College he received also in 1885 the degree of D.D. and in 1899 the degree of D.C.L. In 1902 he received the degree of D.D. from Yale University, and in 1909 the degree of LL.D. from

228

Wesleyan University. In 1901 he declined the call to become Professor of Pastoral Theology in the General Theological Seminary. He was elected Bishop of Vermont June 22, 1893, but declined the election.

He was a member of the American Philological Association, its Secretary from 1873 to 1878, and its President in 1892; of the American Oriental Society; of the Society of Biblical Literature and Exegisis; of the American Historical Association; the American Association for the Advancement of Science; the Connecticut Historical Society; the Connecticut Library Association—its President in 1894; the New Haven Colony Historical Society; the New London County Historical Society; the American Antiquarian Society; and of the Society of Colonial Wars.

He was a Trustee of the Wadsworth Athenaeum; the Watkinson Library; the Colt Bequest; the Hartford Good Will Club; the Russell Library; Ridgefield School; and Trinity College.

Among Dr. Hart's publications may be mentioned: Satires of Juvenal, 1873; Satires of Persius, 1875; Bishop Seabury's Communion Office, with notes, 1874; 2nd ed., 1883; Mozarabic Liturgy, 1877; Somnium Scipionis, 1887; Maclear's Instruction for Confirmation and First Communion, 1895; In Memoriam: Samuel Colt and Caldwell Hart Colt, 1898; History of American Prayer Book in Frere's Proctor, 1901; Short Daily Prayers for Families, 1902; History of the American Book of Common Prayer, 1910; Faith and the Faith, (Bohlen Lectures), 1914; Archbishop Cranmer and the Prayer Book, 1915; The Witness of the Church (Paddock Lectures), 1916; sermons and historical addresses published and unpublished; articles in Appleton's Dictionary of American Biography and in other works; contributions to periodicals; editions of college catalogues, journals of conventions, etc.

This necessarily brief account of Dr. Hart may well be closed with a quotation from the minute adopted by the Faculty of Trinity College. "The Faculty of Trinity College, mindful of the long and distinguished career of their former colleague, the late Rev. Dr. Samuel Hart, desire to place on record their high appreciation of his profound scholarship, his singular gifts as a teacher, his unswerving loyalty to his Alma Mater.... In the midst of grief at the loss of a faithful and dearly beloved friend, the Faculty recall, as the highest good, Dr. Hart's lofty ideals and his unblemished Christian character.... May he rest in peace; and may light perpetual shine upon him."

The funeral service was held in Holy Trinity Church, Middletown, and the interment was in the family plot at Saybrook Point. Memorial services were held in the Church of the Good Shepherd and in other churches about the Diocese. Dr. Hart was indeed a good and a great man, and it may truly be said of him that in all things he was found faithful.

MEMORIALS OF THE DEAN

DR. HART'S CAREER IN OUTLINE

Samuel Hart was born at Saybrook, Conn., June 4, 1845. He was instructed for a time by Rev. Peter L. Shepard, of our Berkeley class of '55, later attended the Episcopal Academy at Cheshire, and entered Trinity College in 1862, being graduated there with the distinction of *Optimus* in 1866. For the next three years he was a student of the Berkeley Divinity School, doing most thorough work, as always, in spite of manifold interruptions calling him to teach in Trinity College, whenever any member of that Faculty was in any way disabled, and the writer of these lines can well remember how he wondered when young Mr. Hart could possibly do his studying and reading for the work of the Divinity School. In 1869 Mr. Hart was ordered Deacon, and proceeded to his Master of Arts Degree,—the writer remembers also the admiration with which elders spoke of the "Master's Oration," on *"The Age of Synthesis,"* which Mr. Hart delivered on that Commencement Day. "Clear as crystal" is a comment which the writer heard from one whose judgment he specially revered. As Deacon, Mr. Hart was drawn at once into the service of Trinity College in a more permanent way. The

Rev. Dr. John T. Huntington, then Professor of Greek, had a quick eye and a warm heart. He had seen the brilliant promise of this young scholar, and had a vision of what it might mean to the College to secure him as one of its Faculty. So Professor Huntington discovered that he was in need of rest, and offered to assign a large part of his salary to the maintenance of a tutor in Greek, if the Trustees would appoint Mr. Hart to such a position. The young tutor made himself soon an indispensable part of the College life. The position of Secretary of the Faculty gravitated to him by natural process, so accurate was he, and so neat, and so beautifully fair were the records that he kept in that graceful chirography of his. From 1870 to 1873 he was assistant professor of mathematics, and full professor from 1873 to 1883, enjoying a brief leave of absence, with care of the American Church in Paris, in 1878–9. He was Professor of Latin, 1883–1899, for there was nothing that he could not teach and teach masterfully, if he gave his mind to it, and really he seemed to give his mind to most things. He went to the Berkeley Divinity School as Professor of Doctrinal Theology and Prayer Book in 1899, serving as Vice-Dean till 1908, and as Dean from 1908 to his death.

Dr. Hart received the degree of D. D. from Trinity College in 1885, and from Yale University in 1892. Trinity gave him its D. C. L. in 1899, and Wesleyan University its LL. D. in 1909. He has been Registrar of the Diocese of Connecticut since 1874; Custodian of the Standard Prayer Book of the Church since 1886, six years before we had one for him to take into his custody; Secretary of the House of Bishops from 1892; Historiographer and Registrar of the Church from 1898. He was a member of the American Philological Association (Secretary, 1883-8, President, 1892); of the American Oriental Society; of the Society of Biblical Literature and Exegesis; of the American Historical Association; of the American Association for the Advancement of Science; of the Connecticut Historical Society (its President since 1900); of the Connecticut Library Association (its President in 1894); of the New Haven Colony Historical Society; of the New London County Historical Society; of the American Antiquarian Society; of the Society of Colonial Wars; of Phi Beta Kappa (Senator since 1892); and of the Psi Upsilon College Fraternity. Dr. Hart was also a Trustee of the Wadsworth Athenaeum, the Watkinson Library, the Colt Bequest, and Trinity College, and President of the Trustees of the Good Will Club, the Russell Library, and the Ridgefield School. As Editor and Author he published Satires of Juvenal, 1873; Satires of Persius, 1875; Bishop Seabury's Communion Office, with notes, 1874; Maclear's Instruction for Confirmation and Holy Communion, 1895; History of the American Prayer Book in Frere's Procter in 1901 (also in raised type for the blind); Short Prayers for Families, 1902; History of American Book of Common Prayer, 1910; Faith and the Faith (Bohlen Lectures), 1914; Paddock Lectures, 1916; and many sermons, addresses, and encyclopedia articles. No cold outline, like this, can convey any impression of the "spirit in the wheels" which pervaded and vitalized all these manifold activities and gave them an immensity of value. Those who know the informing spirit will be glad to read over the crowded details, and think what a wealth they stand for.

THE LAST DAYS

BY THE REV. PROFESSOR W. P. LADD

Dr. Hart always spoke of a person seventy years of age as a young man. But to us who had been with him day by day he had for the past two years begun to show signs of decreasing vigour. His eyes troubled him. His voice lacked the old-time strength. His walk was less sure. And he spoke of certain internal troubles which gave him considerable pain. His work, and especially his task in the last weeks of editing the Report of the General Convention, wore upon him. But characteristically he stuck to his schedule and refused to rest.

On the Monday and Tuesday mornings following Quinquagesima Sunday we noticed in him an unusual shortness of breath, and it was most distressing to watch him struggling through his part in the Chapel service. Tuesday noon I spoke to Bishop Acheson of the Dean's condition and he agreed to seek him out at once to try to persuade him to go for a vacation. An hour after word came of the fatal illness. The Dean had been sitting at his desk when he was attacked with a slight cerebral hemorrhage. Dr. Calef and certain Hartford specialists were summoned. From Tuesday until Sunday morning the doctors and nurses, his sister Mrs. Bailey, and groups of students two at a time day and night attended faithfully and lovingly upon him.

The doctors thought best that few should enter the sick-room. Once the Dean sent for me. It was to remind me of certain details as to the order of the Lenten services and to thank me for looking after the

welfare of the School during his disability. Bishop Acheson offered to administer the Holy Communion; but he said he would wait until Sunday. He was in excellent spirits, frequently joking. His breathing was often labored and he seemed to suffer but the doctor assured us he did not. The hemorrhage was absorbed. But serious complications developed in the internal organs. And he gradually failed. There was in fact a quite general break-down of the whole physical system.

On Saturday night when I was summoned again to his bedside it was known that the Dean was near his end. He was delirious, and thought himself conducting a Church service and preaching. At a pause in his sermon I spoke to him. He recognized me and shook my hand. I said it was a privilege to be allowed to see him. His answer was, joking, "I am not much to see." When I stepped back he charged the nurses to show me the way out. This bit of courtesy was his last conscious act. It was just past midnight. Fifteen minutes afterwards I knelt at the death bed with the nurses, two students, and his sister, and said the commendatory prayer. In the last moments he had thought himself once more in church, and his last earthly words were "The Lord bless you all!"

THE FUNERAL
BY THE REV. PROFESSOR ANTHON T. GESNER

At an early hour on Wednesday, February 28th, the body of our beloved Dean, clad in surplice and stole, was brought under escort of the Faculty and students into the choir of St. Luke's Chapel. Upon the casket, which was encased in black broadcloth with cross extending its entire length, was laid a green wreath of ivy taken from the Chapel walls, a tribute of love from the professors and students of Berkeley. A similar wreath was hung upon the Dean's stall, which was draped in black. In harmony with former custom, funeral lights were set at the head and foot of the coffin. The Eucharist was celebrated at 7 o'clock by the Suffragan Bishop, assisted by Professor Ladd, and at noon, a large company of Alumni and Clergy of the Diocese having arrived, the full Litany (with the Commendatory Prayer from the Office for the Visitation of the Sick) was said by the Rev. Dr. Lucius Waterman of the Class of '76, and then, as the Chapel bell tolled, the casket was borne reverently to the Church of the Holy Trinity. Under the general supervision of the Suffragan Bishop, the details of the procession and seating of those in attendance were carefully arranged for by the Master of Ceremonies, Mr. E. Kent Hubbard, assisted by Professor Cady of Wesleyan University.

The first procession, which included a notable company of representatives of institutions and learned societies of this State, formed in the Parish House, and shortly after one o'clock entered the Church through the door of the Sacristy, led by Professors of the Divinity School.

As the second procession, which included the Bishops, the Rector of the Parish, the members of the Standing Committee, and other attending Clergymen, passed up the central aisle towards the Chancel, the Rev. Dr. Storrs O. Seymour, '61, President of the Standing Committee, read with emotion the sentences of the Burial Office.

The Lesson was read by the Rt. Rev. Thomas F. Davies, D. D., Bishop of the Diocese of Western Massachusetts, after which was sung the 414th hymn, "Guide me, O Thou Great Jehovah."

The Creed and Prayers were said by the Rev. George T. Linsley, '88, Rector of the Church of the Good Shepherd, Hartford, and Bishop Brewster read the concluding prayer and pronounced the benediction.

The full parish choir of forty voices, under the direction of Mr. William B. Davis, led the congregation in the singing of the chants and hymns, of which there were several especially dear to Dr. Hart.

At the conclusion of the service in the Church, the casket was placed in the hearse, and accompanied by the members of Dr. Hart's family and household, and near friends, conveyed to Saybrook, together with a large company of mourners, occupying two special cars on the afternoon train. This company was met by automobiles at the station, where the procession re-formed and moved down the main street of the historic town, passing Grace Church, while the bell tolled, and halting at the gate of the Cemetery, where the casket was tenderly lifted from the hearse, and borne by the pall-bearers to the family plot, which is just within the gate, and shaded by trees of evergreen.

Bishop Brewster, standing at the head of the grave, and Bishop Acheson at the foot, read the Committal and Prayers, while Dr. Hart's lifelong friend, Dr. Seymour, dropped the earth upon the coffin. When Bishop Brewster pronounced the benediction, the hymn "Rock of Ages" was sung by the students, and we turned with sad hearts from all that was mortal of one of the best of men.

A few flakes of snow fell during the service, as if to cover with a fitting pall, one whose life had been of the purest type.

THOSE IN ATTENDANCE AT THE FUNERAL

Besides the Trustees of the Berkeley Divinity School and a great number of the clergy of this and other Dioceses, a large company representing many institutions and organizations of the Church and State, with which Dr. Hart had been connected during his life time, were present at the Dean's funeral.

The General Theological Seminary sent several representatives, the Faculty of Trinity College attended in a body, and many members of the Wesleyan University were in the funeral procession, together with a delegation of undergraduates from both these colleges, representing the Psi Upsilon Fraternity. The Pastors and Clergymen of several of the Churches of Middletown, and representatives of the Connecticut Historical Society, the Middlesex County Historical Society, the Wadsworth Atheneum, the Board of Directors of the Hartford Hospital, the Watkinson Farm School, and the Good Will Club, were in attendance in impressive numbers. Ex-Governor Baldwin of Connecticut, former Governor Frank B. Weeks, and former Secretary of State Charles G. R. Vinal, and many of others of prominence in the State were present.

Bishop Lines of Newark, a Trustee of Berkeley and President of the Alumni Association, through a delay of train, was unable to take part in the service, but was present in the congregation and at the grave.

The floral tributes, which were of great number and beauty, were arranged in the vestibule of the Church, and later carried to Saybrook and placed about the grave, attesting the respect and honor in which Dr. Hart was held by a multitude of people who mourned his departure from this life in which he has been so active.

A SHEAF OF MEMORIES
DR. HART AS AN UNDERGRADUATE
BY MR. B. HOWELL GRISWOLD, OF THE CLASS OF '66, TRINITY COLLEGE

While I am glad to contribute my mite to any offering of affection to the memory of Dr. Hart of the class of '66, Trinity College, after more than fifty years one feels unable to do full justice to the "boy" and one's own feelings. "Sam," as he was affectionately called by all the boys, both in and outside of his class, was modest and to a certain extent retiring. He was a hard student and, while not especially identified with the games or other activities, physical, social or musical, of college life, he was by no means a recluse and was frequently a guest at entertainments of the hospitable families of Hartford. The regard and affection in which he was held showed itself by the absence of any envy of his position as having obtained the highest standing of the whole student body, and when at the close of the course it was announced that he had gained the distinction of "*Optimus*," and had also exceeded the highest marks of any student of previous years as well as during his course, the greatest pleasure was evinced by all, and all felt that he deserved his honors. I have been fortunate in keeping in touch with him by occasional meetings and by correspondence. His letters invariably showed his affectionate friendship, which I always highly valued. He was the Life Secretary, and I am the Life President of the Class of '66, which helped to keep us in close touch all these years.

Baltimore, Md., March 17, 1917.

DR. HART AS A YOUNG TEACHER
BY THE REV. LUCIUS WATERMAN, D. D.

I entered Trinity College in 1867. I think that it was not until 1868, but I am sure that it was before the end of my Freshman year, that our Professor of Mathematics fell ill, and Mr. Samuel Hart came to take his place. From that time on there was a succession of disabilities of teachers in one department or another, and always it was Mr. Hart who came to fill the breach. By the end of my Sophomore year Mr. Hart was fully established as a permanent member of the teaching staff. And what a teacher he was! I think that he worked his classes harder than any other member of the Faculty. I am sure that he taught them more. Some of the other men in that Faculty taught me much, and did some things for me that were greater than teaching. But none of them equalled Mr. Hart in photographing his ideas on the sensitive plate of a student's mind, and making a clear and indelible picture there. A young man once said to me of a great teacher in the Middle West, "He puts his learning in neat packages, and puts them away on shelves in my mind, and I can go and take down one of those packages any

time. It's right there ready, and I can even remember what he said, and how he looked when he said it." That describes fairly the method of my two greatest teachers of the "instructor" as distinguished from the "educator" type, Bishop Williams and Dr. Hart. And perhaps I may say now that Dr. Hart was larger and deeper than that other superlatively great teacher, while his clearness and power of impressive impartation were about the same.

Then Mr. Hart was made deacon and priest, and his sermons began to be a great power in my life. I can recall vividly some of those sermons, the one in which he brought together the parables of the Pounds and the Talents,—"To every man according to his several ability," and "That he might see how much every man had gained by trading," or the one about the hardening of Pharaoh's heart. Hearing that sermon was an event in my life. I can still remember, by the way, a passage in that sermon where the young preacher spoke of men who think that "falsehood in College is not lying, and that stealing in College is not dishonesty." Or again there was the sermon in one Advent Season on Eternal Punishment, which Bishop Williams was to have preached, but could not on account of illness, and Mr. Hart took the Bishop's memoranda of the line of argument, and wrote the sermon. I at least felt, much as I admired Bishop Williams, that we had not lost value by the exchange.

And then how busy Mr. Hart was, how loaded with work, and how ready he was to undertake anything more that would be of help to some one. I apologized, one evening, for interrupting, and he said, with his grave smile, that he had read somewhere,—how wonderful was his reading and his apt remembering !—that interruptions in work were gifts from God, and must be taken as opportunities. This young man, less than six years my senior, became to be an object not only of admiration, but of veneration.

Returning to the young teacher in his beginnings, I would remark that he was never weak in discipline. A distinguished gentleman told me not long since of how Mr. Hart discovered him and a future bishop matching pennies during a recitation hour, and "his language was painfully severe." And the same narrator gave me an example of Professor Hart's thoroughness and masterfulness. He came back to College one summer, when Mr. Hart had been teaching natural science, and Mr. Hart mentioned with satisfaction that "we have performed successfully every experiment but one in Ganot's Physics." "Thorough" was the motto of his life.

DR. HART AND THE CARE OF THE CHURCHES
BY THE REV. D. RUSS JUDD

[The editor has seen a letter from the rector of St. Andrew's, Thompsonville, from which he has asked Mr. Judd's permission to print a few words, written with no thought of publication, which may serve as a sample of Dr. Hart's living service to church after church, and of how his love and generous service drew out the love and gratitude of many in return.]

Dr. Hart is very dear to us here. This would have been his twentieth consecutive visit in Holy Week. . . . There are people in the parish who can remember back a great many years, who think that he has come every year that they can remember, though not always in Holy Week. Years ago, when asking Dr. Hart to come to us, I begged him to be lenient with me for asking him every year. His reply was: "Never mention it again, for I should not think I had kept Lent, if I did not go to St. Andrew's."

Dr. Hart seemed to think it his duty, as I know it was his pleasure, to minister to the smaller churches of Connecticut. In fact, many a place with no church, and no possibility of a church, was ministered to with comparative regularity by Dr. Hart.

. . . . He was an interesting preacher. But he was far more than that. He was the kind and interested friend, with a word of love for the old, help for the young, given in his genial, kindly manner; a hint as to an easy way to master the catechism, or something of that kind, for the child. From the time that he entered the church till he left it, the people, old and young, felt him to be their friend.

DR. HART AND THE CHURCH MISSIONS PUBLISHING CO.
BY THE REV. SAMUEL R. COLLADAY

Among Dr. Hart's multitudinous extra cares a place of considerable importance must be given to those which came to him through his connection with the Church Missions Publishing Company. This began

with its inception in 1891. In fact those who started it would hardly have dared to do so, had it not been for the encouragement and help he gave them. He became the first Vice-President, the Presiding Bishop being ex-officio President, and continued in that office until his death. He never missed a meeting of the board; and for many years he personally revised the manuscript of every publication that was issued. At all times his deep and unflagging interest, his broad and thorough knowledge of the Church's missionary work, his wise counsels, and his unfailing courtesy, made his presence in the Company a tower of strength on which the other members gratefully leaned.

Surely it is not amiss to believe, with one of the members of the Board, that, "Dr. Hart's strong, devoted personality, his constant thought of this work among the many other interests he possessed, cannot be put out like the flame of a candle. Even in the rest of Paradise—who knows how or in what manner—his help may be given us."

At a special meeting of the Company, held on March 8th, an appropriate, but confessedly inadequate Minute was passed to record the Company's realization of "irreparable loss." The above note is largely taken from this Minute.

We thank God for the great privilege that has been ours in his help and friendship. "May he rest in peace, and may light perpetual shine upon him."

DR. HART AND THE NURSES' GUILD
BY MISS EDITH BEACH, SECRETARY OF THE HARTFORD BRANCH G. ST. B.

Dr. Hart has been so much to the Hartford Branch of the Guild of St. Barnabas that it is difficult adequately to express, in any way, its obligations to him.

He had, for many years, done the work of a Chaplain in the Hartford Hospital when, early in 1892, the work of this Guild for Nurses was brought to his notice, and on the 15th of March of that year, he organized the Hartford Branch. From that time he was unwearying in his services for it, never missing a meeting unless more important duties intervened and none who have had the privilege of listening to his words of counsel and help can forget them. Deeply spiritual as as they were and setting forth the teachings of the Church, in its yearly round, they were at the same time eminently practical, pointing out where the help and strength were to be found in which to live the daily round and to do the common task.

His further generous gift of time in carrying on the business meetings and joining in the social side of the Guild, with his genial goodwill and ready interest, made each member know and feel him as a friend, and one to go to in special times of need. Many of the members will say what one nurse has written, "Dr. Hart's death is a great sorrow to all of us who belong to the Guild, and to me it is a great grief and a feeling that I have lost a personal friend."

May we all strive to live as he has taught us by his example and word.

A STORY FROM THE MIDDLESEX HOSPITAL

A young man was lying in a bed in one of the wards, very ill and weak. Dr. Hart coming in saw him, and went to him, laying his hand on his head, and saying some comforting words. Then he knelt and said some prayers. After he went out, the patient asked, "Who is that man?" The nurse told him, and he said. "No one has ever done such a thing for me before."

DR. HART AS SECRETARY OF THE HOUSE OF BISHOPS
BY THE RT. REV. T. F. DAVIES, BISHOP OF WESTERN MASSACHUSETTS

No one who has sat in the House of Deputies at the General Convention since 1892 is ever likely to forget the arrival of messages from the House of Bishops. The coming of one was a distinct event. The business of the House stopped while Dr. Hart walked up the passage and presented the message. His figure and walk became familiar, but there was always something in his bearing that added dignity to the incident. His whole presence denoted the ecclesiastic, for he was of a distinctly priestly type. The Oxford cap in his hand, to me, always symbolized the scholar, the man of solid and accurate learning. A look at his face and expression might well have made a by-stander exclaim: "There goes a man of thoroughly upright and righteous life!" Several deputies have said to me: "It is worth coming to the General Convention

just to see Dr. Hart bring in a message!'' If the House of Deputies ever failed to attach due weight to messages from the Bishops, it was not because of the way those messages were delivered.

I am too young in the House of Bishops to have many reminiscences of Dr. Hart there. Quiet attention to duty, modesty, accuracy, cheerfulness, courtesy and a certain exquisiteness always marked his work. I should add humor also. Twice I have served on a committee, the whole work of which was ordinarily left to Dr. Hart. At this last Convention, on informing me of my appointment, he smilingly added: '' I hope we shall not disagree.''

Since he has gone from us, two sentences from the recent Bohlen Lectures keep recurring to me: '' The life which finds its inspiration in that tone of devotion and work for the Master which our Book of Common Prayer so wonderfully commends and inculcates is the life of faith and sacrament, the eternal life which is already for the believer a real and enduring possession '' (page 134). Certainly it had long been *his* possession! The other is this: '' In our private devotions as we prepare for the reception of the greatest of sacraments, and in the worship of the congregation as we draw near in faith, we pass beneath the simple phrasing of our own prayers or above the dignified utterance of our historic liturgy, to know who it is whose voice speaks to our souls and why we are following the guidance of His voice '' (page 135). So it seems to me that even in the constant performance of the duties of the office of Secretary, in recording resolutions and amendments, Dr. Hart passed beneath the routine and had constantly in mind whose work it was he was doing and whose Kingdom he was serving.

DR. HART AS THE FACULTY SAW HIM
BY THE REV. PROFESSOR W. P. LADD

Our memory most vividly pictures Dr. Hart where he would most like to be remembered—in chapel. Always present, always punctual, with his even, resonant voice taking part in reading, response, and hymn, year after year following the familiar lessons in the Hebrew and Greek texts with unflagging interest, supplying for the absent or forgetful student or professor, watching over the execution of all the carefully thought out details of the service as a robin over the flight of the young fledgling, it was as true of him as of any Bible character that his chief delight was to minister in the sanctuary of the Lord. We of the Faculty inevitably fell behind his high standard. We were at times late or absent, broke rubrics, forgot the proper omissions or insertions, worst of all, we mispronounced. But I hope his constant, kindly watchfulness improved us. And it was a good thing that so much was expected of us, a good thing to have served under one upon whom we felt had come down the spirit of Williams and Seabury, of Butler and Laud, and the judicious Hooker, one who was so truly the custodian of the Prayer Book ideal.

Again we think of the Dean at his desk. His genial welcome bespeaks infinite leisure. The orderly desk seems to indicate that he has before him some small task which he may turn to after your departure. He chats or jokes or advises gravely with you as if your business were his sole concern. Only when one came to know Dr. Hart well did one realize his extraordinary genius for work. His schedule of teaching was always heavy, and at one time or another he taught every subject in the divinity curriculum. But teaching was his recreation. He attended, himself, to all the administrative details of his office, always refusing proffered aid. He received innumerable letters—from prospective students, from alumni, from perplexed vestrymen seeking advice, from busy bishops desiring to be set right on difficult points of Church History or Canon Law; and every letter received a prompt answer in his own handwriting. Besides, there was the work for General Convention, the constant attendance upon trustee and committee meetings, the preparation of historical sermons for ever-recurring centennials and sesquicentennials, the writing of books. Nor was Sunday, with its services and hospital visitations, ever a day of rest. He did not spare himself, and his mind naturally worked accurately and rapidly. Therefore he ever seemed less busy than he was. In the thirteen years in which I was his colleague I never saw him hurried or knew him to be behind in anything he had to do. It was a fitting climax to such a life to have worked hard up to the very end, as he did, and to have died in harness.

Of the Dean in the class room and as a teacher it is for his students rather than for us of the faculty to speak in detail. But two things impressed us. One was his breadth of theological and intellectual sympathy. Outsiders sometimes spoke of Dr. Hart as the typical conservative, fixed immovably in a certain high and dry theology which

was assumed to have prevailed in Connecticut a generation or more ago. To us such an estimate seemed absurd. He was constantly and to the last taking up with new ideas and dropping old ones. He seemed sometimes even to love change for its own sake. And this quality was perhaps bound up with the second thing—his love for young men. This was his ruling passion. It was said of a celebrated French writer much sought out by the great that he never asked the name of a caller, but only his age. Something similar might be said of the Dean. Frequently wearied with the great ecclesiastical functions which his presence so greatly adorned, ill at ease sometimes at gatherings of important people, he was always happy when associating with groups of students whether in the class room or outside. And his devotion they appreciated and returned. Few American teachers can have enjoyed such a popularity with so many successive generations of college and seminary students. Nor did age wither or diminish this extraordinary power.

It was, in fact, in his social relations with students and faculty that the Dean was at his best. His photograph may carry to future generations something of the impression of a great personality which he made upon all whom he met. But no report can do justice to the charm he exercised in acquaintance and conversation. His talk brimmed over with good things. The late Lord Acton had the habit, it is said, of supplying his callers with paper and pencil that they might take notes of his conversation. The Dean's modesty and sense of humor would have been enough to save him from any similar act. But while he talked, one often felt the impulse to write. And one professor at least (now a bishop) used on retiring from the Dean's study to record in his card catalogue interesting facts and stories gleaned in the course of a call. There was no other '' table talk '' like the Dean's. As one listened one was always pleased and frequently amazed at the flow of wit, and apt anecdote, and bits of out-of-the-way erudition. Yet with him conversation never degenerated into brilliant monologue. It did not ramify, and overspread, and kill off the budding efforts of the lesser brethren. It was brief, direct, stimulating, replete with easy openings for others. And in his talk, as in all his social relations, he was the soul of courtesy.

Such a man is a privilege to have known, but a humiliation to attempt to describe.

DR. HART WITH HIS STUDENTS
BY THE REV. C. D. FAIRMAN, '15

As we knelt in chapel on the day of his burial, and made our prayer for him who was our master and father, the sense of personal loss came to me in this way: I can never go to Sammy with my troubles any more. (I am sure not even bishops will mind my calling him ''Sammy.'' Any one who doesn't think of him as ''Sammy'' doesn't love him.)

I have been out of Berkeley two years, but I've always held to the privilege which we all felt was ours, of turning to Dr. Hart in time of trouble. I have had ''many fathers,'' but there are certain things for which Dr. Hart had the only final and comforting answer. This sense of filial dependence is to me probably most characteristic of ''Dr. Hart with his students.'' I think many who read this will agree. His study door had no terrors for us; rather it was an invitation for us to come in and talk. We had many harrowing, and seemingly insurmountable problems. Have I money for next term? How can I believe this article of faith and not fly in the face of the Hibbert Journal? Must I go to Rome? Am I truly called to the ministry? With such burdens we would go to him with a kind of joy, for we knew beforehand his cheering wisdom and the comfort he would bring us. After you had consumed about two hours of his time, and he had stocked you with new courage, and like an angel, had cut the burden from your shoulders, then he would squeeze your hand and say, ''God bless you my boy,—be good, and don't forget your prayers.'' It was funny, but you had tears in your eyes. And the point is, you did try to be sensible, and you tried to see what praying would do.

There are many things for which we students treasure his memory. In his classes, and in private talks, he was never dogmatic, never cocksure. Most firmly he believed and taught that, '' before all things it is necessary that [we] hold the Catholic Faith,'' and he fought valiantly, both in living and teaching, to keep that Faith '' whole and undefiled:'' but his charity,—something in him which stood out always as the '' mind of Christ,''—forbade his daring to pronounce upon brethren weak in the faith ''that without doubt they shall perish everlastingly.'' Some of us, with a taste for heresy-hunting were annoyed at what we called his '' non-committal '' attitude. But we see now that he was the true teacher of teachers and trainer of pastors, and he knew, what I for

one have learned by sad experience since, that the way of a shepherd is to lead, and not drive.

His was a sane, lucid, and joyful theology, given out with subtle accuracy of statement, cautious and fearless at once,— he was the true apologist. The real test of his teaching is that it helps us now.

I have said that we chiefly miss him as one to whom we would turn for advice and support. Yet in the great fundamental truths of our religion we shall not need his support, because already he has planted in us that strong living and growing faith which was his.

We felt that underneath that inquiring, many-sided mind of his there was a rock-built foundation, and that every stone had been tested; tested not in any academic fashion, but by the test of life. His life was so obviously built upon his faith. Every feature of his encyclopedic knowledge, his boyish enthusiasm for the whole of life, the breadth and charity of his points of view, his simple, apostolic piety, his humor and humanity;—all these were "living stones up-builded" upon the Rock of his faith.

Now, as then, when we think of that life, built upon such a faith, it is for us the pragmatic test,—it works. And so beneath all our doubts and problems is a fair portion of that strong faith which the master built up under us.

And because his creed was expressed in his *life*,—was a living and compelling *personality*,—he drew us to him by the many human ways in which that faith was expressed in him,—until he became our *father*.

That, I think, is our best and truest remembrance of him. He whom the Church honors as Priest and Doctor, he whose learning is acknowledged by many colleges and societies,—to us students he shall always be "our Sammy," because we love him. And he has a special benediction which is our very own: "God bless you my boys; and don't forget your prayers."

A
List of Books from the Library
of the late
REV. SAMUEL HART, D.D., D. Can. L., LL.D.
[91] added to the
Library of Trinity College

The Rev. Samuel Hart, D.D., D. Can. L., LL.D., a graduate of Trinity College in the Class of 1866, died at Middletown, February 25, 1917. With his accustomed care he left notes for the guidance of his sister, Mrs. Melville Knox Bailey, the sole heir and executrix, in disposing of his valuable library of some six thousand volumes. Among the institutions remembered by Dr. Hart in this way were the General Convention of the Episcopal Church, the Diocese of Connecticut, the Wadsworth Athenaeum, Yale University, the Berkeley Divinity School, and Trinity College. Naturally, though the number of volumes distributed in this way was relatively small, yet they included many of the more important and valuable items.

Through the kindness of Mrs. Bailey, the Library of Trinity College was permitted to select from the books that remained such as it was desired to purchase. In this way, the College acquired from the library of her honored, distinguished, and beloved alumnus a considerable number of works, chiefly in the fields of his favorite studies, Theology and the Classics, that it is believed Dr. Hart would rejoice to see in the Library of his Alma Mater. The total number of volumes received is 852; of these 554 are bound, 175 unbound, and 123 are pamphlets. The list of books designated for the College by Dr. Hart includes 179 bound and 85 unbound volumes. Those purchased, then, number 375 bound, 90 unbound, and 123 pamphlets.

The purpose of this publication is to preserve in convenient form a list of the books in the College Library acquired either by gift or purchase from Dr. Hart's library.

The titles designated for the College by Dr. Hart are:

The Church Quarterly Review, the set of Teubner Latin Classics, Publications of the New Paleographical Society, Paléographie des Classiques Latins, the editions and translations of Juvenal, publications of the Egypt Exploration Fund, and all Trinity College publications, both bound and unbound.

All other titles in the list were purchased.

ARTHUR ADAMS,
Librarian.

July 16, 1917.

THEOLOGICAL WORKS.

Abbott, E. A. Johannine grammar. 1906.
Allard, Paul. Le Christianisme et l'Empire Romain de Néron à Théodose; 2e ed. 1897. Unbound.
Allen, Ethan. Clergy in Maryland of the Protestant Episcopal Church. 1860.
Analecta liturgica, pars II: Thesaurus hymnologicus. 1888.
Angus, Samuel. Environment of early Christianity. 1915.
Antiquitatum Liturgicarum Arcana. 1605. 3v.
Armenian liturgy translated into English. 1867.
Armenian liturgy translated into English by F. James Issaverdenz. 2d ed. 1873.
Assemanus, J. A. Codex Liturgicus. 1749. 6v.
Bacon, B. W. The Fourth Gospel in research and debate. 1910.
Barnes, A. S. The Early Church in the light of the monuments. 1913.
Bate, H. N. History of the church to A. D. 325. 1908.
Batiffol, Pierre. Anciennes littératures Chrétiennes: la littérature Grecque. 1897. Unbound.
Batten, L. W. The Old Testament from the modern point of view. 1899.
Bennet, W. H., and Adeney, W. F. A Biblical Introduction. 1907.
Beroldus. Beroldus; sive, Ecclesiae Ambrosianae Mediolanensis kalendarium et ordines saec XII; edidit Marcus Magistretti. 1894. Unbound.
Bethune-Baker, J. F. Introduction to the early history of Christian doctrine. 1903.
Bethune-Baker, J. F. Nestorius and his teaching. 1908.
Bible. English. Expositor's Bible; ed. by Rev. W. R. Nicoll. n.d. 6v.
Bible. The Holy Byble... authorized and appointed to be read in the churches. 14th ed. of the Bishop's Bible. 1585.
Bible. O. T. Apocrypha. 1895.
Bible. O. T. Apocrypha ed. by Rev. C. J. Ball; variorum reference ed. n.d.
Bible. O. T. Prophetic books. The minor prophets; with a commentary by Rev. E. B. Pusey. 1877.
Bingham, Joseph. Origines ecclesiasticae; or, The antiquities of the Christian church. 1829. 9v.
Box, G. H. Virgin Birth of Jesus. 1916.
Briggs, C. A. Theological Symbolics. 1914.
Bright, William. Canons of the first four general councils. 1892.
Bright, William. Notes on the canons of the first four general councils. 1882.
Bright, William. Some aspects of primitive church life. 1898.
Burrage, Champlin. The early English dissenters. 1912. 2v.
Cabrol, Fernand, et LeClercq Henri. Dictionnaire D'Archéologie Chrétienne et de Liturgie. No. 1-37. 1903-1916. Unbound.
Carter, J. B. Religion of Numa. 1906.
Chase, F. H. Confirmation in the Apostolic age. 1909.
Chevalier, Ulysse. Poésie liturgique du Moyen age. 1893. Unbound.
Church of England. Book of Common Prayer and administration of the sacraments... in eight languages. 1825.
Church of England. Book of Common Prayer... ed. by G. W. Sprott. 1871.
Church of England. Book of Common Prayer, and the Scottish liturgy. 1912.

Church of England. A form of prayer issued by special command of his Majesty George III., London 1776. 1898.

Church of England. Official year-book. 1915-1916. 2v.

Church of England. Preces privatae in studiosorum gratiam collectae... 1854.

Churchman's missionary atlas. 1912.

Clark, Samuel. Bible atlas of maps and plans. 6th ed. 1900.

Clement, Saint. Κλημεντος Προς Κορινθιους Επιστολη Πρωτη. 1633.

Cobb, W. F. Mysticism and the creed. 1914.

Contentio veritatis: essays in constructive theology, by six Oxford tutors. 1902.

Daniel, Evan. The Prayer-book. n.d.

Daniel, H. A., ed. Thesaurus hymnologicus. 1855-56. 5v. in 2.

Dashiell, T. G. Digest of proceedings of conventions and councils of the diocese of Virginia. 1883.

Dearmer, Percy. Everyman's history of the Prayer-book. 1915.

Catholic Church. Definitions of the Catholic faith and canons of discipline of the first four general councils. 1867.

Denzinger, H. J. D., ed. Enchiridion symbolorum definitionum et declarationum. 10th ed. 1908.

Dore, J. R. Old Bibles; an account of the early versions of the English Bible; 2d ed. 1888.

Dowden, John. Further studies in the Prayer-book. 1908.

Dowden, John. The workmanship of the Prayer-book. 1899.

Doyle, J. B. The Church in Eastern Ohio; a history. 1914.

Durandus, Ursin. Rationale divinorum officiorum. 1589.

Edersheim, Alfred. The Temple: its ministry and services as they were at the time of Christ. 1874.

Edward VI. King Edward the Sixth on the Supremacy. ed. by Robert Potts. 1874.

Foote, H. W. Annals of King's Chapel. 1882-96. 2v.

Forsyth, P. T. The Person and Place of Jesus Christ. n.d.

Foundations: a statement of Christian belief in terms of modern thought, by seven Oxford men. 1913.

Fourth Gospel: essays by Ezra Abbot, A. P. Peabody and Bishop Lightfoot. 1891.

French Protestant Church of Charleston, S. C. Liturgy or forms of divine service. 4th ed. 1853.

Gandolphy, Peter, ed. An exposition of liturgy; 2d ed. 1815.

Garvie, A. E. A handbook of Christian apologetics. 1913.

Gayford, S. C. The future state. 1905.

Goode, William. Nature of Christ's presence in the Eucharest. 1856. 2v.

Goodrich, Wallace. Syllabus of course of lectures upon the ritual music of the Protestant Episcopal Church in the United States of America. 1912.

Gore, Charles. The Body of Christ. 1907.

Gore, Charles. The Incarnation of the Son of God. 1891.

Gray, A. R. An introduction to the study of Christian apologetics. 1912.

Hall, A. C. A. The doctrine of the Church. 1909.

Hall, A. C. A. Companion to the Prayer-book. 1902.

Hall, A. C. A. Notes on the use of the Prayer-book. 1896.

Hardman, J. W. Our Prayer-book in history, literature and church lore. 1890.

Harford, George, and Stevenson, Morley, eds. Prayer-book dictionary. 1912.

Hart, Samuel. The Book of Common Prayer. 1910.

Hart, Samuel, tr. Mozarabic liturgy for the first Sunday in Advent, translated with notes. 1877.

Hart, Samuel, ed. Representative citizens of Connecticut; ed. ed luxe. 1916.

Hart, Samuel. The Witness of the Church. 1916.

Hartford, First Church of Christ. Historical catalogue of the first church in Hartford, 1633-1885. 1885. Unbound.

Hastings, James, Selbie, J. A. and Lambert, J. C. eds. Dictionary of the Apostolic Church. 1916. v. 1

Hawks, F. L. Contributions to the ecclesiastical history of the United States of America. 1836-39. 2v.

Hayes, C. W. The diocese of Western New York. 1904.

Hedley, J. C. Holy Eucharist. 1907.

Hodges, George. The early church. 1915.

Hobart, W. K. The medical language of St. Luke. 1882.

Holdsworth, W. W. Gospel origins. 1913.

Holy Orthodox Church. Book of needs. 1894.

Holy Orthodox Church. Ferial Menaion. 1900.

Holy Orthodox Church. The general Menaion or book of services. 1899.

Illingworth, J. R. The Gospel miracles. 1915.

Illustrious Church of Sarum. Services... with rubrical directions. 3d ed. n.d.

Inge, W. R. Faith and its psychology. 1910.

Jones, Maurice. The New Testament in the twentieth century. 1914.

Julian, John, ed. Dictionary of hymnology. 1892.

Kelley, D. O. History of the diocese of California. 1915.

Kinsman, F. J. Catholic and Protestant. 1913.

Kinsman, F. J. Principles of Anglicanism. 1910.

Knox, William. Observations upon the liturgy. 1789.

Lacey, T. A. A Roman diary, and other documents relating to the papal inquiry into English ordinations. 1910.

Laud, William. Relation of the conference between William Laud and Mr. Fisher, the Jesuit: 4th ed. 1686.

Legg, J. W. Comparative study of the time in the Christian liturgy at which the elements are prepared and set on the Holy Table. 1892.

L'Estrange, Hamon, comp. Alliance of divine offices, exhibiting all the liturgies of the Church of England. 1659.

Liber precum ecclesiae Cathedralis Christi Oxon. 1689.

Lightfoot, J. B. S. Clement of Rome. 1869.

Lloyd's clerical directory. 1913.

Luckock, H. M. Divine liturgy. 1889.

Maclean, A. J., tr. East Syrian daily offices. 1894.

Marshall, Charles, and Marshall, W. W. The Latin Prayer Book of Charles II. 1882.

Martene, Edmund, ed. De antiquis ecclesiae ritibus libri tres. 1783. 4v.

Martinucci, Pio. Manuale sacrarum caeremoniarum 1869-72. 3v.

Mason, A. J. The conditions of our Lord's life on earth. 1896.

Mason, A. J. The Church of England and Episcopacy. 1914.

Mason, A. J., ed. The mission of St. Augustine to England according to the original documents. 1897.

Maude, J. H. History of the Book of Common Prayer. 1899.

Mercer, S. A. B., tr. and ed. Extra-Biblical sources for Hebrew and Jewish history. 1913.

Milligan, William. The Resurrection of our Lord. 1884.

Milligan, William. The Resurrection of the dead. 1894.

Moberly, R. C. Reason and religion. 1896.

Moffatt, James. The theology of the Gospels. 1913.

Mombert, J. I. Handbook of the English versions of the Bible. 1890.

Mone, F. J., ed. Hymni Latini medii aevi. 1853-55. 3v.

Moore, E. C. An outline of the history of Christian thought since Kant. 1912.

Montgomery, J. A. The Samaritans. 1907.

Morin, D. G., ed. Anecdota Maredsolana. 1893-97. v. 1-2, v. 3, pt. 1-2. 4v. Unbound.

Mortimer, A. G. Catholic faith and practice; 3d ed. 1898. 2v.

Mozarabic collects. 1881.

Mozley, J. B. A treatise on the Augustinian doctrine of predestination. 1878.

Muratori, L. A. Liturgia Romana vetus. 1728. 2v.

Neale, J. M., comp. Hymni ecclesiae e breviariis quibusdam et missalibus. 1851.

Neale, J. M. Original sequences, hymns, and other verses. 1866.

Neale, J. M. Sermons on the Blessed Sacrament. 1900.

Nicetas, Saint. Nicetas of Remesiana: his life and works ed. by A. E. Burn. 1905.

Nielsen, Fredrik. The history of the Papacy in the XIXth century. 1906. 2v.

Old Catholic Church. The Offices of the Old Catholic Church: a Prayer-book done into English. 1876.

Ollard, S. L., and Crosse, Gordon. eds. Dictionary of English church history. 1912.

Ottley, R. L. Doctrine of the Incarnation. 1896. 2v.

Overton, J. H. The Anglican revival. 1898.

Paget, Francis. Introduction to the fifth book of Hooker's Treatise of the Laws of Ecclesiastical Polity. 1899.

Palmer, William. Supplement to the first three editions of Origines Liturgicae. 1845. Unbound.

Peile, J. H. F. Ecclesia discens. 1909.

Pemberton, J. H. The coronation service. 1902.

Perry, W. S. The connection of the Church of England with early American discovery and colonization. 1863.

Peters, Samuel. A history of the Rev. Hugh Peters. 1807.

Potter, Horatio. A sermon preached at the consecration of Right Rev. Henry A. Neely, D. D. 1867.

Presbyterian Church in the United States. Book of Common Worship. 1906.

Protestant Episcopal Church in the United States. Alterations and additions in the Book of Common Prayer. 1889. Official copy.

Protestant Episcopal Church in the United States. Notification to the dioceses of the alterations and additions in the Book of Common Prayer of the Protestant Episcopal Church in the United States. 1886.

Protestant Episcopal Church in the United States. Book of Common Prayer ... together with the Psalter or Psalms of David. 1892.

Protestant Episcopal Church in the United States. The Daily Service. 1874.

Protestant Episcopal Church in the United States. Gemeinschaftliches Gebetbuch. 1904.

Protestant Episcopal Church in the United States. Report of the joint committee appointed to prepare a standard Book of Common Prayer. 1893.

Protestant Episcopal Church in the United States. General Convention Journal. 1892.

Protestant Episcopal Church in the United States in 1893.

Protestant Episcopal Church in the United States of America. Diocese of Virginia. Addresses and historical papers before the centennial council. 1885.

Protestant Episcopal Historical Society. Collections ... for year 1851. 2v.

Pullan, Leighton. The teaching of our Lord. 1908.

Pusey, E. B. Daniel the prophet. 1880.

Ragg, Lonsdale. Evidences of Christianity. 1909.

Ramsay, W. M. Was Christ born at Bethlehem? 1898.

Renan, Ernest. L'Antechrist; 3d éd. 1873.

Renan, Ernest. Le livre de Job; 4e éd. 1882.

Renan, Ernest. Saint Paul. 1869.

Rigg, J. M. St. Anselm of Canterbury. 1896.

Robinson, J. A., and James, M. R. The Gospel according to Peter, and the Revelation of Peter. 1892.

Robinson, C. H. History of Christian missions. 1915.

Rose-Troup, Frances. The Western Rebellion of 1549; an account of the insurrections of Devonshire and Cornwall against the religious innovations of Edward VI. 1913.

Sacred Books of the East. Ed. by F. Max Müller. 1897-1901. 12v.

Sanday, William. Christologies, ancient and modern. 1910.

Sanday, William. Criticism of the Fourth Gospel. 1905.

Sanday, William. The conception of priesthood in the Early Church; 2d ed. 1899.

Sanday, William, ed. Different conceptions of priesthood and sacrifice. 1900.

Sayce, A. H. Patriarchal Palestine. 1895.

Seabury, Samuel. Discourses on several subjects. 1815.

Seabury, W. J. Notes on the Constitution of 1901. Unbound.

Smith, W. R. Lectures on the religion of the Semites, first series; the fundamental institutions: new ed. 1894.

Smyth, Piazzi. Our inheritance in the Great Pyramid. 1874.

Sparrow, Anthony. A rationale upon the Book of Common Prayer of the Church of England. 1684.

Sprott, G. W. The worship and offices of the Church of Scotland. 1882.

Srawley, J. H. The epistles of St. Ignatius. 1910.

Stewart, Balfour, and Tait, P. G. The unseen universe. 1875.

Stone, Darwell. Outlines of Christian dogma. 1900.

Swete, H. B. The last discourse and prayer of our Lord. 1913.

Swete, H. B. The forgiveness of sins. 1916.

Temple, E. L. Twentieth century outlook upon Holy Scripture. 1913.

Updike, D. B., comp. On the dedications of American churches. 1891. Unbound.

Updike, Wilkin. History of the Episcopal Church in Narragansett, R. I. 2d ed. 1907. 3v.

Wallace, A. R. Man's place in the universe. 1904.

Webb, Walter. Guide for Seminarians. 1887.

Wells, C. L. Manual of early ecclesiastical history. 1912.

Williams, George. The Orthodox Church of the East in the 18th century. 1868.

Wordsworth, Charles. Some remarks on Bishop Lightfoot's Dissertation on the Christian Ministry; 2d ed. 1884.

Workman, H. B. Christian thought to the Reformation. 1911.

CLASSICAL AUTHORS

Aeschylus. Χοηφοροι: the 'Choephori'; ed. by A. W. Verrall. 1893.

Ammianus Marcellinus. Rerum gestarum libri qui supersunt; recensuit V. Gardthausen. 1874-75. 2v. in 1.

Ampelius. Liber memorialis; recognovit Eduardus Woelfflin. 1873. (Bound with Frontinus' Strategematon)

Anthimus. De observatione ciborum epistula; edidit Valentinus Rose. 1877. (Bound with Censorinus' De die natali liber)

Aristophanes. The birds; tr. by Cary. 1824.

Ausonius. Opuscula; recensuit Rudolfus Peiper. 1886.

Augustine, Saint. Episcopi de civitate Dei libri XXII, recognovit B. Dombart. 1877. 2v.

Avienus. Aratea; edidit Alfredus Breysig. 1882. (Bound with Juvenal's Satirarum libri quinque)

Bährens, Emil, ed. Fragmenta poetarum Romanorum. 1886.

Bährens, Emil, ed. Poetae Latini minores. 1879-81. 5v. in 2.

Bährens, Emil, ed. XII panegyrici Latini. 1874.

Boethius. Commentarii in librum Aristotelis Περι Ερμηνειας; recensuit Carolus Meiser. 1877-80. 2v. in 1.

Boethius. Philosophiae consolationis libri quinque; recensuit Rudolfus Peiper. 1871.

Branat, Samuel, comp. Eclogae poetarum Latinorum. 1881. (Bound with Catullus' Carmina)

Caesar. Belli civilis libri III; recognovit Bernardus Dinter. 1889.

Caesar. Belli Gallici libri VII; recognovit Bernardus Dinter. 1890.

Caesar. Commentarii; recognovit Bernardus Dinter. 1890.

Cassius Felix. De medicina; editus a Valentino Rose. 1879.

Catullus. Carmina; recensuit Lucianus Mueller. 1885.

Celsus. De medicina libri octo; recensuit C. Daremberg. 1859.

Censorinus. De die natali liber; recensuit Fridericus Hultsch. 1867.

Chatelain, Emile. Paléographie des Classiques Latins. 1884-1900. 2pts and plates.

Cicero. Scripta quae manserunt omnia; recognovit C. F. W. Mueller. 1880-90. 4v. in 9.

Cicero. Somnium Scipionis. 1883.

Commodian. Carmina; recognovit Ernestus Ludwig. 1878.

Curtius Rufus. Historiarum Alexandri Magni Macedonis libri qui supersunt; recognovit Theodorus Vogel. 1884.

Dares Phrygius. De excidio Troiae historia; recensuit Ferdinandus Meister. 1873. (Bound with Sallust's Catilina)

Dictys Cretensis. Ephemeridos belli Troiani libri sex; recognovit Ferdinandus Meister. 1872. (Bound with Sallust's Catalina)

Dracontius. Carmina minora; edidit Fridericus de Duhn. 1873. (Bound with Juvenal's Satirarum libri quinque)

Euripides. Ausgewählte tragödien, erklaert von F. G. Schöne. 1851. v. 1. Unbound.

Eusebius. Ιςτοριας Εκκλησιαςτικης. Introduction by William Bright. 1872.

Eutropius. Breviarium ab urbe condita; recognovit Franciscus Ruehl. 1887. (Bound with Frontinus' Strategematon)

Florus. Epitomae de Tito Livio bellorum omnium annorum DCC libri duo; recognovit Carolus Halm. 1872. (Bound with Frontinus' Strategematon)

Frontinus. Strategematon libri quattuor; edidit Gottholdus Gundermann. 1888.

Gaius. Institutionum iuris civilis commentarii quattuor; ed. 5. edidit P. E. Huschke. 1886.

Gellius, Aulus. Noctium Atticarum libri XX. ex recensione Martini Hertz. 1886. 2v. in 1.

Heydenreich, Eduard ed. Incerti auctores de Constantino Magno eiusque matre Helena libellus. 1879.

Hieronymus. De viris inlustribus liber; ex recensione Guilelnii Herdingii. 1879. (Bound with Commodianus' Carmina)

Horace. Carmina; recensuit Lucianus Mueller. 1889.

Horace. Oden und epoden, erklärt von C. W. Nauck; 7. aufl. 1871. Unbound.

Horace. Opera; illustravit C. G. Mitscherlich. 1800. 2v.

Horace. Opera omina; instruxit Guil. Dillenburger. 1860.

Horace. Q. Horatius Flaccus, erklärt von Hermann Schütz. 1880-81. 2v. Unbound.

Horace. Satiren, erklärt von L. F. Heindorf; 3.aufl. 1859. Unbound.

Hultsch, Friedrich, ed. Metrologicorum scriptorum reliquiae. 1864-66. 2v. in 1.

Huschke, P. E., ed. Iurisprudentiae anteiustinianae quae supersunt; ed. 5. 1886.

Hyginus. Liber de munitionibus castrorum; ex recensione Guilelnii Gemoll. 1879. (Bound with Frontinus' Strategematon)

Julius Valerius. Res gestae Alexandri Macedonis; recensuit Bernardus Kuebler. 1888.

Justinian, emperor. Novellae quae vocantur; edidit C. E. Zachariae. 1881. 2v.

Justinus. Trogi Pompei historiarum Philippicarum epitoma; recensuit Iustus Ieep. 1885.

Juvenal. Argumenta satyrarum Juvenalis per Antonium Mancinellum. 1501.

Juvenal. Sixteen satyrs, with notes by Sir Robert Stapylton. 1647.

Juvenal. Mores hominum, with comment by Sir Robert Stapylton. 1660.

Juvenal. Decimus Junius Juvenalis and Aulus Persius Flaccus; tr. by Barten Holydaz. 1673.

Juvenal. D. Junii Juvenalis and Auli Persii Flacci satyrae. 1684.

Juvenal. D. Junii Juvenalis et A. Persii Flacci satirae; interpretatione ac notis illustravit Ludovicus Prateus. 1684.

Juvenal. Satyrae, accedit Auli Persii Flacci satirarum liber; Isaacus Casaubonus recensuit. 1695.

Juvenal. Satirae, ad codices Parisinos recensitae a N. L. Achaintre. 1810. 2v.

Juvenal. Sexdecim satirae, quibus plurima subjuixit additamenta N. E. Lemaire. 1823-30. 3v.

Juvenal. Satirae XVI, recensitae a G. A. Ruperti, quibus adjectae sunt A. Persii Flacci satirae. 1825. 2v.

Juvenal. Decimi Junii Juvenalis et Auli Persii Flacci satirae expurgatae; curavit F. P. Leverett. 1831.

Juvenal. Decimi Junii Juvenalis et Auli Persii Flacci satirae expurgatae; curavit F. P. Leverett. 1833.

Juvenal. Satirae, cum commentariis C. F. Heinrichii. 1839. 2v. Unbound.

Juvenal. Satires of Juvenal and Persius, with English notes by C. W. Stocker; 2d ed. 1839.

Juvenal. Saturarum libri V; ex recensione Ottonis Iahnii. 1851. v. 1.

Juvenal. Satires of Juvenal, Persius, Sulpicia, and Lucilius; tr. by Rev. Lewis Evans. 1852.

Juvenal. Satires of Juvenal and Persius, with English notes by Charles Anthon. 1857.

Juvenal. Satires; tr. by Francis Hodgson. 1807.

Juvenal. Saturae, edidit Otto Ribbeck. 1859. Unbound.

Juvenal. Satirae XVI, with English notes by Herman Prior. 1862.

Juvenal. Decii Junii Juvenalis et A. Persii Flacci satirae, with a commentary by A. J. Macleane; 2d ed. 1867.

Juvenal. Satirae XIII: thirteen satires of Juvenal, with notes and introduction by G. A. Simcox. 1867.

Juvenal. Satires, with English notes by T. H. S. Escott. 1869.

Juvenal. Thirteen satires, with a commentary by J. E. B. Mayor. 1869-72. 2v. Unbound.

Juvenal. Thirteen satires, with English notes by Rev. A. J. Macleane; abridged with additions by Rev. Samuel Hart. 5 copies, besides interleaved copy with original manuscript notes by Dr. Hart. 1873.

Juvenal. Satirae XIII: thirteen satires, with notes by G. A. Simcox; 2d ed. 1873.

Juvenal. Thirteen satires, with English notes by Rev. A. J. Macleane; abridged with additions by Rev. Samuel Hart; 2d ed. 1875.

Juvenal. Thirteen satires, with a commentary by J. E. B. Mayor; 2d ed. 1875-78. 2v.

Juvenal. Thirteen satires, with English notes by Rev. A. J. Macleane; abridged with additions by Rev. Samuel Hart; 3d ed. 1878.

Juvenal. Satirarum libri quinque, ex recognitione C. F. Hermanni. 1890.

Juvenal. Saturarum libri V; mit erklaerenden anmerkungen von Ludwig Friedlaender. 1895. 2v. Unbound.

Juvenal. Satires; tr. with explanatory and classical notes. 1769.

Juvenal. Satires; tr. with explanatory and classical notes. 1777.

Juvenal. Dec. Iunius Iuvenalis von den wahren adel. 1796. (Bound with the 1501 edition of Juvenal)

Juvenal. Satires; tr. into English verse by Charles Badham. 1814.

Juvenal. Satyrs of Decimus Junius Juvenalis and of Aulus Persius Flaccus; tr. by Dryden. 1735.

Juvenal. Satires; tr. into English verse by William Gifford. 1803. 2v.

Juvenal. Thirteen satires; tr. by Alexander Leeper. 1882.

Juvenal. Satirae, with a literal English prose translation by J. D. Lewis. 1873.

Juvenal. New and literal translation of Juvenal and Persius, with notes by Rev. M. Madan. 1789. 2v.

Juvenal. Satires; ed. by T. B. Lindsay. 1890.

Juvenal. Juvenal and Persius, literally tr. by William Smart. 1829.

Juvenal. Satires, with translation by John Stirling. 1760.

Juvenal. Thirteen satires; tr. by H. A. Strong and Alexander Leeper. 1882.

Juvencus. Libri evangeliorum III; recognovit Carolus Marold. 1876. (Bound with Commodianus' Carmina)

Livy. Ab urbe condita liber I, erklärt von Moritz Müller. 1875. Unbound.

Livy. Ab urbe condita liber II, erklärt von Moritz Müller. 1878. Unbound.

Livy. Ab urbe condita liber VII, erklärt von Franz Luterbacher. 1889. Unbound.

Livy. Ab urbe condita libri; recognovit Wilh. Weissenborn. 1887-89. 6v. in 3.

Lucretius. De rerum natura, libri sex; recognovit Iacobus Bernaysius. 1890.

Macrobius. Macrobius; Franciscus Eyssenhardt recognovit. 1868.

Marcellus. De medicamentis liber; edidit Georgius Helmreich. 1889.

Martial. Epigrammaton libri; recognovit Walther Gilbert. 1886.

256

Martianus Capella. Martianus Capella; Franciscus Eyssenhardt recensuit. 1866.

Minucius Felix. Octavius; emendavit et praefatus est Aemilius Baehrens. 1867. (Bound with Commodianus' Carmina)

Namatianus. De reditu suo libri II; recensuit et praefatus est Lucianus Meuller. 1870. (Bound with Juvenal's Satirarum libri quinque)

Nepos. Cornelius Nepos, erklaert von Karl Nipperdey; 7.aufl. 1878. Unbound.

Nepos. Vitae, post Carolum Halmium, recognovit Alfredus Fleckeisen. 1890. (Bound with Sallust's Catilina)

New Palcographical Society. Facsimiles of ancient manuscripts, etc., first and second series. 1903-15. Indices, first series. 1914.

Olcott, G. N. Thesaurus linguae latinae epigraphicae. 1904-11. v. 1, fasc. 1-19. Unbound.

Orelli, J. D., ed. Eclogae poëtarum Latinorum. 1833. Unbound.

Orosius. Historiarum adversum paganos libri VII; ex recensione Caroli Zangemeister. 1889.

Ovid. P. Ovidius Naso, ex Rudolphi Merkelii recognitione, ed. by R. Ehwald. 1888-90. 3v. in 2.

Persius. Satires, tr. into English prose by John Senhouse. 1730.

Persius. Aulus Persius Flaccus; textum recensuit Franciscus Passon. 1808.

Persius. Satyrae. 1601.

Persius. Satyras sex; edidit G. F. Sebaldus. 1765.

Persius. Aulus Persius Flaccus, von Franz Passon. 1809: pt. 1.

Persius. Satirae, ad codices Parisinos recensitae a N. L. Achaintre. 1812.

Persius. Satirae; recensuit Fredericus Plum. 1827.

Persius. Satirarum liber, cum Isaaci Casauboni notis, auxit Fridericus Deubner. 1833. Unbound.

Persius. Satirarum liber; edidit Otto Iahn. 1843. (Bound with Juvenal's Saturarum libri V)

Persius. Satiren, berichtigt und erklaert von C. F. Heinrich. 1844. Unbound.

Persius. Satirarum liber; ed. by A. Pretor. 1868.

Persius. Satires, with English notes by Rev. Samuel Hart. 1875. 2 copies; also an interleaved copy with manuscript notes.

Persius. Satires; ed. by B. L. Gildersleeve. 1875.

Persius. Satirae sex; recensuit E. G. Weber. 1876.

Persius. Satirarum libri; ex recensione C. F. Hermanni. 1881. (Bound with Juvenal's Satirarum libri quinque)

Persius. Satires, with English notes by Rev. Samuel Hart. 1896.

Persius. Satires, translated. 1833.

Persius. Satires, tr. into English verse; 2d ed. 1751. 2 copies.

Persius. Satyres; tr. by Edmund Burton. 1752. 2 copies.

Persius. Satires; tr. by William Drummond. 1803.

Persius. Satires; tr. into English verse by William Gifford. 1821.

Persius. Satires; tr. by Rev. F. Howes. 1809. 2 copies.

Peter, Hermann, ed. Historicorum Romanorum fragmenta. 1883.

Peter, Hermann, ed. Scriptores historiae Augustae. 1884. 2v. in 1.

Phaedrus. Fabulae Aesopiae; recognovit Lucianus Mueller. 1890. (Bound with Catullus' Carmina)

Plautus. Aulularia; sive, Querolus; edidit Rudolphus Peiper. 1875. (Bound with Juvenal's Satirarum libri quinque)

Plautus. Ausgewählte komödien, erklaert von A. O. F. Lorenz. 1876. v. 4. Unbound.

Plautus. Comoediae; ex recognitione Alfredi Fleckeiseni. 1885-90. 2v. in 1.

Pliny, the younger. Epistularum libri novem, Epistularum ad Traianum liber; Panegyricus; recognovit Henricus Keil. 1889.

Pliny, the younger. Plinii Secundi quae fertur, una cum Garglii Martialis medicina, edita a Valentino Rose. 1875.

Pomponius Mela. De chorographia libri tres; recognovit Carolus Frick. 1880. (Bound with Censorinus' De die natali libri)

Porphyris. Commentarii in Q. Horatium Flaccum; recensuit Gulielmus Meyer. 1874.

Propertius. Elegiae; recensuit Lucianus Mueller. 1880. (Bound with Catullus' Carmina)

Quintilian. Institutionis oratoriae libri duodecim; recensuit Eduardus Bonnell. 1884-89. 2v. in 1.

Raoul, M. L. V., tr. Les trois satiriques latins, tr. en vers français. 1842. 2v.

Riese, Alexander, ed. Anthologia latina. 1869-70. 2v. in 1.

Sallust. Catalina, Iugurtha, ex historiis, orationes et epistulae; edidit Adam Eussner. 1889.

Schulze, K. P., ed. Römische elegiker; 2.aufl. 1884. Unbound.

Scribonius Largus. Conpositiones; edidit Georgius Helmreich. 1887. (Bound with Censorinus' De die natali libri)

Seneca. Tragoediae; recensuerunt Rudolfus Peiper et Gustavus Richter. 1867.

Silius Italicus. Punica; edidit Ludovicus Bauer. 1890. v. 1.

Soranus. Gynaeciorum; recognitis a Valentino Rose. 1882.

Statius. Silvae, recensuit Aemilius Baehrens; Achilleis et Thebais, recensuit Philippus Kohlmann. 1876-84. 2v. in 1.

Suetonius. Quae supersunt omnia; recensuit C. L. Roth. 1886.

Tacitus. Cornelius Tacitus; erklärt von Karl Nipperdey; 4. verb. aufl. 1879-80. 2v. Also copy of v. 2, 1852. Unbound.

Tacitus. Historiarum libri qui supersunt; schulausgabe von Carl Heraeus. 1875-77. 2v. Unbound.

Tacitus. Libri qui supersunt, quartum recognovit Carolus Halm. 1889. 2v. in 1.

Tacitus. Opera quae supersunt; recensuit J. G. Orellius. 1859. v. 1.

Terence. Comoediae; recensuit Alfredus Fleckhausen. 1890.

Terence. Comoediae; recensuit Richardus Bentleius. 1846. Unbound.

Terence. Die comödien, erklärt von A. Spengel. 1875-79. 2v. Unbound.

Terence. Phormio; recensuit Carolus Dziatzko; tr. into English prose by M. H. Morgan. 1894. Unbound.

Tibullus. Libri quattuor; recensuit Lucianus Mueller. 1885. (Bound with Catullus' Carmina)

Ulpian. Quae vulgo vocantur fragmenta; ed. 5, edidit P. E. Hischke. 1886. (Bound with Censorinus' De die natali liber)

Varro. Rerum rusticarum libri tres; recognovit Henricus Keil. 1889.

Valerius Flaccus. Argonauticon, libri octo; recognovit Aemilius Baehrens. 1875.

Valerius Maximus. Factorum et dictorum memorabilium libri novem, cum Iulii Paridis et Ianvarii Nepotiani epitomis; iterum recensuit Carolus Kempf. 1888.

Varro. Rerum rusticarum libri tres, recognovit Henricus Keil. 1889.

Vegetius. Epitoma rei militaris; recensuit Carolus Lang. 1885.

Velleius Paterculus. Ex historiae Romanae libris duobus quae supersunt; edidit Carolus Halm. 1876. (Bound with Frontinus' Strategematon)

Virgil. Opera, recognovit Otto Ribbeck. 1889.

Virgil. Virgilii Maronis grammatici opera; edidit Iohannes Huemer. 1886.

TRINITY COLLEGE PUBLICATIONS

Harding, Alfred, Jr., ed. Songs of Trinity College. 1915. 2 copies.

Seabury College. Collection of pamphlets. 1816-1854.

Trinity College. Addresses 1831-54, 1856-86. 2v.

257

Trinity College. Bulletin 1900-1911. 2v.
Trinity College. Catalogue 1824-1913. 7v.
Trinity College. Catalogue 1869-97. 2v.
Trinity College. Catalogue 1862-3.
Trinity College. Miscellany. Catalogues, addresses, bulletins, etc.
Trinity College. Reports. 1881-1900.
Trinity Ivy. v. 14-34, 36-38, 40-42, 44. 1887-1901, 1903-1907, 1909-1914, 1916-1917.
Trinity Ivy. 1873-85. 2v.
Trinity Sketches. Selections from the "Trinity Tablet" 1887-1894. 1894.
Trinity Verse; a second compilation from the "Trinity Tablet" 1868-1895. 1895.

MISCELLANEOUS WORKS

Abbot, E. A. Latin prose through English idiom. 1878.
Alexander, A. B. D. Christianity and Ethics. 1914.
American Oriental Society. Journals. 2-31, 32 pt. 1. v. 30-32. Unbound.
American Oriental Society. Proceedings 1874, 1879-92. Unbound.
American School of Classical Studies in Rome. Supplementary papers, v. 1. 1905.
Bates, A. C. Connecticut statute laws: a bibliographical list of editions of Connecticut laws. 1900. Unbound.
Beers, J. B. & Company. Map of Connecticut. 1886.
Bolles, J. R. The Rogerenes. 1904.
Bonola, Roberto. Non-Euclidean geometry. 1912.
Bretschneider, C. A. Die geometrie und die geometer vor Euclides. 1870. Unbound.
Cajori, Florian. Teaching and history of mathematics in the United States. 1890. Unbound.
College catalogs. Miscellaneous.
Crothers, S. M. Humanly speaking. 1912.
Curtis, E. A. One hundred quatrains from the Rubáiyát of Omar Khayyám; a rendering in English verse. 1899.
Directory of foreign students in the United States and Canada. 1916.
Egypt exploration fund. Memoirs.
   no. 21 Petrie, W. M. F. Royal tombs of the earliest dynasties, pt. 2. 1901.
   no. 22 Petrie, W. M. F. Abydos, pt 1. 1902.
   no. 24 Petrie, W. M. F. Abydos, pt 2. 1903.
   no. 26 Petrie, W. M. F. Ehnarya. 1905.
   no. 28 Naville, Edouard. The XIth dynasty temple at Deir el-Bahari, pt 1. 1907.
   no. 29 Naville, Edouard. The temple of Deir el-Bahari, pt. 6. 1908.
   no. 30 Naville, Edouard. The XIth dynasty temple at Deir el-Bahari, pt 2. 1910.
   no. 31 Ayrton, E. R., and Loat, W. L. S. Pre-dynastic cemetery at El-Mahasna. 1911.
Gocher, W. H. Wadsworth; or, The Charter Oak. 1904.
Hartford, Conn. Driving road chart of the City of Hartford. n. d.
Henshaw, J. P. K. Memoir of the life of Richard Channing Moore. 1842.
Hough, L. H. Athanasius: the hero. 1906.
Jarvis, Mrs. Elizabeth Miller. A memorial of. 1881.
Massachusetts. (Colony). Court of Assistants. Record of Court of Assistants of the Colony of Massachusetts Bay, ed. by John Noble. 1901.
Mendes, H. P. The Earl of Beaconsfield, K. G. 1904.
Oneida Historical Society at Utica. Year book for 1905.
Paulsen, Friedrich. A system of ethics. 1908.
Pynchon, T. R. Lectures given by Dr. Pynchon taken down by Dr. Hart while in college. 1866. Manuscript.
Psi Upsilon Fraternity. Songs. 1891.
Rand, Benjamin, comp. The classical moralists. 1909.
Rand, Benjamin, comp. Modern classical philosophers. 1908.
Shea, George. Memoir concerning the Seabury commemoration ... printed from manuscript ... 1893.

Skinner, John. Amusements of leisure hours. 1809.
Slattery, C. L. Alexander Viets Griswold Allen, 1841-1908. 1911.
Taylor, J. M. Witchcraft delusion in colonial Connecticut. 1908.
Trumbull, J. H., ed. The true-blue laws of Connecticut and New Haven and the false blue-laws invented by the Rev. Samuel Peters. 1876.
Weems, M. L. Life of George Washington. 1810.
Wister, Owen. The Pentecost of calamity. 1915.

PERIODICALS

American Quarterly Church Review, v. 10, no. 3, v. 11, no. 2-3, v. 12, no. 5. Oct. 1857, July-Oct. 1858, Jan. 1860. Unbound.
Church Quarterly Review, v. 1-82. Oct. 1875-July, 1916. Unbound.
Connecticut Churchman. v. 1-8. 1906-1914. 2v.
Hibbert Journal, v. 14, no. 4. July, 1916. Unbound.
Journal of Biblical Literature, v. 31-35. Sept. 1912-June, 1916. Unbound.
Journal of Egyptian Archaeology, v. 1, pt 1. Jan. 1914; v. 2-3. 1915-16. Unbound.
Journal of Theological Studies, v. 1-18. Oct. 1899-Oct. 1916. Unbound.
Phi Beta Kappa Key, v. 1-2. Nov. 1910-May, 1916. v. 2 unbound.
Scottish Church Review, v. 1-2. Feb. 1884-Dec. 1885. Unbound.

PAMPHLETS

Anglican Orders. Bound pamphlets on Anglican Ordinations occasioned by the Encyclical of Leo XIII.
Arbuthnot manuscripts: a description. n. d.
Bates, A. C. An early Connecticut engraver and his work. 1906.
Blatchford, Robert. Chetham College (England). 1910. (First Bodleian booklet)
Briggs, C. A. Virgin birth of our Lord. 1909.
Catholic Church. Festum Jesu Christi natal itium pie celebrandum indicunt Academiae Albertinae... 1837.
Ceremonies to be observed at the royal coronation of ... King George IV. 1821.
Charter of the corporation of Trinity Church defended against the attacks of a late pamphlet: Reprint of original of 1813. 1846.
Church Historical Society. Publications, no. 1-24, 29-31, 33-36, 40-53, 55-58, 60-63, 66-73, 75-77, 79, 82-84, 87-88, 91-94.
Cincinnati, Society of. Historical sketches. 1907.
Cicero. Cato Maior, erklärt von Julius Sommerbrodt; 9.aufl. 1881.
Cicero. Laelius, erklärt von C. W. Nauck; 8.aufl. 1879.
Cicero. Laelius, erklärt von Gustav Lahmeyer; 3.aufl. 1875.
Cicero. Scipio's Dream; ed. by Samuel Hart. 1887.
Connecticut. Society of Colonial Wars in. Addresses delivered before the Society. 1895.
Connecticut. Society of Colonial Wars in. Conquest of Cape Breton, 1745. 1895.
Cummins, G. D. The Prayer-book: a basis of unity. 1867.
Daughters of American Revolution (Connecticut). Yearbook. 1916-17.
Dewick, E. S. On a manuscript pontifical of a Bishop of Metz of the 14th century. 1895.
Dore, J. R. On some early printed editions of the English Bible. n. d.
Emott, James. Revision of the Common Prayer. 1884.
Frere, W. H. Bibliotheca musico-liturgica... 1894.
Gore, Charles. Lux Mundi; preface to the 16th ed. together with an appendix on the Christian doctrine of sin. 1890.
Greer, D. H. Order of service for the consecration of St. Thomas' Church ... N. Y. 1916.

Hazen, A. W. The first decade of the Middlesex County Historical Society, Middletown, Connecticut. 1901-1911: Address of the President. 1911.

Hoadly, C. J. Hiding of the charter. 1900.

Hobart, J. H. The Christian Bishop approving himself unto God... 1827.

Hobart, J. H. Corruptions of the Church of Rome contrasted with certain Protestant errors. 1818.

Hobart, J. H. Principles of the Churchman stated and explained. 1819.

Hobart, J. H. The United States of America compared with some European countries particularly England. 1825.

Hart, Samuel. Connecticut's first quarter century. 1912.

Hart, Samuel. Dr. Samuel Johnson and the beginnings of the church in Connecticut. 1907.

Hart, Samuel. Episcopal bank and Bishop's fund. 1914.

Hart, Samuel. Fundamental orders and the charter. 1912.

Hart, Samuel. Suggestions as to revision of the Table of Lessons. 1911.

Huiginn, E. J. V. Graves of Miles Standish and other pilgrims. 1892.

Jarvis, S. F. Office of institution of Samuel Farmer Jarvis as rector of St. Paul's Church. 1820.

John Fitch; the first... to invent... steam propulsion of vessels through water. 1912.

Jubilee College. The Motto. v. 2. no. 6. March 30, 1852.

Juvenalis Redivivus: a poem. 1863.

Legg, J. W. Black scarf of modern church dignitaries and the grey almuce of mediaeval canons. 1892.

Legg, J. W. Some imitations of Te Deum. 1891.

Lux Mundi. Preface to the 10th edition... on the Christian doctrine of sin. 1890.

Mathewson, A. M. Graves of signers of Declaration of Independence from Connecticut. 1909.

Mead, K. C. William Tully of Connecticut 1785-1859. 1916.

Miscellanea Historica. Collection of pamphlets relating to historical matters. Bound in 7v.

Miscellanea Scholastica. Collection of pamphlets relating to College and University matters. Bound in 11v.

Montgomery, James. Grounds of the Christian's love to the church. 1822.

Muirson, George, and Sharpe, John. Earliest services of the Church of England. n. d.

Nettleship, Henry. Suggestions introductory to a study of the Aeneid. 1875.

Pius IX, Pope. Examination of the first dogmatic constitution. 1870.

Potter, H. Pastoral letter to the clergy of the diocese of New York... 1865.

Protestant Episcopal Church in the United States. Address to their brethren of the laity. 1859.

Protestant Episcopal Church in the United States. Proceedings of the Domestic and Foreign Missionary Society. 1823.

Protestant Episcopal Church in the United States. Domestic and Foreign Missionary Society. Proceedings of the Board of Directors. 1831.

Protestant Episcopal Church in the United States. New York. Journal of the proceedings of the annual convention. 1817.

Responsio archiepiscoporum Angliae ad litteras apostolicas Leonis Papae XIII. 1897.

Stone, Samuel. Catechism, reissued from the original edition printed in 1684. Acorn Club pub. no. 1. 1899.

Supplementary report of the joint commission on marginal readings in the Bible to the general convention of 1901 on the books of the Apocrypha. 1901.

Tacitus. Dialogus de oratoribus, erklärt von Georg Andresen; 2.aufl. 1879.

Tacitus. Das leben des Agricola; schulausgabe von A. Draeger; 3.aufl. 1879.

What ought the diocese to do? Considerations addressed to the churchmen of the diocese of New York by a layman. 1845.

Herwologia Anglica. 1620. Title-page.

GIFTS

A set of the works of Chrysostom from Dr. Hart's library which he had requested might go after his death to the School library has been received from his sister and the executor of his estate, Mrs. M. K. Bailey, who has besides given from her brother's library several rare liturgical works and the parts so far issued of the Oxford English Dictionary. She has also presented to the School certain furnishings which were in the Dean's house, and several notes for collection which have brought in a considerable sum of money.

A fine framed photographic portrait of the late Dean was in May presented to the School by the students and now hangs in the staircase of the library directly opposite the portrait of Bishop Williams.

An enlarged snap-shot framed of Dr. Hart was at the same time presented to the School by J. M. Yamazaki, '13, and now hangs in the School Refectory.

TO REMAIN AT TRINITY.

DR. HART DECLINES THE CALL TO VERMONT.

Thinks It His Duty to Remain With the College—Tributes From Bishop Williams and President Smith.

The Rev. Samuel Hart, D. D., of Trinity College, who was elected bishop of Vermont on June 22 to succeed the late Bishop Bissell, has decided to decline the honorable office and to remain at Trinity College, where his wide field of usefulness is recognized by all. Dr. Hart notified Dr. J. Isham Bliss of Burlington, Vt., who presided at the diocesan convention, of his decision Saturday night.

Dr. Hart told a COURANT reporter yesterday that much as he appreciated the high and honorable office tendered, the good-will of the clergymen of Vermont and their kindness to him, he felt it to be his duty to remain at Trinity College. His decision is final. Dr. G. Williamson Smith, president of Trinity, when seen by a reporter of THE COURANT yesterday, said that he was very glad Dr. Hart had decided to remain. He spoke of Dr. Hart in the most complimentary terms. In addition to being an admirable professor of the Latin language, said Dr. Smith, Dr. Hart's services are invaluable to the college in many ways. His familiarity with the history of the college for the past forty years, his acquaintance with the alumni, and his general knowledge of everything pertaining to Trinity, would make his retirement a great loss. In fact, if he had decided to leave it would take two professors to do the work he performed with such assiduous, unselfish devotion to the college, much of it as a labor of love. Dr. Smith said that much as he desired Professor Hart to remain, he had not discussed the subject with him as he much rather desired that he make his decision apart from any personal influence.

A few days ago in talking with a COURANT reporter Bishop Williams, whose appreciation of Dr. Hart's eminent services to the Diocese of Connecticut is well-known, spoke in complimentary terms of Dr. Hart's services to the church and Trinity College and his far-reaching influence in the community. At that time, although the bishop preferred not to be quoted, he said that without knowing Dr. Hart's views on the subject he thought it quite probable that he would decide to remain at Trinity.

A friend of Trinity, much interested in its prosperity and also in the welfare of the Episcopal church in this diocese, said before Dr. Hart's decision was made known, that it was the earnest wish of every churchman and friend of Trinity that Dr. Hart remain. The diocese of Vermont would limit Dr. Hart's field of usefulness, and although the church there would undoubtedly gain much, the Connecticut diocese and the college would lose the services of a man preeminently adapted to the positions which he had so long filled. The Diocese of Vermont is one of very limited growth.

The late Bishop Bissell during his twenty-five years' episcopacy confirmed 3,000 persons, but the church during that time gained only 1,400 communicants, showing that the young people moved away from the state. He thought that to place Dr. Hart over that diocese was simply to circumscribe the field of usefulness of an energetic, capable man, whose services were of great benefit to the larger, more prosperous and more rapidly growing community of Connecticut.

SAMUEL HART

AND

THE CALL TO

BE BISHOP OF

VERMONT

~~EPISCOPALIANISM~~ IN VERMONT.

A CENTURY OF CHURCH HISTORY.

Its Steady and Considerable Increase Within the Late Bishop Bissell's Episcopate.

In accordance with the expressed wishes of the late Bishop Bissell, whose 25th anniversary would have been celebrated at the annual diocesean convention but for his death, a historical sketch of the Protestant Episcopal church in Vermont was delivered by the rector, Rev. W. H. Collins, in St Michael's Episcopal church at Brattleboro last Sunday, and these extracts will indicate its character and contents:—

The history of the Episcopal church in the diocese of Vermont naturally divides itself into three distinct periods: The first comprising the time from its organization in 1790 to the year 1832, when Vermont, separating itself from its connection with the eastern diocese, became an independent diocese and chose Rt Rev Dr J. H. Hopkins for its first bishop; the second covering the duration of his episcopate from 1832 to 1868; the third from 1868, when the late Rt Rev Dr W. H. A. Bissell became its second bishop to the present year when he entered paradise. . . .

One of the most interesting accounts of the early period may be found in "Thompson's Vermont," as written by Rt Rev Dr Carlton Chase, the first bishop of New Hampshire, who before his elevation to the episcopate was a presbyter in this diocese. It contains an account of missionary work done in Vermont before the organization of the church was accomplished, going back to the years 1767 and 1768, when hundreds of men, women and children received holy baptisms, and the sheep scattered throughout the wilderness were cared for by two devoted clergymen of the church of England, having the apostolic spirit and engaging in apostolic labors. But so weak and feeble was the church in those early days that upon the occasion of its first convention held in Arlington in 1790, there were present only two clergymen, and laymen representing eight parishes. Bishop Chase's words will show the condition of the church a century ago: "With only 10 or 12 parishes, not one of which could wholly support a clergyman, held in contempt by the strong and independent sects around her, she abode quietly in the possession of her primitive and apostolic principles, with no available resources, no order of learned men to maintain the grounds of her faith, worship and discipline; almost crushed beneath prejudice, how could she increase? And yet in those days of weakness, there were earnest, steadfast men, clergy, some, laymen, many, who stood shoulder to shoulder and with the help of God kept alive the cause of the church."

The Eastern diocese, so called, was formed in 1809. It consisted of a confederation of the states of Massachusetts, New Hampshire, Rhode Island and Vermont, for the purpose of securing Episcopal oversight. Rev Dr Griswold was elected as its bishop in 1811, and continued to exercise jurisdiction over Vermont until 1832, when, as has been mentioned, Bishop Hopkins assumed sole charge of the diocese. Among the interesting facts to be found relating to the early history of the church in Vermont are those pertaining to the litigations arising from the bequests of the English "society for propagating the gospel in foreign parts," by which certain lands were given to the church in Vermont chiefly for the support and maintenance of its clergy. This subject has been treated in an able maner by the senior warden of this parish, K. Haskins, who contributed the article entitled "A summary of the early legal struggles of the church in Vermont," published in the Centennial Journal of the year 1890. . . . Among the sources of information concerning the history of the church none are more valuable than the work entitled "The Documentary History of the Church in Vermont." The preparation and publication of this volume were a labor of love on the part of three of our diocesan clergy. Through their patent research, documents have been brought to light, which not only supply the many defects of our early journals, but as it is expressed in the preface, "serve to illustrate the character of the men who figured in those early days in the history of the church in this country, so that the vast amount of information to be found in the work is by no means of interest only to Vermont church men, but to all churchmen throughout the United States."

When Bishop Hopkins was consecrated in 1832 there were 13 presbyters, 14 church buildings, 24 organized parishes and 1112 communicants. At the time of our late bishop's consecration in 1868, there were 31 church edifices, 13 rectories, the Vermont Episcopal institute and trust funds, all aggregating over $312,000. In 1890, when the centennial convention took place, there were 50 church edifices, 25 rectories, the institute and Bishop Hopkins hall, the Episcopal residence in Burlington; trust funds and lands, amounting in all to about $600,000; and since the year 1890, there have been proportional gains. In the year 1868 there were 40 parishes and missions, 24 clergy, 1668 families, comprising 6278 individuals; with 2361 communicants and 1889 Sunday-school pupils and teachers; while the offerings for that year, exclusive of salaries, were over $5000. In 1890 there were 53 parishes and missions, 34 clergy, over 2000 families with over 8000 individuals, 4000 communicants, over 2000 Sunday-school pupils and teachers, while the offerings for that year amounted to over $15,000, exclusive of salaries.

It is by comparing the statistics given above, which were compiled by one of our clergy three years since, and therefore are in reality an underestimate of our present strength, with the meager facts obtainable for the year 1832, that we gain some idea of the growth of the church in Vermont during the last 60 years. But in no other equal period of time has such progress been made as during the past 25 years, which covers the period of our late bishop's episcopate; and while the growth and prosperity of individual parishes may seem small to us, we have reason to thank God, and take courage for what has been accomplished through his blessing, when we view the work of the church in this diocese as a whole. We recall the arduous labors of our predecessors, the manifold difficulties of their task, their personal sacrifices and all that they endured for Christ's sake, and while returning our hearty thanks for their good examples of faith and practice, we believe that we are called to surpass them in faith and diligence, to further the work they so well undertook and carried on; called, by the spirit of the living God, to earnest prayers and watchfulness, to never ceasing effort, that in our day and generation we may be instrumental in manfully doing our part "in breaking down the kingdom of sin, satan and death, until the whole of Christ's dispersed sheep, being gathered into one fold may become partakers of everlasting life through the same Jesus Christ our Lord."

Dr. Hart Elected Bishop.

The Rev. Dr. Samuel Hart, professor of Latin at Trinity college, was elected bishop of the Episcopal church, Vermont, at Burlington yesterday. Dr. Hart is one of the most popular professors on the faculty, and greatly beloved by the students. It has long been expected that he would be made bishop, and while the students grieve at the loss of Dr. Hart as professor, they congratulate him upon the new field of labor that is opened to, him.

Vermont has elected a successor to the late beloved Diocesan, and the choice has fallen upon the Rev. Samuel Hart, D. D., one of the best-known and most-honored of our clergy. As professor in Trinity College, Hartford, Dr. Hart has made a record which entitles him to the highest position within the gift of the Church, and there ne has won the love and confidence of a host of Churchmen. As a prominent member of the committee on the revision of the Prayer Book, he is probably more widely known. In that work, his accurate scholarship and patient attention and courtesy won the admiration of the House of Deputies and were of great service to the Church.

Dr. Hart's Call.

The choice of Rev. Dr. Samuel E. Hart for bishop of Vermont will be regarded both in a pleasant and unpleasant light by Trinity college and by Hartford people generally. It is a delight to the friends of Dr. Hart to have him thus honored. It is an honor which he abundantly deserves for he is a delightful and scholarly Christian gentleman of marked ability and faithfulness to his work.

But much as Hartford may be pleased to have him called to higher offices it is unpleasant to think that the change involves a loss to those among whom he

has lived and labored for so many years. He has become so deeply rooted in Trinity, he is so popular that transplanting becomes an unpleasant task.

If Dr. Hart decides to accept the flattering invitation, however, he will always be sure that he has left a host of warm friends in Hartford. But Trinity will not let him go without a struggle.

REV. SAMUEL HART, D. D.,

OF HARTFORD, CT., BISHOP BISSELL'S SUCCESSOR.

A Majority Vote Cast on the Fourth Ballot—Committee Chosen to Notify Dr. Hart of His Election — Biographical Sketch of the New Bishop—Convention Adjourned.

The final business session of the 103d annual convention of the Episcopal church of the diocese of Vermont opened at 9 o'clock yesterday morning. The committee, consisting of Revs. Walker, Atwell and Randall and Messrs. Haskins and Stone, appointed Wednesday evening to consider some plan for liquidating the deficit in the fund for missions, reported, recommending that the several parishes be assessed 10 per cent on the basis of the apportionment made by the missionary committee for the convention year 1892-1893. The report was accepted and adopted. Mr. Dewey moved that 500 copies of the constitution and canons be printed in pamphlet form; Rev. Mr. Randall moved that the constitution and canons be also printed in the journal of the convention; both motions prevailed. An effort was made to reconsider the vote by which the selection of the time and place of the next meeting was left to the new bishop, but a motion to that effect was lost. A committee of three, consisting of Revs. Goddard and Lewis and Mr. Temple, was appointed to consider the advisability of adopting rules of order of business at annual conventions, to consult with the new bishop and to report at the next convention. The convention was brought to a close with prayers and the benediction by Rev. Dr. Bliss.

The special convention for the election of a bishop was called to order at 2 o'clock by Rev. Dr. J. Isham Bliss, chairman of the standing committe. Secretary Canfield read the call and called the roll. It appeared that 27 of the 29 clergymen entitled to vote for bishop were present. The 42 parishes were represented by 82 lay delegates.

Rev. John Anketell of Fair Haven and Rev. A. S. Brown of Brattleboro gave reasons why they thought their names should appear on the roll. It appeared that Mr. Anketell received his transfer from the diocese of New York last March and Mr. Brown was ordained deacon six months ago. Dr. Bliss stated that in making up the roll the committee held that neither Mr. Anketell nor Mr. Brown had been canonically a resident of the diocese for a year and that they were therefore not entitled to vote for bishop. He ruled accordingly. Thomas H. Canfield of Burlington was elected secretary.

Dr. Bliss then addressed the convention. He referred to the convention which elected Bishop Bissell 25 years ago and said that of the clergy who answered to their names at that convention, but five were now alive. Dr. Bliss referred to the responsibility which rested upon the delegates. He was glad to say that there seemed to be great singleness of purpose in the task. The man chosen as bishop should be a man who properly represents the principles of the church. He should be a learned man, of positive character and of influence among all people. He should be a man of strong will but of kind manner. He should be able to give an impetus to the principal need of this diocese at this time,—church missions and education.

Rev. E. H. Randall of Poultney offered a resolution that "when the convention shall proceed to the election of a bishop only those entitled to vote shall be allowed seats in the church." The resolution was adopted by a vote of 53 to 42 and those who had hoped to witness the impressive ceremony left the church. A number from out of town expressed their disapproval of the unusual action of the convention in strong terms.

ELECTION OF BISHOP.

By general consent no nominating speeches were made. Rev. B. W. Atwell of Shelburne, Rev. A. H. Wheeler of Island Pond, E. P. Gilson of Rutland and C. S. Forbes of St. Albans were appointed tellers for the clergy and Rev. D. L. Sanford of Bellows Falls, Rev. J. C. Flanders of Manchester, C. E. Parker of Vergennes, and E. C. Woodworth of Arlington, were appointed tellers for the laity. Ballots were cast for Rev. Dr. W. J. Harris of Rutland, Rev. W. B. Walker of Bennington, Rev. L. A. Arthur of Detroit, Mich.; Rev. W. H. Dennison of Roxbury, Penn.; Rev. Thomas Davenport of Memphis, Tenn.; Rev. Dr. J. I. Carey of Saratoga, N. Y.; Rev. Dr. D. C. Roberts of Concord, N. H.; Rev. Dr. G. M. C. Fiske of Providence, R. I.; and Rev. Dr. Samuel Hart of Hartford, Ct.

Four ballots were taken, resulting as follows:

VOTE OF THE CLERGY.

Hart	8	11	13	15
Fiske	8	8	8	8
Roberts	3	2	1	3
Carey	5	4	3	8
Dennison	2	2	1	
Harris	1			
Totals	27	27	26	27

VOTE OF THE LAITY.

Hart	30	31	38	41
Fiske	10	15	15	12
Roberts	13	13	13	10
Carey	19	17	11	12
Arthur	3			
Davenport	3	3	2	4
Walker	4			
Totals	82	89	79	79

When the result of the fourth ballot was announced it appeared that Rev. Samuel Hart, D. D., of Hartford, Conn., had received a majority of the votes cast by both the clergy and the laity and his election was announced by Rev. Dr. Bliss. The election was made unanimous and the clerical and lay delegates signed the testimonial of Rev. Dr. Hart's election. A committee consisting of Rev. Dr. J. L. Bliss of Burlington, Rev. Dr. A. B. Flanders of St. Albans, L. G. B. Cannon of Burlington and E. L. Temple of Rutland was appointed to inform Dr. Hart of his election. They will go to Hartford to-day to perform the agreeable duty. The convention then adjourned.

THE NEW BISHOP.

Samuel Hart, D. D., who was yesterday elected bishop of the Episcopal diocese of Vermont, was born in Saybrook, Conn., in 1845, and is therefore 48 years of age. His father was a clergyman. Dr. Hart, who is unmarried, never had charge of a parish. He graduated from Trinity college in 1866 and after a course of study at the Berkeley Divinity school at Middletown,

Conn., was ordained by Bishop Williams. He has been for several years a professor in Trinity college. He is secretary of the House of Bishops, has been for several years a member of the general convention of the Episcopal church and has taken a prominent part in the revision of the prayer-book. He is recognized as one of the best scholars in the liturgy of the church in the country. He is said to be modest and unassuming, but a man of knowledge, thorough in everything. He is exceedingly popular with young men, the students at Trinity continually seeking him for advice.

The name of Rev. Dr. Bliss of this city had been frequently mentioned in connection with the vacant office, but he declined to be considered as a candidate. Many were heard to remark that he would make an excellent bishop and a prominent lay delegate from the east side of the State said that were Dr. Bliss 10 years younger he would have been elected in spite of himself.

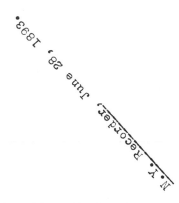

BISHOP-ELECT HART.

Dr. Hart of Trinity College, Hartford, probably never knew how many friends he had until he was elected to the Bishopric of Vermont. For many years a teacher of preachers, he has impressed them quite as much by his character, as by his learning, and has therefore exerted a wide influence upon men who are themselves influential. Dr. Hart has never got on the scholastic side of the "town and gown" fence, but has hustled around in civic matters like a good citizen. Incredible as it may seem to some scholars, he has even voted in local elections without losing caste. So the chances are he will make a good Bishop of the Brooks order, if he concludes to go

Burlington, Vt., June 23, 1893.

N. Y. Recorder, June 23, 1893.

241

LAST EDITION.

Hartford Post, June 23, 1893.

DR. HART'S GREAT HONOR.

Called to the Bishopric of Vermont

BY A UNANIMOUS VOTE AT YESTERDAY'S CONVENTION.

Dr. Hart Talks to a "Post" Reporter on the Subject.

HE MODESTLY REQUESTED HIS FRIENDS NOT TO USE HIS NAME.

Yesterday afternoon at a special convention held a Burlington, the Episcopal diocese of Vermont elected Rev. Samuel Hart, D.D., of this city to the bishopric of the diocese on the fourth ballot. The vote was then made unanimous.

Twenty-seven out of the twenty nine clergymen entitled to vote were present. Forty-two parishes were represented by eighty-two lay delegates.

The convention was called to order at 2 o'clock by Rev. Dr. J. Isham Bliss, who addressed the convention concerning the special business before it in electing a successor to Bishop Bissell. When the time came for the vote to be taken the church was cleared of all those who were not entitled to vote. No nominating speeches were made. The candidates before the convention were Rev. Messrs. W. J. Harris of Rutland, W. B. Walker of Bennington, L. A. Arthur of Detroit, Mich., W. H. Dennison of Roxbury, Pa., Thomas Davenport of Memphis, Tenn., Dr. J. S. Carey of Saratoga, N. Y., Dr. D. C. Roberts of Concord, N. H., Dr. G. M. C. Fiske of Providence, R. I., and Dr. Samuel Hart of this city.

A committee consisting of Rev. Dr. J. T. Bliss of Burlington, Rev. Dr. A. B. Flanders of St. Albans, L. G. B. Cannon of Burlington and E. L. Temple of Rutland were appointed to notify Dr. Hart of his election. They will arrive in this city this afternoon or evening.

DR. HART HIGHLY ESTEEMED.

Professor Hart is much esteemed by Episcopalians the country over and he has been very prominent in the councils of the church. He has been a member of the general convention since 1886 and is at present secretary of the House of Bishops. He has been among the foremost of the revisers of the prayerbook and at present is custodian of the standard prayerbook. He is esteemed as one of the best scholars in the history of the church in the country.

TALKS FOR "THE POST."

This morning a POST reporter called on Prof. Hart at his rooms in Trinity college building and had a most pleasant interview with him. He said that his election was somewhat of a surprise. Word reached him by telegram last evening concerning the unanimous action of the convention. "About a week ago," he said, "I was made aware that several friends were interested in my election and I requested that they desist in their endeavors. I supposed that that settled it. Consequently when the telegram informing me of my election reached me last evening I was somewhat surprised."

In answer to an inquiry regarding his probable treatment of so unanimous a call he said that he would say nothing until he had seen the committee appointed by the convention to confer with him.

Prof. Hart is very popular at Trinity and every effort will be made by both faculty and students to induce him to remain.

The report that a meeting of the college would be held today to take measures looking to inducing Prof. Hart to reject the election of Bishop of Vermont, is without foundation. Such a meeting would be well nigh useless as many of the students have gone to their homes.

MEETING OF TRINITY FACULTY.

A meeting of the faculty of the college was held this morning, but it was not called to take action on the election of Prof. Hart. It was the last meeting of the faculty for the collegiate year and the matter of conferring degrees was the principal occupation of the meeting.

AN HONORABLE CAREER.

Rev. Samuel Hart, D. D., was born in Saybrook, this state in 1845, his father being Judge Henry Hart of the probate court. He graduated from Trinity in 1866 at the age of 21, at which time he was valedictorian of his class and attained the unusual honor, termed "optimus" or highest in scholarship in every subject. He was ordained by Bishop Williams after completing a two years' course at the Berkley Divinity school at Middletown.

The same year he became a tutor in Greek at Trinity. He was elected assistant professor of mathematics two years later in 1870. In 1873 he became Seabury professor of mathematics and astronomy. Dr. Hart has held the chair of the Latin language since 1888. For a quarter of a century he has been an esteemed, able and eminently successful member of the Trinity faculty, with the exception of the year 1878 when the college removed to its present building and he was abroad touring in Europe.

Dr. Hart is second senior professor, President Pynchon being first. Dr. Hart received the degree of D. D. in 1885. He is the registrar of this diocese.

BISHOP-ELECT HART.

Not Certain That He Will Accept the High Office in the Church.

[Special Dispatch to the Boston Herald.]

HARTFORD, Ct., June 23, 1893. It is by no means certain that Rev. Samuel Hart, D. D., of this city, who was yesterday elected bishop of the diocese of Vermont at the special Episcopal convention held in Burlington, Vt., will accept the high office in the church to which he is called.

In an interview, today, Prof. Hart said that he had not yet arrived at any decision, and would not until after the anticipated visit of the committee from the convention, who are expected here tonight or tomorrow.

They will formally notify him of his election, and several days may elapse before he announces his determination.

It is learned that it was intimated to him several days ago that his name might be presented for the vacant bishopric, and that

REV. SAMUEL HART, D. D.

Boston Herald, June 23, 1893.

then, having requested that the matter be not carried any further, he supposed his name would not be brought before the convention.

The students of Trinity College are arranging a meeting with the object of a formal request that he remain with the institution.

He has been so closely identified with the management of the college for many years that the trustees and faculty will unite in urging him to remain, and the people of Hartford, by whom he is widely known and respected, will join in requesting him to refuse the bishopric and continue his residence here.

242

DR. HART CHOSEN BISHOP.

Wise Choice of the Vermont Diocese.

TRINITY COLLEGE THREATENED WITH A GREAT LOSS.

The Election at Burlington, Vt., Yesterday—A Majority on the Fourth Ballot and Vote Made Unanimous.

BURLINGTON, Vt., June 22.—In the special Episcopal convention for the election of a bishop of the diocese of Vermont to-day, the Rev. Samuel Hart, D. D., of Hartford, Conn., was elected on the fourth ballot.

The convention was called to order at 2 o'clock by the Rev. Dr. J. Isham Bliss, and on roll-call it was found that twenty-seven out of twenty-nine clergymen entitled to vote were present, forty-two parishes being represented by eighty-two lay delegates.

Before proceeding to an election, Dr. Bliss addressed the convention concerning the gravity of the question before it in the choice of Bishop Bissell's successor. Only those entitled to vote were allowed seats in the church during the election.

By general consent, no nominating speeches were made. Ballots were cast for the Rev. Messrs. W. J. Harris of Rutland, W. B. Walker of Bennington, L. A. Arthur of Detroit, Mich., W. H. Dennison of Roxbury, Pa., Thomas Davenport of Memphis, Tenn., Dr. J. S. Carey of Saratoga, N. Y., Dr. D. C. Roberts of Concord, N. H., D. G. M. C. Fiske of Providence, R. I., and Dr. Samuel Hart of Hartford, Conn.

Dr. Hart received a majority on the fourth ballot and his election was made unanimous. A committee consisting of the Rev. Dr. J. I. Bliss of Burlington, the Rev. Dr. A. B. Flanders of St. Albans, L. G. B. Cannon of Burlington and E. L. Temple of Rutland was appointed to inform Dr. Hart of his election and will go to Hartford to-morrow to perform its duty.

Dr. Hart was born in Saybrook in 1845. His father was Judge Henry Hart of the probate court. Professor Hart graduated from Trinity in 1866, valedictorian of his class and attaining the peculiar Trinity honor called optimus, or highest in scholarship in every subject. After the two years' course in Berkeley Divinity School at Middletown he was ordained by Bishop Williams.

The same year, 1868, he entered upon a tutorship at Trinity in Greek. In 1870 he was elected assistant professor of mathematics, in 1873 becoming Seabury professor of mathematics and astronomy. Since 1883 Dr. Hart has occupied the chair of the Latin language and literature. At the close of the present college year, therefore, Dr. Hart completes a quarter century of continuous service on the Trinity faculty, with but one interruption. In 1878, the year that the college was removed into its present buildings, he went abroad and spent about a year in Europe. Dr. Hart is second senior professor, being excelled only by ex-President Pynchon in length of service. He received the degree of D. D. in 1885.

Professor Hart has been very prominent in the councils of the Episcopal Church, being a member of the general convention since 1886, and at present holding the secretaryship of the House of Bishops. He has taken a prominent part in the revision of the prayerbook and is custodian of the standard prayerbook. He is recognized as one of the best scholars in the liturgy of the church in the country. He is also the registrar of this diocese.

The feeling among the students last night was that a meeting would be held to-day, at which efforts would be made to induce Dr. Hart to remain at Trinity. Dr. Hart's popularity both among faculty and students is so genuine and heartfelt that he will be overwhelmed with petitions not to leave Hartford when the news becomes generally known to-day.

DR. HART.

Vermont's Episcopal convention has made a very wise choice in electing for the Bishop of that diocese the Rev. Dr. SAMUEL HART of Trinity College. If the question of his acceptance were viewed only in the light of his personal feeling, interest, or ambition, very likely the decision of his friends would probably be unanimous in the affirmative. It is not, however, a question for others to answer; its decision must ultimately rest in the personal court of the individual conscience chiefly concerned. And even in the Church it is held to be a laudable ambition, or perhaps we should say, a laudable Christian aspiration, to attain to higher, more commanding official positions of honor and usefulness. If in reaching a personal decision in such a case, any man has ever been more governed by a strictly religious and conscientious motive than that which will rule Dr. Hart in deciding this question — a question of duty — that now comes to him, we know not who it may have been. It can only be hoped that for the sake of Trinity, and of his many sincere and admiring friends in Hartford, Dr. Hart will elect to stay where he is—with his alma mater, where he is best known and loved. His acceptance of this honor tendered from Vermont would mean a sad loss to Trinity College. It would also mean a loss to hundreds of his friends outside of Trinity and, many of them, outside of the Episcopal Church. And they are persons whose approval means something. His hearty, wholesome, and contagious vivacity and unfailing good-nature are characteristic of the man.

He would be sadly and very seriously missed in and about the College. Though still but 48 years of age, and in the very prime of life, Dr. Hart has gained an influence and a real power for good, in all that concerns the College and its best interests, that in other instances is reached, if reached at all, only in the ripe fullness of years, after an almost life-long service at the post of duty. With the single and signal exception of President Smith himself, no other man on the Faculty of Trinity could so ill be spared. His ability is many-sided, wonderfully varied. In most instances a man is distinctively strong only in one, or at most in two directions: Nature is not apt to be lavish of her gifts in equipping the individual character at all points. But Dr. Hart is an exception to prove the rule; his graduation honors, in 1866, included not only the position of valedictorian of his class, but the Trinity honor called optimus, or highest in scholarship in every subject. The TIMES has found him a valuable aid even in the record and study of so seemingly light and passing a matter as the phenomena of the weather. But it is in higher fields that he is more widely known.

Nobody can hesitate as to his sincere devotion to the interests of his denomination. In the councils of the Church he has been prominent. He is the secretary, to-day, of the House of Bishops. The genuineness of his zeal for the Church is as undoubted as was that of the good Bishop Burgess—and it is shown in almost the same gentle and self-effacing way. He would become, no doubt, that power, as a Bishop, that is the sure heritage of a nature which unites marked ability and zeal with perfect genuineness, and a sincerity as modest in its manifestation as it is real in its substance.

But we do not feel like being reconciled to the loss of such a man as Dr. Hart. Neither the College nor his friends in Hartford can afford to lose him.

PROF. HART AND THE BISHOPRIC.

The election of Dr. Hart to the bishopric of Vermont threatens to remove a man whom neither Trinity College nor Hartford can afford to lose. For many years a teacher of earnestness, skill and devotion, he has brought to his professional work

243

PROFESSOR HART.

that which in the modern conception of education outranks everything; namely, character. His influence for good in this way upon well-nigh a generation of undergraduates has been great, incalculable. Nobody we can think of has, in his daily habit and converse, given out more of sweetness and light whether in his scholastic work or his social life,—and this without ostentation or even consciousness of the atmosphere of purity and high purpose which surrounded him. To fine natural gifts he has added much scholarship, resulting in a rounded culture to which his ability to fill several widely different positions at Trinity is practical testimony. In his wider relations to Hartford, too, Prof. Hart has made himself universally respected and been a *persona grata* because of his courteous gentleness and enjoyable social gifts. He has taken a genuine interest in city doings of various kinds and THE COURANT has long valued him as a contributor and a friend. His ability and zeal in the ecclesiastical affairs of his college and his church at large have been marked and that there is a peculiar fitness in his selection for the high office to which he has been called, is patent. Nevertheless, we cannot but hope that he will stay where he has done so much and is so highly esteemed, for men of his stamp are few and far between in this world.

APPOINTMENT OF BISHOPS.

To the Editor of The Times:

For one I cannot agree with the editorial in yesterday's TIMES concerning Dr. Hart's election. In late Episcopal elections we have seen how difficult it is to secure the ablest men for the office of bishop. Men of experience and ability, men who have shown themselves worthy of the highest office by their faithfulness, and their work in the past, these are the men that we need for the bishopric. A great deal of undue pressure has been brought to bear upon great men who have been called to be chief executors in the Church, urging them to remain in the positions which they have held so well. Many dangerous precedents have been set in this way, and the Church has regretfully been obliged to pass by the best men and to call compromise men to be her leaders. If the Episcopal office is more than a perfunctory one, if it is one of essential overseership and leadership, by all means let us have our most able men for Bishops, and let us not through misguided sentiment, be obliged to elect men whom we can *afford* to lose from the positions which they hold. The excellent work that Dr. Hart has done at Trinity College, is one proof of his fitness for the Bishopric. AN ALUMNUS OF TRINITY.

There is truth in what our correspondent says in regard to the selection of the ablest men for Bishops in the great and influential and respected Episcopal church. But "Alumnus" overlooks another matter of great importance.

Trinity College has its position in the country. It is a growing institution—if not a rapidly-growing, yet an advancing institution of learning. Now, when a new and greater future seems to be opening for the college, able men are needed there. Professor Hart occupies a very important position in the college, and his usefulness there is great—perhaps greater and of more real usefulness than it could be were he made Bishop of Vermont. It is a small church up there, with few

members; but it needs a capable Bishop in Vermont, and one can be selected who can be better spared from his present surroundings than can Professor Hart.

Other and wider fields of official usefulness in the Church will open to Professor Hart, in case he should ever consent to relinquish his place in Trinity College.

MAY NOT BE A BISHOP.

Professor Hart Has Not Yet Made Up His Mind.

HARTFORD, Conn., June 23.—It is said to be by no means certain that the Rev. Samuel Hart, D. D., of this city, who was Friday elected Bishop of the Diocese of Vermont at the special Episcopal Convention held in Burlington, Vt., will accept the high office in the church to which he is called.

Professor Hart says that he has not yet arrived at any decision, and will not until after the anticipated visit of the Committee from the Convention.

They will formally notify him of his election, and several days may elapse before he announces his determination. It is learned that it was intimated to him several days ago that his name might be presented for the vacant Bishopric, and that then, having requested that the matter be not carried any further, he supposed his name would not be brought before the Convention.

The students of Trinity College are arranging a meeting with the object of a formal request that he remain with the institution. He has been so closely identified with the management of the College for many years that the Trustees and Faculty will unite in urging him to remain, and the people of Hartford, by whom he is widely known and respected, will join to urge him to refuse the Bishopric and continue his residence here.

Phila., June 25, 1893

MAY DECLINE THE BISHOPRIC.

PROFESSOR HART HAS NOT YET MADE UP HIS MIND ON THE QUESTION.

HARTFORD, Conn., June 24.—It is said to be by no means certain that the Rev. Samuel Hart, D. D. of this city, who was yesterday elected Bishop of the Diocese of Vermont at the special Episcopal Convention held in Burlington, Vt., will accept the high office in the Church to which he is called.

Professor Hart says that he has not yet arrived at any decision, and will not until after the anticipated visit of the Committee from the Convention, who are expected here to-day. They will formally notify him of his election, and several days may elapse before he announces his determination. It is learned that it was intimated to him several days ago that his name might be presented for the vacant Bishopric, and that then, having requested that the matter be not carried any further, he supposed his name would not be brought before the Convention.

The students of Trinity College are arranging a meeting with the object of a formal request that he remain with the institution. He has been so closely identified with the management of the College for many years that the Trustees and Faculty will unite in urging him to remain, and the people of Hartford, by whom he is widely known and respected, will join to urge him to refuse the Bishopric and continue his residence here.

Phila. Evg. Telegraph
June 24, 1893.

Students Ask Prof. Hart to Remain.

On Monday the students of Trinity College, as an expression of their regard for Professor Samuel Hart and in the hope in a measure to influence him to refuse the bishopric of Vermont, to which he was recently elected, drew up the following memorial, which was universally signed:

To the Reverend Samuel Hart, D.D.:

We have heard with deep interest of your election to the bishopric of Vermont, and wish now to express to you our congratulation on the honor received. We cannot refrain from telling you of the great respect and affection which you are held by the student body, and of the irreparable loss we should suffer should you feel called to accept:

Not only have you been a faithful professor, but above all, a true friend to every one of us. In case of sickness you have greatly aided; in case of trouble or discouragement you have always counseled and cheered; in short, we have gone to you for almost everything, and have always received what we asked for, if it was in your power to give it. We appreciate most highly the good you have done, in various ways, in connection with the chapel.

We sincerely hope for the good of the college and our own individual good that you will see your way clear to remain and labor among us.

DR. HART TO STAY.

It is very good news that Professor Samuel Hart has decided not to go to Vermont. Good news for Hartford and Connecticut, we mean. Of course it will be very afflictive news to the Green Mountain churchmen, who showed such excellent judgment in the choice of a bishop and who now find themselves compelled to resume their quest. We condole with them in their disappointment, and wish them better luck next time. But his college and town and state had a prior claim on Dr. Hart, and in keeping him they are only keeping their own. He is needed down here for home consumption. Trinity College wouldn't seem like Trinity College nor Hartford like Hartford without him.

VACANT VERMONT BISHOPRIC.

Dr. Hart's Declination Makes a Special Convention Necessary.

A Burlington, Vt., dispatch says that the news that the Rev. Dr. Samuel Hart had declined the office of bishop of the Episcopal diocese of Vermont was received there with regret, though it was not entirely unexpected.

The Rev. Dr. Bliss, rector of St. Paul's church, Burlington, and president of the standing committee, has called a meeting of that committee, to be held to-day. At that time a call for another special convention will be formulated, but, under the canons of the diocese, it cannot be held for at least a month after the call has been issued.

The Rev. Dr. George McClellan Fiske of Providence, R. I., stood next to Dr. Hart on the four ballots taken in the June convention. Next to him came the Rev. J. I. Carey of Saratoga, N. Y., followed by the Rev. Dr. D. C. Roberts of Concord, N. H. All of these gentlemen will have supporters in the next convention, and it is possible that a selection may be made from one of the number.

"Dr. Samuel Hart's decision not to accept his election as Episcopal bishop of Vermont," says a Rutland dispatch, "was a keen disappointment to all church people in this section, regardless of creed. His fitness for the place led all to hope that he would accept. It is thought here that Dr. Carey of Saratoga will be selected for the position."

SPECIMENS OF HART'S
CORRESPONDENCE ON
CONNECTICUT HISTORY:

LETTERS FROM HISTORIAN
JAMES SHEPARD, ESQ.,
OF NEW BRITAIN

244

New Britain, Conn.
Dec. 19, 1904.

[94]

Rev Samuel Hart D.D.
Middletown Conn.

My Dear Doctor Hart

Yours of Nov. 30th came duly to hand enclosing my abstract of the old laws. You are at perfect liberty to copy the same if you wish - and I can return it to you any time as I have two copies. With my other work I have to go slow on Church History and besides I am much hamppered by trouble with my eyes by reason of which I am forbidden to use my eyes at all by artificial light, so it will be a long time before I am ready to print. I also want to make thorough work and glean all that can be reached. While the Church here is the main object I shall publish any item of general interest that I can find even if it does not relate specifically to the Church here.

It takes all the poetry out of the W[m] Pitkin et al petition to think that they were not Episcopalians. William Pitkin and Nicholas Olmstead were in this country as early as 1637. Their original petition is very hard to read, but Stiles' Windsor Vol. 1 under an "Episode in Church History" prints it in full and comments on the same. In Walker's History of the first Church Hartford, this same W[m] Pitkin with others (four of whom were not on the petition—One was Jonathan Gilbert) ask to be admitted to communion and full fellowship on account of their Church covenant in Eng. The Windsor petitioners made a similar request to Mr. Wareham of Windsor according to Stiles. In my notes, I put "Episcopalians" down as shorter than "Church of England" and it never occurred to me that it could ever mean any thing but Episcopalians. I shall have to change it.

As to the article in the Jarvis Centenary to which I called your attention, I have written the author Dr. Seymour of Litchfield and he says that the information referred to as to Roger Searle was contained in a little diocesan paper from Ohio or Southern Ohio, but he did not find it readily at hand. I have written to the Regis-

trar of the Diocese of Southern Ohio— also to Mr. Williams Dean of the Cathedral asking if they could send me a copy of the Diocesan paper containing this account of Mr Searles work in Ohio—but so far I have no reply. Do you have any such Ohio paper in your Library? I understood at first from Mr Seymours article that Roger Searle was a missionary of the Society for the Promotion of Christian Knowledge, but on second reading he does not quite say so and from what I learn I think he had no connection with this Society. According to Sword's Almanac he was however one of the directors of the Prayer Book & Bibble Society of Conn., that preceeded the C K. Society.

In the reprint of the journal I have also found an unreported reference to the church in Berlin. Under Southington in Parish reports 1815, (as I remember) the Rev. Asa Cornwall reports officiating occasionally at Berlin and other parishes. I return by Adams Express prepaid the "Church Cyclopaedia" and thank you very much for the loan of the same. I kept it longer than I should expecting to buy a copy and so did not copy what I wanted, but the publishers have none on hand and I have not found it elsewhere.

I shall very soon put together such notes as I have about Rev Roger Searle.

Yours truly

James Shepard.

New Britain, Conn., May 3, 1905
Rev. Dr. Samuel Hart.

My Dear Sir

My Roger Searle article was published in the Old Northwest Genealogical Quarterly for April 1905 but as yet I have only one copy of it. In due time I shall have a copy to present to you.

In following up the report in the Journal of the Convention that the Rev. Asa Cornwall officiated occasionally at Berlin, his grandson the Rev. N. Ellsworth Cornwall of Stratford Conn. has sent me two old sermons, saying I

need not return them if they are of interest to me. One was delivered at Berlin Sept. 11 1814, and the other at Berlin Dec. 11. 1818. "pro Mrs. Deming." The last is of especial interest as it was at the funeral of Mrs Lucina, wife of Mr. Elizur Deming, the most active of any family at Christ Church Worthington. It was at their house that all the meetings and services were held before the church was ready for use, and after that, the key of the Church was kept at this Deming house. One sermon has ten endorsements on it from 28 Feb. 1813 to April 16, 1826, and the other 12, from Feb 18, 1818 to Oct. 24 1832, all of the places being in Connecticut. I shall not want to keep these sermons, but if you would like to have them deposited in the archives of the Diocese I shall be glad to send them to you, after a while, with Mr. Cornwall's consent.

The Presbyterian Synod of New York & Philadelphia and Delegates from the Association of Conn. & other Colonies held conventions annually from 1766 to 1775, for the sole purpose of opposing the establishment of an Episcopate in America. Dr. Beardsley in his history of the Church in Conn. and Bishop Perry in his Church history, briefly refer to this Convention. Dr Smalley of New Britain was on the Committee to write a letter to the Dissenters in London, and to all the pastors in America to show them what a calamity it would be to have a Bishop in America.

Was not this the first general convention of any religious body ever held in America when any attempt was made to have the several colonies or provinces represented in the Convention? I have been unable, so far, to find any prior general convention. Of course I know of the Boston Synod in the early years of 1600 and other Conventions by colonies, but I do not call them general conventions in the sense that this 1766 convention was. They sent invitations to all the colonies where there were Presbyterians, Congregationalists or Dutch Reform Churches so it was a general convention of all Non Episcopal Churches although N. Y. & Philadelphia and Connecticut are the only Colonies named in the name of the Convention.

Miss Mary Amelia Hart of Arlington N. Y. has kindly loaned me 93 of the Rev. Seth Hart's sermons. I am tabulating the endorsements thereon and expect to publish them in my account of

Seth Hart. Their value is shown by the fact that they show he had charge of the Church at Meriden for about 5 years, 1795 to summer or fall of 1800, and yet his name is not mentioned in the records of the church at Meriden. One sermon marked Newington, June 3, 1798 Miss Hart misread for Jan 3, 1798, and thinking it was his first sermon at Newington told me I might give it to you for the Diocese if I would give her a type written copy of it. Christ Church voted April 19, 1798 to hire Mr. Seth Hart and the first sermon as I read the endorsements was the first Sunday after the 19th viz. April 22, 1798. I have sent Miss Hart a type written copy of this sermon and asked her if I should forward the original to you. When I am through with it. She says no doubt they will all eventually be given to the Diocese and I suggested to her that if she did not do so in her life time that she put a clause to that effect in her will. I shall keep these old sermons a few days longer and then return them to Miss Hart.

Yours truly

James Shepard.

New Britain, Conn., July 8, 1905

Rev. Samuel Hart D.D.
  Middletown, Conn.

Dear Dr. Hart

I send you today by Adams Express two sermons by the Rev. Asa Cornwall, presented by his grandson Rev. N. E. Cornwall, of Stratford, Conn. Also two sermons by the Rev. Seth Hart and copies of his letters to his wife in 1797, both presented by his granddaughter, Miss Mary Amelia Hart of Arlington, N. Y. and all of them for the Diocese of Conn.

As you told me you had never been to St. Matthews Church, East Plymouth, I also send you a photograph of the Church and two views of its communion service and baptismal basin. This pewter belonged to the old Church at New Cambridge and I believe is described with the names of the donors in the old records of the Church which you have. At any rate Mr. Welton in reply to my question in the fall of 1903 as to its history sent me an extract from his copy of the old records, describing this pewter, and naming the donors but I cannot just now put my hands on his letter. I shall today send Mr. Welton

a picture of the Church and one of the photos of the service.

As I remember the accounts, this old Church was one of the last that were consecrated by Bishop Seabury in 1795, and Bishop Griswold was ordained by him in the old Church the day of the Consecration. Mr. Griswold was the Rector of St. Matthews, hence the memmorial window a part of which shows in one of the views. The key to the Church and the pewter are kept by Mrs. Ann Brooks, an old lady who lives directly opposite the Church.

My church history progresses some but slowly.
Yours truly
James Shepard.

New Britain, Conn., Sept. 29, 1905.

Rev Samuel Hart D.D.
  Berkeley Divinity School
  Middletown Conn.

My Dear Dr. Hart,

Many thanks for copy of the 1905 journal of the convention and also for the detached leaves therefrom.

I was particularly glad to see that you had 14 vols. of The (old) Churchman. I am searching all the old church papers I can find and later, (but not for some time yet,) I shall want to examine these, if I do not find them elsewhere--nearer to me.

Mr. Bodley and myself are trying to borrow a set of the Journals of the Convention of the Rev. Mr. Harriman, 1820 to date and I shall go over every page of them. In case the set is not complete we will examine the missing ones elsewhere.

I have very deliberately compared my type written copy of the records of Christ Church, Worthington with the original and found many minor errors. Believe the copy as I Now have it is correct in every thing but spelling. I did not try to follow that. I enclose a list of all the corrections that are important.
Yours truly
James Shepard.

[Attachment: "Amendments to copy of 'Records of Christ Church Wethersfield & Berlin, Conn. 1797-1827.'"]

New Britain, Conn., Nov. 15, 1905.
Rev. Samuel Hart D.D.
  Middletown Conn.

My Dear Dr. Hart,

I enclose a copy of St Michael's Bulletin, Naugatuck with a historical sketch. Also a newspaper sketch of the Church at Bethany for which I have no further use and not wanting to destroy them send them to you to use as you see fit.

The Rev. Seth Hart endorsed many sermons before 1794 as preached at Gunntown and after that date some were Gunntown and others Salem. When Thomas J. Davis was made Priest in 1832, he was called as of Salem Bridge. From the sketch of the Naugatuck Church and these facts, I suppose that what is now Millville, in the town of Naugatuck, was first called Gunntown and then Salem and that the present Naugatuck center was called Salem Bridge. The Rev. Thomas J. Davis was also rector of the Church at Bethany and I got the newspaper sketch on that account but that period, 1832, is skipped.

I have been through all the Journals of the Connecticut Convention page by page. When I struck the lists of Ordinations in the Journals for 1865 and 1866, I thought I could add to them and so made the enclosed typescript of ordinations that I gleaned from the Middletown Gazette. By later Journals I found that you had these names, but the date was May 5, but still later I found that you had discovered the error in date so now all I can add is, perhaps, the fact that they were published in the Middletown paper at the time of the June Convention in 1815. The Convention I beleive was on the 7th so no doubt the ordinations were on the 6. That of Humphreys was printed the 9th but perhaps the printer put in the 6 bottom side up. I notice also that some of the names are a little different.

I had also found the list of Bishop Hobarts work in Conn in the Christian Journal before I saw your notice that Mr Hooper had found the same. I have a copy of it.

If one is to search for Episcopal items early in Conn. in secular papers, I think from what I have seen that the New Haven Journal is the best paper. When I read the Journals I found what I suppose an explanation for this, that is, that Mr. Green the Editor was a delegate from New Haven to the Conven-

tion and thus suppose that the Editors were Episcopalians. I have looked in only a few years of the Journal about 1798 to 1800.

The steple of Christ Church Worthington was blown down on the evening of Sept 3, 1821, and that of the church in Middletown the same time. The Methodist Church was also partly unroofed and the Episcopal Church at Norfolk had the front blowed in and the organ destroyed.

I scanned all the Registrar's reports closely for possible sources of information. I would like soon to examine the files of the (old) Churchman 1831 etc Also the mss. records of the Episcopal Society of Barkhampstead 1784-1834. The Typescript History of St Michael's Naugatuck by Gardner, and Bailey's copy of Farmington baptisms from the New Haven (Trinity) church records. I presume this last is with Mr. Bissell at the Capitol and if so I can find it without troubling you. Such Church periodicals as I can find at Trinity I shall examine, (the early ones) but I think they do not have the (old) Churchman 1831 etc.

I think I have run down the Stratford school and will write it up. It was kept several years and Joseph Brown the School Master was paid by the S.P.G. There was also one of their schools at Groton. The law of 1842, if enforced, was sufficient to have suppressed these Episcopal Schools but it is said to have been aimed at "The Shepherd's Tent" in New London and the Episcopal schools went right on as if no law had been passed. Perhaps they had the sanction of the Selectmen.

The Rev. John Read, Congregational Minister at Stratford, 1702 to 7, is the first person in Conn. whose name I have learned, to go over to the Episcopal Church. He became a Lawyer--settled in Boston and was a communicant at the King's Chapel.

Yours truly

James Shepard.

[Attachment: "Additions to the list of Ordinations in Journals for 1865 and 1866...."]

New Britain, Conn., Dec. 18, 1905.
Rev. Samuel Hart D.D.
  Middletown, Conn.
My Dear Dr. Hart,
  By the same mail I send you Samuel Griswold's Sermon No 1, which his

granddaughter Mrs. Chapman says I may give to you for the Diocesan Archives. She also loaned me one other sermon for inspection and which I return to her.

I have long thought that Rev. Samuel Griswold, who as a candidate for Holy orders read service and sermons at Christ Church Worthington, during Rev. James Kilbourn's absence in the summer of 1802 succeeded Mr. Kilbourn and remained in charge until he settled at Great Barington some time in 1804. I am corroborated now to the extent of finding that he preached at "Berlin" Feb. 18, 1804 and March 19, 1804, apparently giving them monthly service. I have also thought that Rev. James Kilbourn had charge of the church in Granby when he was at Christ Church, Worthington. The sermon I send you shows that Mr. Griswold preached at least one sermon at Granby at the time that he was taking Mr. Kilbourn's place in the summer of 1802 from which I infer that Granby was also Mr. Kilbourns charge, taken in connection with the fact that he Kilbourn then resided at Granby and was the fina[n]cial agent who finished building the church there. Mr. Griswold preached in many different places in Conn. before 1805 as appears from endorsements on his sermons.

In an addition to one of his sermons he several times indicates the word "world" by a circle enclosing a cross, thus-- ⊕   The Rev. Seth Hart indicated the same by a circle enclosing a dot, thus-- ⊙. Was this then a standard symbol or did they stumble upon it from the spherical form of the world? Mr. Griswold officiated part of the time at Barkhampstead while he was at Great Barrington and most of the time from 1821 to 1828.

Yours truly

James Shepard.

New Britain, Conn., Nov. 15, 1907.
My Dear Dr. Hart,
  I thank you for the many favors received from time to time and not acknowledged before this, Registrars report--Historical papers etc.

I am sending you by Express prepaid for the Diocese a bound copy of my compilation of the endorsements on your Kinsman's sermons, "Mr. Seth Hart" and the "Rev. Seth Hart." I intended this for my St. Mark's, but finally left it out. It is the only thing I omitted that I thought could be of any possible

use to any one. I give one copy also to the Conn. Historical Society and as Mr. Bodley says I make it thus a matter of "Church and State."

I also send you Heald's Sketch of Trinity Parish Tariffville, Conn.; Baileys sketch of Trinity Church, Branford, Conn; McManus' Story of St. Paul's, Medina, Ohio.; and Sylvester Smith's sketch of the Methodist Episcopal Church in New Haven. If you want these for the Diocese you are welcome to them and if you do not then you are welcome to them and may dispose of them as you please. These came to me for use in preparing my St. Mark's History and I have no further use for them.

Sincerely yours--
James Shepard

Rev. Samuel Hart D.D.
Middletown, Conn

139 Lake Street New Britain, Conn.
May 25, 1915

My Dear Dr Hart

The record book and envelope relating to the Churches at New Cambridge and East Plymouth came to hand Saturday.

The record book was a great surprise to me for I supposed that it was lost beyond all prospects' of recovery.

I find I have quite a task on them. I will return them as soon as I can, but it may be quite a while yet.

Yours truly

James Shepard.

139 Lake St.
New Britain, Conn. July 5, 1916

My Dear Dr. Hart.

Replying to your favor of the 3rd inst. the only manuscript or document relating to St. Peters that I ever had from yourself or the Diocese is the diary of the Rev. Roger Searle. There was a loose sheet in [it] giving on one side the names of the members of St Matthews and on the other those of St Peters. I have had this twice, first when I was preparing S[a]int Marks History and last about a year ago when I made excerpts concerning St. Matthews, returning it to you after a few weeks. The first time I borrowed it you went to Hartford for it but the last time I think you had it at Middletown. I have

never seen the volume of accounts belonging to St Peters. I trust that you will soon be able to locate both of them.

As I wrote you before, the 1830 Journal of Convention gives Rev Joseph T. Clark as Rector of St Peters and St Matthews as the successor of Rev. Robert William Harris. I supposed that they were St Matthews Rectors and proceeded for a while on that basis. I afterwards learned from one of the Potter papers you loaned me that the Journal was in error as to the St. Matthews end, hence I have no use for the enclosed sketches of these two Minister[s]. The facts as to Mr Harris can be easily found but I was a long time searching for the birth and parentage of the Rev. Mr Clark. If you care to retain these sketches you are at liberty to make any use of them you may see fit.

I am in hopes of having Mr Seymour soon close a contract for publishing my New Cambridge St Matthews history.

I was pained recently to learn of the long continued illness of the Rev Joseph Hooper.

Very truly yours

James Shepard

Rev. Samuel Hart D.D.
Middletown, Conn.

SCRAPBOOK [95]

249

WAS FOUNDED IN 1794.

EPISCOPAL ACADEMY IN CHESHIRE.

Many Prominent People Present at the Commemoration To-day—The Historical Address by Rev. Edwin S. Lines of New Haven—President Dwight and Many Others Speak.

[96]

Cheshire, June 21.— THIS is a big day for Cheshire in general and for the Episcopal academy in particular, in that to-day is the 100th anniversary of the birthday of that well-known school for boys which has been carefully nurtured and cherished under the espionage of the Protestant Episcopal church of the diocese of Connecticut. The day, as far as weather is concerned, is all that could be desired. The thermometer was sufficiently high to render the heat uncomfortable, but the sun was hidden a greater part of the day in clouds, and a cool breeze blew over the academy grounds to the great comfort of the three hundred and odd guests.

The hundred or more out-of-town people who attended the reception last night were reinforced this morning by about 200. A special train from New Haven arrived at 9:55, in time for the morning exercises. The celebration of the day was begun by religious services in St. Peters' church. This was followed by a historical and commemorative address by Rev. E. S. Lines, of New Haven. Rev. James Stoddard, formerly of New Britain, but now principal of the academy, delivered an address of welcome. The assemblage then resolved itself into a sort of an eulogistic body and for several minutes there were remarks of regret that the Rt. Rev. John Williams, of Middletown, bishop of the Connecticut diocese, was unable to be present. He was to have spoken on "The Academy and its Relations to the Diocese."

Other addresses were made by Rev. Samuel Hart, D. D., president of Trinity college, Hon. Benjamin Stark of New London and C. Larue Munson. of Philadelphia. President Timothy Dwight, of Yale, was present and made remarks, and Prof. Andrew W. Phillips, of Yale, who is one of the trustees of the school, and who is considered one of its staunchest supporters, made congratulatory remarks. Dr. Robert Horton, the aged ex-principal, although nearly blind and unable to see with the eye the festivities of the day, was present and spoke feelingly of his connection with the institution and its career.

Governor Morris is expected this afternoon, and will probably make an address. The number of graduates of the school who returned to be present in the celebration, was somewhat small-

Rev. Dr. S. J. Horton.

er than was expected. Some of the older classes, however, were represented, and at dinner, which was served at 1 o'clock and during the hour prior to the afternoon session, there was a reunion. The celebration was very successful, and the outlook for the institution, while it is not at the zenith of its career, is encouraging.

Rev. E. S. Lines' Address.

Rev. E. S. Lines' address was as follows:

We meet here to-day to celebrate the completion of a century since the establishment of the diocesan school of Connecticut. At the diocesan convention held in New Haven in the month of June, 1794, it was voted to establish this school and to ask the members of the church in Connecticut for the money with which to do it. It had been a project long in the minds of Connecticut churchmen. They had known the worth of an educated clergy and of institutions of learning in which they might be trained. But there had been no means with which to establish schools or colleges. If modest churches could be built and clergy be supported they must be content. Few traces of the prosperity of the middle of the Eighteenth century were left, after the war of independence, in which so many Connecticut churchmen were on the wrong side. To open churches and to provide for the ordinary ministrations of the clergy, to learn how to go on in poverty and weakness, with aid from the mother church withdrawn, in the face of deepened prejudice and hostility,—was the task to which Bishop Seabury and his fellow churchmen set themselves with courage and self sacrifice which we can hardly appreciate.

The vision of a church college or school in Connecticut never quite vanished. From his coming back from England and Scotland, rich in ancient foundations, the mind of our first bishop was upon the establishment of a school under the care of the diocese of Connecticut. The training of a learned clergy was to be the first office of such a school. As early as 1770, Dr. Samuel Johnson had written from Stratford to the secretary of the Society for the Propagation of the Gospel of "a design I have entertained of holding a little academy or resource for young students of divinity, to prepare them for holy orders; the design of which is chiefly to improve them in classical learning, Latin and Greek, to teach them Hebrew, and direct and assist them in studying divinity; and before they go if not graduated otherwise, I would procure them the degree of M. A. at the college at New York."

Bishop Seabury's desire for the school is shown in an extract from a letter to the bishop of Edinburgh in 1788. "We are also endeavoring to establish an academy for the education of our own clergy, etc.; and perhaps, if we can raise £1,400 or £1,500 sterling by subscription in the course of the winter, of which we have good hopes, to set it a-going in the course of the next summer; and flatter ourselves that by making it a general school for fitting young men for the various occupations of life,

Rev. James Stoddard, M. A., Principal.

Horton Hall, the New Academy.

it will support itself." In the following year, 1789, Bishop Seabury wrote to Bishop White that a convention of lay delegates from the several congregations was to be called to consider the practicability of instituting an Episcopal academy in the state. So it would appear that the founding of the school was under consideration several years before it was accomplished. Even while such great matters as the very organization of the church, the adaptation of the "Book of Common Prayer," and all pertaining to diocesan administration were unsettled and the cause of anxiety, the necessity of the church school was strongly felt. Churchmen were thinking of it as necessary for the well being of the church. There must be a school which churchmen could call their own and in which their clergy could be educated. If we could reproduce the circumstances and feeling of the time we would doubtless see that they judged aright. The church was fighting then for the right to live against prejudice and suspicion of which we happily have little knowledge. In the enjoyment of the fruits of the victory

Mr. Woodbury, Head Master.

won, it ill becomes us to forget those who won the victory for us through hardship and self sacrifice.

At a convocation at East Haddam in February, 1792, the subject of the establishing of the academy was considered and it was "voted that the several clergy make enquiry of their neighboring towns, and see what can be done towards erecting an Episcopal academy and report to the next convention." Two years were to pass, however, before action was taken, which assured the founding of the school. At the convention of 1794, held in Trinity church, New Haven, the business relating to the academy had the first place. On the first day of the session a committee with Rev. Mr. Bowden as chairman, was appointed to prepare an address to the members of the church in the state, pointing out the importance of establishing the academy. They were to provide subscription papers for the purpose of obtaining money. The committee reported the next day that more time was required for the business committed to them and a standing committee was appointed to address the members of the church, to present a plan of the academy and to obtain money. The action of this convention made the definite beginning of the diocesan school of Connecticut—the point from which we count our history, the event which suggests this centennial anniversary. If it be said that we are anticipating by two years the proper celebration of the 100th anniversary of

the establishment of the school in its own building in Cheshire, we reply that the school was already in existence, waiting to be transferred here. The names of that committee ought to live in honor among us. They were men of high position in church and state alike. They are the men through whose efforts the hopes of Connecticut churchmen were realized. They were Rev. Drs. Mansfield and Hubbard, Rev. Mr. Baldwin, Hon. Jonathan Ingersoll, Messrs. Elias Shipman, S. W. Johnson, J. L. Wooster, John Nichols, Ebenezer Baldwin. The majority of the committee were graduates of Yale college and men of large influence in Connecticut.

The committee prosecuted their work with diligence and at the convention in 1795 proposals from various towns for the establishment of the academy were received and a committee to report upon them was appointed. They laid before the convention proposals from the towns of Wallingford and Cheshire. The response of the church people was so generous as to assure the establishment of the academy. A choice among places desiring the school must be made. A new committee of nine persons, with Rev. Dr. Bela Hubbard of Trinity church, New Haven, as chairman, was appointed to receive proposals from the towns of Cheshire, Wallingford and Stratford only, up to July 1, 1795, "at which time the committee shall meet at Maj. Bellamy's tavern, in Hamden," and there and then decide to establish the academy in the place considered most eligible. The town of Stratford was brought into consideration with Cheshire and Wallingford because of the importance of the mother parish and because Rev. John Bowden had already a school there. The existence of the diocesan school was assured and Rev. Messrs. Bowden and Baldwin and S. W. Johnson were appointed a committee to frame a code of laws "and also to form a constitution for the academy upon the most liberal and beneficial plan." This convention at Stratford, in 1795, was the last at which Bishop Seabury presided. He died before the academy was fully established in Cheshire, but not before the mind of the Connecticut church people had been fully declared, and his long and cherished purpose was in process of fulfilment.

At that conference in Maj. Bellamy's tavern, in Hamden, July 1, 1795, Cheshire prevailed against Wallingford and Stratford and obtained the prize of the new academy. There was no better place for a school than this fair country town, lying upon these beautiful hills, a town of good name, wealth and refinement for those days, in which the Episcopal church had long been established. Midway between the great routes of travel between New Haven and Hartford, and New Haven and Litchfield, it was itself easy of access. The people of Cheshire were generous and the honor of having the first of our diocesan institutions came to them. The corner-stone of the old academy building was laid April 28, 1796, with Masonic honors, and it was completed in the autumn at a cost of £702 lawful money. In the Connecticut "Courant" of May 4, 1796, you will read of the laying of the cornerstone by Temple lodge, F. and A. M., with the procession from their lodge room, of the "well adapted discourse" of Rev. Reuben Ives, of "the pertinent observations" of Rev. Tillotson Bronson, and the return from the services to partake with the proprietors of "a festive entertainment." Rev. Reuben Ives, rector of St. Peter's church, was probably most influential in bringing the academy to Cheshire. He was one of the most useful of our early clergy. On that day he bade those engaged in the work, not discouraged by difficulties "look forward unto the distant good" they were promoting. That was a great day for the church in Connecticut, although in our eyes, the day of small things.

But before the Academy building was finished or its first principal elected a school had been opened in Cheshire by Rev. Tillotson Bronson, who says in his advertisement that he will teach, besides the common school branches, higher mathematics, surveying, navigation and dead languages if desired. He adds "As the subscriber understands reading and construing the French language, two or three French gentlemen might find their account in spending a few months in Cheshire to instruct in their own language and to be instructed in English."

The Diocesan convention was held in Cheshire, June 1 1796. Rev. Mr. Jarvis had declined the election as bishop at the special convention in May and Rev. Richard Mansfield presided. The constitution of the Academy was adopted. Trustees were chosen by the convention. "Female education might be attended to under this institution." The

The Old Chapel and School.

course of studies included those of a college course and provision was made that lectures might be delivered in Divinity, law or physic. Pupils were to attend public worship where parents and guardians directed. In the list of trustees you will find the most eminent of the clergy and laymen in the diocese. Rev. John Bowden was unanimously elected principal. He was probably the most scholarly Connecticut presbyter. Born in Ireland, 45 years before, he had been an assistant minister of Trinity church, New York city, and rector of the church in Norwalk. His voice had failed and from 1792 he had taught a school in Stratford. The high regard of his brethren was shown in his election as bishop of Connecticut in this same year. It was doubtless well understood that he would be the principal of the new academy. He had all the votes in the convention and on the very day of his election he sent his advertisement of his readiness to receive pupils to the "Connecticut Courant." Dr. Bowden took large and distinguished part in the theological controversy of the time, and was plainly held in high esteem by churchmen upon both sides of the Atlantic.

Dr. Bowden in December, 1796, made his formal announcement of the opening of the academy. Some extracts from the advertisement are interesting. "The system of education to be pursued in this seminary is as extensive as that of any college on the continent. Besides a learned, a common English education, will be particularly attended to, as being the most useful to the generality of youth; English grammar, reading, spelling and pronouncing with propriety deserve the utmost regard and it is the determination of the subscriber that they shall be taught with unremitting care and assiduity."

To prevent or remove misapprehension which may arise from the name, Episcopal academy, it is stated that "the greater part of the trustees are laymen, and they may be of any denomination whatever and four of them actually are Presbyterians. * * * The pupils who do not belong to the Episcopal church will not be obliged to attend her service, but that mode of worship which their parents or guardians prefer."

"The public may be assured that all will be fair, candid and liberal."

"It does not accord either with the disposition of the subscriber or with the character of modesty to insinuate that any extraordinary literary advantages will attend the institution. The plan of education he flatters himself is good, but whether it will be executed, time alone can determine. * * * Attention and fidelity will not be wanting."

"To those who are not acquainted with the town of Cheshire, it may be expedient to observe, that it is situated in a pleasant and healthful country, about 14 miles from New Haven. The road to it is good—the necessaries and conveniences of life are abundant, and the manners of the people afford as few temptations to vice as can be reasonably expected where the population is considerable."

"To those who wish well to every well meant endeavor to cultivate the human mind, who entertain the pleasing hope of seeing a general diffusion of literature throughout the community—who, loving science themselves are desirous that all should love it—to those persons, there needs no apology for instituting the Episcopal academy. As much has been done and is still doing to throw light upon the human mind, the founders of this institution hope that they will be favored with public countenance for endeavoring to contribute a few rays to the general illumination."

In the year following the formal opening of the academy, Dr. Bowden "informs the public that by the constitution of the Episcopal academy, females are admitted. They will be instructed in reading, writing, arthmetic, English grammar, geography, astronomy, the figures of rhetoric, and the French language. Due attention will be paid to them and they will be under the immediate tuition of the principal." Before the school is a year old, "the professor of the French language in the Cheshire academy informs the public that he proposes opening a dancing school in the town of Cheshire," in which "the minuet, country dances and cotillions" will be taught. The proprietors are within the year finding a reward for their investment. William Law will sell an excellent farm "within a mile of the meeting house, church and academy," and to the statement that "the situation is itself airy and salubrious, its prospect extensive and diversified,, is added the statement that it is "within reach of a flourshing academy."

The school made a good beginning under Dr. Bowden. His reputation as an instructor was established. The one institution of the churchmen of Connecticut was meeting the expectations of its founders. Rev. Dr. Smith was requested to visit New York and solicit donation for the school in 1797. "The grand levy of the church in the state" was asked for next year in order to ascertain what sum might be obtained for a fund for the school. In 1799 the convention voted that one or more agents should be appointed "to go to Europe for the purpose of soliciting donations for the academy." They were to go when the trustees should be possessed of unappropriated funds sufficient to pay their expenses, and apparently that time did not come.

Dr. Bowden was principal for six years. Resigning in 1802, Rev. Dr. William Smith was chosen in his place. It may here be noted that from 1799 to 1803, Bishop Jarvis lived at Cheshire, having removed thither that he might place his son under Dr. Bowden's instruction. His son was the distinguished Dr. Samuel Farmar Jarvis of later years. Dr. Bowden became the professor of moral philosophy in Columbia college and died in office in 1817. Upon Dr. Smith's election as principal measures were taken to increase the funds of the school by a lottery. The legislature granted a lottery in 1802 for $15,000 and after many delays $12,000 were received from it. Dr. Smith was ambitious and the desire to make a college out of the academy became strong. The convention of 1804 recommended the trustees to "apply to the legislature at their next session for a charter empowering them to give degrees in the arts, divinity and law and to enjoy all other privileges usually granted to colleges." The song of degrees has ever had charms for the clergy. The school was often called in the early days Seabury college,—the name doubtless expressing the hope or wish of the one using it. The writer may be permitted to say that he wishes that the academy had borne the name of the Seabury Diocesan school.

Again in 1810 by vote of the convention the trustees were requested to prefer a petition to the next general assembly of the state of Connecticut, praying that said academy may be constituted a college by the name and style of the Episcopal college of Connecticut, with all the powers, privileges, and immunities of a college." The same request was made the next year, 1811, but all in vain. The Connecticut legislature might grant the Episcopal academy a lottery, but not the power to confer degrees.

The academy did not prosper under Dr. Smith. A very unfavorable report of its condition was presented to the convention in 1805 and the next year Dr. Smith resigned in a rather ungracious way. He was born in Scotland and was a man of learning and of skill in controversy. He lacked steadfastness. He was musical without doing much for harmony in the places where he worked. "The Office of Institution of Ministers" in the "Book of Common Prayer" was prepared by him. He lived until 1821, part of the time officiating in Connecticut and part of the time in New York.

Rev. Tillotson Bronson was at once elected principal. He was born in Plymouth, Conn., 1762, and was graduated at Yale college in 1786. In the 10 years between the opening of his school in Cheshire and his election as principal in 1806, he had been rector of St. John's church, Waterbury. He was a teacher of much experience and a man of large influence in the diocese. For 20 years he was the principal of the academy and under him for nearly the whole period it prospered. In 1819 Dr. Bronson reported to the convention that the average number of students during his administration had been 60. From the founding of the school 28 of its students had taken holy orders and about 90 had entered various colleges. The number entering the practice of law and medicine could not be determined. Dr. Bronson had the services of assistants like Rev. Asa Cornwall, whose names ought not to be forgotten. Many of the clergy of the first half of this century received their whole school and college training in the academy in these years. The brief sketch of many a faithful minister little known, informs us that the academy was his college. The diocese and whole church owe a larger debt to the academy and than is commonly recognised.

The convention held in October, 1819, at the time of Bishop Brownell's consecration received extended reports from the academy. A financial statement is made expressing the unhappy purpose of putting all the funds of the school, then amounting to $13,000, into bank stock as soon as possible. The course of study is given at length and shows enlargement. Morning prayers were attended at the academy about sunrise throughout the year. One of the visitors at the examinations, Rev. Mr. Noble, reports himself greatly pleased at what he saw and heard. One observation which he makes has occurred to others,—"Few men are born to be eminent scholars."

There is more in the way of qualification in the visitor's praise than could be wished. "When it is recollected that only a small proportion of the students continue in the academy over two years one cannot form an unfavorable judgment of the literary acquisitions here obtained.. * * * The classic taste which is formed at this institution is, in my opinion, when circumstances are taken into consideration, much more correct than could be expected, and the young gentlemen who are sent here, only want that length of time which is allotted to a collegiate course, to form a taste for literature, as pure and chaste as that which is acquired at our colleges." There were two boys here about that time whose future work was to fill large place in the history of the country—Andrew H. Foote and Gideon Welles—the grand admiral who opened the way through the western rivers into the heart of the confederacy and the secretary of the navy through our great civil war. Their letters written during the stormy days of the rebellion speak of the unbroken friendship begun here in the academy. If we could but read the history closer there would be more friendships begun at Cheshire like this to record. There are

other men who have done large work for church and state, looking back with tenderness to their school days in Cheshire. It is the school of Admiral Andrew H. Foote and of Secretary Gideon Welles, and it a fact to stir the pride of all who have been students here.

During the last years of Dr. Bronson's life the academy lost ground. The charter for Washington college, or as we know it, Trinity college, was granted in 1823, and the interest of Connecticut churchmen was divided. They had their own college at last and the academy must take a subordinate place. It was natural that the institution of higher rank should become the center of interest. With advancing years Dr. Bronson lost something of his former power. In the failure of the Eagle bank of New Haven, in 1825, the academy, with the bishop's fund and many parishes lost large sums. The diocesan school after 30 years of prosperity was to see evil days.

Dr. Bronson resigned in 1826 and soon after died. Temporary provision was made but no satisfactory principal was found. Rev. Henry M. Mason was for a time in charge of the academy and of St. Peter's church. But the number of pupils decreased and in 1829 the project of removing the school from Cheshire and entire reorganization was considered. In that year Bishop Brownell said in his address to the convention that "the board of trustees had sought in vain to obtain a suitable person for principal and that it seemed doubtful whether under existing circumstances the school could be put in successful operation. The funds which remained must be sacredly applied to the purpose for which they were given—the education of youth under the auspices of the church." The placing of the remaining funds at interest, until the sum lost by the failure of the Eagle bank was made up, was suggested by him. The convention voted that the charge of St. Peter's parish and of the academy ought not to be given to the same person. But within the year, Rev. Christian F. Cruse was called to the charge of church and academy. He remained so short a time that his name hardly need appear among the principals of the school. In 1832 Rev. Bethel Judd, D. D., was electd principal. He held that office for three years only. He was graduated at Yale college in 1797, and after leaving Connecticut he became president of St. John's college, Maryland, dying in 1858. He appears t. have had little interest in the academy and the trustees appear to have met but once while he was principal. He introduced manual training but not much came of it. I have been told that wooden bedsteads were among the articles upon which the boys were to show their skill. Very likely boys who were called out of bed at sunrise throughout the year for prayers counted a bedstead an article of furniture of little importance and had no interest in their manufacture. At least manual labor did not succeed and Dr. Judd's administration was not prosperous. The old academy building was, however, repaired and remodeled. From a report made to the convention in this year of 1835, it would appear that the funds of the academy now amounted to above $8,000. Dr. Beardsley has called the 10 years following Dr. Bronson's death the dark age of the academy. It surely led in those years but a feeble life, for lack of a principal of force and perseverance.

New hope came in 1836 in the election of Rev. Allen C. Morgan, born in New London in 1802 and graduated at Yale college with distinction in 1826. Dr. Beardsley has written of him—his instructor and friend—with affection and enthusiasm. He seemed for the academy a most fortunate choice. Everything opened with great promise. The number of pupils increased to 60. Changes in the constitution of the school, giving the trustees the power to elect the principal and other rights were made. The school was newly ordered under an enthusiastic, wise, experienced teacher and all looked forward to a larger, more useful life for the academy. But before two years were gone Mr. Morgan died, in his 37th year, most deeply mourned. Again the prospects of the school were clouded. Bishop Brownell, who had congratulated the convention upon the prosperity of the school under Mr. Morgan, in 1838 speaks of his death as a peculiar affliction to a great company of people to whom he had endeared himself, and as a great loss to the institution over which he had presided with distinguished ability.

The Rev. E. E. Beardsley, Trinity college, 1832 to whom the thoughts of all of us go to-day and whenever we think of St. Peter's church and he was at once chosen principal of the school. With great wisdom and faithfulness, as in all things, he administered the trust and the school went on prosperously without the break which one might have expected at Mr. Morgan's death. Dr. Beardsley took full charge of the academy for some years, ministering to the parish gratuitously and so enabling the parish to build the new church. In the address delivered by hm upon the fiftieth anniversary of the school in 1844, Dr. Beardsley says that the average number of boys under instruction in the six years of his administration has been 52 and that 350 different pupils have been in the school. We think of the period of Dr. Beardsley's service here as a time of substantial growth. The impression left upon the mind of one who reads the history is that of a quiet, wise administration, making for character and good scholarship. One change in the school is ever to be associated with Dr. Beardsley. Up to this time, the pupils had found their homes about the town. The rate of board was modest, $1.75 and $2.00 per week. It was the old idea of the academy to which pupils came to study and recite. Dr. Beardsley purchased a large house and received a number of pupils into his family. I suppose that the bringing of the pupils together in the house of the principal and under his full and immediate charge dates from that time.

Rev. Seth B. Paddock, rector of Christ church, Norwich, a graduate of Yale college in 1820, became principal in the autumn of 1844, when Dr. Beardsley resigned to become rector of St. Peter's church. Dr. Paddock's two distinguished sons, the late bishops of Massachusetts and Washington, were already students in Trinity college. Dr. Paddock died in office in 1852. He found 53 pupils and then the number arose to above 70, averaging rather more than 60. He had as assistants one or more young men from Trinity college, among them the honored Dr. Charles A. Lindsley of New Haven. Dr. Paddock's reports in the diocesan journals have an old time flavor, as when in 1849, "he respectfully solicits his brethren of the clergy and friends of the church to aid him by their prayers and patronage to carry out the designs of the pious founders of the institution."

Rev. Hilliard Bryant, rector of St. Peter's church had assisted Dr. Paddock in the latter part of his service as principal and was in charge while the transfer was made to his successor, Rev. Edward Ballard, who continued in office until 1858. He was from the diocese of Massachusetts and after his res- ignation he went to Maine and became superintendent of schools in that state. He died in 1870. The academy was well attended in his time, the number of pupils rising as high as 70. He was a kindly, warm hearted man of gentle manners and disposition. In 1855 he reported the purchase of the house and property adjoining the academy, long occupied by the principal and boarding pupils.

From 1858 to 1861 Rev. John H. Babcock was principal. The number of pupils rose from 30 or 40 to 40 or 50, but the school did not prosper. In 1861 there was little left save the old academy building and the old frame house upon the corner which was burned in 1873.

I come now to speak of the longest term of service as principal of the academy, and of its most prosperous days as regards attendance of pupils and increase in buildings. Because these changes have taken place within the memory of most of us, it is less necessary to speak of them in detail. Dr. Horton came to Cheshire with 14 boys from Windham where he had a school, January 1, 1862. It must have required great courage to make a beginning here in midwinter. The school was practically suspended. There were but the old academy building and the old frame house upon the corner, ill adapted for a boarding house for pupils. Dr. Horton was graduated at Trinity college in 1843 and his experience had fitted him for the hard task before him. He knew how to get boys and how to get along with boys. He had large knowledge of the practical concerns of life and power to manage and direct. He had tact and perseverance. Immediately boys were drawn towards the school. It was in the midst of the war and the introduction of military discipline and uniform and drill made an attractive feature in the school. The old dwelling house grew too small and was enlarged. The moderate funds of the academy of about $5,000 were supplemented by Dr. Horton from the receipts of the school, and a large addition was built upon the north side, full three stories in height. The Junior house across the street—Beardsley hall—made possible the separation of the younger from the older boys. Soon through the generosity of Mr. Slater, Bronson hall stood beside the old academy with its chapel, school room and recitation rooms. Other improvements came, too numerous to be named. Dr. Horton gathered about him strong teachers. I may be pardoned for naming Profs. Woodbury, Phillips and Fuller of my own time, to whom many of us, well on in middle life, owe a great debt. The school grew and prospered and boys came from all parts of the country, from the West Indies, from South and Central America. There were more than a hundred boarding pupils and the school went on doing good work in a quiet, well ordered way.

On September 25, 1873, the fire swept away the group of wooden buildings in which the principal and the older pupils lived and where all were fed. There was nothing left of the group of buildings upon the corner. It was just at the beginning of a new and promising school year and the emergency required courage and great wisdom. Dr. Horton carried the school through that critical time, but the school never quite recovered from it. The fund of the academy and the insurance received, amounting in all to $15,000 were put into the new building which cost $30,000, so leaving a debt of $15,000. The new building was completed in the summer of 1874 and named Horton hall. The change from the old buildings was a great gain. The addition of the large field east of the board-

ing house must also be noted. In a sermon preached 15 years after coming to Cheshire Dr. Horton said that about 800 pupils had been in the school. Fifteen more years of service were to be added and then Dr. Horton resigned his trust. And now, he walks among us, the old principal of the academy,—the principal who knew in some mysterious way what all the boys were doing. For 30 years and so longer than any one before him, he was the head of our Diocesan school. A great company of boys have come and gone in these 30 years. They were watched over and kept in health. They were uniformly well taught. They were well fed. Religion was presented to them in a reasonable, scriptural way. They are widely scattered now and the Doctor and the Academy and Cheshire and St. Peter's church keep their places in their minds and hearts and hold them up to their work. Many of them must feel a great debt of gratitude to the doctor for what he did for them. All wish for him an age of quietness and peace. His name is bound in with nearly one-third of the century of the life of the school. It is too soon to say how these 30 years will appear in the history of the academy. It is happily not too late to recognize the work of Dr. Horton.

And now we turn to the future. There is a new principal at the head of the academy, a Connecticut man born and bred, one of our own presbyters, well equipped for his work. He is in his place by appointment of the diocese of Connecticut, the representative of us all, with the right to look to all of us for support. The school belongs to the diocese of Connecticut and its prosperity is her gain. The trustees have been obliged to incur large financial obligations in order to make the buildings suitable for their purpose in a time when the demands in respect to equipment are very great. Again, Trinity college, as is fitting gives us our principal and other colleges are represented in the instruction. Mr. Stoddard has with great courage and self-sacrifice undertaken the work. A good beginning has been made. The change of administration has been brought about without the break so often noted in the history of the school. The demands upon the principal are greater than ever before. I do not know how any man could have done more than Mr. Stoddard to set the school towards the future in a good way. More has been done in the way of renewal and improvement than can be here described. The equipment of the school commands respect. We believe that the future has more for the academy in the way of usefulness and reputation than the past. We believe that the oldest of our diocesan institutions will not fall behind the later born in the work for sound learning and true religion. Mr. Stoddard must give us a strong, enlightened, far-seeing leadership and Connecticut churchmen must stand behind him. The changes which had to be made have come at a time of general depression and discouragement in the country, but we must pluck up courage and push on. I do not believe that the diocese of Connecticut will fail to meet the obligation of the time or sacrifice her great opportunity.

Great changes have come in education and new methods must be followed. Cities and towns have schools of high rank as they had not a generation ago. But there is a place still for the diocesan school of high order in discipline and instruction. An old foundation with an honorable history and traditions is a rich part of the inheritance of the diocese of Connecticut.

The possibilities of the school and duty towards it never came to me so forcibly—if the personal reference may be pardoned —as when standing in Rugby school field and on Harrow Hill, I thought of the place and power of the English public school. I am sure that the task of building up this school ought to come to us as Christian men and good citizens as of great dignity. It becomes us to have large purposes and high courage. A great school of sound learning and reasonable

religion is worth working for and making sacrifices for. The secondary education of the school has hardly kept pace with the higher education of the college and the opportunity to do much for good learning is here.

Nearly a hundred years ago, Rev. Reuben Ives, faithful rector of St. Peter's church, spoke of the distant good to be thought of in laying this foundation. Fifty years ago Dr. Beardsley spoke of the coming up of the future sons of the church, a half century gone to celebrate this anniversary. And to-day we send our thoughts still forward to the distant good and we think of an unbroken succession of sons of this school and of the church as coming up to celebrate their anniversaries. For it will mean good for church and state to have the boys come up to Cheshire to be trained and taught, while looking out as their fathers did upon these ranges of glorious hills stretching away toward the sea. Boys will come and go out to do their work as men in the great world. And still the Hanging hills will tempt the far wandering boy and the Sleeping Giant will keep his place before the boy's wondering eyes. So may this ancient school remain a witness for religion and for learning, for discipline and training. So may the prayers and hopes of the fathers be fulfilled

THREE EPISCOPAL CHURCHES TO CELEBRATE THIS YEAR

Memorial Church of the Holy Trinity, St. Peter's, Cheshire, and Christ Church, Tashua.

[1910]

FEATURES OF THEIR HISTORY.

Three of the Protestant Episcopal churches in the diocese of Connecticut will have anniversaries of marked interest this year. The Memorial Church of the Holy Trinity in Westport will reach its semi-centennial, April 16. St. Peter's church at Cheshire and Christ church at (Tashua), Trumbull, were founded 150 years ago. The anniversary of the Cheshire church will occur June 29. The founding of Christ church at Tashua took place in 1760. Grace church at Long Hill in Trumbull was begun in 1836. For ten years it constituted a part of the parish at Tashua. It was then admitted into union with the convention as a separate organization. Christ church was consecrated by Bishop Seabury June 8, 1795. Bishop Hobart visited it in 1817 and confirmed a class of 82 persons. The Rev. L. H. Sheffield is present rector. The history of this ancient church will be a source of fruitful inquiry.

St. Peter's in Cheshire.

St. Peter's church in Cheshire was founded in 1760. Joseph Moss was influential in assembling neighbors in the place at the house of Zachariah Ives as far back as 1751 and acted as a lay reader. In that year the Rev. Ichabod Camp organized an Episcopal society from this band of neighbors. The Rev. Samuel Andrews began his work at St. Peter's. During the previous year Joseph Moss bought the property on which the place of worship was erected. He was aided in the project by Henry Brooks, sr., Zachariah Ives, Benjamin Lewis, Amos Matthews, Ebenezer Tuttle, Moses Tuttle and Isaac Tyler. Mr. Moss was parish clerk for many years. He died July 10, 1775 at the age of 62.

In 1770 a second church building

was erected, occupying the site where the present church stands. A new brick church was consecrated August 1, 1840, during the rectorship of the Rev. Eben E. Beardsley. The first church was opened for services in December, 1760, with services and a sermon by the Rev. Mr. Scovill. The church that was consecrated in 1840 has received many benefactions from communicants and friends. In 1881 it was the recipient of artistic furnishings and memorial windows. The bell was given by Mrs. P. S. Beers and daughters, Mrs. N. S. Platt and Mrs. M. N. Chamberlain. In 1888, George A. Jarvis of Brooklyn, N. Y., shared in the erection of a new tower of stone and brick, 70 feet in height. The cornerstone was laid by Bishop John Williams, July 11, 1889. The rector at that time was the Rev. J. Frederick Sexton, now of New Haven.

Rectors of St. Peter's.

In 1786, Samuel Andrews withdrew from the rectorship and removed to Nova Scotia. He was succeeded in 1788 by the Rev. Reuben Ives, son of Zachariah Ives and a graduate of Yale. Mr. Ives died October 17, 1836. His rectorship at St. Peter's was concluded in 1820. In that year Dr. Bronson, principal of the Cheshire Academy, and Assistant Principal Cornwall began preaching in St. Peter's, Rector Cornwall continuing in the church until 1828. The rectors from that time until 1834 were Henry M. Mason, C. F. Cruse and the Rev. Dr. Judd. The Rev. Eben E. Beardsley began his rectorship in 1835. He was principal of the academy. He remained with the church until 1840, when he was succeeded by the Rev. William F. Morgan. The Rev. Frederick Miller was the successor of Mr. Morgan and continued in the field until 1843. Mr. Beardsley was recalled and was rector until 1848. During the last sixty years the rectors of St. Peter's have included the Rev. Joseph H. Nichols, the Rev. Hilliard Bryant, who was rector during the Civil War; the Rev. Julius H. Ward, the Rev. E. M. Pecke, the Rev. W. B. Buckingham, the Rev. O. H. Raftery and the Rev. J. Frederick Sexton. The Rev. Mr. Raftery has been located at Portland for a number of years. He is a graduate of Trinity college. The Rev. Dr. Sanford J. Horton, who became principal of the Cheshire academy, January 1, 1862, was greatly interested in the prosperity of St. Peter's. Dr. Horton graduated from Trinity in 1843. The present rector of the church, the Rev. Frank S. Morehouse, is also a graduate of Trinity and of the General Theological seminary in New York. He was a student under Professor Beckwith at both of these institutions.

Ordained in England.

In 1767, seven years after the founding of St. Peter's, Abraham Beach, who was born in Cheshire, and Richard Samuel Clarke embarked for England, where they received ordination. Mr. Beach graduated from Yale in the class of 1757. He died in 1828.

Holy Trinity at Westport.

Memorial church of the Holy Trinity at Westport was begun in 1860 by Richard Henry Winslow and was completed by Mrs. Mary Fitch Winslow in 1862. On the fourteenth of February, 1860, R. H. Winslow, J. Morse, D. G. Townsend, N. Cleaveland, M. L. Mason, J. E. Perring, James Gardner, E. M. Lees, J. R. Nichols, E. S. Downs,

254

J. F. Bulkley, Samuel Gorham 2d and J. C. Cotter met at the residence of John Cleaveland with the view of organizing a second Episcopal church in Westport. Nehemiah Cleaveland was chosen moderator and M. L. Mason clerk. Nehemiah Cleaveland and Myron L. Mason were elected wardens; R. H. Winslow, Francis Burritt, E. S. Downs, John Cleaveland, D. J. Townsend and William Wood vestrymen; R. H. Winslow treasurer and James R. Nichols clerk. The Rev. John Purves was invited April 24 to become rector and the invitation was accepted April 26. In May R. H. Winslow, Francis Burritt and Daniel J. Townsend were appointed a committee with power on the erection of a stone church. The site selected by the committee was the Wakeman place, which had been an inn in the days of the Revolution. Washington passed a night there in September, 1780, while returning from Hartford where he had been in conference with Count Rochambeau. When the old inn was demolished in 1860 a French crown piece of an early date in the eighteenth century was found. It was in a notable state of preservation.

Death of R. H. Winslow.

R. H. Winslow, chairman of the committee having the erection of the church in charge, died February 14, 1861. Francis Burritt, also a member of the building committee, died in April of that year. Under the fostering care of Mrs. Winslow, who was a Norwich woman, the work of construction was carried to completion in 1862. It was consecrated under the name of the Memorial Church of the Holy Trinity.

Rectors of the Church.

The Rev. John Purves, who accepted the rectorship, April 20, 1860, discontinued his work in February, 1862. He was succeeded in October of that year by the Rev. William H. Benjamin, who remained until the spring of 1864, when he resigned. The Rev. John Eaton Smith became rector, January 1, 1865, and held the position until June, 1870. His death occurred in September. The Rev. Lawrence S. Stevens was appointed rector in October, 1870, and continued his ministrations until April 1875. The Rev. Alonzo Norton Lewis, who graduated at Yale in 1852, became rector of the church July 1, 1875. He had received an honorary degree from Trinity and was a man of ability and distinction in the church. He was a classmate of Colonel Homer B. Sprague of the Thirteenth connecticut.

The Rev. Kenneth MacKenzie is the rector of the church at present. The date of the bishop's consent to the founding of the parish was April 16, 1860. The semi-centennial anniversary will not be observed until the day of the consecration, which will take place June 30, 1913.

Richard Henry Winslow.

Richard Henry Winslow, who was one of the originators of the church, was born in Albany, N. Y., September 16, 1806, and was a Mayflower descendant. He was a nephew of Leonard Corning, American consul at Maranham, Brazil, and spent his early life in that country and in Europe. In 1832 he became a member of stock exchange in New York and amassed a fortune. He established his residence in Westport and in 1858 was a member of the general assembly from that town. A. Homer Byington was a member from Norwalk and is one of

the few men now living who was in the house with Mr. Winslow in 1858. In 1859 Mr. Winslow was the candidate for lieutenant-governor on the democratic ticket. He was elected senator from the old Tenth district in 1860. His colleagues in the senate included Elisha Johnson of Hartford; John W. Stoughton of South Windsor, A. B. Mygatt of New Milford, Ephraim H. Hyde of Ellington and Natham A. Baldwin of Milford. The Hon. O. H. Perry of Southport was speaker of the house. The death of Senator Winslow, which occurred February 14 1861, was deeply felt by the church and town of which he was a leading representative.

GARDINER OR STYLES?
[97]
Question as to the Name of the First White Child Born in Connecticut—Interesting Facts.

Deputy Comptroller F. Clarence Bissell makes the following interesting contribution to the discussion as to the name of the first white child born in Connecticut:

The following epitaph appears upon a table monument of Connecticut brownstone, about 6 feet by 3 feet, in the Center church cemetery of this city:

> Here lyeth the body of
> Mr. David Gardiner of Gardiners Island.
> Deceased Ivly 10, 1689
> In the Fifty Fovrth year of his age
> Well sick dead in one hovrs space
> Engrave the remembrance of death on
> thine heart whenas thov dost see
> how swiftly hovrs depart
> Born at Saybrook, April 29, 1636.
> The first white child born in Connecticut.

The last three lines of this inscription are of modern appearance and were not included in the copy of this inscription as given by John Warner Barber in his Connecticut Historical Collections in 1836 (p. 59). Neither does the copy of this inscription given in "Lion Gardiner and His Descendants," C. C. Gardiner, St. Louis, 1890 (p. 89) include these final lines. When were they added to the original inscription, by whom and by what authority?

An ancient manuscript referred to in this latter work (p. 3), which, according to the author, "contains strong internal evidence of having been written by him" (Lion Gardiner the father of David), declares that he———"Dwelt at Saybrooke Fort four years, it is at the mouth of the Connecticut River, of which I was commander, and there was born to me a son named David, 1636, the 29th of April, the first born in that place,"———. Note that Barber quotes this date incorrectly as 1635 in his copy of this manuscript (p. 60), but the family historian invariably calls it 1636. This appears to settle the fact that David Gardiner was "the first" (son or child?) "born in that place."

In the manuscript "Diary of the Rev. John Sharpe, Chaplain to his Majesty's Forces in the Fort of New York" (manuscript No. 4,123 in Pennsylvania Historical Society Collections) is the following entry, "1710, Jan. 26th. To Long hill, preached Eph. 5, 15, 16, a congregation of 200 the greater part whereof had never heard the Common Prayer; 27th, Baptized Isaac Styles the first man child born in the Colony of Connecticut, a man of 80 years of age. Visited one Zachary a sick person. Dined at Dr. Johnson's and returned to Stratford."

In "Documentary History of the Protestant Episcopal church in the United States of America, Connecticut," Hawkes & Perry, 1862 (p. 42), in "An Account of the Sufferings of the Members of the Church of England at Stratford," 1710, signed by the church wardens, etc., appears———"The Rev. Mr. Sharpe, who was near a month amongst us, and took much pains, and baptized many, amongst whom was an aged man, said to be the first man-child born in the colony of Connecticut"———. It is evident from this that he was considered by himself and neighbors as the first man-child born in Connecticut. It may be noted in this connection that he (Isaac Styles) was one of the petitioners to the bishop of London from Stratford, April 1, 1707, printed in the latter publication. In "The Stiles family in America, Genealogies of the Connecticut family," H. R. Stiles, Jersey City, 1895, (p. 407), after quoting the above from Sharpe's diary, the editor adds a note found in the handwriting of Savage, the compiler of the New England Genealogical Dictionary: "Of course, if the first male-child born in Connecticut he would not be more than 76, instead of 80 years. Perhaps his mental faculties in Jan. 1710-11, were infirm, so that he might not judge rightly of his own age; and the Rev. officiating priest was perhaps too ignorant of the history to correct his venerable catechumen's error."

Who was the first white child born within the present limits of Connecticut?

Two Questions Answered.
(Chief Justice Simeon E. Baldwin in (Congregationalist.)

I. "Why do you value Congregationalism?" Because it subjects the individual to no authority except the particular church to which he may belong, and that church to no authority except that which is divine, and as to this leaves it to be its own interpreter.

II. "How can it be made more efficient in New England?" By taking on more warmth and color, and by closer association between the different churches of its order through a greater centralization of advisory right. Gowns for the ministers, responses in Scripture reading by the congregation, chorus choirs, particularly if vested, give warmth and color. Substituting local associations for councils, as recommended by the national council, gives more centralization. Universal recognition that a weekly prayer meeting, while helpful to some, is uncongenial to others, and that each church member in this is his own judge of what best suits his character and temperament, would remove a stumbling block in the way of many and shut a door which has taken many into the Episcopal church who really prefer the Congregational order, with its greater freedom of faith and simplicity of worship.

WHAT THE REDCOATS DID
WHEN THEY INVADED ESSEX.
Reminiscences of the War of 1812
Told By One Who Had Them
First Hand.
BRAVE OLD DEACON POST.

255

Pautapaug settlement, (now Essex,) at the time of the invasion by the British redcoats on the morning of April 9, 1814, was on a point of land 100 rods long, between the North and South coves. Most of the houses were located on this point, where Main street was laid out. They numbered about twenty, but within a circuit of a mile there were eighty or 100 more. The population was about 800. In 1816 a new street was laid out, north of and parallel to Main street, (it is called New street at the present time.) To this point the river is generally open in the winter, except in extremely cold weather. In the old days vessels laid up here and goods were deposited, while the river was closed above. The village suffered much from the restrictive system and the succeeding war of 1812, particularly by a visit from the vessels of the British squadron then blockading a part of the United States fleet in New London harbor. Ship building was then carried on at "The Point," at which many privateers were fitted out to prey on British commerce, in ships coming over with goods of all kinds to supply the British army and navy on and about the New England coast. These light draught vessels could dodge out and in the river, thus evading the heavy armed vessels of the British, as the depth of water would not allow the latter to cross the bar at the river's mouth.

The business of ship building was commenced at Pautapaug by John Tucker in 1720, but was not extensively carried on for some years. In 1775 the ship Oliver Cromwell of twenty-four guns was built at this place by Uriah Hayden. For ten or fifteen years before the war of 1812-14 from 1,200 to 2,000 tons of shipping were annually launched from "The Point" and the yards in the neighborhood. Business commenced to thrive after the Revolutionary war. The British knew that there were vessels building at Pautapaug Point, and they knew that it was a depository for goods captured from their vessels by the privateers, and that there was quite a fleet of vessels in the Connecticut river which they could not get at unless they took to small boats. A council was held on board the English fleet to consider a boat expedition up the river to Pautapaug. Captain William Coot, who was an officer in the fleet, was well acquainted with the Point, and with some of the people, as he had visited the place before the war. To him was given command of the expedition.

To allay suspicion of the people at Saybrook and along the Sound shore, several vessels got under way and for several days cruised up and down the coast. Then on a dark night they hove to off the mouth of the Connecticut river, showing no lights, and manned two cutters and two barges, armed with 12-pound cannonades, and 250 men and proceeded up the river, with muffled rowlocks and without a glimmer on board. At that time the fort at Saybrook was not fully manned, and a very poor lookout was kept. If the soldiers had been on their guard they would have discovered the boats creeping by them, as they rowed close inshore. Captain Coot, knowing the condition at the fort, therefore thought that the closer they kept to it the least likelihood there was of being seen, and so it proved, for not anyone at Saybrook Point knew that the boats had passed up the river. It was the intention of the officers on the boats to arrive at Pautapaug before daylight, but there sprung up a strong northerly wind, and as there was some freshet in the river, it retarded their progress so much that they did not arrive at the Point till about 8 a. m.

The British were soon discovered by people living near the river, and they speedily gave the alarm through the village. Captain Coot knew that there were only a few able-bodied men at home, as they were away in the American army. On landing he gave orders not to molest any of the people, unless the troops were interfered with. All the arms were stacked on the dock under guard of ten men, thus showing that Coot was confident that he would have little trouble from the people of the village. People living on the main street closed their houses and many of them went to the home of friends on the outskirts of the village. If there had been fifteen or twenty resolute men in the place they could have captured the guns and placed Captain Coot and his men in a bad fix.

The redcoats broke into the brick store of Samuel Hayden, located near where they landed. The store was full hogsheads, tierces and puncheons of West India rum, molasses, tobacco and a large quantity of other goods taken from British vessels by our privateers and stored there. The barrels of rum were rolled into the street and the heads knocked in, allowing the liquor to run into the river. Coot gave strict orders that no liquor should be saved or drank by the men, as he knew that if they did he could not control them, but as he could not be everywhere at once, the men took advantage of it and some of them got so full that they had to be carried on board their boats when they left. This was told the writer by an eye-witness.

At this time there were a number of vessels in the different coves and one ship of 400 tons, ready to launch at the New City yard. Thirty or forty redcoats patrolled the streets, and the rest were at the different ship yards destroying all the shipping, both large and small, that they could find. When Coot built a fire under the new ship at New City to burn her, old Captain Jude Pratt, who was the principal owner begged Captain Coot not to destroy his vessel as it would ruin him, but Coot was obstinate and gave orders to destroy everything on the premises. At this juncture Captain Pratt conceived a new idea. He sought Coot and gave him a Masonic sign which the latter promptly returned and then gave orders to his men to put out all the fires. This vessel was the only one saved.

There was a man in the village who had the true spirit of 76 in his blood. He was Deacon Reuben Post, who lived at New City. As soon as he heard of the arrival of the British he got out his old Kings arm, loaded it with several slugs and marched down towards where the enemy was reported to be. Now the old deacon was no more afraid of the redcoats than he was of a red-combed rooster. He longed to get shot at them. Reaching the head of Main street he found several of his townsmen gathered there and he stopped to ask where he could find the enemy, but he was finally persuaded not to carry out his warlike intention, as it would only call down on the heads of innocent people the vengeance of the British. He was told for the first time that Captain Coot, on landing, had assured the people that no one would be molested, if they did not interfere with him. Upon that the old deacon marched home.

After destroying all the vessels they could find except three or four which they took with them, the British prepared to leave, as Cootwell knew that if he tarried much longer there would be more men on the Point imbued with the old deacon's spirit and he might have a battle on his hands. An old resident of the Point, Captain Glover, owned a small sloop, by which he earned a living for himself and family in fishing and freighting. He begged Captain Coot not to burn her, as she was all he had. The captain took compassion on the old man and told him if he would pilot them out of the river he would not destroy the sloop. Captain Glover consented, in order to save his vessel. At sundown the marauders left the Point. A crowd was assembling, and there were too many of them to suit Coot. The boats dropped down the river and stopped in Ayres's bay about dark. There the British burned several vessels that they had carried with them. Just why they did this no one except themselves knew.

At midnight they crept across the river and followed the east side down, as Coot mistrusted that there might be some guns on Ferry Point by this time, and sure enough there were. The news of the invasion of Pautapaug reached Guilford. The patriots there raised a company of thirty men, and, with two ten-pound field pieces, arrived at Ferry Point at dark, to head them off before they got out of the river. There was at that time part of a battery of ten-pound field guns at Guilford; they mustered a company, and, with horses attached to the guns, arrived at Ferry Point (a half-mile above the present drawbridge) just after dark, where they threw up entrenchments. (Some marks of these can be seen yet.) Scouts informed them when the British left Pautapaug Point. The invaders could be plainly seen from Ferry Point when they burned their prizes in Ayres's bay. This bay is formed by Ayres's Point and Ferry Point, a distance of perhaps a quarter of a mile, and a very quiet place, where it is said Captain Kidd anchored many times.

After the British got under way the Guilford men opened fire on them. It was so dark they could not see the boats very well, but they continued to blaze away. On Captain Glover's return to Essex he reported that several of the enemy were killed and wounded. When the British vessels were reported sailing up the coast, some of the vessel owners thought they were up to mischief, so they ran their vessels up the river, some into Hamburgh cove and others into Chester creek, thereby saving those crafts. It was said years after that Captain Coot said that it was so late in the day when he got through his job at Essex that he dared not remain any longer in the river, as in all probability he would have been stopped, although he had reason to believe that he would find a number of vessels stowed away in the coves and creeks above.

At this time the men from the British fleet landed on the different islands on the Sound, carried away thousands of sheep, poultry and pigs, etc., to stock their larder. After the war Captain Coot had the temerity to visit Pautapaug, but he met with a very cool reception and was warned to leave.

Uriah Hayden, who built the Oliver Cromwell of twenty-four guns, has descendants living in Essex at the present time. Although the British were often on our coast during the war, destroying and carrying off everything

they could find, in consequence of which many conflicts took place, it is worthy of note that no American belonging to Middletown or Saybrook was killed excepting Charles Dolph of Saybrook, who lost his life January 15, 1815, in retaking a sloop from the privateer Boxer of Lisbon. (Mr. Dolph's descendants are living in Essex.)

It is stated in the statistical account of Middlesex county of 1816, that the amount of property destroyed in this invasion of Pautapaug by the British was about $160,000, the sum of $60,000 falling on the people of the Point; that twenty-two vessels were burned, and much other property destroyed. The amount stated doesn't seem reasonable to the writer. The vessels of those days were small, anywhere from 25 to 400 tons, and they couldn't average more than $2,000 each. Where the $100,000 comes in we are unable to see. There were storehouses on the dock, which stand there now, one standing back of the steamboat dock, now removed. These were filled with rum, molasses, tobacco and goods of all kinds. This property was all destroyed or carried off. Notwithstanding all this we cannot believe that the loss amounted to $160,000.   H. C. A.

Essex, March 20.

THE HISTORICAL ASPECT OF THE AMERICAN CHURCHES.

This is the title of an address delivered by the Dean of Westminster in Sion College, on the 17th day of March, 1879, and printed in full in the June number of *Macmillan's Magazine*. It was evidently inspired by the recent visit of that dignitary to this country, and all readers of religious history will be interested in its perusal, and admire the skill and felicity with which he has grouped together the "American Churches," and touched with a few bold outlines their historical aspects.

A traveller in search of local and general information is apt to pick up many things which lie loosely in the minds of people, and often have only a vague traditionary authority. Some statements in this address must be received *cum grano salis,* and others will not bear the test of careful and thorough investigation. For example, Dean Stanley, in doing honor to the memory of John Eliot, commonly styled *the apostle of the Indians,* speaks of him as one "whose translation of the Bible into their language remains as the monument both of his own gigantic effort and the sole record of their tongue, and also of the friendly relations which the Church of England then maintained with its separated children. It was supported by the Society for the Propagation of the Gospel—' the venerable society,' as the Americans call it—and by Sion College."

Whatever Sion College may have done, it is not correct to say that his "gigantic effort" was supported by the venerable Society for the Propagation of the Gospel. Eliot was born at Nasing, England, in 1604, and, emigrating to this country, was settled, in 1631, as minister of the church in Roxbury, Mass., where he died May 20th, 1690. How much

aid the venerable society—had it been in existence—might have given to his zealous work for the moral and spiritual welfare of the Indians is not conceivable. But his work was practically ended long before its charter was granted; for it was not until the 16th of June, 1701, that "King William III., of glorious memory, was graciously pleased to erect and settle a corporation, with perpetual per cent. on their share capital, and possess a high reputation for probity of manufacture. The most important of these is perhaps the Industrial Co-operative Society of Oldham, founded in 1850-1. From very small beginnings it has gradually extended its operations, until in 1874 it divided a dividend of £40,000—equivalent to about $200,000—among its shareholders. The total turnover is about £250,000 a year, and it forms a kind of bank for other co-operative societies.

The Sun mill, another co-operative society of Oldham, has a share capital of £100,000.

In France co-operation has developed itself mainly in the form of production. In Paris alone there were at one time one hundred productive societies. One of these was a pianoforte manufactory, which started with a capital next to nothing, and in ten months' time had acquired a capital of nearly 83,000 francs. Another was the Association Remquet, for carrying on the printing business, which, at the expiration of ten years, divided on the there was a valid succession. But who that knows the history of the Institution Office will be willing to accept in their intended bearings the words which follow?

"To his (Seabury's) influence also must be attributed that singular office in the American Prayer Book, happily not obligatory, the one exception to its general tone on which we shall presently enlarge—the Office of Institution of the Clergy—containing every phrase relating to ministerial functions which, both from the English and American Prayer Books, had been carefully excluded—' altar,' ' sacerdotal,' ' apostolic succession.' This office, although now hardly ever used in the American Episcopal Church, yet remains, we will not say as a ' dead fly, causing the ointment to stink,' but, at any rate, as a mark of the influence which Seabury's spirit continued to exercise after his death."

Bishop Seabury died suddenly, February, 1796, and if there be any evidence that he ever suggested or thought of the Office for the Institution of Ministers, we have failed in our researches to find it. It is true, the office owes its origin to Connecticut, and it was prepared, at the request of the convention of the diocese, by the Rev. William Smith, D.D., one of its clergy, nearly four years after the death of the bishop, but not formally accepted by that body until 1804.

Printed copies of it had been previously transmitted to the several bishops in the United States, and to the Standing Committees of those States in which there were no bishops; and the General Convention of 1804 prescribed it, and set it forth with alterations in 1808, the title being changed from "In

godly conversation, having a competency of knowledge in the principles of religion." The earliest struggles for Episcopacy in Connecticut were not begun until a later date, and they were based on the validity of orders. Men crossed the ocean to obtain what they could not receive in America, and it would have been strange inconsistency in them to ask for the privilege of communing with a body whose government and discipline they had ceased to recognize.   E. E. B.

duction" to "Institution," and its use made to depend upon recommendation, and not upon requisition. Thus, while Seabury could have had no part in compiling the office, the influence of his spirit appears to have had less to do with its incorporation into the Book of Common Prayer than the final action of the house of bishops in 1808, when only two members were present—White, of Pennsylvania, and Claggett, of Maryland.

In another part of the address is this extraordinary statement: "In the State archives at Hartford there is still to be seen a petition from the Episcopal clergy of Connecticut urging the governor of the State to use his

influence in inducing the Congregationalists to allow them access to the Eucharist." Has not the dean made a mistake here, and substituted a petition of laymen, signing themselves "professors of the Protestant Christian religion, members of the Church of England," and declaring their grievances, that they were not under the care of those who "administered in a due manner" the sacraments of Baptism and the Lord's Supper? Such a petition was preferred in the latter part of the seventeenth century, and the ministers and churches in the colony were recommended "to consider whether it be not their duty to *entertain* all such persons, who are of an honest and

BISHOP WILLIAMS' JOHNNY CAKE

(By the late Bishop of Connecticut.)

A forgetful old Bishop
All broken to pieces
Neglected to dish up
For one of his nieces
A receipt for "Corn Pone"
The best ever known,
So he hastens to repair his sin of omission
And hopes that in view of his shattered condition
His suit for forgiveness he humbly may urge.
So here's the receipt and it comes from Lake George:
Take a cup of corn meal
(And the meal should be yellow,)
Add a cup of wheat flour
For to make the corn mellow,
Of sugar a cup, white or brown at your

pleasure,
The color is nothing—the point is the measure.
And now comes a troublesome thing to indite,
For the rhyme and the reason they trouble me quite,
For after the sugar, the flour and the meal,
Comes a cup of sour cream; but unless you should steal
From your neighbors I fear you will never be able
This item to put upon your cook's table;
For, "sure and indeed," in all towns I remember
Sour cream is as scarce as June bugs in December.
So here an alternative, nicely contrived,
Is suggested your mind to relieve,
And showing how you, without stealing at all,
The ground that seemed lost may retrieve:
Instead of sour cream, take one cup of milk—
"Sweet milk!" What a sweet phrase to utter!
And to make it cream like, put into the cup
Just three tablespoonfuls of butter.
Cream of tartar, one teaspoonful—rules dietetic—
How near I wrote it down tartar emetic!
But no, cream of tartar it is without doubt;
And so the alternative makes itself out,
Of soda the half of a teaspoonful add,
Or else your poor corn cake will go to the bad;
Two eggs must be broken without being beat,
Then of salt a teaspoonful your work will complete.
Twenty minutes of baking are needed to bring
To the point of perfection this "awful good thing."
To eat at the best this remarkable cake,
You should fish all day long on the royal named lake,
With the bright water glancing in glorious light,
And beauties unnumbered bewildering your sight
On mountain and lake, in water and sky,
And then when the shadows fall down from on high
Seek Sabbath day point as the light fades away,
And end with this feast the angler's long day.
Then, then you will find without any question
That an appetite honest doth wait on digestion.

ANCIENT BALLAD OF A BLACK SNAKE.
POISONED A MAN UP SPRINGFIELD WAY.
Was A Popular Song In New England For Years.

AN ANCIENT WARNING TO ALL YOUNG MEN.

Maybe there are some of the older "Courant" readers who have heard sung the ballad of Springfield Mountain. It is a ballad that has the distinction of being the only genuine New England ballad which received the popular approval of the people to anywhere near the extent that ballads are supposed to receive. It is truly American in its story, was founded on an actual occurrence, and has been sung with variations almost numberless. One of the forms as brief as any is the following, and it was sung with a refrain after each two lines:—
On Springfield Mountain there did dwell
A lovely youth, I knew him well.

One Friday morning he did go
Down in the meadow for to mow.

He had not moved across the field
Before a black snake bit his heel.

When he received this deadly wound
He dropped his scythe right on the ground.

They took him to his Sally dear,
Which made him feel quite wondrous queer.

Oh, Johnny, dear, why did you go
Down in the meadow for to mow?

Oh, Sally, dear, and don't you know
'Tis daddy's grain and must be mowed?

At last he died, gave up the ghost,
To Abraham's bosom he did post.

Now all young men, a warning take,
And avoid the bite of a big black snake.

J. G. Holland in his "History of Western Massachusetts," published in Springfield in 1855, says that the origin of the song was in Wilbraham, Mass. Timothy Merrick died there as a result of a snake bite, August 6, 1761. A gravestone marks the place where he is buried and a young woman to whom he was engaged to be married was supposed to be the author of the verses, which were the original version from which the variations sprang. The original version began:—
On Springfield Mountains there did dwell
A likely youth was known full well.
Leftenant Merrick's only son,
A likely youth near twenty-one.

From the original version there grew up many variations. In some of them it is "Leftenant Curtis's son" who suffered the fatal wound and in one "Leftenant Carter" is the man that appears. The wider apart the variations went the greater was the particularity of detail. The words were sung to a tune, and as the addition of a few lines only meant the singing of the tune over again, composition was simple. One version described in detail the lonesomeness of the poor young man's death. An example of this interpretation follows:—
He looked around but looked in vain;
No one came nigh for to ease his pain.
So he made up his mind his time had come,
And laid his head on a cold stun.

Not satisfied with the pathos of a solitary death scene, some of the rhymsters sought to make more of a plot to the tale and they eagerly seized hold of the unfortunate lady love of the victim as a fit subject for more doggerel. How the young woman entered into the funeral is shown in the following specimen:—
He took the reptyle in his hand
And straightway went to Molly Bland.
Oh, Molly, Molly, her you see
A pizen sarpent that bit me.

Then Molly Bland she squatted down,
And sucked the pizen from the wound;
And oh, she had a rotten tooth,
The venom soon affected both.

The death of Molly gave occasion for ingenuity as to the fate of the couple after death. It is too bad that the mower was gathered in by the scythe of Death so tragically, but the old song must have given a lot of fun to the old-time rhymsters.

THE PRESIDENT'S BLUNDER.

It was enough to have the monument at Provincetown a hundred feet higher than anything in Plymouth. But the President of the United States came with a fleet of iron-clads, landed, mounted the rostrum, and called the Mayflower band Puritans. That is enough to make Colonial genealogists and the New England historian turn up their coat collars. If there is one thing that the Mayflower descendant abhors it is to hear the Pilgrims called Puritans. Here is the President speaking, in a great public address, of Provincetown as "the shrine of Puritanism" and of the people as "sons of Puritans." O ye shades of BREWSTER and BRADFORD!

Plymouth has now a suspicion that the authority of the President is not unassailable on all historical and literary matters. He has violated their sanctuary; he is ignorant of a fundamental Colonial distinction. What he may say about the Irish Sagas will no longer interest them; no partisan feeling will they show about nature stories, and Dr. LONG may be right for aught they care; indeed, is there not some question about what did and did not happen at San Juan Hill?

The distinction is an important one. It is a real historical difference and not a mere verbal one. The Pilgrims and Puritans represented two distinct tendencies. The Pilgrims were separatists from the Church of England and had sojourned many years in Holland, whence they came to America. The Puritans tried to purify the English Church; they rallied and came from England to New England. The Pilgrims settled in Plymouth; the Puritans in Boston and Salem. The Pilgrims never persecuted persons for differing religious beliefs. MILES STANDISH was said to be at heart a Catholic. The Puritans were religious bigots and carried their fanaticism into their politics. The compact that the Pilgrims signed in the Mayflower cabin in the Harbor of Provincetown is a model of liberalism. How did the President dare to make a speech at Provincetown and not know these facts?

FIFTY YEARS AGO
SATURDAY, MAY 18, 1861.—

A patriotic demonstration took place in the town of Old Saybrook, Ct., made particularly interesting by the antiquity of the place and its various revolutionary relics and reminiscences. A fine flagstaff was raised upon the spot which had given birth to the old Saybrook platform, and but a short distance from the old fort built by the first settlers of the place.

The services were prefaced by the raising of the flag by Deacon Sill (91 yrs.), a colonel of the war of 1812, and the patriarch of the place. A prayer and addresses were then made by Rev. Messrs. McCall, Loper and Gallup, the intervals being appropriately filled by national songs. In conclusion the old men of the village were called upon and short and telling speeches made.

258

CHARLES HEMENWAY ADAMS.

In the death this morning of Charles Hemenway Adams there passes from this life a man of high intellectual endowment, who had been an indefatigable worker in the newspaper field for almost all his mature life, and was most highly esteemed by those who knew best the quality of his work, the extraordinary range of his information, and his masterly use of language to convey thought. Graduated from Yale in the class of 1866, he passed, after a few years on the Springfield Republican and the New York Sun, to the Hartford Courant as an editorial writer, remaining there until serious illness compelled his retirement a year or two ago. He never recovered from the attack, but for a considerable time wrote at intervals, and found his chief pleasure in that limited continuance of the habit of a lifetime. Until this illness he had been for many years absorbed in the newspaper to a degree not easily to be understood by those who have had no experience of the hold such work takes on a man who is meant by nature for it, the real delight that goes with the most strenuous effort that will forever remain anonymous. That is one of the mysteries of newspaper work which those not born to it cannot understand. And he was certainly to that manner born.

Personally Mr. Adams was a delightful companion among the few with whom he had intimate relations. He was a mine of information. His reading was very wide, and it was thoroughly digested. He was impatient of ignorance, and bitter against false logic. To an unusual degree he had facts at his command when he sat down to work. As a writer he was rather solid than brilliant, but he was never dull. He gave his life to hard work without prospect of personal distinction outside the small field in which he was personally known, and he found delight in his work. These things are not unusual in the newspaper world, and perhaps the fact that this is so adds a genuine dignity to work that is avowedly done for the day, and for the most part destined to be forgotten the day after. It is seed sown by the wayside, but sometimes it bears fruit, and the better the sowing the greater the chance that something will come of it.

In brief, Mr. Adams belonged to a school that has largely passed away, but which still holds among some newspapers which are not the least influential and respected. It had at least the merit of sincerity and of respect for reason above any passion of the moment.

FUNERAL OF CHARLES HEMMENWAY ADAMS

[98]

Verses Written by Him on Death of General Sherman Read.

The funeral of Charles Hemmenway Adams, for thirty-four years an editorial writer on "The Courant" and for many years associate editor, was held at the home of his sister, Mrs. F. Will Hallock, No. 122 Derby avenue, Derby, at 2:30 o'clock yesterday afternoon. The gathering of friends included Dr. G. A. Shelton of Shelton, who was a classmate of Mr. Adams's in the Yale class of 1866; and three associates of Mr. Adams for years on the staff of "The Courant," Watson Robertson Sperry, Charles W. Burpee and C. L. Sherman. The Rev. Charler W. Coulter of Stony Creek, a young man in whom Mr. Adams took an interest, officiated and after a reading of the Scriptures and a prayer in which he spoke with deep sincerity of the value of Mr. Adams's life work, he read the following beautiful verses, written by Mr. Adams on the death of Gen. William Tecumseh Sherman:—

The strenuous day is past;
　The march, the fight.
The bugle sounds at last
　Lights out. Good night.

The sky is white with stars;
　The tents gleam white.
Tired captain from the wars,
　Sleep through the night.

Sleep till the shadows take
　Their endless flight;
Until the morning break,
　Good night! Good night!

The bearers were Mr. Adams's Hartford newspaper associates and members of his family. The burial was in Oak Cliff Cemetery, Derby, by the side of his mother, whom he tenderly cared for, for many years, in this city. There were many wreaths and loose flowers, and a wealth of roses from his former associates and "The Courant."

Mr. Adams was buried very quietly yesterday by those who loved him. His face, thinned by illness, was familiar, and yet with the purely intellectual lines in it strongly marked The weather, which was fitful early in the day, became settled and bright with the light of the sun as he was laid away among his kindred in the Derby cemetery. His grave was made on the gentle slope of one of those beautiful hills of the Naugatuck valley. If he had been among the living grouped about his final resting place he would have liked the simplicity of what was done and the sincerity with which the farewell words were spoken. The sadness of it was softened by the great hope which the Christian feels when death steps in. It was the end of a long day's work, well and faithfully done; and his friends felt, as they strolled back to the cares of the living, that the old friend they had left behind deserved his rest.

FIFTY YEARS AGO

FRIDAY, AUG. 16, 1861.—

A serious affray occurred at Saybrook, Conn., in the afternoon. A number of prominent secession sympathizers of the state had called a "peace meeting," to commence at 3 p.m., when a "peace" flag was to be raised, and several speeches were to be made. Among the speakers who were announced, and on hand, was W. W. Eaton of Hartford. The fact becoming known in New Haven, about 90 residents of that city came up on the morning train. On reaching Saybrook, the boys marched in procession to the flagstaff, upon which it was rumored a flag was to be raised, surrounded it and immediately proceeded to hoist the Stars and Stripes. Judge Colyer of Hartford, with others, undertook to prevent the Stars and Stripes from being raised, and cut the halyards, and, it is said, also made an attempt to use the knife upon some of the New Haven boys, when a desperate affray commenced between the secession sympathizers and unionists, which resulted in Judge Colyer having one of his cheeks dreadfully cut, and the great peace advocate of Saybrook faring little better. Mr. Eaton was deterred from making his prepared speech; and, quiet being restored, Capt. Jos. R. Hawley, of the returned 1st regt., whose bravery at Bull Run had been frequently alluded to, made a capital union speech, which was enthusiastically received by the assemblage. About 40 of the New Haven boys returned home in the evening, while 50 remained to watch movements for the night and take care of the flagstaff so that no flag should be raised upon it. The flag which the secession sympathizers intended to raise was a white one, with the word "Peace" inscribed thereon.

BISHOP FERGUSON DIES.

[99]

First Negro to Hold Office in Episcopal Church—Dined in Richmond by Bishop Potter.

New York, August 4.—The Right Rev. Samuel D. Ferguson, bishop of Liberia and West Africa, and the first negro member of the House of Bishops of the Protestant Episcopal Church of America, is dead at his home in Monrovia, Liberia, according to a cable received yesterday by the Domestic and Foreign Mission Society of the Protestant Episcopal Church, 281 Fourth avenue.

He was in his seventy-fifth year and for more than thirty years had been a noted figure in his church, coming here frequently to attend conferences, during which he was highly honored. In 1907 the late Bishop Henry C. Potter of New York entertained him at dinner in Richmond, Va., for which he was severely criticised throughout the south.

Bishop Ferguson was born in Charleston, S. C., and emigrated with his parents to Liberia when 6 years old. He was educated in the mission schools and was an excellent student, giving early promise of being a leader among his people. In 1862 he was appointed a teacher and began his studies for the ministry. Three years later he was admitted to the church as a deacon, being appointed a priest in 1868. As a priest his work attracted attention and he was soon suggested for further advancement.

The House of Bishops assembled in New York in 1884 and elected him

missionary bishop of Cape Palmas and its adjacent territory, the diocese later being changed to that of Liberia and West Africa. On June 24, 1885, his consecration took place in Grace church, New York. During the same year he received the honorary degree of D. D. from Kenyon college and in 1893 Liberia college conferred on him the degree of D. C. L.

Bishop Ferguson came here to attend the 300th anniversary of the Episcopal Church in America in 1907 and it was said then that he would be the first negro to sit in the chancel of St. Paul's church, the church which Jefferson Davis and General Robert E. Lee attended in Richmond, Va. He was then the ranking missionary bishop of his church, having succeeded Bishop C. C. Penick, who resigned as bishop of Cape Palmas in 1883. After Bishop Fenwick's resignation church decided to send no more white men to Central Africa under present conditions, and Bishop Ferguson's appointment was commended for his tact in the face of the race prejudice in the south. When he attended the convention in Boston in 1904 he was made much of, but made no application for quarters through the hospitality committee when called upon to attend the convention in Richmond. He corresponded with the Rev. C. L. Somers, rector of the negro church of St. Philip and was entertained by William C. Scott, a negro barber.

Robert N. Jackson.

Robert Nesmith Jackson, first and only president of the Middlesex Banking company of this city died at the home of his sister Mrs. Harriet F. Giraud, 194 Washington street, about 1:30 this morning, aged 70 years. He had been in poor health for several years, but was able to attend to his business affairs until about six months ago. His health caused relatives serious anxiety. At times he suffered greatly, but bore pain with marvelous patience and submission.

Mr. Jackson was born at Paris, France, March 11, 1845, the son of Hon. Ebenezer and Hannah Sage Jackson. His early education was received at various private schools. He entered St. Paul's school, Concord, New Hampshire, in 1856, and graduated in 1860. He was engaged in the manufacturing business a short time in Middletown and then in New York with the old firm of William B. Cooper & Co., commission and shipping merchants. Afterwards he became a member of the firm of Hubbard & Jackson, in the real estate business in Chicago, where he remained until the great fire. Then he returned to Middletown, where he resided until his death. Mr. Jackson organized and built up from small beginnings the Middlesex Banking company, and was its only president, serving for 40 years. He was married June 1, 1876, at Terre Haute, Ind., to Miss Sarah Ewing Law, daughter of Commodore Richard Law, United States navy. They had two sons, Eben and Richard Law Jackson, and two daughters, Mrs.

W. Blair Roberts, of Dallas, South Dakota, and Mrs. Frederick Wiggin, of New Haven, all of whom with Mrs. Jackson survive. He also leaves a brother, Charles E. Jackson and four sisters, Mrs. Giraud and the Misses Selina, Katherine and Margaret Jackson.

Mr. Jackson was for a number of years a vestryman of the Church of the Holy Trinity, of which he had been a faithful member and communicant from his boyhood. He was a trustee of the Berkeley Divinity school. As president of Indian Hill cemetery, he was untiring in the improvement and beautification of that lovely spot. The cemetery will be an enduring monument of his fine taste and good judgment. The work of development of that cemetery was commenced by his father, who was one of his predecessors in the office, the late Dr. Alsop only intervening. Mr. Jackson was a member of the Massachusetts Society of the Cincinnati, representing his great grandfather, General Michael Jackson, of the Continental line.

The funeral will be attended at the Church of the Holy Trinity Tuesday afternoon, at 2:30. Burial will be in Indian Hill cemetery.

GIVES ANCIENT HISTORY OF WITTER HOMESTEAD

Bits of early history of old families in Preston and stories of the old Witter homestead which was recently destroyed by fire, were related Wednesday night by Henry W. Beckwith, of New Haven, connected with Brown, Martin & Co., Inc., investment brokers.

Mr. Beckwith, who is a direct descendant of the Downer and Witter families who located in Preston in the latter part of the sixteenth century told of the history and the Downer and Witter families of which a granddaughter, Miss Mary A. Witter of Norwich is a descendant.

In the interview Mr. Beckwith said: To the best of my recollection Penobscot street got its name from the Penobscot Indians who came down from Maine by canoes sometime between 1785 and 1790 and landed along this coast. A group of them came to a landing just above what is now Preston bridge. According to a story told me by my aunt, Mrs. Juliet D. Ackley, now dead, smallpox broke out among this group of Indians and they were forced to remain here.

At that time my great-grandfather, Dr. Avery Downer, and his father Dr. Joshua Downer, were practicing physicians in Preston City. As the other doctors in Norwich were afraid to associate with the Indians, fearing a spread of smallpox among their patients, Dr. Downer and his father attended them.

It is my belief that Penobscot street got its name from the fact that these Indians had stopped in that vicinity during their illness. Dr. Avery Downer, practiced medicine in Preston City for many years from 1782 until the time of his death about 1854. He was a Revolutionary War veteran and was the next to the last survivor of those who witnessed the scenes following the battle of Fort Griswold.

The other survivor was a man named Gallup who lived in New York state at that time.

Dr. Downer entered the Revolutionary war and studied medicine with his father. He received a license to practice and become surgeon of the 8th Connecticut Regiment. He later married Abagail Mott, daughter of General Mott. General Mott's wife was Abigail Rossiter, daughter of Rev. Mr. Possiter, a graduate of Yale, who was a pastor of the Congregational church at Preston City. General Mott was a military man long before the Revolutionary war and had held the position of a lieutenant under the crown, being stationed at Crown Point and at Ticonderoga.

At the beginning of the Revolutionary war he entered the army and was sent by the government to Ticonderoga to put the fort in repair, he being an engineer. Dr. Downer and General Mott are both buried in the Preston City cemetery. Of these families there remains but one descendant living today in Norwich, Miss Mary A. Witter, granddaughter of Avery Downer, now residing at the Johnson Home. There were other descendants but they went west where they made their homes.

Speaking of the old Witter homestead property at Hallville which recently burned to the ground, he said: Miss Mary A. Witter is the only surviving member of the old Witter family who built the homestead where they lived for years. Miss Witter in her younger days lived in the old homestead and is familiar with many of the stories connected with the Witter family's early history.

The old Witter property on which stood the homestead which burned down a couple of weeks ago, was purchased from the town of Preston in 1692 by Ebenezer Witter, who was deacon and original organizer of the Preston City church. He is buried in the Avery cemetery and the stone marking his grave is well preserved. His wife, Dorothy Morgan Witter, is buried beside him. He died in 1712 and the stone marking his grave is the second oldest in the cemetery.

Ebenezer Witter's wife's family lived in Preston City, going there from Wethersfield, this state. Ebenezer Witter also owned what is now Matthewson's Mill, this being the place where he first settled. The Witter property, at his death, went to his son, Ebenezer, who sold it to his son, Jacob Witter, who owned a tavern in Norwich Town. From Jacob Witter the property went to his nephew, Jonah Witter, in 1785.

Ebenezer, the second, had a son Nathan, who went to Brooklyn, Conn., in 1775 and settled about two miles from the center of the present town of Brooklyn. Nathan's son Jonah later acquired the old Witter homestead, and was the last of the family to live in the original house which stood east of the brick house recently destroyed by fire. In 1800 he built the brick house mentioned. The bricks used for the construction of the house were brought from Providence by boat, landed near what is now Dawley's lumber yard and carted from there to Preston. The corners of the building were faced with brown stone, as were the arches above the doors and windows. This stone was carted 40 miles by ox team from Portland, Conn. The building, when completed, was one of the finest in this section of the country.

260

The hallway ran from the front to the rear of the house. The wainscoting and front stairways were of solid mahogany. The rooms were cozy and there was an open fireplace in each room. The building had a dormer roof and the attic was constructed as a hall where in the old days socials and entertainments, dances, etc., were held.

Jonah Witter lived there until his death and then the property went to his son, Lucas Witter, and at his death to his son, Lucas, and following his death the property went to Miss Mary A. Witter, now living in Norwich. Miss Mary A. Witter's mother was before her marriage Miss Emily Downer, and Miss Witter's father was Lucas Witter.

The Witter homestead was a landmark on the Westerly road for years. It passed from the Witter family about 1902. Much of the furniture which was purchased in New York and Philadelphia is now scattered among the descendants of the family.

Until quite recently the original paper on the attic walls remained, evidently having been removed after the house passed from the Witter family.

It is of interest to note that among the descendants of the Jonah Witter family are Samuel Hart, dean of Berkeley Divinity school, John H. Hewitt, professor at Williams College, and others prominent today in the life of Norwich.

ABOUT BEDS.

Those of the Daddies and Granddaddies Fondly Remembered.

(Hartford Letter to Shore Line Times.)

If Parson Whitfield of Guilford and Parson Hooker of this city could revisit their respective settlements they would doubtless be surprised at the progress toward luxury which has been made since their time. Some of the inventions would be beyond their understanding while others would easily commend themselves, but, assuming the good men were incarnated in the flesh once more, they would discover that beds—couches they are called in poems—have not changed much from their time. Once, between the time of Hooker and the time of Taft, sleeping was a luxury; but we have left that state far behind and are now in the dark ages when invention is seeking for the most adamant brand of bed. To be sure, nobody has got out a stamped-steel mattress but its coming, and a lot of testimonials will be given it by various physicians, as that profession is more busily engaged in rendering life uncomfortable than any other just now. As a matter of fact, Comfort was found in most farmhouse chambers from, say, 1800 to 1870; at about that date the factory-made mattress came in and Comfort went out.

Up to the 70's the construction of a bed was a fine art. It began with the heavy wooden framework pierced with holes through which a rope was run so as to form nice little squares. Upon this was piled a "tick," a great striped bag, the size of the bed, stuffed with rye straw generally, but sometimes with corn husks which sounded a sort of automatic alarm the instant one attempted to climb upon the bed. If the farmerfolk were not careful in the selection of the husks, now and then the end of a corncob would get mixed in—making a hard and unyielding knob which generally proved annoying for a year or until the tick was refilled. But upon this tick was placed another filled with feathers and comfort, a section of Paradise confined in a striped cotton covering. The patrician form of feather bed was the one made of geese feathers stripped from the protesting fowls against their painfully audible protests. The geese were "picked" once a year and they did not like it any more than the farmer's boy liked to have his hair cut, but, like him, they had to take their medicine. When sufficient feathers had been accumulated to fill a tick the bed was completed save for its linen sheets in summer, sometimes woolen ones in winter, and always the gay quilts that grandmother pieced and which are being collected by idle and sinfully rich females from the cities.

Now, when the bed thus made and covered was ready, its prospective occupant climbed on a chair or mounted to the bureau and plunged into it as one might dive into deep water. There was no lying awake and tossing about in an attempt to adapt one's body to the contour of the mattress, or praying Heaven to send daylight and release from misery.

Why did this end? Possibly because the doctors said that sleeping on feathers was unhealthy (horrible fiction that it was) or because the older folk with good judgment died off. The next step was the fatal one of making a mattress and terming it a bed. First off, the old bed-cords went into the discard and a lattice-work of wood was put in and on this was placed a mattress stuffed with excelsior or kindling wood. It was abominable—a torture of the Spanish inquisition—and not a person can be found to say a good word for it now. Those mattresses are still made, but they are chiefly useful at the factory where they are made as increasing the fire hazard there. Various things make work for the fire department but there is nothing that can get it on a keen jump quicker than a fire in one of these factories. From the advent of the mattress the only progress has been in the line of refining the torture, and it is now down to a nice point. The mattresses are stuffed with cotton and indorsed by doctors, stuffed with hair and indorsed by more doctors, and stuffed with the Lord knows what, possibly pig iron, and indorsed by still more doctors. They are braced and cantilevered and reinforced-factory construction and slow-burning and all that—but no human body can dint one enough so that even a micrometer will detect the depression. Of course there is a breed growing up which has never slept in an old-fashioned bed and which therefore supposes that the modern outrage is the proper thing to support a tired man's frame during the hours in which he is supposed to sleep. By and by the West will arrive at the Japanese conception of a bed which consists of a floor covered by matting with a block of wood for a pillow. Of course that may be luxury for a Jap. But in time some sane man or woman will construct an old-fashioned feather bed such as a human being can rest in. And then the world will begin to grow sane again, and will go to bed early because the process means luxury and not torture, rest and not misery, peace and not pain, comfort and not cruelty.

THE DIOCESE OF CONNECTICUT.

The secretary of the Convention of the Protestant Episcopal Church in the Diocese of Connecticut, the Rev. Melville K. Bailey of Branford, has just published the journal of the last convention, which was held at St. John's Church in this city on the 10th and 11th of June last, with the usual appendices containing parochial statistics, reports, etc. We have already given, from advance sheets, the principal items in the statistics of the Hartford parishes. The following figures are gathered from the statistics of the diocese:

The whole number of Episcopal parishes and churches in Connecticut is 145, and there are 29 other chapels and missions, making in all 174 regular congregations. The clergymen are 195—one bishop, 179 presbyters and fifteen deacons, of whom, however, twenty are not resident in the diocese. The whole number of families reported by 156 parishes and missions is 17,717; the whole number of communicants registered is 24,887, of whom 1,370 had been admitted during the year, showing an increase of 6 per cent. in the number of communicants, although confirmations were held during the year in but eighty-three places. Baptisms during the year are reported in 138 parishes and missions to the number of 2,344 —nearly one to every ten communicants— 1,838 being baptisms of infants and 506 of adults. There were 630 marriages and 1,624 burials during the year. The number of teachers in Sunday schools is reported as 1,953. The number of scholars is 16,596.

Coming to items of income and contributions, we find that nearly $275,000 was expended for parochial support during the year, an average of about $1,785 for each parish and mission reporting; about $25,000 of this sum was income from property, the rest being pew rents and offerings. The offerings for all purposes within the parishes were a little over $422,000, and those for objects without the parishes were $54,000, making the total amount of contributions about $476,000, or nearly $20 for each communicant. Adding the amount of income from property, the grand total of income and contributions for the year is nearly $501,500.

A study of the statistics of the parishes of the Episcopal church in Connecticut in connection with the published figures of population as determined by the census of 1890 is full of interest, especially when the figures of this year are compared with those of 1880. The diocese is divided into six archdeaconries, following county lines, Tolland county being joined with Hartford and Windham county with New London. In the six counties outside of the New London archdeaconries— that is to say, in the first, second and fourth congressional districts—there are but three towns having at present a population of 2,000 in which there is not a parish of the Episcopal Church: Berlin, Southington and Haddam. In the last two, however, there are organized missions; so that Berlin is the only town of 2,000 inhabitants outside of the New London archdeaconry in which there are not regular services. In Fairfield county, there is no town of 1,000 inhabitants without

a parish. In New Haven county, Madison is the only town of 1,000 inhabitants without a parish, and there services are held regularly in connection with the parish in Clinton. In the New London archdeaconry there are seven towns of 2,000 inhabitants in which there is no Episcopal church; but in some cases, as for instance, Waterford, there are churches near by in adjoining towns.

The statement was made not long since that the decrease of population in the hill towns of Connecticut was seriously weakening the Episcopal church in certain regions of the state. But the official figures show that, unless it be in a few special instances, this is not the case. Litchfield is the typical hill county of the state; and of its twenty-six towns, nineteen have fewer inhabitants now than they had in 1880. In twelve of these nineteen towns there are parishes; and but four of these report fewer communicants than they had ten years ago. On the other hand, some towns which have suffered great loss in population, have increased very largely in the number of communicants. Litchfield has lost nine per cent. from its population, but the number of communicants in its four parishes has increased 25 per cent., and there is now one communicant for every nine inhabitants. Salisbury has lost 462 from its 3,715 inhabitants, but has added 70 to its 125 communicants. Taking the whole county, there has been in ten years a gain of less than two per cent. in the population and a gain of over twenty-three per cent. in the number of communicants in the Episcopal parishes. The strongest parish in the county is at Watertown, where out of 2,324 inhabitants, 322, or one in seven, are reckoned as communicants in Christ Church.

Coming to a different part of the state, we find that in Hartford County the population has increased in the past ten years by about one-seventh; the number of communicants in the Episcopal parishes has increased from 3,243 to 4,490, or more than one-half. In this city the increase has been from 1,465 to 2,120, or in about the same ratio as in the rest of the county. By far the largest increase reported is in the town of Manchester, where for the 54 communicants of 1880 there are now 310, the population meanwhile having increased a little over twenty-seven per cent. In New Britain the population has increased by 36 per cent.; but the number of communicants has increased from 180 to 321, or by 78 per cent. On the other hand, the town of East Windsor has lost 136 from its 3,019 inhabitants of ten years ago; but the two parishes of Broad Brook and Warehouse Point report 185 communicants where there was 150 in 1880; in Windsor, though the town has lost 103 inhabitants, Grace Church has gained 16 communicants; and in Newington, where the population has decreased by over forty per cent., the number of communicants has increased by over fifty per cent. In the whole of Hartford county the ratio of communicants to the population is about as one to 32; ten years ago it was about as one to 39.

While the counties east of Hartford show less strength than this in the Episcopal church, those to the west and the south show greater strength. Thus the ratio of communicants to the population in Litchfield county is one to 19; in Fairfield county one

to 23; and in Middlesex county, one to 26. The corresponding ratio for the whole state is about one to 30, if we may assume that the complete returns will give us a population of 740,000. With this same assumption, we find that the population of the state has increased nearly 16 per cent. in ten years; and in the same time the increase in the number of communicants in the diocese has been from 20,249 to 24,887, or nearly 23 per cent. At present, the Episcopal Church appears to be stronger in Brookfield than in any other town of the state; for there, the population being exactly 1,000, St. Paul's Church reports 220 communicants.

Using the latest available figures of the state board of registration, it would appear that the Episcopal clergy of Connecticut baptize each year a number of infants equal to ten per cent. of those born in the state, solemnize twelve per cent. of the marriages, and officiate at twelve per cent. of the burials.

The Bi-Centenary of the S.P.G. and 175th Anniversary of Trinity Church, Southport, Conn.

[101]

Old Trinity church, in the town of Fairfield, has now an event in retrospect that its members will ever take pleasure in recalling. Thursday, Nov. 22, dawned propitiously, and the result was that the commemoration services were largely attended by clergy and laity, not only from the immediate vicinity, but from all over the state. At eight o'clock there was a celebration of the Holy Communion, the Bishop of Delaware officiating. The chief service of the day was at 10:30. The sermon was preached by the Rt. Rev. Bishop of Albany, from Jer. vi. 16: "Thus saith the Lord, stand ye in the ways, and see, and ask for the old paths, wherein is the good way, and walk therein, and ye shall find rest for your souls."

The preacher dwelt upon the stability and excellence of the old paths, showing wherein they are the only "good way," and dwelt at length upon the faithful adherence to them that characterized the long record of Trinity parish. The bishop of the diocese then celebrated the Holy Communion, being assisted by Bishops Coleman, and W. A. Leonard. The offertory was devoted to the Venerable Society for the Propagation of the Gospel as a thank-offering. At one o'clock an ample repast was served in the parish house to the clergy and guests by the women of the parish.

The afternoon service, at three o'clock, was even more largely attended than the morning. It was conducted by Archdeacon Louis N. Booth, of Fairfield county, who represented the bishop of the diocese. The first address was made by Bishop Coleman, and was upon the work of the Venerable Society in the world. He said:

"The first charter for the propagation of the Gospel was granted by Queen Elizabeth to Sir Humphrey Gilbert, in 1583, who was given permission to plant the Christian religion in 'all places convenient.' The same permission was granted in the charter given to the Venerable Society for the Propagation of the Gospel in Foreign Parts in 1701. The charter gave permission to plant the Gospel in all places convenient, but the meaning of the word was enlarged considerably, and the Gospel was planted in many places peculiarly inconvenient."

than 20 separate and distinct races among the pupils of that school, all under systematic instruction. That will show you that the term world-wide or catholic is deservedly applied to the Society, whose bi-centenary we are commemorating."

The second address brought the work of the Venerable Society nearer home, for the subject of that was the work of the Society in the American colonies. It had been assigned to Bishop Leonard, who prefaced his remarks with a few words of interest. He said that he was a son of Trinity parish. He had been born in the borough, had been baptized in old Trinity, called "The Church on the Hill," which edifice preceded the present structure, had been brought up in the Sunday-school of the present church, was related for over a century to some warden or vestryman of the church, and now came back as a son to a mother, to lay his service of gratitude at her feet.

He said that a desultory and slow missionary work had gone on for a century and a half before the Venerable Society was organized under letters patent. After the Society had been chartered it was taken in hand by Sir Richard Bulkley, an ancestor of not a few then in the congregation of Trinity, and with three other colleagues the work was undertaken and carried on successfully. He gave an outline of the scope and limits of the work, and gave a few figures to show how well it was carried on. In 1741, less than forty years after the Society had been chartered, he said, there had been built under its direction nearly 100 churches, thousands of Bibles and Books of Common Prayer had been given away, and 70 persons were constantly employed by the Society, which was

"Two missionaries, Keith and Talbot, were sent out soon after the Society was chartered, to what is now the United States of America, and that was the principal field first taken up. In 1703 the work was extended into Newfoundland, in 1712 to the Windward Islands." The speaker then gave a list of the various places where the work of the Society had been taken up throughout the world, chronologically arranged from the time of the granting of its charter to the present day.

In concluding his address, the bishop said: "Since the charter was first granted $32,500,000 have been expended in the carrying on of the work, and the annual income of the Society is now about $850,000. Wonderful progress has been made in the work all over the world, but especially is India to be noted. In Burmah there is a school containing not less than 700 pupils, and there are no less

practically the first missionary Society of the mother Church.

The difficulties which were encountered by the early missionaries, their struggles with the Indians and negroes, and with the early whites, many of whom had sunken to a moral plane nearly as low as that of their wild neighbors, were vividly sketched by the speaker, who gave also a brief outline of the particular work which the Society had done in each state where its assistance had been asked. The Venerable Society was aiding 77 missions along the Atlantic coast at the time when, through the termination of the Revolutionary War, it felt bound to withdraw its aid.

The address which perhaps brought the work of the Venerable Society home with more directness to the auditors was the third, that delivered by the Rev. Dr. Hart, of Middletown, who spoke on the debt of Connecti-

cut to the Venerable Society. He said in substance:

"The debt of Connecticut to the Venerable Society may best be shown by a rapid survey of the early Church history of the colony. It began in one sense with the visit of the Society's first missionaries, Keith and Talbot, to New London on a Sunday in 1702, when they were courteously received by the minister, Mr. Saltonstall, afterward Governor, and preached in his meeting-house. In 1706, the Rev. Mr. Muirson, with Colonel Caleb Heathcote "fully armed," rode from Rye, through Fairfield to Stratford, and in the next year an organization was effected in the latter place, including some Fairfield or Southport people; but they had no settled minister until 1722. That was the memorable year in which seven of the leading young ministers of the Congregational order, including the rector and the tutor of Yale College, declared their doubtfulness of the validity of Presbyterian orders; and four of them determined to sail for England, when they applied to the Archbishop of Canterbury for ordination and to the Society for the Propagation of the Gospel for encouragement and material help in their work. From their action began the peculiar history of the Church in Connecticut, with its clergy almost entirely of its own sons, men of high character and good learning, who crossed the sea to seek authority to minister in holy things and returned to labor among their own people. In fifty-two years forty-three Connecticut men, all college graduates, went abroad for ordination: two lost their lives before arriving in England, and four others before they could reach home; seven returned to work elsewhere, and the other thirty devoted themselves to work here, forming nearly the whole body of clergymen in the colony. The Venerable Society did not seek for places in which to establish parishes, nor did it furnish men for the places where men were needed; but it gave the aid of its modest stipends of not more than £60 sterling each, it supplied books, and above all it gave encouragement and counsel. And thus arose the type of sober and strong Churchmanship, a result of which was seen in the fact that at the end of a half century one-fourteenth part of the inhabitants of the colony were attached to the Church of England. It met with opposition, of course; but it was always respected; and largely in consequence of action taken by the Fairfield Churchmen it received really generous treatment from the civil authority. The labors of those clergymen whose names are on the roll of the Venerable Society were untiring and unselfish, they established parishes which soon became, and are to-day centres of Church work and progress; they met the needs of earnest and sober-minded people; they gave a tone to the Church in this land, as by their action at the close of the Revolution they maintained for it the ministry and the faith; the consideration of that which they did tells us of our debt to the Venerable Society—a debt the more blessed and the more gratefully acknowledged as it is one which can never be repaid in kind."

[102]

THE CENSUS AND THE GROWTH OF THE CHURCH.

The publication of the statistics of the population of Connecticut as determined by the census of this year 1900 gives occasion for a comparison of the numerical growth of the Church with that of the State. And as the data are at hand which were derived from a similar comparison ten years ago, the results may be perhaps more interesting, if not more valuable.

Two things should be remembered: First, that the increase of the population of Connecticut during the past ten years has been in considerable part from the immigration of persons who would not naturally fall under the immediate influence of our Church; and, secondly, that whereas in 1890 the parishes reported the whole number of communicants registered, in 1900 they reported the number of actual communicants or those still under the care of the rectors or ministers; and this change, causing in the last year an apparent loss of more than 1,500 communicants, will keep our comparison from being overmuch to the Church's advantage.

To begin with, let us take the figures for the whole state and diocese. In the decade from 1880 to 1890, the population of the state increased from 622,700 to 746,258, or nearly 20 per cent.; the number of communicants in the diocese increased from 20,249 to 24,887, or nearly 23 per cent.; and in 1890 there was almost exactly one communicant for every 30 inhabitants. In 1900, the population of the state is 908,355, having increased 21.7 per cent. in ten years; the number of communicants in the diocese is 30,868, showing an increase of more than 24 per cent. in the decade; and the ratio of communicants to population is nearer 1 to 29 than 1 to 30. This shows a steady and uniform growth in the Church, giving an increase of over 50 per cent. in twenty years.

The greatest strength of the Church is still in those counties which lie wholly or partially to the west of the Connecticut River. In Fairfield county, one person in every 21 is a communicant; in Litchfield county two persons in every 41; in New Haven county, one in 27; in Hartford county, not quite one in 33; in Middlesex county, as in Fairfield, one in 21. Ten years ago, there were two towns of 2,000 inhabitants in these five counties in which there was not a Church parish or regularly constituted mission—Berlin and Southington. Now these are both occupied; and Cromwell is the only town of 2,000 inhabitants within these counties—or, for that matter, in the first, second, and third Congressional districts—which has not regular services. Every other town of 1,000 inhabitants in the five counties is occupied, except Cornwall in Litchfield county, Madison in New Haven county, and Avon, Burlington, Granby, Rocky Hill and South Windsor in Hartford county; but of these, Burlington and Avon are supplied by Collinsville parish and Granby by Tariffville parish, the church in each case being near the border-line of towns. Every town in Fairfield county has a parish, except two of fewer than 700 inhabitants each. Across the river, there are three towns in New London county and three in Windham county, having over 2,000 inhabitants each, in which we have no parish or mission.

Ten years ago, a good deal was said as to the decay of the hill towns and the weakening of the Church in them. A study of the statistics of Litchfield county, the typical hill-country of Connecticut, showed that, for the most part, even where there was a decrease of population there was a gain in the number of communicants. In 1890, of the twenty-six towns in this county, nineteen had fewer inhabitants than they had in 1880; in twelve of these there were parishes; and but four of these had fewer communicants than they had ten years before. The past ten years, from 1890 to 1900, show a decrease of population in but 10 towns of the county, four of which are occupied by the Church; and in three of these the number of communicants has increased. The largest town in the county is Torrington, which has more than doubled its population in ten years; here the number of communicants has increased more than 150 per cent. In Winchester, another manufacturing town, the population has increased about 24 per cent., but the communicant roll has increased more than 100 per cent.; while in Salisbury, an agricultural town, where the population has gained but 2 per cent., the number of communicants has doubled. In these two cases it may well be noted, the rectors have been in charge of their cures for twenty and seventeen years respectively.

In Fairfield county, there are some notable instances of growth. Brookfield, the banner town of the diocese, which ten years ago reported 220 of its 989 inhabitants as communicants, now reports 241 out of 1,046, or almost one in four; and a glance at the map will show that few of these can be living without the town limits. Newtown, Trumbull, and Westport have more than one-tenth of the population enrolled as communicants; and in the last named town, where the population has increased by about 8 per cent., there are nearly 38 per cent. more communicants than there were ten years ago. Bethel has lost about 2 per cent. in population, and gained 20 per cent. in communicants; Stamford has added 20 per cent. to the number of its inhabitants, and over one-third to the number of its communicants. And in Bridgeport, in which the number of inhabitants has increased from 49,000 to 71,000, the number of communicants has increased from 1,900 to 2,300.

In New Haven, where the growth of the population has been from 81,000 to 109,000, and this largely, as in Bridgeport, from immigration, the Church has nearly 4,000 communicants where ten years ago she had 3,200, a gain of 25 per cent. Meriden has increased the communicant roll from 673 to 1,122, while her population has advanced from 25,400 to 28,700—67 per cent. against 13. In Branford, the Church's per cent. of increase has been 39, that of the town 28; in Naugatuck, the percentages are 45 and 60. North Haven, which ten years ago had about one communicant in every 12 persons, has now, with a population increased by 300, one in every 9 persons. And the little town of Bethany has 82 communicants in a population of 517.

In Middlesex county, Middletown has grown by 15 per cent. in population, and the two parishes have added 45 per cent. to their communicant rolls; Portland has lost 830 inhabitants and gained 40 communicants; in old Saybrook the population has decreased by 4 per cent. and the number of communicants has increased by over 19 per cent.

There are encouraging figures from the statistics of the part of the diocese on the east of the river. New London county has in ten years gained less than 8 per cent. in population; but the Church has gained nearly 21 per cent. in the number of communicants; and in Tolland county, where the population has diminished in every town but three, our three parishes, all in declining towns, have gained about one-sixth in the number of communicants.

These are some of the numerical proofs of the growth of the Church in Connecticut. Some examples of decline might be adduced; but none would set aside the general impression made by the study of the statistics for towns as different in location and in the occupation of the inhabitants as are those which have been named. *** A comparison of data in the Journal of 1889 with those given by the State Board of Health for the same year shows that the Church clergymen of Connecticut solemnize nearly 12 per cent. of the marriages in the State, officiate at nearly 13 per cent. of the burials, and baptize each year a number of infants amounting to about 8 per cent. of the children born in the year. ***

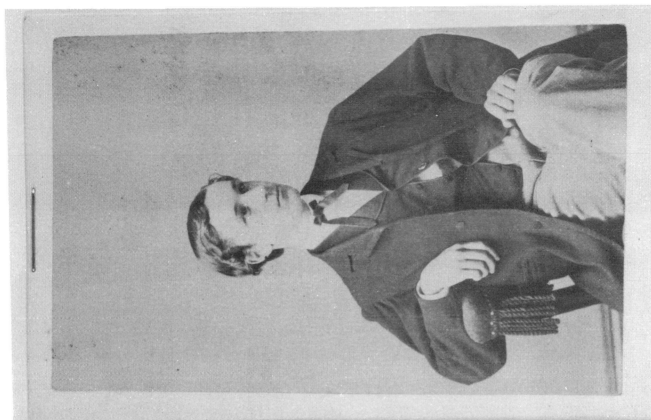

R. J. GEMMILL, PHOTOGRAPHER,
Opposite the Post Office, Hartford, Conn.

Samuel Hart

266

NOTES

[1] The first draft was written on the backs of Trinity College circulars of 1894. The second or fair draft, which I use herein, must have been made <u>ca</u>. 1899, shortly after Hart joined the faculty of the Berkeley Divinity School. (In the revision he says he hopes to know Middletown better than he does at the time he delivers his address.

[2] This paper seems to have been intended for the Connecticut Historical Society in or about 1900, when Hart became its president.

[3] Delivered in December, 1890, the date being inferred from the letter to Hart from Dr. Eben Edwards Beardsley (Dec. 16, 1890), edited at the end of this address. (The letter was found with the MS.)

[4] I date the MS. about 1904 because its last pages are inscribed on Berkeley Divinity School flyers announcing the 50th Annual Ordination on June 7, 1904.

[5] It seems to have been delivered before some board of education. Internal evidence points to 1896 as the date of the original composition. Excisions indicate that it was delivered a second time a few years later.

[6] Delivered at Baltimore on Jan. 13, 1907; then at the Long Island Church Club on Jan. 23, 1911; finally at Stafford Springs, March 17, 1911.

[7] From a newspaper clipping. The emended manuscript and a typescript survive along with the later material on Samuel Peters.

[8] I have omitted the beginning and ending of the surviving corrected typescript because they are homiletical rather than historical.

[9] From a typescript, at the end of which are genealogical charts of the early episcopal succession in America. Laid in (and reprinted herewith) is a letter to Hart from Warren R. Dix.

[10] The three parts are taken from <u>In Memoriam. Samuel Colt and Caldwell Hart Colt</u>.... Illustrated by Clifton Johnson. [Springfield, Mass.], 1898. (It contains an excellent pictorial description of both the Church of the Good Shepherd and its memorial parish house. The following historical sketch was prepared by the present compiler for the rededication of the church on March 21, 1976:)

RECTORS:
Henry Wells Nelson, D.D., 1866-1876; John Henry Watson, 1877-1893; Cornelius Gardner Bristol, 1893-1901; George Thomas Linsley, D.D., 1901-1932; Cramer Clark Cabaniss, 1932-1955; Kenneth Walter Cameron, <u>Locum Tenens</u>, 1955-1956; Joseph Ash Johnson, 1956-1963; William Nelson Penfield, 1964-1965; Richard Cockrell, 1966-1971; Edward Blaine Gever, Jr., 1972-- ASSISTANTS:
Corwin Carlyle Roach, 1929-1930; Cramer Clark Cabaniss, 1930-1932; William Conrad Hamm, 1932-1937; George James Karney, 1959-1963; William Nicholas Persing, 1963-1972; Sherrill Scales, Jr., 1973-1975.

This parish originated during the Civil War (1859-1864) as a union Sunday School, which met one day a week in the Charter Oak Hall Building at the bottom of Colt's Meadow—the rent for which was paid by a patriotic civic organization known as the "Sons of Temperance." For some reason, the project was offered to St. John's Episcopal Church (then of Hartford but now in West Hartford), possibly because it was currently engaged in several missionary enterprises--one of them in East Hartford--and possibly because it was the only parish in the vicinity that had an assistant (the Rev. Henry Wells Nelson) who could be spared for part-time work in the meadows. One suspects, of course, that Mrs. Elizabeth (Hart) Colt, widow of Colonel Samuel Colt (who had died on January 10, 1862) had something to do with the change of auspices and with a plan for eventually creating an Anglican parish on her estate.

With an initial budget of $300 a year, Fr. Nelson rearranged the room at Charter Oak Hall, setting up a temporary altar and beginning services for adults on May 22, 1864—two months after Ulysses S. Grant had become Commander-in-Chief of the Union Armies. Colt weapons, meanwhile, were helping to bring the War to a conclusion.) A year later, the Rector of St. John's (the Rev. William Croswell Doane, later Bishop of Albany) reported to the Diocesan Convention that what had been a miscellaneous group of non-denominational children had now become instructed Episcopalians--thirty-eight having been baptized and ten confirmed within the first twelve months of Fr. Nelson's "special work." The parish was officially organized on July 18, 1866, as the Church of the Good Shepherd, but the architect's plans for a building indicated that Mrs. Colt had first considered calling it the "Church of the Holy Innocents." A few months later its foundations were laid, and, on September 4, 1867, the cornerstone was placed with special ceremonies. Fr. Nelson, meanwhile, had assumed the title of Rector on August 27, 1866, thereafter giving full time to the work until September 11, 1876, when he accepted a post in the Diocese of Western New York under Bishop Arthur Cleveland Coxe, once Rector of St. John's, Hartford.

The parish experienced its first catastrophe in the great flood which swept over the meadows in the spring of 1936, requiring extensive redecoration and replacement of damaged furniture and fabrics. Being on higher ground, the Caldwell Hart Colt Parish House, which had formally opened on September 10, 1896, was temporarily used for services. The second catastrophe (apart from some intervening floods) was the gradual subsiding of the meadows under the heavy weight of stone, imperiling the tower and threatening permanent ruin to the whole structure. After the last service had been held in the church on January 1, 1974, the Parish House once again became the meeting place of the faithful. During the following twenty-seven months, thanks

to modern engineering skill, the foundation was strengthened, and the church building was made ready for another phase of its history, which was introduced by a Service of Thanksgiving and Rededication on the first day of spring, March 21, 1976.

[11] From a MS. sermon entitled "The Seed Growing Secretly. Sesquicentenary of Horseneck Chapel" and bearing the number 317. A typescript, probably intended for the press, survives in the Connecticut Historical Society.

[12] From an undated typescript in the Diocesan Archives. I assume it was written in 1897, when Andrews died.

[13] Apparently intended for a dictionary or encyclopedia ca. 1900, for which year Hart gives the population or census.

[14] At the close of the Civil War, Dr. Eben Edwards Beardsley, Registrar of the Diocese of Connecticut, sent a questionnaire to all Episcopal parishes and missions, seeking information in preparation for his projected History. The parish in Old Saybrook asked young Samuel Hart, just graduating from Trinity College, Hartford, to complete it. Hart himself later became Registrar.

[15] From Diocese of Connecticut: The Jarvis Centenary...27 October 1897 and the Consecration of the Bishop Coadjutor Elect ...28 October 1897, Trinity Church, New Haven. [New Haven, 1897], pp. 56-72. Hart was responsible for only Part II, or the last half, of the "Century of Church Life." His address was reported in full in the Hartford Daily Courant, Oct. 28, 1897, p. 12.

[16] Hartford (Case, Lockwood & Brainard), 1881. Only the Hart pieces in this anonymous volume are reproduced here: pp. 33-34, 51-53, 55-60, 79-81, 85-87.

[17] I have abridged the "Historical Sketch" and "Notes" because of their great length. Scholars will wish to handle the volume itself for the complete annotations, which occupy pages 27-72.

[18] The Election of Bishop Seabury: A Sermon Preached in Christ Church, Hartford ...April 1, 1883. Hartford (Case, Lockwood & Brainard), 1883.

[19] The Consecration of Bishop Seabury: A Sermon Preached in Grace Church, Saybrook, on...Nov. 16, 1884, and in St. James's Church, New London, on the following Sunday. Hartford (Case, Lockwood & Brainard), 1884.

[20] The Episcopate of Bishop Seabury: A Sermon Preached in Christ Church, Middle Haddam, on...August 2, 1885, and in Trinity Church, Branford, on the following Sunday. Hartford (Case, Lockwood & Brainard), 1885.

[21] From Saybrook's Quadrimillennial: Commemoration of the 250th Anniversary of the Settlement of Saybrook, Nov. 27, 1885. Hartford, 1886, pp. 8-20. Offprints were circulated with the pages numbered 1-13.

[22] Bishop Seabury's Communion Office: An Historical Sermon Preached in Grace Church, Newington, on...September 26, 1886. Hartford (Case, Lockwood & Brainard), 1886.

[23] A part of the "Round Robin Series" issued by the Junior Auxiliary Publishing Co., Hartford, Conn., Dec., 1897. It was Publication no. 26.

[24] A Humble Master: A Sermon in Memory of the Rt. Rev. John Williams...Preached in...Middletown...19 February 1899. Middletown (Felton & King), 1899. Front cover: In Memory of Bishop Williams.

[25] Trinity College Bulletin, II, nos. 1-2 (1901-1903). A MS. and a typescript survive in the Diocesan Archives along with newspaper reports, one from the Hartford Courant of Nov. 14, 1901. The address was delivered on either Nov. 11 or Nov. 12, 1901.

[26] Pages 17-21 of Lucy Cushing Jarvis, ed., Sketches of Church Life in Colonial Connecticut. New Haven (Tuttle, Morehouse, & Taylor), 1902. The Diocesan Archives owns (in thick outline form) Hart's "The Debt of Connecticut to the Venerable Society," first delivered (apparently from outline) on Nov. 21, 1900, but not included here. For another published sketch on the work of the S.P.G. in Connecticut, see Hart's paper drawn from the outline, see pages 261-262 of the present volume.

[27] An Address Commemorative of John Brocklesby, LL.D., Late Professor Emeritus in Trinity College. By Appointment of the Association of the Alumni. Hartford (Case, Lockwood & Brainard), 1889.

[28] In New Haven Colony Historical Society Transactions, VII (1907), pp. 120-128. It was "Read January 27, 1902."

[29] Connecticut Public Library Document, no. 5-1904, whole no. 47.

[30] Historical Papers Relating to the Henry Whitfield House, Guilford, Conn. (Reprinted by Vote of the Trustees.) n.p., n.d., pp. 27-31. Hart's address appears in a section entitled: "Papers Read at the Formal Opening of the State Historical Museum in the Henry Whitfield House, Sept. 21, 1904." The address seems to have appeared earlier in a State publication on pages 10-14.

[31] From Norris Galpin Osborn, ed., Men of Mark in Connecticut. Ideals of American Life Told in Biographies and Autobiographies. Introd. chapter by Samuel Hart. (5 vols.) Hartford, 1906-1910, vol. I (1906), pp. 9-17.

[32] Pp. 17-22 of Gurdon Wadsworth Russell's An Account of Some of the Descendants of John Russell The Emigrant from Ipswich, England, who came to Boston, New England, Oct. 3, 1635...with some Sketches of the Allied Families of Wadsworth, Tuttle, and Beresford. Ed. Edwin Stanley Welles. Hartford, 1910.

[33] From a small booklet issued by the parish. Hart's MS. survives in the Diocesan Archives as well as the text issued in the Hartford Times of Nov. 6, 1910. I have omitted the first two paragraphs, which are homiletical. The sermon text was Ezra 5:16.

[34] Published both as a separate leaflet and in the Trinity Parish Record, VII, no. 6 (May, 1912), pp. 6-7.

[35] First delivered before the Middlesex County Historical Society of Middletown,

268

Conn., May 22, 1912, and reported in The Penny Press. It was probably read before the New Haven Colony Historical Society, for it appeared in its Papers, VIII (1914), pp. 238-254, which are here reproduced.

[36] In The Phi Beta Kappa Key, II, no. 3 (March, 1914), pp. 111-115. On pp. 101-102 of this same issue is a biographical sketch headed: "Dr. Samuel Hart, Trinity '66."

[37] New-England Historical and Genealogical Register, LXX, no. 1 (Jan., 1916), pp. 51-55.

[38] In Dr. Samuel Johnson and the Beginnings of the Church in Connecticut: An Address...and a Sermon. n.p., [1907].

[39] Report of the Celebration of the Centennial of the Incorporation of the Town of Marlborough, Aug. 23d and 25th 1903. Compiled by Mary Hall. Hartford (Case, Lockwood & Brainard), 1904, pp. 68-70.

[40] This text of "General Robert Sedgwick" appears in the Society of Colonial Wars in Connecticut: Proceedings, II (1909), no. 10, pp. 161-184. The Diocese of Connecticut owns a MS. and a typescript; the Connecticut Historical Society has a 60-page MS.

[41] From newspaper clippings, on one of which is penciled the date, Jan. 11, 1906. Dr. Parker was pastor in Hartford for sixty years.

[42] Mrs. Elizabeth Hart Colt, a booklet reprinted from the Parish of the Good Shepherd, published in Hartford, late fall, 1905. Hart's "Memorial Sermon" (which I have excerpted here) appears on pp. 12-22; his obituary notice, published in The Churchman of Sept. 2, 1905, appears on pp. 23-25 of the booklet.

[43] This biographical sketch is a kind of preface (pp. 3-7) to In Memoriam. Poems by the late Rev. Robert Clarkson Tongue, ed. Minnie Wyatt Tongue. [Meriden, Conn.: Journal Pub. Co., ca. 1905]. Tongue had died on Dec. 15, 1904.

[44] The Connecticut Magazine, VII, no. 1 (March-April, 1901), pp. 264-272.

[45] Bishop Seabury and Connecticut Churchmanship: A Sermon Preached before the Convention of the Diocese of Connecticut in St. John's Church, Hartford, June 9th 1896. New Haven (Ptd. for the Convention), 1896. I have omitted section one, which is entirely homiletical. The text was John 4:34-38.

[46] From the New England Magazine, o.s. IV, no. 3, or n.s. I, no. 5 (May, 1886), pp. 393-408. It was reprinted in J. Hammond Trumbull, The Memorial History of Hartford County, Connecticut, 1633-1884. (2 vols.), Boston, 1886, I, pp. 435-444.

[47] Taken from the Watertown News, Nov. 1, 1915, pp. 3, 5, 7-8. Hart delivered his sermon on Oct. 17, 1915. His original MS. is in the Diocesan Archives. I have here omitted the beginning, which is entirely homiletical, an exposition of text: Psalm 48:12-13.

[48] This and the following article, "The Bishop's Fund," are reprinted from the Connecticut Churchman, IX, nos. 1-2 (Oct.-Nov., 1914); they were also printed as a separate.

[49] This review probably appeared in a Hartford newspaper in 1885, after the publication of Edwin Emerson Johnson's Life After Death and Other Sermons, Hartford (Brown & Gross), 1885. A second edition appeared in 1886.

[50] A clipping probably from a Hartford paper. Hart has cancelled the sixth line and inserted it below where it makes sense.

[51] This clipping, probably from a Hartford paper, I date ca. 1886. Prof. Johnson died at Hartford on April 30, 1883.

[52] From the Hartford Courant, Sat., Sept. 1, 1888, p. 4.

[53] From The Churchman, Aug. 11, 1894, pp. 153-154. I add (from a later issue of The Churchman) James Gammack's addenda to Hart's observations. Franklin Bowditch Dexter delivered his address "On Some Social Distinctions at Harvard and Yale Before the Revolution" at the annual meeting of the American Antiquarian Society on Oct. 21, 1893. It was published in the Proceedings of that organization and then reprinted separately at Worcester, Mass., Press of Charles Hamilton, 1894.

[54] The Churchman, Dec. 29, 1894.

[55] Hartford Daily Courant, Aug. 16, 1895, p. 4. Hart's address was delivered on August 15.

[56] Hartford Daily Courant, Nov. 2, 1895, which contains a picture of the memorial tablet not reproduced here. The service was held on Nov. 1, All Saints' Day.

[57] The Churchman, Feb. 15, 1896, pp. 205-206.

[58] The first clipping, from the Hartford Daily Times of Feb. 14, 1896, is apparently a reprint of an article that originally appeared in the New York Herald. The second was written by Hart at Hartford on Feb. 15 [1896], it seems as a response to the first at the invitation of the Hartford Times. The third is an article by Melville Knox Bailey, reprinted from the Deep River New Era, Nov. 13 and 27, 1942.

[59] Hart's long article is here preceded by the editorial of the same date: Hartford Daily Courant, July 22, 1896.

[60] The Churchman, Nov. 13, 1897.

[61] From an unidentified newspaper clipping, which I date ca. 1900.

[62] Hartford Daily Courant, Oct. 20, 1900, p. 8. Hart's memorial sketch probably begins at the bar following the first paragraph.

[63] Hartford Daily Courant [or Times], June 22, 1904.

[64] An unidentified clipping, probably from the Hartford Daily Courant, ca. July 12, 1904. Bp. Huntington had died on July 11.

[65] Hartford Daily Courant [or Times], Oct. 7, 1904. Pynchon died in New Haven on Oct. 6, aged 81 years, 8 months and 17 days. Hart's memoir begins after the bar following the first two paragraphs.

[66] Hart's original MS. in the Diocesan Archives is dated Aug. 5, 1905. The reproduced clipping is from an unidentified news-

paper, published probably in Newtown. (Two additional clippings, not by Hart but probably appearing in the same issue, are included here.)

[67] The Hartford Department of Parks reports that the date of the unveiling was April 26, 1906. The clipping reproduced herewith must derive from a Hartford paper of Friday, April 27, 1906, or thereabouts.

[68] According to Appletons' Cyclopaedia, Andrews was a clergyman born in Danbury, Conn., July 21, 1817. He was graduated at Williams College in 1839 and became a lawyer. Subsequently ordained into the ministry of the Congregational Church, he later became a tutor at Trinity College, Hartford. Finally, he adopted the Irvingite doctrines and became, in 1868, a pastor of the Catholic Apostolic Church in Hartford, dying in 1906. The clipping reproduced herewith probably appeared in October of that year.

[69] The Diocesan Archives owns the original MS. and a corrected typescript. The address was delivered in the Congregational Church, on Palisado Green, Windsor, Conn., Nov. 26, 1907, under the auspices of the Connecticut Daughters of the American Revolution. Ellsworth was Chief Justice of the Supreme Court under President George Washington. The title of Hart's address in the program was "Oliver Ellsworth, the Christian Citizen."

[70] The celebration was on May 7, 1908. The clipping reprinted here may have appeared in a Hartford paper of that date.

[71] Hartford Times, June [?5], 1908. Hart's address was delivered on the fifth. A similar report appears in the Hartford Daily Courant of June [?6], 1908, p. 16.

[72] The following editorial on "The Saybrook Platform" was published in a Hartford paper (according to Hart's penciled note) on Sept. 9, 1908. Because it announced the forthcoming bicentennial at Old Saybrook (in which Hart was to participate along with the Rev. Dr. Llewellyn Pratt, of Norwich) on Sept. 29, 1908, and because Hart carefully preserved clippings of that celebration, I include here everything he thought worthy of preservation.

[73] Hartford Daily Times, Oct. 30, 1909.

[74] Ca. 1910. From a Hartford newspaper clipping, pp. 11-12.

[75] Hartford Daily Times, [?May], 1910. From an old clipping.

[76] Delivered May 15, 1911. From the Norwalk Hour, May 16, 1911, pp. 7 and 12.

[77] Delivered Oct. 15, 1911. From the Waterbury American, Oct. 17, 1911, p. 5.

[78] Delivered Oct. 13, 1911. Clipping taken from the Bristol Press, Oct. 16, 1911.

[79] Delivered Jan. 6, 1912. Text is taken from a newspaper clipping of Jan. 7 or 8, page 10. See also a text in Parish of the Good Shepherd, XVIII, no. 2 (Jan., 1912), pp. 1 and 4.

[80] Delivered June 1, 1912. From the Danbury Evening News, June 1, 1912, pp. 4-5. I have appended other historical materials from the long article, which began on p. 3. For another account, see the Hartford Daily Times of the same date.

[81] From a [?Middletown] newspaper, Thursday morning, Jan. [?], 1913. An undated typescript survives in the Diocesan Archives.

[82] I give first Hart's complete address (delivered May 27, 1913), found in the Hartford Courant of ca. May 28, on p. 22. Following it is the preliminary announcement of the celebration at Saybrook Point from the same newspaper, May 27.

[83] Hart sent the biographical portion of the following clipping to the Hartford Courant ca. Dec. 23, 1913.

[84] Clipping from the Hartford Courant ca. April 2, 1914.

[85] From the Hartford Daily Times, June 23, 1915.

[86] Delivered March 19, 1916. From the Hartford Daily Courant, March 20, 1916.

[87] Delivered Sept. 23, 1904. My text is from Hart's corrected typescript now in the Diocesan Archives--a presentation copy to the D. A. R. of Bristol, inscribed to that organization on Oct. 13, 1911. The Diocese also owns the original MS. accompanied by correspondence, etc. For newspaper reports, see the Hartford Courant of Sept. 24, 1904.

[88] Delivered June 21, 1894. My text is taken from the corrected typescript in the Diocesan Archives, which also owns the original MS.

[89] See Trinity College Bulletin, n.s. XV, no. 3 (July, 1918), pp. 19-22. This issue is devoted to necrology covering the years 1916-1918.

[90] See Berkeley Divinity School Bulletin, no. 28 (April, 1917), pp. 8-22.

[91] Trinity College Bulletin, n.s. XIV, no. 3 (July, 1917), pp. 1-22.

[92] Berkeley Divinity School Bulletin, no. 29 (August, 1917), p. 9.

[93] Materials on the following five pages are taken from the Hart Collection in the Diocesan Archives.

[94] These letters by James Shepard are filed under his name in the Diocesan Archives--probably a gift from Samuel Hart to the Diocese.

[95] In the Hart Collection of the Diocesan Archives--a folder of loose historical and biographical clippings which Hart collected for reference. (I have selected only typical examples for this volume.)

[96] New Haven Evening Register, June 21, 1894, pp. 1 and 3.

[97] An undated clipping from the Hartford Times, ca. May 28, 1906. The identical text appeared simultaneously in the Willimantic Daily Chronicle.

[98] The three clippings on Charles Hemenway Adams, of the Hartford Courant, are all unidentified, except the second, which is from a Hartford paper dated Aug. 31, 1915. [99] Ferguson died Aug. 3, 1916.

[100] Hartford Courant, Sept. 1, 1890.

[101] From The Churchman (1900), p. 695. For Hart's earlier paper on the S.P.G. see note 26 above and pages 100-101 above, to which it refers. [102] Ibid., 719-720.